Lecture Notes in Computer Science

Vol. 49: Interactive Systems. Proceedings 1976. Edited by A. Blaser and C. Hackl. VI, 380 pages. 1976.

Vol. 50: A. C. Hartmann, A Concurrent Pascal Compiler for Minicomputers. VI, 119 pages. 1977.

Vol. 51: B. S. Garbow, Matrix Eigensystem Routines – Eispack Guide Extension. VIII, 343 pages. 1977.

Vol. 52: Automata, Languages and Programming. Fourth Colloquium, University of Turku, July 1977. Edited by A. Salomaa and M. Steinby. X, 569 pages. 1977.

Vol. 53: Mathematical Foundations of Computer Science. Proceedings 1977. Edited by J. Gruska. XII, 608 pages. 1977.

Vol. 54: Design and Implementation of Programming Languages. Proceedings 1976. Edited by J. H. Williams and D. A. Fisher. X, 496 pages. 1977.

Vol. 55: A. Gerbier, Mes premières constructions de programmes. XII, 256 pages. 1977.

Vol. 56: Fundamentals of Computation Theory. Proceedings 1977. Edited by M. Karpiński. XII, 542 pages. 1977.

Vol. 57: Portability of Numerical Software. Proceedings 1976. Edited by W. Cowell. VIII, 539 pages. 1977.

Vol. 58: M. J. O'Donnell, Computing in Systems Described by Equations. XIV, 111 pages. 1977.

Vol. 59: E. Hill, Jr., A Comparative Study of Very Large Data Bases. X, 140 pages. 1978.

Vol. 60: Operating Systems, An Advanced Course. Edited by R. Bayer, R. M. Graham, and G. Seegmüller. X, 593 pages. 1978.

Vol. 61: The Vienna Development Method: The Meta-Language. Edited by D. Bjørner and C. B. Jones. XVIII, 382 pages. 1978.

Vol. 62: Automata, Languages and Programming. Proceedings 1978. Edited by G. Ausiello and C. Böhm. VIII, 508 pages. 1978.

Vol. 63: Natural Language Communication with Computers. Edited by Leonard Bolc. VI, 292 pages. 1978.

Vol. 64: Mathematical Foundations of Computer Science. Proceedings 1978. Edited by J. Winkowski. X, 551 pages. 1978.

Vol. 65: Information Systems Methodology, Proceedings, 1978. Edited by G. Bracchi and P. C. Lockemann. XII, 696 pages. 1978.

Vol. 66: N. D. Jones and S. S. Muchnick, TEMPO: A Unified Treatment of Binding Time and Parameter Passing Concepts in Programming Languages. IX, 118 pages. 1978.

Vol. 67: Theoretical Computer Science, 4th GI Conference, Aachen, March 1979. Edited by K. Weihrauch. VII, 324 pages. 1979.

Vol. 68: D. Harel, First-Order Dynamic Logic. X, 133 pages. 1979.

Vol. 69: Program Construction. International Summer School. Edited by F. L. Bauer and M. Broy. VII, 651 pages. 1979.

Vol. 70: Semantics of Concurrent Computation. Proceedings 1979. Edited by G. Kahn. VI, 368 pages. 1979.

Vol. 71: Automata, Languages and Programming. Proceedings 1979. Edited by H. A. Maurer. IX, 684 pages. 1979.

Vol. 72: Symbolic and Algebraic Computation. Proceedings 1979. Edited by E. W. Ng. XV, 557 pages. 1979.

Vol. 73: Graph-Grammars and Their Application to Computer Science and Biology. Proceedings 1978. Edited by V. Claus, H. Ehrig and G. Rozenberg. VII, 477 pages. 1979.

Vol. 74: Mathematical Foundations of Computer Science. Proceedings 1979. Edited by J. Bečvář. IX, 580 pages. 1979.

Vol. 75: Mathematical Studies of Information Processing. Proceedings 1978. Edited by E. K. Blum, M. Paul and S. Takasu. VIII, 629 pages. 1979.

Vol. 76: Codes for Boundary-Value Problems in Ordinary Differential Equations. Proceedings 1978. Edited by B. Childs et al. VIII, 388 pages. 1979.

Vol. 77: G. V. Bochmann, Architecture of Distributed Computer Systems. VIII, 238 pages. 1979.

Vol. 78: M. Gordon, R. Milner and C. Wadsworth, Edinburgh LCF. VIII, 159 pages. 1979.

Vol. 79: Language Design and Programming Methodology. Proceedings, 1979. Edited by J. Tobias. IX, 255 pages. 1980.

Vol. 80: Pictorial Information Systems. Edited by S. K. Chang and K. S. Fu. IX, 445 pages. 1980.

Vol. 81: Data Base Techniques for Pictorial Applications. Proceedings, 1979. Edited by A. Blaser. XI, 599 pages. 1980.

Vol. 82: J. G. Sanderson, A Relational Theory of Computing. VI, 147 pages. 1980.

Vol. 83: International Symposium Programming. Proceedings, 1980. Edited by B. Robinet. VII, 341 pages. 1980.

Vol. 84: Net Theory and Applications. Proceedings, 1979. Edited by W. Brauer. XIII, 537 Seiten. 1980.

Vol. 85: Automata, Languages and Programming. Proceedings, 1980. Edited by J. de Bakker and J. van Leeuwen. VIII, 671 pages. 1980.

Vol. 86: Abstract Software Specifications. Proceedings, 1979. Edited by D. Bjørner. XIII, 567 pages. 1980

Vol. 87: 5th Conference on Automated Deduction. Proceedings, 1980. Edited by W. Bibel and R. Kowalski. VII, 385 pages. 1980.

Vol. 88: Mathematical Foundations of Computer Science 1980. Proceedings, 1980. Edited by P. Dembiński. VIII, 723 pages. 1980.

Vol. 89: Computer Aided Design - Modelling, Systems Engineering, CAD-Systems. Proceedings, 1980. Edited by J. Encarnacao. XIV, 461 pages. 1980.

Vol. 90: D. M. Sandford, Using Sophisticated Models in Resolution Theorem Proving.
XI, 239 pages. 1980

Vol. 91: D. Wood, Grammar and L Forms: An Introduction. IX, 314 pages. 1980.

Vol. 92: R. Milner, A Calculus of Communication Systems. VI, 171 pages. 1980.

Vol. 93: A. Nijholt, Context-Free Grammars: Covers, Normal Forms, and Parsing. VII, 253 pages. 1980.

Vol. 94: Semantics-Directed Compiler Generation. Proceedings, 1980. Edited by N. D. Jones. V, 489 pages. 1980.

Vol. 95: Ch. D. Marlin, Coroutines. XII, 246 pages. 1980.

Vol. 96: J. L. Peterson, Computer Programs for Spelling Correction: VI, 213 pages. 1980.

Vol. 97: S. Osaki and T. Nishio, Reliability Evaluation of Some Fault-Tolerant Computer Architectures. VI, 129 pages. 1980.

Vol. 98: Towards a Formal Description of Ada. Edited by D. Bjørner and O. N. Oest. XIV, 630 pages. 1980.

Vol. 99: I. Guessarian, Algebraic Semantics. XI, 158 pages. 1981.

Vol. 100: Graphtheoretic Concepts in Computer Science. Edited by H. Noltemeier. X, 403 pages. 1981.

Vol. 101: A. Thayse, Boolean Calculus of Differences. VII, 144 pages. 1981.

Vol. 102: J. H. Davenport, On the Integration of Algebraic Functions. 1–197 pages. 1981.

Vol. 103: H. Ledgard, A. Singer, J. Whiteside, Directions in Human Factors of Interactive Systems. VI, 190 pages. 1981.

Vol. 104: Theoretical Computer Science. Ed. by P. Deussen. VII, 261 pages. 1981.

Vol. 105: B. W. Lampson, M. Paul, H. J. Siegert, Distributed Systems – Architecture and Implementation. XIII, 510 pages. 1981.

Vol. 106: The Programming Language Ada. Reference Manual. X, 243 pages. 1981.

Lecture Notes in Computer Science

Edited by G. Goos and J. Hartmanis

139

J. Uhl S. Drossopoulou
G. Persch G. Goos M. Dausmann
G. Winterstein W. Kirchgässner

An Attribute Grammar for the Semantic Analysis of Ada

Springer-Verlag
Berlin Heidelberg New York 1982

Authors
Jürgen Uhl
Sophia Drossopoulou
Guido Persch
Gerhard Goos
Manfred Dausmann
Georg Winterstein
Walter Kirchgässner
Institut für Informatik II der Universität
Postfach 6380, 7500 Karlsruhe 1, Germany

CR Subject Classifications (1979): 3.1, 3.2, 3.4

ISBN 3-540-11571-4 Springer-Verlag Berlin Heidelberg New York
ISBN 0-387-11571-4 Springer-Verlag New York Heidelberg Berlin

Printed in Germany

Printing and binding: Beltz Offsetdruck, Hemsbach/Bergstr.
2145/3140-543210

Preface

Attribute grammars are an established tool for the formal specification of the semantics of a programming language and also the specification of the language's compiler. This book contains an attribute grammar specifying the static semantics of Ada, together with an explanatory introduction.

This attribute grammar, which we shall call the AG, completely describes the semantics of Ada, as published in July 1980. The AG was extensively tested with the help of an equivalent automatically generated Pascal program. From this specification we systematically developed the semantic analysis part of our Ada compiler front-end.

Part A of this volume describes the development of the AG. It contains a survey of the tasks of semantic analysis within a front-end, the use of attribute grammars for the specification of static semantics and semantic analysis, and the procedure for writing the AG.

Part B is a rationale for the AG: the three main tasks of semantic analysis are described, the main attributes are introduced, their use, their dependencies and their types are outlined.

Part C contains the AG itself.

We are particularly indebted to Brigitte Hutt, Uwe Kastens and Erich Zimmermann, without whose support the present work could not have been carried out: They provided the tools for the systematic and efficient use of attribute grammars, and they readily and frequently advised us on the design of the AG.

This research was partially supported by the Bundesamt für Wehrtechnik und Beschaffung under Contract No. E/F61D/90104/95031.

Table of Contents

PART A : DEVELOPMENT OF THE AG

PART A:

DEVELOPMENT

OF THE AG

1. Introduction and Survey

1.1. Survey of the Karlsruhe Ada Compiler Front-End

Ada is a new system programming language designed by a team led by J. D. Ichbiah on behalf of the American Department of Defense.

In April 1979 an Ada Implementation Group was established at the University of Karlsruhe for developing a compiler front-end for Ada. This front-end should analyze Ada source programs (Revised Ada [Ada80]) and translate them into an intermediate language (from which a machine dependent back-end may then generate code). The front-end should be machine independent, written in Ada itself (for bootstrap purposes) and run on a SIEMENS 7700 under the operating system BS2000.

When this project started, only a preliminary form of Ada existed [Ada79]. In order to gain experience in implementing Ada we started by writing a front-end for preliminary Ada. Preliminary Ada-0 [Dau79], a subset of Ada, was defined as the bootstrap language and a compiler was implemented. The intermediate language AIDA [Dau80] was defined. SEPAREE [Dau81], a system supporting separate compilation for Ada, was developed. The semantic analysis part of the preliminary front-end was based on a preliminary version of the Formal Definition [FD80] of the language designed at INRIA. This description was incomplete at that time; we therefore had to fill the gaps and then transform this specification into an executable program. In summer 1980 a front-end for preliminary Ada was running. Further information about this front-end can be found in [GoWi80].

In July 1980 the Revised Reference Manual for Ada was published [Ada80], and we started with the design of a front-end for this language.

A revised bootstrap language, Ada-0 [Per81a], was defined and a compiler was written. Ada-0 is essentially Ada, except that it does not comprise overloading, derived types, real numbers, tasks and generics. On the other hand, Ada-0 provides for exception handling and separate compilation, both important for the implementation of compilers.

Due to the increasing interest in a common intermediate language for Ada, Diana [Diana81], a Descriptive Intermediate Attributed Notation for Ada was designed in January 1981 by teams from Karlsruhe, Carnegie-Mellon-University, Intermetrics and Softech. Diana is an attributed tree. It reflects the abstract syntactic structure of an Ada program together with the additional information gained by lexical and semantic analysis.

This time we adopted a different approach to semantic analysis: We wrote an attribute grammar specifying the static semantics of Ada. This specification was automatically translated into an equivalent Pascal program [KaZi80], and could thus be extensively tested. After several iterations of testing and modifying the AG, we systematically transformed the AG into equivalent Ada programs. They were integrated as the semantic analysis part with the scanner, the parser, and the separate compilation system to form the front-end of the compiler.

The front-end for Revised Ada was first running in Dezember 1981.

1.2. Tasks and Modularization of the Front-End

The Reference Manual for Ada [Ada80] and the definition of Diana [Diana81] determine the input-output behaviour of the front-end: The input to the front-end is an Ada compilation unit in its textual form; its output is the Diana representation of this compilation unit with all semantic attributes. Any inconsistencies between the Ada source program and the rules of the language which are detectable at compile time must be found and reported.

The front-end must recognize the lexical tokens, the syntactic structure of the program and then analyze its meaning. Due to the complicated visibility rules, the concepts of overloading, generics and the demand of rigorous type checking, even across the boundaries of compilation units, the front-end has mainly to deal with the semantic analysis compared to that lexical analysis and parsing are of minor interest.

In [GoWi81] the modularization of a compiler for Ada is discussed with particular emphasis on the modularization of the compiler front-end.

Such an Ada front-end mainly consists of:

- the scanner (lexical analysis), which analyzes the input text and recognizes all lexical tokens of Ada. The scanner uses a finite automaton as the underlying model.
- the parser (syntactic analysis), which generates from the sequence of lexical units the equivalent Diana Parse Tree with all lexical attributes (for example identifier codes). Syntactic analysis is achieved by a table-driven LR(1)-method. The tables (including error recovery) were automatically generated by the parser generator system PGS ([Denc77] and [Denc80]) from a context-free grammar which is equivalent to that given in Appendix E of [Ada80] and satisfies the LALR(1)-condition [Per81b]. The parser also contains a complete error recovery system [Roe78] which corrects any syntactic error by deleting from or inserting symbols into the program. Thus it is guaranteed, that the Diana Parse Tree output by the parser always corresponds to a syntactically correct (but sometimes semantically meaningless) Ada program.

- the semantic analyzer, which reports any statically detectable error in the Ada program and calculates the semantic attributes required by Diana. It starts with the program representation by a Diana Parse Tree and adds the semantic attributes to this tree. These attributes convey information about the meaning of several language elements to subsequent compiler phases or to other tools of an Ada programming environment.

The front-end has, therefore, two internal interfaces: the list of lexical units as output by the scanner and the structure tree as output by the parser.

The structure tree represents the abstract syntax with the lexical information. Its structure is described in Appendix II of [Diana81] and it is called the **Diana Parse Tree**.

The output of semantic analysis is the structure tree with lexical and semantic attributes. This abstract data type is defined in Ch.2 of [Diana81] and it is called the **Diana Tree**.

The difference between the Diana Tree and the Diana Parse Tree is that the first has in addition semantic attributes some ambiguities are resolved whose resolution requires semantic information, e.g. a name followed by an association list in parentheses is resolved in different kinds of nodes for function call, procedure call, entry call, indexed, conversion and slice (cf. 3.1.4 in [Diana81]).

The structure of the front-end is shown in Figure 1.

1.3. Tasks of Semantic Analysis

Semantic analysis mainly deals with name analysis (overloading resolution), type-checking and context-conditions. It determines the meaning of the language elements in the program, and checks their correct use.

The meaning of a language element consists of information computed at compile time (static semantics), and of its interpretation at run time (dynamic semantics). It is thus clear that for example the identity of a name (overloading resolution) is part of static semantics, whereas the handler to be executed when an exception is raised belongs to dynamic semantics.

```
             Ada  source
                  |
          +-------V-------+
          |               |
          |    scanner    |
          |               |
          +---------------+
                  |

             Lexical tokens

                  |
                  V
          +---------------+
          |               |
          |    parser     |
          |               |
          +---------------+
                  |

            Diana Parse Tree

                  |
          +-------V-------+
          |               |
          |   semantic    |
          |   analyzer    |
          |               |
          +---------------+
                  |
                  V

              Diana  Tree
```

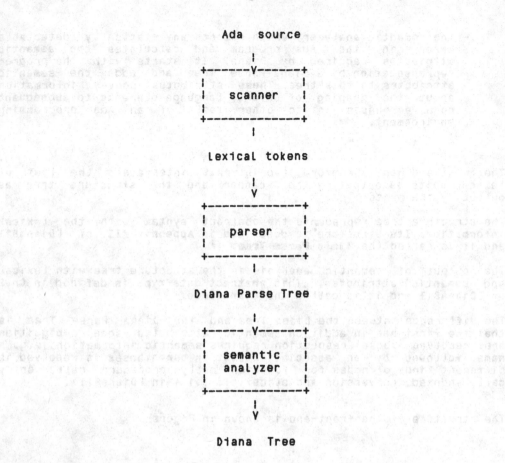

Figure_1: Structure of the front-end

The exact division of the semantics into static and dynamic is ultimately an engineering task of the compiler designer. In some cases the boundary is not clear, and then some strategy must be developed for its definition.

The information to be computed by semantic analysis can be classified into the information to be passed to subsequent compiler phases and the information needed for checking of language rules. Of course, some information may be used for both purposes.

1.4. Formal Specification of Semantic Analysis

The task of analysis for such a complex language as Ada must be treated in a systematic manner. As we saw in 1.2, lexical and syntactic analysis were specified formally and then their implementation was developed in a systematic way. The tools we have used are widely accepted. They belong to the state of the art of compiler construct, and they have proven the merits of formal specifications.

Semantic analysis is a much more complex task, and therefore, the demand for an "organized" procedure is more urgent. We could either keep our fingers crossed and start programming, or first develop a formal specification and then transform this specification into an equivalent Ada program.

The first method would certainly never lead to an understandable, correct and complete semantic analyzer. Therefore a decision has to be made which method to use for the specification of semantic analysis. Parallel to our work, a group at INRIA developed a formal definition of Ada [FD80] in a denotational style and the University of Denmark, together with the Danish Datamation Centre, also developed a formal description of Ada [BjOe80], expressed in the Vienna Development Method. Both were incomplete at the time when we started our work.

Instead of trying to produce a specification in a similar way, or to complete one of the above specifications, we decided to write our own in the form of an attribute grammar.

The reasons for this decision were as follows:

Attribute grammars describe the properties of a language and the relationships of these properties, whereas denotational semantics in any form describe more than this, and are, therefore, much too powerful.

Attribute grammar specifications are rigorous and readable because they do not specify any part of the implementation, for example the tree traversal and function calling hierarchies.

A specification by an attribute grammar is very near to the behaviour of a compiler, i.e. the attribution of a tree.

Attribute grammars are easy to modify.

The specification can proceed in an "incremental" way, i.e. we can start with the specification of the basic concepts and gradually extend the specification. Thus, at first, we need not take the whole language into account.

Attribute grammars allow the formalized description of usual compiler techniques (for example definition tables). We need not learn new techniques; we can use the old an well established methods but in a formal way and can, in addition, check their correct usage.

Several properties of attribute grammars can be proven, e.g. completeness, consistency, well-definedness. Also it is possible to derive algorithms which implement a specification given by an attribute grammar.

We have already had experience with attribute grammar specifications. Several attribute grammars have been developed at our Institute (cf. 3) and we had experience in expressing usual high level programming language concepts like scope rules and typing.

We have at our disposal the GAG-system [KaZi80] which facilitates the development of attribute grammar specifications, produces information about the properties of an attribute grammar, and even automatically generates an equivalent Pascal program. The availability of this tool was of great importance to us:

- The information about attribute dependencies, type compatibility, completeness of attribute definition was an important aid during the first stages of the development of the AG.

- The automatic calculation of an attribute evaluation strategy freed us from any considerations about the number of passes, attribute evaluation order, tree traversals and assignment of attributes to phases or passes. These decisions are not related to the task of semantic analysis; they belong to the implementation strategy. If the "specificator" would also take them into account, he would probably confuse these implementation considerations with the pure semantic specification. A later revision or optimization of the specification may change the dependencies of the attributes and the old decisions may become invalid under the new situation.

- It is particulary important that the methods of the GAG-system are based on ordered attribute grammars (OAG) [Kast80] and not on multi-pass grammars. Our experience during the development of the AG coincided with the experience made in similar projects: when an attribute grammar is well defined it already satisfies the condition of OAG or it can very easily be transformed to satisfy it. On the other hand, the class of OAG is not too large, and it allows an efficient implementation.

- With the automatic generation of an equivalent Pascal program we were able to test our specification at a very early phase, even when it was still incomplete, and to discover errors which would have been difficult to correct later on.

1.5. Specification of Semantic Analysis with Attribute Grammars

1.5.1 Attribute Grammars

Attribute grammars were introduced in 1968 by Knuth [Knuth68], [Knuth71]. An extensive theory has evolved on that subject, and attribute grammars have been used in several projects.

Attribute grammars (as defined formally in [Kast80], and with the terminology of [GoWa82]) consist of:

- a **context-free grammar**
- a set of **attributes** for each symbol of the context-free grammar
- **attribution rules** establishing the value of every attribute according to the syntactic production in which it appears and in terms of the values of other attributes of symbols in the same production
- **conditions** involving attributes of one production. If a given condition is not satisfied by the attribute values of a particular subtree, a specific error message is given

Attributes are generally classified as **synthesized**, **inherited** and **intrinsic**. Synthesized attributes are calculated when their nonterminal appears on the left hand side of a production, inherited attributes are calculated when their nonterminal appears on the right hand side of the production, intrinsic attributes are predefined. One can visualize synthesized attributes as "going up the tree" and inherited attributes as "going down the tree". The values of intrinsic attributes are determined in advance, i.e. during lexical analysis or parsing (for example the textual position, or the string representing an identifier are intrinsic attributes).

An attribute grammar is **well-defined**, if all non-intrinsic attributes for each structure tree are effectively computable (i.e. there are no circular dependencies among attributes, and every attribute value is defined by an attribution rule).

Attribute grammars describe the attribution of structure trees and the consistency conditions of the attribute values. Attributes serve to distribute the information in the tree, conditions serve to express the semantic checks.

1.5.2. General Strategies in Specifying Static Semantics with an Attribute Grammar

Attributes should reflect the concepts of the language. In most high level programming languages it is possible to declare entities, and to use them later on. Language rules restrict the way in which those entities may be used.

Therefore, we provide attributes to transfer information from the definition point (defining occurrence) of the entity to the point of its application (applied occurrence), attributes to distinguish the applied occurrences, and possibly also additional attributes to check the consistency of the input program with the rules of the language.

An attribute 'environment' represents all information about declared entities. The 'environment' is the equivalent to the definition table (possession or symbol table), it may be considered as a data base with descriptions of entities. When a new entity is declared, the environment is enriched by the information about the new entity. Block structure and all elements affecting the visibility of identifiers (scope rules) should also be reflected in the 'environment' attribute.

An attribute 'meaning' reflects the identity of applied occurrences (identification of names or expressions). The 'meaning' depends on the 'environment' (declared entities, hiding etc.) and on the 'meanings' of the inner and outer context. The 'environment' sometimes depends on the 'meaning' (for example type names in object declarations).

The rules of the language are reflected in relationships between attribute values. If these relationships are not satisfied, a specific error message will be given, stating the violated language rule. In most cases these relationships are based on the values of the attributes 'environment' and 'meaning', sometimes, however, additional attributes must be introduced for this purpose.

1.5.3. From Static Semantics Specification to Semantic Analysis Specification

Specifying semantic analysis of a language is not the same as specifying static semantics of this language.

The static semantics is part of the definition of the language. Static semantics is concerned with establishing the meaning of every element in the program and with finding out whether or not the program is correct. (It might be viewed as an acceptor which only states "correct" or "erroneous" for any input program).

The semantic analysis is part of a compiler. It must therefore support the programmer: it must generate intelligible error messages stating the exact error in the program, and it should not show some side effect caused by the error. In case of erroneous input, it must provide for error recovery and must allow to resume the analysis in order to find further errors. In particular, error recovery should minimize the probability of duplicate error messages and avalanche errors. Semantic analysis must also support the work of subsequent compiler phases: it must furnish them with the information they need, in an appropriate form. The semantic analysis is a program executed very often: it must, therefore, be efficient.

We are convinced that the best way to specify the semantic analysis is by starting with the specification of the static semantics without any consideration of error recovery and efficiency. Only when this part of the specification is almost complete, we extend the specification to include these considerations, too. (This is in accordance with the general strategy to specify the "logical" behaviour of a very complex system in a first stage, and to modify the specification in a second stage so as to describe a system with additional qualities, such as efficiency etc.)

1.5.4. Partitioned Attribute Grammars

The GAG-system [KaZi80] can be used in its full power, only if the attribute grammar is a partitionable attribute grammar.

Partitioned attribute grammars are defined in [GoWa82]. A **partition** of the attributes is a classification of the attributes A(X) of each symbol X into classes A1(X), A2(X), ..., Am(X). A **partitioned** attribute grammar is an attribute grammar together with such a partition that the attributes of each symbol can be evaluated in the order given by this classification. An attribute grammar is **partitionable**, if such a classification exists.

Partitionable attribute grammars were first introduced under the name of arranged orderly attribute grammars in [Kast80], together with a particular algorithm to construct such a classification. If this classification leads to a partitioned attribute grammar, then the grammar is called **ordered** (OAG), [Kast80].

One can organize this classification so that for all symbols X, A1(X) contains inherited, A2(X) synthesized, ..., A2*i-1(X) contains inherited, A2*i(X) synthesized attributes. (The classes may also be empty.) From such a partition of the attributes a table-driven algorithm can be derived controlling the tree traversal and attribute evaluation. The **attribution algorithm** consists of actions in the form of:

- evaluate an attribute from the current production
- visit the production corresponding to the i-th symbol on the right hand side of the current production (son i)
- visit the production to which the symbol on the left hand side of the current production belongs (father)

For a given attribute grammar and its particular attribute

dependencies a local tree walk rule consisting of these operations is calculated for each production. It is applied to each tree node derived by the corresponding production.

Tree traversals need not proceed in passes through the tree, rather it may locally oscillate between nodes or complete attribute evaluation may take place for some subtrees before others are visited.

1.5.5. GAG: Generator for Attribute Grammars

As we have already mentioned, we used the GAG-system for the development and testing of the AG.

The GAG-system consists of two phases:

- the analysis phase
- the generation phase.

The analysis phase checks the syntax and semantics of the input ALADIN program (cf. 1.6). The semantic checks comprise the amount of type checking which is required by ALADIN. If the input is a correct ALADIN program, then attribute dependencies are evaluated and analyzed, to check whether the given attribute grammar is ordered.

If the attribute grammar is ordered, the generation phase produces for the specification an equivalent analyzer in Pascal. In particular, it produces a partition of the attribute grammar using the algorithm from [Kast80]. It generates a table for the visit sequences, an implementation of the attributes and their types, and it transforms the attribution rules and functions into Pascal programs (functions and procedures). Furthermore, it applies some optimization techniques on the generated programs. All programs are embedded into an analyzer frame to form a running Pascal program.

1.6. ALADIN: A Language for Attribute Grammar Definitions

The input language for the GAG-system is ALADIN, (A Language for Attribute Definitions) [Kast79]. ALADIN was especially developed for the formulation of static semantics with attribute grammars. It is an applicative language with strong typing, and has data types similar to those of Pascal and ALGOL 68 (integer, boolean, string, enumeration types, structures, discriminated union) and a list concept. The attribution rules are grouped together with the productions.

The data types supported by ALADIN are essentially those required by compilers: various tables containing several kinds of entries for every item. Strong typing enforces the security of the analyzer.

ALADIN is self-explanatory for people who are familiar with ALGOL 68 and Ada. A complete Reference Manual for ALADIN is given in [Kast79]. In this chapter we shall give an informal, short introduction covering only those features of ALADIN which we used in the AG. This chapter is therefore neither complete, nor absolutely precise.

A specification in ALADIN consists of:

- comments
- type definitions
- constant definitions
- symbol and attribute definitions
- productions with attribution rules and conditions
- function definitions

Comments

Comments start with '%' and end with the end of the line.

Types

ALADIN offers the predefined types INT, BOOL, SYMB (symbols of the specified language), CHAR and STRING with the usual semantics. Additional types may be defined, i.e. : scalar and range types and the composite types set, record, union and list.

Scalar, range, and record type definitions have the form:

```
TYPE type_1 : ( scalar_1, ..., scalar_n );
TYPE type_2 : [ scalar_j  :  scalar_k ];
TYPE type_3 : STRUCT ( comp_1, ..., comp_k : type_1 ,
                       ...
                       comp_n, ..., comp_m : type_j );
```

Aggregates of type type_3 may be written in the form: type_3(exp_1, expr_2, ..., expr_m), where expr_1, ..., expr_k are values of type type_1, ... expr_n, ..., expr_m are values of type type_j.

Union types of ALADIN reflect the discriminated union concept of ALGOL 68. A union type definition has the form:

```
TYPE type_1 : UNION ( type_2, type_3, ..., type_n );
```

The type type_1 "unites" the types type_2, ..., type_n. It may have any value of type type_2 <u>or</u> type_3 <u>or</u> ... type_n.

Types may also be lists of other types:

```
TYPE type_1 : LISTOF type_2;
```

<u>Expressions</u>

Expressions consist of operators, function calls, constants, IF-expressions, CASE-expressions, Type-tests, Symbol-tests (in productions), parameters (in functions) or attribute names (in the syntactic productions).

The operators =, =/ are defined for all values; +, - are defined for integer; NOT, AND, OR, XOR for boolean; and the functions HEAD, TAIL, FRONT, LAST, EMPTY and the concatenation operand + for list types.

IF-expressions have the form:

```
IF <boolean_expr_1>
THEN <expr_2>
ELSE <expr_3>
FI
```

CASE-expressions are possible over scalar or union type values. For an expression expr_1 of the scalar type type_1 we can write:

```
CASE <expr_1> OF
scalar_1 : ... : scalar_k : <expr_2 >;
 ...
scalar_l : ... : scalar_m : <expr_j  >
OUT                         <expr_j+1>
ESAC
```

where scalar_1, ..., scalar_m all belong to the scalar type type_1. The OUT-part is required only when the listed scalars scalar_1, ..., scalar_m do not cover the whole type type_1.

For union types the CASE-expression is according to the special type of a value. For an expression expr_1 of the type type_1 which unites type_2, ..., type_n we write:

```
CASE <expr_1> OF
IS type_2 : ... IS type_k : <expr_2  >;
 ...
IS type_l : ... IS type_m : <expr_j  >
OUT                         <expr_j+1>
ESAC
```

Here also,the OUT-part must appear exactly if the sequence type_2, ..., type_m does not cover all types united in type_1. In type-tests we can also ask the united type of an expression expr_1 of type type_1:

```
<expr_1> IS type_k
```

is true if expr_1 is of the united type type_k. And we can also assert that an expression must be of a certain united type:

```
<expr_1> QUA type_k
```

An expression may be immediately followed by a condition. The following expression:

```
( <expr_1>
  CONDITION
     <boolean_expr_2>
  MESSAGE
     "<message_1>" )
```

has the value of expr_1; but if the boolean_expr_2 is false, then message_1 is generated.

Symbol and Attribute Declarations

Attributes of a certain type are associated to the nonterminals and terminals of the language

```
TERM t_1   : attr_1, attr_2, ..., attr_j : type_1,
             ...
             attr_n, ...                 : type_m;
```

(in the AG all attributes of a terminal are intrinsic) and

```
NONTERM A : attr_1, attr_2, ... : type_1,
            ...
            attr_n, ...         : type_n;
```

(in the AG the attributes of nonterminals are either synthesized or inherited).

Constant Declarations

Constant definitions allow a shortened notation for values which are used often:

```
CONST const1 : <expr_1>;
```

expr_1 determines the type and the value of the constant. This expression may contain previously defined constants, function calls and all operators available in ALADIN.

Productions, Attribution Rules and Conditions

The syntactic productions are followed by several attribution rules and conditions on attribute values in arbitrary order. The general form is:

```
RULE r_j :
    Y    ::=  X1   X2  ...  Xn
STATIC
    Xi.attr_j := <expr_1> ;
    Y .attr_k := <expr_2> ;
        ...
    TRANSFER attr_q, ..., attr_s ;
        ...
    CONDITION
        <boolean_expr_3>
    MESSAGE
        "<message1>";
        ...
END;
```

r_j introduces a name for this rule. Such a rule name can be used later on to reference the corresponding production, e.g. in symbol tests (see below).

The attribution rules have generally the form of "assignments". In the example above it is established that the value of the attribute attr_j of the nonterminal Xi is identical to the value of expr_1. Sometimes attributes are passed over unchanged from the nonterminal of the left hand side Y to the nonterminals of the right hand side X1, ..., Xn or vice versa. In this case, TRANSFER allows a shortened notation. Instead of writing: Y.attr_q := Xl.attr_q (where Xl is the only symbol on the right hand side possessing an attribute called attr_q), we can write:

```
TRANSFER attr_q;
```

And instead of writing: Xj.attr_s := Y.attr_s; (for all Xj on the right hand side of the production with an attribute called attr_s), we can use the shorter notation:

```
TRANSFER attr_s;
```

If a symbol A appears more than once in the syntactic production, then we distinguish between the different occurrences through an index: A[k] means the k-th occurrence of A in the production.

The expressions in the attribution rules may depend on attributes from the given syntactic production, constants, symbol tests, function calls, inner and outer attributes.

Symbol tests give information about the structure of the tree; they have the form:

```
Xj IS r_k      resp.      Y IS r_k
```

and return true if the node belonging to Xj is further derived according to the production r_k, resp. if the father node of Y is derived according to production r_k.

Inner attributes allow us to refer to attributes of the tree "below", outer attributes allow us to refer to attributes of the tree "above" the current production.

```
Xi CONSTITUENT Z.attr_j
```

means the attribute attr_j of the first node marked with Z in the tree under Xi, whereas

```
Xi CONSTITUENTS Z.attr_j
```

means the list of the attributes attr_j of all nodes marked with Z in the tree under Xi (in the postfix representation of the derivation tree). And

```
INCLUDING Z.attr_j
```

means the attribute attr_j of the nearest node marked with Z above the current production.

Function Declarations

Functions are used for recursively defined expressions or frequently used evaluations. They have the form:

```
FUNCTION func_1 ( p_1, ..., p_j : type_1,
                  ...
                  p_n, ..., p_m : type_m) type_r :

        <expr_1>
```

where the parameters are p_1, ..., p_j with type type_1 etc., the result of the function is the value of expr_1 and it is of type type_r. The expression may be arbitrarily complex but it may only depend on the parameters or on constants. Other functions may be called and all operators are possible (according to the operands' types). Very often, the functions are recursive (for list operations).

The description of ALADIN in this chapter was by no means complete: the discrimination of attributes as synthesized and inherited in their definition, the set types, the operators IN, MOD, /, *, >=, <=, the more rigorous notation of recursions in the productions, the distinction of attribution rules into static and dynamic semantics and special rules for subsets of the language, and the very powerful concept of lists with keys were omitted. The semantics of the features we introduced were outlined only in such detail as we believe it is necessary to understand our AG.

1.7. An Example

In the following example we give an attribute grammar specification in ALADIN of a language in which variables of type boolean or integer can be declared. The semantic analysis must check that variables are either of type integer or boolean, and that no identifier may appear in a declaration if it was previously declared. The syntax of this language is:

```
DECL_S     ::= DECL  DECL_S
DECL       ::= ID  ':'  TYPE_SPEC
ID         ::= id
TYPE_SPEC  ::= ID
```

We need attributes containing all relevant information about previously declared identifiers; and attributes to transfer the information about the type and designator of a variable. We need attributes to represent the information about the variables already declared: their identifier and their type.

The domains of the attributes are defined by the types:

```
TYPE type_kind    : ( bool_type, int_type, error_type );
TYPE description  : STRUCT( designator : SYMB,
                            type_desc  : type_kind);
TYPE environment  : LISTOF description;
```

Some values will be used quite often (for example the designator for 'integer' and 'boolean'), we declare the constants:

```
CONST  int_desi    : SYMB ('integer');
CONST  bool_desi   : SYMB ('boolean');
```

We can now declare the symbols and their attributes. Attributes are not variables, they are identificators for values. If the value of some attribute is to be "changed", then we must provide for a second attribute to contain the "changed" value, for example in DECL the attribute env_in contains the declaration information just __before__, the attribute env_out contains the declaration information just __after__ the declaration:

```
NONTERM DECL       : env_in,
                     env_out : environment;

NONTERM DECL_S     : env_in,
                     env_out : environment;

NONTERM ID         : desi    : SYMB,
                     env_in  : environment;

NONTERM TYPE_SPEC  : type    : type_kind,
                     env_in  : environment;
```

The nonterminal DECL has an attribute env_in and an attribute env_out of type environment, etc. The attribute env_in contains the information about all variables declared before the current element, env_out contains the information about all variables declared up to the end of the current element. TYPE_SPEC.type means the type expressed by TYPE_SPEC, ID.desi is the designator of ID.

The attributes of terminals are intrinsic:

```
   TERM  id : desi       : SYMB;
```

(In this case, desi is already calculated by the lexical analysis and is passed over to the semantic analysis by the parser).

The attribution rules (the rules according to which the attributes are calculated) are given along with the production:

```
     RULE r_1 :
        DECL ::=  ID  ':'  TYPE_SPEC
     STATIC

        TRANSFER env_in;

        DECL.env_out :=
            environment (description
                            (ID.desi,
                             TYPE_SPEC.type)) +
            DECL.env_in;

     END;
```

Here the old environment (env_in, describing the variables declared before this DECL) supplemented by the description of the new variable becomes the new environment (env_out, describing the variables declared up to the end of this DECL). DECL.env_in is an inherited attribute whereas DECL.env_out is a synthesized attribute.

```
     RULE r_2 :
        ID   ::=  id
     STATIC

        TRANSFER desi;

        CONDITION
        IF (ID IS r_1) THEN
           NOT (id_already_declared
                  (ID.desi,
                   ID.env_in))
        ELSE TRUE
        FI
           MESSAGE
           "this identifier was already declared";

     END;
```

```
FUNCTION id_already_declared (desi : SYMB,
                              env  : environment) BOOL:
   IF EMPTY (env) THEN
      FALSE
   ELSE IF desi = HEAD (env).desi THEN
      TRUE
   ELSE id_already_declared (desi,
                             TAIL (env))
   FI FI;
```

For the nonterminal ID and the terminal id the attribute desi is identical (TRANSFER desi). ID.desi is a synthesized attribute. If the production r_2 stands for the name of a declared entity in r_1 (ID IS r_1) then we must check whether an identifier with the same designator has already been declared. In such a case the error message from above is generated.

```
RULE r_3 :
   TYPE_SPEC ::= ID
STATIC

   TRANSFER env_in;

   TYPE_SPEC.type :=
      IF ID.desi = int_desi THEN
         int_type
      ELSE IF ID.desi = bool_desi THEN
         bool_type
      ELSE (error_type
            CONDITION FALSE
               MESSAGE
               "the name of a type expected")
      FI FI;

END;
```

The attribute TYPE_SPEC.type is calculated depending on ID.desi. If ID.desi is not the designator of a type (integer, or boolean), then the error value error_type is assigned to TYPE_SPEC.type and an error message is generated.

```
RULE r_4 :
   DECL_S     ::=   DECL   DECL_S
STATIC
   DECL.env_in        := DECL_S[1].env_in;
   DECL_S[2].env_in   := DECL.env_out;
   DECL_S[1].env_out  := DECL_S[2].env_out;
END;
```

The environment is "threaded" through the subtrees: The env_in of the first declaration (DECL) is the same as that of the whole declaration sequence (DECL_S[1]). The env_in of the rest of the declarative sequence (DECL_S[2]) is the env_out of the first declaration(DECL). env_out at the end of the declaration sequence (DECL_S[1]) is identical to the env_out of the tail of the declaration sequence (DECL_S[2]). We show these dependencies in Figure 2.

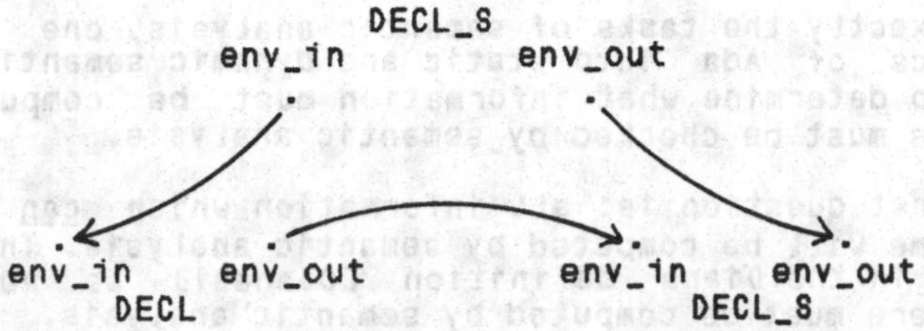

Figure 2: Environment Attribute Dependencies

2. Procedure for the AG

2.1. Semantic Analysis for Ada

In order to determine exactly the tasks of semantic analysis, one has to split the semantics of Ada into static and dynamic semantics. Particularly, we have to determine what information must be computed and which language rules must be checked by semantic analysis.

The strategy for the first question is: all information which can be computed at compile time will be computed by semantic analysis. These decisions are reflected in the Diana definition [Diana81] as well. All attributes given there must be computed by semantic analysis.

The second question is directly answered by the Ada Reference Manual, section 1.6: Any rule that uses the terms "legal", "allowed", "must", "may only" must be checked at compile time, and therefore belongs to the static semantics. Any rule that may lead to the raising of the predefined exceptions CONSTRAINT_ERROR, ..., TASKING_ERROR belongs to the dynamic semantics.

The AG specifies semantic analysis of a single compilation unit. Separate compilation is not described within the AG, rather an already existing separate compilation system [Dau81] is integrated into the front-end. Also the generation of Diana is not formally described (see 2.2).

In some cases the AG additionally checks rules belonging to dynamic semantics, but then only a warning is generated (for example if a task calls an entry of its own).

Many Ada elements with very complicated dynamic semantics possess quite simple static semantics, for example exceptions, tasks etc. On the other hand it was not trivial to describe:

- determination of all properties of newly declared entities
- derived types
- expression analysis (overloading resolution)
- scope and hiding rules
- generics
- machine representation specifications

A comparison with the solutions offered for those problems in the two other formal specifications of Ada static semantics, [FD80] and [Bjoe80], (as far as those problems were attacked in these definitions) proves that the problems are not caused by attribute grammars as a description method, but by the difficulties inherent in the language.

2.2. Diana and the AG

In 1.2. we have already mentioned that the semantic analysis takes a Diana Parse Tree and generates a Diana Tree. This is also reflected in the AG: the syntax of the productions in the AG is a prefix notation of the Diana Parse Tree.

The Diana Tree contains all information which is computed by semantic analysis and passed through this interface to further compiler phases. It differs from the Diana Parse Tree in two points:

- It resolves syntactic ambiguities.
- It contains semantic and code attributes.

Syntactic ambiguities arise from the fact that some syntactic structures cannot be distinguished by a parser without having knowledge about meanings of the structures. E.g. a name followed by an association list can be a function call, a procedure call, an entry call, an indexed expression, a slice or a conversion.

Semantic attributes are used to carry information about the meanings of a Diana structure to other compiler phases. Code attributes (or machine dependent attributes) are introduced in Diana (cf. [Diana81] ch. 3.4.1) to record values of representation attributes which are needed to evaluate static expressions. The code attributes are assumed to be computed by machine dependent modules, see 2.4, they are not further discussed in this book.

Mostly, the semantic attributes of Diana have no direct counterpart in the AG: the attributes calculated by the AG are not in the form required by Diana. This is due to the fact that Diana has tree valued attributes, which are difficult to express in attribute grammars. Therefore the AG does not formally specify their computation, rather it contains comments which indicate the actions to produce the Diana Tree.

The transformation of the Diana Parse Tree into its final form and the computation of semantic attributes are implemented in a special module of the front-end which is called Diana Generation.

2.3. Development of the AG

In order to write an attribute grammar for a language, one must define accurately <u>which</u> language is to be described.

We started with the Reference Manual for Ada [Ada80], the Implementors' Guide [IG80] and the Formal Definition [FD80]. The Implementors' Guide [IG80] gives supplementary explanations and a set of tests with their effect; the Formal Definition [FD] is a denotational-like description of the semantics of the language but it was incomplete at that time.

Some problems still arose during our work, concerning <u>what</u> exactly Ada <u>is</u>. We found out that the Reference Manual was incomplete and even ambiguous in some points. At the same time several discussions and meetings on the semantics of the language took place. We kept track of all development in this field and made our decisions as near to the Reference Manual as possible. Most of these problems have been solved in the course of the Ada Validation Facility. The solutions we suggested were very often accepted.

We first described the static semantics of Ada without consideration of the tasks specific to semantic analysis: error recovery and efficiency. Later on we tried to extend the AG so as to comprise these aspects too. This method proved successful: For example, the attributes at_expected and at_context (cf. 7.5, 7.6) were introduced only in a later stage for the optimization of overloading resolution. Error recovery in the AG was a very bulgy work, nevertheless it could be achieved as an extension of the AG and did not require any "change of philosophy". Thus, the extension from a specification for the static semantics of Ada to a specification for the process of semantic analysis with efficiency and error recovery considerations came out very naturally.

In the course of his Master's thesis J. Uhl wrote the main part of the AG and also a documentation presenting a classification of the concepts of Ada and their representation in the AG [Uhl81]. The AG was then further developed, and it was validated in a careful "walk-through" by a mixed group of people, only some of whom were directly involved in the development of the AG.

An implementation of the AG in Pascal was automatically generated by the GAG-system [KaZi80] and it was tested. For this purpose we used about one thousand test programs. These tests comprise tests written by people directly involved in the development of the AG ("white box" tests), tests written by people not directly involved in the development of the AG ("black box" tests), and all test sets for Ada we were able to get from outside.

The Pascal analyzer generated by GAG takes about 1 MBytes of program storage and it analyzes 5 lines of Ada input per second.

Since this performance was sufficient for our goals (testing) we did not try to improve it any further.

2.4. Completeness and Parametrization of the AG

The AG is complete except for the following two points:

- parametrization with machine dependent modules
- incomplete specifications

Here we discuss the reasons for these points; in AG0.2 of Part C we give the functions of the AG where the specification is incomplete.

Parametrization with machine dependent modules

Although in 1.2 it looks as if the semantic analysis in the Ada front-end were machine-independent, still, due to some properties of Ada, semantic analysis requires some interaction with machine dependent modules:

- some entities from the package STANDARD describing elementary data types and operations available on the target machine
- the target machine arithmetic according to whose accuracy the static expressions must be evaluated
- the storage allocator to determine the representation of data types and objects needed for the calculation of static representation attributes in the program

The fact that semantic analysis requires several pieces of information from machine dependent modules which normally belong to the compiler back-end, is reflected in the AG by several functions and constants which are not completely specified and are marked by: '% >MACHINE<'.

Incomplete Specifications

Some relationships cannot be expressed with an acceptable effort in ALADIN, although their implementation is easily carried out. In these cases the front-end behaves correctly, but the AG is incomplete.

These relationships are:

The generation of arbitrary but unique integer values is allowed in ALADIN only in productions, and not within function bodies.

The comparison of the "structure" of names (i.e. that p.x + p.y is the same as x + y if x and y are declared in a package called p, as needed for the comparison of subprogram specifications) would require a very complicated structure of the 'meaning' attribute. Instead, the AG calls incompletely specified functions, which are completed in the implementation.

The functions which are incompletely specified in the AG are indicated by the comment: '% > INCOMPLETE <'.

2.5. Implementation of the AG in Ada

After all the test programs, among them all those we could get from the Ada Compiler Validation Capability, had passed the generated Pascal version of the analyzer, we started the final implementation of the AG in Ada. The Ada programs are derived from the attribute grammar specification in a systematic manner similar to the automated generation process of the GAG-system. (This ensures that the final semantic analyzer is equivalent to the specification and can easily be maintained together with it. In fact the AG serves as a documentation of the Ada implementation.)

All test programs were input to this front-end as well. The Ada implementation of the AG takes about 700 KByte of program storage. Together with the Diana Generation and connected to the separate compilation system, it builds a separate phase within the front-end. This phase takes about 2.1 MByte of program and data storage. The front-end analyzes 25 lines of Ada per second.

2.6. Adaptability to Ada'82

In contrast to the DoD's first plans, which anticipated that Ada would be standardized by the end of 1980, the language is still undergoing small refinements.

From what we now know about Ada'82, we believe that by some minor changes the AG could be modified so as to describe the semantics for Ada'82. For example, in chapter 3.3 of [Dro82] we describe how the Ada'82 rules about use clauses can be specified (by omitting the attributes at_allowed2 and at_with_use, cf. 7).

Note that independently of the amount of changes, we need not reconsider the attribute evaluation order, because these considerations are not part of the specification, and because an evaluation strategy is automatically computed by the GAG-system.

3. Comparison of the AG with other Attribute Grammars

At our Institute attribute grammars were written for other languages as well. We compare the attribute grammars for Pascal, LIS [LIS78] (a predecessor of Ada with separate compilation and representation specifications, without overloading, tasks and generics) and Pearl [Pearl80] (a very complex language for real time processing), with our AG for Ada:

	Pascal	PEARL	LIS	Ada
input lines	2.600	13600	14500	22000
class of AG	OAG	OAG	OAG	OAG
max. number of visits to symbol from ancestor	4	4	2	4
person-months	4	24	18	18
specification complete	YES	YES	YES	YES
error handling included	YES	NO	NO	YES
specification tested	YES	NO	NO	YES

Table 1: Comparison of Attribute Grammars

Every one of these attribute grammars was developed with its specific purpose:

The Pascal attribute grammar [KAZ81] was developed as an example to demonstrate that efficient analyzers for real life languages can be generated automatically by the GAG-system.

The attribute grammar for Pearl [Pearl80] was developed to serve as the language's standard. Now, this attribute grammar constitutes the official definition of Pearl.

The attribute grammar for LIS was developed in parallel to a compiler front-end for this language with the aim of constituting a formal specification of the static semantics of LIS. During its development several large gaps in the reference manual of LIS were uncovered which were then taken into account in the language's revisions. The specification could be analyzed (with respect to formal correctness and consistency), but it could not be tested, because the GAG-system was not sufficiently developed at this time. Nevertheless the attribute grammar served for the systematic development of the semantic analysis part of the front-end. The experience was absolutely satisfactory, and now the attribute grammar will be tested and completed in order to comprise error handling too.

An important remark from the table above is the small number of visits to a node from its ancestor. This number gives an upper bound for the oscillation process within the tree while calculating attributes. Although the attribute grammars were originally written without any consideration of the resulting number of visits, this number is still low (another indication that specifications should primarily concentrate on the logical properties and consider efficiency only at the end).

We also notice that all attribute grammars are partitionable and not LAG(k) (attributes computable in k left to right passes through the tree). None of these attribute grammars could be easily transformed into an equivalent LAG.

4. Experience with Attribute Grammars

Attribute grammars proved to be a very convenient tool for the specification of semantic analysis.

Because all dependencies are expressed over the attribute dependencies, and nothing is said about passes, tree traversals or function calling hierarchies, changes are very easily made, and the "specifier" concentrates on the concepts of the language reflected in the attributes and does not mix the rules of the language with particularities of his implementation.

The specification proceeded in stages, and during this procedure, new attributes were introduced and the old dependencies became more complicated. E.g. the attribute at_env_in (described in 6.1) was primarily computable during the first visit to a node. Five months later, we introduced the attribute at_user_reps (described in 6.8) in order to specify also the concept of representation specifications given by the programmer. A new situation emerged: at_env_in depends now on at_user_reps; at_user_reps may be calculated during the first, at_env_in during the second visit to a node. This change came quite unexpectedly, through an aspect of Ada which we did not think would have such global impacts on semantic analysis. But, as no decision depended on the visits and evaluation order of the attributes, this new situation did not affect the further procedure of the specification.

After completing a particular phase in the development of the specification we could ensure that the AG was well-defined at this stage. Then we extended and modified it so as to describe more concepts of the language, or improved algorithms. With the help of the GAG-system we could even test the AG in these in-between stages.

Another advantage of using attribute grammars to specify static semantics is that the correctness of the specification can easily be tested at a very early stage of its development. On the one hand attribute grammars are readable and understandable, so that one can ascertain oneself whether it is a correct specification. Several properties of the AG can be checked by the analysis part of the GAG-system. On the other hand the GAG-system generates a semantic analyzer in Pascal automatically from the specification. Various test programs can then be input to the generated analyzer to check its reaction. These results also allow a conclusion about the correctness of the specification.

P A R T B:

R A T I O N A L E F O R T H E A G

Introduction

In Part B we discuss the AG in more detail. In Ch. 5 we describe the tasks and the resulting structure of the AG. In Ch. 6, 7 and 8 we introduce the attributes and methods used for these tasks. In Ch. 9 we outline the types of the attributes.

In the following discussion we often speak of attribute, language elements, entities, syntactic units and shall also use such words as before, after, preceding and following.

The word attribute always means an attribute in the sense of attribute grammars, and whenever we speak of some attribute, we mean the <u>value</u> of this attribute. We sometimes say that attribute at_1 is <u>modified</u> (for example a description in the attribute at_env_in is updated). This means that some other attribute at_2 is evaluated as a modification of the value of at_1.

We use the term Ada attribute, when we mean attributes as defined by Ada.

By language element we mean <u>any</u> part of the Ada input program, for example a declaration, an expression, a discriminant part, a case statement. Note that a language element may be part of another language element, for example an expression may be part of a statement. Entities are used in the sense of the definition in 3.1 in [Ada80], i.e. anything that can be declared or named in a program, for example objects, subprograms, generic packages, labels. Syntactic unit is any syntactically bracketed form in an Ada program, for example a discriminant part, a record type, a body, a block, an accept statement, a case statement.

The words before, after, preceding and following (in conjunction with the Ada input program) are used in the sense of <u>textual</u> precedence or succession. (In Ada the textual order is very important, for example identifiers may not be used before their declaration, representation specifications may not be given after the use of some Ada representation attribute.)

In order to illustrate the methods, we show parts of the AG and explain the intention. We mainly show the attribution rules and the type definitions, because we consider these parts as the more important ones. We also describe in short the effect of some functions, but do not go into particulars about constant declarations, attribute declarations or function bodies.

As the values of attributes depend on many aspects (cf. the attribute at_allowed1 in 7.1, 7.5, 7.6, 8.5.3), sometimes a lot of function calls and parameters appear in the attribution rule of one attribute in the AG. In the examples given in this rationale we only show those parts of the attribution rules reflecting the aspects, which are important for the subject currently discussed, and we omit the remainder. These omissions are denoted by "...". The complete specification can be found in Part C. Syntactic productions (with some attribution rules) are referenced by the rule number. Functions are ordered alphabetically.

In Appendix A1 we give a short description of the meaning of the attributes of the AG. (The meaning of the functions can be deduced from the comments preceding the function bodies in AG6, part C.) In Appendix A2 we list the occurrences of the attributes in this rationale.

For readability reasons naming conventions are used within the AG. Attributes start with "at_", types start with "tp_", functions start with "f_", "cf_" or "ch_", constants start with "c_", scalars start with "sc_" and the components of a struct (record) type have the prefix "s_" (cf. AG0.1).

5. Overall Structure of the AG

5.1. Main Semantic Tasks

The semantic analysis of our front-end must:

- check the consistency of the source program with the definition of the language and give appropriate messages for illegal input

- inform subsequent compiler phases about the meaning of the components of the program, i.e. generate the Diana tree with the semantic attributes as described in the Diana definition

In Ada, as in most other high level programming languages, the programmer can:

- declare some entity

- use some entity

Consequently, information is collected by:

- elaboration of declarations:

  For every declaration all information about the declared entity must be collected and kept, in order to be used when the entity appears in some other place.

- analysis of names and expressions:

  The entities are always used in the form of a name, possibly within an expression. The semantic analysis must determine which entity is meant, taking into account all rules about visibility, overloading, etc.

In the following we shall discuss the three tasks of semantic analysis within the AG:

- declaration elaboration

- name and expression analysis

- semantic checks

In attribute grammars, information is contained in attributes. The semantic tasks described above evaluate some attribute by using other attributes; some of the attributes used are evaluated by other semantic tasks. We may say that the semantic tasks communicate via attributes.

In the following figure we show the dependencies between the semantic tasks and the attributes which build their interfaces. The attributes appearing in this figure (and all remaining of the AG as well) will be briefly introduced in 5.2, and discussed in more detail in 6 to 9.

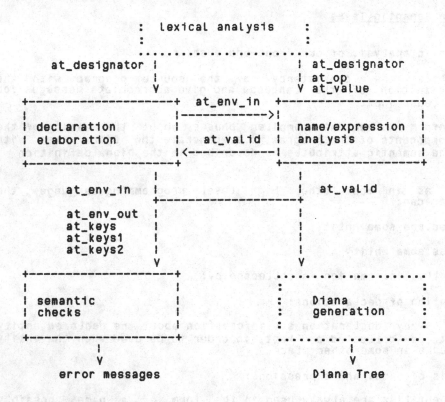

```
                    : lexical analysis       :
                    :                        :
                    ..........................
     at_designator  |                        | at_designator
                    |                        | at_op
                    V                        V at_value
  +-------------------+  at_env_in  +-------------------+
  |                   |------------>|                   |
  | declaration       |             | name/expression   |
  | elaboration       |  at_valid   | analysis          |
  |                   |<------------|                   |
  +-------------------+             +-------------------+
                    |                        |
        at_env_in   |                        | at_valid
                    +------------------------+
        at_env_out  |                        |
        at_keys     |                        |
        at_keys1    |                        |
        at_keys2    |                        |
                    V                        V
  +-------------------+             .....................
  |                   |             :                   :
  | semantic          |             :  Diana            :
  | checks            |             :  generation       :
  |                   |             :                   :
  +-------------------+             .....................
           |                                 |
           V                                 V
     error messages                     Diana Tree
```

The semantic checks use the attributes at_env_in, at_env_out, at_keys1, at_keys2 and at_keys which are calculated by declaration elaboration and the attribute at_valid which is calculated by name and expression analysis. The Diana Generation uses at_env_in from declaration elaboration and at_valid from name and expression analysis.

The above figure reflects the structure of the AG: Lexical analysis does not belong to the AG (at_designator, at_op and at_value are intrinsic attributes). The Diana Generation (as pointed out in 2.1) does not belong to the AG either.

5.2. Classes of Attributes

Various language elements possess properties of the same kind (as for example a selected component or a name followed by an association list both possess the property meaning). This is expressed in the AG by the naming of the attributes, as for instance, at_valid, at_env_in are attributes of EXP, APPLY, GENERAL_ASSOCS :

```
NONTERM EXP            :  at_env_in   : tp_env,
                          at_valid    : tp_descr_set ,
          ...

NONTERM APPLY          :  at_env_in   : tp_env,
                          at_valid    :tp_descr_set,
          ...

NONTERM GENERAL_ASSOCS :  at_env_in   : tp_env,
                          at_valid    : tp_assoc_list,
          ...
```

The type of the identically named attributes may differ, as for example the attribute APPLY.at_valid and the attribute GENERAL_ASSOCS.at_valid have different types, but, nevertheless, they both express the meaning (after the completion of overloading resolution) of the subexpression (of APPLY, or GENERAL_ASSOCS respectively).

In the sections 6. to 9. we introduce the attributes of the AG, discuss their meaning, their interdependencies and their types. In Appendix A1 we shortly outline the meaning of each attribute and indicate the semantic task the attribute belongs to and its use (output or internal). According to the semantic task in which the attributes are involved and whether they are output by lexical analysis or only used for the transfer of information computed by other semantic tasks, the attributes are classified as follows:

Lexical Analysis

Output : at_designator, at_op, at_value

The attributes at_designator, at_op and at_value denote an identifier, an operator of Ada or a value. They are provided by lexical analysis. They are intrinsic attributes.

Declaration Elaboration

Input : at_designator, at_valid

Internal : at_env,
at_labels, at_loops_blocks,
at_pos, at_char,
at_impl_descrs, at_impl_subprs,
at_user_rep, at_user_reps

Output : at_env_in, at_env_out, at_keys, at_keys1, at_keys2

Name_and_Expression_Analysis

```
Input    : at_env_in, at_designator, at_op, at_value

Internal : at_context,
           at_expected,
           at_allowed1, at_with_use, at_allowed2,
           at_expected_in, at_expected_out

Output   : at_valid
```

Semantic_Checks

```
Input    : at_env_in, at_env_out, at_keys, at_keys1, at_keys2,
           at_valid

Internal : at_first_select, at_select_state,
           at_is_exp, at_init,
           at_others_allowed,
           at_empty,
           at_is_last,
           at_is_item,
           at_unconstrained,
           at_has_range,
           at_positional_allowed,
           at_return_required,
           at_encl_unit,
           at_usable,
           at_block_no,
           at_is_operator, at_param_no,
           at_no_decls, at_no_code_stms,
           at_first_stm
           at_discrim_allowed
Output   : none
```

Semantic checks do not calculate information necessary for other semantic tasks. They generate error messages if the Ada program is illegal. Therefore they do not deliver any output attributes. The internal attributes for the semantic checks contain information only about the structure of a language element without considering its meaning.

<u>Information Transfer</u>

Input : at_valid, at_designator, at_keys

Internal : none

Output : at_designators,
at_def,
at_comp, at_comps, at_discriminants,
at_variant, at_variants, at_type, at_dscrt_ranges,
at_names, at_choices, at_assoc, at_assocs,
at_header, at_spec, at_rename,
at_instantiation,
at_rep, at_reps

The last class comprises those attributes, that do not contain any new information. They simply transfer the information from one place of the tree (where it is computed by some semantic task) to another place of the tree (where it is used by some semantic task). The values of these attributes are used by the three main semantic tasks. But as their evaluation is trivial, we did not mention them in the preceding figure, and we will not discuss them any further.

6. Declaration Elaboration

Declaration elaboration has to collect all information offered in a declaration and to keep it until it is needed for name and expression analysis. In other words, declaration elaboration transfers information from the defining to the applied occurrence of an entity.

The environment contains for every declared entity one description with all its static properties. It also reflects the block structure and visibility rules, so that identification can be achieved (by the corresponding functions) according to the visibility rules of Ada.

We sometimes distinguish between the declarations before the current position (at_env_in, 6.1), after the current position (at_env_out, 6.1) and an intermediate environment attribute (at_env, 6.3). In Ada the complete definition of an entity may proceed through several (textually separated) declarations. A declaration either introduces a new entity, or it gives supplementary information about an entity which was previously introduced. The keys attribute (at_keys, 6.2) denotes the entities meant in the current declaration. Entities are represented by their descriptions. We may, therefore, as well say that the keys k1 denote the descriptions d1, meaning that k1 denote the entities which are represented by the descriptions d1. The new environment (at_env_out) is generated from the old environment (at_env_in) either by adding new descriptions (when the declaration introduces new entities) or by modifying an old description (when the declaration gives additional information about old ones). The descriptions which are added/modified are denoted by at_keys. In subprogram bodies we determine to which specification the body belongs in two stages, therefore we have two keys attributes (at_keys1, at_keys2, 6.3).

Some elements of Ada induce implicit declarations. Label, loop or block names are implicitly declared at the end of the declarative part of the enclosing block or body, numeric and derived type definitions may cause an implicit type declaration, derived type definitions in addition cause the derivation of subprograms. declaration of the instantiated entity. Descriptions for these entities are kept in attributes (at_labels and at_loops_blocks in 6.4, at_impl_descrs in 6.6, at_impl_subprs in 6.7) and are entered in the environment.

Semantic analysis must sometimes know about the machine representation of an entity. Machine representation may not be calculated before the last representation specification which affects the representation of this entity has been analyzed. An attribute (at_user_reps, 6.8) indicates the entities for which representation specifications follow in the program. Depending on this attribute the machine representation of an entity may be calculated or not.

In the remainder of this chapter we discuss the attributes used in declaration elaboration in more detail.

6.1. at_env_in, at_env_out

The purpose of declaration elaboration is to collect all information necessary for name and expression analysis. The environment attribute holds a single description for each entity which is declared so far and whose scope encloses the current position. It also contains the necessary information to support the identification according to the visibility rules. The environment is used in identification (cf. r_123 in 7.1), overloading resolution (cf. r_125 in 7.1 and 7.2) and all kinds of checks.

Each nonterminal (except DESIGNATOR and ID) possesses an inherited environment attribute (at_env_in), with the information about all preceding declarations in whose scope the nonterminal lies. In the case of names, expressions and statements, (where no new entities are introduced) the environment is passed over unchanged to the next language element:

```
RULE r_084
   APPLY ::= apply NAME GENERAL_ASSOCS
STATIC
   TRANSFER at_env_in;
```

In all places where an entity may be declared or new information is given about a previously declared entity, a new environment attribute at_env_out is evaluated from at_env_in.

```
RULE   r_016 :
   DECL                 ::= subtype ID CONSTRAINED
STATIC

   CONSTRAINED.at_env_in :=
                 ... (  ...
                        DECL.at_env_in );

   DECL.at_env_out         :=
                 ... (  ...
                        CONSTRAINED.at_type    ,
                        CONSTRAINED.at_env_in );
```

The new environment (at_env_out) contains the description of the new entity in addition to all descriptions from the old environment (at_env_in). It is passed to the remaining declarative sequence:

```
RULE   r_021 :
   DECLS                ::= DECL  DECLS
STATIC
   DECL.at_env_in        := DECLS[1].at_env_in;
   DECLS[2].at_env_in    := DECL.at_env_out;
   DECLS[1].at_env_out   := DECLS[2].at_env_out;
```

These dependencies are shown in the following figure:

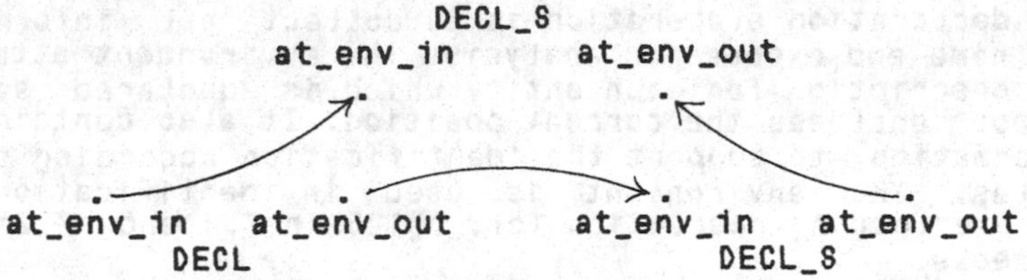

The new environments are evaluated similarly for discriminants (r_075), variants (r_079), declarations and representation specifications (r_021), and for declarative items (r_048).

Use clauses affect the visibility of identifiers, and therefore affect the environment:

```
RULE   r_197 :
  USE                   ::= use   NAMES
STATIC
  USE.at_env_out := f_add_imported_descrs
                        ( ...
                          NAMES.at_names,
                          USE.at_env_in );
```

Sometimes, the information about all entities from a declarative part (at_env_out) is used for some other attribute:

```
RULE   r_171 :
  HEADER                ::= procedure PARAM_S
STATIC
  HEADER.at_header   := tp_procedure (... PARAM_S.at_env_out);
```

The block structure of an Ada program influences identification and hiding. Therefore, it must be reflected in the environment attribute. We must know the syntactic unit enclosing the current position in the Ada program. We must also know in which part of this unit we are (for example in the declarative part, in the statements or in an exception handler of a block, in the discriminant part or in the components of a record type):

```
RULE   r_057 :
  TYPE_DECL             ::= type ID VAR_DECL_S TYPE_SPEC
STATIC
  VAR_DECL_S.at_env_in := f_empty_local_encl_state
                            ( ...
                              TYPE_DECL.at_keys,
                              sc_in_discr_part,
                              ID.at_env_in);
```

f_empty_local_state creates a new declarative part for the discriminants and it registers the type (denoted by TYPE_DECL.at_keys) as the enclosing unit. It also registers that we are in the discriminant part (sc_in_discr_part).

In package specifications (r_176), subprogram headers (r_190), generic parts (r_245), analogous considerations apply.

In several cases in Ada visibility of identifiers stretches over textually separated areas. In package, subprogram and task bodies all entities from the specification (and the generic parameters, if it was a generic package or subprogram) are directly visible. Therefore in the AG, the environment at the beginning of a body is supplemented by all declarations from the specification (and possibly by the generic parameters).

```
RULE   r_141 :
   BLOCK_STUB          ::= BLOCK
STATIC
   BLOCK.at_env_in :=  ...
      f_new_local
        (f_make_local
          ( ...
             BLOCK_STUB.at_keys,
             BLOCK_STUB.at_env_in) );
```

BLOCK_STUB.at_keys refers to the corresponding package specification (cf. 6.2). The function f_make_local returns the descriptions of the generic parameters (if the package specification was a generic) and the descriptions of the entities declared in the visible and private part of the package specification. The function f_new_local opens a new declarative part in which it enters the descriptions returned by f_make_local.

The entries from a task specification must be visible in the task body (r_212).

6.2. at_keys

In Ada the declaration of some entity may take place in several (textually separated) stages. First, an entity is introduced (e.g. private type declaration, subprogram specification) and its definition may be later completed with additional information (e.g. full type declaration, subprogram body).

Accordingly, in the AG a description is introduced in the environment and later on, when the declaration is completed, the description for this entity is updated with the additional information. The attribute at_keys denotes the entities which are introduced or whose definitions are completed by the current declaration.

We must distinguish three cases when elaborating a declaration. First, it follows from the syntax that a new entity is introduced, for example in package specifications. Second it follows from the syntax or the designator of the declaration that additional information is provided for some already introduced entity, for example in package bodies (syntax) or constant declarations (designator). In the third, and most difficult case, it can be decided only after analysis of the declaration whether it introduces a new entity or it provides additional information for a previously introduced one, for example in subprogram bodies. In the remainder of 6.2 we discuss the first and the second case, whereas in 6.3 we explain the third case.

```
RULE r_173:
  PACKAGE_DECL ::= package_decl ID PACKAGE_DEF
STATIC
  PACKAGE_DECL.at_keys := f_gen_keys ;
     % f_gen_keys is a function generating a new key

  PACKAGE_DEF.at_env_in := f_add_descr
                               ( ...
                                ID.at_designator,
                                PACKAGE_DECL.at_keys ,
                                sc_package,
                                PACKAGE_DECL.at_env_in)
```

A package specification always introduces a new package, therefore, at_keys is a new key (f_gen_key), i.e. no description denoted by PACKAGE_DECL.at_keys exists in PACKAGE_DECL.at_env_in. The environment for PACKAGE_DEF contains all previous declarative information (from PACKAGE_DEF.at_env_in) and in addition a new description of a package (sc_package) with the designator ID.at_designator (f_add_descr). PACKAGE_DECL.at_keys denotes this new description.

Component declarations (r_004), number declarations (r_015), variable declarations (r_073), subprogram specifications (r_190), task specifications (r_211), parameter declarations (r_179 - r_181) always introduce one or more new entities. In these cases too, at_keys contains as many new keys as new entities are introduced (object, number, component and parameter declarations may introduce more than one entity) and at_env_out has the value of at_env_in augmented by the new descriptions denoted by at_keys.

In the following figure we visualize the attribute dependencies for a package specification:

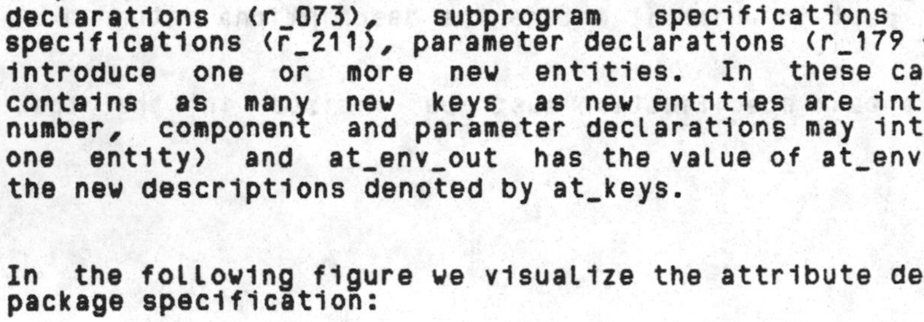

```
RULE  r_178  :
  PACKAGE_BODY  ::=  package_body  ID  BLOCK_STUB
STATIC
  PACKAGE_BODY.at_keys := f_prev_defs
                          ( ...
                          ID.designator,
                          sc_package,
                          PACKAGE_BODY.at_env_in);
  BLOCK_STUB.at_env_in := f_update_add_descrs
                          ( ...
                          PACKAGE_BODY.at_keys,
                          ID.designator,
                          PACKAGE_BODY.at_env_in);
  PACKAGE_BODY.at_env_out := f_mark_body_prov
                             (PACKAGE_BODY.at_keys,
                              BLOCK_STUB.at_env_in);
```

If the package body is preceded by a corresponding package specification, then PACKAGE_BODY.at_keys denotes the corresponding description in the environment (PACKAGE_BODY.at_env_in), otherwise it denotes a new description (f_prev_defs). BLOCK_STUB.at_env_in is evaluated from PACKAGE_BODY.at_env_in in the first case by updating the description of the package (denoted by PACKAGE_BODY.at_keys), in the second case by entering a new description denoted by PACKAGE_BODY.at_keys (f_update_add_descrs). In PACKAGE_BODY.at_env_out we indicate that a body has been given for the package denoted by PACKAGE_BODY.at_keys (f_mark_body_prov).

Constant declarations (r_014), type declarations (r_057), subprogram bodies (r_195), task bodies (r_212) either introduce one or more new entities, or complete previous declarations. In these cases (as in package bodies discussed above), the attribute at_keys is calculated by searching in at_env_in for entities with the same identifier and of the same nature. If such an entity is found, then this one is updated, else a new description is added to the environment.

In the following figure we show the attribute dependencies for package bodies (r_178, r_141):

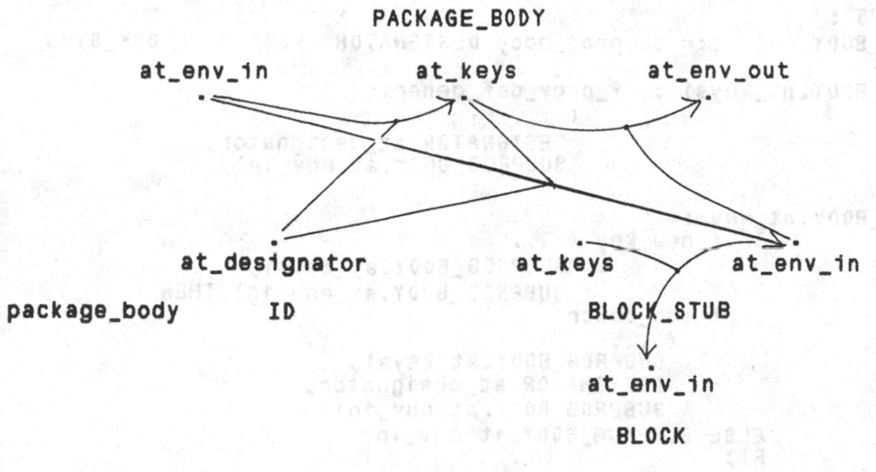

6.3. at_keys1, at_keys2, at_env

In the case of subprogram bodies the determination of the corresponding subprogram specification is more difficult because of the possibility of subprogram overloading. We can decide whether the subprogram body is the body of a generic subprogram by comparing the subprogram designators (because generic subprograms cannot be overloaded). However, in order to decide whether it is the body of a non generic subprogram, we must compare the headers (i.e. formal parts and the result). As a consequence, the decision about which specification the subprogram belongs to, is based upon the information from the analysis of the HEADER. However, if the subprogram body corresponds to a generic subprogram specification, then the environment of the HEADER must also contain all the generic parameters. Therefore, the decision about which specification the body belongs to, is split into two stages: SUBPROG_BODY possesses two key attributes, SUBPROG_BODY.at_keys1 denotes the corresponding generic specification, if any. SUBPROG_BODY.at_keys2 denotes the corresponding subprogram specification (generic or not), if any.

In the following discussion, we use the term: k1 is a new key in environment env1, meaning that a description for the subprogram denoted by k1 is not contained in the environment env1. Assume that S is the subprogram whom the body belongs to.

If S has a previous generic subprogram specification, then:
- SUBPROG_BODY.at_keys1 is an old key in SUBPROG_BODY.at_env_in
- SUBPROG_BODY.at_keys1 = SUBPROG_BODY.at_keys2

If S has a previous non generic subprogram specification, then:
- SUBPROG_BODY.at_keys1 is a new key in SUBPROG_BODY.at_env_in
- SUBPROG_BODY.at_keys2 =/ SUBPROG_BODY.at_keys1
- SUBPROG_BODY.at_keys2 is an old key in SUBPROG_BODY.at_env_in

If S has no previous subprogram specification, then:
- SUBPROG_BODY.at_keys1 is a new key in SUBPROG_BODY.at_env_in
- SUBPROG_BODY.at_keys2 = SUBPROG_BODY.at_keys1

Let us now consider the attribution rules for these attributes (at_env is an auxiliary attribute):

```
RULE   r_195 :
   SUBPROG_BODY      ::= subprog_body DESIGNATOR  HEADER  BLOCK_STUB
STATIC
   SUBPROG_BODY.at_keys1 := f_prev_def_generic
                              ( ...
                               DESIGNATOR.at_designator,
                               SUBPROG_BODY.at_env_in);

   SUBPROG_BODY.at_env :=
                 IF f_new_key ( ...
                               SUBPROG_BODY.at_keys1,
                               SUBPROG_BODY.at_env_in) THEN
                    f_add_descr
                       ( ...
                        SUBPROG_BODY.at_keys1,
                        DESIGNATOR.at_designator,
                        SUBPROG_BODY.at_env_in)
                 ELSE SUBPROG_BODY.at_env_in
                 FI;
```

```
HEADER.at_env_in :=  f_new_local
                        (f_make_local1
                            ( ...
                              SUBPROG_BODY.at_keys1,
                              SUBPROG_BODY.at_env_in),
                          SUBPROG_BODY.at_keys1,
                          SUBPROG_BODY.at_env);

SUBPROG_BODY.at_keys2 :=
         IF f_new_key ( ...
                          SUBPROG_BODY.at_keys1,
                          SUBPROG_BODY.at_env_in) THEN
            f_prev_def_subpr
               ( ...
                 DESIGNATOR.at_designator,
                 HEADER.at_header,
                 SUBPROG_BODY.at_env_in)
         ELSE SUBPROG_BODY.at_keys1
         FI;

BLOCK_STUB.at_env_in :=
     IF f_new_key ( ...
                      SUBPROG_BODY.at_keys1,
                      SUBPROG_BODY.at_env_in) THEN
        f_add_local_descrs
           (...
            DESIGNATOR.at_designator,
            SUBPROG_BODY.at_keys2,
            HEADER.at_header,
            SUBPROG_BODY.at_env_in)
     ELSE f_update_descrs_by_keys
             ( ...,
              SUBPROG_BODY.at_keys2,
              sc_in_body,
              SUBPROG_BODY.at_env_in)
     FI;

BLOCK_STUB.at_keys := SUBPROG_BODY.at_keys2;

SUBPROG_BODY.at_env_out :=
       f_update_descrs_by_keys
          ( ...,
           SUBPROG_BODY.at_keys2,
           sc_complete,
           BLOCK_STUB,at_env_in);
```

If S is a generic subprogram, (i.e. a generic subprogram specification with the same identifier as ID.at_designator precedes the current position) then SUBPROG_BODY.at_keys1 denotes the generic specification. Otherwise SUBPROG_BODY.at_keys1 is a new key (f_prev_def_generic). In the first case SUBPROG_BODY.at_env is identical to SUBPROG_BODY.at_env_in, in the second case it contains in addition to the descriptions from SUBPROG_BODY.at_env_in a new description for S denoted by SUBPROG_BODY.at_keys1 (f_add_descr). HEADER.at_env_in has a new declarative part enclosed in S. This declarative part already contains the generic parameters of S, if any. The function f_make_local1 returns the (possibly empty) list of generic parameters. f_local opens a new declarative part enclosed by S (SUBPROG_BODY.at_keys1) and containing any generic parameters (from f_make_local1). If S is a generic subprogram, then SUBPROG_BODY.at_keys1 and SUBPROG_BODY.at_keys2 are identical. If S is not a generic subprogram, (i.e. SUBPROG_BODY.at_keys1 is a new key), then it is either a non generic subprogram for which a specification and no body is previously given, or it is a new subprogram. The function f_prev_def_subpr searches the previous declarations (in SUBPROG_BODY.at_env_in) for a specification with the same header (HEADER.at_header) and the same designator (DESIGNATOR.at_designator). If no such subprogram exists, then SUBPROG_BODY.at_keys2 is a new key. Accordingly, BLOCK_STUB.at_env_in is evaluated either by updating (f_update_descrs_by_keys) the old description for S in SUBPROG_BODY.at_env_in (the one denoted by SUBPROG_BODY.at_keys2) or by adding (f_add_local_descrs) a new description for S (also denoted by SUBPROG_BODY.at_keys2). In SUBPROG_BODY.at_env_out the fact that a body for S has been given is indicated in the description denoted by SUBPROG_BODY.at_keys2 (f_update_descrs_by_keys).

6.4. at_labels, at_loops_blocks

The labels of an Ada program are implicitly declared at the end of the declarative part of the innermost enclosing subprogram, task or package body. The loop and block identifiers are implicitly declared at the end of the declarative part of the innermost enclosing block or body. Therefore, we keep two attributes: at_labels contains all label identifiers appearing in the same body. at_loops_blocks contains all loop and block identifiers appearing in the same block, together with the information about whether it is a block or a loop (r_159).

```
RULE   r_157
   STM      ::=  labeled   ID    STM
STATIC

   STM[1].at_labels ::= ... ( ... ID.at_designator )
                             + STM[2].at_labels ;
```

Labels must be carried to the innermost enclosing body, whereas block and loop names need only be carried to the innermost block or body:

```
RULE   r_151
   STM     ::=  BLOCK
STATIC
   TRANSFER at_labels;

   STM.at_loops_blocks := c_no_bl_lab_loops;
```

The descriptions for the loop and block identifiers are entered in the environment as soon as a nonterminal BLOCK is encountered The descriptions for the labels are entered in the environment only if BLOCK belongs to a subprogram, package or task body, but not if BLOCK is a STM (r_151 where at_context = sc_block). The function f_declare_implicit adds to the environment one description for each one of the labels, blocks or loops, and marks in these descriptions that their declaration was an implicit one (cf. s_state in 9.2.1.4).

```
RULE   r_140 :
   BLOCK ::= block ITEM_S  STM_S  ALTERNATIVE_S
STATIC
   STM_S.at_env_in :=
         f_declare_implicit
            ( ...
            IF BLOCK.at_context = sc_stm THEN
               BLOCK.at_loops_blocks
            ELSE BLOCK.at_loops_blocks + BLOCK.at_labels
            FI,
            ITEM_S.at_env_out);
```

6.5. at_pos, at_char

The position of an enumeration literal within its enumeration type declaration is important for the calculation of some Ada attributes (like SUCC, PRED). The attribute at_pos indicates this position.

If enumeration types contain character literals, then strings may be built over the character literals of those types. The attribute at_char indicates whether an enumeration literal list contains any characters:

```
RULE   r_036 :
   ENUM_LITERAL          ::= id

RULE   r_037 :
   ENUM_LITERAL          ::= char

RULE   r_038 :
   ENUM_LITERALS         ::= ENUM_LITERAL ENUM_LITERALS
STATIC
   ENUM_LITERALS[2].at_pos  := ENUM_LITERALS[1].at_pos + 1;
   ENUM_LITERALS[1].at_char := ENUM_LITERALS[2].at_char OR
                               (ENUM_LITERAL IS r_037);
```

6.6. at_impl_descrs

In Ada some type declarations implicitly introduce other types, cf. [Ada80] 3.3 : "The declaration of ... derived types, numeric types and array types has the effect of specifying a constraint for a type defined by an underlying unconstrained type definition. The identifier introduced by a type declaration containing such a type definition is the name of a subtype of the (anonymous) unconstrained type." Also, enumeration type declarations, besides introducing a type also introduce the enumeration literals.

Implicitly declared types and enumeration literals are described by the attribute at_impl_descrs and entered in the environment.

In type declarations a new key is generated for the description of the anonymous implicitly declared type (if the type definition is a constrained array, a float or integer type, or a derived type with a constraint):

```
RULE   r_057 :
   TYPE_DECL  ::=  type  ID  VAR_DECL_S  TYPE_SPEC
STATIC
   TYPE_SPEC.at_keys := CASE TYPE_SPEC OF
                        r_061 : r_062 : r_065 : r_066 : f_gen_keys
                        OUT TYPE_DECL.at_keys
                        ESAC;
```

The new description in at_impl_descrs is denoted by TYPE_SPEC.at_keys:

```
RULE   r_066 :
   TYPE_SPEC          ::= integer RANGE
STATIC
   TYPE_SPEC.at_impl_descrs :=
           ...          ( ...
                          sc_anonymous,
                          TYPE_SPEC.at_keys,
                          ...,
                          tp_derived
                             (f_valid_predef_int
                                 ( RANGE.at_valid,
                                   TYPE_SPEC.at_env_in))
   TYPE_SPEC.at_type := tp_constrained
                           ( ...
                            TYPE_SPEC.at_keys,
                            RANGE.at_valid);
```

TYPE_SPEC.at_impl_descrs contains the description of an anonymous type derived from an INTEGER type from the package STANDARD; this type is determined by f_valid_predef_int so that it contains the values given in the range (RANGE.at_valid). The type described by TYPE_SPEC.at_type is a subtype of this anonymous type (denoted by TYPE_SPEC.at_keys), it is constrained by the given range (RANGE.at_valid), and is denoted by TYPE_DECL.at_keys.

Similar attribution rules apply for array (r_061), derived (r_062) and float (r_065) types.

For a type declaration (r_057) we distinguish three cases :
- the declaration introduces a new type
- the declaration completes a previously declared (incomplete or private) type and
- the declaration introduces an implicitly declared type of which the completed type is a subtype.

The first and second case are described above. The third case causes complications, especially for private types : The description of the private type can neither be completed by the subtype description nor by that of the implicit base type. The first solution is invalid because type referencing keys always refer to a base type. The second solution does not imply the constraint of the private type to objects of this type declared previous to the completion or to other entities refering to the private type (subtypes, derived types, access types, ...).

The solution of the problem is, to complete the private type description with the implicitly declared base type and to adjust all references of the private type to the newly implied constraint (f_adjust_local_env).

The same problem arises for instantiations if a constrained actual type is associated to an (unconstrained) formal type. It is solved by using the same method as for private and incomplete types (cf. f_adjust_generics and 7.7).

An enumeration type declaration introduces the enumeration type and also the enumeration literals. The descriptions of the enumeration literals are also collected in at_impl_descrs:

```
RULE   r_038 :
   ENUM_LITERALS      ::= ENUM_LITERAL ENUM_LITERALS
STATIC
   ENUM_LITERALS[1].at_impl_descrs :=
                  ...   ( ...
                          ENUM_LITERAL.at_designator,
                          tp_enum_literal
                            ( ...
                              ENUM_LITERALS[1].at_pos
                            ) +
                ENUM_LITERALS[2].at_impl_descrs;


RULE   r_063 :
   TYPE_SPEC          ::= enum_literal_s ENUM_LITERALS
STATIC
   TYPE_SPEC.at_impl_descrs:= ENUM_LITERALS.at_impl_descrs;
```

All the implicit descriptions are entered in the environment (cf. r_057 in 6.7, and r_073 for the implicit array type declarations which are possible in variable declarations).

6.7. at_impl_subprs

Derived type declarations may implicitly introduce new subprograms (cf. [Ada80] chapter 3.4). The descriptions for those subprograms are contained in the attribute at_impl_subprs:

```
RULE   r_057 :
   TYPE_DECL           ::= type ID VAR_DECL_S  TYPE_SPEC
STATIC
   TYPE_SPEC.at_impl_subprs :=
      ...
         IF NOT (TYPE_SPEC IS r_062) THEN % derived type
            c_empty_descrs
         ELSE f_impl_subprs
               ( ...
                  TYPE_SPEC.at_keys,
                  TYPE_SPEC.at_impl_descrs,
                  TYPE_DECL.at_env_in)
         FI
```

(In contrast to other attributes which are used in further productions besides the one in which they are calculated, the attribute at_impl_subprs is local to r_057.)

The descriptions of all implicitly declared types, enumeration literals and subprograms are entered in the environment:

```
RULE   r_057 :
   TYPE_DECL           ::= type ID VAR_DECL_S  TYPE_SPEC
STATIC
   TYPE_DECL.at_env_out :=
      f_add_local_descrs
         ( ...
           TYPE_SPEC.at_impl_subprs,
           f_add_local_descrs(
              TYPE_SPEC.at_impl_descrs,
              TYPE_SPEC.at_env_in      ));
```

6.8. at_user_reps

An Ada program may contain representation specifications for types, which the compiler must take into account for the mapping into the machine representations (type mapping). The program may also contain Ada representation attributes (for example SIZE) which may even have static values. No representation specification for a type may appear after an Ada representation attribute of an entity whose representation depends on the representation of this type.

The AG, therefore calls the functions for the type mapping for all entities for which representation specifications or Ada representation attributes appear. It also checks that no Ada representation attribute or specification for an entity e1 appears before a representation specification for an entity e2, if the representation of e1 depends on the representation of e2.

For the type mapping the AG must call machine dependend functions (cf. 2.4). These functions in particular deliver the values for the Ada representation attributes (if they are static) and check whether the representation specifications are consistent with the type declarations. (For example that the value given in SIZE is not too small, etc.)

The attribute at_user_reps denotes the types for which representation specifications are given at some later point of the Ada program. The representation of a type may be calculated only if this type does not depend on any type denoted in the attribute at_user_reps.

```
RULE    r_057 :
   TYPE_DECL            ::= type VAR_DECL_S TYPE_SPEC
STATIC
   TYPE_DECL.at_env_out :=
        ...
        f_update_repr
           ( ...
            TYPE_DECL.at_keys,
            INCLUDING DECL.at_user_reps,
            TYPE_SPEC.at_env_in);
```

The function f_update_repr compares the currently declared type with the types from DECL.at_user_reps and thus knows whether a representation specification for this type exists later on in the program. In this case, it marks the representation part of the description, so that no reference may be made to it by any representation attribute (cf. in 9.2.1.3 the component s_repr and the type tp_repr_state).

When the last representation specification of a type is analyzed, the machine representation for this type (and any type depending on this type) is calculated, according to all given representation specifications. If the representation specification is not the last one, then the information about this specification must be entered into the description of the type.

```
RULE   r_266 :
   REP        ::= record_rep  NAME  EXP_VOID  COMP_REP_S
STATIC
   REP.at_env_out :=
        ...
        f_calculate_repr
           (NAME.at_valid,
            f_update_repr
               (NAME.at_valid,
                REP.at_user_reps,
                f_enter_rep
                   (NAME.at_valid,
                    COMP_REP_S.at_reps,
                    REP.at_env_in)));
```

The function f_enter_rep adds the representation information (COMP_REP_S.at_reps) to the description of the record type given by NAME.at_valid. f_update_repr compares this type with the types used in later representation specifications (REP.at_user_reps) and thus finds out whether further representation specifications for this type follow. If this is not the case, f_calculate_repr computes the machine representation for this type (if it does not depend on other types for which representation specifications follow) and also for all entities depending on it (if those entities themselves do not depend on further types for which representation specifications follow in the program).

When an Ada representation attribute appears in the program, then the machine representations of all types on which the Ada attribute depends, is calculated. If this Ada attribute depends on a type with a representation specification following (f_new_repr_state), then an error message is generated:

```
RULE   r_122 :
   NAME                 ::= attribute NAME ID
STATIC
   CONDITION
   ...
   IF f_is_repr_attribute (ID.at_designator) THEN
      CASE f_new_repr_state
              (NAME[2].at_valid ,
               f_calculate_repr
                  (NAME[2].at_valid,
                   NAME[1].at_env_in)) OF
      ...
      sc_user_rep : FALSE
      OUT TRUE
      ESAC
   ELSE TRUE
   FI
      MESSAGE
      "repr attribute conflicts with later repr specification";
```

6.9. at_user_rep

at_user_reps is a synthesized attribute and its value is transmitted from the end to the beginning of every declarative part. At every representation specification the identifier of the type is registered in the attribute at_user_rep:

```
RULE   r_265 :
   REP                  ::= simple_rep NAME EXP
STATIC
   REP.at_user_rep := NAME.at_user_rep;
```

Compare also r_266, for record type representations.

All these type names must be known by the type declarations preceding the representation specifications.

```
RULE   r_048 :
   ITEMS                ::= ITEM ITEMS
STATIC
   ITEMS[1].at_user_reps := ITEMS[2].at_user_reps +
                            ITEM.at_user_rep    ;
   ITEM.at_user_reps     := ITEMS[2].at_user_reps ;
```

The same applies for representation specifications or declarations (r_023 - r_026).

The dependencies of the rules r_048, r_049, r_042, and r_043 are illustrated in the following figure:

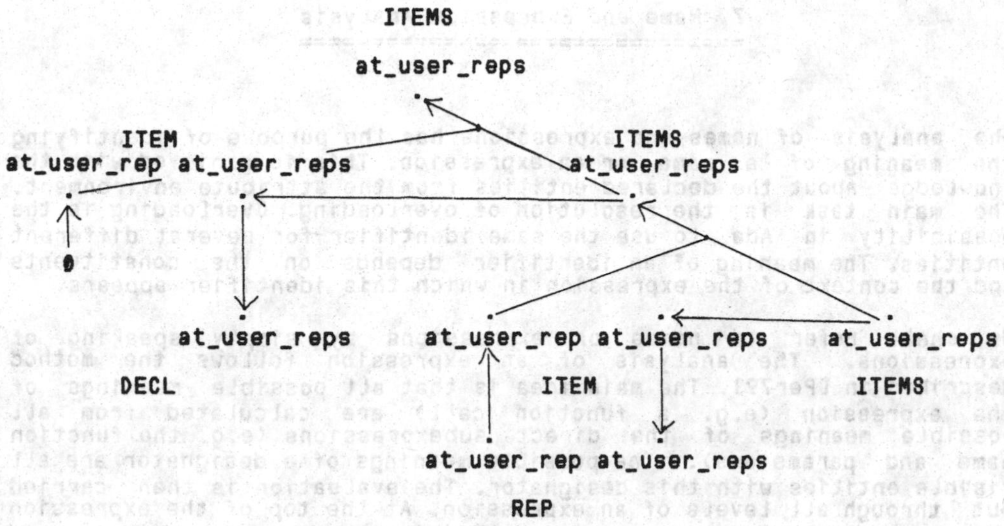
ITEMS
at_user_reps
ITEM
at_user_rep
at_user_reps
ITEMS
at_user_reps
at_user_reps
at_user_rep
at_user_reps
at_user_reps
DECL
ITEM
ITEMS
at_user_rep
at_user_reps
REP

7. Name and Expression Analysis

The analysis of names and expressions has the purpose of identifying the meaning of a name or an expression. This is achieved with the knowledge about the declared entities from the attribute environment. The main task is the resolution of overloading. Overloading is the possibility in Ada to use the same identifier for several different entities. The meaning of an identifier depends on the constituents and the context of the expression in which this identifier appears.

We shall refer to names or expressions by simply speaking of expressions. The analysis of an expression follows the method described in [Per79]. The main idea is that all possible meanings of the expression (e.g. a function call) are calculated from all possible meanings of the direct subexpressions (e.g. the function name and parameters). The possible meanings of a designator are all visible entities with this designator. The evaluation is then carried out through all levels of an expression. At the top of the expression there should be only one meaning, otherwise the expression is invalid or ambiguous. From this unique meaning the meanings of the subexpressions are derived. These meanings are also unique, if the meaning at the whole expression is unique. This is repeated over all expression levels as well.

For the analysis of an expression the entities which are made directly visible by use clauses are only taken into account if the expression has no meaning otherwise. We use the term imported entities for the entities made directly visible by use clauses.

The attribute at_valid (7.4) contains the final meaning of an expression. Its value depends on the attribute at_allowed2 of this expression. The attribute at_allowed1 (7.1) contains all possible meanings of an expression without consideration of the imported entities. The attribute at_allowed2 (7.3) contains all possible meanings of an expression, taking the imported entities into account, if necessary. The information, whether the imported entities must be considered is carried by the attribute at_with_use (7.2).

The above attributes completely describe the semantics of overloading resolution. However, in order to optimize this process, we introduce additional attributes. The knowledge about the type expected from an expression (at_expected, 7.5), or the knowledge about the nature (for example subtype indication, procedure or entry call) expected from a name (at_context, 7.6) sometimes enables us to restrict the possible meanings and thus save storage (less meanings kept in at_allowed1 and at_allowed2) and time (less combinations in the compound expressions to be considered). In other cases we know in advance the list of entities (at_expected_in and at_expected_out in 7.7) which must be given actual values by an association list. This information allows overloading resolution at a lower level, and instead of the usual three attributes for the meaning (at_allowed1, at_allowed2 and at_valid), only one attribute (at_valid, cf. 7.8) is needed.

Our method was, first to specify the static semantics without any further consideration, and then to modify the specification to make the semantic analysis more efficient. This extension of the specification came out very smoothly. In particular, the concept of required type (at_expected) which is used for overloading resolution in [BjOe80], very naturally emerged as an optimization of the original method for overloading resolution [Per79]. It is important to notice, that attribute grammars allow to express such optimizations by formal specifications.

In the following we discuss the various attributes in greater detail.

7.1. at_allowed1

at_allowed1 contains all possible meanings without regarding the imported entities.

```
RULE   r_123 :
   NAME           ::=  DESIGNATOR
STATIC
   NAME.at_allowed1 :=
         ...
         f_identify
           (DESIGNATOR.at_designator,
            NAME.at_env_in)
```

For compound expressions the attribute at_allowed1 depends on the attributes at_allowed1 of the components of the expression. It is evaluated by various functions named f_allowed_xyz, where xyz depends on the nature of the compound expression.

```
RULE   r_125 :
   NAME              ::=  selected   NAME  DESIGNATOR
STATIC
   NAME[1].at_allowed1 := ...
                              f_allowed_selected
                                (NAME[2].at_allowed1,
                                 DESIGNATOR.at_designator,
                                 NAME[1].at_env_in)
```

Compare also the attribution rules for at_allowed1 in the productions r_081 to r_135 for compound expressions.

7.2. at_with_use

If no meaning is found for the whole expression without consideration of the imported entities, then the expression must be analyzed once again, this time also considering the imported entities for all constituents of the expression:

```
RULE   r_150 :
   STM           ::= assign NAME EXP
STATIC
   NAME.at_with_use := f_use_required (NAME.at_allowed1);
```

The attribute at_with_use indicates whether the expression must be analyzed again with consideration of the imported entities.

```
RULE   r_125 :
   NAME          ::=   selected   NAME   DESIGNATOR
STATIC
   TRANSFER at_with_use;
```

7.3. at_allowed2

The new possible meanings are described by at_allowed2. at_allowed2 is equal to at_allowed1 if the use clauses need not be considered (i.e. at_with_use = FALSE), otherwise it is calculated the same way as at_allowed1, but by regarding in addition the imported entities.

First, the identification of the designators is possibly repeated, this time also considering the imported entities (f_identify_with_use):

```
RULE   r_123 :
   NAME          ::=   DESIGNATOR
STATIC
   NAME.at_allowed2 :=    ...
         IF NAME.at_with_use THEN
            ...
            f_identify_with_use
               (DESIGNATOR.at_designator,
                NAME.at_env_in)
         ELSE NAME.at_allowed1
         FI;
```

Then all the attributes at_allowed2 are calculated (if necessary) from the values of the at_allowed2 of the subexpressions (again by the functions f_allowed_xyz):

```
RULE   r_125 :
   NAME          ::=   selected   NAME   DESIGNATOR
STATIC
   NAME[1].at_allowed2 :=             ...
                  IF NAME[1].at_with_use THEN
                     f_allowed_selected
                        (NAME[2].at_allowed2,
                         DESIGNATOR.at_designator,
                         NAME[1].at_env_in),
                  ELSE NAME[1].at_allowed1
                  FI
```

7.4. at_valid

At the top of the expression there should be only one single meaning in at_allowed2. This is then the final meaning of the expression:

```
RULE   r_150 :
   STM              ::=    assign   NAME   EXP
STATIC
   NAME.at_valid  := ...  NAME.at_allowed2
```

at_valid expresses the meaning of an expression, it is then computed for the subexpressions:

```
RULE   r_125 :
   NAME                  ::=   selected   NAME   DESIGNATOR
STATIC
   NAME[2].at_valid   :=  ...
                          f_valid
                             (NAME[1].at_valid,
                              NAME[2].at_allowed2 )
```

For the evaluation of NAME[2].at_valid from NAME[1].at_valid and NAME[2].at_allowed2 - not considering DESIGNATOR.at_designator - the function f_valid uses the component s_origin of the description (meaning) in NAME[1].at_valid. Every description has a component s_origin. s_origin denotes which description (meaning) from the left subexpression is responsible for the description to which s_origin belongs. Compare the s_origin component of tp_descr in 9.2.1.7.

We visualize the attribute dependencies in the next example (we have omitted the attribute at_env_in on which at_allowed1 and at_allowed2 depend):

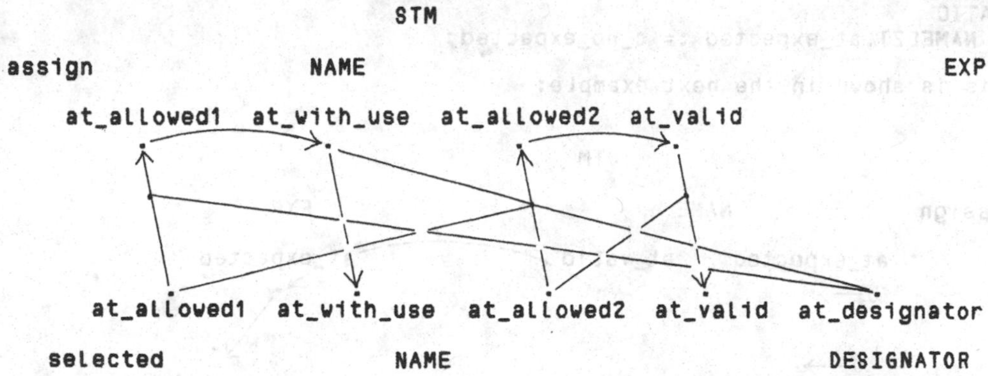

7.5. at_expected

In some contexts an expression is required to be of a certain type. The attribute at_expected denotes the type expected from an expression.

For example, the expression following "while", "if", "elsif" must be of boolean type:

```
RULE   r_149 :
   ITERATION           ::= while EXP
STATIC
   EXP.at_expected     := c_bool;
```

at_expected may depend on the syntactic context (as above) or on a previously calculated expression (for example the right hand side expression in an assignment must have the same type as the named variable). In other cases no specific type (c_no_expected) is expected (for example the named variable in an assignment may have any type):

```
RULE   r_150 :
   STM                 ::= assign NAME EXP
STATIC
   NAME.at_expected := c_no_expected;

   EXP.at_expected := f_object_type1 (... NAME.at_valid);
```

at_expected is propagated to the subexpressions, as far as possible:

```
RULE   r_106 :
   EXP                 ::= parenthesized EXP
STATIC
  TRANSFER at_expected;
```

In some cases, although a specific type may be expected from a compound expression, no information can be derived about the type of a subexpression:

```
RULE   r_125 :
   NAME                ::= selected  NAME  DESIGNATOR
STATIC
   NAME[2].at_expected := c_no_expected;
```

This is shown in the next example:

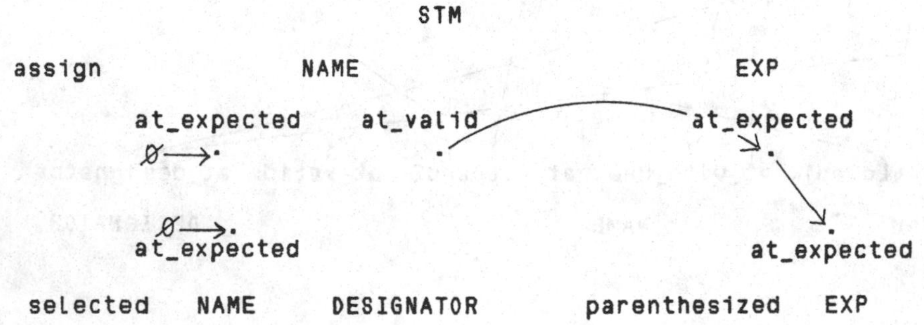

The knowledge about the type expected from an expression is used to make the evaluation of possible meanings more efficient: only meanings compatible with the expected type (f_allowed_expected) are stored in the attribute at_allowed1 or at_allowed2:

```
RULE  r_125 :
  NAME              ::= selected NAME DESIGNATOR
STATIC
  NAME[1].at_allowed1 := f_allowed_expected
                            (f_allowed_selected
                                 (NAME[2].at_allowed1,
                                  DESIGNATOR.at_designator,
                                  NAME[1].at_env_in),
                             NAME[1].at_expected,
                             NAME[1].at_env_in);
  NAME[1].at_allowed2 :=   ...
                     IF NAME[1].at_with_use THEN
                        f_allowed_expected
                           (f_allowed_selected
                               (NAME[2].at_allowed2,
                                DESIGNATOR.at_designator,
                                NAME[1].at_env_in),
                            NAME[1].at_expected,
                            NAME[1].at_env_in)
                     ELSE NAME[1].at_allowed1
                     FI;
```

We show the dependencies in an example (We omit the attribute at_env_in on which at_allowed1, at_allowed2 depend. We also omit the attribute at_valid, because it does not directly depend on at_expected):

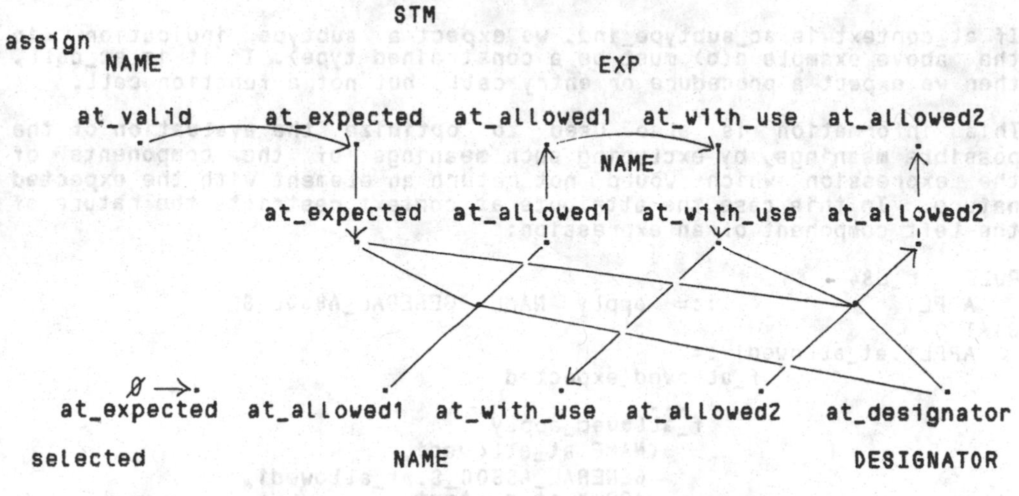

7.6. at_context

The attribute at_context gives information about the context in which an expression appears. It indicates the kind of an expression, whether a string is an aggregate, or an operator name, whether a subtype indication appears within an access type definition, whether a name is a choice of an aggregate or a call, whether a name stands for the value of an attribute or for the attribute itself.

In Ada, the same syntactic form is used for many semantically different elements (for example a(b) may be a subprogram or entry call, an array component, an indexed entry family, a type mark with constraint, a type conversion, or a slice). However, sometimes the outer context of a name gives the information about the kind of the name.

```
RULE  r_007 :
   CONSTRAINED        ::= NAME
STATIC
   NAME.at_context := sc_subtype_ind ;
```

or:

```
RULE  r_152 :
   STM                ::= NAME
STATIC
   NAME.at_context := sc_call;
```

The attribute at_context is passed over to subtrees as long as possible:

```
RULE  r_124 :
   NAME               ::= APPLY
STATIC
   TRANSFER at_context ;
```

If at_context is sc_subtype_ind, we expect a subtype indication (in the above example a(b) must be a constrained type). If it is sc_call, then we expect a procedure or entry call, but not a function call.

This information is also used to optimize the evaluation of the possible meanings, by excluding such meanings of the components of the expression which would not return an element with the expected nature. In this case the attribute at_context restricts the nature of the left component of an expression:

```
RULE  r_084 :
   APPLY              ::=  apply  NAME  GENERAL_ASSOC_S
STATIC
   APPLY.at_allowed1 :=
                  f_allowed_expected
                     ( ...
                      f_allowed_apply
                         (NAME.at_allowed1,
                          GENERAL_ASSOC_S.at_allowed1,
                          APPLY.at_context,
                          APPLY.at_env_in),
                      APPLY.at_expected,
                      APPLY.at_env_in);
```

Here, if the context is sc_call, only such meanings from NAME.at_allowed1 are considered, that denote a procedure or entry whereas, if the context is sc_subtype_ind, only types and subtypes are considered.

In the production of APPLY at_context indicates whether a string is the name of an operator and not a string literal:

```
RULE   r_084 :
  APPLY              ::=  apply NAME GENERAL_ASSOC_S
STATIC
  NAME.at_context    := ... sc_string_is_name ;
```

7.7. at_expected_in, at_expected_out

Very often when a certain entity e1 is used, it must be followed by a list of associations (a1, ..., an), i.e. a list of (actual) entities corresponding to some (formal) entities attached to e1: In subprogram or entry calls there must be an actual parameter for every formal parameter, in aggregates a value for every component of the array or record must be given, in discriminant constraints a value for each discriminant has to be provided, etc. The list of formal entities for which an actual value must be given is unique for each entity. But in most cases the name for e1 may be ambiguous, so that the association list itself is used in overloading resolution of the whole expression and affects the meaning of the name.

In two cases the association list does not influence the meaning of the name. In generic instantiations and record type representations the name itself must be unambiguous. The actual generic parameters resp. the record components in the record type representation, depend on the meaning of the name (at_valid).

The attribute at_expected_in is the list of generic formal parameters for which an association has not been given before the current association has been considered. at_expected_out contains the generic formal parameters for which no value has been given after the end of the association list. The same applies for record type representations where the remaining record components are evaluated.

In a generic instantiation at_expected_in contains the complete list of the generic parameters of the generic entity which is instantiated (NAME.at_valid):

```
RULE   r_259 :
  INSTANTIATION   ::=  instantiation NAME GENERIC_ASSOC_S
STATIC
  GENERIC_ASSOC_S.at_expected_in  :=
                   f_generic_params (NAME.at_valid);
```

The dependencies are shown in the following figure:

In r_266 the components of the record type build the at_expected_in for the following list of component representations.

After a generic association, the corresponding generic formal parameter is deleted from the expected list (f_choices_out). If the current parameter is a type, then any occurrence of the formal type in the remaining formal generic parameter list must be replaced by the actual type (f_adjust_generics):

```
RULE  r_257 :
   GENERIC_ASSOCS      ::= GENERIC_ASSOC GENERIC_ASSOCS
STATIC
   GENERIC_ASSOC.at_expected_in:=GENERIC_ASSOCS[1].at_expected_in;

   GENERIC_ASSOCS[2].at_expected_in :=
      f_adjust_generics
         (f_choices_out (GENERIC_ASSOC.at_valid.s_choices,
                         GENERIC_ASSOC.at_expected_in),
          GENERIC_ASSOC.at_valid,
          GENERIC_ASSOC.at_env_in);

   GENERIC_ASSOCS[1].at_expected_out :=
              GENERIC_ASSOCS[2].at_expected_out;
```

The dependencies are shown in the following figure:

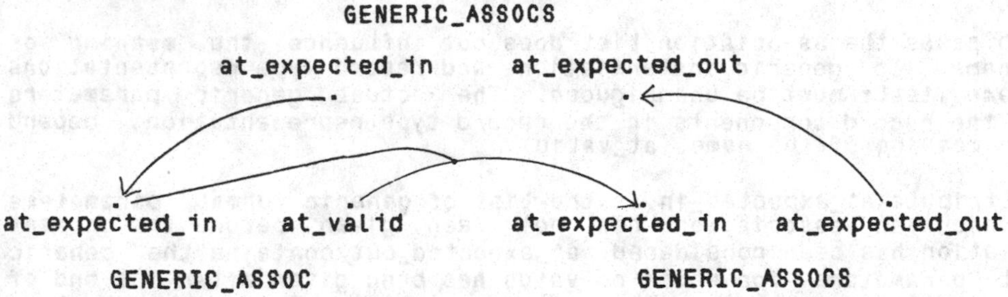

In r_262 similar dependencies exist for the record components in a record type representation.

The attribute at_expected_in is, in particular, used to determine at_context for APPLY: whether the actual parameter must be subtype indication or an object (function call, type conversion, etc.).

The meaning of a generic association (GENERIC_ASSOC.at_valid) depends on the remaining formal generic parameters (GENERIC_ASSOC.at_expected_in) and the possible meanings of the actual generic parameter.

```
RULE  r_255 :
   GENERIC_ASSOC             ::=    ACTUAL
STATIC

   GENERIC_ASSOC.at_valid   :=
             f_generic_allowed_expected
               ( ...
                 GENERIC_ASSOC.at_expected_in,
                 ACTUAL.at_allowed2,
                 GENERIC_ASSOC.at_env_in);
```

The function f_generic_allowed_expected compares the possible meanings of the actual parameter (ACTUAL.at_allowed2) with the current formal generic parameter (GENERIC_ASSOC.at_expected_in), and thus resolves overloading for the meaning of ACTUAL. The meaning found is the final one for the association (therefore the nonterminal

GENERIC_ASSOC has no further attributes at_allowed1, at_allowed2 and at_with_use). In named generic associations (r_255) the meaning of an association is calculated in a similar way. We can now complete the previous figure (omitting at_env_in on which GENERIC_ASSOC.at_valid depends):

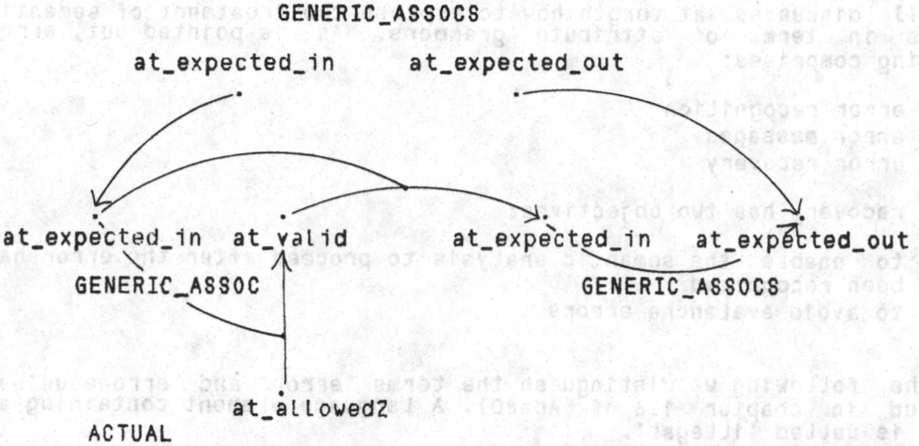

The meaning of a list of generic associations is collected in r_257 (and also used to update at_expected_in, cf. r_257 in 7.7). Then, possibly together with the default parameters, it is used to calculate the generic instantiation (f_expand_instantiation).

8. Semantic Checks and Error Handling

8.1. General Strategies

[KAZ81] discusses at length how to express the treatment of semantic errors in terms of attribute grammars. As is pointed out, error handling comprises:

- error recognition
- error messages
- error recovery

Error recovery has two objectives:

- to enable the semantic analysis to proceed after the error has been recognized
- to avoid avalanche errors

In the following we distinguish the terms 'error' and 'erroneous' as defined in chapter 1.6 of [Ada80]. A language element containing an error is called 'illegal'.

8.1.1. Error Recognition

For every rule from [Ada80] concerning static semantics, the AG contains one or more restrictions on the attribute values. An appropriate error message is generated in the case of violation of this restriction. Such conditions are preceded by a comment indicating the rule and chapter in [Ada80] which it refers to. For example %C 4.3/3 indicates the third rule of chapter 4.3. (aggregates): "all positional component association must be given first".

8.1.2. Error Messages

Error messages should exactly state the rules violated by the program. The best way to do this is to use the corresponding text of the reference manual. In addition, no more than one message per error should be generated. However, our AG sometimes gives several error messages for one error. This is done so for reasons of documentation: every condition expresses the rule it checks by giving an error message, even if a function evaluating the boolean expression of this condition generates more specific error messages. An implementation, however, should not generate the unspecific error message if it is ensured that in all cases a specific error message is produced.

8.1.3. Error Recovery

Error recovery has primarily the purpose of enabling the continuation of the analysis. The consistency of internal data used in further parts of the analysis must be ensured. Thus, the parser always outputs a Diana Parse Tree corresponding to a syntactically correct Ada program. The semantic analysis ensures that its data correspond to semantically correct programs only as far as this data is needed to continue semantic analysis. For example, it need not provide a body for a package for which the programmer forgot to give one. On the other hand, if a subtype indication in a variable declaration does not denote a type, some error recovery must be provided, because this subtype indication will probably be used if this variable appears later on in the program. The care for consistent data is supported by two features of ALADIN: strong typing, and the fact that every expression (and thus every attribute) has a defined value. The strong typing rules are checked by the GAG system at the time of the analysis of the AG. It ensures, that any expression which appears in the AG has the type (and the structure) anticipated. The fact that every attribute has a defined value guarantees that no attribute will be used before it is evaluated, even if the value of this attribute is involved in some semantic error.

However, the AG makes more restrictive assumptions on the structure of its internal data than are explicitly expressed by ALADIN. These assumptions are reflected by the use of list-operators (HEAD, TAIL), which assume that a list contains at least one element, and by the use of type qualification which assumes, that an object of a union type is of one special of the united types. Some of those assumptions are based on the fact that the production rules do not express all restrictions which apply to the Diana Parse Tree. For example TYPE_SPEC in VAR_DECL (r_073) may only be derived to CONSTRAINED (r_058) or to array type definition (r_061). Other assumptions are based on the structure of the AG itself (for example if the nature of a description is sc_subtype, then its denotation must be tp_constrained; cf. 9.2.1, and AGD.3 in Part C). For security, maintainance and documentation purposes, in some of these places, which we anticipate that they can never be reached, the error message "compiler error" is given. These error messages should never occur. They will not be discussed any further.

Error recovery should lead to as few avalanche errors as possible. For example, it is superfluous to generate an error message stating that an expression is meaningless, if this has already been reported for a subexpression. Also, error messages arising from the fact that an entity is used whose declaration was semantically illegal (for example the use of a variable with an undefined type) are superfluous. On the other hand, if some undefined identifier is used more than once, then an error message is generated every time.

Avalanche error messages are avoided by special error values, which do not cause any further error messages.

8.2. Classes of Errors

According to the nature of errors, we classify them into structural errors, errors concerned with declaration elaboration and errors concerned with name and expression analysis. We further classify the checks required by the language into the following twelve classes. The first class contains all structural errors. The second to the sixth contain the errors concerning declaration elaboration. The senventh to the twelfth class are errors concerned with name and expression analysis.

1. Structural Errors

Some language rules are not concerned with the meaning of a language element, but only with the place where it may appear (for example private type declarations are only allowed in the visible part of a package specification, or in generic parts). These checks could also be achieved by a more restrictive (and very complicated) context-free grammar for Ada. However, this would be confusing, because only conflicts with the grammar given in [Ada80] should be reported as syntax errors. Instead, we look for these errors by simple structural checks.

2. Errors Concerning Declaration Elaboration

Completeness of Declarations

At the end of a package specification, a body, or a block all declarations must be "completed", i.e. private types, deferred constants and incomplete types must be completed, bodies must be given for subprograms, tasks, or packages.

Matching of Declarations

Rules request the matching of the discriminant part in private and complete type declarations, the matching of formal and actual generic parameters, the matching of the renaming specification and the renamed entity.

Hiding

No declaration may hide an entity declared in the same declarative part.

Linearity in Declarations

No recursive type definitions are allowed without an intermediate access type, and Ada representation attributes must not be used before a representation specification.

Compatibility of Constraints

Constraints must be equal or more restrictive than earlier constraints on the same type. For arrays and records constraints are only allowed for unconstrained types.

3. Errors concerning Name and Expression Analysis

Expected Nature of an Entity

In some contexts entities must have a particular nature, for example in a generic instantiation a generic package or subprogram is required.

Expected Qualities of an Entity

In some contexts entities must have certain qualities, for example the complete type for a private type must be a type allowing assignment.

Unique Meaning

Every expression must have a unique meaning, otherwise it is either meaningless or ambiguous.

Usability and Dependencies of Entities

For all forms of declarations, except those of subprograms, packages, and tasks, an identifier can only be used as a name of a declared entity once the elaboration of the entity is completed. A subprogram, package, or task identifier can be used as a name of the corresponding entity as soon as the identifier is introduced. Generic parameters, subprogram parameters, record components, discriminants must not depend on other entities from the same generic part, formal part, or record type declaration. Also the transfer of control via exit and goto statements is restricted.

Completeness of Expressions

Aggregates, calls, instantiations, and constraints must be complete, in the sense that an actual value must be provided for every component, parameter without default, discriminant, or index.

Syntactic Form of Expressions

Association lists must have specific forms according to their kind, for example discrete ranges must not appear as formal parameters in subprogram calls, whereas slices may contain discrete ranges. This can not be checked by syntax analysis because of the inherent syntactic ambiguity of these language elements.

Most of the rules from above do not affect the proceeding of semantic analysis and therefore do not require error recovery. These errors are only stated without any further actions. Some of the checks from the third (matching of declarations, cf. 8.4.2) and seventh (expected nature, cf. 8.5.1) class require error recovery and some do not. The ninth class (unique meaning, cf. 8.5.3) requires error recovery.

Now we will examine these checks in detail:

8.3. Structural Errors

For these checks we only need to inspect the structure of the Ada program. A lot of attributes are used to transfer the information about the productions of the language elements preceding and/or following the current position. The attributes for these checks are not needed in further analysis.

8.3.1. at_positional_allowed

Positional associations are not allowed after the occurrence of at least one named association. The attribute at_positional_allowed indicates whether or not a named parameter has appeared in the association list till now:

```
RULE   r_094 :
   COMP_ASSOC              ::=  NAMED
```

and

```
RULE   r_097 :
   COMP_ASSOCS             ::= COMP_ASSOC  COMP_ASSOCS
STATIC
   COMP_ASSOCS[2].at_positional_allowed :=
           COMP_ASSOC[1].at_positional_allowed  AND
           NOT (COMP_ASSOC IS r_094) ;
   %C 4.3/3
   CONDITION
   COMP_ASSOCS[1].at_positional_allowed OR
   (COMP_ASSOC IS r_094)
      MESSAGE
      "positional component association must occur first";
```

at_positional_allowed is used in the same way in other association lists (r_114 and r_257).

8.3.2. at_is_last

The choice "others" may only appear as the last choice in an aggregate, a variant part, a case statement or an exception handler. The attribute at_is_last for a choice indicates whether this choice is the last one in the whole construction. Otherwise, the choice "others" is illegal (r_092). The attribute at_is_last is also defined for all nonterminals from which a choice can be derived. It indicates whether a variant is the last one in the variant list (r_079), whether a component association (r_097) or association (r_114) is the last one, whether an alternative (r_138) is the last in exception handlers or in a case statement. The last choice in the last variant (r_077), resp. in alternative (r_136) etc. is then the last choice of the whole language element.

8.3.3. at_empty

Discriminant parts are only allowed in private, limited private, incomplete and record type declarations. The attribute at_empty indicates whether the discriminant part is empty, i.e. whether a discriminant part is given at all (r_076), and:

```
RULE   r_057 :
   TYPE_DECL          ::= type  ID  VAR_DECL_S  TYPE_SPEC
STATIC
   %C 3.7./5
   CONDITION
   VAR_DECL_S.at_empty        OR
   (TYPE_SPEC IS r_067)       OR     % record , incomplete
   ...                               % private , limited private
      MESSAGE
      "no discriminants allowed"
```

8.3.4. at_unconstrained

Unconstrained arrays are only allowed as explicit type declarations. Therefore, if an index appears in the discrete range list (r_032, r_033) of an array type definition in an object declaration (r_061), it is an error.

8.3.5. at_has_range

A range constraint is required in a fixed point type declaration, but not in an accuracy constraint (r_064, r_040).

8.3.6. at_init

In a discriminant list, either all or none of the discriminants may have an initialization. at_init indicates whether all, none or only some of the discriminants were initialized (r_075, r_076). In the latter case (r_057) an error message is generated.

8.3.7. at_encl_unit

Some elements are only allowed within particular units, for example return statements are only allowed within subprogram bodies. The attribute at_encl_unit contains the information about the kind and state of the innermost enclosing body or specification:

```
RULE  r_177  :
  PACKAGE_SPEC    ::= package_spec  DECL_S  DECL_REP_S
STATIC
  DECL_S.at_encl_unit      ::= ...(sc_package, sc_visible);
  DECL_REP_S.at_encl_unit ::= ...(sc_package, sc_private);
```

The attribute at_encl_unit is also used to denote that the current language element is enclosed by a subprogram header (r_170, r_171), a subprogram body (r_195), a package body (r_178), an accept statement (r_204), a task body (r_212). The information from the attribute at_encl_unit is then used to check that private or limited private type declarations may only appear in the visible part of a package (r_071, r_072), that return statements may only appear within subprogram bodies or accept statements (r_161), that return statements with an expression may only appear within a function (r_161), that functions may have parameters only of mode in (r_180, r_181), that raise statements without a name may only appear within an exception handler (r_236), and that no out parameters are allowed as generic parameters (r_181).

In contrast to the environment attribute which completely describes the block structure, at_encl_unit does not regard the enclosing blocks and loops.

8.3.8. at_return_required

A function body should always be terminated by a return statement, otherwise the program is erroneous (in the sense of [Ada80] 1.6). Therefore, every statement which could cause the function to be left is marked with at_return_required:

```
RULE  r_141  :
   BLOCK_STUB              ::=  BLOCK
STATIC
   BLOCK.at_return_required :=
              BLOCK.at_encl_unit.nature = sc_function ;
```

The last statement from a sequence of statements leading out of a function body is also marked (r_164, r_136, r_140, r_143, r_157, r_158). If the last statement of such a list is not a return or a raise statement, then a warning is generated (r_150, r_152, etc).

8.3.9. at_is_operator, at_param_no

For operator overloading special rules must be obeyed. The inherited attribute at_is_operator conveys to the HEADER the information about whether the HEADER belongs to some operator declaration (r_190, r_195). If so, then no default values for the parameters are allowed (r_179). The synthesized attribute at_param_no counts how many parameters are in a parameter list (r_183, r_184); in operator overloading for 'NOT', one single parameter is required, for '+' or '-' one or two, otherwise two parameters are required (r_190 and r_195).

8.3.10. at_block_no

Body stubs are only allowed in the outermost declarative part. The inherited attribute at_block_no counts the enclosing blocks (r_223, r_140, r_178, r_195, r_044, r_045). A stub is only allowed if at_block_no = 1 (r_142).

8.3.11. at_first_select, at_select_state

A selective wait must contain at least one alternative starting with an accept statement, it must not contain more than one alternative beginning with a terminate, etc. The synthesized attribute at_first_select indicates whether a statement list starts with an accept statement, a delay statement, a terminate or is empty (r_198). The synthesized attribute at_select_state indicates which types of select alternatives have already appeared:

```
RULE  r_199 :
   SELECT_CLAUSES       ::= SELECT_CLAUSE  SELECT_CLAUSES
STATIC
   SELECT_CLAUSES[1].at_select_state :=
     ... (SELECT_CLAUSE.at_first_select,
          SELECT_CLAUSES[2].at_select_state);
```

All the rules about the types of the select alternatives can then be checked by comparing at_select_state with the type of the current SELECT_CLAUSE (r_199 and r_201).

8.3.12. at_no_code_stms, at_no_decls, at_empty

Code statements may only appear in code procedures. Such procedures may only contain use clauses, pragmas and code statements. The synthesized attribute at_no_code_stms is TRUE if none of the preceding statements is a code statement (r_267). If this is not the case, then the current statement must be a code statement too (r_164). Code statement sequences may only appear within procedure bodies (r_140). Such code procedures must not contain any declarations (r_140 with at_no_decls from r_048, r_049), nor any exception handlers (r_140 and at_empty from r_138).

8.3.13. at_is_item

The pragmas SUPPRESS and OPTIMIZE may only appear in declarative parts. The attribute at_is_item indicates whether the current position is in a declarative part and helps to check the above rule (r_219).

8.3.14. at_is_exp

Type conversions are syntactically described as expressions, whereas all other language elements summarized by APPLY are names. at_is_exp is used to check that APPLY is an expression (EXP ::= NAME ::= APPLY) if APPLY denotes a type conversion.

8.4. Errors Concerning Declaration Elaboration

8.4.1. Completeness of Declarations

Here we inspect the environment resulting at the end of the visible or private part of a package (r_177) or the declarative part of a block (r_140):

```
RULE  r_177 :
  PACKAGE_SPEC          ::= package_spec DECL_S  DECL_REP_S
STATIC
  %C 3.8/2
  CONDITION
  ch_all_types_completed ( ... DECL_S.at_env_out)
     MESSAGE
     "missing full declarations for incomplete types";
```

Declarative parts of blocks or bodies must also be complete (r_140).

A corresponding package specification must have been given before a package body (cf. 6.3 for f_new_key):

```
RULE  r_178 :
  PACKAGE_BODY          ::= package_body ID BLOCK_STUB
STATIC

  CONDITION
  NOT (f_new_key ( ... PACKAGE_BODY.at_keys ,
                       PACKAGE_BODY.at_env_in))
     MESSAGE
     "missing package specification for package body";
```

8.4.2. Matching of Declarations

After deciding that a particular declaration must match with another one, the checking is achieved by functions of the form ch_matching_xyz (where xyz stands for the kind of the entities which must match). The next example shows private or incomplete type completions (cf. 6.3 for f_new_key):

```
RULE r_057 :
   TYPE_DECL         ::= type ID VAR_DECL_S  TYPE_SPEC
STATIC
   %C 7.4.1/3, C 3.8/4
   CONDITION
   IF f_new_key( ... TYPE_DECL.at_keys, TYPE_DECL.at_env_in) THEN
      TRUE
   ELSE ch_matching_discr_parts
          (TYPE_SPEC.at_type,
           f_type ( ... TYPE_DECL.at_keys,
                        TYPE_DECL.at_env_in))
   FI
      MESSAGE
      "the discriminant part of private (or incomplete) type
       and complete type should match"
```

In other cases these checks must take place parallel to expression analysis, because overloading resolution and possibly error correction take place in the same course:

```
RULE  r_196 :
   RENAME            ::= rename NAME
STATIC
   NAME.at_valid := ...  f_valid_renamed
                           (NAME.at_allowed2,
                            RENAME.at_keys,
                            RENAME.at_env_in);
```

The function f_valid_renamed selects from the meanings in NAME.at_allowed2 those matching the specification in the renaming declaration. This information is obtained from RENAME.at_keys. It also checks the matching rules and gives appropriate error messages. If the entities in NAME.at_allowed2 are of a different nature to that of the specification in the renaming declaration (for example an object renaming a subprogram) then f_valid_renamed returns an appropriate error value.

Similar checks are carried out for the actual and corresponding formal generic parameter (r_255).

8.4.3. Hiding

The elaboration of entities takes place in many, sometimes textually separated stages (as we saw in 6 and as suggested by the description in [Ada80] 3.10). To avoid multiple checks of the rule forbidding declarations to hide entities from the same declarative part, we check for it only in the last stage, when the elaboration is completed (for example at the end of a variable declaration, at the complete declaration of some private type, at the end of a subprogram specification). The function f_update_descrs_by_keys is always used in declarations and it checks this rule when the declaration is completed (s_nature=sc_complete, cf. tp_nature in 9.2.1).

Due to the fact that the enumeration literals are not introduced in several stages (cf. end of 6.6), this check can be carried out directly in the production introducing the enumeration literal:

```
RULE   r_038 :
   ENUM_LITERALS     ::= ENUM_LITERAL ENUM_LITERALS
STATIC
   %C 8.3/1
   CONDITION
   ch_local_hiding
      ( ...
       ENUM_LITERAL.at_designator,
       INCLUDING TYPE_SPEC.at_env_in)
      MESSAGE
      "THIS enum literal hides entity from same decl-part";
```

8.4.4. Linearity of Declarations

Recursive type declarations without an intermediate access type are forbidden in Ada. Every type declaration is therefore checked to see whether it is recursive (ch_no_recursion). In this case, several condition and attribute evaluations would lead to infinite loops. So they must be suppressed for recursively defined types. For example the implicitly declared subprograms are not evaluated:

```
RULE   r_057 :
   TYPE_DECL            ::= type ID VAR_DECL_S  TYPE_SPEC
STATIC
   TYPE_SPEC.at_impl_subprs :=
     IF ch_no_recursion ( ...
                         TYPE_DECL.at_keys,
                         TYPE_SPEC.at_type,
                         TYPE_DECL.at_env_in) THEN
       ...
     ELSE (c_empty_descrs
           %C 3.3/2
           CONDITON FALSE MESSAGE
              "recursive type specification without
              intermediate  access type illegal")
```

For representation specifications compare also the discussion about at_user_reps in 6.9.

8.4.5. Compatibility of Constraints

Compatibility of constraints must be checked whenever a certain type is further constrained, i.e. in the context of APPLY if it is a constrained type (by the function f_valid_assocs) in the context of allocators (r_100) and in r_005:

```
RULE   r_005 :
  CONSTRAINED_1        ::= constrained NAME CONSTRAINT
STATIC
  %C 3.3/1, 3.6.1/1, 3.7.2/3, 3.5.7/3, 3.6.1/2, 3.5.9/4
  %C 3.5.7/4
  CONDITION
  ch_constraint (NAME.at_valid,
                 CONSTRAINT.at_valid,
                 CONSTRAINED_1.at_env_in)
     MESSAGE
     "illegal constraint";
```

8.5. Errors Concerning Name and Expression Analysis

8.5.1. Expected Nature of an Entity

These checks use the value of the attribute at_valid. In some cases one need only ask whether the attribute at_valid denotes an entity of the expected nature. In these cases the condition is checked after at_valid was evaluated, and it does not affect its value, as in:

```
RULE   r_155 :
  STM                  ::= exit NAME_VOID EXP_VOID
STATIC
  %C 5.7/1
  CONDITION
  CASE c_valid : NAME_VOID.at_valid OF
  IS tp_descr_set : ( ... c_valid.s_nature = sc_loop)
  OUT TRUE
  ESAC
     MESSAGE
     "a loop name expected here";
```

In other places the attribute at_valid must have a particular nature and its evaluation is interwoven with this check:

```
RULE   r_007 :
  CONSTRAINED          ::= NAME
STATIC
  NAME.at_valid := cf_unique_type_descr (NAME.at_allowed2);
```

NAME must denote some type. cf_unique_type_descr (among other things, cf. 8.5.4) checks that NAME.at_allowed2 denotes some type; if this is not the case, NAME.at_allowed2 is replaced by the error value c_error_type_descr_set which does not cause any avalanche errors. Even if objects of such a type occur in expressions, no superfluous error messages are generated.

Similarly, the names in use clauses must denote packages. The function f_add_imported_descrs which elaborates a use clause assumes that its first parameter is a list of packages. Therefore we take into account only those entities denoted by NAMES which are packages (cf_packages):

```
RULE   r_197 :
   USE                    ::= use NAMES
STATIC
   USE.at_env_out := f_add_imported_descrs
                        (cf_packages (NAMES.at_names),
                         USE.at_env_in);
```

Here the function cf_packages selects out of NAMES.at_names only those denoting a package and gives an error message for each of the remaining elements.

8.5.1.1. at_first_stm

The first sequence of statements in a conditional entry call must be an entry call. For this check STM_S has the synthesized attribute at_first_stm stating the nature of the first statement in the list:

```
RULE   r_205 :
   STM                    ::= cond_entry STM_S  STM_S
STATIC
   %C 9.7.2/1
   CONDITION
   STM_S[1].at_first_stm = sc_entry_call
     MESSAGE
     "first statement after select in a
     conditional entry call must be entry_call";
```

Analogous conditions apply for timed entry calls (r_209).

8.5.1.2. at_others_allowed

The choice "others" is allowed in aggregates only under special conditions (cf. [Ada80] 4.3.2). The attribute at_others_allowed indicates whether the choice "others" may appear (r_110), and is then used for the check (r_099).

8.5.2. Expected Qualities of an Entity

These checks occur after the evaluation of the attribute at_valid:

```
RULE   r_150 :
   STM                  ::= assign NAME EXP
STATIC
   %C 3.2/3, C 3.7.1/4, C 6.2/1, C 7.4.2/1, C 6/2
   CONDITION
   ch_is_assign_allowed (NAME.at_valid,
                         STM.at_env_in )
       MESSAGE
       "assignment forbidden for this NAME";
```

Also a positive static real range and a positive static real/integer expression is expected in fixed/float types (r_040, r_041), a static integer range is required in integer types (r_066), the type in a variable declaration must allow assignment (r_073), etc.

8.5.3. Unique Meaning

When some part of a compound expression is found to be meaningless, an error message is generated. No further error messages are given for expressions containing a meaningless one. This means that a particular check takes place every time some new attribute at_allowed2 is calculated:

```
RULE   r_123 :
   NAME                 ::= DESIGNATOR
STATIC
   NAME.at_allowed2 :=
       cf_not_empty (IF NAME.at_with_use THEN
                        f_allowed_expected
                           (f_identify_with_use
                              (
                               DESIGNATOR.at_designator,
                               NAME.at_env_in),
                     ELSE NAME.at_allowed1
                     FI);
```

The function cf_not_empty returns its input parameter unaltered if this parameter contains at least one meaning, otherwise it generates an error message and returns the error value c_error_descr_set. All functions f_allowed_xyz (the functions computing the at_allowed1/at_allowed2 attribute from the at_allowed1/at_allowed2 attributes of the subexpressions) return the same error value c_error_descr_set if one of the constituents has already the error value c_error_descr_set. Thus, as soon as some part of an expression is found to be meaningless, an error message for this part is generated, and the analysis of the expression above is skipped practically, thus avoiding further redundant error messages.

```
RULE   r_125 :
   NAME                 ::= selected NAME DESIGNATOR
STATIC
   NAME[1].at_allowed2 :=
           cf_not_empty (IF NAME[1].at_with_use THEN
                            f_allowed_expected
                              ( ...
                                f_allowed_selected
                                  (NAME[2].at_allowed2,
                                   DESIGNATOR.at_designator,
                                   NAME[1].at_env_in),
                         ELSE NAME[1].at_allowed1
                         FI);
```

If the expression is meaningless, then this will be detected by cf_not_empty during the evaluation of the at_allowed2 attribute of some subexpression. at_allowed2 might still be ambiguous, i.e. it could contain more than one possible meanings:

```
RULE r_150 :
   STM    ::= assign NAME EXP
STATIC
   NAME.at_valid := cf_unique_descr ( ...
                                     NAME.at_allowed2 );
```

The function cf_unique_descr checks that NAME.at_allowed2 has not more than one meaning. Otherwise it returns only one of these and generates an error message.

8.5.4. Usability and Dependencies of Entities

The use of entities which are already introduced is generally forbidden in three cases: if the declaration of the entity is still incomplete (cf. [Ada80] 3.1), if illegal dependencies are introduced (cf. [Ada80] 3.7.1, 6.1 and 12.1), or if control is transferred illegally via exit or goto statements (cf. [Ada80] 5.7 and 5.9).

These rules can only be checked when the meaning of the applied occurence has been identified.

The first case is checked by the function ch_usable (called by cf_unique_descr, alredy discussed in 8.5.1) with the aid of the component s_state (cf. 9.2.1.4) of a description, which is equal to sc_id_established when an identifier is introduced.

The second case is checked by the function ch_dependencies (also called from cf_unique_descr). For this purpose ch_dependencies uses the information about the unit enclosing the current position (s_enclosing in the environment, cf. 9.2), and the unit enclosing the entity (s_enclosing in descriptions, cf. 9.2.1.8). Due to the fact, that dependency on a discriminant name is sometimes allowed and sometimes not, we need also the attribute at_discrim_allowed (8.5.4.1).

The third case is checked with the aid of the attribute at_usable (8.5.4.2).

A special case of the second rule is the dependency of record components from discriminants.

8.5.4.1. at_discrim_allowed

at_discrim_allowed indicates whether an entity may depend on a discriminant:

```
RULE  r_052 :
   RANGE                ::= range  EXP  EXP
STATIC
   EXP[1].at_valid := cf_unique_descr
                         (...
                          RANGE.at_valid.s_lower_bound,
                          RANGE.at_discrim_allowed,
                          NAME.at_env_in);
```

Dynamic arrays in record types must depend on discriminants (r_032).

The function cf_unique_type_descr (introduced in 8.5.1) checks that a name denotes a type (8.5.1) that the name is unique (8.5.3) and that no illegal dependencies exist. As type names never depend on discriminants, no parameter is required, indicating whether discriminant dependencies are allowed.

8.5.4.2. at_usable

Special rules forbid the transfer of control between some syntactic units via goto statements. The attribute STM.at_usable contains the label names from this sequence of statements, which must not be used in goto statements appearing outside this statements sequence. The function f_make_usable marks in STM_S.at_env_in that these targets may be used inside STM_S:

```
RULE  r_140 :
   BLOCK           ::= block  ITEM_S  STM_S  ALTERNATIVE_S
STATIC
   STM_S.at_env_in := f_make_usable (STM_S.at_usable,
                                     ITEM_S.at_env_out);

   ALTERNATIVE_S.at_env_in := ITEM_S.at_env_out;
```

Label names which are not made usable are illegal in goto statements (r_156). Similar conditions apply for exit statements (r_155).

In the above rule (r_140) in STM_S.at_env_in the targets appearing in the exception handlers (ALTERNATIVE_S) are not usable (thus the jump into an exception handler is forbidden), and in ALTERNATIVE_S.at_env_in the targets appearing in the sequence of statements (STM_S) are not visible (thus prohibiting a jump from the exception handler back to the statements of the block or body). Note that the targets appearing in STM_S resp. ALTERNATIVE_S are visible in ALTERNATIVE_S resp. STM_S but they are are not usable.

The rules (cf. [Ada80] Ch. 5.9) forbidding the transfer of control from one of the sequences of statements of an if statement (r_143, r_144), case statement or exception handler (r_136, r_138), select statement (r_198), to another sequence of statements, is expressed in this way. Illegal transfer of control out of a body or accept statement is checked by the function ch_control without the aid of at_usable.

8.5.5. Completeness of Expressions

Some of these restrictions are related to overloading resolution. For example, the completeness of the actual parameter list is information used in overloading resolution of the subprogram name. In those cases, where the completeness of the expression affects the meaning of the whole expression, it cannot be checked separately and no specific error messages can be given. However, in the cases where completeness of the expression does not affect the meaning, the rule can be checked explicitly after the meaning of the expression has been established (i.e. at_valid has been calculated).

```
RULE r_099 :
   EXP                 ::= aggregate COMP_ASSOCS
STATIC
   %C 4.3/1, C 4.3/2, C 4.3/4, C 4.3.2/2, C 13.3/2, C 13.3/3
   CONDITION
   ch_aggreg (COMP_ASSOCS.at_valid,
              EXP.at_valid,
              EXP.at_env_in)
      MESSAGE
      "wrongly built aggregate";
and
RULE r_259 :
   INSTANTIATION  ::= instantiation NAME GENERIC_ASSOC_S
STATIC
   %C 12.3/2
   CONDITION
   ch_have_default (GENERIC_ASSOC_S.at_expected_out)
      MESSAGE
      "actual parameters missing";
```

8.5.6. Syntactic Form of Expressions

When semantic analysis has resolved the syntactic ambiguity inherent in the APPLY (i.e. a name followed by a bracketed expression or association list), the syntax of APPLY must be checked: Type conversions must contain one single expression, slices must contain one single discrete range, indexed components must contain a list of expressions, in named parameter associations in subprogram calls no more than one formal parameter may appear in a named parameter association. These functions are accomplished by the functions ch_syntax_converted, ch_syntax_slice, ch_syntax_indexed, ch_syntax_params, which are called by f_allowed_apply according to the nature of the expression.

9. Attribute Types

In this chapter we describe the types of the attributes introduced in the previous chapters (6, 7, 8), in order to illustrate the way in which their information is represented We omit simple attribute types (INT or BOOL).

9.1. at_keys, at_keys1, at_keys2 : tp_key_list

```
TYPE tp_key                    : UNION (INT);
TYPE tp_key_list               : LISTOF tp_key;
```

tp_key is introduced to provide the unique access to descriptions in the environment. Every declared entity is represented by a description in the environment. We say "a key denotes an entity" or "a key denotes a description". The key can be used to retrieve information about this entity from the environment. The function f_select_by_key accesses the description from the environment wich has (is denoted by) a given key. The use of a key in descriptions is further discussed in 9.2.1.2.

The attributes at_keys, at_keys1 and at_keys2 are lists of keys. They denote those descriptions from the environment which have one of the key values in their list. The attributes at_keys, at_keys1, at_keys2 denote the description(s) of the entity (entities) which are currently declared. In some declarations (for example type declarations) only a single entity is declared. In other declarations (for example variable declarations) one or more entities can be declared. For technical reasons at_keys, at_keys1, at_keys2 are lists for all nonterminals, although for some nonterminals (for example SUBPROG_BODY) these lists always contain exactly one element.

9.2. at_env, at_env_in, at_env_out : tp_env

The environment reflects all knowledge about the declared entities, their scope and visibility. Every entity has its own description. We distinguish between the entities declared in the current syntactic unit (block, body, record, generic part, formal part, visible part, private part), and those declared globally to the current position. The descriptions for the former entities are contained in the component s_local, those for the latter in the component s_global. The block structure is reflected in the environment: the component s_enclosing denotes the enclosing language element. The environment also keeps track of the package names which appeared in enclosing use clauses (s_imported).

```
TYPE tp_descr_list : LISTOF tp_descr;

TYPE tp_env        : STRUCT (s_imported  : tp_key_list,
                             s_global,
                             s_local     : tp_descr_list,
                             s_enclosing : tp_key);
```

9.2.1. tp_descr

All knowledge about an entity is kept in a record of type tp_descr, called a description. Descriptions are used for entities in the environment, as well as for values (e.g. numeric literals, function results etc.) within name and expression analysis (cf. tp_descr_set in 9.7). In the latter case we speak of value descriptions. Descriptions have the following structure:

```
TYPE tp_descr : STRUCT (s_designator : tp_designator,
                        s_key        : tp_key,
                        s_repr       : tp_repr,
                        s_state      : tp_state,
                        s_nature     : tp_nature,
                        s_den        : tp_den
                        s_origin     : tp_origin,
                        s_enclosing  : tp_key);
```

9.2.1.1. s_designator

s_designator is either the code given by lexical analysis, or anonymous for implicit declarations, or an error value.

```
TYPE tp_designator : UNION (SYMB, tp_anonymous,
                            tp_error_designator);
```

9.2.1.2. s_key

This component gives the unique key (cf. 9.1) by which the description may be referred to, if it is a description in the environment. The component s_key for value descriptions has a special value (c_key). All other subcomponents of a description which are of the type tp_key denote entities for which a description exists in the environment.

9.2.1.3. s_repr

s_repr contains all information about the representation of an entity: the list of representation specifications already given for this entity (s_reps), the representation state (s_rep_state), i.e. whether the representation has already been computed, further representation specifications which follow in the program, etc.:

```
TYPE tp_repr       : STRUCT (s_rep_state : tp_rep_state,
                             s_reps      : tp_rep_list);

TYPE tp_rep_state : (
   sc_start_rep      ,
         % no representation specifications follow or precede

   sc_user_rep       ,
         % representation specifications follow

   sc_static_rep     ,
         % representation specifications precede
         % representation statically evaluable

   sc_dynamic_rep    ,
         % representation specifications precede
         % representation dynamically evaluable

   sc_incomplete rep );
         % no representation specifications follow or precede
         % entity depends on incomplete or private type
```

__9.2.1.4. s_state__
s_state is the state of an entity during the several stages of its completion:

```
TYPE tp_state : (
   sc_id_established,
         % when the identifier is introduced

   sc_deferred   , sc_incompl_private,
   sc_incomplete, sc_spec_complete   ,
         % when the declaration is finished,
         % but still must be completed in a later one

   sc_in_body    , sc_in_handler,
   sc_in_visible, sc_in_private,
   sc_in_formal_part, sc_in_generic_part,
   sc_in_record , sc_in_discr_part,
         % when the entity encloses the current declarations
         % or statements

   sc_complete,
         % when the declaration is completed, and
         % no later "completion" is allowed

   sc_implicitly_declared,
         % when the description belongs to an implicitly
         % declared subprogram; the subprogram may be
         % redeclared by a later explicit declaration

   sc_void_state ,
         % when the description belongs to a value

   sc_error_state);
         % when it is an error
```

The component s_state serves for:

- usability checks
- dependency checks
- completeness checks

9.2.1.5. s_nature

s_nature is the nature of the entity

```
TYPE tp_nature : ( sc_constant, sc_variable , sc_number,
                   sc_value   , sc_converted_var,
                   sc_in, ...
                   sc_function, ...
                   sc_label   , ...
                   sc_void_nature  ,
                   sc_error_nature );
```

All natures, except sc_value, sc_converted_var, sc_void_nature, sc_error_nature correspond to entities explicitly or implicitly declared in the environment.

9.2.1.6. s_den

s_den contains most of the information about an entity. It reflects the structure of that part of the Ada program which declares the entity, sometimes enriched with additional information.

```
TYPE tp_den : UNION (tp_object , tp_type_den , tp_constrained ,
                     tp_subpr  , tp_entry    , tp_entry_family,
                     tp_package, tp_generic  , tp_enum_literal,
                     tp_dummy  , tp_dummy_aggr, tp_operation  ,
                     tp_void   );
```

In 9.2.1.6.1 to 9.2.1.6.13 we shortly outline the types unified in tp_den.

9.2.1.6.1. tp_object

tp_object is the denotation for descriptions of variables, constants, values, type conversion of a variable, in, out, in out parameters, and discriminants. Objects are characterized by their subtype (s_type) and their initial value (s_init):

```
TYPE tp_object  : STRUCT (s_type : tp_constrained,
                          s_init : tp_init);
```

The subtype indication (s_type) contains the information about the base type (s_base_type denotes the base type, never a subtype) and the constraint which applies to this object (s_constraint). If the subtype indication in an object declaration does not contain an explicit constraint, but the subtype name denotes a constrained subtype, then this constraint is contained in the component s_den.s_type.s_constraint of the descriptions of the object.

```
TYPE tp_constrained : STRUCT( s_base_type  : tp_key,
                              s_constraint : tp_constraint);
```

The kind (literal, static, dynamic, no expression) of the

initialization (s_exp_kind) and the value (s_value), if statically evaluable, are also given for objects.

```
TYPE tp_init  : STRUCT (s_value    : tp_value,
                        s_exp_kind : tp_exp_kind);
```

9.2.1.6.2. tp_type_den
tp_type_den is the denotation for types. It contains the information from the type definition (s_type) and a list of subprograms applicable to this type (s_derivable_subprogs):

```
TYPE tp_type_den : STRUCT (s_type                : tp_type     ,
                           s_derivable_subprogs : tp_key_list );

TYPE tp_type     : UNION (tp_fixed, tp_float, ...  );
```

The component s_derivable_subprogs denotes all explicitly declared subprograms which will be derived if this type is derived.

9.2.1.6.3. tp_constrained
tp_constrained is the denotation of subtypes. If a subtype declaration does not contain an explicit constraint, but a constraint is inherited from the subtype name in the subtype indication, this constraint is contained in the denotation of the subtype (cf.9.2.1.6.1).

9.2.1.6.4. tp_subpr
tp_subpr is the denotation for functions and procedures (not generic, cf. 9.2.1.6.7). It consists of the information from the header (s_spec), supplementary information about the definition (s_def), and a special indication whether the subprogram is an operator from the package STANDARD (s_op, cf. 9.2.1.6.12).

```
TYPE tp_subpr : STRUCT( s_spec : tp_header,
                        s_def  : tp_subpr_def,
                        s_op   : tp_op);
```

For technical reasons, during the elaboration of an entry or entry family their denotation is of type tp_subpr and the s_spec component is of type tp_entry or tp_entry_family. After completion of the declaration the denotation of the entry or entry family (at_env_out in r_190) is of the type tp_entry (9.2.1.6.5) or tp_entry_family (9.2.1.6.6).

```
TYPE tp_header : STRUCT (tp_function, tp_procedure,
                         tp_entry   , tp_entry_family);
```

The component s_def indicates that the subprogram renames another one (tp_rename), or that it is an instantiation of a generic subprogram (tp_instantiation). In addition, if it is a formal generic subprogram parameter, s_def indicates whether it has a default (tp_key), no default (tp_no_default), or a box (tp_box) initialization.

```
TYPE tp_subpr_def : UNION( tp_rename,  tp_instantiation, tp_key,
                           tp_no_default, tp_box,        tp_void);
```

9.2.1.6.5. tp_entry
tp_entry is used for entries. It only reflects the declaration of the entry (parameter list), without additional information.

```
TYPE tp_entry : STRUCT( s_params : tp_descr_list );
```

9.2.1.6.6. tp_entry_family
tp_entry_family also only reflects the declaration of an entry family.

```
STRUCT tp_entry_family : STRUCT ( s_dscrt_range : tp_dscrt_range,
                                  s_entry       : tp_entry);
```

9.2.1.6.7. tp_package
tp_package is used for (non-generic) packages. We keep track of all implicit or explicit declarations from its visible part (s_visible), of the declarations from the visible and private part (s_pack_spec) which are then made visible in the package body, of the use clauses appearing within the package specification (s_imported), and whether a body has been given (s_body_prov).

```
TYPE tp_package : STRUCT (s_visible,
                          s_pack_spec : tp_descr_list,
                          s_imported  : tp_key_list,
                          s_body_prov : BOOL);
```

(The component s_state = sc_complete in the description of a package only denotes that no body is required for this package. Packages sometimes do not need a body, whereas tasks and subprograms always require one, generic instantiation and renaming excluded. Therefore for packages we need a special component (s_body_prov) indicating that a body is provided. In subprograms and tasks s_state = sc_complete means that a body was given)

9.2.1.6.8. tp_generic
tp_generic is the denotationn of generic subprograms or packages. It only reflects the generic declaration. The component s_den of tp_generic is of type tp_package or tp_subpr.

```
TYPE tp_generic : STRUCT ( s_generic_params : tp_descr_list,
                           s_den            : tp_den);
```

9.2.1.6.9. tp_enum_literal
tp_enum_literal indicates the type of an enumeration literal (s_type), its position within the enumeration type (s_pos) and whether it is a character literal (s_char):

```
TYPE tp_enum_literal : STRUCT( s_type : tp_key,
                               s_pos  : INT,
                               s_char : BOOL);
```

9.2.1.6.10. tp_dummy_aggr
tp_dummy_aggr is used for the analysis of multidimensional aggregates, because no explicit type for the inner aggregates is known.

```
Type tp_dummy_aggr   : STRUCT ( s_assocs : tp_assoc_list );
```

9.2.1.6.11. tp_dummy

tp_dummy is used in the case of choices which are not directly visible (names of record components in aggregates) and formal parameters (in parameter associations). This context is indicated by at_context = sc_id_not_visible (cf. 7.6). The dummy denotation is necessary to avoid the error message "unknown identifier" and also to indicate that the association consists of the identifier only (and not the 'meaning') of the choice and the actual parameter.

```
TYPE tp_dummy : (sc_dummy);
```

9.2.1.6.12. tp_operation

tp_operation is used for the descriptions of predefined operators, according to the rules from [Ada80 ch. 4.4]. For these operators we need not keep the whole information about their specification, as in tp_subpr (9.2.1.6.4), because this information directly follows from the values in tp_operation:

```
TYPE tp_operation : ( s_op : tp_op );

TYPE tp_op        : ( sc_in_op, sc_not_in_op, ....
                      sc_ui_minus1_op,
                          % the universal integer unary minus
                      .....
                      sc_no_predef_op,
                          % a user-defined operator

                      sc_no_op    );
                          % not an operator
```

9.2.1.6.13. tp_void

tp_void is only used during the elaboration of a declaration, before the analysis of the specific information about the entity.

```
TYPE tp_void : ( sc_void );
```

9.2.1.7. s_origin

s_origin is used to facilitate the evaluation of the attribute at_valid of the left subexpression of a compound expression. For this purpose the at_allowed2 of the left subexpression and at_valid of the compound expression are used. The component s_origin from the description in at_valid denotes the one description from the at_allowed2 of the left subexpression, which is "responsible" for the meaning in the description in at_valid.

```
TYPE tp_origin       : UNION (tp_entity_orig, tp_type_orig,
                              tp_no_orig);

TYPE tp_entity_orig : STRUCT (s_descr : tp_descr);

TYPE tp_type_orig   : STRUCT (s_key   : tp_key);

TYPE tp_no_orig     : (sc_no_orig);
```

s_origin has the value sc_no_origin for descriptions which do not belong to compound expressions. (cf. also the attribution rule for at_valid in r_125 from chapter 7.4). If the left subexpression has a value description (for example the expression 1+2), then s_origin denotes the type of the subexpression (tp_type_orig), otherwise s_origin denotes the entity from the subexpression itself (tp_entity_orig).

9.2.1.8. s_enclosing

s_enclosing denotes the enclosing syntactic unit (for example for a record component it denotes the corresponding record type description).

9.3. at_user_reps, at_user_rep : tp_designator_list

at_user_reps and at_user_rep indicate the types, for which representation specifications follow in the same declarative part. For this purpose the designators of these types are enough information (because no overloading of type names is allowed, and the types for which representation specifications are given must be declared in the same declarative part).

9.4. at_impl_descrs, at_impl_subprs : tp_descr_list

The implicitly declared subprograms, types, and enumeration literals must be entered in the environment. Therefore they are represented by a list of descriptions.

9.5. at_labels, at_loops_blocks, at_usable : tp_bl_lab_loops

In order to effect the implicit declaration of the labels, block or loop identifiers, only the identifier and its nature (sc_block, sc_label or sc_loop) of each one must be known. at_usable gives the list of block names which may be used in goto and exit statements.

```
TYPE tp_bl_lab_loop  : STRUCT (s_designator : tp_designator,
                               s_nature     : tp_nature);

TYPE tp_bl_lab_loops : LISTOF tp_bl_lab_loop ;
```

9.6. at_allowed1, at_allowed2, at_valid: tp_descr_set

The attributes at_allowed1, at_allowed2, and at_valid are of different types (tp_descr_set, tp_assoc_list, tp_actual. tp_comp_assoc, tp_constraint, tp_fixed, ...) depending on the nonterminal the attribute belongs to. If this is a name or expression, they are of type tp_descr_set. For all other nonterminals the these attributes have the structure of the corresponding language element in which names and expressions are represented by components of type tp_descr_set. tp_descr_set is used in name and expression analysis. A name may have several meanings and we need a special description for each. The list of all these possible meanings is contained in s_descrs. Literals may have a type and all types derived from this type. Instead of keeping one description for every type, we note in an additional component of tp_descr_set that this entity may have the types appearing in the component s_den.s_type.s_base_type of each description in s_descrs, as well as all types derived from them. Similarly, in the case of an allocator, the object may have any type accessing the type given after **new**, and instead of listing all these types, we mark the second component of tp_descr_set.

```
TYPE tp_descr_set  : STRUCT (s_descrs : tp_descr_list,
                             s_add    : tp_additional);

TYPE tp_additional : (sc_add_deriv, sc_add_access, sc_no_add);
```

The attribute at_valid contains the unique meaning of an expression, i.e. LENGTH(... at_valid.s_descrs) = 1 and at_valid.s_add = sc_no_add. Therefore, at_valid could be of the type tp_descr instead of tp_descr_set, but for technical reasons, it is easier if at_valid has the same type as the attributes at_allowed1 and at_allowed2.

9.7. at_context : tp_context

The attribute at_context contains information about the outer context of a name or an expression. This information is useful in order to determine the language element which is meant by an entity followed by a parenthesized list of associations.

```
TYPE tp_context : ( sc_subtype_ind    ,
                        % subtype indication expected

                    sc_attr_name      ,
                        % the attribute is followed by an index

                    sc_call           ,
                        % procedure or entry call

                    sc_string_is_name,
                        % this string is an operator

                    sc_id_not_visible,
                        % identifiers may denote
                        % formal parameter (in param. assocs.),
                        % or record components (in aggregates);
                        % they may be not directly visible

                    sc_access         ,
                        % within access type specification

                    sc_no_special     );
```

9.8. at_expected : tp_key_void

The attribute at_expected indictes the type expected from a name or expression - if such a unique type is known. Accordingly, it denotes this type, or it is void.

```
TYPE tp_key_void : UNION ( tp_key, tp_void );
```

9.9. at_expected_in, at_expected_out : tp_descr_list

In generic associations (or component associations in a record type representation) at_expected_in and at_expected_out are lists of remaining generic parameters (record components). Therefore they are lists of descriptions.

9.10. at_init : tp_mixed_init

The attribute at_init gives information about the initialization of discriminants: sc_init means that all discriminants up to now have an initialization, sc_not_init means that all discrimininants up to now do not have an initialization, sc_mixed denotes the mixed case.

```
TYPE tp_mixed_init : (sc_init, sc_not_init, sc_mixed );
```

9.11. at_encl_unit : tp_encl_unit

at_encl_unit gives the kind and state of the innermost enclosing block or specification:

```
TYPE tp_encl_unit : STRUCT (s_nature : tp_nature,
                            s_state  : tp_state);
```

9.12. at_first_select : tp_select_type

This contains the types of the select alternatives:

```
TYPE tp_select_type : (sc_accept, sc_terminate, sc_delay,
                       sc_other , sc_empty);
```

9.13. at_select_state : tp_select_state

This attribute indicates the types of select alternatives which have already been encountered:

```
TYPE tp_select_state : STRUCT (s_accept   , s_delay ,
                               s_terminate, s_else  : BOOL);
```

9.14. at_first_stm : tp_stm_type

The attribute at_first_stm is used to check the rules which require that the first statement in conditional or timed entry calls must be an entry call:

```
TYPE tp_stm_type : ( sc_entry_call,
                      % first stm in this list is entry call
                     sc_other_stms);
```

APPENDIX

A1. Attributes and their Meaning

Here we give in alphabetical order the names of all attributes of the AG together with their meaning and their use within the three semantic tasks (cf. 5.1).

at_allowed1: all possible meanings of an expression without consideration of the imported entities (internal to name and expression analysis)

at_allowed2: all possible meanings of an expression, if necessary with consideration of the imported entities (internal to name and expression analysis)

at_assoc: (information transfer)

at_assocs: (information transfer)

at_block_no: the number of enclosing blocks (internal to semantic checks)

at_char: whether a character literal appears in a list of enumeration literals (internal to declaration elaboration)

at_choices: (information transfer)

at_comp: (information transfer)

at_comps: (information transfer)

at_context: information about the outer context of an expression determining the nature of the expression (internal to name and expression analysis)

at_def: (information transfer)

at_designator: output of lexical analysis

at_designators: (information transfer)

at_discrim_allowed: whether references to discriminants of enclosing records are allowed (internal to semantic checks)

at_discriminants: (information transfer)

at_dscrt_ranges: (information transfer)

at_empty: whether a discriminant part or exception part is given, or not (internal to semantic checks)

at_encl_unit: the state and nature of the enclosing body or specification (internal to semantic checks)

at_env: intermediate environment containing descriptions of all entities declared until now and an incomplete description for the currently declared entity (internal to declaration elaboration)

at_env_in: environment containing descriptions of all entities declared until now, except the currently declared entities (if any) (output of declaration elaboration)

at_env_out: environment containing descriptions of all entities declared up to now, including the currently declared entities and any implicitly introduced types, subprograms or literals (output of declaration elaboration)

at_expected: the expected type of an expression (internal to name and expression analysis)

at_expected_in: the remaining generic parameters (resp. components) in an instantiation (resp. record type representation specification), before the current association (resp. component representation) (internal to name and expression analysis)

at_expected_out: the unspecified generic parameters (resp. components) in an instantiation (resp. record type representation) (internal to name and expression analysis)

at_first_select: the type of the first statement in a list of statements (whether it is an accept, terminate, else or delay) (internal to semantic checks)

at_first_stm: the nature of the first statement in a list of statements; (internal to semantic checks)

at_has_range: whether a fixed point constraint includes a range constraint (internal to semantic checks)

at_header: (information transfer)

at_impl_descrs: list of descriptions for implicitly declared enumeration literals, array types, or derived types (internal to declaration elaboration)

at_impl_subprs: descriptions of the subprograms derived by a derived type declaration (internal to declaration elaboration) at_init: whether in a discriminant part all, some, or none of the discriminants are initialized (internal to semantic checks)

at_instantiation: (information transfer)

at_is_exp: instead of a name also an expression may appear (internal to semantic checks)

at_is_item: whether a pragma may appear in a declarative part (internal to semantic checks)

at_is_last: whether a choice (association, case alternative, exception handler, variant) is the last one in the corresponding expression (association list, case statement, exception part or variant part) (internal to semantic checks)

at_is_operator: whether a header belongs to some operator declaration (internal to semantic checks)

at_keys, at_keys1, at_keys2: unique access to the currently declared entities (output of declaration elaboration)

at_labels: the labels appearing within the current body (internal to declaration elaboration)

at_loops_blocks: the loop or block identifiers appearing within the current body or block (internal to declaration elaboration)

at_names: (information transfer)

at_no_code_stms: whether code statements follow (internal to semantic checks)

at_no_decls: whether a list of declarative items contains only use clauses and pragmas (internal to semantic checks)

at_op: output of lexical analysis

at_others_allowed: whether the choice "others" is allowed in an array aggregate (internal to semantic checks)

at_param_no: the number of parameters in a header (internal to semantic checks)

at_pos: position of an enumeration literal in the enumeration type declaration (internal to declaration elaboration)

at_positional_allowed: whether positional associations may appear (internal to semantic checks)

at_rename: (information transfer)

at_rep: (information transfer)

at_reps: (information transfer)

at_return_required: whether a return statement is required at the end of the current statement resp. statement list (internal to semantic checks)

at_select_state: the types of select alternatives up to now (internal to semantic checks)

at_spec: (information transfer)

at_type: (information transfer)

at_unconstrained: whether an array type definition is an unconstrained array (internal to semantic checks)

at_usable: labels appearing in the following statements (internal to semantic checks)

at_user_rep: the identifier of the type appearing in a length, record, or enumeration type representation specification (internal to declaration elaboration)

at_user_reps: identifiers of the types appearing in length, record, or enumeration type representation specifications in the same declarative part following the current position (internal to declaration elaboration)

at_valid : the unique meaning of the expression (output of name and expression analysis)

at_value: output of lexical analysis

at_variant: (information transfer)

at_variants: (information transfer)

at_with_use : whether imported entities must be taken into account (internal to name and expression analysis)

A2. Attributes and their Ocurrence in the Rationale

Here we give the attributes of the AG in alphabetic order together with an index to the chapters of the rationale where this attribute is discussed. The first column contains the name of the attribute, the second contains the index of the chapters where the meaning and use of this attribute is described. The third column contains the index of the chapter where the type of the attribute is given.

at_allowed1	7.1	9.6
at_allowed2	7.3	9.6
at_assoc		
at_assocs		
at_block_no	8.3.10	
at_char	6.6	
at_choices		
at_comp		
at_comps		
at_context	7.6	9.7
at_def		
at_designator		
at_designators		
at_discrim_allowed	8.5.4.1	
at_discriminants		
at_dscrt_ranges		
at_empty	8.3.3, 8.3.12	
at_encl_unit	8.3.7	9.11
at_env	6.3	9.2
at_env_in	6.1	9.2
at_env_out	6.1	9.2
at_expected	7.5	9.8
at_expected_in	7.7	9.9
at_expected_out	7.7	9.9
at_first_select	8.3.11	9.12
at_first_stm	8.5.1.1	9.14
at_has_range	8.3.5	
at_header		
at_impl_descrs	6.6	9.4
at_impl_subprs	6.7	9.4
at_init	8.3.6	9.10
at_instantiation		
at_is_exp	8.3.14	
at_is_item	8.3.13	
at_is_last	8.3.2	
at_is_operator	8.3.9	
at_keys	6.2, 6.7	9.1
at_keys1	6.3	9.1
at_keys2	6.3	9.1
at_labels	6.4	9.5
at_loops_blocks	6.4	9.5
at_names		
at_no_code_stms	8.3.12	
at_no_decls	8.3.12	
at_op		
at_others_allowed	8.5.1.2	
at_param_no	8.3.9	
at_pos	6.5	

at_positional_allowed	8.3.1	
at_rename		
at_rep		
at_reps		
at_return_required	8.3.8	
at_select_state	8.3.11	9.13
at_spec		
at_type		
at_unconstrained	8.3.4	
at_usable	8.5.4.2	9.5
at_user_rep	6.9	9.3
at_user_reps	6.10	9.3
at_valid	7.4, 7.7	9.6
at_value		
at_variant		
at_variants		
at_with_use	7.2	

P A R T   C:

T H E   A G

AG0. Introduction

AG0.1 Conventions Used in the AG

Naming Conventions

Due to the length of the AG, and in order to increase readability, we used the following naming conventions: [Kast-79]:

Names of

- types start with **tp_**
- components start with **s_**
- scalars start with **sc_**
- constants start with **c_**
- attributes start with **at_**
- productions start with **r_**
- parameters start with **p_**
- functions start with **f_**, **ch_** or **cf_**
- symbols have no prefix

Functions

- starting with **f_** calculate a new value and sometimes perform elementary error recovery.
- starting with **ch_** return boolean values. They check language rules and their value is used for the generation of error messages.
- starting with **cf_** check for violation of language rules and perform error recovery.

Some function names only differ in a last additional number (e.g. f_allowed_converted and f_allowed_converted1 or f_base_type and f_base_type1). This means either that f_...1 is called within f_... (e.g. for list processing), or that the two functions generally have the same effect and only differ in the type of their parameters

Nonterminals and reserved words in ALADIN are written in upper case letters, all other identifiers are written in lower case letters.

The attributes which logically contain the same kind of information, have the same name, even if their type is different (cf. Appendix 1 of Part B).

Structure_of_Syntactic_Rules_and_Attribution_Rules

The general format of rules is

```
   RULE  r_<rule_number>
      <syntactic_rule>
      [% - restrictions imposed by diana (need not be checked)]
      [% - relation to the concrete Ada syntax]
   [STATIC
      <attribution_rules, including conditions>]
      [% - evaluation rules for semantic diana attributes]
   END;
```

Error_Messages

Each rule of Ada which can be tested at compile time, is checked in the AG by one or more CONDITIONs. These conditions are preceded by a comment of the form: **%C x/y** where x denotes the chapter of the Reference Manual [Ada80], and y denotes a rule mentioned in this chapter. E.g. **%C 6.5/1** means the first rule in the chapter 6.5 Function Subprograms: "only functions may have parameters of mode in".

Compiler_Errors

In the AG we make several assumptions about values of attributes, which are not explicitly expressed by the attribute types in ALADIN. E.g. if the nature of a description is sc_type, then its denotation must be tp_type_den. Such assumptions are documented in two different ways :

- by the call of predefined ALADIN operators ,(e.g. HEAD, TAIL) or by type qualification (QUA)
- by CONDITIONs producing the error message "compiler error"

In AG0.3 we describe some assertions about attributes or components of the type tp_descr.

Warnings

Errors which belong to the dynamic semantics, but which the AG can discover are reported as well. These messages are preceded by "W:", which indicates that a warning is to be issued.

AGO.2. Completeness and Parametrization of the AG

Here we give the functions whose bodies are not completely specified in the AG (cf. 2.4).

Parametrization

- Evaluation of static expressions:

  f_eval
  f_eval_converted
  f_eval_function
  f_eval_indexed
  f_eval_less_equal
  f_eval_less_equal1
  f_eval_membership
  f_eval_selected
  f_eval_short_circuit
  f_eval_exp

- Type mapping (evaluation of machine dependent representation attributes)

  f_tm_map_derived
  f_tm_map_subtype
  f_tm_map_type

- Values from the package STANDARD:

  c_max_int_value
  c_min_int_value
  c_max_digits_value
  c_min_priority_value
  c_max_priority_value

Incomplete

- Tree structure comparison

  f_tree_same_constraint
  f_tree_same_value

The functions and constants reflecting the parametrization with the machine dependent part are indicated by the comment: % >MACHINE< , the incomplete functions are indicated by the comment: % >INCOMPLETE<

AGD.3. Assertions about the Structure of Descriptions

Here we describe some relationships which must be satisfied for components of a description. This list is not complete, it merely serves to explain the intention of some components of tp_descr.

The relationships are expressed with a notation similar to ALADIN.

Relationships between s_nature and s_den of tp_descr

```
IF s_state  = sc_complete THEN

  CASE s_nature OF
  sc_constant           :
  sc_variable           :
  sc_in                 :
  sc_in_out             :
  sc_out                :
  sc_number             :
  sc_rec_comp           :
  sc_discriminant       :
  sc_converted_var      :      s_den IS tp_object

  sc_type               :      s_den IS tp_type_den

  sc_subtype            :      s_den IS tp_constrained

  sc_function           :      s_den QUA tp_subpr
                                  .s_header IS tp_function

  sc_procedure          :      s_den QUA tp_subpr
                                  .s_header IS tp_procedure

  sc_generic_function   :
  sc_generic_procedure  :      s_den IS tp_generic

  sc_entry              :      s_den IS tp_entry

  sc_entry_family       :      s_den IS tp_entry_family

  sc_package            :      s_den IS tp_package   OR
                               s_den IS tp_generic

  sc_common_op          :
  sc_predefined_op      :
  sc_universal_op       :      s_den IS tp_operation

  sc_task               :      s_den IS tp_object

  sc_exception          :
  sc_label              :
  sc_block              :
  sc_loop               :      s_den IS tp_void

  sc_enum_literal       :      s_den IS tp_enum_literal
```

```
  sc_void_nature        :   s_den IS tp_void
  sc_error_nature       :   s_den  IS tp_object
  ESAC
FI
```

Relationships_between_s_nature_and_s_key_of_tp_descr

```
CASE s_nature OF

sc_value                :       s_key  =  c_key

OUT                     :       s_key  =/ c_key

ESAC
```

Relationships_between_s_state_and_s_nature_or_s_den

```
CASE s_state OF

sc_deferred              :  s_nature = sc_constant

sc_incompl_private          s_nature = sc_type  AND
                          ( s_den QUA tp_type_den IS tp_private  OR
                            s_den QUA tp_type_den IS tp_l_private )

sc_complete_generic      :  s_nature = sc_in         %
                            s_nature = sc_out        %  generic
                            s_nature = sc_type       %
                            s_nature = sc_function   % parameters
                            s_nature = sc_procedure  %

sc_in_init               :  s_den IS tp_object

sc_incomplete            :  s_nature  IS sc_type AND
                           (s_den QUA tp_type_den
                              IS tp_incompl_type)

sc_spec_complete         :   (s_nature = sc_type   AND
                              s_den QUA tp_type_den IS tp_task_spec)
                                                              OR
                              s_nature = sc_function          OR
                              s_nature = sc_generic_function  OR
                              s_nature = sc_procedure         OR
                              s_nature = sc_generic_procedure OR
                              s_nature = sc_generic_package   OR
                              s_nature = sc_label             OR
                              s_nature = sc_block             OR
                              s_nature = sc_loop
```

```
sc_in_body                 :  s_nature = sc_loop                OR
                              s_nature = sc_block               OR
                              s_nature = sc_function            OR
                              s_nature = sc_generic_function    OR
                              s_nature = sc_procedure           OR
                              s_nature = sc_generic_procedure   OR
                              s_nature = sc_package

sc_in_handler              :  s_nature = sc_block               OR
                              s_nature = sc_function            OR
                              s_nature = sc_generic_function    OR
                              s_nature = sc_procedure           OR
                              s_nature = sc_generic_procedure   OR
                              s_nature = sc_package

sc_in_generic_part         :  s_nature = sc_void_nature        AND
                              s_den   IS tp_void

sc_record                  :   s_nature = sc_type              AND
                               s_den   IS tp_void

sc_in_formal_part          :  (s_nature = sc_function           OR
                               s_nature = sc_generic_function   OR
                               s_nature = sc_procedure          OR
                               s_nature = sc_generic_procedure  OR
                               s_nature = sc_package             )
                                                               AND
                               s_den   IS tp_void
sc_in_discr_part           :   s_nature = sc_type              AND
                               s_den IS tp_void

sc_in_visible              :  (s_nature = sc_type               OR
                                                  % task type
                               s_nature = sc_package             )
                                                               AND
                               s_den IS tp_void

sc_in_private              :   s_nature = sc_package           AND
                               s_den IS tp_void

sc_void_state              :   s_nature = sc_void_nature

ESAC
```

```
%%%%%%%%%%%%%%%%%%%%%%%%%%%%%%%%%%%%%%%%%%%%%%%%%%%%%%%%%%%%%%%%%%%%%%%
%                                                                     %
% AG1 Attribute Types                                                 %
%                                                                     %
%%%%%%%%%%%%%%%%%%%%%%%%%%%%%%%%%%%%%%%%%%%%%%%%%%%%%%%%%%%%%%%%%%%%%%%
%                                                                     %
%  In this chapter the types of the attributes are given in alphabetic %
%  order                                                              %
%                                                                     %
%  Most of these types describe the structure of the environment-     %
%  attributes (definition table). The type of such attributes is      %
%  tp_env.                                                            %
%                                                                     %
%%%%%%%%%%%%%%%%%%%%%%%%%%%%%%%%%%%%%%%%%%%%%%%%%%%%%%%%%%%%%%%%%%%%%%%
TYPE tp_access          : STRUCT (s_accessed : tp_constrained);

                          % Constraints imposed on accessed objects
                          % may be represented as constraint of
                          % s_accessed as well as constraint of the
                          % access type (cf. f_allowed_all and
                          % ch_constraint).
TYPE tp_actual          : UNION (tp_descr_set, tp_dscrt_range);

TYPE tp_additional      : (sc_add_deriv, sc_add_access, sc_no_add);

TYPE tp_address_spec    : STRUCT (s_address : tp_descr_set);

TYPE tp_anonymous       : (sc_anonymous);

TYPE tp_array           : STRUCT (s_indices     : tp_dscrt_range_list,
                                  s_comp_type   : tp_constrained);

                          % s_indices is a list of elements of
                          % type tp_index. Tp_array always denotes
                          % an unconstrained array type.
                          % Constraint arrays are represented
                          % as subtypes of unconstrained
                          % arrays (cf. tp_constraint).
TYPE tp_assoc           : UNION (tp_comp_assoc, tp_dscrt_range);

TYPE tp_assoc_list      : LISTOF tp_assoc;

TYPE tp_assoc_list_void : UNION (tp_assoc_list, tp_void);

TYPE tp_bl_lab_loop     : STRUCT (s_designator  : tp_designator,
                                  s_key         : tp_key,
                                  s_nature      : tp_nature);
TYPE tp_bl_lab_loops    : LISTOF tp_bl_lab_loop;

TYPE tp_block_context   : (sc_block_stub, sc_stm);

TYPE tp_box             : (sc_box);

TYPE tp_choice          : UNION (tp_others, tp_dscrt_range,
                                 tp_descr, tp_descr_set);
```

```
                                    % tp_descr_set is used in case of array
                                    % aggregates.
                                    % tp_descr denotes the entity (parameter or
                                    % record component) referred to in a
                                    % procedure/function/entry call,
                                    % instantiation or record aggregate.
TYPE tp_choice_context   : (sc_handler, sc_case, sc_variant, sc_named);

TYPE tp_choice_list      : LISTOF tp_choice;

TYPE tp_choice_list_void : UNION (tp_choice_list, tp_void);

TYPE tp_comp             : UNION (tp_variant_part, tp_descr_list,
                                  tp_descr, tp_void);

                                    % in tp_record, one component declaration
                                    % introducing several entities (originally
                                    % described by tp_descr_list) is described
                                    % by a list of components each introducing
                                    % one entity (tp_descr).

TYPE tp_comp_assoc       : STRUCT (s_choices : tp_choice_list,
                                   s_actual  : tp_descr_set);

TYPE tp_comp_assoc_void  : UNION (tp_comp_assoc, tp_void);

TYPE tp_comp_list        : LISTOF tp_comp;

TYPE tp_comp_list_void   : UNION (tp_comp_list, tp_void);

TYPE tp_comp_rep         : STRUCT (s_comp         : tp_key,
                                   s_relative     : tp_descr_set,
                                   s_range_constr : tp_range_constr);

TYPE tp_comp_rep_list    : LISTOF tp_comp_rep;

TYPE tp_constrained      : STRUCT (s_base_type  : tp_key,
                                   s_constraint : tp_constraint);

                                    % s_base_type always refers to a type
                                    % description, never to a subtype.
                                    %
                                    % For s_constraint the indicated type of
                                    % constituents of the constraint is
                                    % irrelevant, i.e. it is never taken into
                                    % account. Only the values are regarded.

TYPE tp_constraint       : UNION (tp_range_constr, tp_fixed, tp_float,
                                  tp_dscrt_range_list, % index_constrain
                                  tp_assoc_list, %discriminant_constrain
                                  tp_void);

TYPE tp_context          : (sc_subtype_ind, sc_no_special,
                            sc_attr_name, sc_call, sc_string_is_name,
                            sc_id_not_visible, sc_access);

TYPE tp_controlled_rep   : (sc_controlled_rep);
```

```
TYPE tp_den               : UNION (tp_object,
                                   tp_type_den,
                                   tp_constrained,
                                   tp_subpr,
                                   tp_entry,
                                   tp_entry_family,
                                   tp_package,
                                   tp_generic,
                                   tp_enum_literal,
                                   tp_dummy,
                                   tp_dummy_aggr,
                                   tp_operation,
                                   tp_void);

TYPE tp_den_same          : UNION (tp_den, tp_same);

TYPE tp_derived           : STRUCT (s_parent_type : tp_key);

                               % s_parent_type always refers to a base
                               % type. A type derived from a subtype
                               % is represented as a subtype
                               % whose base type is derived from the
                               % corresponding base type.

TYPE tp_descr             : STRUCT (s_designator  : tp_designator,
                                    s_key         : tp_key,
                                    s_repr        : tp_repr,
                                    s_state       : tp_state,
                                    s_nature      : tp_nature,
                                    s_den         : tp_den,
                                    s_origin      : tp_origin,
                                    s_enclosing   : tp_key);

TYPE tp_descr_list        : LISTOF tp_descr;

TYPE tp_descr_list_list   : LISTOF tp_descr_list;

TYPE tp_descr_list_void   : UNION (tp_descr_list, tp_void);

TYPE tp_descr_set         : STRUCT (s_descrs    : tp_descr_list,
                                    s_add       : tp_additional);

                               % describes a set of descriptions
                               % containing s_descrs and additionally
                               % those described by s_add.

TYPE tp_descr_set_void    : UNION (tp_descr_set, tp_void);

TYPE tp_descr_void        : UNION (tp_descr, tp_void);

TYPE tp_descrs_list       : LISTOF tp_descr_set;

TYPE tp_designator        : UNION (SYMB, tp_anonymous,
                                   tp_error_designator);

TYPE tp_designator_list   : LISTOF tp_designator;

TYPE tp_dscrt_range       : UNION (tp_constrained, tp_range,
                                   tp_index);
```

```
TYPE tp_dscrt_range_list: LISTOF tp_dscrt_range;

TYPE tp_dummy           : (sc_dummy);

TYPE tp_dummy_aggr      : STRUCT (s_assocs : tp_assoc_list);

TYPE tp_encl_unit       : STRUCT (s_nature : tp_nature,
                                  s_state  : tp_state);

TYPE tp_entity_orig     : STRUCT (s_descr : tp_descr);

TYPE tp_entry           : STRUCT (s_params : tp_descr_list);

TYPE tp_entry_family    : STRUCT (s_dscrt_range : tp_dscrt_range,
                                  s_entry       : tp_entry);

TYPE tp_enum_literal    : STRUCT (s_type : tp_key,
                                  s_pos  : INT,
                                  s_char : BOOL);

TYPE tp_enum_rep        : LISTOF INT;

TYPE tp_enum_type       : STRUCT (s_literals  : tp_key_list,
                                  s_char      : BOOL);

TYPE tp_env             : STRUCT (s_imported    : tp_key_list,
                                  s_global,
                                  s_local       : tp_descr_list,
                                  s_enclosing   : tp_key);

TYPE tp_error_designator: (sc_error_designator);

TYPE tp_error_type      : (sc_error_type);

TYPE tp_exception       : (sc_constraint_error, sc_numeric_error);

TYPE tp_exp_kind        : (sc_literal, sc_static, sc_not_static,
                           sc_no_exp);

TYPE tp_fixed           : STRUCT (s_delta : tp_descr_set,
                                  s_range : tp_range);

TYPE tp_float           : STRUCT (s_digits : tp_descr_set,
                                  s_range  : tp_range);

TYPE tp_formal_type     : (sc_formal_discrt, sc_formal_fixed,
                           sc_formal_float, sc_formal_integer);

TYPE tp_function        : STRUCT (s_params : tp_descr_list,
                                  s_result : tp_constrained);

TYPE tp_generic         : STRUCT (s_generic_params : tp_descr_list,
                                  s_den            : tp_den);

TYPE tp_generic_header  : UNION (tp_header, tp_package);

TYPE tp_header          : UNION (tp_function, tp_procedure,
                                 tp_entry, tp_entry_family);

TYPE tp_incompl_type    : STRUCT (s_discriminants : tp_descr_list);
```

```
TYPE tp_index            : STRUCT (s_type : tp_constrained);

TYPE tp_init             : STRUCT (s_value    : tp_value,
                                   s_exp_kind : tp_exp_kind);

TYPE tp_instantiation    : STRUCT (s_name   : tp_descr,
                                   s_assocs : tp_assoc_list);

TYPE tp_int_list         : LISTOF INT;

TYPE tp_integer          : STRUCT (s_range : tp_range);

TYPE tp_key              : UNION (INT);

TYPE tp_key_list         : LISTOF tp_key;

TYPE tp_key_void         : UNION (tp_key, tp_void);

TYPE tp_l_private        : STRUCT (s_discriminants : tp_descr_list);

TYPE tp_length_spec      : STRUCT (s_kind : tp_length_spec_kind,
                                   s_val : tp_descr_set);

TYPE tp_length_spec_kind: (sc_obj_size, sc_collection_size,
                           sc_task_size, sc_actual_delta);

TYPE tp_map              : STRUCT (s_old,
                                   s_new : tp_descr);

TYPE tp_map_list         : LISTOF tp_map;

TYPE tp_mixed_init       : (sc_init, sc_not_init, sc_mixed);

TYPE tp_nature           : (sc_constant, sc_variable, sc_in, sc_in_out,
                           sc_out, sc_number, sc_value, sc_rec_comp,
                           sc_discriminant, sc_converted_var,
                           sc_type, sc_subtype,
                           sc_function, sc_procedure,
                           sc_generic_function, sc_generic_procedure,
                           sc_entry, sc_entry_family,
                           sc_common_op, sc_predefined_op,
                           sc_universal_op,
                           sc_package, sc_task,
                           sc_exception,
                           sc_enum_literal,
                           sc_label, sc_block, sc_loop,
                           sc_void_nature, sc_error_nature);

TYPE tp_nature_same      : UNION (tp_nature, tp_same);

TYPE tp_no_default       : (sc_no_default);

TYPE tp_no_orig          : (sc_no_orig);

TYPE tp_no_val           : (sc_no_val);

TYPE tp_object           : STRUCT (s_type : tp_constrained,
                                   s_init : tp_init);
```

```
TYPE tp_object_def          : UNION (tp_descr, tp_rename, tp_void);

TYPE tp_op                  :
       (sc_in_op, sc_not_in_op,
        sc_and_then_op, sc_or_else_op,
        sc_not_op, sc_and_op, sc_or_op, sc_xor_op,
        sc_co_not_op, sc_co_and_op, sc_co_or_op, sc_co_xor_op,
        sc_co_minus_op, sc_co_plus_op, sc_co_abs_op,
        sc_co_mult_op, sc_co_div_op, sc_co_exp_op,
        sc_co_concat_op,
        sc_co_equal_op, sc_co_n_equal_op,
        sc_co_less_op, sc_co_le_equal_op,
        sc_co_greater_op, sc_co_gr_equal_op,
        sc_ui_minus1_op, sc_ui_plus1_op, sc_ui_abs_op, sc_ui_plus_op,
        sc_ui_minus_op, sc_ui_mult_op, sc_ui_div_op, sc_ui_exp_op,
        sc_ui_rem_op, sc_ui_mod_op,
        sc_si_minus1_op, sc_si_plus1_op, sc_si_abs_op, sc_si_plus_op,
        sc_si_minus_op, sc_si_mult_op, sc_si_div_op, sc_si_exp_op,
        sc_si_rem_op, sc_si_mod_op,
        sc_i_minus1_op, sc_i_plus1_op, sc_i_abs_op, sc_i_plus_op,
        sc_i_minus_op, sc_i_mult_op, sc_i_div_op, sc_i_exp_op,
        sc_i_rem_op, sc_i_mod_op,
        sc_li_minus1_op, sc_li_plus1_op, sc_li_abs_op, sc_li_plus_op,
        sc_li_minus_op, sc_li_mult_op, sc_li_div_op, sc_li_exp_op,
        sc_li_rem_op, sc_li_mod_op,
        sc_ur_minus1_op, sc_ur_plus1_op, sc_ur_abs_op, sc_ur_plus_op,
        sc_ur_minus_op, sc_ur_mult_op, sc_ur_div_op, sc_ur_exp_op,
        sc_ur_ui_mult_op, sc_ui_ur_mult_op, sc_ur_ui_div_op,
        sc_sf_minus1_op, sc_sf_plus1_op, sc_sf_abs_op, sc_sf_plus_op,
        sc_sf_minus_op, sc_sf_mult_op, sc_sf_div_op, sc_sf_exp_op,
        sc_f_minus1_op, sc_f_plus1_op, sc_f_abs_op, sc_f_plus_op,
        sc_f_minus_op, sc_f_mult_op, sc_f_div_op, sc_f_exp_op,
        sc_lf_minus1_op, sc_lf_plus1_op, sc_lf_abs_op, sc_lf_plus_op,
        sc_lf_minus_op, sc_lf_mult_op, sc_lf_div_op, sc_lf_exp_op,
        sc_fi_minus1_op, sc_fi_plus1_op, sc_fi_abs_op, sc_fi_plus_op,
        sc_fi_minus_op, sc_fi_mult_op, sc_fi_div_op,
        sc_fi_i_mult_op, sc_fi_i_div_op,
        sc_i_fi_mult_op,
        sc_concat_op,
        sc_no_op, sc_no_predef_op);

TYPE tp_operation           : STRUCT (s_op : tp_op);

TYPE tp_op_list             : LISTOF tp_op;

TYPE tp_origin              : UNION (tp_entity_orig, tp_type_orig,
                                     tp_no_orig);

TYPE tp_others              : (sc_others);

TYPE tp_pack_rep            : (sc_pack_rep);

TYPE tp_package             : STRUCT (s_visible,
                                      s_pack_spec : tp_descr_list,
                                      s_imported  : tp_key_list,
                                      s_body_prov : BOOL);

TYPE tp_package_def         : UNION (tp_instantiation, tp_rename,
                                     tp_package);
```

```
TYPE tp_private          : STRUCT (s_discriminants : tp_descr_list);

TYPE tp_procedure        : STRUCT (s_params : tp_descr_list);

TYPE tp_range            : UNION (tp_range_constr, tp_void);

TYPE tp_range_constr     : STRUCT (s_lower_bound,
                                   s_upper_bound : tp_descr_set);

TYPE tp_range_val        : STRUCT (s_min, s_max : INT);

TYPE tp_range_val_list   : LISTOF tp_range_val;

TYPE tp_real_val         : (sc_real_val); %>MACHINE<

TYPE tp_record           : STRUCT (s_descrs : tp_descr_list,
                                   s_comps  : tp_comp_list);

                           % s_descrs is a list of all components
                           % of the record, inluding the discriminants
                           % and implicitly declared (array) types
                           % whereas s_comps represents the structure
                           % of the record (without the discriminants)

TYPE tp_record_rep       : STRUCT (s_align     : tp_descr_set,
                                   s_comp_reps : tp_comp_rep_list);

TYPE tp_rename           : STRUCT (s_descr    : tp_descr);

TYPE tp_rename_void      : UNION (tp_rename, tp_void);

TYPE tp_rep_state        : (sc_start_rep,
                            sc_user_rep,
                            sc_static_rep,
                            sc_dynamic_rep,
                            sc_incompl_rep);

TYPE tp_repr             : STRUCT (s_rep_state : tp_rep_state,
                                   s_reps      : tp_rep_list);

TYPE tp_rep              : UNION (tp_length_spec, tp_enum_rep,
                                  tp_record_rep, tp_address_spec,
                                  tp_controlled_rep, tp_pack_rep);

TYPE tp_rep_list         : LISTOF tp_rep;

TYPE tp_repr_same        : UNION (tp_repr, tp_same);

TYPE tp_same             : (sc_same);

TYPE tp_select_state     : STRUCT (s_accept,
                                   s_delay,
                                   s_terminate,
                                   s_else      : BOOL);

TYPE tp_select_type      : (sc_accept, sc_delay, sc_terminate,
                            sc_other, sc_empty);

TYPE tp_state            : (sc_id_established, sc_implicitly_declared,
                            sc_deferred, sc_incompl_private,
```

```
                              sc_complete_generic, sc_in_init,
                              sc_incomplete, sc_complete ,sc_spec_complete,
                              sc_in_body, sc_in_handler,
                              sc_in_generic_part,sc_in_record,
                              sc_in_formal_part, sc_in_discr_part,
                              sc_in_visible, sc_in_private,
                              sc_error_state, sc_void_state);

TYPE tp_state_same        : UNION (tp_state, tp_same);

TYPE tp_stm_type          : (sc_entry_call, sc_other_stms);

TYPE tp_string_val        : LISTOF SYMB;

TYPE tp_subpr             : STRUCT (s_spec : tp_header,
                                    s_def  : tp_subpr_def,
                                    s_op   : tp_op);

                              % s_spec IS tp_function OR tp_procedure

TYPE tp_subpr_def         : UNION (tp_rename, tp_void, tp_box,
                                   tp_instantiation, tp_no_default,
                                   tp_key);

                              % tp_key is used to refer to the original
                              % of an implicitly derived subprogram or
                              % to the default of a generic parameter

TYPE tp_task_def          : UNION (tp_rename, tp_constrained);

TYPE tp_task_spec         : STRUCT (s_visible : tp_descr_list);

TYPE tp_type              : UNION (tp_fixed, tp_float, tp_integer,
                                   tp_incompl_type, tp_universal,
                                   tp_record, tp_array, tp_derived,
                                   tp_access, tp_enum_type, tp_private,
                                   tp_l_private, tp_constrained,
                                   tp_formal_type, tp_task_spec,
                                   tp_void, tp_error_type);

TYPE tp_type_den          : STRUCT (s_type           : tp_type,
                                    s_derivable_subprogs
                                                     : tp_key_list);

                              % within tp_type_den, tp_constrained
                              % is not used for s_type.

TYPE tp_type_orig         : STRUCT (s_key : tp_key);

                              % always refers to a base type

TYPE tp_type_range        : UNION (tp_constrained, tp_range_constr);

TYPE tp_universal         : (sc_universal);

TYPE tp_user_reps         : LISTOF tp_designator;

TYPE tp_use_decide        : UNION (tp_choice, %includes descr_set, range,
                                   tp_fixed, tp_float);
```

```
TYPE tp_value              : UNION (INT, tp_real_val,
                                    tp_assoc_list, % for aggregate values
                                    tp_string_val,
                                    tp_no_val, tp_exception);

TYPE tp_variant            : STRUCT (s_choices : tp_choice_list,
                                     s_comps   : tp_comp_list);

TYPE tp_variant_list       : LISTOF tp_variant;

TYPE tp_variant_part       : STRUCT (s_discr    : tp_key,
                                     s_variants : tp_variant_list);

TYPE tp_void               : (sc_void);
```

```
%%%%%%%%%%%%%%%%%%%%%%%%%%%%%%%%%%%%%%%%%%%%%%%%%%%%%%%%%%%%%%%%%%%%%%%%%%%%%%%
%                                                                             %
% AG2. Constants                                                              %
%                                                                             %
%%%%%%%%%%%%%%%%%%%%%%%%%%%%%%%%%%%%%%%%%%%%%%%%%%%%%%%%%%%%%%%%%%%%%%%%%%%%%%%
%                                                                             %
%  In general constants are used for two purposes:                            %
%     - to give a name to construct with a certain meaning                    %
%       (e.g. the standard environment is named c_standard)                   %
%     - to have an abbreviation for a construct, which is often               %
%       used ,possibly in different contexts and with a different             %
%       meaning (e.g. constants used in error cases to provide a              %
%       consistent result)                                                    %
%                                                                             %
%  Descriptions for entities, which are (explicitly or implicitly)            %
%  predefined in Ada (e.g. package STANDARD, arithmetic operators) are        %
%  contained in the constant c_start_env.                                     %
%                                                                             %
%%%%%%%%%%%%%%%%%%%%%%%%%%%%%%%%%%%%%%%%%%%%%%%%%%%%%%%%%%%%%%%%%%%%%%%%%%%%%%%

%------------------------------------------------------------------------------
%                                                                             -
% 2.1. Designators                                                            -
%                                                                             -
%------------------------------------------------------------------------------

CONST c_standard_desi              : 'standard';
CONST c_bool_desi                  : 'bool';
CONST c_true_desi                  : 'true';
CONST c_false_desi                 : 'false';
CONST c_x_desi                     : 'x';
CONST c_y_desi                     : 'y';
CONST c_not_desi                   : 'not';
CONST c_and_desi                   : 'and';
CONST c_or_desi                    : 'or';
CONST c_xor_desi                   : 'xor';
CONST c_float_desi                 : 'float';
CONST c_int_desi                   : 'integer';
CONST c_plus_desi                  : '+';
CONST c_minus_desi                 : '-';
CONST c_abs_desi                   : 'abs';
CONST c_mult_desi                  : '*';
CONST c_div_desi                   : '/';
CONST c_rem_desi                   : 'rem';
CONST c_mod_desi                   : 'mod';
CONST c_exp_desi                   : '**';
CONST c_equal_desi                 : '=';
CONST c_n_equal_desi               : '/=';
CONST c_greater_desi               : '>';
CONST c_gr_equal_desi              : '>=';
CONST c_less_desi                  : '<';
CONST c_le_equal_desi              : '<=';
CONST c_char_desi                  : 'character';
CONST c_char_a_desi                : 'a';
CONST c_char_b_desi                : 'b';
CONST c_char_c_desi                : 'c';
CONST c_lc_a_desi                  : 'lc_a';
CONST c_ascii_desi                 : 'ascii';
CONST c_string_desi                : 'string';
CONST c_concat_desi                : '&';
```

```
CONST c_natural_desi           : 'natural';
CONST c_priority_desi          : 'priority';
CONST c_duration_desi          : 'duration';
CONST c_system_desi            : 'system';
CONST c_system_name_desi       : 'system_name';
CONST c_name_desi              : 'name';
CONST c_storage_desi           : 'storage';
CONST c_memory_size_desi       : 'memory_size';
CONST c_min_int_desi           : 'min_int';
CONST c_max_int_desi           : 'max_int';
CONST c_constr_error_desi      : 'constraint_error';
CONST c_num_error_desi         : 'numeric_error';
CONST c_sel_error_desi         : 'select_error';
CONST c_stor_error_desi        : 'storage_error';
CONST c_task_error_desi        : 'tasking_error';
CONST c_address_desi           : 'address';
CONST c_base_desi              : 'base';
CONST c_size_desi              : 'size';
CONST c_first_desi             : 'first';
CONST c_last_desi              : 'last';
CONST c_image_desi             : 'image';
CONST c_val_desi               : 'val';
CONST c_value_desi             : 'value';
CONST c_pos_desi               : 'pos';
CONST c_pred_desi              : 'pred';
CONST c_succ_desi              : 'succ';
CONST c_delta_desi             : 'delta';
CONST c_act_delta_desi         : 'actual_delta';
CONST c_bits_desi              : 'bits';
CONST c_large_desi             : 'large';
CONST c_mach_rounds_desi       : 'machine_rounds';
CONST c_digits_desi            : 'digits';
CONST c_mantissa_desi          : 'mantissa';
CONST c_emax_desi              : 'emax';
CONST c_small_desi             : 'small';
CONST c_epsilon_desi           : 'epsilon';
CONST c_mach_radix_desi        : 'machine_radix';
CONST c_mach_mantissa_desi     : 'machine_mantissa';
CONST c_mach_emin_desi         : 'machine_emin';
CONST c_mach_emax_desi         : 'machine_emax';
CONST c_mach_overfl_desi       : 'machine_overflows';
CONST c_length_desi            : 'length';
CONST c_range_desi             : 'range';
CONST c_constrained_desi       : 'constrained';
CONST c_position_desi          : 'position';
CONST c_first_bit_desi         : 'first_bit';
CONST c_last_bit_desi          : 'last_bit';
CONST c_stor_size_desi         : 'storage_size';
CONST c_terminated_desi        : 'terminated';
CONST c_failure_desi           : 'failure';
CONST c_count_desi             : 'count';
CONST c_controlled_desi        : 'controlled';
CONST c_include_desi           : 'include';
CONST c_inline_desi            : 'inline';
CONST c_interface_desi         : 'interface';
CONST c_list_desi              : 'list';
CONST c_optimize_desi          : 'optimize';
CONST c_pack_desi              : 'pack';
CONST c_stor_unit_desi         : 'storage_unit';
CONST c_suppress_desi          : 'suppress';
```

```
%----------------------------------------------------------------------
%                                                                     -
%     2.2. Constants for error values and abbreviations               -
%                                                                     -
%----------------------------------------------------------------------
%                                                                     -
%     The constants are given in such an order, that no forward       -
%     references occur.                                               -
%                                                                     -
%----------------------------------------------------------------------

CONST c_standard           : f_gen_key;

CONST c_system             : f_gen_key;

CONST c_unaccessible       : f_gen_key;

CONST c_designator         : sc_anonymous;

CONST c_empty_enum_rep     : tp_enum_rep ();

CONST c_empty_reps         : tp_rep_list ();

CONST c_empty_user_reps    : tp_user_reps (tp_designator_list ());

CONST c_start_repr         : tp_repr (sc_start_rep, c_empty_reps);

CONST c_no_origin          : tp_origin (sc_no_orig);

CONST c_no_bl_lab_loops    : tp_bl_lab_loops ();

CONST c_compare_designators   : tp_designator_list
                                 (c_equal_desi, c_n_equal_desi,
                                  c_less_desi, c_le_equal_desi,
                                  c_greater_desi, c_gr_equal_desi);

CONST c_key                : f_gen_key;

CONST c_enclosing          : c_key;

CONST c_constrained        : tp_constrained (c_key,
                                             sc_void);

CONST c_descr              : tp_descr (c_designator,
                                       c_key,
                                       c_start_repr,
                                       sc_complete,
                                       sc_void_nature,
                                       sc_void,
                                       c_no_origin,
                                       c_enclosing);

CONST c_descr_set          : f_descr_set2 (c_descr);

CONST c_designators        : tp_designator_list ();

CONST c_empty_descrs       : tp_descr_list ();
```

```
CONST c_empty_descr_set : f_descr_set3 (c_empty_descrs);

CONST c_empty_keys          : tp_key_list ();

CONST c_entry_den           : tp_den (tp_entry (c_empty_descrs));

CONST c_entry_descr_set     : f_descr_set4
                                 (sc_entry,
                                  c_entry_den);

CONST c_error_key           : f_gen_key;

CONST c_error_type_key      : f_gen_key;

CONST c_error_type_den      : tp_type_den (sc_error_type,
                                           c_empty_keys);

CONST c_error_type          : tp_constrained (c_error_type_key,
                                              sc_void);

CONST c_error_init          : tp_init (sc_no_val,
                                       sc_literal);

CONST c_error_obj_den       : tp_object (c_error_type,
                                         c_error_init);

CONST c_error_descr         : f_descr
                                (sc_error_designator,
                                 c_error_key,
                                 c_start_repr,
                                 sc_error_state,
                                 sc_error_nature,
                                 c_error_obj_den,
                                 c_unaccessible);

CONST c_error_descr_list    : tp_descr_list (c_error_descr);

CONST c_error_descr_set     : f_descr_set2 (c_error_descr);

CONST c_error_assoc         : tp_assoc (tp_comp_assoc
                                         (tp_choice_list
                                           (tp_choice
                                             (c_error_descr_set)),
                                          c_error_descr_set));

CONST c_error_assocs        : tp_assoc_list (c_error_assoc);

CONST c_error_header        : tp_header (tp_procedure
                                           (c_error_descr_list));

CONST c_error_pack_den      : tp_package (c_empty_descrs,
                                          c_empty_descrs,
                                          c_empty_keys,
                                          FALSE);

CONST c_error_range         : tp_range_constr
                                (c_error_descr_set,
                                 c_error_descr_set);

CONST c_error_dscrt_range   : tp_constrained
```

```
                                (c_error_type_key,
                                 c_error_range);

CONST c_error_task_den        : tp_type_den (tp_task_spec
                                                (c_empty_descrs),
                                             c_empty_keys);

CONST c_error_type_descr      : f_descr
                                (sc_error_designator,
                                 c_error_type_key,
                                 c_start_repr,
                                 sc_error_state,
                                 sc_type,
                                 tp_type_den (sc_error_type,
                                              c_empty_keys),
                                 c_unaccessible);

CONST c_no_type_key           : f_gen_key;

CONST c_no_type_descr         : f_descr
                                (sc_anonymous,
                                 c_no_type_key,
                                 c_start_repr,
                                 sc_complete,
                                 sc_type,
                                 tp_type_den (sc_error_type,
                                              c_empty_keys),
                                 c_unaccessible);

CONST c_error_type_descr_set  : f_descr_set2 (c_error_type_descr);

CONST c_error_type_range      : tp_type_range (c_error_type);

CONST c_exception_descr_set   : f_descr_set4
                                  (sc_exception,
                                   tp_den (sc_void));

CONST c_function_den          : tp_den (tp_subpr
                                          (tp_function (c_empty_descrs,
                                                        c_constrained),
                                           tp_subpr_def (sc_void),
                                           sc_no_op) );

CONST c_function_descr_set    : f_descr_set4
                                  (sc_function,
                                   c_function_den);

CONST c_init                  : tp_init (sc_no_val, sc_not_static);

CONST c_no_expected           : tp_key_void (sc_void);

CONST c_no_init               : tp_init (sc_no_val, sc_no_exp);

CONST c_no_type               : tp_constrained (c_no_type_key, sc_void);

CONST c_package_den           : tp_den
                                  (tp_package (c_empty_descrs,
                                               c_empty_descrs,
                                               c_empty_keys,
                                               TRUE));
```

```
CONST c_package_descr_set       : f_descr_set4
                                     (sc_package,
                                      c_package_den);

CONST c_proc_den                : tp_den (tp_subpr
                                            (tp_procedure
                                               (c_empty_descrs),
                                             tp_subpr_def (sc_void),
                                             sc_no_op));

CONST c_proc_descr_set          : f_descr_set4
                                     (sc_procedure,
                                      c_proc_den);

CONST c_task_descr_set          : f_descr_set4
                                     (sc_task,
                                      tp_den (sc_void));


%-----------------------------------------------------------------------
%                                                                      -
%  2.3. Unaccessible Entities                                          -
%                                                                      -
%-----------------------------------------------------------------------
%                                                                      -
%  This chapter contains the description of entities, not explicitly   -
%  declared in the STANDARD package, but logically equivalent to such  -
%  entities (E.g. operator descriptions for "=", "/="; descriptions    -
%  for universal types etc.)                                           -
%                                                                      -
%-----------------------------------------------------------------------
%.......................................................................
%                                                                      .
%  2.3.1. Universal Access                                             .
%                                                                      .
%.......................................................................

CONST c_any_access          : f_gen_key;

CONST c_any_access_descr :
         f_unaccessible_descr
            (sc_anonymous,
             c_any_access,
             sc_type,
             tp_type_den
               (sc_universal,
                c_empty_keys));
%.......................................................................
%                                                                      .
%  2.3.2. Universal Integer                                            .
%                                                                      .
%.......................................................................

CONST c_univ_int                      : f_gen_key;

CONST c_univ_int_abs                  : f_gen_key;

CONST c_univ_int_div                  : f_gen_key;
```

```
CONST c_univ_int_minus1        : f_gen_key;

CONST c_univ_int_minus         : f_gen_key;

CONST c_univ_int_mod           : f_gen_key;

CONST c_univ_int_mult          : f_gen_key;

CONST c_univ_int_plus          : f_gen_key;

CONST c_univ_int_plus1         : f_gen_key;

CONST c_univ_int_real_mult     : f_gen_key;

CONST c_univ_int_rem           : f_gen_key;

CONST c_univ_int_constr        : tp_constrained (c_univ_int,
                                                  sc_void);

CONST c_univ_int_descr :
        f_unaccessible_descr
          (sc_anonymous,
           c_univ_int,
           sc_type,
           tp_type_den
             (sc_universal,
              c_empty_keys));

CONST c_univ_int_plus1_descr :
        f_unaccessible_descr
          (c_plus_desi,
           c_univ_int_plus1,
           sc_universal_op,
           f_standard_function1
               (c_univ_int_plus1,
                c_univ_int_constr,
                c_univ_int_constr,
                sc_ui_plus1_op));

CONST c_univ_int_minus1_descr :
        f_unaccessible_descr
          (c_minus_desi,
           c_univ_int_minus1,
           sc_universal_op,
           f_standard_function1
               (c_univ_int_minus1,
                c_univ_int_constr,
                c_univ_int_constr,
                sc_ui_minus1_op));

CONST c_univ_int_abs_descr :
        f_unaccessible_descr
          (c_abs_desi,
           c_univ_int_abs,
           sc_universal_op,
           f_standard_function1
               (c_univ_int_abs,
                c_univ_int_constr,
                c_univ_int_constr,
```

```
          sc_ui_abs_op));

CONST c_univ_int_plus_descr :
      f_unaccessible_descr
        (c_plus_desi,
         c_univ_int_plus,
         sc_universal_op,
         f_standard_function2
             (c_univ_int_plus,
              c_univ_int_constr,
              c_univ_int_constr,
              c_univ_int_constr,
              sc_ui_plus_op));

CONST c_univ_int_minus_descr :
      f_unaccessible_descr
        (c_minus_desi,
         c_univ_int_minus,
         sc_universal_op,
         f_standard_function2
             (c_univ_int_minus,
              c_univ_int_constr,
              c_univ_int_constr,
              c_univ_int_constr,
              sc_ui_minus_op));

CONST c_univ_int_mult_descr :
      f_unaccessible_descr
        (c_mult_desi,
         c_univ_int_mult,
         sc_universal_op,
         f_standard_function2
             (c_univ_int_mult,
              c_univ_int_constr,
              c_univ_int_constr,
              c_univ_int_constr,
              sc_ui_mult_op));

CONST c_univ_int_div_descr :
      f_unaccessible_descr
        (c_div_desi,
         c_univ_int_div,
         sc_universal_op,
         f_standard_function2
             (c_univ_int_div,
              c_univ_int_constr,
              c_univ_int_constr,
              c_univ_int_constr,
              sc_ui_div_op));

CONST c_univ_int_rem_descr :
      f_unaccessible_descr
        (c_rem_desi,
         c_univ_int_rem,
         sc_universal_op,
         f_standard_function2
             (c_univ_int_rem,
              c_univ_int_constr,
              c_univ_int_constr,
              c_univ_int_constr,
```

```
            sc_ui_rem_op));

CONST c_univ_int_mod_descr :
        f_unaccessible_descr
          (c_mod_desi,
           c_univ_int_mod,
           sc_universal_op,
           f_standard_function2
               (c_univ_int_mod,
                c_univ_int_constr,
                c_univ_int_constr,
                c_univ_int_constr,
                sc_ui_mod_op));

%.....................................................................
%
%  2.3.3. Universal Real
%
%.....................................................................

CONST c_univ_real_abs             : f_gen_key;

CONST c_univ_real_div             : f_gen_key;

CONST c_univ_real_int_mult        : f_gen_key;

CONST c_univ_real_int_div         : f_gen_key;

CONST c_univ_real_minus1          : f_gen_key;

CONST c_univ_real_minus           : f_gen_key;

CONST c_univ_real_mult            : f_gen_key;

CONST c_univ_real_plus1           : f_gen_key;

CONST c_univ_real_plus            : f_gen_key;

CONST c_univ_real                 : f_gen_key;

CONST c_univ_real_constr          : tp_constrained (c_univ_real,
                                                     sc_void);

CONST c_univ_real_descr :
        f_unaccessible_descr
          (sc_anonymous,
           c_univ_real,
           sc_type,
           tp_type_den
             (sc_universal,
              c_empty_keys));

CONST c_univ_real_plus1_descr :
            f_unaccessible_descr
              (c_plus_desi,
               c_univ_real_plus1,
               sc_universal_op,
               f_standard_function1
                   (c_univ_real_plus1,
                    c_univ_real_constr,
```

```
                c_univ_real_constr,
                sc_ur_plus1_op));

CONST c_univ_real_minus1_descr :
      f_unaccessible_descr
        (c_minus_desi,
         c_univ_real_minus1,
         sc_universal_op,
         f_standard_function1
             (c_univ_real_minus1,
              c_univ_real_constr,
              c_univ_real_constr,
              sc_ur_minus1_op));

CONST c_univ_real_abs_descr :
      f_unaccessible_descr
        (c_abs_desi,
         c_univ_real_abs,
         sc_universal_op,
         f_standard_function1
             (c_univ_real_abs,
              c_univ_real_constr,
              c_univ_real_constr,
              sc_ur_abs_op));

CONST c_univ_real_plus_descr :
      f_unaccessible_descr
        (c_plus_desi,
         c_univ_real_plus,
         sc_universal_op,
         f_standard_function2
             (c_univ_real_plus,
              c_univ_real_constr,
              c_univ_real_constr,
              c_univ_real_constr,
              sc_ur_plus_op));

CONST c_univ_real_minus_descr :
      f_unaccessible_descr
        (c_minus_desi,
         c_univ_real_minus,
         sc_universal_op,
         f_standard_function2
             (c_univ_real_minus,
              c_univ_real_constr,
              c_univ_real_constr,
              c_univ_real_constr,
              sc_ur_minus_op));

CONST c_univ_real_mult_descr :
      f_unaccessible_descr
        (c_mult_desi,
         c_univ_real_mult,
         sc_universal_op,
         f_standard_function2
             (c_univ_real_mult,
              c_univ_real_constr,
              c_univ_real_constr,
              c_univ_real_constr,
              sc_ur_mult_op));
```

```
CONST c_univ_real_div_descr :
        f_unaccessible_descr
          (c_div_desi,
           c_univ_real_div,
           sc_universal_op,
           f_standard_function2
               (c_univ_real_div,
                c_univ_real_constr,
                c_univ_real_constr,
                c_univ_real_constr,
                sc_ur_div_op));

CONST c_univ_real_int_mult_descr :
        f_unaccessible_descr
          (c_mult_desi,
           c_univ_real_int_mult,
           sc_universal_op,
           f_standard_function2
               (c_univ_real_int_mult,
                c_univ_real_constr,
                c_univ_int_constr,
                c_univ_real_constr,
                sc_ur_ui_mult_op));

CONST c_univ_int_real_mult_descr :
        f_unaccessible_descr
          (c_mult_desi,
           c_univ_int_real_mult,
           sc_universal_op,
           f_standard_function2
               (c_univ_int_real_mult,
                c_univ_int_constr,
                c_univ_real_constr,
                c_univ_real_constr,
                sc_ui_ur_mult_op));

CONST c_univ_real_int_div_descr :
        f_unaccessible_descr
          (c_div_desi,
           c_univ_real_int_div,
           sc_universal_op,
           f_standard_function2
               (c_univ_real_int_div,
                c_univ_real_constr,
                c_univ_int_constr,
                c_univ_real_constr,
                sc_ur_ui_div_op));
%............................................................................
%
%  2.3.4. Universal Fixed
%
%............................................................................

CONST c_univ_fixed          : f_gen_key;

CONST c_univ_fixed_descr  :
         f_unaccessible_descr
           (sc_anonymous,
            c_univ_fixed,
```

```
            sc_type,
            tp_type_den
              (sc_universal,
               c_empty_keys));
%.........................................................................
%                                                                        .
%  2.3.5. Universal Common Operators                                     .
%                                                                        .
%.........................................................................
%                                                                        .
%  Common operators include all operators which are predefined in        .
%  chapter 4.4 of the Reference Manual, and which are not generally      .
%  implicitly declared by the mechanism of derived subprograms for       .
%  derived types. The common operators comprise the comparison           .
%  operators, fixed point operators and exponentiation.                  .
%                                                                        .
%.........................................................................

CONST c_common_abs              : f_gen_key;

CONST c_common_and              : f_gen_key;

CONST c_common_concat           : f_gen_key;

CONST c_common_div              : f_gen_key;

CONST c_common_equal            : f_gen_key;

CONST c_common_exp              : f_gen_key;

CONST c_common_greater          : f_gen_key;

CONST c_common_gr_equal         : f_gen_key;

CONST c_common_less             : f_gen_key;

CONST c_common_le_equal         : f_gen_key;

CONST c_common_minus            : f_gen_key;

CONST c_common_mult             : f_gen_key;

CONST c_common_not              : f_gen_key;

CONST c_common_n_equal          : f_gen_key;

CONST c_common_or               : f_gen_key;

CONST c_common_plus             : f_gen_key;

CONST c_common_xor              : f_gen_key;

CONST c_common_designators : tp_designator_list
                             (c_not_desi, c_and_desi, c_or_desi,
                              c_xor_desi, c_abs_desi,
                              c_minus_desi, c_plus_desi, c_mult_desi,
                              c_div_desi, c_exp_desi,
                              c_concat_desi) +
                              c_compare_designators;
```

```
CONST c_common_ops            : tp_op_list
                               (sc_co_not_op, sc_co_and_op, sc_co_or_op,
                                sc_co_xor_op, sc_co_abs_op,
                                sc_co_minus_op, sc_co_plus_op,
                                sc_co_mult_op,
                                sc_co_div_op, sc_co_exp_op,
                                sc_co_concat_op,
                                sc_co_equal_op, sc_co_n_equal_op,
                                sc_co_less_op, sc_co_le_equal_op,
                                sc_co_greater_op, sc_co_gr_equal_op);

CONST c_common_keys           : tp_key_list
                               (c_common_not, c_common_and, c_common_or,
                                c_common_xor, c_common_abs,
                                c_common_minus, c_common_plus,
                                c_common_mult,
                                c_common_div, c_common_exp,
                                c_common_concat,
                                c_common_equal, c_common_n_equal,
                                c_common_less, c_common_le_equal,
                                c_common_greater, c_common_gr_equal);
%.......................................................................
%
%  2.3.6. Descriptions of all Unaccessible Entities
%
%.......................................................................

CONST c_unaccessible_descrs : tp_descr_list
                                (c_any_access_descr,
                                 c_univ_fixed_descr,
                                 c_univ_int_descr,
                                 c_univ_int_plus1_descr,
                                 c_univ_int_minus1_descr,
                                 c_univ_int_abs_descr,
                                 c_univ_int_plus_descr,
                                 c_univ_int_minus_descr,
                                 c_univ_int_mult_descr,
                                 c_univ_int_div_descr,
                                 c_univ_real_descr,
                                 c_univ_real_plus1_descr,
                                 c_univ_real_minus1_descr,
                                 c_univ_real_abs_descr,
                                 c_univ_real_plus_descr,
                                 c_univ_real_minus_descr,
                                 c_univ_real_mult_descr,
                                 c_univ_real_div_descr,
                                 c_error_descr,
                                 c_error_type_descr,
                                 c_no_type_descr) +
                              f_common_descrs (c_common_designators,
                                               c_common_keys,
                                               c_common_ops);

CONST c_unaccessible_descr    : f_descr
                                (sc_anonymous,
                                 c_unaccessible,
                                 c_start_repr,
                                 sc_in_body,
                                 sc_package,
                                 tp_package
```

```
                         (c_unaccessible_descrs,
                          c_empty_descrs,
                          c_empty_keys,
                          TRUE),
                        c_error_key);

%--------------------------------------------------------------------------
%                                                                        -
%    2.4. Package STANDARD                                               -
%                                                                        -
%--------------------------------------------------------------------------
%                                                                        -
%    All descriptions from build the visible part of the package         -
%    STANDARD.                                                           -
%                                                                        -
%--------------------------------------------------------------------------


%..........................................................................
%                                                                        .
% 2.4.1 Implementation dependent Values                                  .
%                                                                        .
%..........................................................................


CONST c_max_int_value         : tp_value (INT (1000));    >MACHINE<
CONST c_min_int_value         : tp_value (INT (-1000));   >MACHINE<
CONST c_max_digits_value      : tp_value (INT (1000));    >MACHINE<
CONST c_min_float_value       : tp_value (tp_real_val (sc_real_val));
CONST c_max_float_value       : tp_value (tp_real_val (sc_real_val));
CONST c_dur_delta_value       : tp_value (tp_real_val (sc_real_val));
CONST c_min_dur_value         : tp_value (tp_real_val (sc_real_val));
CONST c_max_dur_value         : tp_value (tp_real_val (sc_real_val));
CONST c_min_priority_value    : tp_value (INT (10));      >MACHINE<
CONST c_max_priority_value    : tp_value (INT (10));      >MACHINE<


%..........................................................................
%                                                                        .
% 2.4.2 Descriptions of the entities in Package STANDARD                 .
%                                                                        .
%..........................................................................


% .  .  .  .  .  .  .  .  .  .  .  .  .  .  .  .  .  .  .  .  .  .  .  .  .
%                                                                        .
% 2.4.2.1 Boolean                                                        .
```

```
CONST c_bool                  : f_gen_key;
CONST c_true                  : f_gen_key;
CONST c_false                 : f_gen_key;
CONST c_and                   : f_gen_key;
CONST c_or                    : f_gen_key;
CONST c_not                   : f_gen_key;
CONST c_xor                   : f_gen_key;

CONST c_bool_constr           : tp_constrained (c_bool, sc_void);
CONST c_bool_descr            :
              f_standard_descr
                 (c_bool_desi,
                  c_bool,
                  sc_type,
                  tp_type_den
                      (tp_enum_type
                         (tp_key_list (c_false, c_true),
                          FALSE),
                       tp_key_list
                         (c_and,
                          c_not,
                          c_or,
                          c_xor)));

CONST c_false_descr :
           f_standard_descr
             (c_false_desi,
              c_false,
              sc_enum_literal,
              tp_enum_literal (c_bool, 0, FALSE));

CONST c_true_descr  :
           f_standard_descr
             (c_true_desi,
              c_true,
              sc_enum_literal,
              tp_enum_literal (c_bool, 1, FALSE));

CONST c_not_descr   :
           f_standard_descr
             (c_not_desi,
              c_not,
              sc_predefined_op,
              f_standard_function1
                    (c_not,
                     c_bool_constr,
                     c_bool_constr,
                     sc_not_op));

CONST c_and_descr   :
           f_standard_descr
             (c_and_desi,
              c_and,
              sc_predefined_op,
              f_standard_function2
                    (c_and,
                     c_bool_constr,
                     c_bool_constr,
                     c_bool_constr,
                     sc_and_op));
```

```
CONST c_or_descr :
        f_standard_descr
          (c_or_desi,
           c_or,
           sc_predefined_op,
           f_standard_function2
                (c_or,
                 c_bool_constr,
                 c_bool_constr,
                 c_bool_constr,
                 sc_or_op));

CONST c_xor_descr :
        f_standard_descr
          (c_xor_desi,
           c_xor,
           sc_predefined_op,
           f_standard_function2
                (c_xor,
                 c_bool_constr,
                 c_bool_constr,
                 c_bool_constr,
                 sc_xor_op));

%. . . . . . . . . . . . . . . . . . . . . . . . . . . . . . . . . . . .
%                                                                      .
% 2.4.2.2 Integer                                                      .
%                                                                      .
%. . . . . . . . . . . . . . . . . . . . . . . . . . . . . . . . . . . .

CONST c_int_abs                  : f_gen_key;
CONST c_int_div                  : f_gen_key;
CONST c_int_minus1               : f_gen_key;
CONST c_int_minus                : f_gen_key;
CONST c_int_mod                  : f_gen_key;
CONST c_int_mult                 : f_gen_key;
CONST c_int_plus                 : f_gen_key;
CONST c_int_plus1                : f_gen_key;
CONST c_int_rem                  : f_gen_key;
CONST c_int                      : f_gen_key;
CONST c_max_int                  : f_gen_key;
CONST c_min_int                  : f_gen_key;

CONST c_int_1_init               : tp_init (1, sc_literal);

CONST c_int_constr               : tp_constrained (c_int, sc_void);

CONST c_max_int_descr            :
        tp_descr
          (c_max_int_desi,
           c_max_int,
           c_start_repr,
           sc_complete,
           sc_number,
           tp_object
             (tp_constrained (c_univ_int, sc_void),
```

```
                tp_init (c_max_int_value, sc_literal)),
              c_no_origin,
              c_system);

CONST c_min_int_descr          :
         tp_descr
           (c_min_int_desi,
            c_min_int,
            c_start_repr,
            sc_complete,
            sc_number,
            tp_object
              (tp_constrained (c_univ_int, sc_void),
               tp_init (c_min_int_value, sc_literal)),
            c_no_origin,
            c_system);

CONST c_1_int_descr            :
       f_standard_descr
         (sc_anonymous,
          f_gen_key,
          sc_value,
          tp_object (c_int_constr,
                     c_int_1_init));

CONST c_int_constr1            : tp_constrained (c_int,
                                   tp_range_constr
                                   (f_descr_set2 (c_1_int_descr)
                                    f_descr_set2
                                       (c_max_int_descr)));

CONST c_int_descr              :
       f_standard_descr
           (c_int_desi,
            c_int,
            sc_type,
            tp_type_den
              (tp_integer
                 (tp_range_constr
                     (f_descr_set2 (c_min_int_descr),
                      f_descr_set2 (c_max_int_descr))),
               tp_key_list
                 (c_int_plus1,
                  c_int_minus1,
                  c_int_abs,
                  c_int_plus,
                  c_int_minus,
                  c_int_mult,
                  c_int_div,
                  c_int_rem,
                  c_int_mod)));

CONST c_int_plus1_descr                     :
       f_standard_descr
         (c_plus_desi,
          c_int_plus1,
          sc_predefined_op,
          f_standard_function1
            (c_int_plus1,
             c_int_constr,
```

```
                c_int_constr,
                sc_i_plus1_op));

CONST c_int_minus1_descr                                    :
        f_standard_descr
          (c_minus_desi,
           c_int_minus1,
           sc_predefined_op,
           f_standard_function1
               (c_int_minus1,
                c_int_constr,
                c_int_constr,
                sc_i_minus1_op));

CONST c_int_abs_descr                                       :
        f_standard_descr
          (c_abs_desi,
           c_int_abs,
           sc_predefined_op,
           f_standard_function1
               (c_int_abs,
                c_int_constr,
                c_int_constr,
                sc_i_abs_op));

CONST c_int_plus_descr                                      :
        f_standard_descr
          (c_plus_desi,
           c_int_plus,
           sc_predefined_op,
           f_standard_function2
               (c_int_plus,
                c_int_constr,
                c_int_constr,
                c_int_constr,
                sc_i_plus_op));

CONST c_int_minus_descr                                     :
        f_standard_descr
          (c_minus_desi,
           c_int_minus,
           sc_predefined_op,
           f_standard_function2
               (c_int_minus,
                c_int_constr,
                c_int_constr,
                c_int_constr,
                sc_i_minus_op));

CONST c_int_mult_descr                                      :
        f_standard_descr
          (c_mult_desi,
           c_int_mult,
           sc_predefined_op,
           f_standard_function2
               (c_int_mult,
                c_int_constr,
                c_int_constr,
                c_int_constr,
                sc_i_mult_op));
```

```
CONST c_int_div_descr                   :
        f_standard_descr
          (c_div_desi,
           c_int_div,
           sc_predefined_op,
           f_standard_function2
               (c_int_div,
                c_int_constr,
                c_int_constr,
                c_int_constr,
                sc_i_div_op));

CONST c_int_rem_descr                   :
        f_standard_descr
          (c_rem_desi,
           c_int_rem,
           sc_predefined_op,
           f_standard_function2
               (c_int_rem,
                c_int_constr,
                c_int_constr,
                c_int_constr,
                sc_i_rem_op));

CONST c_int_mod_descr                   :
        f_standard_descr
          (c_mod_desi,
           c_int_mod,
           sc_predefined_op,
           f_standard_function2
               (c_int_mod,
                c_int_constr,
                c_int_constr,
                c_int_constr,
                sc_i_mod_op));

%. . . . . . . . . . . . . . . . . . . . . . . . . . . . . . . . . . . .
%
% 2.4.2.3 Float
%
%. . . . . . . . . . . . . . . . . . . . . . . . . . . . . . . . . . . .


CONST c_float                    : f_gen_key;
CONST c_float_abs                : f_gen_key;
CONST c_float_div                : f_gen_key;
CONST c_float_minus1             : f_gen_key;
CONST c_float_minus              : f_gen_key;
CONST c_float_mult               : f_gen_key;
CONST c_float_plus1              : f_gen_key;
CONST c_float_plus               : f_gen_key;

CONST c_float_constr             : tp_constrained (c_float, sc_void);

CONST c_max_float_descr          :
        f_standard_descr
          (sc_anonymous,
            f_gen_key,
```

```
          sc_value,
          tp_object (c_float_constr,
                     tp_init (c_max_float_value, sc_literal)));

CONST c_min_float_descr          :
        f_standard_descr
          (sc_anonymous,
          f_gen_key,
          sc_value,
          tp_object (c_float_constr,
                     tp_init (c_min_float_value, sc_literal)));

CONST c_max_digits_descr         :
        f_standard_descr
          (sc_anonymous,
          f_gen_key,
          sc_value,
          tp_object
            (c_int_constr,
            tp_init (c_max_digits_value, sc_literal)));

CONST c_float_descr                                   :
        f_standard_descr
          (c_float_desi,
          c_float,
          sc_type,
          tp_type_den
               (tp_float
                   (f_descr_set2 (c_max_digits_descr),
                    tp_range_constr
                        (f_descr_set2 (c_min_float_descr),
                         f_descr_set2 (c_max_float_descr))),
             tp_key_list
               (c_float_plus1,
                c_float_minus1,
                c_float_abs,
                c_float_plus,
                c_float_minus,
                c_float_mult,
                c_float_div)));

CONST c_float_plus1_descr                             :
           f_standard_descr
             (c_plus_desi,
              c_float_plus1,
              sc_predefined_op,
              f_standard_function1
                  (c_float_plus1,
                   c_float_constr,
                   c_float_constr,
                   sc_f_plus1_op));

CONST c_float_minus1_descr                            :
        f_standard_descr
          (c_minus_desi,
           c_float_minus1,
           sc_predefined_op,
           f_standard_function1
               (c_float_minus1,
                c_float_constr,
```

```
                c_float_constr,
                sc_f_minus1_op));

CONST c_float_abs_descr                                         :
        f_standard_descr
          (c_abs_desi,
           c_float_abs,
           sc_predefined_op,
           f_standard_function1
               (c_float_abs,
                c_float_constr,
                c_float_constr,
                sc_f_abs_op));


CONST c_float_plus_descr                                        :
        f_standard_descr
          (c_plus_desi,
           c_float_plus,
           sc_predefined_op,
           f_standard_function2
               (c_float_plus,
                c_float_constr,
                c_float_constr,
                c_float_constr,
                sc_f_plus_op));

CONST c_float_minus_descr                                       :
        f_standard_descr
          (c_minus_desi,
           c_float_minus,
           sc_predefined_op,
           f_standard_function2
               (c_float_minus,
                c_float_constr,
                c_float_constr,
                c_float_constr,
                sc_f_minus_op));

CONST c_float_mult_descr                                        :
        f_standard_descr
          (c_mult_desi,
           c_float_mult,
           sc_predefined_op,
           f_standard_function2
               (c_float_mult,
                c_float_constr,
                c_float_constr,
                c_float_constr,
                sc_f_mult_op));

CONST c_float_div_descr                                         :
        f_standard_descr
          (c_div_desi,
           c_float_div,
           sc_predefined_op,
           f_standard_function2
               (c_float_div,
                c_float_constr,
                c_float_constr,
```

```
            c_float_constr,
            sc_f_div_op));

%. . . . . . . . . . . . . . . . . . . . . . . . . . . . . . . . . . . . . . . . . . . .
%                                                                                      .
% 2.4.2.4 Character                                                                    .
%                                                                                      .
%. . . . . . . . . . . . . . . . . . . . . . . . . . . . . . . . . . . . . . . . . . . .

CONST c_char_a              : f_gen_key;
CONST c_char_b              : f_gen_key;
CONST c_char_c              : f_gen_key;
CONST c_char                : f_gen_key;

CONST c_char_constr         : tp_constrained (c_char, sc_void);

CONST c_char_a_descr        :
        f_standard_descr
          (c_char_a_desi,
           c_char_a,
           sc_enum_literal,
           tp_enum_literal (c_char, 0, TRUE));

CONST c_char_b_descr        :
        f_standard_descr
          (c_char_b_desi,
           c_char_b,
           sc_enum_literal,
           tp_enum_literal (c_char, 1, TRUE));

CONST c_char_c_descr        :
        f_standard_descr
          (c_char_c_desi,
           c_char_c,
           sc_enum_literal,
           tp_enum_literal (c_char, 2, TRUE));

CONST c_char_descr          :
        f_standard_descr
          (c_char_desi,
           c_char,
           sc_type,
           tp_type_den
               (tp_enum_type
                   (tp_key_list (c_char_a, c_char_b, c_char_c),
                    TRUE),
                c_empty_keys));


%. . . . . . . . . . . . . . . . . . . . . . . . . . . . . . . . . . . . . . . . . . . .
%                                                                                      .
% 2.4.2.5 Package ASCII                                                                .
%                                                                                      .
%. . . . . . . . . . . . . . . . . . . . . . . . . . . . . . . . . . . . . . . . . . . .

CONST c_ascii       : f_gen_key;

CONST c_lc_a_descr :
          tp_descr
```

```
            (c_lc_a_desi,
             f_gen_key,
             c_start_repr,
             sc_complete,
             sc_constant,
             tp_object
               (tp_constrained (c_char, sc_void),
                tp_init (0, sc_static)),
             c_no_origin,
             c_ascii);

CONST c_ascii_descr :
            tp_descr
              (c_ascii_desi,
               c_ascii,
               c_start_repr,
               sc_complete,
               sc_package,
               tp_package
                 (tp_descr_list (c_lc_a_descr),
                  c_empty_descrs,
                  c_empty_keys,
                  TRUE),
               c_no_origin,
               c_standard);



%. . . . . . . . . . . . . . . . . . . . . . . . . . . . . . . . . . . . . .
%
% 2.4.2.6 Predefined Types and Subtypes
%
%. . . . . . . . . . . . . . . . . . . . . . . . . . . . . . . . . . . . . .

CONST c_natural               : f_gen_key;
CONST c_string                : f_gen_key;
CONST c_priority              : f_gen_key;
CONST c_duration              : f_gen_key;

CONST c_string_constr         : tp_constrained (c_string, sc_void);

CONST c_string_descr          :
        f_standard_descr
          (c_string_desi,
           c_string,
           sc_type,
           tp_type_den
             (tp_array
                (tp_dscrt_range_list (tp_index (c_int_constr1)),
                 c_char_constr),
              c_empty_keys));

CONST c_natural_descr         :
        f_standard_descr
          (c_natural_desi,
           c_natural,
           sc_subtype,
           c_int_constr1);
```

```
CONST c_dur_constr            : tp_constrained (c_duration, sc_void);

CONST c_min_dur_descr         :
      f_standard_descr
        (sc_anonymous,
         f_gen_key,
         sc_value,
         tp_object (c_dur_constr,
                    tp_init (c_min_dur_value, sc_literal)));

CONST c_max_dur_descr         :
      f_standard_descr
        (sc_anonymous,
         f_gen_key,
         sc_value,
         tp_object (c_dur_constr,
                    tp_init (c_max_dur_value, sc_literal)));

CONST c_dur_delta_descr       :
      f_standard_descr
        (sc_anonymous,
        f_gen_key,
        sc_value,
        tp_object
          (c_float_constr,
           tp_init (c_dur_delta_value, sc_literal)));

CONST c_duration_descr        :
      f_standard_descr
        (c_duration_desi,
        c_duration,
        sc_type,
        tp_type_den
          (tp_fixed
             (f_descr_set2 (c_dur_delta_descr),
              tp_range_constr
                 (f_descr_set2 (c_min_dur_descr),
                  f_descr_set2 (c_max_dur_descr))),
           c_empty_keys));

CONST c_pri_constr            : tp_constrained (c_priority, sc_void);

CONST c_min_priority_descr    :
      f_standard_descr
        (sc_anonymous,
        f_gen_key,
        sc_value,
        tp_object
          (c_pri_constr,
           tp_init (c_min_priority_value, sc_literal)));

CONST c_max_priority_descr    :
      f_standard_descr
        (sc_anonymous,
        f_gen_key,
        sc_value,
        tp_object
          (c_pri_constr,
           tp_init (c_max_priority_value, sc_literal)));
```

```
CONST c_priority_descr          :
        f_standard_descr
          (c_standard_desi,
           c_standard,
           sc_subtype,
           tp_constrained
             (c_int,
              tp_range_constr
                  (f_descr_set2 (c_min_priority_descr),
                   f_descr_set2 (c_max_priority_descr))));


%. . . . . . . . . . . . . . . . . . . . . . . . . . . . . . . . . . . . . .
%
% 2.4.2.7 Predefined Exceptions
%
%. . . . . . . . . . . . . . . . . . . . . . . . . . . . . . . . . . . . . .


CONST c_constr_error            : f_gen_key;
CONST c_num_error               : f_gen_key;
CONST c_sel_error               : f_gen_key;
CONST c_stor_error              : f_gen_key;
CONST c_task_error              : f_gen_key;

CONST c_constr_error_descr      :
        f_standard_descr
          (c_constr_error_desi,
           c_constr_error,
           sc_exception,
           tp_den (sc_void));

CONST c_num_error_descr         :
        f_standard_descr
          (c_num_error_desi,
           c_num_error,
           sc_exception,
           tp_den (sc_void));

CONST c_sel_error_descr         :
        f_standard_descr
          (c_sel_error_desi,
           c_sel_error,
           sc_exception,
           tp_den (sc_void));

CONST c_stor_error_descr        :
        f_standard_descr
          (c_stor_error_desi,
           c_stor_error,
           sc_exception,
           tp_den (sc_void));

CONST c_task_error_descr        :
        f_standard_descr
          (c_task_error_desi,
           c_task_error,
           sc_exception,
```

```
        tp_den (sc_void));


%. . . . . . . . . . . . . . . . . . . . . . . . . . . . . . . . . . . . . . . . . . . .
%                                                                                      .
% 2.4.2.8 Package SYSTEM                                                               .
%                                                                                      .
%. . . . . . . . . . . . . . . . . . . . . . . . . . . . . . . . . . . . . . . . . . . .

CONST c_system_name_enum           : f_gen_key;
CONST c_system_name                : f_gen_key;

CONST c_system_name_enum_descr :
        tp_descr
          ('ARBITRARY',
           c_system_name_enum,
           c_start_repr,
           sc_complete,
           sc_enum_literal,
           tp_enum_literal
             (c_system_name,
              0,
              FALSE),
           c_no_origin,
           c_system);

CONST c_system_name_descr :
        tp_descr
          (c_system_name_desi,
           c_system_name,
           c_start_repr,
           sc_complete,
           sc_type,
           tp_type_den
             (tp_enum_type
                (tp_key_list (c_system_name_enum),
                 FALSE),
              c_empty_keys),
           c_no_origin,
           c_system);

CONST c_name_descr :
        tp_descr
          (c_name_desi,
           f_gen_key,
           c_start_repr,
           sc_complete,
           sc_constant,
           tp_object
             (tp_constrained (c_system_name, sc_void),
              tp_init (0, sc_static)),
           c_no_origin,
           c_system);

CONST c_memory_size_descr :
        tp_descr
          (c_memory_size_desi,
           f_gen_key,
```

```
            c_start_repr,
            sc_complete,
            sc_number,
            tp_object
              (tp_constrained (c_univ_int, sc_void),
               tp_init (256000, sc_literal)),
            c_no_origin,
            c_system);

CONST c_storage_descr :
         tp_descr
           (c_storage_desi,
            f_gen_key,
            c_start_repr,
            sc_complete,
            sc_number,
            tp_object
              (tp_constrained (c_univ_int, sc_void),
               tp_init (32, sc_literal)),
            c_no_origin,
            c_system);

CONST c_system_descr          :
        f_standard_descr
          (c_system_desi,
           f_gen_key,
           sc_package,
           tp_package
             (tp_descr_list
                (c_system_name_descr,
                 c_name_descr,
                 c_storage_descr,
                 c_memory_size_descr,
                 c_min_int_descr,
                 c_max_int_descr),
              c_empty_descrs, c_empty_keys, TRUE));


%.......................................................................
%
% 2.4.3 Description of the Package STANDARD
%
%.......................................................................

CONST c_standard_descrs        : tp_descr_list
                 (c_true_descr,
                  c_false_descr,
                  c_bool_descr,

                  c_not_descr,
                  c_and_descr,
                  c_or_descr,
                  c_xor_descr,

                  c_int_descr,

                  c_int_plus1_descr,
                  c_int_minus1_descr,
                  c_int_abs_descr,
```

```
                 c_int_plus_descr,
                 c_int_minus_descr,
                 c_int_mult_descr,
                 c_int_div_descr,
                 c_int_rem_descr,
                 c_int_mod_descr,

                 c_max_digits_descr,
                 c_float_descr,

                 c_float_minus1_descr,
                 c_float_plus1_descr,
                 c_float_abs_descr,
                 c_float_minus_descr,
                 c_float_plus_descr,
                 c_float_mult_descr,
                 c_float_div_descr,

                 c_char_descr,
                 c_char_a_descr,
                 c_char_b_descr,
                 c_char_c_descr,
                 c_ascii_descr,

                 c_string_descr,

                 c_natural_descr,
                 c_dur_delta_descr,
                 c_duration_descr,
                 c_system_descr,

                 c_constr_error_descr,
                 c_num_error_descr,
                 c_sel_error_descr,
                 c_stor_error_descr,
                 c_task_error_descr);

CONST c_standard_descr          : f_descr
                                    (c_standard_desi,
                                     c_standard,
                                     c_start_repr,
                                     sc_in_body,
                                     sc_package,
                                     tp_package
                                         (c_standard_descrs,
                                          c_empty_descrs,
                                          c_empty_keys,
                                          TRUE),
                                     c_unaccessible);
```

```
%-----------------------------------------------------------------------
%                                                                      -
% 2.5. Start Environment                                               -
%                                                                      -
%-----------------------------------------------------------------------
%                                                                      -
% The environment with which any compilation unit is initialized       -
%                                                                      -
%-----------------------------------------------------------------------


CONST c_start_env                : f_env
                                    (c_empty_keys,
                                     tp_descr_list (c_unaccessible_descr)+
                                     c_unaccessible_descrs +
                                     tp_descr_list (c_standard_descr),
                                     c_standard_descrs,
                                     c_standard);
```

```
%%%%%%%%%%%%%%%%%%%%%%%%%%%%%%%%%%%%%%%%%%%%%%%%%%%%%%%%%%%%%%%%%%%%%%%%%
%                                                                       %
% AG3. Terminals and their Attributes                                   %
%                                                                       %
%%%%%%%%%%%%%%%%%%%%%%%%%%%%%%%%%%%%%%%%%%%%%%%%%%%%%%%%%%%%%%%%%%%%%%%%%

TERM abort              :;
TERM accept             :;
TERM access             :;
TERM address            :;
TERM aggregate          :;
TERM allocator          :;
TERM all                :;
TERM alternative_s      :;
TERM alternative        :;
TERM and_then           :;
TERM apply              :;
TERM array              :;
TERM assign             :;
TERM assoc              :;
TERM attribute          :;
TERM binary             :;
TERM block              :;
TERM box                :;
TERM case               :;
TERM char               : at_designator : SYMB;
TERM choice_s           :;
TERM code               :;
TERM comp_rep_s         :;
TERM comp_rep           :;
TERM comp_unit          :;
TERM cond_clause        :;
TERM cond_entry         :;
TERM constant           :;
TERM constrained        :;
TERM context            :;
TERM decl_rep_s         :;
TERM decl_s             :;
TERM delay              :;
TERM derived            :;
TERM dscrt_range_s      :;
TERM entry              :;
TERM enum_literal_s     :;
TERM exception          :;
TERM exit               :;
TERM fixed              :;
TERM float              :;
TERM formal_discrt      :;
TERM formal_fixed       :;
TERM formal_float       :;
TERM formal_integer     :;
TERM for                :;
TERM function           :;
TERM general_assoc_s    :;
```

```
TERM generic_assoc_s      :;
TERM generic_param_s      :;
TERM generic              :;
TERM goto                 :;
TERM id_s                 :;
TERM id                   : at_designator : SYMB;
TERM if                   :;
TERM in_op                :;
TERM in_out               :;
TERM index                :;
TERM instantiation        :;
TERM integer              :;
TERM in                   :;
TERM item_s               :;
TERM l_private            :;
TERM labeled              :;
TERM loop                 :;
TERM membership           :;
TERM name_s               :;
TERM named_stm            :;
TERM named                :;
TERM no_default           :;
TERM not_in               :;
TERM null_access          :;
TERM null_comp            :;
TERM null_stm             :;
TERM number_decl          :;
TERM numeric_literal      : at_value : tp_value;
TERM or_else              :;
TERM others               :;
TERM out                  :;
TERM package_body         :;
TERM package_decl         :;
TERM package_spec         :;
TERM param_assoc_s        :;
TERM param_s              :;
TERM parenthesized        :;
TERM pragma_s             :;
TERM pragma               :;
TERM private              :;
TERM procedure            :;
TERM qualified            :;
TERM raise                :;
TERM range                :;
TERM record_rep           :;
TERM record               :;
TERM rename               :;
TERM return               :;
TERM reverse              :;
TERM select_clause_s      :;
TERM select_clause        :;
TERM selected             :;
TERM select               :;
TERM simple_rep           :;
TERM stm_s                :;
TERM string               : at_designator : SYMB;
TERM stub                 :;
TERM subprog_body         :;
TERM subprog_decl         :;
TERM subtype              :;
```

```
TERM subunit            ;
TERM task_body          ;
TERM task_decl          ;
TERM task_spec          ;
TERM terminate          ;
TERM timed_entry        ;
TERM type               ;
TERM use                ;
TERM var_decl_s         ;
TERM var_decl           ;
TERM variant_part       ;
TERM variant_s          ;
TERM variant            ;
TERM void               ;
TERM while              ;
TERM with               ;
```

```
%%%%%%%%%%%%%%%%%%%%%%%%%%%%%%%%%%%%%%%%%%%%%%%%%%%%%%%%%%%%%%%%%%%%%%%%%%%%%%%%
%
% AG4. Nonterminals and their Attributes
%
%%%%%%%%%%%%%%%%%%%%%%%%%%%%%%%%%%%%%%%%%%%%%%%%%%%%%%%%%%%%%%%%%%%%%%%%%%%%%%%%
%
% The nonterminals of the attribute grammar together with their
% attributes are given in alphabetic order.
%
%%%%%%%%%%%%%%%%%%%%%%%%%%%%%%%%%%%%%%%%%%%%%%%%%%%%%%%%%%%%%%%%%%%%%%%%%%%%%%%%


NONTERM ACCESS_CONSTRAINT : at_allowed1,
                            at_allowed2,
                            at_valid               : tp_assoc_list,
                            at_discrim_allowed     : BOOL,
                            at_with_use            : BOOL,
                            at_others_allowed      : BOOL,
                            at_env_in              : tp_env;
NONTERM ACTUAL            : at_expected            : tp_key_void,
                            at_allowed1,
                            at_allowed2,
                            at_valid               : tp_actual,
                            at_discrim_allowed     : BOOL,
                            at_with_use            : BOOL,
                            at_context             : tp_context,
                            at_others_allowed      : BOOL,
                            at_env_in              : tp_env;
NONTERM ALTERNATIVE       : at_env_in              : tp_env,
                            at_context             : tp_choice_context,
                            at_expected            : tp_key_void,
                            at_choices             : tp_choice_list,
                            at_labels,
                            at_loops_blocks        : tp_bl_lab_loops,
                            at_return_required     : BOOL,
                            at_is_last             : BOOL,
                            at_encl_unit           : tp_encl_unit;
NONTERM ALTERNATIVES      : at_env_in              : tp_env,
                            at_context             : tp_choice_context,
                            at_expected            : tp_key_void,
                            at_choices             : tp_choice_list,
                            at_labels,
                            at_loops_blocks        : tp_bl_lab_loops,
                            at_encl_unit           : tp_encl_unit,
                            at_return_required     : BOOL;
NONTERM ALTERNATIVE_S     : at_env_in              : tp_env,
                            at_context             : tp_choice_context,
                            at_expected            : tp_key_void,
                            at_choices             : tp_choice_list,
                            at_labels,
                            at_loops_blocks        : tp_bl_lab_loops,
                            at_encl_unit           : tp_encl_unit,
                            at_empty               : BOOL,
                            at_return_required     : BOOL;
NONTERM APPLY             : at_expected            : tp_key_void,
```

```
                              at_allowed1,
                              at_allowed2,
                              at_valid                  : tp_descr_set,
                              at_with_use               : BOOL,
                              at_context                : tp_context,
                              at_is_exp                 : BOOL,
                              at_user_rep               : tp_user_reps,
                              at_env_in                 : tp_env;
NONTERM ASSOC               : at_expected_in            : tp_descr_list,
                              at_allowed2               : tp_comp_assoc,
                              at_valid                  : tp_comp_assoc,
                              at_others_allowed         : BOOL,
                              at_env_in                 : tp_env;
NONTERM BINARY_OP           : at_op                     : tp_op;
NONTERM BLOCK               : at_env_in                 : tp_env,
                              at_loops_blocks           : tp_bl_lab_loops,
                              at_labels                 : tp_bl_lab_loops,
                              at_context                : tp_block_context,
                              at_return_required        : BOOL,
                              at_encl_unit              : tp_encl_unit,
                              at_block_no               : INT;
NONTERM BLOCK_STUB          : at_env_in                 : tp_env,
                              at_keys                   : tp_key_list,
                              at_encl_unit              : tp_encl_unit,
                              at_block_no               : INT;
NONTERM CHOICE              : at_allowed1,
                              at_allowed2,
                              at_valid                  : tp_choice,
                              at_expected               : tp_key_void,
                              at_with_use               : BOOL,
                              at_context                : tp_choice_context,
                              at_env_in                 : tp_env;
NONTERM CHOICES             : at_allowed1,
                              at_allowed2,
                              at_valid                  : tp_choice_list,
                              at_context                : tp_choice_context,
                              at_expected               : tp_key_void,
                              at_with_use               : BOOL,
                              at_env_in                 : tp_env,
                              at_is_last                : BOOL;
NONTERM CHOICE_S                                        : at_allowed1,
                              at_allowed2,
                              at_valid                  : tp_choice_list,
                              at_context                : tp_choice_context,
                              at_expected               : tp_key_void,
                              at_with_use               : BOOL,
                              at_env_in                 : tp_env,
                              at_is_last                : BOOL;
NONTERM COMP                : at_comp                   : tp_comp,
                              at_env_in,
                              at_env_out                : tp_env;
NONTERM COMP_ASSOC          : at_allowed1,
                              at_allowed2               : tp_assoc,
                              at_valid                  : tp_assoc,
                              at_others_allowed         : BOOL,
                              at_with_use               : BOOL,
                              at_env_in                 : tp_env,
                              at_is_last                : BOOL;
NONTERM COMP_ASSOCS         : at_allowed1,
                              at_allowed2               : tp_assoc_list,
```

```
                                  at_valid                  : tp_assoc_list,
                                  at_others_allowed         : BOOL,
                                  at_with_use               : BOOL,
                                  at_env_in                 : tp_env,
                                  at_positional_allowed     : BOOL;
NONTERM COMP_REP                : at_env_in                 : tp_env,
                                  at_expected_in            : tp_descr_list,
                                  at_rep                    : tp_comp_rep;
NONTERM COMP_REPS               : at_env_in                 : tp_env,
                                  at_expected_in            : tp_descr_list,
                                  at_reps                   : tp_comp_rep_list;
NONTERM COMP_REP_S              : at_env_in                 : tp_env,
                                  at_expected_in            : tp_descr_list,
                                  at_reps                   : tp_comp_rep_list;
NONTERM COMP_UNIT               : at_env                    : tp_env;
NONTERM CONTEXT                 : at_env_in,
                                  at_env_out                : tp_env;
NONTERM CONTEXT_ELEMS           : at_env_in,
                                  at_env_out                : tp_env;
NONTERM CONTEXT_ELEM            : at_env_in                 : tp_env;
NONTERM COND_CLAUSE             : at_env_in                 : tp_env,
                                  at_labels,
                                  at_loops_blocks           : tp_bl_lab_loops,
                                  at_encl_unit              : tp_encl_unit,
                                  at_return_required        : BOOL;
NONTERM COND_CLAUSES            : at_env_in                 : tp_env,
                                  at_labels,
                                  at_loops_blocks           : tp_bl_lab_loops,
                                  at_encl_unit              : tp_encl_unit,
                                  at_return_required        : BOOL;
NONTERM CONSTRAINED             : at_type                   : tp_constrained,
                                  at_discrim_allowed        : BOOL,
                                  at_env_in                 : tp_env;
NONTERM CONSTRAINED_1           : at_type                   : tp_constrained,
                                  at_discrim_allowed        : BOOL,
                                  at_env_in                 : tp_env;
NONTERM CONSTRAINED_VOID        : at_type                   : tp_constrained,
                                  at_env_in                 : tp_env;
NONTERM CONSTRAINT              : at_allowed1,
                                  at_allowed2               : tp_constraint,
                                  at_valid                  : tp_constraint,
                                  at_expected               : tp_key_void,
                                  at_with_use               : BOOL,
                                  at_discrim_allowed        : BOOL,
                                  at_env_in                 : tp_env;
NONTERM DECL                    : at_env_in,
                                  at_env_out                : tp_env,
                                  at_user_reps              : tp_user_reps,
                                  at_keys                   : tp_key_list,
                                  at_is_item                : BOOL,
                                  at_encl_unit              : tp_encl_unit;
NONTERM DECLS                   : at_env_in,
                                  at_env_out                : tp_env,
                                  at_user_reps              : tp_user_reps,
                                  at_encl_unit              : tp_encl_unit;
NONTERM DECL_S                  : at_env_in,
                                  at_env_out                : tp_env,
                                  at_user_reps              : tp_user_reps,
                                  at_encl_unit              : tp_encl_unit;
NONTERM DECL_REP                : at_env_in,
```

```
                            at_env_out          : tp_env,
                            at_user_reps        : tp_user_reps,
                            at_user_rep         : tp_user_reps,
                            at_encl_unit        : tp_encl_unit;
NONTERM DECL_REPS         : at_env_in,
                            at_env_out          : tp_env,
                            at_user_reps        : tp_user_reps,
                            at_encl_unit        : tp_encl_unit;
NONTERM DECL_REP_S        : at_env_in,
                            at_env_out          : tp_env,
                            at_user_reps        : tp_user_reps,
                            at_encl_unit        : tp_encl_unit;
NONTERM DESIGNATOR        : at_designator       : tp_designator;
NONTERM DSCRT_RANGE       : at_valid            : tp_dscrt_range,
                            at_discrim_allowed  : BOOL,
                            at_env_in           : tp_env;
NONTERM DSCRT_RANGES      : at_dscrt_ranges     : tp_dscrt_range_list,
                            at_env_in           : tp_env,
                            at_unconstrained    : BOOL;
NONTERM DSCRT_RANGE_S     : at_dscrt_ranges     : tp_dscrt_range_list,
                            at_env_in           : tp_env,
                            at_unconstrained    : BOOL;
NONTERM DSCRT_RANGE_VOID  : at_valid            : tp_dscrt_range,
                            at_env_in           : tp_env;
NONTERM ENUM_LITERAL      : at_designator       : tp_designator;
NONTERM ENUM_LITERALS     : at_impl_descrs      : tp_descr_list,
                            at_pos              : INT,
                            at_char             : BOOL,
                            at_designators      : tp_designator_list;
NONTERM EXCEPTION_DEF     : at_env_in           : tp_env,
                            at_keys             : tp_key_list;
NONTERM EXP               : at_expected         : tp_key_void,
                            at_allowed1,
                            at_allowed2         : tp_descr_set,
                            at_valid            : tp_descr_set,
                            at_context          : tp_context,
                            at_others_allowed   : BOOL,
                            at_with_use         : BOOL,
                            at_env_in           : tp_env;
NONTERM EXP_VOID          : at_valid            : tp_descr_set_void,
                            at_expected         : tp_key_void,
                            at_others_allowed   : BOOL,
                            at_discrim_allowed  : BOOL,
                            at_env_in           : tp_env;
NONTERM FIXED             : at_allowed1,
                            at_allowed2         : tp_fixed,
                            at_valid            : tp_fixed,
                            at_with_use         : BOOL,
                            at_env_in           : tp_env,
                            at_has_range        : BOOL;
NONTERM FLOAT             : at_allowed1,
                            at_allowed2         : tp_float,
                            at_valid            : tp_float,
                            at_with_use         : BOOL,
                            at_env_in           : tp_env;
NONTERM FORMAL_SUBPROG_DEF: at_def              : tp_subpr_def,
                            at_env_in           : tp_env;
NONTERM FORMAL_TYPE_SPEC  : at_type             : tp_type;
NONTERM GENERAL_ASSOC     : at_allowed1,
                            at_allowed2         : tp_assoc,
```

```
                                  at_valid                  : tp_assoc,
                                  at_discrim_allowed        : BOOL,
                                  at_others_allowed         : BOOL,
                                  at_with_use               : BOOL,
                                  at_env_in                 : tp_env,
                                  at_is_last                : BOOL;
NONTERM GENERAL_ASSOCS          : at_allowed1,
                                  at_allowed2               : tp_assoc_list,
                                  at_valid                  : tp_assoc_list,
                                  at_discrim_allowed        : BOOL,
                                  at_others_allowed         : BOOL,
                                  at_with_use               : BOOL,
                                  at_env_in                 : tp_env,
                                  at_positional_allowed     : BOOL;
NONTERM GENERAL_ASSOC_S         : at_allowed1,
                                  at_allowed2               : tp_assoc_list,
                                  at_valid                  : tp_assoc_list,
                                  at_discrim_allowed        : BOOL,
                                  at_others_allowed         : BOOL,
                                  at_with_use               : BOOL,
                                  at_env_in                 : tp_env;
NONTERM GENERIC                 : at_env_in,
                                  at_env,
                                  at_env_out                : tp_env,
                                  at_keys                   : tp_key_list;
NONTERM GENERIC_ASSOC           : at_valid                  : tp_comp_assoc,
                                  at_expected_in            : tp_descr_list,
                                  at_env_in                 : tp_env;
NONTERM GENERIC_ASSOCS          : at_valid                  : tp_assoc_list,
                                  at_expected_out,
                                  at_expected_in            : tp_descr_list,
                                  at_env_in                 : tp_env,
                                  at_positional_allowed     : BOOL;
NONTERM GENERIC_ASSOC_S         : at_valid                  : tp_assoc_list,
                                  at_expected_out,
                                  at_expected_in            : tp_descr_list,
                                  at_env_in                 : tp_env;
NONTERM GENERIC_HEADER          : at_env_in                 : tp_env,
                                  at_header                 : tp_generic_header,
                                  at_is_operator            : BOOL;
NONTERM GENERIC_PARAM           : at_env_in,
                                  at_env_out                : tp_env,
                                  at_encl_unit              : tp_encl_unit;
NONTERM GENERIC_PARAMS          : at_env_in,
                                  at_env_out                : tp_env,
                                  at_encl_unit              : tp_encl_unit;
NONTERM GENERIC_PARAM_S         : at_env_in,
                                  at_env_out                : tp_env;
NONTERM HEADER                  : at_env_in                 : tp_env,
                                  at_header                 : tp_header,
                                  at_encl_unit              : tp_encl_unit,
                                  at_param_no               : INT,
                                  at_is_operator            : BOOL;
NONTERM INSTANTIATION           : at_instantiation          : tp_instantiation,
                                  at_env_in                 : tp_env;
NONTERM ID                      : at_designator             : tp_designator;
NONTERM IDS                     : at_designators            : tp_designator_list,
                                  at_param_no               : INT;
NONTERM ID_S                    : at_designators            : tp_designator_list,
                                  at_param_no               : INT;
```

```
NONTERM ITEM              : at_env_in,
                            at_env_out               : tp_env,
                            at_user_rep              : tp_user_reps,
                            at_user_reps             : tp_user_reps,
                            at_no_decls              : BOOL,
                            at_encl_unit             : tp_encl_unit,
                            at_block_no              : INT;
NONTERM ITEMS             : at_env_in,
                            at_env_out               : tp_env,
                            at_user_reps             : tp_user_reps,
                            at_no_decls              : BOOL,
                            at_encl_unit             : tp_encl_unit,
                            at_block_no              : INT;
NONTERM ITEM_S            : at_env_in,
                            at_env_out               : tp_env,
                            at_no_decls              : BOOL,
                            at_encl_unit             : tp_encl_unit,
                            at_block_no              : INT;
NONTERM ITERATION         : at_env_in,
                            at_env_out               : tp_env,
                            at_keys                  : tp_key_list;
NONTERM MEMBERSHIP_OP     : at_op                    : tp_op;
NONTERM NAME              : at_expected              : tp_key_void,
                            at_user_rep              : tp_user_reps,
                            at_allowed1,
                            at_allowed2              : tp_descr_set,
                            at_valid                 : tp_descr_set,
                            at_context               : tp_context,
                            at_with_use              : BOOL,
                            at_env_in                : tp_env;
NONTERM NAMES             : at_names                 : tp_descr_list,
                            at_env_in                : tp_env;
NONTERM NAME_S            : at_names                 : tp_descr_list,
                            at_env_in                : tp_env;
NONTERM NAME_VOID         : at_valid                 : tp_descr_set_void,
                            at_context               : tp_context,
                            at_expected              : tp_key_void,
                            at_env_in                : tp_env;
NONTERM NAMED             : at_allowed1,
                            at_allowed2              : tp_assoc,
                            at_valid                 : tp_assoc,
                            at_discrim_allowed       : BOOL,
                            at_with_use              : BOOL,
                            at_others_allowed        : BOOL,
                            at_env_in                : tp_env,
                            at_is_last               : BOOL;
NONTERM OBJECT_DEF        : at_expected              : tp_key_void,
                            at_valid                 : tp_object_def,
                            at_discrim_allowed       : BOOL,
                            at_env_in                : tp_env,
                            at_keys                  : tp_key_list,
                            at_is_exp                : BOOL;
NONTERM PACKAGE_DEF       : at_def                   : tp_package_def,
                            at_env_in                : tp_env,
                            at_keys                  : tp_key_list;
NONTERM PACKAGE_DECL      : at_env_in,
                            at_env_out               : tp_env,
                            at_keys                  : tp_key_list;
NONTERM PACKAGE_SPEC      : at_spec                  : tp_package,
                            at_env_in                : tp_env;
```

```
NONTERM PACKAGE_BODY       : at_env_in,
                             at_env_out             : tp_env,
                             at_keys                : tp_key_list,
                             at_block_no            : INT;
NONTERM PARAM              : at_env_in,
                             at_env_out             : tp_env,
                             at_keys                : tp_key_list,
                             at_param_no            : INT,
                             at_encl_unit           : tp_encl_unit;
NONTERM PARAMS             : at_env_in,
                             at_env_out             : tp_env,
                             at_param_no            : INT,
                             at_encl_unit           : tp_encl_unit;
NONTERM PARAM_S            : at_env_in,
                             at_env_out             : tp_env,
                             at_encl_unit           : tp_encl_unit,
                             at_param_no            : INT;
NONTERM PARAM_ASSOC        : at_env_in              : tp_env,
                             at_assoc               : tp_comp_assoc;
NONTERM PARAM_ASSOC_S,
        PARAM_ASSOCS       : at_env_in              : tp_env,
                             at_assocs              : tp_assoc_list;
NONTERM PRAGMA,
        PRAGMAS,
        PRAGMA_S           : at_env_in,
                             at_env_out             : tp_env;
NONTERM RANGE              : at_allowed1,
                             at_allowed2            : tp_range_constr,
                             at_valid               : tp_range,
                             at_expected            : tp_key_void,
                             at_with_use            : BOOL,
                             at_discrim_allowed     : BOOL,
                             at_env_in              : tp_env;
NONTERM RANGE_VOID         : at_allowed1,
                             at_allowed2            : tp_range,
                             at_valid               : tp_range,
                             at_with_use            : BOOL,
                             at_env_in              : tp_env;
NONTERM RECORD             : at_comps               : tp_comp_list,
                             at_env_in,
                             at_env_out             : tp_env;
NONTERM RENAME             : at_rename              : tp_rename,
                             at_keys                : tp_key_list,
                             at_env_in              : tp_env;
NONTERM REP                : at_env_in,
                             at_env_out             : tp_env,
                             at_user_rep            : tp_user_reps,
                             at_user_reps           : tp_user_reps,
                             at_keys                : tp_key_list;
NONTERM SHORT_CIRCUIT_OP   : at_op                  : tp_op;
NONTERM SELECT_CLAUSE      : at_env_in              : tp_env,
                             at_labels,
                             at_loops_blocks        : tp_bl_lab_loops,
                             at_encl_unit           : tp_encl_unit,
                             at_return_required     : BOOL,
                             at_first_select        : tp_select_type;
NONTERM SELECT_CLAUSES     : at_env_in              : tp_env,
                             at_labels,
                             at_loops_blocks        : tp_bl_lab_loops,
                             at_select_state        : tp_select_state,
```

```
                                 at_encl_unit             : tp_encl_unit,
                                 at_return_required       : BOOL;
NONTERM SELECT_CLAUSE_S        : at_env_in                : tp_env,
                                 at_labels,
                                 at_loops_blocks          : tp_bl_lab_loops,
                                 at_select_state          : tp_select_state,
                                 at_encl_unit             : tp_encl_unit,
                                 at_return_required       : BOOL;
NONTERM STM                    : at_env_in                : tp_env,
                                 at_usable,
                                 at_labels,
                                 at_loops_blocks          : tp_bl_lab_loops,
                                 at_encl_unit             : tp_encl_unit,
                                 at_return_required       : BOOL;
NONTERM STMS                   : at_env_in                : tp_env,
                                 at_first_stm             : tp_stm_type,
                                 at_usable,
                                 at_labels,
                                 at_loops_blocks          : tp_bl_lab_loops,
                                 at_encl_unit             : tp_encl_unit,
                                 at_return_required       : BOOL,
                                 at_no_code_stms          : BOOL,
                                 at_first_select          : tp_select_type ;
NONTERM STM_S                  : at_env_in                : tp_env,
                                 at_first_stm             : tp_stm_type,
                                 at_usable,
                                 at_labels,
                                 at_loops_blocks          : tp_bl_lab_loops,
                                 at_encl_unit             : tp_encl_unit,
                                 at_return_required       : BOOL,
                                 at_no_code_stms          : BOOL,
                                 at_first_select          : tp_select_type ;
NONTERM SUBPROG_DEF            : at_def                   : tp_subpr_def,
                                 at_env_in                : tp_env,
                                 at_keys                  : tp_key_list;
NONTERM SUBPROG_DECL           : at_env_in,
                                 at_env,
                                 at_env_out               : tp_env,
                                 at_header                : tp_header,
                                 at_keys                  : tp_key_list;
NONTERM SUBPROG_BODY           : at_env_in,
                                 at_env,
                                 at_env_out               : tp_env,
                                 at_keys1,
                                 at_keys2                 : tp_key_list,
                                 at_block_no              : INT;
NONTERM SUBUNIT_BODY           : at_env_in                : tp_env,
                                 at_keys                  : tp_key_list;
NONTERM TASK_DEF               : at_env_in                : tp_env,
                                 at_keys                  : tp_key_list,
                                 at_impl_descrs           : tp_descr_list,
                                 at_def                   : tp_task_def;
NONTERM TASK_SPEC              : at_env_in                : tp_env,
                                 at_keys                  : tp_key_list,
                                 at_spec                  : tp_task_spec;
NONTERM TASK_BODY              : at_env_in,
                                 at_env_out               : tp_env,
                                 at_keys                  : tp_key_list,
                                 at_block_no              : INT;
NONTERM TYPE_DECL              : at_env_in,
```

```
                          at_env_out              : tp_env,
                          at_keys                 : tp_key_list,
                          at_encl_unit            : tp_encl_unit;
NONTERM TYPE_SPEC       : at_type                 : tp_type,
                          at_keys                 : tp_key_list,
                          at_env_in               : tp_env,
                          at_discriminants        : tp_descr_list,
                          at_impl_descrs,
                          at_impl_subprs          : tp_descr_list,
                          at_encl_unit            : tp_encl_unit;
NONTERM TYPE_RANGE      : at_allowed1,
                          at_allowed2             : tp_type_range,
                          at_valid                : tp_type_range,
                          at_expected             : tp_key_void,
                          at_with_use             : BOOL,
                          at_env_in               : tp_env;
NONTERM UNIT_BODY       : at_env_in               : tp_env,
                          at_keys                 : tp_key_list;
NONTERM USE             : at_env_in,
                          at_env_out              : tp_env;
NONTERM VAR_DECL        : at_env_in,
                          at_env_out              : tp_env,
                          at_discrim_allowed      : BOOL,
                          at_keys                 : tp_key_list,
                          at_init                 : tp_mixed_init;
NONTERM VAR_DECLS       : at_env_in,
                          at_env_out              : tp_env,
                          at_init                 : tp_mixed_init;
NONTERM VAR_DECL_S      : at_env_in,
                          at_env_out              : tp_env,
                          at_init                 : tp_mixed_init,
                          at_empty                : BOOL;
NONTERM VARIANT         : at_variant              : tp_variant,
                          at_expected             : tp_key_void,
                          at_env_in,
                          at_env_out              : tp_env,
                          at_is_last              : BOOL;
NONTERM VARIANTS        : at_variants             : tp_variant_list,
                          at_expected             : tp_key_void,
                          at_env_in,
                          at_env_out              : tp_env;
NONTERM VARIANT_S       : at_variants             : tp_variant_list,
                          at_expected             : tp_key_void,
                          at_env_in,
                          at_env_out              : tp_env;
```

```
%%%%%%%%%%%%%%%%%%%%%%%%%%%%%%%%%%%%%%%%%%%%%%%%%%%%%%%%%%%%%%%%%%%%%%%%%%%%%
%                                                                           %
% AG5. Syntactic Rules and Attribute Calculation                            %
%                                                                           %
%%%%%%%%%%%%%%%%%%%%%%%%%%%%%%%%%%%%%%%%%%%%%%%%%%%%%%%%%%%%%%%%%%%%%%%%%%%%%
%                                                                           %
% CONDITIONS (i.e. checks of semantic Ada rules) are prefixed by a          %
% comment denoting the place where this rule appears in the Ada             %
% Reference Manual [Ada80], e.g. C.3.2/1 means the first rule given in      %
% [Ada80].                                                                  %
% The syntactic rules belonging to the same chapter from the                %
% Ada Reference Manual are grouped together. Within those                   %
% groups the rules are ordered according to the alphabetic order            %
% of the nonterminal on the left hand side of the rule.                     %
%                                                                           %
%%%%%%%%%%%%%%%%%%%%%%%%%%%%%%%%%%%%%%%%%%%%%%%%%%%%%%%%%%%%%%%%%%%%%%%%%%%%%


%---------------------------------------------------------------------------
%                                                                          -
% 5.2. Lexical Elements                                                    -
%                                                                          -
%---------------------------------------------------------------------------


%- - - - - - - - - - - - - - - - - - - - - - - - - - - - - - - - - - - - -
RULE   r_001 :
ID                        ::= id
STATIC

   ID.at_designator := id.at_designator

END;
```

```
%------------------------------------------------------------------------
%                                                                       -
% 5.3. Declarations and Types                                           -
%                                                                       -
%------------------------------------------------------------------------


%- - - - - - - - - - - - - - - - - - - - - - - - - - - - - - - - - - - -
RULE   r_002 :
COMP                    ::= null_comp
STATIC

   COMP.at_comp    := sc_void;

   COMP.at_env_out := COMP.at_env_in

END;
%- - - - - - - - - - - - - - - - - - - - - - - - - - - - - - - - - - - -
RULE   r_003 :
COMP                    ::= variant_part NAME VARIANT_S '%'
STATIC

   TRANSFER at_env_in, at_env_out;

   NAME.at_expected     := c_no_expected;

   NAME.at_context      := sc_no_special;

   NAME.at_with_use     := f_use_required (NAME.at_allowed1);

   NAME.at_valid        := cf_unique_descr
                              (NAME.at_allowed2,
                               TRUE,
                               NAME.at_env_in);

   %C 3.7.3/4
   CONDITION
      ELEM_IN_LIST (f_head_descr (NAME.at_valid),
                    INCLUDING TYPE_SPEC.at_discriminants)
      MESSAGE
      "the name of a disciminant of the record expected";

   VARIANT_S.at_expected := f_object_type1
                               (f_head_descr (NAME.at_valid).s_den);

   %C 3.7.3/1
   CONDITION
   ch_exhaustive_choices (f_obj_constrained1
                            (f_head_descr (NAME.at_valid)),
                          f_variant_choices (VARIANT_S.at_variants),
                          COMP.at_env_in)
      MESSAGE
      "each choice for the disrim-type must appear exactly once";

   COMP.at_comp := tp_variant_part
                      (f_head_descr (NAME.at_valid).s_key,
                       VARIANT_S.at_variants);

END ;
%- - - - - - - - - - - - - - - - - - - - - - - - - - - - - - - - - - - -
```

```
RULE    r_004 :
COMP                    ::= VAR_DECL
STATIC

   TRANSFER at_env_in, at_env_out;

   VAR_DECL.at_discrim_allowed := FALSE;

   COMP.at_comp := f_select_by_keys (VAR_DECL.at_keys,
                                     VAR_DECL.at_env_out);

END;
%- - - - - - - - - - - - - - - - - - - - - - - - - - - - - - - - - - - - - -
RULE    r_005 :
CONSTRAINED_1           ::= constrained NAME CONSTRAINT
STATIC

   TRANSFER at_env_in, at_discrim_allowed;

   NAME.at_expected   := c_no_expected;

   NAME.at_context    := sc_no_special;

   NAME.at_with_use   := f_use_required (NAME.at_allowed1);

   NAME.at_valid      := cf_unique_type_descr (NAME.at_allowed2);

   CONSTRAINT.at_expected :=
      IF f_is_scalar_type
           (f_select_by_key
               (f_base_type (f_head_descr (NAME.at_valid)),
                CONSTRAINED_1.at_env_in),
            CONSTRAINED_1.at_env_in) THEN
         f_base_type (f_head_descr (NAME.at_valid))
      ELSE c_no_expected      % no valid constraint;
                              % checked in ch_valid_constraint
      FI;

   CONSTRAINT.at_with_use := f_valid_constraint
                                (NAME.at_valid,
                                 CONSTRAINT.at_allowed1,
                                 CONSTRAINED_1.at_env_in) IS tp_void;

   CONSTRAINT.at_valid :=
      CASE c_constr :
            f_valid_constraint
               (NAME.at_valid,
                CONSTRAINT.at_allowed2,
                CONSTRAINED_1.at_env_in) OF
      IS tp_void : (f_error_constraint (CONSTRAINT.at_allowed2)
                   CONDITION FALSE
                      MESSAGE "illegal constraint")
      OUT c_constr
      ESAC;

   %C 3.3/1, 3.6.1/1, 3.7.2/3, 3.5.7/3, 3.6.1/2, 3.5.9/4
   %C 3.5.7/4
   CONDITION
   ch_constraint (NAME.at_valid,
                  CONSTRAINT.at_valid,
```

```
                CONSTRAINED_1.at_env_in)
      MESSAGE "illegal constraint";

   CONSTRAINED_1.at_type :=
      tp_constrained
         (f_base_type
            (f_head_descr (NAME.at_valid)),
          CONSTRAINT.at_valid);

   %C 3.3.1, C 3.6.1/1     checked only in r_084 because CONSTRAINT
   %                       can only mean range or accuracy constraint
   %C 3.8/3 similarly, need only be checked at r_007
   %C 3.3/3 checked by cf_unique_type_descr

   %
   % Diana Generation:
   %
   %     Set SM_BASE_TYPE, SM_TYPE_STRUCT using NAME.at_valid
   %     Set SM_CONSTRAINT using NAME.at_valid and CONSTRAINT.at_def
   %
END;
%- - - - - - - - - - - - - - - - - - - - - - - - - - - - - - - - - - -
RULE   r_006:
CONSTRAINED            ::= CONSTRAINED_1
STATIC

   TRANSFER

END;
%- - - - - - - - - - - - - - - - - - - - - - - - - - - - - - - - - - -
RULE   r_007:
CONSTRAINED                 ::= NAME
   %
   %  especially NAME ::= APPLY  is index- / discriminant constraint
   %
STATIC

   TRANSFER at_env_in;

   NAME.at_expected := c_no_expected;

   NAME.at_context := IF CONSTRAINED IS r_059 THEN
                         sc_access
                      ELSE sc_subtype_ind
                      FI;

   NAME.at_with_use := f_use_required (NAME.at_allowed1);

   NAME.at_valid := cf_unique_type_descr (NAME.at_allowed2);

   %C 3.6.1/4
   CONDITION
   CASE f_encl_descr (CONSTRAINED.at_env_in).s_state  OF
   sc_in_record :
      ch_static_discrim_array (NAME.at_valid,
                               CONSTRAINED.at_env_in)
   OUT TRUE
   ESAC
      MESSAGE
      "dynamic arrays in records must directly depend on discriminants"
```

```
   CONSTRAINED.at_type :=
      f_gen_constrained
         (f_head_descr (NAME.at_valid),
          sc_void);

   %
   % Diana Generation:
   %
   %     Transform NAME into a constrained with a name and an
   %     index/discriminant constraint.
   %     Set SM_TYPE_STRUCT, SM_BASE_TYPE using NAME.at_valid
   %     Set SM_CONSTRAINT using NAME.at_valid
   %
END;
%- - - - - - - - - - - - - - - - - - - - - - - - - - - - - - - - - - -
RULE   r_008 :
CONSTRAINED_VOID        ::= void
STATIC

   CONSTRAINED_VOID.at_type := c_constrained;

END;
%- - - - - - - - - - - - - - - - - - - - - - - - - - - - - - - - - - -
RULE   r_009:
CONSTRAINED_VOID        ::= CONSTRAINED
STATIC

   TRANSFER;

   CONSTRAINED.at_discrim_allowed := FALSE;

END;
%- - - - - - - - - - - - - - - - - - - - - - - - - - - - - - - - - - -
RULE   r_010 :
CONSTRAINT              ::= FIXED
STATIC

   TRANSFER at_env_in, at_with_use;

   CONSTRAINT.at_allowed1 := FIXED.at_allowed1;

   CONSTRAINT.at_allowed2 := FIXED.at_allowed2;

   FIXED.at_valid := CONSTRAINT.at_valid QUA tp_fixed;

END;
%- - - - - - - - - - - - - - - - - - - - - - - - - - - - - - - - - - -
RULE   r_011 :
CONSTRAINT              ::= FLOAT
STATIC

   TRANSFER at_env_in, at_with_use;

   CONSTRAINT.at_allowed1 := FLOAT.at_allowed1;

   CONSTRAINT.at_allowed2 := FLOAT.at_allowed2;

   FLOAT.at_valid := CONSTRAINT.at_valid QUA tp_float;

   %
```

```
   % Diana Generation:
   %
   %    Set SM_TYPE_STRUCT of FLOAT using SM_TYPE_STRUCT of
   %    enclosing constrained node.
   %
END;
%- - - - - - - - - - - - - - - - - - - - - - - - - - - - - - - - - - - -
RULE   r_012 :
CONSTRAINT              ::= RANGE
STATIC

   TRANSFER at_env_in, at_expected, at_with_use, at_discrim_allowed;

   CONSTRAINT.at_allowed1 := RANGE.at_allowed1;

   CONSTRAINT.at_allowed2 := RANGE.at_allowed2;

   RANGE.at_valid := CONSTRAINT.at_valid QUA tp_range_constr;

END;
%- - - - - - - - - - - - - - - - - - - - - - - - - - - - - - - - - - - -
RULE   r_013 :
DECL                    ::= constant ID_S '%' TYPE_SPEC OBJECT_DEF
   %
   %  TYPE_SPEC ::= CONSTRAINED  or
   %  TYPE_SPEC ::= array ...
   %
   %  OBJECT_DEF is not RENAME
   %
STATIC

   TRANSFER at_encl_unit;

   DECL.at_keys := f_prev_defs (ID_S.at_designators,
                                sc_constant,
                                DECL.at_env_in);

   TYPE_SPEC.at_keys := IF TYPE_SPEC IS r_058 THEN
                           c_empty_keys                          %CONSTRAINED
                        ELSE f_gen_keys                          %array
                        FI;

   TYPE_SPEC.at_env_in :=
      f_update_add_descrs (DECL.at_keys,
                           ID_S.at_designators,
                           sc_id_established,
                           sc_constant,
                           sc_void,
                           DECL.at_env_in);

   TYPE_SPEC.at_discriminants := c_empty_descrs;

   %A 7.4/3
   CONDITION
      ch_deferred_constants (DECL.at_keys,
                             TYPE_SPEC.at_type QUA tp_constrained,
                             OBJECT_DEF.at_valid IS tp_descr,
                             DECL.at_env_in);

   TYPE_SPEC.at_impl_subprs := c_empty_descrs;
```

```
OBJECT_DEF.at_expected :=
   TYPE_SPEC.at_type QUA tp_constrained.s_base_type;

OBJECT_DEF.at_discrim_allowed := FALSE;

OBJECT_DEF.at_env_in :=
  f_update_descrs_by_keys
     (DECL.at_keys,
      c_start_repr,
      sc_in_init,
      sc_constant,
      tp_object
         (TYPE_SPEC.at_type QUA tp_constrained,
          c_init),
      TYPE_SPEC.at_env_in);

OBJECT_DEF.at_keys := DECL.at_keys;

%C 3.2/1, C 7.4/1
CONDITION
CASE OBJECT_DEF.at_valid OF
IS tp_descr : ch_is_assign_allowed_for_type
               (TYPE_SPEC.at_type,
                DECL.at_env_in)
OUT TRUE
ESAC
   MESSAGE
   "initialization forbidden";

DECL.at_env_out :=
   f_add_local_descrs
      (TYPE_SPEC.at_impl_descrs, % implicitly declared array type
       CASE c_def : OBJECT_DEF.at_valid OF
       IS tp_descr:              %initialized constant
          f_update_descrs_by_keys
             (DECL.at_keys,
              sc_same,
              sc_complete,
              sc_same,
              tp_object                      % for unconstrained arrays
                                             % gain constrained from
                 (tp_constrained             % initialization expression
                     (TYPE_SPEC.at_type QUA tp_constrained
                          .s_base_type,
                      CASE c_constr: TYPE_SPEC.at_type QUA
                          tp_constrained.s_constraint OF
                      IS tp_void :
                          CASE c_array :
                             f_type
                                (TYPE_SPEC.at_type
                                    QUA tp_constrained.s_base_type,
                                 OBJECT_DEF.at_env_in)  OF
                          IS tp_array :
                             f_make_index_constr
                                (c_array.s_indices,
                                 c_def.s_den QUA tp_object
                                      .s_init,
                                 OBJECT_DEF.at_env_in)
                          OUT c_constr
                          ESAC
```

```
                    OUT c_constr
                    ESAC),
                 tp_init
                    (f_object_init1 (c_def).s_value,
                     CASE c_exp_kind : f_object_value_kind1
                        (c_def) OF
                     sc_literal : sc_static
                     OUT c_exp_kind
                     ESAC)),
              OBJECT_DEF.at_env_in)
     OUT IF f_private_from_same_decl_part
              (TYPE_SPEC.at_type,
               OBJECT_DEF.at_env_in) THEN
            f_update_descrs_by_keys
               (DECL.at_keys,
                sc_same,
                sc_deferred,
                sc_same,
                sc_same,
               OBJECT_DEF.at_env_in)
         ELSE %error
            f_update_descrs_by_keys
               (DECL.at_keys,
                sc_same,
                sc_complete,
                sc_same,
                sc_same,
                OBJECT_DEF.at_env_in)
         FI
     ESAC);

%C 3.6/1, C 3.7.2/4
CONDITION
   IF f_is_array_type1 (TYPE_SPEC.at_type, DECL.at_env_out) THEN
      TRUE  %constrained by initialization
   ELSE
      f_no_unconstr_arr_rec (TYPE_SPEC.at_type,
                             DECL.at_env_out)
   FI
   MESSAGE
   "unconstrained arr/rec types illegal in obj/comp declarations";

%C 3.2/4, C 3.2/1, C 7.4/3
CONDITION
   f_private_from_same_decl_part (TYPE_SPEC.at_type,
                                  DECL.at_env_out) OR
   (OBJECT_DEF.at_valid IS tp_descr)
   MESSAGE
   "constant not initialized";

%
% Diana Generation:
%
%    Set SM_OBJ_TYPE of all ID_S to TYPE_SPEC
%    Set SM_OBJ_DEF of all ID_S to OBJECT_DEF
%    Initialize SM_ADDRESS of all ID_S with void
%
%    If it is a deferred constant determine the full
%    declaration and adjust SM_OBJ_DEF and SM_TYPE_SPEC.
%
```

```
END;
%- - - - - - - - - - - - - - - - - - - - - - - - - - - - - - - -
RULE   r_014 :
DECL                    ::= VAR_DECL
STATIC

   TRANSFER;

   VAR_DECL.at_discrim_allowed := FALSE;

END;
%- - - - - - - - - - - - - - - - - - - - - - - - - - - - - - - -
RULE   r_015 :
DECL                    ::= number_decl ID_S '%' EXP
STATIC

   DECL.at_keys         := f_gen_keylist (ID_S.at_designators);

   EXP.at_expected      := c_no_expected;

   EXP.at_context       := sc_no_special;

   EXP.at_env_in        := f_add_descrs (ID_S.at_designators,
                                         DECL.at_keys,
                                         sc_id_established,
                                         sc_number,
                                         sc_void,
                                         DECL.at_env_in);

   EXP.at_with_use      := f_use_required (EXP.at_allowed1);

   EXP.at_valid         := cf_unique_descr
                              (EXP.at_allowed2,
                               FALSE,
                               EXP.at_env_in);

   %C 3.2/5
   CONDITION
     ch_literal_exp (EXP.at_valid)
     MESSAGE
     "a literal expression required";


   EXP.at_others_allowed := FALSE;

   DECL.at_env_out :=
      f_update_descrs_by_keys
         (DECL.at_keys,
          c_start_repr,
          sc_complete,
          sc_number,
          tp_object
             (f_head_descr (EXP.at_valid).s_den
                 QUA tp_object. s_type,
              f_object_init (EXP.at_valid)),
         EXP.at_env_in);

   %
   % Diana Generation:
   %
```

```
   %    Set SM_INIT_EXP of all ID_S to EXP
   %    Set SM_OBJ_TYPE of all ID_S using EXP.at_valid
   %
END;
%- - - - - - - - - - - - - - - - - - - - - - - - - - - - - - - - - - - - - -
RULE   r_016 :
DECL                  ::= subtype ID CONSTRAINED
STATIC

   DECL.at_keys :=                                  % only for improvement
                                                    % of error handling
      f_prev_defs (tp_designator_list (ID.at_designator),
                   sc_type,
                   DECL.at_env_in);

   %C 7.4.1/1
   CONDITION
      f_new_key (HEAD (DECL.at_keys),
                 DECL.at_env_in)
      MESSAGE
"no subtype declaration allowed for private/incomplete type completion"

   CONSTRAINED.at_discrim_allowed := FALSE;

   CONSTRAINED.at_env_in :=
      f_update_add_descrs
         (DECL.at_keys,
          tp_designator_list (ID.at_designator),
          sc_id_established,
          sc_subtype,
          sc_void,
          DECL.at_env_in);

   DECL.at_env_out :=
      f_update_descrs_by_keys (DECL.at_keys,
                               c_start_repr,
                               sc_complete,
                               sc_subtype,
                               CONSTRAINED.at_type,
                               CONSTRAINED.at_env_in);

   %
   % Diana Generation:
   %
   %    Set SM_TYPE_SPEC of ID to CONSTRAINED
   %
END;
%- - - - - - - - - - - - - - - - - - - - - - - - - - - - - - - - - - - - - -
RULE   r_017 :
DECL                  ::= TYPE_DECL
STATIC

   TRANSFER

END;
%- - - - - - - - - - - - - - - - - - - - - - - - - - - - - - - - - - - - - -
RULE   r_018 :
DECL                  ::= USE
STATIC
```

```
   DECL.at_keys := c_empty_keys;

   TRANSFER;

END;
%- - - - - - - - - - - - - - - - - - - - - - - - - - - - - - - - - - - -
RULE   r_019 :
DECL                    ::= PRAGMA
STATIC

   TRANSFER at_env_in, at_env_out;

   DECL.at_keys     := c_empty_keys;

END;
%- - - - - - - - - - - - - - - - - - - - - - - - - - - - - - - - - - - -
RULE   r_020:
DECLS                   ::=
STATIC

   DECLS.at_env_out := DECLS.at_env_in;

END;
%- - - - - - - - - - - - - - - - - - - - - - - - - - - - - - - - - - - -
RULE   r_021 :
DECLS                   ::= DECL  DECLS
STATIC

   TRANSFER at_user_reps, at_encl_unit;

   DECL.at_is_item := FALSE;

   DECL.at_env_in := DECLS[1].at_env_in;
   DECLS[2].at_env_in := DECL.at_env_out;
   DECLS[1].at_env_out := DECLS[2].at_env_out;

END;
%- - - - - - - - - - - - - - - - - - - - - - - - - - - - - - - - - - - -
RULE   r_022 :
DECL_S                  ::= decl_s DECLS
STATIC

   TRANSFER

END;
%- - - - - - - - - - - - - - - - - - - - - - - - - - - - - - - - - - - -
RULE   r_023 :
DECL_REP                ::= DECL
STATIC

   TRANSFER;

   DECL.at_is_item := FALSE;

   DECL_REP.at_user_rep := c_empty_user_reps;

END;
%- - - - - - - - - - - - - - - - - - - - - - - - - - - - - - - - - - - -
RULE   r_024 :
```

```
DECL_REP              ::= REP
STATIC

   TRANSFER at_env_in, at_env_out, at_user_reps, at_user_rep;

END;
%- - - - - - - - - - - - - - - - - - - - - - - - - - - - - - - - - - -
RULE   r_025:
DECL_REPS             ::=
STATIC

   DECL_REPS.at_user_reps := c_empty_user_reps;

   DECL_REPS.at_env_out := DECL_REPS.at_env_in;

END;
%- - - - - - - - - - - - - - - - - - - - - - - - - - - - - - - - - - -
RULE   r_026 :
DECL_REPS             ::= DECL_REP DECL_REPS
STATIC

   TRANSFER at_encl_unit;

   DECL_REPS[1].at_user_reps := DECL_REPS[2].at_user_reps +
                                DECL_REP.at_user_rep;

   DECL_REP.at_env_in := DECL_REPS[1].at_env_in;
   DECL_REP.at_user_reps := DECL_REPS[2].at_user_reps;

   DECL_REPS[2].at_env_in := DECL_REP.at_env_out;
   DECL_REPS[1].at_env_out := DECL_REPS[2].at_env_out;

END;
%- - - - - - - - - - - - - - - - - - - - - - - - - - - - - - - - - - -
RULE   r_027 :
DECL_REP_S            ::= decl_rep_s DECL_REPS
STATIC

   TRANSFER

END;
%- - - - - - - - - - - - - - - - - - - - - - - - - - - - - - - - - - -
RULE   r_028 :
DSCRT_RANGE           ::= CONSTRAINED
STATIC

   TRANSFER at_env_in, at_discrim_allowed;

   %C 3.6/2, 5.4/4
   CONDITION
      f_is_discrete_type
         (f_select_by_key
             (CONSTRAINED.at_type.s_base_type,
              DSCRT_RANGE.at_env_in),
           DSCRT_RANGE.at_env_in)
      MESSAGE
      "a discrete type expected here";

   DSCRT_RANGE.at_valid    := CONSTRAINED.at_type;
```

```
END;
%- - - - - - - - - - - - - - - - - - - - - - - - - - - - - - - - - - - - -
RULE   r_029 :
DSCRT_RANGE          ::= RANGE
STATIC

   TRANSFER at_env_in, at_discrim_allowed;

   RANGE.at_expected := c_no_expected;

   RANGE.at_with_use := f_use_required (RANGE.at_allowed1);

   DSCRT_RANGE.at_valid     := f_valid_dscrt_range (RANGE.at_allowed2,
                                                    RANGE.at_env_in);

   %C 3.6/2, 5.4/4
   CONDITION
      f_is_discrete_type
          (f_select_by_key
              (DSCRT_RANGE.at_valid QUA tp_constrained .s_base_type,
               DSCRT_RANGE.at_env_in),
           DSCRT_RANGE.at_env_in)
     MESSAGE
     "a discrete type expected here";

   RANGE.at_valid := DSCRT_RANGE.at_valid QUA tp_constrained
                     .s_constraint QUA tp_range_constr;

END;
%- - - - - - - - - - - - - - - - - - - - - - - - - - - - - - - - - - - - -
RULE   r_030 :
DSCRT_RANGE          ::= index NAME
STATIC

   TRANSFER at_env_in;

   NAME.at_expected := c_no_expected;

   NAME.at_context := sc_no_special;

   NAME.at_with_use := f_use_required (NAME.at_allowed1);

   NAME.at_valid := cf_unique_type_descr (NAME.at_allowed2);

   %C 3.6/2
   CONDITION
      f_is_discrete_type (f_head_descr (NAME.at_valid),
                          DSCRT_RANGE.at_env_in)
     MESSAGE
     "a discrete type expected here";

   DSCRT_RANGE.at_valid :=
      tp_index
         (f_constrained
            (f_head_descr (NAME.at_valid).s_key,
             DSCRT_RANGE.at_env_in));

END;
%- - - - - - - - - - - - - - - - - - - - - - - - - - - - - - - - - - - - -
RULE   r_031:
```

```
DSCRT_RANGES          ::=
STATIC

   DSCRT_RANGES.at_unconstrained := FALSE;          % does not matter

   DSCRT_RANGES.at_dscrt_ranges  := tp_dscrt_range_list ();

END;
%- - - - - - - - - - - - - - - - - - - - - - - - - - - - - - - - - - -
RULE   r_032 :
DSCRT_RANGES          ::= DSCRT_RANGE DSCRT_RANGES
STATIC

   DSCRT_RANGES[1].at_unconstrained := DSCRT_RANGE IS r_030;
                            % Syntax ensures that no mixed form possible

   TRANSFER at_env_in;

   DSCRT_RANGE.at_discrim_allowed := TRUE;

   DSCRT_RANGES[1].at_dscrt_ranges :=
      tp_dscrt_range_list (DSCRT_RANGE.at_valid)  +
      DSCRT_RANGES[2].at_dscrt_ranges;

   %C 3.6.1/4
   CONDITION
      CASE f_encl_descr (DSCRT_RANGES[1].at_env_in).s_state  OF
      sc_in_record :
         ch_static_discrim_range (DSCRT_RANGE.at_valid,
                                  DSCRT_RANGE.at_env_in)
      OUT TRUE
      ESAC
      MESSAGE
      "dynamic arrays in records must directly depend on discriminants"

END;
%- - - - - - - - - - - - - - - - - - - - - - - - - - - - - - - - - - -
RULE   r_033 :
DSCRT_RANGE_S         ::= dscrt_range_s DSCRT_RANGES
STATIC

   TRANSFER;

END;
%- - - - - - - - - - - - - - - - - - - - - - - - - - - - - - - - - - -
RULE   r_034 :
DSCRT_RANGE_VOID      ::= DSCRT_RANGE
STATIC

   TRANSFER at_valid, at_env_in;

   DSCRT_RANGE.at_discrim_allowed := FALSE;

END;
%- - - - - - - - - - - - - - - - - - - - - - - - - - - - - - - - - - -
RULE   r_035 :
DSCRT_RANGE_VOID      ::= void
STATIC

   DSCRT_RANGE_VOID.at_valid := sc_void;
```

```
END;
%- - - - - - - - - - - - - - - - - - - - - - - - - - - - - - - - -
RULE   r_036 :
ENUM_LITERAL           ::= id
STATIC

   ENUM_LITERAL.at_designator := id.at_designator;

END;
%- - - - - - - - - - - - - - - - - - - - - - - - - - - - - - - - -
RULE   r_037 :
ENUM_LITERAL           ::= char
STATIC

   ENUM_LITERAL.at_designator := char.at_designator;

END;
%- - - - - - - - - - - - - - - - - - - - - - - - - - - - - - - - -
RULE   r_038 :
ENUM_LITERALS           ::= ENUM_LITERAL ENUM_LITERALS
STATIC

   ENUM_LITERALS[1].at_designators :=
      tp_designator_list( ENUM_LITERAL.at_designator )
      +    ENUM_LITERALS[2].at_designators;

   %C 3.5.1/1
   CONDITION
   NOT ( ELEM_IN_LIST(ENUM_LITERAL.at_designator,
                      ENUM_LITERALS[2].at_designators))
      MESSAGE
      "Enumeration literals must be distinct.";
  %RECOVER delete (ENUM_LITERAL)

   %C 8.3/1
   CONDITION
      ch_local_hiding
         (ENUM_LITERAL.at_designator,
          tp_enum_literal (c_key, 0, FALSE),
          c_key,
          f_local (INCLUDING (TYPE_SPEC.at_env_in)),
          INCLUDING TYPE_SPEC.at_env_in)
      MESSAGE
      "THIS enum literal hides entity from same decl-part";

  ENUM_LITERALS[2].at_pos   := ENUM_LITERALS[1].at_pos + 1;

  ENUM_LITERALS[1].at_impl_descrs :=
     tp_descr_list
        (f_descr
           (ENUM_LITERAL.at_designator,
            f_gen_key,
            c_start_repr,
            sc_complete,
            sc_enum_literal,
            tp_enum_literal
               (HEAD (INCLUDING TYPE_SPEC.at_keys),
                ENUM_LITERALS[1].at_pos,
                ENUM_LITERAL IS r_037),
```

```
           f_enclosing (INCLUDING TYPE_SPEC.at_env_in))) +
      ENUM_LITERALS[2].at_impl_descrs;

   ENUM_LITERALS[1].at_char := ENUM_LITERALS[2].at_char OR
                               (ENUM_LITERAL IS r_037);

   %
   % Diana Generation:
   %
   %    Set SM_POS, initialize SM_REP of ENUM_LITERAL using
   %    ENUM_LITERALS[1].at_pos
   %
END;
%- - - - - - - - - - - - - - - - - - - - - - - - - - - - - - -
RULE   r_039 :
ENUM_LITERALS          ::=
STATIC

   ENUM_LITERALS.at_designators := tp_designator_list();

   ENUM_LITERALS.at_impl_descrs := c_empty_descrs;

   ENUM_LITERALS.at_char        := FALSE;

END;
%- - - - - - - - - - - - - - - - - - - - - - - - - - - - - - -
RULE   r_040 :
FIXED                  ::= fixed EXP RANGE_VOID
STATIC

   FIXED.at_has_range := RANGE_VOID IS r_053;

   TRANSFER at_env_in, at_with_use;

   EXP.at_expected := c_no_expected;

   EXP.at_context := sc_no_special;

   FIXED.at_allowed1 := tp_fixed (EXP.at_allowed1,
                                  RANGE_VOID.at_allowed1);

   FIXED.at_allowed2 := tp_fixed (EXP.at_allowed2,
                                  RANGE_VOID.at_allowed2);

   EXP.at_valid :=  cf_unique_descr (FIXED.at_valid.s_delta,
                                     FALSE,
                                     FIXED.at_env_in);

   %C 3.5.9/1
   CONDITION
      EXP.at_valid =/ c_error_descr_set AND
      ch_static_real (EXP.at_valid) AND
      ch_is_positive (EXP.at_valid)
      MESSAGE
      "a positive static real expression expected after DELTA";

   EXP.at_others_allowed := FALSE;

   RANGE_VOID.at_valid := FIXED.at_valid.s_range;
```

```
   %
   % Diana Generation:
   %
   %     Initialize SM_SIZE with void
   %     Initialize SM_ACTUAL_DELTA, SM_BITS with values given
   %     by machine dependent type mapping
   %
END;
%- - - - - - - - - - - - - - - - - - - - - - - - - - - - - - - - - - - - - -
RULE   r_041 :
FLOAT                    ::= float EXP RANGE_VOID
STATIC

   TRANSFER at_env_in, at_with_use;

   EXP.at_expected := c_no_expected;

   EXP.at_context := sc_no_special;

   FLOAT.at_allowed1 := tp_float (EXP.at_allowed1,
                                  RANGE_VOID.at_allowed1);

   FLOAT.at_allowed2 := tp_float (EXP.at_allowed2,
                                  RANGE_VOID.at_allowed2);

   EXP.at_valid := cf_unique_descr (FLOAT.at_valid.s_digits,
                                    FALSE,
                                    FLOAT.at_env_in);

   %C 3.5.7/1
   CONDITION
      EXP.at_valid =/ c_error_descr_set AND
      ch_static_int (EXP.at_valid, FLOAT.at_env_in) AND
      ch_is_positive (EXP.at_valid)
      MESSAGE
      "a static integer positive expression required after DIGITS";

   EXP.at_others_allowed := FALSE;

   RANGE_VOID.at_valid := FLOAT.at_valid.s_range;

   %
   % Diana Generation:
   %
   %     Initialize SM_SIZE to void
   %
END;
%- - - - - - - - - - - - - - - - - - - - - - - - - - - - - - - - - - - - - -
RULE   r_042 :
ITEM                     ::= DECL
STATIC

   TRANSFER at_encl_unit, at_env_in, at_env_out, at_user_reps;

   ITEM.at_no_decls := (DECL IS r_018) OR (DECL IS r_019);
                                % USE     OR           PRAGMA

   DECL.at_is_item := TRUE;

   ITEM.at_user_rep := c_empty_user_reps;
```

```
END;
%- - - - - - - - - - - - - - - - - - - - - - - - - - - - - - - - - - - - -
RULE   r_043 :
ITEM                    ::= REP
STATIC

   TRANSFER at_env_in, at_env_out, at_user_rep, at_user_reps;

   ITEM.at_no_decls := FALSE;

END;
%- - - - - - - - - - - - - - - - - - - - - - - - - - - - - - - - - - - - -
RULE   r_044 :
ITEM                    ::= PACKAGE_BODY
STATIC

   TRANSFER at_env_in, at_env_out, at_block_no;

   ITEM.at_no_decls := FALSE;

   ITEM.at_user_rep := c_empty_user_reps;

END;
%- - - - - - - - - - - - - - - - - - - - - - - - - - - - - - - - - - - - -
RULE   r_045 :
ITEM                    ::= SUBPROG_BODY
STATIC

   TRANSFER at_env_in, at_env_out, at_block_no;

   ITEM.at_no_decls := FALSE;

   ITEM.at_user_rep := c_empty_user_reps;

END;
%- - - - - - - - - - - - - - - - - - - - - - - - - - - - - - - - - - - - -
RULE   r_046 :
ITEM                    ::= TASK_BODY
STATIC

   TRANSFER at_env_in, at_env_out, at_block_no;

   ITEM.at_no_decls := FALSE;

   ITEM.at_user_rep := c_empty_user_reps;

END;
%- - - - - - - - - - - - - - - - - - - - - - - - - - - - - - - - - - - - -
RULE   r_047:
ITEMS                   ::=
STATIC

   ITEMS.at_no_decls := TRUE;

   ITEMS.at_user_reps := c_empty_user_reps;

   ITEMS.at_env_out := ITEMS.at_env_in;
```

```
END;
%- - - - - - - - - - - - - - - - - - - - - - - - - - - - - - - - -
RULE   r_048 :
ITEMS                    ::= ITEM ITEMS
STATIC

   TRANSFER at_encl_unit, at_block_no;

   ITEMS[1].at_no_decls := ITEM.at_no_decls AND ITEMS[2].at_no_decls;

   ITEMS[1].at_user_reps := ITEMS[2].at_user_reps +
                            ITEM.at_user_rep;

   ITEM.at_env_in := ITEMS[1].at_env_in;
   ITEM.at_user_reps      := ITEMS[2].at_user_reps;

   ITEMS[2].at_env_in := ITEM.at_env_out;
   ITEMS[1].at_env_out := ITEMS[2].at_env_out;

END;
%- - - - - - - - - - - - - - - - - - - - - - - - - - - - - - - - -
RULE   r_049 :
ITEM_S                   ::= item_s ITEMS
   %
   %  declarative_items
   %     representation_specifications
   %        program_components
   %
STATIC

   TRANSFER;

END;
%- - - - - - - - - - - - - - - - - - - - - - - - - - - - - - - - -
RULE   r_050 :
OBJECT_DEF               ::= EXP_VOID
STATIC

   OBJECT_DEF.at_is_exp := EXP_VOID IS r_108;

   TRANSFER at_env_in, at_discrim_allowed;

   EXP_VOID.at_expected := OBJECT_DEF.at_expected;

   EXP_VOID.at_others_allowed := FALSE;

   OBJECT_DEF.at_valid :=
      CASE c_allowed : EXP_VOID.at_valid OF
      IS tp_void : tp_object_def (sc_void);
      IS tp_descr_set    : f_head_descr (c_allowed)
      ESAC;

END;
%- - - - - - - - - - - - - - - - - - - - - - - - - - - - - - - - -
RULE   r_051 :
OBJECT_DEF               ::= RENAME
STATIC

   TRANSFER at_keys;

   OBJECT_DEF.at_is_exp := FALSE;
```

```
   RENAME.at_env_in := f_update_descrs_by_keys
                          (OBJECT_DEF.at_keys,
                           sc_same,
                           sc_id_established,
                           sc_same,
                           sc_same,
                           OBJECT_DEF.at_env_in);

   OBJECT_DEF.at_valid := RENAME.at_rename;

END;
%- - - - - - - - - - - - - - - - - - - - - - - - - - - - - - - - - - -
RULE   r_052 :
RANGE                  ::= range EXP EXP
STATIC

   TRANSFER at_env_in, at_expected, at_with_use;

   EXP[1].at_context := sc_no_special;

   EXP[2].at_context := sc_no_special;

   RANGE.at_allowed1  := tp_range_constr (EXP[1].at_allowed1,
                                           EXP[2].at_allowed1);

   RANGE.at_allowed2 := IF RANGE.at_with_use THEN
                           tp_range_constr (EXP[1].at_allowed2,
                                            EXP[2].at_allowed2)
                        ELSE RANGE.at_allowed1
                        FI;

   EXP[1].at_valid := cf_unique_descr
                         (RANGE.at_valid QUA tp_range_constr
                              .s_lower_bound,
                          RANGE.at_discrim_allowed,
                          RANGE.at_env_in);

   EXP[1].at_others_allowed := FALSE;

   EXP[2].at_valid := cf_unique_descr
                         (RANGE.at_valid QUA tp_range_constr
                              .s_upper_bound,
                          RANGE.at_discrim_allowed,
                          RANGE.at_env_in);

   EXP[2].at_others_allowed := FALSE;

   %
   % Diana Generation:
   %
   %    Set SM_BASE_TYPE using RANGE.at_valid
   %
END;
%- - - - - - - - - - - - - - - - - - - - - - - - - - - - - - - - - - -
RULE   r_053 :
RANGE_VOID             ::= RANGE
STATIC
```

```
   TRANSFER at_valid, at_env_in, at_with_use;

   RANGE_VOID.at_allowed1 := RANGE.at_allowed1;

   RANGE_VOID.at_allowed2 := RANGE.at_allowed2;

   RANGE.at_expected := c_no_expected;

   RANGE.at_discrim_allowed := FALSE;

END;
%- - - - - - - - - - - - - - - - - - - - - - - - - - - - - - - - - - -
RULE   r_054 :
RANGE_VOID             ::= void
STATIC

   RANGE_VOID.at_allowed1 := sc_void;

   RANGE_VOID.at_allowed2 := RANGE_VOID.at_allowed1;

END;
%- - - - - - - - - - - - - - - - - - - - - - - - - - - - - - - - - - -
RULE   r_055 :
RECORD                 ::= COMP RECORD
STATIC

   COMP.at_env_in        := RECORD[1].at_env_in;

   RECORD[2].at_env_in := COMP.at_env_out;

   RECORD[1].at_comps :=
      f_make_comps (COMP.at_comp) + RECORD[2].at_comps;

   RECORD[1].at_env_out := RECORD[2].at_env_out;

END;
%- - - - - - - - - - - - - - - - - - - - - - - - - - - - - - - - - - -
RULE   r_056 :
RECORD                 ::=
STATIC

   RECORD.at_comps := tp_comp_list ();

   RECORD.at_env_out := RECORD.at_env_in;

END;
%- - - - - - - - - - - - - - - - - - - - - - - - - - - - - - - - - - -
RULE   r_057 :
TYPE_DECL              ::= type ID VAR_DECL_S '%' TYPE_SPEC
   %
   %  TYPE_SPEC is not CONSTRAINED
   %
   %  TYPE_SPEC ::= FORMAL_TYPE_SPEC  <=>
   %  TYPE_DECL is GENERIC_PARAM
   %
STATIC

   TRANSFER at_encl_unit;
```

```
%C 3.7.1/5
CONDITION
VAR_DECL_S.at_empty                              % discriminants empty
OR (TYPE_SPEC IS r_067)                          % or record
OR (TYPE_SPEC IS r_070)                          % or incomplete
OR (TYPE_SPEC IS r_071)                          % or private
OR (TYPE_SPEC IS r_072)                          % or limited private
   MESSAGE
   "No discriminants allowed.";
%C 3.7.1/7
CONDITION
VAR_DECL_S.at_init =/ sc_mixed
   MESSAGE
   "Either none or all discriminants must be initialized.";

TYPE_DECL.at_keys      := f_prev_defs
                          (tp_designator_list (ID.at_designator),
                           sc_type,
                           TYPE_DECL.at_env_in);

TYPE_SPEC.at_env_in :=
   IF f_new_key (HEAD (TYPE_DECL.at_keys), TYPE_DECL.at_env_in) THEN
      f_add_descr (ID.at_designator,
                   HEAD (TYPE_DECL.at_keys),
                   sc_id_established,
                   sc_type,
                   sc_void,
                   TYPE_DECL.at_env_in)
   ELSE TYPE_DECL.at_env_in
   FI;

VAR_DECL_S.at_env_in := f_empty_local_encl_state
                          (HEAD (TYPE_DECL.at_keys),
                           sc_in_discr_part,
                           TYPE_SPEC.at_env_in);

TYPE_SPEC.at_keys :=
   IF NOT f_new_key (HEAD (TYPE_DECL.at_keys),
                     TYPE_DECL.at_env_in) THEN
      TYPE_DECL.at_keys
   ELSE CASE TYPE_SPEC OF
       %array   derived  float    integer
        r_061:  r_062:   r_065:   r_066: f_gen_keys
        OUT  TYPE_DECL.at_keys
        ESAC
   FI;

TYPE_SPEC.at_discriminants  = f_local (VAR_DECL_S.at_env_out);

%C 7.4.1/3, C 3.8/4
CONDITION
IF f_new_key (HEAD (TYPE_DECL.at_keys), TYPE_DECL.at_env_in) THEN
   TRUE
ELSE ch_matching_discr_parts
       (TYPE_SPEC.at_type,
        f_type (HEAD (TYPE_DECL.at_keys),
                TYPE_DECL.at_env_in))
FI
   MESSAGE
   "discr parts of priv/incompl type and full decl should match";
```

```
%C 7.4/2
CONDITION
IF f_new_key (HEAD (TYPE_DECL.at_keys), TYPE_DECL.at_env_in) THEN
   TRUE
ELSE NOT (TYPE_SPEC.at_type IS tp_incompl_type)
FI
   MESSAGE "Complete type specification expected";

%C 7.4/2
CONDITION
IF f_new_key (HEAD (TYPE_DECL.at_keys), TYPE_DECL.at_env_in) THEN
   TRUE
ELSE CASE f_type (HEAD (TYPE_DECL.at_keys),
                  TYPE_DECL.at_env_in) OF
     IS tp_private : IS tp_l_private :
        f_encl_state (TYPE_DECL.at_env_in) = sc_in_private
     OUT TRUE
     ESAC
FI
   MESSAGE "Completion of private type must occur in private part";

TYPE_SPEC.at_impl_subprs :=
   IF NOT ch_no_recursion
            (IF TYPE_SPEC.at_type IS tp_constrained THEN
                HEAD (TYPE_SPEC.at_keys)
             ELSE HEAD (TYPE_DECL.at_keys)
             FI,
             IF TYPE_SPEC.at_type IS tp_constrained THEN
                HEAD (TYPE_SPEC.at_impl_descrs).s_den
                   QUA tp_type_den.s_type
             ELSE TYPE_SPEC.at_type
             FI,
          TYPE_DECL.at_env_in) THEN
   (c_empty_descrs
    %C 3.3/2
    CONDITION FALSE  MESSAGE
    "recursive type def without interm access type erroneous")
   ELSE IF NOT (TYPE_SPEC IS r_062  OR       % derived (including
                (TYPE_SPEC IS r_065) OR      %  float and integer)
                (TYPE_SPEC IS r_066)) THEN
      IF TYPE_SPEC IS r_060 THEN         % FORMAL_TYPE_SPEC
         CASE TYPE_SPEC.at_type QUA tp_formal_type OF
         sc_formal_integer :
            f_impl_subprs
              (HEAD (TYPE_DECL.at_keys),
               c_int,
               TYPE_DECL.at_env_in);
         sc_formal_float :
            f_impl_subprs
              (HEAD (TYPE_DECL.at_keys),
               c_float,
               TYPE_DECL.at_env_in)
         OUT c_empty_descrs
         ESAC
      ELSE c_empty_descrs
      FI
   ELSE f_impl_subprs
          (IF TYPE_SPEC.at_type IS tp_constrained THEN
              HEAD (TYPE_SPEC.at_keys)
           ELSE HEAD (TYPE_DECL.at_keys)
           FI,
```

```
            IF TYPE_SPEC.at_type IS tp_constrained THEN
               HEAD (TYPE_SPEC.at_impl_descrs) .s_den
                  QUA tp_type_den .s_type
            ELSE TYPE_SPEC.at_type
            FI QUA tp_derived .s_parent_type,

            TYPE_DECL.at_env_in)
      FI FI;

   TYPE_DECL.at_env_out :=
      IF NOT ch_no_recursion
            (IF TYPE_SPEC.at_type IS tp_constrained THEN
                HEAD (TYPE_SPEC.at_keys)
             ELSE HEAD (TYPE_DECL.at_keys)
             FI,
             IF TYPE_SPEC.at_type IS tp_constrained THEN
                HEAD (TYPE_SPEC.at_impl_descrs).s_den
                   QUA tp_type_den.s_type
             ELSE TYPE_SPEC.at_type
             FI,
             TYPE_DECL.at_env_in) THEN
         f_update_descrs_by_keys
            (TYPE_DECL.at_keys,
             c_start_repr,
             sc_complete,
             sc_type,
             c_error_type_den,
             TYPE_SPEC.at_env_in)
      ELSE
         f_update_repr
          (HEAD (TYPE_DECL.at_keys),
           INCLUDING DECL.at_user_reps,
           f_enter_subprs
            (IF TYPE_SPEC IS r_062 THEN    % derived
                f_further_derivable (TYPE_SPEC.at_impl_subprs)
             ELSE c_empty_keys
             FI,
             IF NOT f_new_key
                     (HEAD (TYPE_DECL.at_keys),
                      TYPE_DECL.at_env_in) THEN
                HEAD (TYPE_DECL.at_keys)
             ELSE IF TYPE_SPEC.at_type IS tp_constrained THEN
                HEAD (TYPE_SPEC.at_keys)
             ELSE HEAD (TYPE_DECL.at_keys)
             FI FI,
             f_add_local_descrs
              (TYPE_SPEC.at_impl_subprs,
               IF f_new_key (HEAD (TYPE_DECL.at_keys),
                             TYPE_DECL.at_env_in) THEN
                  f_add_local_descrs
                     (TYPE_SPEC.at_impl_descrs,
                      f_update_descrs_by_keys
                         (TYPE_DECL.at_keys,
                          c_start_repr,
                          CASE TYPE_SPEC.at_type OF
                          IS tp_incompl_type : sc_incomplete;
                          IS tp_private :
                          IS tp_l_private : sc_incompl_private;
                          IS tp_task_spec : sc_spec_complete
                          OUT               sc_complete
                          ESAC,
```

```
                    IF TYPE_SPEC.at_type IS tp_constrained THEN
                       sc_subtype
                    ELSE sc_type
                    FI,
                    IF TYPE_SPEC.at_type IS tp_constrained THEN
                       TYPE_SPEC.at_type QUA tp_constrained
                    ELSE
                       tp_type_den
                          (TYPE_SPEC.at_type,
                           c_empty_keys)
                    FI,
                    TYPE_SPEC.at_env_in))
         ELSE IF TYPE_SPEC.at_type IS tp_constrained THEN
            f_add_descr
               (sc_anonymous,
                HEAD (TYPE_DECL.at_keys),
                sc_complete,
                sc_type,
                HEAD (TYPE_SPEC.at_impl_descrs)
                  .s_den,
                f_adjust_local_env
                   (HEAD (TYPE_DECL.at_keys),
                    f_descr
                       (ID.at_designator,
                        f_gen_key,
                        c_start_repr,
                        sc_complete,
                        sc_subtype,
                        TYPE_SPEC.at_type QUA tp_constrained,
                        f_enclosing (TYPE_DECL.at_env_in)),
                    TYPE_SPEC.at_env_in))
         ELSE f_add_local_descrs
                 (TYPE_SPEC.at_impl_descrs,
                  f_update_descr_by_key
                     (HEAD (TYPE_DECL.at_keys),
                      sc_same,
                      IF TYPE_SPEC.at_type IS tp_task_spec THEN
                         sc_spec_complete
                      ELSE sc_complete
                      FI,
                      sc_same,
                      tp_type_den
                         (TYPE_SPEC.at_type,
                          c_empty_keys),
                      TYPE_SPEC.at_env_in))
         FI FI)))
   FI;

%C 7.4.1/2
CONDITION
IF f_new_key (HEAD (TYPE_DECL.at_keys), TYPE_DECL.at_env_in) THEN
   TRUE
ELSE IF NOT ch_no_recursion
               (HEAD (TYPE_DECL.at_keys),
                IF TYPE_SPEC.at_type IS tp_constrained THEN
                   HEAD (TYPE_SPEC.at_impl_descrs).s_den
                      QUA tp_type_den.s_type
                ELSE TYPE_SPEC.at_type
```

```
                    FI,
                    TYPE_DECL.at_env_in) THEN
      TRUE
   ELSE IF
      f_type (HEAD (TYPE_DECL.at_keys),
              TYPE_DECL.at_env_in) IS tp_private THEN
      ch_is_assign_allowed_for_type
         (TYPE_SPEC.at_type,
          TYPE_DECL.at_env_out)
   ELSE TRUE
   FI FI FI
      MESSAGE
      "assignment/equality must be available for  private types";

   %C 7.4.1/4
   CONDITION
   IF f_new_key (HEAD (TYPE_DECL.at_keys), TYPE_DECL.at_env_in) OR
      NOT ch_no_recursion (HEAD (TYPE_DECL.at_keys),
                           TYPE_SPEC.at_type,
                           TYPE_DECL.at_env_in) THEN
      TRUE
   ELSE NOT f_is_unconstr_arr
            (f_select_by_key
               (HEAD (TYPE_DECL.at_keys),
                TYPE_DECL.at_env_out),
             TYPE_DECL.at_env_out)
   FI
      MESSAGE
"Unconstrained array type not allowed for completion of a private type"

   %C 3.3/2  in TYPE_DECL.at_impl_subprs

   %
   % Diana Generation:
   %
   %    Set SM_TYPE_SPEC of ID to TYPE_SPEC. If TYPE_SPEC is a
   %    private, limited private or incomplete type determine
   %    the type declaration which completes the given one and
   %    adjust SM_TYPE_SPEC of ID.
   %
   %    IF TYPE_SPEC is a record, private or limited private
   %    then set SM_DISCRIMINANTS of TYPE_SPEC to VAR_DECL_S.
   %
END;
%- - - - - - - - - - - - - - - - - - - - - - - - - - - - - - - - -
RULE   r_058 :
TYPE_SPEC              ::= CONSTRAINED
STATIC

   TRANSFER at_env_in;

   CONSTRAINED.at_discrim_allowed := FALSE;

   TYPE_SPEC.at_impl_descrs := c_empty_descrs;

   TYPE_SPEC.at_type := CONSTRAINED.at_type;

END;
%- - - - - - - - - - - - - - - - - - - - - - - - - - - - - - - - -
```

```
RULE   r_059 :
TYPE_SPEC              ::= access CONSTRAINED
STATIC

   TRANSFER at_env_in;

   CONSTRAINED.at_discrim_allowed := FALSE;

   %C 3.3/2
   CONDITION
      NOT (CONSTRAINED.at_type.s_base_type =
           HEAD (INCLUDING TYPE_DECL.at_keys))
      MESSAGE
      "recursive type def without interm access type erroneous";

   TYPE_SPEC.at_impl_descrs := c_empty_descrs;

   TYPE_SPEC.at_type := tp_access (CONSTRAINED.at_type);

   %
   % Diana Generation:
   %
   %    Initialize SM_SIZE, SM_STORAGE_SIZE with void
   %    Initialize SM_CONTROLLED with false
   %
END;
%- - - - - - - - - - - - - - - - - - - - - - - - - - - - - - - - -
RULE   r_060 :
TYPE_SPEC              ::= FORMAL_TYPE_SPEC
STATIC

   TRANSFER;

   TYPE_SPEC.at_impl_descrs := c_empty_descrs;

END;
%- - - - - - - - - - - - - - - - - - - - - - - - - - - - - - - - -
RULE   r_061 :
TYPE_SPEC              ::= array DSCRT_RANGE_S '%' CONSTRAINED
STATIC

   TRANSFER at_env_in;

   %C 3.6/1
   CONDITION
   (TYPE_SPEC IS r_057)    % type declaration
   OR NOT (DSCRT_RANGE_S.at_unconstrained)
      MESSAGE
      "Unconstrained array type definition not allowed.";

   CONSTRAINED.at_discrim_allowed := FALSE;

   %C 3.7.2/4
   CONDITION
      CONSTRAINED.at_type.s_constraint =/ sc_void OR
      f_no_unconstr_arr_rec
         (CONSTRAINED.at_type,
          TYPE_SPEC.at_env_in)
      MESSAGE
      "component type must be constrained";
```

```
   TYPE_SPEC.at_impl_descrs :=
        IF HEAD (DSCRT_RANGE_S.at_dscrt_ranges) IS tp_index THEN
           c_empty_descrs
        ELSE tp_descr_list
                (f_descr
                     (sc_anonymous,
                      HEAD (TYPE_SPEC.at_keys),
                      c_start_repr,
                      sc_complete,
                      sc_type,
                      tp_type_den
                         (tp_array
                             (f_make_index_list
                                 (DSCRT_RANGE_S.at_dscrt_ranges),
                              CONSTRAINED.at_type),
                          c_empty_keys),
                      f_enclosing (TYPE_SPEC.at_env_in)))
        FI;

   TYPE_SPEC.at_type :=
        IF HEAD (DSCRT_RANGE_S.at_dscrt_ranges) IS tp_index THEN
           IF NOT (TYPE_SPEC IS r_057) THEN     % type_decl
              c_error_type
           ELSE
              tp_array
                 (DSCRT_RANGE_S.at_dscrt_ranges,
                  CONSTRAINED.at_type)
           FI
        ELSE tp_constrained
                (HEAD (TYPE_SPEC.at_keys),
                 DSCRT_RANGE_S.at_dscrt_ranges)
        FI;

   %
   % Diana Generation:
   %
   %    Initialize SM_SIZE with void
   %    Initialize SM_PACKING with false
   %
END ;
%- - - - - - - - - - - - - - - - - - - - - - - - - - - - - - - - - - - - -
RULE  r_062 :
TYPE_SPEC             ::= derived CONSTRAINED
STATIC

   TRANSFER at_env_in;

   CONSTRAINED.at_discrim_allowed := FALSE;

   TYPE_SPEC.at_impl_descrs :=
      IF CONSTRAINED.at_type.s_constraint IS tp_void THEN
         c_empty_descrs
      ELSE tp_descr_list
              (f_descr
                   (sc_anonymous,
                    HEAD (TYPE_SPEC.at_keys),
                    c_start_repr,
                    sc_complete,
                    sc_type,
                    tp_type_den
```

```
                (tp_derived (CONSTRAINED.at_type
                                   .s_base_type),
                     c_empty_keys),
                  f_enclosing (TYPE_SPEC.at_env_in)))
    FI;

   TYPE_SPEC.at_type :=
      IF CONSTRAINED.at_type.s_constraint IS tp_void THEN
        tp_derived
           (CONSTRAINED.at_type.s_base_type)
      ELSE tp_constrained (HEAD (TYPE_SPEC.at_keys),
                          CONSTRAINED.at_type.s_constraint)
      FI;

   %
   % Diana Generation:
   %
   %    Derive sm_attributes from parent type (CONSTRAINED.at_def)
   %    If it is a derived fixed type, set SM_ACTUAL_DELTA
   %    to value given by machine dependent type mapping.
   %    If it is a derived enumeration or record type, compute
   %    new SM_TYPE_STRUCT of CONSTRAINED.
   %
END;
%- - - - - - - - - - - - - - - - - - - - - - - - - - - - - - - -
RULE   r_063 :
TYPE_SPEC              ::= enum_literal_s ENUM_LITERALS '%'
STATIC

   ENUM_LITERALS.at_pos := 0;

   TYPE_SPEC.at_impl_descrs := ENUM_LITERALS.at_impl_descrs;

   TYPE_SPEC.at_type            :=
      tp_enum_type (f_keys (TYPE_SPEC.at_impl_descrs),
                    ENUM_LITERALS.at_char);

   %
   % Diana Generation:
   %
   %    Initialize SM_SIZE of TYPE_SPEC with void
   %    Set SM_OBJ_TYPE of all ENUM_LITERALS to TYPE_SPEC
   %
END;
%- - - - - - - - - - - - - - - - - - - - - - - - - - - - - - - -
RULE   r_064 :
TYPE_SPEC              ::= FIXED
STATIC

   TRANSFER at_env_in;

   %C 3.5.9/2
   CONDITION
   FIXED.at_has_range
      MESSAGE
      "A range constraint is required in a fixed point type definition";

   FIXED.at_with_use := f_use_required (FIXED.at_allowed1);

   FIXED.at_valid := tp_fixed (FIXED.at_allowed2.s_delta,
```

```
                         f_valid_range_constr
                            (FIXED.at_allowed2.s_range,
                             TYPE_SPEC.at_env_in));

   TYPE_SPEC.at_impl_descrs := c_empty_descrs;

   TYPE_SPEC.at_type := FIXED.at_valid;

   %C 3.5.9/3
   CONDITION
      FIXED.at_valid.s_range =/ c_error_range AND
      ch_static_real_range (FIXED.at_valid.s_range)
      MESSAGE
      "a static real range required";

END;
%- - - - - - - - - - - - - - - - - - - - - - - - - - - - - - - - - - -
RULE  r_065 :
TYPE_SPEC       ::= FLOAT
STATIC

   TRANSFER at_env_in;

   FLOAT.at_with_use := f_use_required (FLOAT.at_allowed1);

   FLOAT.at_valid := tp_float (FLOAT.at_allowed2.s_digits,
                          f_valid_range_constr
                             (FLOAT.at_allowed2.s_range,
                              TYPE_SPEC.at_env_in));

   TYPE_SPEC.at_impl_descrs :=
      tp_descr_list
         (f_descr
            (sc_anonymous,
             HEAD (TYPE_SPEC.at_keys),
             c_start_repr,
             sc_complete,
             sc_type,
             tp_type_den
                (tp_derived
                   (f_valid_predef_float
                      (FLOAT.at_valid,
                       TYPE_SPEC.at_env_in)),
             c_empty_keys),
          f_enclosing (TYPE_SPEC.at_env_in)));

   TYPE_SPEC.at_type := tp_constrained
                           (HEAD (TYPE_SPEC.at_keys),
                            FLOAT.at_valid);

   %C 3.5.7/2
   CONDITION
      FLOAT.at_valid.s_range = c_error_range OR
      ch_static_real_range (FLOAT.at_valid.s_range)
      MESSAGE
      "a static real range required";

   %
   % Diana Generation:
   %
```

```
   %     Set SM_TYPE_STRUCT of FLOAT using TYPE_SPEC.at_keys
   %
END;
%- - - - - - - - - - - - - - - - - - - - - - - - - - - - - - - - - -
RULE   r_066 :
TYPE_SPEC          ::= integer RANGE
STATIC

   TRANSFER at_env_in;

   RANGE.at_expected := c_no_expected;

   RANGE.at_with_use := f_use_required (RANGE.at_allowed1);

   RANGE.at_valid := f_valid_range_constr (RANGE.at_allowed2,
                                           TYPE_SPEC.at_env_in);
   %C 3.5.4/2
   CONDITION
      ch_non_null_range (RANGE.at_valid)
      MESSAGE
      "a non null range required in integer type definitions";

   %C 3.5.4/2
   CONDITION
      ch_static_int_range (RANGE.at_valid, TYPE_SPEC.at_env_in)
      MESSAGE
      "a static integer range required";

   RANGE.at_discrim_allowed := FALSE;

   TYPE_SPEC.at_impl_descrs :=
      tp_descr_list
         (f_descr
            (sc_anonymous,
             HEAD (TYPE_SPEC.at_keys),
             c_start_repr,
             sc_complete,
             sc_type,
             tp_type_den
                (tp_derived
                   (f_valid_predef_int
                      (RANGE.at_valid QUA tp_range_constr,
                       TYPE_SPEC.at_env_in)),
                 c_empty_keys),
             f_enclosing (TYPE_SPEC.at_env_in)));

   TYPE_SPEC.at_type := tp_constrained
                           (HEAD (TYPE_SPEC.at_keys),
                            RANGE.at_valid QUA tp_range_constr);

   %
   % Diana Generation:
   %
   %    Set SM_TYPE_STRUCT using TYPE_SPEC.at_impl_descrs
   %    Initialize SM_SIZE with void
   %
END;
%- - - - - - - - - - - - - - - - - - - - - - - - - - - - - - - - - -
RULE   r_067 :
```

```
TYPE_SPEC              ::= record RECORD '%'
STATIC

   RECORD.at_env_in :=
      f_new_local (TYPE_SPEC.at_discriminants,
                   HEAD (INCLUDING TYPE_DECL.at_keys),
                   f_update_descrs_by_keys
                     (INCLUDING TYPE_DECL.at_keys,
                      sc_same,
                      sc_in_record,
                      sc_same,
                      sc_same,
                      TYPE_SPEC.at_env_in));

   TYPE_SPEC.at_impl_descrs := c_empty_descrs;

   TYPE_SPEC.at_type := tp_record (f_local (RECORD.at_env_out),
                                   RECORD.at_comps);
   %
   % Diana Generation:
   %
   %    Initialize SM_SIZE with void
   %    Initialize SM_PACKING with false
   %
END;
%- - - - - - - - - - - - - - - - - - - - - - - - - - - - - - - - - - - -
RULE r_068 :
TYPE_SPEC              ::= TASK_SPEC
STATIC

   TRANSFER at_env_in, at_keys;

   TYPE_SPEC.at_impl_descrs := c_empty_descrs;

   TYPE_SPEC.at_type         :=  TASK_SPEC.at_spec;

END;
%- - - - - - - - - - - - - - - - - - - - - - - - - - - - - - - - - - - -
RULE   r_069 :
TASK_SPEC              ::= task_spec DECL_REP_S '%'
   %
   %  DECL_REP_S are only entries or pragmas
   %
STATIC

   DECL_REP_S.at_encl_unit := tp_encl_unit (sc_task, sc_void_state);

   DECL_REP_S.at_env_in :=
      f_update_encl_state (sc_in_visible,
                           f_new_local
                              (c_empty_descrs,
                               HEAD (TASK_SPEC.at_keys),
                               TASK_SPEC.at_env_in));

   TASK_SPEC.at_spec := tp_task_spec
                           (f_local
                              (DECL_REP_S.at_env_out));
   %
   % Diana Generation:
   %
   %    Initialize SM_BODY, SM_ADDRESSS, SM_STORAGE_SIZE with void
```

```
END;
%- - - - - - - - - - - - - - - - - - - - - - - - - - - - - - - - - - -
RULE   r_070 :
TYPE_SPEC              ::= void
STATIC

   TYPE_SPEC.at_impl_descrs := c_empty_descrs;

   TYPE_SPEC.at_type := tp_incompl_type
                        (TYPE_SPEC.at_discriminants);

END;
%- - - - - - - - - - - - - - - - - - - - - - - - - - - - - - - - - - -
RULE   r_071 :
TYPE_SPEC              ::= private
STATIC

   %C 7.4/1
   CONDITION
   (TYPE_SPEC.at_encl_unit.s_state = sc_in_visible)
   OR (TYPE_SPEC.at_encl_unit.s_state = sc_in_generic_part)
      MESSAGE
      "Private type definition only allowed in package or generic part";

   TYPE_SPEC.at_impl_descrs := c_empty_descrs;

   TYPE_SPEC.at_type := tp_private (TYPE_SPEC.at_discriminants);

END;
%- - - - - - - - - - - - - - - - - - - - - - - - - - - - - - - - - - -
RULE   r_072 :
TYPE_SPEC              ::= l_private
STATIC

   %C 7.4/1
   CONDITION
   (TYPE_SPEC.at_encl_unit.s_state = sc_in_visible)
   OR (TYPE_SPEC.at_encl_unit.s_state  = sc_in_generic_part)
      MESSAGE
      "Private type definition only allowed in package or generic part";

   TYPE_SPEC.at_impl_descrs := c_empty_descrs;

   TYPE_SPEC.at_type := tp_l_private (TYPE_SPEC.at_discriminants);

END;
%- - - - - - - - - - - - - - - - - - - - - - - - - - - - - - - - - - -
RULE   r_073 :
VAR_DECL               ::= var_decl ID_S '%' TYPE_SPEC OBJECT_DEF
   %
   %  TYPE_SPEC ::= CONSTRAINED  or
   %  TYPE_SPEC ::= array ...
   %
STATIC

   TRANSFER at_discrim_allowed;

   TYPE_SPEC.at_encl_unit := tp_encl_unit (sc_procedure, sc_void_state);
```

```
VAR_DECL.at_init := IF OBJECT_DEF.at_is_exp THEN
                        sc_init
                    ELSE
                        sc_not_init
                    FI;

VAR_DECL.at_keys  := f_gen_keylist (ID_S.at_designators);

TYPE_SPEC.at_keys := IF TYPE_SPEC IS r_058 THEN
                         c_empty_keys
                     ELSE f_gen_keys
                     FI;

TYPE_SPEC.at_env_in :=
   f_add_descrs (ID_S.at_designators,
                 VAR_DECL.at_keys,
                 sc_id_established,
                 sc_variable,
                 sc_void,
                 VAR_DECL.at_env_in);

TYPE_SPEC.at_discriminants := c_empty_descrs;

TYPE_SPEC.at_impl_subprs := c_empty_descrs;

OBJECT_DEF.at_expected :=
   TYPE_SPEC.at_type QUA tp_constrained .s_base_type;

OBJECT_DEF.at_env_in :=
   f_update_descrs_by_keys
      (VAR_DECL.at_keys,
       c_start_repr,
       sc_in_init,
       CASE f_encl_state (VAR_DECL.at_env_in) OF
       sc_in_record : sc_rec_comp;
       sc_in_discr_part : sc_discriminant
       OUT sc_variable

       ESAC,
       tp_object
          (TYPE_SPEC.at_type QUA tp_constrained,
           c_no_init),
       TYPE_SPEC.at_env_in);

OBJECT_DEF.at_keys := VAR_DECL.at_keys;

%C 3.2/1, C 3.6.3/1, C 7.4/1
CONDITION
   IF OBJECT_DEF.at_valid IS tp_descr THEN
       ch_is_assign_allowed_for_type (TYPE_SPEC.at_type,
                                      OBJECT_DEF.at_env_in)
   ELSE TRUE
   FI
   MESSAGE
   "illegal initialization";

%C 3.6/1 checked in r_061;

VAR_DECL.at_env_out :=
   f_update_descrs_by_keys
```

```
    (VAR_DECL.at_keys,
     sc_same,
     sc_complete,
     sc_same,
     sc_same,
     IF OBJECT_DEF.at_valid IS tp_void THEN
        OBJECT_DEF.at_env_in
     ELSE f_update_descrs_by_keys
           (VAR_DECL.at_keys,
            sc_same,
            sc_same,
            CASE c_def : OBJECT_DEF.at_valid OF
            IS tp_rename :  c_def.s_descr.s_nature
            OUT sc_same
            ESAC,
            tp_object
              (TYPE_SPEC.at_type QUA tp_constrained,
               CASE c_def : OBJECT_DEF.at_valid OF
               IS tp_descr :
                  c_init;
               IS tp_rename :
                  c_def.s_descr.s_den QUA tp_object .s_init
               OUT c_no_init
               ESAC),
            f_add_local_descrs
              (TYPE_SPEC.at_impl_descrs,
               OBJECT_DEF.at_env_in))
     FI);

   %C 3.6/1, C 3.7.2/4
   CONDITION
      f_no_unconstr_arr_rec (TYPE_SPEC.at_type,
                             VAR_DECL.at_env_out)
      MESSAGE
      "unconstrained arr/rec types illegal in obj/comp declarations";

   %C 3.7.1/1
   CONDITION
      f_encl_state (VAR_DECL.at_env_in) =/ sc_in_discr_part OR
      f_is_discrete_type1 (TYPE_SPEC.at_type,
                           VAR_DECL.at_env_out)
      MESSAGE
      "discriminants must have discrete type";

   %
   % Diana Generation:
   %
   %     Set SM_OBJ_TYPE of all ID_S to TYPE_SPEC.
   %     In contexts of discriminants or record components
   %     set SM_INIT_EXP of all ID_S to OBJECT_DEF,
   %     otherwise set SM_OBJ_DEF of all ID_S to OBJECT_DEF,
   %     and initialize SM_ADDRESS of all ID_S with void.
   %
   %     If it is a renaming declaration, transform the kind
   %     of the ID_S according to OBJECT_DEF.at_allowed1
   %
END;
%- - - - - - - - - - - - - - - - - - - - - - - - - - - - - - -
RULE   r_074:
VAR_DECLS            ::=
```

```
STATIC

   VAR_DECLS.at_init := sc_init;          % does not matter

   VAR_DECLS.at_env_out := VAR_DECLS.at_env_in;

END;
%- - - - - - - - - - - - - - - - - - - - - - - - - - - - - - - - - - - -
RULE   r_075 :
VAR_DECLS                  ::= VAR_DECL VAR_DECLS
STATIC

   VAR_DECLS[1].at_init :=
      IF (VAR_DECLS[2] IS r_074) OR
         (VAR_DECL.at_init = VAR_DECLS[2].at_init) THEN
         VAR_DECL.at_init
      ELSE
         sc_mixed
      FI;

   VAR_DECL.at_env_in := VAR_DECLS[1].at_env_in;
   VAR_DECL.at_discrim_allowed := TRUE;

   VAR_DECLS[2].at_env_in := VAR_DECL.at_env_out;
   VAR_DECLS[1].at_env_out := VAR_DECLS[2].at_env_out;

END;
%- - - - - - - - - - - - - - - - - - - - - - - - - - - - - - - - - - - -
RULE   r_076 :
VAR_DECL_S                 ::= var_decl_s VAR_DECLS
STATIC

   TRANSFER;

   VAR_DECL_S.at_empty := VAR_DECLS IS r_074;

END;
%- - - - - - - - - - - - - - - - - - - - - - - - - - - - - - - - - - - -
RULE   r_077 :
VARIANT                    ::= variant CHOICE_S '%' RECORD '%'
STATIC

   TRANSFER at_env_in;

   CHOICE_S.at_is_last := VARIANT.at_is_last;

   CHOICE_S.at_context := sc_variant;

   CHOICE_S.at_expected := VARIANT.at_expected;

   CHOICE_S.at_with_use := FALSE; %irrelevant;

   CHOICE_S.at_valid := cf_unique_choices
                           (CHOICE_S.at_allowed2,
                            VARIANT.at_env_in);

   %C 3.7.3/2
   CONDITION ch_static_choices (CHOICE_S.at_valid)
   MESSAGE  "choices must be static";
```

```
   VARIANT.at_variant := tp_variant (CHOICE_S.at_valid,
                                     RECORD.at_comps);

   VARIANT.at_env_out := RECORD.at_env_out;

END;
%- - - - - - - - - - - - - - - - - - - - - - - - - - - - - - - - - -
RULE   r_078:
VARIANTS               ::=
STATIC

   VARIANTS.at_variants := tp_variant_list ();

   VARIANTS.at_env_out  := VARIANTS.at_env_in;

END;
%- - - - - - - - - - - - - - - - - - - - - - - - - - - - - - - - - -
RULE   r_079 :
VARIANTS               ::= VARIANT VARIANTS
STATIC

   VARIANT.at_is_last := VARIANTS[2] IS r_078;

   VARIANT.at_env_in       := VARIANTS[1].at_env_in;

   VARIANTS[2].at_env_in := VARIANT.at_env_out;
   VARIANTS[1].at_variants :=
      tp_variant_list (VARIANT.at_variant) +
      VARIANTS[2].at_variants;

   VARIANTS[1].at_env_out := VARIANTS[2].at_env_out;

   TRANSFER at_expected;

END;
%- - - - - - - - - - - - - - - - - - - - - - - - - - - - - - - - - -
RULE   r_080 :
VARIANT_S              ::= variant_s VARIANTS
STATIC

   TRANSFER;

END;
```

```
%-----------------------------------------------------------------------
%
% 5.4. Names and Expressions
%
%-----------------------------------------------------------------------

%- - - - - - - - - - - - - - - - - - - - - - - - - - - - - - - - - - - -
RULE   r_081 :
ACCESS_CONSTRAINT      ::= GENERAL_ASSOC_S
STATIC

   TRANSFER at_allowed1, at_allowed2, at_valid, at_env_in, at_with_use,
            at_others_allowed, at_discrim_allowed;

END;
%- - - - - - - - - - - - - - - - - - - - - - - - - - - - - - - - - - - -
RULE   r_082 :
ACTUAL                 ::= EXP
STATIC

   TRANSFER at_expected, at_context, at_env_in,at_with_use,
            at_others_allowed;

   ACTUAL.at_allowed1 := tp_actual (EXP.at_allowed1);

   ACTUAL.at_allowed2 := tp_actual (EXP.at_allowed2);

   EXP.at_valid :=
      IF ACTUAL.at_valid IS tp_dscrt_range THEN
         EXP.at_allowed2   %EXP.at_allowed2 denotes type and is unique
      ELSE cf_unique_descr (ACTUAL.at_valid QUA tp_descr_set,
                            ACTUAL.at_discrim_allowed,
                            ACTUAL.at_env_in)
      FI;

END;
%- - - - - - - - - - - - - - - - - - - - - - - - - - - - - - - - - - - -
RULE   r_083 :
ACTUAL                 ::= CONSTRAINED_1
STATIC

   TRANSFER at_env_in;

   CONSTRAINED_1.at_discrim_allowed := FALSE;

   ACTUAL.at_allowed1 :=
      IF ACTUAL.at_context = sc_subtype_ind OR
         (ACTUAL.at_context = sc_access) THEN
           f_descr_set
             (c_key,
              sc_subtype,
              CONSTRAINED_1.at_type,
              sc_no_add)
      ELSE tp_actual (CONSTRAINED_1.at_type)
      FI;

   ACTUAL.at_allowed2 := ACTUAL.at_allowed1;

END;
```

```
RULE   r_084 :
APPLY                  ::= apply NAME GENERAL_ASSOC_S '%'
   %
   %  comprises indexed, slice, procedure-, function-, entry- call,
   %  type conversion, subtype with index-/ discriminant constraint
   %  and operator calls (except short circuit and membership).
   %
STATIC
   TRANSFER at_env_in, at_with_use, at_user_rep;

   NAME.at_expected := c_no_expected;

   NAME.at_context := IF NAME IS r_122 THEN      % attribute
                         sc_attr_name
                      ELSE sc_string_is_name
                      FI;

   CONDITION
      NOT (APPLY.at_context = sc_call AND
           EMPTY (GENERAL_ASSOC_S.at_allowed1))
      MESSAGE
      "too few parameters for procedure/entry call";

   APPLY.at_allowed1 :=
     f_allowed_expected
       (IF NAME IS r_122 THEN
           f_allowed_attr_apply
              (NAME.at_allowed1,
               LAST (NAME CONSTITUENTS ID.at_designator) QUA SYMB,
               GENERAL_ASSOC_S.at_allowed1,
               APPLY.at_env_in)
        ELSE f_allowed_apply
                (NAME.at_allowed1,
                 GENERAL_ASSOC_S.at_allowed1,
                 APPLY.at_context,
                 APPLY.at_env_in)
        FI,
        APPLY.at_expected,
        APPLY.at_env_in);

   APPLY.at_allowed2 :=
      cf_not_empty
      (IF APPLY.at_with_use THEN
          f_allowed_expected
             (IF NAME IS r_122 THEN
                 f_allowed_attr_apply
                    (NAME.at_allowed2,
                     LAST (NAME CONSTITUENTS ID.at_designator)
                        QUA SYMB,
                     GENERAL_ASSOC_S.at_allowed2,
                     APPLY.at_env_in)
              ELSE f_allowed_apply
                      (NAME.at_allowed2,
                       GENERAL_ASSOC_S.at_allowed2,
                       APPLY.at_context,
                       APPLY.at_env_in)
              FI,
              APPLY.at_expected,
              APPLY.at_env_in)
      ELSE APPLY.at_allowed1
      FI);
```

```
NAME.at_valid := cf_unique_descr
                    (IF NAME IS r_122 THEN                  %attribute
                        NAME.at_allowed2
                     ELSE f_valid
                             (APPLY.at_valid,
                              NAME.at_allowed2.s_descrs)
                     FI,
                     FALSE,
                     APPLY.at_env_in);

%C KA/2
CONDITION
   IF APPLY.at_context = sc_call THEN
      NOT (f_own_entry (NAME.at_valid,
                        APPLY.at_env_in))
   ELSE TRUE
   FI
   MESSAGE
   "WARNING : task calls entry of its own";

%C 3.9/2
CONDITION
   CASE f_encl_state (APPLY.at_env_in) OF
   sc_in_handler : sc_in_body : TRUE
   OUT CASE c_den : f_head_descr (NAME.at_valid).s_den OF
       IS tp_entry : IS tp_subpr :
          (f_head_descr (NAME.at_valid).s_state=sc_complete) OR
          (f_head_descr
               (NAME.at_valid).s_state=sc_implicitly_declared)
       OUT TRUE
       ESAC
   ESAC
   MESSAGE
   "calls to subpr/entries illegal before their body in decl.parts";

%C 6.1/1
CONDITION
   f_encl_state (APPLY.at_env_in) =/ sc_in_formal_part
   OR (NOT f_is_user_defined_funct (f_head_descr (NAME.at_valid),
                                    APPLY.at_env_in))
   MESSAGE
   "no calls to user-defined functions allowed in formal parts";

%C SYNTAX
CONDITION
APPLY.at_context = sc_subtype_ind OR
(f_head_descr(NAME.at_valid).s_nature =/ sc_type AND
(f_head_descr(NAME.at_valid).s_nature =/ sc_subtype)) OR
APPLY.at_is_exp
   MESSAGE "A name (no type converion) expected";

GENERAL_ASSOC_S.at_discrim_allowed :=
   (f_encl_descr (APPLY.at_env_in).s_state  = sc_in_record) OR
   (f_encl_descr (APPLY.at_env_in).s_state  = sc_in_discr_part) AND
   (f_head_descr (APPLY.at_valid).s_den IS tp_constrained);

GENERAL_ASSOC_S.at_valid :=
   IF NAME IS r_122 THEN
      f_valid_attr_param
         (GENERAL_ASSOC_S.at_allowed2,
          NAME.at_allowed2,
```

```
            LAST (NAME CONSTITUENTS ID.at_designator),
            APPLY.at_env_in)
      ELSE f_valid_assocs
             (APPLY.at_valid,
              NAME.at_valid,
              GENERAL_ASSOC_S.at_allowed2,
              APPLY.at_context,
              APPLY.at_env_in)
      FI;

   GENERAL_ASSOC_S.at_others_allowed := FALSE;

   %C  3.3/1 3.7.2/3  checked by ch_constraint in f_valid_assocs

   %C 7.4.2/1 automatically through absense
   %          of =, =/ for l_priv

   %
   % Diana Generation:
   %
   %     Transform APPLY into function_call, procedure_call,
   %     entry_call, attribute_call, indexed, slice or conversion
   %     corresponding to NAME.at_valid and APPLY.at_context.
   %
   %     Transform GENERAL_ASSOC_S into the form appropriate
   %     for the new construct.
   %
   %     If it is transformed into an EXP-node, set
   %     SM_EXP_TYPE and SM_VALUE using APPLY.at_valid.
   %     If it is transformed into a slice node set
   %     SM_CONSTRAINT using NAME.at_valid.
   %
END;
%- - - - - - - - - - - - - - - - - - - - - - - - - - - - - - - - - - -
RULE   r_085 :
ASSOC                ::= assoc ID ACTUAL
STATIC

   TRANSFER at_env_in;


   ACTUAL.at_discrim_allowed := FALSE;

   ACTUAL.at_expected  :=
      IF ASSOC IS r_188 THEN
         c_no_expected          %PARAM_ASSOC
      ELSE                      %GENERIC_ASSOC
        CASE c_den : HEAD (f_select_by_designator00
                            (ID.at_designator,
                             ASSOC.at_expected_in,
                             ASSOC.at_env_in))
                        .s_den OF
        IS tp_object : f_object_type1 (c_den)
        OUT c_no_expected
        ESAC
      FI;
   ACTUAL.at_context :=
      IF ASSOC IS r_188 THEN                  %PARAM_ASSOC
         sc_id_not_visible
      ELSE
```

```
      CASE HEAD (f_select_by_designator00
                    (ID.at_designator,
                     ASSOC.at_expected_in,
                     ASSOC.at_env_in))
               .s_nature OF
       sc_type :
       sc_subtype : sc_subtype_ind;
       sc_predefined_op : sc_common_op :
       sc_universal_op :
       sc_procedure : sc_function : sc_string_is_name
       OUT                          sc_no_special
       ESAC
    FI;

  ACTUAL.at_with_use := f_use_required1 (ACTUAL.at_allowed1);

  ASSOC.at_allowed2 :=
     tp_comp_assoc
       (tp_choice_list
          (IF ASSOC IS r_188 THEN          %PARAM_ASSOC
              tp_choice (f_make_dummy (ID.at_designator,
                                       c_empty_descr_set,
                                       sc_id_not_visible))
           ELSE
              tp_choice
                (HEAD (f_select_by_designator00
                          (ID.at_designator,
                           ASSOC.at_expected_in,
                           ASSOC.at_env_in)))
           FI),
        ACTUAL.at_allowed2 QUA tp_descr_set);

  ACTUAL.at_valid := IF ASSOC IS r_188 THEN  %PARAM_ASSOC
                         c_error_descr_set    %SUPPRESS ERROR MESSAGE
                     ELSE ASSOC.at_valid.s_actual
                     FI;

  ACTUAL.at_others_allowed := FALSE;

  %C 12.1.1/3         checked in  r_257;

  %C 12.1.1/2         checked in  r_257;

  %
  % Diana Generation:
  %
  %    In context of generic_assoc_s, if ACTUAL is a
  %    type name, transform it into a constrained node,
  %    set SM_BASE_TYPE, SM_CONSTRAINT, SM_TYPE_STRUCT of
  %    this new node using ACTUAL.at_valid.
  %
  %    Set SM_DEFN of ID using ASSOC.at_valid
  %
END;
%- - - - - - - - - - - - - - - - - - - - - - - - - - - - - - - - - - - - - - -
RULE   r_086 :
BINARY_OP              ::= SHORT_CIRCUIT_OP
STATIC

  TRANSFER at_op;
```

```
END;
%- - - - - - - - - - - - - - - - - - - - - - - - - - - - - - - - - - - - - -
RULE   r_087 :
CHOICE                    ::= RANGE
STATIC

   TRANSFER at_env_in, at_expected, at_with_use;

   CHOICE.at_allowed1 := CASE c_type : CHOICE.at_expected OF
                          IS tp_key : tp_constrained
                                         (c_type,
                                          f_make_range
                                             (RANGE.at_allowed1,
                                              c_type,
                                              CHOICE.at_env_in))
                          OUT tp_range (RANGE.at_allowed1)
                          ESAC;

   CHOICE.at_allowed2 := CASE c_type : CHOICE.at_expected OF
                          IS tp_key : tp_constrained
                                         (c_type,
                                          f_make_range
                                             (RANGE.at_allowed2,
                                              c_type,
                                              CHOICE.at_env_in))
                          OUT tp_range (RANGE.at_allowed2)
                          ESAC;

   RANGE.at_valid := CASE c_choice :CHOICE.at_valid
                        QUA tp_dscrt_range OF
                     IS tp_range : c_choice
                     OUT c_choice QUA tp_constrained
                             .s_constraint QUA tp_range_constr
                     ESAC;

   RANGE.at_discrim_allowed := FALSE;

END;
%- - - - - - - - - - - - - - - - - - - - - - - - - - - - - - - - - - - - - -
RULE   r_088 :
CHOICE                    ::= CONSTRAINED_1
STATIC

   TRANSFER at_env_in;

   CONSTRAINED_1.at_discrim_allowed := FALSE;

   CHOICE.at_allowed1 := CONSTRAINED_1.at_type;

   CHOICE.at_allowed2 := CHOICE.at_allowed1;

   CONDITION CHOICE.at_expected = sc_void OR
         (CHOICE.at_expected = CHOICE.at_allowed2 QUA tp_constrained
                                     .s_base_type)
      MESSAGE "Discrete range not of appropriate type";

END;
%- - - - - - - - - - - - - - - - - - - - - - - - - - - - - - - - - - - - - -
```

```
RULE   r_089 :
CHOICE                 ::= EXP
STATIC

   TRANSFER at_env_in, at_with_use;

   EXP.at_expected := c_no_expected;

   EXP.at_context       := IF CHOICE.at_context = sc_named THEN
                                sc_id_not_visible
                             ELSE sc_no_special
                             FI;

   CHOICE.at_allowed1 :=
      CASE c_choice : IF CHOICE.at_context = sc_named THEN
                             EXP.at_allowed1
                          ELSE f_make_constrained (EXP.at_allowed1)
                          FI
      OF IS tp_descr_set : f_allowed_expected (c_choice,
                                                   CHOICE.at_expected,
                                                   CHOICE.at_env_in)
         OUT c_choice          % IS tp_constrained
      ESAC;

   CHOICE.at_allowed2 :=
      IF CHOICE.at_with_use THEN
         CASE c_choice : IF CHOICE.at_context = sc_named THEN
                                  EXP.at_allowed2
                             ELSE f_make_constrained (EXP.at_allowed2)
                             FI  OF
         IS tp_descr_set : cf_not_empty
                               (f_allowed_expected
                                     (c_choice,
                                      CHOICE.at_expected,
                                      CHOICE.at_env_in))
         OUT c_choice     % IS tp_constrained
         ESAC
      ELSE CHOICE.at_allowed1
      FI;

   CONDITION CASE c_choice : CHOICE.at_allowed2
             OF IS tp_constrained :
                   CHOICE.at_expected = sc_void OR
                   (c_choice.s_base_type = CHOICE.at_expected)
                OUT TRUE
             ESAC
      MESSAGE "Discrete range not of appropriate type";

   EXP.at_valid := CASE c_choice : CHOICE.at_valid OF
                      IS tp_descr_set    : c_choice;
                      IS tp_dscrt_range  : EXP.at_allowed2;
                            %EXP.at_allowed2 denotes type and is unique
                      IS tp_descr        : f_descr_set2 (c_choice)
                      OUT (c_error_descr_set CONDITION FALSE MESSAGE
                                                 "compiler error")
                      ESAC;

   EXP.at_others_allowed := FALSE;

END;
```

```
%- - - - - - - - - - - - - - - - - - - - - - - - - - - - - - - - - - - - -
RULE   r_090 :
CHOICE                  ::= others
STATIC

   CHOICE.at_allowed1 := sc_others;

   CHOICE.at_allowed2 := CHOICE.at_allowed1;

END;
%- - - - - - - - - - - - - - - - - - - - - - - - - - - - - - - - - - - - -
RULE   r_091:
CHOICES                 ::=
STATIC

   CHOICES.at_allowed1 := tp_choice_list ();

   CHOICES.at_allowed2 := tp_choice_list ();

END;
%- - - - - - - - - - - - - - - - - - - - - - - - - - - - - - - - - - - - -
RULE   r_092 :
CHOICES                 ::= CHOICE CHOICES
STATIC

   TRANSFER at_is_last, at_env_in, at_expected, at_context;

   %C 3.7.3/4, 4.3/2, 5.4/2, 11.2/1
   CONDITION
   NOT (CHOICE IS r_090)                         % it is not others
   OR ((CHOICES[2] IS r_091)                     % it appears alone
   AND (CHOICES[1] IS r_093 )
   AND (CHOICES[1].at_is_last))                  % as last choice
      MESSAGE
      "OTHERS can only appear alone and as last choices.";

   CHOICES[1].at_allowed1 :=
      tp_choice_list (CHOICE.at_allowed1) +
      CHOICES[2].at_allowed1;

   CHOICES[2].at_with_use := CHOICES[1].at_with_use;

   CHOICES[1].at_allowed2 :=
      tp_choice_list (CHOICE.at_allowed2) +
      CHOICES[2].at_allowed2;

   CHOICES[2].at_valid := TAIL (CHOICES[1].at_valid);

   %C 11.2/3
   CONDITION
      IF CHOICE.at_context  = sc_handler AND
         (CHOICE.at_valid IS tp_descr_set) THEN
         CASE f_head_descr (CHOICE.at_valid QUA tp_descr_set)
              .s_nature OF
         sc_exception : sc_error_nature : TRUE
         OUT FALSE
         ESAC
      ELSE TRUE
      FI
      MESSAGE
```

```
    "handler must be chosen by exception names";

   CHOICE.at_with_use := CASE CHOICES[1].at_context OF
                           sc_handler: sc_case : sc_variant :
                              f_use_required (CHOICE.at_allowed1)
                           OUT CHOICES[1].at_with_use
                           ESAC;

   CHOICE.at_valid     := HEAD (CHOICES[1].at_valid);

END;
%- - - - - - - - - - - - - - - - - - - - - - - - - - - - - - - - - - -
RULE   r_093 :
CHOICE_S                 ::= choice_s CHOICES
STATIC

   TRANSFER;

END;
%- - - - - - - - - - - - - - - - - - - - - - - - - - - - - - - - - - -
RULE   r_094 :
COMP_ASSOC               ::= NAMED
STATIC

   TRANSFER at_env_in, at_allowed1, at_with_use, at_allowed2, at_valid,
            at_others_allowed, at_is_last;

   NAMED.at_discrim_allowed := FALSE;

END;
%- - - - - - - - - - - - - - - - - - - - - - - - - - - - - - - - - - -
RULE   r_095 :
COMP_ASSOC               ::= EXP
STATIC

   TRANSFER at_env_in, at_with_use, at_others_allowed;

   EXP.at_expected := c_no_expected;

   EXP.at_context := sc_no_special;

   COMP_ASSOC.at_allowed1 := tp_comp_assoc (tp_choice_list (),
                                            EXP.at_allowed1);

   COMP_ASSOC.at_allowed2 := IF EXP.at_with_use THEN
                                tp_comp_assoc (tp_choice_list (),
                                               EXP.at_allowed2)
                             ELSE COMP_ASSOC.at_allowed1
                             FI;

   EXP.at_valid :=
      cf_unique_descr (COMP_ASSOC.at_valid
                          QUA tp_comp_assoc .s_actual,
                       FALSE,
                       COMP_ASSOC.at_env_in);

END;
%- - - - - - - - - - - - - - - - - - - - - - - - - - - - - - - - - - -
RULE   r_096 :
```

```
COMP_ASSOCS             ::=
STATIC

   COMP_ASSOCS.at_allowed1 := tp_assoc_list ();

   COMP_ASSOCS.at_allowed2 := tp_assoc_list ();

END;
%- - - - - - - - - - - - - - - - - - - - - - - - - - - - - - -
RULE   r_097 :
COMP_ASSOCS             ::= COMP_ASSOC COMP_ASSOCS
STATIC

   TRANSFER at_env_in, at_with_use, at_others_allowed;

   COMP_ASSOC.at_is_last := COMP_ASSOCS[2] IS r_096;

   COMP_ASSOCS[2].at_positional_allowed :=
      COMP_ASSOCS[1].at_positional_allowed AND
      NOT (COMP_ASSOC IS r_094);                       % named

   %C 4.3/3
   CONDITION
   COMP_ASSOCS[1].at_positional_allowed
   OR (COMP_ASSOC IS r_094)                            % named
      MESSAGE
      "Positional component associations must occur first.";

   COMP_ASSOCS[1].at_allowed1 :=
      tp_assoc_list (COMP_ASSOC.at_allowed1) +
      COMP_ASSOCS[2].at_allowed1;

   COMP_ASSOCS[1].at_allowed2 :=
      IF COMP_ASSOCS[1].at_with_use THEN
         tp_assoc_list (COMP_ASSOC.at_allowed2) +
         COMP_ASSOCS[2].at_allowed2
      ELSE COMP_ASSOCS[1].at_allowed1
      FI;

   COMP_ASSOCS[2].at_valid := TAIL (COMP_ASSOCS[1].at_valid);

   COMP_ASSOC.at_valid := HEAD (COMP_ASSOCS[1].at_valid);

END;
%- - - - - - - - - - - - - - - - - - - - - - - - - - - - - - -
RULE   r_098 :
EXP                     ::= NAME
STATIC

   TRANSFER at_context, at_expected, at_allowed1, at_allowed2,
            at_with_use, at_valid,    at_env_in;

   %C 6.1/1
   CONDITION
      (f_encl_state (EXP.at_env_in) =/ sc_in_formal_part) OR
      (HEAD (NAME.at_valid.s_descrs).s_nature =/ sc_variable)
      MESSAGE
      "no variables allowed in formal parts";
```

```
END;
%- - - - - - - - - - - - - - - - - - - - - - - - - - - - - - - - - - - - -
RULE   r_099 :
EXP                   ::= aggregate COMP_ASSOCS   '%'
STATIC

   TRANSFER at_env_in, at_with_use, at_others_allowed;

   COMP_ASSOCS.at_positional_allowed := TRUE;

   EXP.at_allowed1 :=  f_add_dummy_aggr
                         (EXP IS r_082  OR        %ACTUAL ::= EXP
                         (EXP IS r_095) OR        %COMP_ASSOC ::= EXP
                         (EXP IS r_131),          %NAMED ::= CHOICES EXP
                        COMP_ASSOCS.at_allowed1,
                        f_allowed_aggregates
                           (EXP.at_expected,
                            COMP_ASSOCS.at_allowed1,
                            EXP.at_env_in));

   EXP.at_allowed2 :=
      cf_not_empty
        (IF EXP.at_with_use THEN
            f_add_dummy_aggr
               (EXP IS r_082  OR              %ACTUAL ::= EXP
               (EXP IS r_095) OR              %COMP_ASSOC ::= EXP
               (EXP IS r_131),                %NAMED ::= CHOICES EXP
              COMP_ASSOCS.at_allowed2,
              f_allowed_aggregates
                  (EXP.at_expected,
                   COMP_ASSOCS.at_allowed2,
                   EXP.at_env_in))
         ELSE EXP.at_allowed1
         FI);

   COMP_ASSOCS.at_valid    := f_valid_aggregate
                                 (EXP.at_valid,
                                  COMP_ASSOCS.at_allowed2,
                                  EXP.at_env_in);

   %C 4.3/1, C 4.3/2, C 4.3/4, C 4.3.2/2, C 13.3/2, C 13.3/3, C 13.3/4
   CONDITION
      ch_aggreg (COMP_ASSOCS.at_valid,
                 EXP.at_valid,
                 EXP.at_env_in)
      MESSAGE
      "wrongly built aggregate";

   %C 4.3.2/2
   CONDITION
      IF NOT EXP.at_others_allowed AND
         f_is_array (HEAD (EXP.at_valid.s_descrs),
                           EXP.at_env_in) THEN
         NOT f_has_others_comp (COMP_ASSOCS.at_valid)
      ELSE TRUE
      FI
      MESSAGE "others-component not allowed";

   %
```

```
  % Diana Generation:
  %
  %    Set SM_EXP_TYPE and SM_VALUE using EXP.at_valid
  %
  %    If not EXP.at_others_allowed then build new constraint
  %    using EXP.at_valid and set SM_CONSTRAINT accordingly.
  %
END;
%- - - - - - - - - - - - - - - - - - - - - - - - - - - - - - - - - - -
RULE   r_100 :
EXP                   ::= allocator NAME ACCESS_CONSTRAINT '%'
STATIC

  TRANSFER at_env_in, at_with_use;

  %C 6.1/1
  CONDITION
     (f_encl_state (EXP.at_env_in) =/ sc_in_formal_part)
     MESSAGE
     "no allocator calls allowed in formal parts";

  NAME.at_expected := c_no_expected;

  NAME.at_context := sc_no_special;

  EXP.at_allowed1 :=
     f_allowed_allocator (EXP.at_expected,
                          NAME.at_allowed1,
                          ACCESS_CONSTRAINT.at_allowed1,
                          EXP.at_env_in);

  NAME.at_valid := cf_unique_type_descr (NAME.at_allowed2);

  %C 3.8/1, C 4.8/5
  CONDITION
     NOT EMPTY (ACCESS_CONSTRAINT.at_allowed2) OR
     CASE c_type : f_type1 (f_head_descr (NAME.at_valid)) OF
     IS tp_constrained :
        IF c_type.s_constraint /= sc_void THEN
           TRUE
        ELSE FALSE
        FI
     OUT FALSE
     ESAC        OR
     CASE c_type : f_parent_base_type2
                   (f_head_descr (NAME.at_valid).s_key,
                    NAME.at_env_in) OF
     IS tp_record : EMPTY (f_discriminants (c_type));
     IS tp_array : FALSE
     OUT TRUE
     ESAC

     MESSAGE
    "for unconstr array/rec types index/discr constraint required";

 EXP.at_allowed2 :=
    cf_not_empty
       (IF EXP.at_with_use THEN
           f_allowed_allocator (EXP.at_expected,
                                NAME.at_allowed2,
```

```
                                   ACCESS_CONSTRAINT.at_allowed2,
                                   EXP.at_env_in)
     ELSE EXP.at_allowed1
     FI);

ACCESS_CONSTRAINT.at_discrim_allowed :=
   (f_encl_descr (EXP.at_env_in).s_state = sc_in_record)  OR
   (f_encl_descr (EXP.at_env_in).s_state = sc_in_discr_part) AND
   f_acc_constr_is_constraint
      (ACCESS_CONSTRAINT.at_allowed2,
       NAME.at_valid,
       EXP.at_env_in);

ACCESS_CONSTRAINT.at_valid :=
   IF f_is_error_descr_set (EXP.at_valid) THEN
      f_error_assocs (ACCESS_CONSTRAINT.at_allowed2)
   ELSE IF EMPTY (ACCESS_CONSTRAINT.at_allowed2) THEN
      tp_assoc_list ()
   ELSE IF f_acc_constr_is_constraint
              (ACCESS_CONSTRAINT.at_allowed2,
               NAME.at_valid,
               EXP.at_env_in) THEN
         (f_make_assocs
            (f_valid_constraint
               (NAME.at_valid,
                ACCESS_CONSTRAINT.at_allowed2,
                EXP.at_env_in))
          %C constraint
          CONDITION
             ch_constraint
                (NAME.at_valid,
                 IT,
                 EXP.at_env_in)
             MESSAGE "illegal constraint")
   ELSE IF f_acc_constr_is_exp
             (ACCESS_CONSTRAINT.at_allowed2,
              NAME.at_valid,
              EXP.at_env_in) THEN
      tp_assoc_list
         (tp_comp_assoc
             (tp_choice_list (),
              f_valid_descr_set
                 (HEAD (ACCESS_CONSTRAINT.at_allowed2)
                      QUA tp_comp_assoc .s_actual,
                  f_base_type
                     (HEAD (NAME.at_valid.s_descrs)),
                  EXP.at_env_in)))
   ELSE f_valid_aggregate1
        (f_base_type
           (HEAD (NAME.at_valid.s_descrs)),
         ACCESS_CONSTRAINT.at_allowed2,
         EXP.at_env_in) QUA tp_assoc_list
   FI FI FI FI;

%C 4.8/2, C 4.3/1, C 4.3/2, C 4.3/3, C 4.3.2/2
CONDITION
   IF f_acc_constr_is_aggreg
        (ACCESS_CONSTRAINT.at_valid,
         NAME.at_valid,
         EXP.at_env_in) THEN
```

```
      %C 4.8/2, C 4.3/1, C 4.3/2, C 4.3/3
      (ch_aggreg (ACCESS_CONSTRAINT.at_valid,
                  EXP.at_valid,
                  EXP.at_env_in)
       CONDITION IT
          MESSAGE
          "wrongly built aggregate") AND
       %C 4.3.2/2
       (IF f_is_unconstr_arr (HEAD (NAME.at_valid.s_descrs),
                              EXP.at_env_in) THEN
          NOT f_has_others_comp (ACCESS_CONSTRAINT.at_valid)
        ELSE TRUE
        FI
       CONDITION IT
          MESSAGE
          "others-component not allowed")
    ELSE TRUE
    FI;

  ACCESS_CONSTRAINT.at_others_allowed :=
    f_is_constr_arr
      (HEAD (NAME.at_valid.s_descrs),
       EXP.at_env_in);

   %
   % Diana Generation:
   %
   %    Transform ACCESS_CONSTRAINT from GENERAL_ASSOC_S to
   %    DSCRT_RANGE_S, EXP, dscrmt_aggregate or void.
   %
   %    Set SM_EXP_TYPE and SM_VALUE of ACCESS_CONSTRAINT if it
   %    became an aggregate using NAME.at_valid.
   %    Set SM_CONSTRAINT of ACCESS_CONSTRAINT if it became an
   %    aggregate or string_literal, using NAME.at_valid.
   %    Set SM_EXP_TYPE and SM_VALUE of EXP using EXP.at_valid.
   %
END;
%- - - - - - - - - - - - - - - - - - - - - - - - - - - - - - - - - -
RULE   r_101 :
EXP                   ::= binary EXP BINARY_OP EXP
STATIC

  TRANSFER at_env_in, at_with_use;

  EXP[2].at_expected  := c_bool;

  EXP[2].at_context := sc_no_special;

  EXP[3].at_expected  := c_bool;

  EXP[3].at_context := sc_no_special;

  EXP[1].at_allowed1  := f_allowed_expected
                           (f_allowed_short_circuit
                              (EXP[2].at_allowed1,
                               EXP[3].at_allowed1,
                               BINARY_OP.at_op,
                               EXP[1].at_env_in),
                               EXP[1].at_expected,
                          EXP[1].at_env_in);
```

```
   EXP[2].at_valid := cf_unique_descr (EXP[2].at_allowed2,
                                       FALSE,
                                       EXP[1].at_env_in);

   EXP[2].at_others_allowed := FALSE;

   EXP[3].at_valid := cf_unique_descr (EXP[3].at_allowed2,
                                       FALSE,
                                       EXP[1].at_env_in);

   EXP[3].at_others_allowed := FALSE;

   EXP[1].at_allowed2 := cf_not_empty
                            (IF EXP[1].at_with_use THEN
                                f_allowed_expected
                                   (f_allowed_short_circuit
                                      (EXP[2].at_allowed2,
                                       EXP[3].at_allowed2,
                                       BINARY_OP.at_op,
                                       EXP[1].at_env_in),
                                    EXP[1].at_expected,
                                    EXP[1].at_env_in)
                             ELSE EXP[1].at_allowed1
                             FI);

    %
    % Diana Generation:
    %
    %    Set SM_EXP_TYPE and SM_VALUE using EXP[1].at_valid
    %
END;
%- - - - - - - - - - - - - - - - - - - - - - - - - - - - - - - - - -
RULE   r_102 :
EXP                  ::=char
STATIC

   EXP.at_allowed1 := f_allowed_expected
                         (f_identify (char.at_designator,
                                      EXP.at_env_in),
                          EXP.at_expected,
                          EXP.at_env_in);

   EXP.at_allowed2 := cf_not_empty
                         (IF EXP.at_with_use THEN
                             f_allowed_expected
                                (f_identify_with_use
                                   (char.at_designator,
                                    EXP.at_env_in),
                                 EXP.at_expected,
                                 EXP.at_env_in)
                          ELSE EXP.at_allowed1
                          FI);

    %
    % Diana Generation:
    %
    %    Set SM_EXP_TYPE, SM_VALUE, SM_DEFN using EXP.at_valid
    %
END;
```

```
%- - - - - - - - - - - - - - - - - - - - - - - - - - - - - - - - - - - -
RULE   r_103 :
EXP                     ::= numeric_literal
STATIC

   EXP.at_allowed1 :=
       f_allowed_expected
          (f_descr_set
              (c_key,
               sc_value,
               tp_object
                  (IF numeric_literal.at_value IS tp_real_val THEN
                      c_univ_real_constr
                   ELSE c_univ_int_constr
                   FI,
                   tp_init (numeric_literal.at_value, sc_literal)),
              sc_no_add),
           EXP.at_expected,
           EXP.at_env_in);

   EXP.at_allowed2 := cf_not_empty (EXP.at_allowed1);

   %
   % Diana Generation:
   %
   %     Set SM_EXP_TYPE, SM_VALUE using EXP.at_valid
   %
END;
%- - - - - - - - - - - - - - - - - - - - - - - - - - - - - - - - - - - -
RULE   r_104 :
EXP                     ::= membership EXP MEMBERSHIP_OP TYPE_RANGE
STATIC

   TRANSFER at_env_in, at_with_use;

   EXP[2].at_expected := c_no_expected;

   EXP[2].at_context := sc_no_special;

   TYPE_RANGE.at_expected := c_no_expected;

   EXP[1].at_allowed1 := f_allowed_expected
                            (f_allowed_membership
                                (f_allowed_exp_in_range
                                    (EXP[2].at_allowed1,
                                     TYPE_RANGE.at_allowed1,
                                     EXP[1].at_env_in),
                                 TYPE_RANGE.at_allowed1,
                                 MEMBERSHIP_OP.at_op,
                                 EXP[1].at_env_in),
                             EXP[1].at_expected,
                             EXP[1].at_env_in);

   EXP[2].at_valid := cf_unique_descr
                         (f_allowed_exp_in_range
                             (EXP[2].at_allowed2,
                              TYPE_RANGE.at_allowed2,
                              EXP[1].at_env_in),
                          FALSE,
                          EXP[1].at_env_in);
```

```
   EXP[2].at_others_allowed := FALSE;

   TYPE_RANGE.at_valid := f_valid_type_range
                              (EXP[2].at_allowed2,
                               TYPE_RANGE.at_allowed2,
                               EXP[1].at_env_in);

   EXP[1].at_allowed2 :=
      cf_not_empty
         (IF EXP[1].at_with_use THEN
             f_allowed_expected
                (f_allowed_membership
                    (f_allowed_exp_in_range
                        (EXP[2].at_allowed2,
                         TYPE_RANGE.at_allowed2,
                         EXP[1].at_env_in),
                     TYPE_RANGE.at_allowed2,
                     MEMBERSHIP_OP.at_op,
                     EXP[1].at_env_in),
                 EXP[1].at_expected,
                 EXP[1].at_env_in)
          ELSE EXP[1].at_allowed1
          FI);

   %
   % Diana Generation:
   %
   %    Set SM_EXP_TYPE, SM_VALUE using EXP[1].at_valid
   %
END;
%- - - - - - - - - - - - - - - - - - - - - - - - - - - - - - - - -
RULE   r_105 :
EXP                     ::= null_access
STATIC

   EXP.at_allowed1 :=
      f_allowed_expected
         (f_descr_set
             (c_key,
              sc_value,
              tp_object
                 (tp_constrained
                     (c_any_access,
                      sc_void),
                  c_no_init),
              sc_no_add),
          EXP.at_expected,
          EXP.at_env_in);

   EXP.at_allowed2 := EXP.at_allowed1;

   %
   % Diana Generation:
   %
   %    Set SM_EXP_TYPE, SM_VALUE using EXP.at_valid
   %
END;
%- - - - - - - - - - - - - - - - - - - - - - - - - - - - - - - - -
RULE   r_106 :
```

```
EXP                       ::= parenthesized EXP
STATIC

   TRANSFER at_env_in, at_expected, at_with_use;

   EXP[1].at_allowed1  := f_allowed_parenthesized
                             (EXP[2].at_allowed1,
                              EXP[1].at_env_in);

   EXP[1].at_allowed2  := cf_not_empty
                            (IF EXP[1].at_with_use THEN
                                  f_allowed_parenthesized
                                    (EXP[2].at_allowed2,
                                     EXP[1].at_env_in)
                             ELSE EXP[1].at_allowed1
                             FI);

  EXP[2].at_valid :=
     cf_unique_descr (f_valid (EXP[1].at_valid,
                               EXP[2].at_allowed2.s_descrs),
                      FALSE,
                      EXP[1].at_env_in);

  EXP[2].at_context := sc_no_special;

  EXP[2].at_others_allowed := FALSE;

   %
   % Diana Generation:
   %
   %    Set SM_EXP_TYPE, SM_VALUE using EXP[1].at_valid
   %
END;
%- - - - - - - - - - - - - - - - - - - - - - - - - - - - - - - -
RULE   r_107 :
EXP                       ::= qualified NAME EXP
STATIC

   TRANSFER at_env_in;

   NAME.at_expected := c_no_expected;

   NAME.at_context := sc_no_special;

   NAME.at_with_use := f_use_required (NAME.at_allowed1);

   NAME.at_valid    := cf_unique_type_descr (NAME.at_allowed2);

   EXP[2].at_with_use := EXP[1].at_with_use;

   EXP[2].at_expected :=
      IF NOT f_is_fixed_type (f_head_descr (NAME.at_valid),
                              EXP[1].at_env_in) THEN
         f_base_type (f_head_descr (NAME.at_valid))
      ELSE c_no_expected
      FI;

   EXP[2].at_context := sc_no_special;

   EXP[1].at_allowed1 := f_allowed_qualified
```

```
                         (EXP[2].at_allowed1,
                          f_head_descr
                             (NAME.at_valid),
                          EXP[1].at_env_in);

   EXP[1].at_allowed2 := cf_not_empty
                         (IF EXP[1].at_with_use THEN
                             f_allowed_qualified
                                (EXP[2].at_allowed2,
                                   f_head_descr
                                      (NAME.at_valid),
                                 EXP[1].at_env_in)
                          ELSE EXP[1].at_allowed1
                          FI);

   EXP[2].at_valid :=
      cf_unique_descr (f_valid (EXP[1].at_valid,
                                EXP[2].at_allowed2.s_descrs),
                       FALSE,
                       EXP[1].at_env_in);

   EXP[2].at_others_allowed :=
      f_is_constr_arr
        (HEAD (NAME.at_valid.s_descrs),
         EXP[1].at_env_in);

   %
   % Diana Generation:
   %
   %    If EXP[2].at_others_allowed then set SM_CONSTRAINT of
   %    EXP[2] using NAME.at_valid.
   %
   %    Set SM_EXP_TYPE, SM_VALUE using EXP[1].at_valid
   %
END;
%- - - - - - - - - - - - - - - - - - - - - - - - - - - - - - - -
RULE  r_108 :
EXP_VOID            ::= EXP
STATIC

   TRANSFER at_expected, at_env_in, at_others_allowed;

   EXP.at_context := sc_no_special;

   EXP.at_with_use := f_use_required (EXP.at_allowed1);

   EXP_VOID.at_valid := tp_descr_set_void (EXP.at_allowed2);

   EXP.at_valid :=
      cf_unique_descr (EXP.at_allowed2,
                       EXP_VOID.at_discrim_allowed,
                       EXP_VOID.at_env_in);

END;
%- - - - - - - - - - - - - - - - - - - - - - - - - - - - - - - -
RULE  r_109 :
EXP_VOID            ::= void
STATIC

   EXP_VOID.at_valid := sc_void;
```

```
END;
%- - - - - - - - - - - - - - - - - - - - - - - - - - - - - - - - - - - - - - - - -
RULE   r_110 :
GENERAL_ASSOC          ::= ACTUAL
STATIC

   TRANSFER at_env_in, at_with_use, at_discrim_allowed;

   ACTUAL.at_expected := c_no_expected;

   ACTUAL.at_context := sc_no_special;

   GENERAL_ASSOC.at_allowed1 :=
      CASE c_actual : ACTUAL.at_allowed1 OF
      IS tp_dscrt_range : c_actual;
      IS tp_descr_set   : tp_comp_assoc (tp_choice_list (),
                                        c_actual)
      ESAC;

   GENERAL_ASSOC.at_allowed2 :=
      IF GENERAL_ASSOC.at_with_use THEN
         CASE c_actual : ACTUAL.at_allowed2 OF
         IS tp_dscrt_range : c_actual;
         IS tp_descr_set   : tp_comp_assoc (tp_choice_list (),
                                           c_actual)
         ESAC
      ELSE GENERAL_ASSOC.at_allowed1
      FI;

   %C 6.4.1/1
   CONDITION
      ch_variable_for_out_in_out (GENERAL_ASSOC.at_valid,
                                  GENERAL_ASSOC.at_env_in)
      MESSAGE
      "THIS actual parameter should be a variable";

   ACTUAL.at_valid :=
      CASE c_valid : GENERAL_ASSOC.at_valid OF
      IS tp_dscrt_range : c_valid;
      IS tp_comp_assoc  : tp_actual (c_valid.s_actual)
      ESAC;

   ACTUAL.at_others_allowed :=
      GENERAL_ASSOC.at_others_allowed OR
      CASE c_valid : GENERAL_ASSOC.at_valid OF
      IS tp_comp_assoc :
         IF EMPTY (c_valid.s_choices) THEN
            FALSE
         ELSE
            CASE c_choice : HEAD (c_valid.s_choices) OF
            IS tp_descr :
               CASE c_choice.s_nature OF
               sc_in: sc_in_out: sc_out:
                  f_is_constr_arr1
                     (c_choice,
                      GENERAL_ASSOC.at_env_in)
               OUT FALSE
               ESAC
            OUT FALSE
```

```
            ESAC
         FI
      OUT FALSE
      ESAC;

END;
%- - - - - - - - - - - - - - - - - - - - - - - - - - - - - - - - - - - -
RULE   r_111 :
GENERAL_ASSOC          ::= RANGE
STATIC

   TRANSFER at_env_in, at_with_use, at_discrim_allowed;

   RANGE.at_expected := c_no_expected;

   GENERAL_ASSOC.at_allowed1 := tp_dscrt_range (RANGE.at_allowed1);

   GENERAL_ASSOC.at_allowed2 := tp_dscrt_range (RANGE.at_allowed2);

   RANGE.at_valid :=
              CASE c_valid : GENERAL_ASSOC.at_valid
                        QUA tp_dscrt_range OF
              IS tp_range :  c_valid
              OUT c_valid QUA tp_constrained .s_constraint
                   QUA tp_range_constr
              ESAC;

END;
%- - - - - - - - - - - - - - - - - - - - - - - - - - - - - - - - - - - -
RULE   r_112 :
GENERAL_ASSOC          ::= NAMED
STATIC

   TRANSFER;

   %C 6.4.1/1
   CONDITION
     ch_variable_for_out_in_out (GENERAL_ASSOC.at_valid,
                                 GENERAL_ASSOC.at_env_in)
     MESSAGE
     "THIS actual parameter should be a variable";

END;
%- - - - - - - - - - - - - - - - - - - - - - - - - - - - - - - - - - - -
RULE   r_113:
GENERAL_ASSOCS         ::=
STATIC

   GENERAL_ASSOCS.at_allowed1 := tp_assoc_list ();

   GENERAL_ASSOCS.at_allowed2 := tp_assoc_list ();

END;
%- - - - - - - - - - - - - - - - - - - - - - - - - - - - - - - - - - - -
RULE   r_114 :
GENERAL_ASSOCS         ::= GENERAL_ASSOC GENERAL_ASSOCS
STATIC

   TRANSFER at_env_in, at_with_use, at_others_allowed,
            at_discrim_allowed;
```

```
   GENERAL_ASSOC.at_is_last := GENERAL_ASSOCS[2] IS r_113;

   GENERAL_ASSOCS[2].at_positional_allowed :=
      GENERAL_ASSOCS[1].at_positional_allowed AND
      NOT (GENERAL_ASSOC IS r_112);                          % named

   %C 6.4/2
   CONDITION
   GENERAL_ASSOCS[1].at_positional_allowed
   OR (GENERAL_ASSOC IS r_112)
      MESSAGE
      "Positional parameters must occur first.";

   GENERAL_ASSOCS[1].at_allowed1 :=
      tp_assoc_list (GENERAL_ASSOC.at_allowed1) +
      GENERAL_ASSOCS[2].at_allowed1;

   GENERAL_ASSOCS[1].at_allowed2 :=
      IF GENERAL_ASSOCS[1].at_with_use THEN
         tp_assoc_list (GENERAL_ASSOC.at_allowed2) +
         GENERAL_ASSOCS[2].at_allowed2
      ELSE GENERAL_ASSOCS[1].at_allowed1
      FI;

   GENERAL_ASSOCS[2].at_valid :=
      TAIL (GENERAL_ASSOCS[1].at_valid);

   GENERAL_ASSOC.at_valid :=
      HEAD (GENERAL_ASSOCS[1].at_valid);

   %
   % Diana Generation:
   %
   %    If GENERAL_ASSOC.at_others_allowed, then set SM_CONSTRAINT
   %    of GENERAL_ASSOC using GENERAL_ASSOC.at_valid.
   %
END;
%- - - - - - - - - - - - - - - - - - - - - - - - - - - - - - - - - - -
RULE   r_115 :
GENERAL_ASSOC_S         ::= general_assoc_s GENERAL_ASSOCS
STATIC

   TRANSFER;

   GENERAL_ASSOCS.at_positional_allowed := TRUE;

END;
%- - - - - - - - - - - - - - - - - - - - - - - - - - - - - - - - - - -
RULE   r_116:
IDS                     ::=
STATIC

   IDS.at_param_no := 0;

   IDS.at_designators := tp_designator_list ()

END;
%- - - - - - - - - - - - - - - - - - - - - - - - - - - - - - - - - - -
RULE   r_117 :
```

```
IDS                   ::= ID IDS
STATIC

   IDS[1].at_param_no := IDS[2].at_param_no + 1;

   IDS[1].at_designators :=
      tp_designator_list (ID.at_designator)  +
        IDS[2].at_designators

END;
%- - - - - - - - - - - - - - - - - - - - - - - - - - - - - - - - - - -
RULE   r_118 :
ID_S                  ::= id_s  IDS
STATIC

   TRANSFER

END;
%- - - - - - - - - - - - - - - - - - - - - - - - - - - - - - - - - - -
RULE   r_119 :
MEMBERSHIP_OP         ::= in_op
STATIC

   MEMBERSHIP_OP.at_op := sc_in_op;

END;
%- - - - - - - - - - - - - - - - - - - - - - - - - - - - - - - - - - -
RULE   r_120 :
MEMBERSHIP_OP         ::= not_in
STATIC

   MEMBERSHIP_OP.at_op := sc_not_in_op;

END;
%- - - - - - - - - - - - - - - - - - - - - - - - - - - - - - - - - - -
RULE   r_121 :
NAME                  ::= all NAME
STATIC

   TRANSFER at_env_in, at_with_use, at_user_rep;

   NAME[2].at_expected := c_no_expected;

   NAME[2].at_context := sc_no_special;

   NAME[1].at_allowed1 := f_allowed_expected
                            (f_allowed_all
                               (NAME[2].at_allowed1,
                                NAME[1].at_env_in),
                             NAME[1].at_expected,
                             NAME[1].at_env_in);
   NAME[1].at_allowed2 :=
      cf_not_empty
         (IF NAME[1].at_with_use THEN
              f_allowed_expected
                  (f_allowed_all
                      (NAME[2].at_allowed2,
                       NAME[1].at_env_in),
                   NAME[1].at_expected,
                   NAME[1].at_env_in)
```

```
        ELSE NAME[1].at_allowed1
        FI);

   NAME[2].at_valid := cf_unique_descr
                            (f_valid_all (NAME[1].at_valid,
                                          NAME[2].at_allowed2),
                             FALSE,
                             NAME[1].at_env_in);
   %
   % Diana Generation:
   %
   %    Set SM_EXP_TYPE, SM_VALUE using NAME[1].at_valid
   %
END;
%- - - - - - - - - - - - - - - - - - - - - - - - - - - - - - - - - - -
RULE   r_122 :
NAME                ::= attribute NAME ID
STATIC

   TRANSFER at_env_in, at_with_use, at_user_rep;

   %C A.1
   CONDITION
      (ID.at_designator =/ c_base_desi)  OR
      (NAME[1] IS r_122)
      MESSAGE
      "the BASE attribute may only appear in other attribute exprs";

   NAME[2].at_expected := c_no_expected;

   NAME[2].at_context := sc_string_is_name;

   NAME[1].at_allowed1 :=
      IF NAME[1].at_context = sc_attr_name THEN
         NAME[2].at_allowed1
      ELSE f_allowed_expected
              (f_allowed_attribute
                  (ID.at_designator QUA SYMB,
                   NAME[2].at_allowed1,
                   NAME[1].at_env_in),
               NAME[1].at_expected,
               NAME[1].at_env_in)
      FI;

   NAME[2].at_valid := cf_unique_descr (NAME[2].at_allowed2,
                                        TRUE,
                                        NAME[1].at_env_in);
   %C 3.8/3
   CONDITION
      f_head_descr (NAME[1].at_valid).s_state =/ sc_incomplete
      OR (NAME[1].at_context = sc_access)
      MESSAGE
      "name of yet incomlete type may only appear after ACCESS";

   %C 13.1/3
   CONDITION
      (NAME[1] IS r_264) OR   %REP ::= address NAME EXP
      (NAME[1] IS r_265) OR   %REP ::= simple_rep NAME EXP
```

```
    IF f_is_repr_attribute (ID.at_designator) THEN
       CASE f_new_repr_state
               (f_head_descr (NAME[2].at_valid).s_key,
                f_calculate_repr
                   (f_head_descr (NAME[2].at_valid).s_key,
                    FALSE,
                    NAME[1].at_env_in)) OF
       sc_incompl_rep:
          (TRUE CONDITION FALSE MESSAGE
               "this repr attr depends on private/incompl types")
       sc_user_rep    : FALSE
       OUT TRUE
       ESAC
    ELSE TRUE
    FI
    MESSAGE
    "forbidden use of repr attr because of later repr spec";

  NAME[1].at_allowed2 :=
    cf_not_empty
      (IF NAME[1].at_with_use THEN
          IF NAME[1].at_context = sc_attr_name THEN
             NAME[2].at_allowed2
          ELSE f_allowed_expected
                 (f_allowed_attribute
                     (ID.at_designator QUA SYMB,
                      NAME[2].at_allowed2,
                      NAME[1].at_env_in),
                  NAME[1].at_expected,
                  NAME[1].at_env_in)
          FI
       ELSE NAME[1].at_allowed1
       FI);

   %
   % Diana Generation:
   %
   %    Set SM_EXP_TYPE, SM_VALUE using NAME[1].at_valid
   %
END;
%- - - - - - - - - - - - - - - - - - - - - - - - - - - - - - - - - -
RULE   r_123 :
NAME                 ::= DESIGNATOR
STATIC

   NAME.at_user_rep := tp_user_reps (DESIGNATOR.at_designator);

   NAME.at_allowed1 :=
     IF DESIGNATOR IS r_169                   %DESIGNATOR ::= string
          AND (NOT (NAME.at_context = sc_string_is_name)) THEN
        f_make_string_aggregate
          (DESIGNATOR.at_designator QUA SYMB,
           NAME.at_expected,
           NAME.at_env_in)
     ELSE  f_make_dummy
             (DESIGNATOR.at_designator,
              f_allowed_expected
                 (f_identify
                    (DESIGNATOR.at_designator,
                     NAME.at_env_in),
```

```
              NAME.at_expected,
              NAME.at_env_in),
          NAME.at_context)
   FI;

NAME.at_allowed2 :=  cf_not_empty
   (IF NAME.at_with_use THEN
       IF DESIGNATOR IS r_169              %DESIGNATOR ::= string
            AND (NOT (NAME.at_context = sc_string_is_name)) THEN
          f_make_string_aggregate
            (DESIGNATOR.at_designator QUA SYMB,
             NAME.at_expected,
             NAME.at_env_in)
       ELSE  f_make_dummy
               (DESIGNATOR.at_designator,
                f_allowed_expected
                   (f_identify_with_use
                       (DESIGNATOR.at_designator,
                        NAME.at_env_in),
                    NAME.at_expected,
                    NAME.at_env_in),
                NAME.at_context)
       FI
    ELSE NAME.at_allowed1
    FI);

%C 3.8/3
CONDITION
   f_head_descr (NAME.at_valid).s_state =/ sc_incomplete
      OR (NAME.at_context = sc_access)
   MESSAGE
   "name of yet incomlete type may only appear after ACCESS";

%C KA/2
CONDITION
   IF NAME.at_context = sc_call THEN
      NOT (f_own_entry (NAME.at_valid,
                        NAME.at_env_in))
   ELSE TRUE
   FI
   MESSAGE
   "WARNING : task calls entry of its own";

%
% Diana Generation:
%
%   1)If DESIGNATOR is a used_id, it is transformed to used_name_id,
%     used_object_id or used_bltn_id depending on NAME.at_valid.
%
%     If it became a used_name_id, set SM_DEFN
%     using NAME.at_valid.
%     If it became a used_object_id, set SM_DEFN,
%     SM_EXP_TYPE, SM_VALUE using NAME.at_valid.
%     If it became a used_bltn_id, set SM_OPERATOR
%     using NAME.at_valid.
%
%   2)If DESIGNATOR is a used_string, it is transformed to
%     used_op, string_literal or used_bltn_op depending on
%     NAME.at_valid.
%
```

```
%     If it became a used_op, set SM_DEFN
%     using NAME.at_valid.
%     If it became a string_literal, set SM_EXP_TYPE, SM_VALUE
%     using NAME.at_valid, if not NAME.at_others_allowed then
%     build new constraint using NAME.at_valid and set
%     SM_CONSTRAINT accordingly.
%     If it became a used_bltn_op, set SM_OPERATOR
%     using NAME.at_valid.
%
END;
%- - - - - - - - - - - - - - - - - - - - - - - - - - - - - - - - -
RULE   r_124 :
NAME                ::= APPLY
STATIC

   TRANSFER at_env_in, at_user_rep, at_expected, at_valid,
            at_allowed1, at_allowed2, at_with_use;

   %C 3.8/3
   CONDITION
      f_head_descr (NAME.at_valid).s_state =/ sc_incomplete
         OR (NAME.at_context = sc_access)
     MESSAGE
    "name of yet incomlete type may only appear after ACCESS";

   APPLY.at_context := IF NAME.at_context = sc_id_not_visible THEN
                           sc_no_special
                       ELSE NAME.at_context
                       FI;

   APPLY.at_is_exp := NAME IS r_098; % EXP ::= NAME

END;
%- - - - - - - - - - - - - - - - - - - - - - - - - - - - - - - - -
RULE   r_125 :
NAME                ::= selected NAME DESIGNATOR
STATIC

   TRANSFER at_env_in, at_with_use;

   NAME[1].at_user_rep := tp_user_reps (DESIGNATOR.at_designator);

   NAME[2].at_expected := c_no_expected;

   NAME[2].at_cbntext := sc_string_is_name;

   NAME[1].at_allowed1 := f_allowed_expected
                             (f_allowed_selected
                                 (NAME[2].at_allowed1,
                                  DESIGNATOR.at_designator,
                                  NAME[1].at_env_in),
                              NAME[1].at_expected,
                              NAME[1].at_env_in);

   NAME[1].at_allowed2 :=
      cf_not_empty
         (IF NAME[1].at_with_use THEN
             f_allowed_expected
                (f_allowed_selected
                    (NAME[2].at_allowed2,
```

```
                DESIGNATOR.at_designator,
                NAME[1].at_env_in),
             NAME[1].at_expected,
             NAME[1].at_env_in)
      ELSE NAME[1].at_allowed1
      FI);

   NAME[2].at_valid := cf_unique_descr
                          (f_valid
                              (NAME[1].at_valid,
                               NAME[2].at_allowed2.s_descrs),
                          FALSE,
                          NAME[1].at_env_in);

   %C 3.8/3
   CONDITION
      f_head_descr (NAME[1].at_valid).s_state =/ sc_incomplete
        OR (NAME[1].at_context = sc_access)
      MESSAGE
     "name of yet incomlete type may only appear after ACCESS";

   %C KA/2
   CONDITION
      IF NAME[1].at_context = sc_call THEN
         NOT (f_own_entry (NAME[1].at_valid,
                           NAME[1].at_env_in))
      ELSE TRUE
      FI
      MESSAGE
      "WARNING : task calls entry of its own";

   %C 4.1.3/4 checked in f_allowed_selected;

   %
   % Diana Generation:
   %
   %  1)If NAME[1] is EXP, set SM_EXP_TYPE and SM_VALUE
   %    using NAME[1].at_valid.
   %
   %  2)If DESIGNATOR is a used_id then it is transformed
   %    to a used_name_id, used_object_id or used_bltn_id
   %    respectively, depending on NAME[1].at_valid and
   %    on the context (if NAME[1] is EXP).
   %
   %    If DESIGNATOR is a used_string then it is transformed
   %    to a used_op or used_bltn_op respectively
   %    depending on NAME[1].at_valid and on the
   %    context (if NAME[1] is EXP).
   %
   %  3)If DESIGNATOR became a used_op or used_name_id or
   %    used_object_id, SM_DEFN of DESIGNATOR is set
   %    using NAME[1].at_valid.
   %    If DESIGNATOR became a used_object_id, SM_EXP_TYPE and
   %    SM_VALUE of DESIGNATOR is set using NAME[1].at_valid.
   %    If DESIGNATOR became a used_bltn_op or used_bltn_id,
   %    SM_OPERATOR of DESIGNATOR is set using NAME[1].at_valid.
   %
   %
END;
%- - - - - - - - - - - - - - - - - - - - - - - - - - - - - - -
```

```
RULE   r_126 :
NAMES                  ::= NAME NAMES
STATIC

   TRANSFER at_env_in;

   NAME.at_expected := c_no_expected;

   NAME.at_context := sc_no_special;

   NAME.at_with_use := f_use_required (NAME.at_allowed1);

   NAME.at_valid := cf_unique_descr (NAME.at_allowed2,
                                     TRUE,
                                     NAME.at_env_in);

   NAMES[1].at_names :=
      NAME.at_valid.s_descrs +
      NAMES[2].at_names;

END;
%- - - - - - - - - - - - - - - - - - - - - - - - - - - - - - - - - - - - - - -
RULE   r_127 :
NAMES                  ::=
STATIC

   NAMES.at_names := c_empty_descrs;

END;
%- - - - - - - - - - - - - - - - - - - - - - - - - - - - - - - - - - - - - - -
RULE r_128 :
NAME_S                 ::= name_s NAMES
STATIC

   TRANSFER

END;
%- - - - - - - - - - - - - - - - - - - - - - - - - - - - - - - - - - - - - - -
RULE   r_129 :
NAME_VOID              ::= NAME
STATIC

   TRANSFER at_env_in, at_context, at_expected;

   NAME.at_with_use := f_use_required (NAME.at_allowed1);

   NAME_VOID.at_valid   := tp_descr_set_void
                           (cf_unique_descr (NAME.at_allowed2,
                                             TRUE,
                                             NAME_VOID.at_env_in));

   NAME.at_valid := NAME_VOID.at_valid QUA tp_descr_set;

END;
%- - - - - - - - - - - - - - - - - - - - - - - - - - - - - - - - - - - - - - -
RULE   r_130 :
NAME_VOID              ::= void
STATIC

   NAME_VOID.at_valid  := sc_void;
```

```
END;
%- - - - - - - - - - - - - - - - - - - - - - - - - - - - - - - - - - -
RULE   r_131 :
NAMED                    ::= named CHOICE_S '%' EXP
STATIC

   TRANSFER at_env_in, at_with_use;

   CHOICE_S.at_is_last := NAMED.at_is_last;

   CHOICE_S.at_context := sc_named;

   CHOICE_S.at_expected := c_no_expected;

   EXP.at_expected := c_no_expected;

   EXP.at_context := sc_no_special;

   NAMED.at_allowed1 := tp_comp_assoc (CHOICE_S.at_allowed1,
                                       EXP.at_allowed1);

   NAMED.at_allowed2 := tp_comp_assoc (CHOICE_S.at_allowed2,
                                       EXP.at_allowed2);

   CHOICE_S.at_valid :=
      cf_unique_choices (NAMED.at_valid QUA tp_comp_assoc .s_choices,
                         NAMED.at_env_in);

   EXP.at_valid :=
      cf_unique_descr (NAMED.at_valid QUA tp_comp_assoc .s_actual,
                       NAMED.at_discrim_allowed,
                       NAMED.at_env_in);

   EXP.at_others_allowed :=
      NAMED.at_others_allowed OR
      CASE c_choice : HEAD (NAMED.at_valid QUA tp_comp_assoc
                            .s_choices) OF
      IS tp_descr :
         CASE c_choice.s_nature OF
         sc_in: sc_in_out: sc_out:
            f_is_constr_arr1
               (c_choice,
                NAMED.at_env_in)
         OUT FALSE
         ESAC
      OUT FALSE
      ESAC;

END;
%- - - - - - - - - - - - - - - - - - - - - - - - - - - - - - - - - - -
RULE   r_132 :
SHORT_CIRCUIT_OP       ::= and_then
STATIC

   SHORT_CIRCUIT_OP.at_op := sc_and_then_op;

END;
%- - - - - - - - - - - - - - - - - - - - - - - - - - - - - - - - - - -
RULE   r_133 :
```

```
SHORT_CIRCUIT_OP        ::= or_else
STATIC

   SHORT_CIRCUIT_OP.at_op := sc_or_else_op;

END;
%- - - - - - - - - - - - - - - - - - - - - - - - - - - - - - - - - - - - - - -
RULE   r_134 :
TYPE_RANGE              ::= RANGE
STATIC

   TRANSFER at_env_in, at_expected, at_with_use;

   TYPE_RANGE.at_allowed1 := RANGE.at_allowed1;

   TYPE_RANGE.at_allowed2 := RANGE.at_allowed2;

   RANGE.at_valid := IF TYPE_RANGE.at_valid = c_error_type_range THEN
                         c_error_range
                     ELSE TYPE_RANGE.at_valid QUA tp_range_constr
                     FI;

   RANGE.at_discrim_allowed := FALSE;

END;
%- - - - - - - - - - - - - - - - - - - - - - - - - - - - - - - - - - - - - - -
RULE   r_135 :
TYPE_RANGE              ::= CONSTRAINED
STATIC

   TRANSFER at_env_in;

   CONSTRAINED.at_discrim_allowed := FALSE;

   TYPE_RANGE.at_allowed1 := CONSTRAINED.at_type;

   TYPE_RANGE.at_allowed2 := TYPE_RANGE.at_allowed1;

END;
```

```
%------------------------------------------------------------------------------
%                                                                            -
% 5.5. Statements                                                            -
%                                                                            -
%------------------------------------------------------------------------------

%- - - - - - - - - - - - - - - - - - - - - - - - - - - - - - - - - - - - - - -
RULE   r_136 :
ALTERNATIVE            ::= alternative CHOICE_S '%' STM_S '%'
STATIC

   TRANSFER at_encl_unit, at_return_required, at_labels,
            at_loops_blocks, at_expected;

   CHOICE_S.at_is_last := ALTERNATIVE.at_is_last;

   CHOICE_S.at_context := ALTERNATIVE.at_context;

   CHOICE_S.at_env_in := ALTERNATIVE.at_env_in;

   CHOICE_S.at_with_use := FALSE; %uninportant;

   CHOICE_S.at_valid := cf_unique_choices
                          (CHOICE_S.at_allowed2,
                           ALTERNATIVE.at_env_in);

   %C 5.4/3
   CONDITION ch_static_choices (CHOICE_S.at_valid) OR
             (ALTERNATIVE.at_context = sc_handler)
      MESSAGE "choices must be static";

   STM_S.at_env_in :=
      f_make_usable
         (STM_S.at_usable,
          ALTERNATIVE.at_env_in);

   ALTERNATIVE.at_choices := CHOICE_S.at_valid;

END;
%- - - - - - - - - - - - - - - - - - - - - - - - - - - - - - - - - - - - - - -
RULE   r_137:
ALTERNATIVES           ::=
STATIC

   ALTERNATIVES.at_labels := c_no_bl_lab_loops;

   ALTERNATIVES.at_loops_blocks := c_no_bl_lab_loops;

   ALTERNATIVES.at_choices := tp_choice_list ();

END;
%- - - - - - - - - - - - - - - - - - - - - - - - - - - - - - - - - - - - - - -
RULE   r_138 :
ALTERNATIVES           ::= ALTERNATIVE ALTERNATIVES
STATIC

  TRANSFER at_encl_unit, at_env_in, at_return_required,
           at_expected, at_context;
```

```
   ALTERNATIVE.at_is_last := ALTERNATIVES[2] IS r_137;

   ALTERNATIVES[1].at_labels :=
      ALTERNATIVE.at_labels + ALTERNATIVES[2].at_labels;

   ALTERNATIVES[1].at_loops_blocks :=
      ALTERNATIVE.at_loops_blocks + ALTERNATIVES[2].at_loops_blocks;

   ALTERNATIVES[1].at_choices :=
                        ALTERNATIVE.at_choices +
                        ALTERNATIVES[2].at_choices;

END;
%- - - - - - - - - - - - - - - - - - - - - - - - - - - - - - - - - - - -
RULE   r_139 :
ALTERNATIVE_S           ::= alternative_s ALTERNATIVES
STATIC

   TRANSFER;

   ALTERNATIVE_S.at_empty := ALTERNATIVES IS r_137;

END;
%- - - - - - - - - - - - - - - - - - - - - - - - - - - - - - - - - - - -
RULE   r_140 :
BLOCK                   ::= block ITEM_S '%'  STM_S '%'  ALTERNATIVE_S '%'
STATIC

   TRANSFER at_return_required;

   ITEM_S.at_block_no := BLOCK.at_block_no + 1;

   ITEM_S.at_encl_unit := BLOCK.at_encl_unit;

   STM_S.at_encl_unit  := BLOCK.at_encl_unit;

   ALTERNATIVE_S.at_encl_unit :=
      tp_encl_unit (BLOCK.at_encl_unit.s_nature, sc_in_handler);

   BLOCK.at_labels := STM_S.at_labels + ALTERNATIVE_S.at_labels;

   BLOCK.at_loops_blocks := STM_S.at_loops_blocks
                            + ALTERNATIVE_S.at_loops_blocks;


   %C 13.8/1
   CONDITION
   STM_S.at_no_code_stms
   OR (BLOCK.at_encl_unit = tp_encl_unit(sc_procedure, sc_in_body))
      MESSAGE
      "Only procedures may contain code statements.";

   %C 13.8/2
   CONDITION
   STM_S.at_no_code_stms OR ITEM_S.at_no_decls
      MESSAGE
      "Only use clauses and pragmas may appear in code procedures.";

   %C 13.8/3
   CONDITION
```

```
   STM_S.at_no_code_stms OR ALTERNATIVE_S.at_empty
      MESSAGE
      "No exception handler may appear in code procedures.";

   ITEM_S.at_env_in := BLOCK.at_env_in;

   %C 7.1/1, C 7.3/1
   CONDITION
   ch_all_bodies_appeared (f_local (ITEM_S.at_env_out))
      MESSAGE
      "missing bodies of specified program units";

   %C 3.8/2
   CONDITION
   ch_all_types_completed (f_local (ITEM_S.at_env_out))
      MESSAGE
      "missing full declarations for incomplete types";

   STM_S.at_env_in :=
      f_make_usable
        (STM_S.at_usable,
         f_declare_implicit
           (f_make_descrs
              (IF BLOCK.at_context = sc_stm THEN
                  BLOCK.at_loops_blocks
               ELSE BLOCK.at_loops_blocks + BLOCK.at_labels
               FI,
               f_enclosing (ITEM_S.at_env_out)),
            ITEM_S.at_env_out));

   ALTERNATIVE_S.at_env_in := f_update_encl_state
                                 (sc_in_handler,
                                  STM_S.at_env_in);

   ALTERNATIVE_S.at_expected := c_no_expected;

   ALTERNATIVE_S.at_context := sc_handler;

   %C 11.2/1
   CONDITION
      ch_alternatives (ALTERNATIVE_S.at_choices);


END;
%- - - - - - - - - - - - - - - - - - - - - - - - - - - - - - - - - -
RULE   r_141 :
BLOCK_STUB            ::= BLOCK
STATIC

   TRANSFER at_encl_unit, at_block_no;

   BLOCK.at_return_required :=
      BLOCK_STUB.at_encl_unit.s_nature = sc_function;

   BLOCK.at_env_in :=
      f_new_imported
        (f_select_by_key (HEAD (BLOCK_STUB.at_keys),
                               BLOCK_STUB.at_env_in),
         f_new_local
           (f_make_local
```

```
              (f_select_by_key (HEAD (BLOCK_STUB.at_keys),
                                BLOCK_STUB.at_env_in).s_den),
           HEAD (BLOCK_STUB.at_keys),
           BLOCK_STUB.at_env_in));

   BLOCK.at_context := sc_block_stub;

END;
%- - - - - - - - - - - - - - - - - - - - - - - - - - - - - - - - -
RULE   r_142 :
BLOCK_STUB          ::= stub
STATIC

   %C 10.2/1
   CONDITION
   BLOCK_STUB.at_block_no = 1
      MESSAGE
      "Subunits are only allowed in outermost declarative part.";

END;
%- - - - - - - - - - - - - - - - - - - - - - - - - - - - - - - - -
RULE   r_143 :
COND_CLAUSE         ::= cond_clause EXP_VOID STM_S '%'
STATIC

   TRANSFER at_encl_unit, at_return_required,
            at_labels, at_loops_blocks;

   EXP_VOID.at_env_in := COND_CLAUSE.at_env_in;

   STM_S.at_env_in := f_make_usable (STM_S.at_usable,
                                     COND_CLAUSE.at_env_in);

   EXP_VOID.at_expected := c_bool;

   EXP_VOID.at_others_allowed := FALSE;

   EXP_VOID.at_discrim_allowed := FALSE;

   %C 3.5.3/1, C 5.3/1    checked through EXP_VOID.at_expected :=
   %                      and cf_unique_descr;

END;
%- - - - - - - - - - - - - - - - - - - - - - - - - - - - - - - - -
RULE   r_144 :
COND_CLAUSES        ::= COND_CLAUSE COND_CLAUSES
STATIC

   TRANSFER at_return_required, at_encl_unit, at_env_in;

   COND_CLAUSES[1].at_labels := COND_CLAUSE.at_labels
                              + COND_CLAUSES[2].at_labels;

   COND_CLAUSES[1].at_loops_blocks := COND_CLAUSE.at_loops_blocks
                                    + COND_CLAUSES[2].at_loops_blocks;

END;
%- - - - - - - - - - - - - - - - - - - - - - - - - - - - - - - - -
RULE   r_145 :
COND_CLAUSES        ::=
```

```
STATIC

   COND_CLAUSES.at_labels := c_no_bl_lab_loops;

   COND_CLAUSES.at_loops_blocks := c_no_bl_lab_loops;

END;
%- - - - - - - - - - - - - - - - - - - - - - - - - - - - - - - - - - -
RULE   r_146 :
ITERATION               ::= for ID DSCRT_RANGE
STATIC

   ITERATION.at_keys := f_gen_keys;

   DSCRT_RANGE.at_discrim_allowed := FALSE;

   DSCRT_RANGE.at_env_in :=
      f_add_descr
         (ID.at_designator,
          HEAD (ITERATION.at_keys),
          sc_id_established,
          sc_constant,
          sc_void,
          ITERATION.at_env_in);

   ITERATION.at_env_out :=
      f_update_descr_by_key
         (HEAD (ITERATION.at_keys),
          c_start_repr,
          sc_complete,
          sc_constant,
          tp_object
             (DSCRT_RANGE.at_valid QUA tp_constrained,
              c_init),
          DSCRT_RANGE.at_env_in);

   %
   % Diana Generation:
   %
   %     Set SM_OBJ_TYPE of ID to DSCRT_RANGE, if DSCRT_RANGE
   %     is a range node, then build constrained node with
   %     this range and a type name determined with
   %     DSCRT_RANGE.at_valid and set SM_OBJ_TYPE of ID
   %     to this new constrained.
   %
END;
%- - - - - - - - - - - - - - - - - - - - - - - - - - - - - - - - - - -
RULE   r_147 :
ITERATION               ::= reverse ID DSCRT_RANGE
STATIC

   ITERATION.at_keys := f_gen_keys;

   DSCRT_RANGE.at_discrim_allowed := FALSE;


   DSCRT_RANGE.at_env_in :=
      f_add_descr
         (ID.at_designator,
          HEAD (ITERATION.at_keys),
```

```
        sc_id_established,
        sc_constant,
        sc_void,
        ITERATION.at_env_in);

   ITERATION.at_env_out :=
      f_update_descrs_by_keys
        (ITERATION.at_keys,
         c_start_repr,
         sc_complete,
         sc_constant,
         tp_object
            (DSCRT_RANGE.at_valid QUA tp_constrained,
             c_init),
         DSCRT_RANGE.at_env_in);

   %
   % Diana Generation:
   %
   %    Set SM_OBJ_TYPE of ID to DSCRT_RANGE, if DSCRT_RANGE
   %    is a range node, then build constrained node with
   %    this range and a type name determined with
   %    DSCRT_RANGE.at_valid and set SM_OBJ_TYPE of ID
   %    to this new constrained.
   %
END;
%- - - - - - - - - - - - - - - - - - - - - - - - - - - - - - - - - - - - -
RULE   r_148 :
ITERATION               ::= void
STATIC

   ITERATION.at_keys    := c_empty_keys;

   ITERATION.at_env_out := ITERATION.at_env_in;

END;
%- - - - - - - - - - - - - - - - - - - - - - - - - - - - - - - - - - - - -
RULE   r_149 :
ITERATION               ::= while EXP
STATIC

   EXP.at_expected   := c_bool;

   EXP.at_context := sc_no_special;

   EXP.at_env_in := ITERATION.at_env_in;

   EXP.at_with_use := f_use_required (EXP.at_allowed1);

   EXP.at_valid       := cf_unique_descr (EXP.at_allowed2,
                                          FALSE,
                                          ITERATION.at_env_in);

   EXP.at_others_allowed := FALSE;

   ITERATION.at_keys := c_empty_keys;

   ITERATION.at_env_out := ITERATION.at_env_in;

   %C 3.5.3/1, C 5.5/3         checked throuh EXP.at_expected := ...
```

```
%                          and cf_unique_descr;

END;
%- - - - - - - - - - - - - - - - - - - - - - - - - - - - - - - - - -
RULE   r_150 :
STM                   ::= assign NAME EXP
STATIC

   TRANSFER at_env_in;

   STM.at_usable := c_no_bl_lab_loops;

   STM.at_labels := c_no_bl_lab_loops;

   STM.at_loops_blocks := c_no_bl_lab_loops;

   %C KA/1
   CONDITION
   NOT STM.at_return_required
      MESSAGE
      "Warning : Return should appear after this statement.";

   NAME.at_expected := c_no_expected;

   NAME.at_context := sc_no_special;

   NAME.at_with_use := f_use_required (NAME.at_allowed1);

   NAME.at_valid := cf_unique_descr (NAME.at_allowed2,
                                     FALSE,
                                     NAME.at_env_in);

   %C 3.2/3, C 3.7.1/4, C 6.2/1, C 7.4.2/1, C 5.2/2
   CONDITION
      ch_is_assign_allowed (NAME.at_valid,
                            STM.at_env_in)
      MESSAGE
      "assignment forbidden for this NAME";

   EXP.at_expected := f_object_type1
                      (HEAD (NAME.at_valid.s_descrs).s_den);

   EXP.at_context := sc_no_special;

   EXP.at_with_use := f_use_required (EXP.at_allowed1);

   EXP.at_valid := cf_unique_descr (EXP.at_allowed2,
                                    FALSE,
                                    STM.at_env_in);

   EXP.at_others_allowed := FALSE;

   % C 5.2./1 checked automatically through cf_unique_descr
   % and EXP.at_expected := .....;

END;
%- - - - - - - - - - - - - - - - - - - - - - - - - - - - - - - - - -
RULE   r_151 :
STM                   ::= BLOCK
STATIC
```

```
    TRANSFER at_return_required, at_labels, at_encl_unit;

    BLOCK.at_block_no := 13;                    % must only be > 1

    STM.at_usable := c_no_bl_lab_loops;

    STM.at_loops_blocks := c_no_bl_lab_loops;

    BLOCK.at_env_in := IF STM IS r_159 THEN
                             STM.at_env_in
                       ELSE f_empty_local_add_global
                                 (f_gen_key,
                                  sc_in_body,
                                  sc_block,
                                  STM.at_env_in)
                       FI;

    BLOCK.at_context := sc_stm;

END;
%- - - - - - - - - - - - - - - - - - - - - - - - - - - - - - - - - - -
RULE   r_152 :
STM                     ::= NAME
STATIC

    STM.at_usable := c_no_bl_lab_loops;

    STM.at_labels := c_no_bl_lab_loops;

    STM.at_loops_blocks := c_no_bl_lab_loops;

    %C KA/1
    CONDITION
    NOT STM.at_return_required
       MESSAGE
       "Warning : Return should appear after this statement.";

    NAME.at_expected := c_no_expected;

    NAME.at_context := sc_call;

    NAME.at_env_in := STM.at_env_in;

    NAME.at_with_use := f_use_required (NAME.at_allowed1);

    NAME.at_valid :=     IF NAME IS r_124 THEN
                              cf_unique_descr (NAME.at_allowed2,
                                               FALSE,
                                               STM.at_env_in)
                         ELSE f_valid
                                 (cf_unique_descr
                                     (cf_not_empty
                                        (f_allowed_proc_entry
                                           (NAME.at_allowed2,
                                            tp_assoc_list (),
                                            STM.at_env_in)),
                                      FALSE,
                                      STM.at_env_in),
                                  NAME.at_allowed2.s_descrs)
```

```
                FI;

  %C KA/2
  CONDITION
     IF (NAME IS r_124) THEN
        TRUE
     ELSE  NOT (f_own_entry (NAME.at_valid, STM.at_env_in))
     FI
  MESSAGE
     "WARNING : task calls entry of its own"

END;
%- - - - - - - - - - - - - - - - - - - - - - - - - - - - - - - - - - - -
RULE   r_153 :
STM                      ::= case EXP ALTERNATIVE_S '%'
STATIC

  TRANSFER at_encl_unit, at_return_required, at_env_in,
           at_labels   , at_loops_blocks;

  STM.at_usable := c_no_bl_lab_loops;

  EXP.at_expected := c_no_expected;

  EXP.at_context := sc_no_special;

  EXP.at_with_use := f_use_required (EXP.at_allowed1);

  EXP.at_valid := cf_unique_descr (EXP.at_allowed2,
                                   FALSE,
                                   EXP.at_env_in);

  %C 5.4/4
  CONDITION
     f_is_discrete_type
        (f_select_by_key
           (f_object_type
              (f_head_descr
                 (EXP.at_valid)),
            STM.at_env_in),
         STM.at_env_in)
     MESSAGE
     "expression after case must be of discrete type";

  EXP.at_others_allowed := FALSE;

  ALTERNATIVE_S.at_context := sc_case;

  ALTERNATIVE_S.at_expected :=
           f_object_type1
              (HEAD (EXP.at_valid.s_descrs).s_den);

  %C 5.4/1
  CONDITION
     ch_exhaustive_choices (f_obj_constrained1
                              (f_head_descr (EXP.at_valid)),
                           ALTERNATIVE_S.at_choices,
                           STM.at_env_in)
    MESSAGE
    "each possible value of expr. must appear once as case label";
```

```
END;
%- - - - - - - - - - - - - - - - - - - - - - - - - - - - - - - - - - - - -
RULE   r_154 :
STM                    ::= if COND_CLAUSES '%'
STATIC

   TRANSFER at_return_required, at_encl_unit, at_labels,
            at_loops_blocks, at_env_in;

   STM.at_usable                         := c_no_bl_lab_loops;

END;
%- - - - - - - - - - - - - - - - - - - - - - - - - - - - - - - - - - - - -
RULE   r_155 :
STM                    ::= exit NAME_VOID  EXP_VOID
STATIC

   TRANSFER at_env_in;

   STM.at_usable := c_no_bl_lab_loops;

   STM.at_labels := c_no_bl_lab_loops;

   STM.at_loops_blocks := c_no_bl_lab_loops;

   NAME_VOID.at_context := sc_no_special;

   NAME_VOID.at_expected := c_no_expected;

   %C 5.7/2
   CONDITION
   IF NAME_VOID IS r_130 THEN                    % void
      f_in_loop                         %REQ: declare anonymous loops
         (f_encl_descr (STM.at_env_in),
          STM.at_env_in)
   ELSE
      TRUE
   FI
      MESSAGE
      "Exit only allowed within a loop";

   %C 5.7/3
   CONDITION
   CASE c_valid : NAME_VOID.at_valid OF
   IS tp_void : TRUE;   %checked by f_in_loop (5.7/2)
   IS tp_descr_set :
        ch_control (f_head_descr (c_valid),
                    f_encl_descr (STM.at_env_in),
                    STM.at_env_in)
   ESAC
      MESSAGE
      "Exit must not transfer control out of a body or accept stm";

   %C 5.7/4
   CONDITION
      CASE c_valid : NAME_VOID.at_valid OF
      IS tp_descr_set : (f_head_descr (c_valid).s_nature = sc_loop)
         OUT TRUE
```

```
      ESAC
      MESSAGE
      "a loop name expected here";

   EXP_VOID.at_expected := c_bool;

   EXP_VOID.at_others_allowed := FALSE;

   EXP_VOID.at_discrim_allowed := FALSE;

   %C 5.7/2, 5.7/3 through fc_enclosing_loop;

   %C 3.5.3/1, C 5.7/1          checked automatically through
   %                            EXP_VOID.at_expected and
   %                            cf_unique_descr;

   %
   % Diana Generation:
   %
   %     Set SM_STM using NAME_VOID.at_valid if NAME_VOID
   %     is not void, otherwise using the enclosing
   %     component of STM.at_env_in.
   %
END;
%- - - - - - - - - - - - - - - - - - - - - - - - - - - - - - - - -
RULE   r_156 :
STM                    ::= goto NAME
STATIC

   TRANSFER at_env_in;

   STM.at_usable := c_no_bl_lab_loops;

   STM.at_labels := c_no_bl_lab_loops;

   STM.at_loops_blocks := c_no_bl_lab_loops;

   NAME.at_expected := c_no_expected;

   NAME.at_context := sc_no_special;

   NAME.at_with_use := f_use_required (NAME.at_allowed1);

   NAME.at_valid := cf_unique_descr (NAME.at_allowed2,
                                     FALSE,
                                     NAME.at_env_in);

   %C 5.9/1
   CONDITION
      f_head_descr (NAME.at_valid).s_nature = sc_label
      MESSAGE
      "Label name expected";

   %C 5.9/2
   CONDITION
   f_head_descr (NAME.at_valid).s_state = sc_complete
      MESSAGE
      "Goto must not transfer control into a compound stm or handler";

   %C 5.9/2
```

```
   CONDITION
   ch_control (f_encl_descr1 (f_head_descr (NAME.at_valid),
                              STM.at_env_in),
               f_encl_descr (STM.at_env_in),
               STM.at_env_in)
      MESSAGE
      "Goto must not transfer control out of a body or accept stm";

END;
%- - - - - - - - - - - - - - - - - - - - - - - - - - - - - - - - - - - - -
RULE   r_157 :
STM                    ::= labeled ID STM
STATIC

   TRANSFER at_encl_unit, at_return_required, at_loops_blocks,
            at_env_in;

   STM[1].at_usable :=
      tp_bl_lab_loops
         (tp_bl_lab_loop (ID.at_designator,
                          f_gen_key,
                          sc_label))
      + STM[2].at_usable;

   STM[1].at_labels := tp_bl_lab_loops (HEAD (STM[1].at_usable))
                       + STM[2].at_labels;

   %
   % Diana Generation:
   %
   %     Set SM_STM of ID to STM[2]
   %     If STM[2] is a NAME then transform it into a
   %     procedure/entry call using STM[2].at_valid.
   %
END;
%- - - - - - - - - - - - - - - - - - - - - - - - - - - - - - - - - - - - -
RULE   r_158 :
STM                    ::= loop ITERATION STM_S '%'
STATIC

   TRANSFER at_encl_unit, at_labels, at_loops_blocks;

   STM_S.at_return_required := FALSE;       % return should be after loo

   STM.at_usable := c_no_bl_lab_loops;

   %C KA/1
   CONDITION
   NOT STM.at_return_required
      MESSAGE
      "Warning : Return should appear after this statement.";

   ITERATION.at_env_in :=  IF STM IS r_159 THEN
                               STM.at_env_in
                           ELSE f_empty_local_add_global
                                  (f_gen_key,
                                   sc_in_body,
                                   sc_loop,
                                   STM.at_env_in)
                           FI;
```

```
   STM_S.at_env_in :=
      f_make_usable (STM_S.at_usable,
                     ITERATION.at_env_out);

END;
%- - - - - - - - - - - - - - - - - - - - - - - - - - - - - - - - - - -
RULE   r_159 :
STM                    ::= named_stm ID STM
STATIC
   %
   %  STM ::= loop ... or
   %  STM ::= block ...
   %
   TRANSFER at_encl_unit, at_return_required, at_labels;

   STM[1].at_usable := c_no_bl_lab_loops;

   STM[1].at_loops_blocks :=
     tp_bl_lab_loops
        (tp_bl_lab_loop
            (ID.at_designator,
             f_gen_key,
             IF STM[2] IS r_158 THEN
                sc_loop
             ELSE sc_block
             FI))
      + STM[2].at_loops_blocks;

   STM[2].at_env_in :=  f_empty_local_encl_state
                          (f_head_descr
                             (f_identify (ID.at_designator,
                                          STM[1].at_env_in))
                                .s_key,
                           sc_in_body,
                           STM[1].at_env_in);
   %
   % Diana Generation:
   %
   %     Set SM_STM of ID to STM[2]
   %
END;
%- - - - - - - - - - - - - - - - - - - - - - - - - - - - - - - - - - -
RULE   r_160 :
STM                    ::= null_stm
STATIC

   STM.at_usable := c_no_bl_lab_loops;

   STM.at_labels := c_no_bl_lab_loops;

   STM.at_loops_blocks := c_no_bl_lab_loops;

   %C KA/1
   CONDITION
   NOT STM.at_return_required
      MESSAGE
      "Warning : Return should appear after this statement.";

END;
%- - - - - - - - - - - - - - - - - - - - - - - - - - - - - - - - - - -
```

```
RULE   r_161 :
STM                     ::= return EXP_VOID
STATIC

   TRANSFER at_env_in;

   STM.at_usable := c_no_bl_lab_loops;

   STM.at_labels := c_no_bl_lab_loops;

   STM.at_loops_blocks := c_no_bl_lab_loops;

   %C 5.8/1, 5.8/4
   CONDITION
   (STM.at_encl_unit.s_nature = sc_function)
   OR (STM.at_encl_unit.s_nature = sc_procedure)
   OR (STM.at_encl_unit.s_nature = sc_entry)
      MESSAGE
      "Return may only appear within function, procedure, accept.";

   %C 5.8/2
   CONDITION
   (STM.at_encl_unit.s_nature = sc_function)
   XOR (EXP_VOID IS r_109)                              % void
      MESSAGE
      "A return statement for a function must include an expression.";
   %RECOVER replace_by (null_stm)

   EXP_VOID.at_expected :=
      CASE c_den : f_encl_except_bl_loop (STM.at_env_in) OF
      IS tp_subpr : CASE c_function : c_den.s_spec OF
                    IS tp_function : c_function.s_result.s_base_type
                    OUT c_no_expected
                    ESAC
      OUT c_no_expected
      ESAC;

   EXP_VOID.at_others_allowed :=
      CASE c_den : f_encl_except_bl_loop (STM.at_env_in) OF
      IS tp_subpr : CASE c_function : c_den.s_spec OF
                    IS tp_function :
                          f_is_array_type1
                             (c_function.s_result,
                              STM.at_env_in) AND
                         (c_function.s_result.s_constraint =/
                          sc_void)
                    OUT FALSE
                    ESAC
      OUT FALSE
      ESAC;

   EXP_VOID.at_discrim_allowed := FALSE;


   %C 5.8/3 checked through overl. resol and EXP_VOID.at_expected ..;

   %C 5.8/4 is checked in f_encl_except_bl_loop;
```

```
   %
   % Diana Generation:
   %
   %     If EXP_VOID is an aggregate or string_literal,
   %     set SM_CONSTRAINT to the function's result type
   %     using enclosing component of the current environment.
   %
END;
%- - - - - - - - - - - - - - - - - - - - - - - - - - - - - - - - - -
RULE   r_162 :
STM                    ::= PRAGMA
STATIC

   TRANSFER at_env_in;

   STM.at_usable := c_no_bl_lab_loops;

   STM.at_labels := c_no_bl_lab_loops;

   STM.at_loops_blocks := c_no_bl_lab_loops;

   %C KA/1
   CONDITION
   NOT STM.at_return_required
      MESSAGE
      "Warning : Return should appear after this statement.";

END;
%- - - - - - - - - - - - - - - - - - - - - - - - - - - - - - - - - -
RULE   r_163:
STMS                   ::=
STATIC

   STMS.at_no_code_stms := TRUE;                         % default

   STMS.at_usable := c_no_bl_lab_loops;

   STMS.at_labels := c_no_bl_lab_loops;

   STMS.at_loops_blocks := c_no_bl_lab_loops;

   STMS.at_first_select := sc_empty;

   STMS.at_first_stm := sc_other_stms;

END;
%- - - - - - - - - - - - - - - - - - - - - - - - - - - - - - - - - -
RULE   r_164 :
STMS                   ::= STM STMS
STATIC

   TRANSFER at_encl_unit, at_env_in;

   STMS[1].at_no_code_stms :=
      NOT (STM IS r_267) AND STMS[2].at_no_code_stms;

   %C 13.8/1
   CONDITION
   (STM IS r_267) XOR                             % code
   STMS[1].at_no_code_stms
      MESSAGE
      "Code procedure may only contain code statements.";
```

```
   STM.at_return_required := STMS[1].at_return_required
                             AND   (STMS[2] IS r_163);

   STMS[2].at_return_required := STMS[1].at_return_required;

   STMS[1].at_usable := STM.at_usable + STMS[2].at_usable;

   STMS[1].at_labels := STM.at_labels + STMS[2].at_labels;

   STMS[1].at_loops_blocks :=
      STM.at_loops_blocks + STMS[2].at_loops_blocks;

   STMS[1].at_first_select :=
      IF STMS[1] IS r_165 THEN                % STM is first
         IF       STM IS r_204 THEN sc_accept
         ELSE IF STM IS r_206 THEN sc_terminate
         ELSE IF STM IS r_207 THEN sc_delay
         ELSE                       sc_other
         FI FI FI
      ELSE
         sc_other
      FI;

   STMS[1].at_first_stm :=
      IF STM IS r_152 THEN
         IF f_head_descr (LAST (STM CONSTITUENTS NAME
               .at_valid)).s_nature = sc_entry THEN
            sc_entry_call
         ELSE sc_other_stms
         FI
      ELSE  sc_other_stms
      FI;

   %
   % Diana Generation:
   %
   %    If STM is a NAME (indexed, selected, used_name_id) then
   %    transform it into entry/procedure call using STM.at_valid.
   %
END;
%- - - - - - - - - - - - - - - - - - - - - - - - - - - - - - - - -
RULE   r_165 :
STM_S                  ::= stm_s  STMS
   %
   %  STMS is not empty
   %
STATIC

   TRANSFER;

END;
```

```
%----------------------------------------------------------------------------
%                                                                          -
% 5.6-7 Subprograms and Packages                                           -
%                                                                          -
%----------------------------------------------------------------------------

%- - - - - - - - - - - - - - - - - - - - - - - - - - - - - - - - - - - - - -
RULE   r_166 :
DECL                  ::= PACKAGE_DECL
STATIC

  TRANSFER

END;
%- - - - - - - - - - - - - - - - - - - - - - - - - - - - - - - - - - - - - -
RULE   r_167 :
DECL                  ::= SUBPROG_DECL
STATIC

  TRANSFER at_env_in, at_env_out, at_keys;

END;
%- - - - - - - - - - - - - - - - - - - - - - - - - - - - - - - - - - - - - -
RULE   r_168 :
DESIGNATOR            ::= ID
STATIC

  DESIGNATOR.at_designator := ID.at_designator;

END;
%- - - - - - - - - - - - - - - - - - - - - - - - - - - - - - - - - - - - - -
RULE   r_169 :
DESIGNATOR            ::= string
STATIC

  DESIGNATOR.at_designator := string.at_designator

END;
%- - - - - - - - - - - - - - - - - - - - - - - - - - - - - - - - - - - - - -
RULE   r_170 :
HEADER                ::= function PARAM_S '%' CONSTRAINED_VOID
STATIC

  PARAM_S.at_encl_unit := tp_encl_unit (sc_function,
                                        IF HEADER.at_is_operator THEN
                                           sc_in_formal_part
                                        ELSE
                                           sc_void_state
                                        FI );

  HEADER.at_encl_unit  := PARAM_S.at_encl_unit;

  HEADER.at_param_no   := PARAM_S.at_param_no;

  PARAM_S.at_env_in :=
     f_update_encl
       (sc_in_formal_part,
        IF HEADER IS r_247 THEN
           sc_generic_function
```

```
        ELSE sc_function
        FI,
        sc_same,
        HEADER.at_env_in);

    CONSTRAINED_VOID.at_env_in := PARAM_S.at_env_out;

    HEADER.at_header :=
      tp_function (f_recent_local
                    (HEADER.at_env_in,
                     PARAM_S.at_env_out),
                  CONSTRAINED_VOID.at_type);

END;
%- - - - - - - - - - - - - - - - - - - - - - - - - - - - - - - - - - - - - - -
RULE   r_171 :
HEADER                  ::= procedure PARAM_S '%'
STATIC

    PARAM_S.at_encl_unit := tp_encl_unit (sc_procedure, sc_void_state);

    HEADER.at_encl_unit := PARAM_S.at_encl_unit;

    HEADER.at_param_no  := 0;

    PARAM_S.at_env_in :=
      f_update_encl
        (sc_in_formal_part,
         IF HEADER IS r_247 THEN
            sc_generic_procedure
         ELSE sc_procedure
         FI,
         sc_same,
         HEADER.at_env_in);

    HEADER.at_header :=
      tp_procedure (f_recent_local
                     (HEADER.at_env_in,
                      PARAM_S.at_env_out));

END;
%- - - - - - - - - - - - - - - - - - - - - - - - - - - - - - - - - - - - - - -
RULE   r_172 :
HEADER                  ::= entry DSCRT_RANGE_VOID PARAM_S '%'
   %
   % only occurs directly within TASK_SPEC
   %
STATIC

    PARAM_S.at_encl_unit := tp_encl_unit (sc_entry, sc_void_state);

    HEADER .at_encl_unit := PARAM_S.at_encl_unit;

    HEADER .at_param_no  := 0;

    DSCRT_RANGE_VOID.at_env_in :=
      f_update_encl
        (sc_id_established,
         IF DSCRT_RANGE_VOID IS r_035 THEN
            sc_entry
         ELSE sc_entry_family
```

```
        FI,
        sc_void,
        HEADER.at_env_in);

   PARAM_S.at_env_in := f_update_encl
                          (sc_in_formal_part,
                           IF DSCRT_RANGE_VOID IS r_035 THEN
                              sc_entry
                           ELSE sc_entry_family
                           FI,
                           sc_void,
                           HEADER.at_env_in);

   HEADER.at_header :=
      IF DSCRT_RANGE_VOID IS r_035 THEN      %DSCRT_RANGE_VOID ::= void
         tp_header (tp_entry
                     (f_local
                        (PARAM_S.at_env_out)))
      ELSE tp_entry_family
           (DSCRT_RANGE_VOID.at_valid,
              tp_entry (f_local (PARAM_S.at_env_out)))
      FI;
END;
%- - - - - - - - - - - - - - - - - - - - - - - - - - - - - - - - - -
RULE   r_173 :
PACKAGE_DECL             ::= package_decl ID PACKAGE_DEF
STATIC

   PACKAGE_DECL.at_keys := f_gen_keys;

   PACKAGE_DEF.at_env_in :=
      f_add_descr
         (ID.at_designator,
          HEAD (PACKAGE_DECL.at_keys),
          sc_id_established,
          sc_package,
          sc_void,
          PACKAGE_DECL.at_env_in);

   PACKAGE_DEF.at_keys := PACKAGE_DECL.at_keys;

   PACKAGE_DECL.at_env_out :=
      CASE c_def : PACKAGE_DEF.at_def OF
      IS tp_instantiation :
         f_expand_instantiation
            (c_def.s_name,
             c_def.s_assocs,
             sc_package,
             HEAD (PACKAGE_DECL.at_keys),
             PACKAGE_DEF.at_env_in)
      OUT f_update_descrs_by_keys
            (PACKAGE_DECL.at_keys,

             c_start_repr,

             IF f_body_required (PACKAGE_DEF.at_def) THEN
                sc_spec_complete
             ELSE sc_complete
```

```
            FI,

            sc_package,

            CASE c_def : PACKAGE_DEF.at_def OF
            IS tp_package   : c_def;
            IS tp_rename    : c_def.s_descr.s_den QUA tp_package
            OUT sc_void % IS tp_instantiation
            ESAC,

            PACKAGE_DEF.at_env_in)
    ESAC;

  %
  % Diana Generation:
  %
  %    Initialize SM_BODY and SM_ADDRESS of ID with void.
  %    Set SM_SPEC of ID to PACKAGE_DEF.
  %
  %    If PACKAGE_DEF is an instantiation, then at_def.s_name
  %    of PACKAGE_DEF denotes the generic package.
  %    Create declarations for the generic parameters and
  %    set SM_ACTUAL_DECL_S of PACKAGE_DEF using PACKAGE_DEF.at_def.
  %    Then perform instantiation of the specification using
  %    PACKAGE_DEF.at_def and set SM_SPEC of ID
  %    to this new specification.
  %
  %    If PACKAGE_DEF is a rename node, then at_def.s_descr
  %    of PACKAGE_DEF denotes the renamed package. Set
  %    SM_SPEC of ID to SM_SPEC of this renamed package.
  %
END;
%- - - - - - - - - - - - - - - - - - - - - - - - - - - - - - - - - -
RULE   r_174 :
PACKAGE_DEF            ::= RENAME
STATIC

  PACKAGE_DEF.at_def := RENAME.at_rename;

  TRANSFER  at_env_in, at_keys;

END;
%- - - - - - - - - - - - - - - - - - - - - - - - - - - - - - - - - -
RULE   r_175 :
PACKAGE_DEF            ::= INSTANTIATION
STATIC

  TRANSFER at_env_in;

  PACKAGE_DEF.at_def := INSTANTIATION.at_instantiation;

END;
%- - - - - - - - - - - - - - - - - - - - - - - - - - - - - - - - - -
RULE   r_176 :
PACKAGE_DEF            ::= PACKAGE_SPEC
STATIC

  PACKAGE_SPEC.at_env_in := f_empty_local_encl_state
                              (HEAD (PACKAGE_DEF.at_keys),
                               sc_in_visible,
```

```
                              PACKAGE_DEF.at_env_in);

   PACKAGE_DEF.at_def := PACKAGE_SPEC.at_spec;

END;
%- - - - - - - - - - - - - - - - - - - - - - - - - - - - - - - - - - - -
RULE   r_177 :
PACKAGE_SPEC            ::= package_spec DECL_S '%' DECL_REP_S '%'
STATIC

   DECL_S.at_encl_unit := tp_encl_unit(sc_package, sc_in_visible);

   DECL_REP_S.at_encl_unit := tp_encl_unit(sc_package, sc_in_private);

   DECL_S.at_user_reps := DECL_REP_S.at_user_reps;

   DECL_S.at_env_in :=
      f_update_encl_state
         (sc_in_visible,
          PACKAGE_SPEC.at_env_in);

   %C 3.8/2
   CONDITION
      ch_all_types_completed (f_local (DECL_S.at_env_out))
      MESSAGE
      "missing full declarations for incomplete types";

   DECL_REP_S.at_env_in := f_update_encl_state
                              (sc_in_private,
                               DECL_S.at_env_out);

   %C 7.4/2, C 7.4/3, C 7.4.1/1
   CONDITION
      ch_all_private_completed
         (f_local (DECL_REP_S.at_env_out))
      MESSAGE
      "missing full decls for private types/deferred consants";

   %C 3.8/2
   CONDITION
      ch_all_types_completed (f_recent_local
                                (DECL_S.at_env_out,
                                 DECL_REP_S.at_env_out))
      MESSAGE
      "missing full declaration for incomplete types";

   PACKAGE_SPEC.at_spec :=
      tp_package
       (f_recent_local (PACKAGE_SPEC.at_env_in,
                        DECL_S.at_env_out),
        f_recent_local (PACKAGE_SPEC.at_env_in,
                        DECL_REP_S.at_env_out),
        f_subtr_n
           (f_imported (DECL_REP_S.at_env_out),
            LENGTH (f_imported (PACKAGE_SPEC.at_env_in))),
        FALSE);

END;
%- - - - - - - - - - - - - - - - - - - - - - - - - - - - - - - - - - - -
RULE   r_178 :
```

```
PACKAGE_BODY           ::= package_body ID BLOCK_STUB
STATIC

   TRANSFER at_block_no;

   BLOCK_STUB.at_encl_unit := tp_encl_unit (sc_package, sc_in_body);

   PACKAGE_BODY.at_keys :=
      f_prev_defs
         (tp_designator_list (ID.at_designator),
          sc_package,
          PACKAGE_BODY.at_env_in);

   %C GAP
   CONDITION
      NOT f_new_key (HEAD (PACKAGE_BODY.at_keys),
                     PACKAGE_BODY.at_env_in)
      MESSAGE
      "missing package specification for package body ";

   BLOCK_STUB.at_env_in :=
      f_update_add_descrs
         (PACKAGE_BODY.at_keys,
          tp_designator_list (ID.at_designator),
          sc_in_body,
          sc_package,
          sc_same,
          PACKAGE_BODY.at_env_in);

   BLOCK_STUB.at_keys := PACKAGE_BODY.at_keys;


   PACKAGE_BODY.at_env_out :=
      f_mark_body_prov
         (PACKAGE_BODY.at_keys,
          BLOCK_STUB.at_env_in);

   %
   % Diana Generation:
   %
   %  1)If it is a generic package, transform ID to
   %    a generic_id and set SM_GENERIC_PARAM_S using
   %    PACKAGE_BODY.at_keys.
   %
   %  2)Adjust SM_BODY of AS_ID (PACKAGE_DECL) to BLOCK_STUB
   %    using PACKAGE_BODY.at_keys.
   %    Set SM_BODY of ID to BLOCK_STUB.
   %    Set SM_SPEC of ID using PACKAGE_BODY.at_keys.
   %    If it is not a generic package, copy the value of SM_ADDRESS
   %    from AS_ID (PACKAGE_DECL) using PACKAGE_BODY.at_keys.
   %
END;
%- - - - - - - - - - - - - - - - - - - - - - - - - - - - - - - - - -
RULE   r_179 :
PARAM                  ::= in ID_S '%' CONSTRAINED EXP_VOID
STATIC

   TRANSFER at_param_no;

   %C 6.7/3
```

```
CONDITION
 (PARAM.at_encl_unit.s_state =/ sc_in_formal_part)
OR (EXP_VOID IS r_109)                              % void
   MESSAGE
   "Default values are not allowed in operator declarations.";
%RECOVER delete  (EXP_VOID)

 PARAM.at_keys := f_gen_keylist (ID_S.at_designators);

 CONSTRAINED.at_discrim_allowed := FALSE;

 CONSTRAINED.at_env_in := f_add_descrs
                            (ID_S.at_designators,
                             PARAM.at_keys,
                             sc_id_established,
                             sc_in,
                             sc_void,
                             PARAM.at_env_in);

 EXP_VOID.at_expected := CONSTRAINED.at_type.s_base_type;


 EXP_VOID.at_others_allowed := FALSE;

 EXP_VOID.at_discrim_allowed := FALSE;

 EXP_VOID.at_env_in := f_update_descrs_by_keys
                          (PARAM.at_keys,
                           c_start_repr,
                           sc_in_init,
                           sc_in,
                           tp_object
                              (CONSTRAINED.at_type,
                               c_no_init),
                           CONSTRAINED.at_env_in);

PARAM.at_env_out :=
   f_update_descrs_by_keys
      (PARAM.at_keys,
       sc_same,
       sc_complete,
       sc_same,
       sc_same,
       CASE c_allowed : EXP_VOID.at_valid OF
       IS tp_void : EXP_VOID.at_env_in;
       IS tp_descr_set :
          f_update_descrs_by_keys
             (PARAM.at_keys,
              sc_same,
              sc_same,
              sc_in,
              tp_object
                 (CONSTRAINED.at_type,
                  f_object_init (c_allowed)),
             EXP_VOID.at_env_in)
       ESAC);

%C 3.2/1, C 3.6.3/1, C 7.4/1
CONDITION
  IF EXP_VOID IS r_108 THEN
```

```
        ch_is_assign_allowed_for_type
           (CONSTRAINED.at_type,
            PARAM.at_env_in)
      ELSE TRUE
      FI
      MESSAGE
      "initialization forbidden for objects of this type";

   %
   % Diana Generation:
   %
   %     Set SM_OBJ_TYPE of all ID_S to CONSTRAINED
   %     Set SM_INIT_EXP of all ID_S to EXP_VOID
   %
END;
%- - - - - - - - - - - - - - - - - - - - - - - - - - - - - - - - - -
RULE   r_180 :
PARAM                 ::= in_out ID_S '%' CONSTRAINED EXP_VOID
   %
   %  EXP_VOID ::= void
   %
STATIC
   TRANSFER at_param_no;
   %C 6.5/1
   CONDITION
   PARAM.at_encl_unit.s_nature =/ sc_function
     MESSAGE
     "A function may only have parameters of mode IN.";

   PARAM.at_keys := f_gen_keylist (ID_S.at_designators);

   CONSTRAINED.at_discrim_allowed := FALSE;

   CONSTRAINED.at_env_in := f_add_descrs
                              (ID_S.at_designators,
                               PARAM.at_keys,
                               sc_id_established,
                               sc_in_out,
                               sc_void,
                               PARAM.at_env_in);

   EXP_VOID.at_expected := CONSTRAINED.at_type.s_base_type;

   %C 9.2/2
   CONDITION
   NOT (f_is_task_type (CONSTRAINED.at_type, PARAM.at_env_in))
      MESSAGE "in out parameters must not be of a task type";

   EXP_VOID.at_others_allowed := FALSE;

   EXP_VOID.at_discrim_allowed := FALSE;

   EXP_VOID.at_env_in :=
      f_update_descrs_by_keys
         (PARAM.at_keys,
          c_start_repr,
          sc_complete,
          sc_in_out,
          tp_object
             (CONSTRAINED.at_type,
              c_no_init),
          CONSTRAINED.at_env_in);
```

```
   PARAM.at_env_out := EXP_VOID.at_env_in;

   %C 6.1/3 checked by the syntax;

   %
   % Diana Generation:
   %
   %     Set SM_OBJ_TYPE of all ID_S to CONSTRAINED
   %
END;
%- - - - - - - - - - - - - - - - - - - - - - - - - - - - - - - - - - - -
RULE   r_181 :
PARAM                ::= out ID_S '%' CONSTRAINED EXP_VOID
   %
   %  EXP_VOID ::= void
   %
STATIC
   TRANSFER at_param_no;
   %C 6.5/1
   CONDITION
   PARAM.at_encl_unit.s_nature =/ sc_function
      MESSAGE "A function may only have parameters of mode IN.";

   %C 12.1.1/1
   CONDITION
   PARAM.at_encl_unit.s_state =/ sc_in_generic_part
      MESSAGE
      "The mode OUT is not allowed for generic parameters.";

   PARAM.at_keys := f_gen_keylist (ID_S.at_designators);

   CONSTRAINED.at_discrim_allowed := FALSE;

   CONSTRAINED.at_env_in := f_add_descrs
                             (ID_S.at_designators,
                              PARAM.at_keys,
                              sc_id_established,
                              sc_out,
                              sc_void,
                              PARAM.at_env_in);

   EXP_VOID.at_expected := CONSTRAINED.at_type.s_base_type;

   %C 9.2/2
   CONDITION
      NOT (f_is_task_type (CONSTRAINED.at_type, PARAM.at_env_in))
      MESSAGE
      "out parameters may not be of task type";

   EXP_VOID.at_others_allowed := FALSE;

   EXP_VOID.at_discrim_allowed := FALSE;

   EXP_VOID.at_env_in := f_update_descrs_by_keys
                          (PARAM.at_keys,
                           c_start_repr,
                           sc_complete,
                           sc_out,
                           tp_object
                              (CONSTRAINED.at_type,
                               c_no_init),
```

```
                              CONSTRAINED.at_env_in);

   PARAM.at_env_out := EXP_VOID.at_env_in;

   %C 6.1/3 checked by the syntax;

   %
   % Diana Generation:
   %
   %    Set SM_OBJ_TYPE of all ID_S to CONSTRAINED
   %
END;
%- - - - - - - - - - - - - - - - - - - - - - - - - - - - - - - - - - - -
RULE   r_182:
PARAMS                  ::=
STATIC

   PARAMS.at_param_no := 0;

   PARAMS.at_env_out := PARAMS.at_env_in;

END;
%- - - - - - - - - - - - - - - - - - - - - - - - - - - - - - - - - - - -
RULE   r_183 :
PARAMS                  ::= PARAM PARAMS
STATIC

   TRANSFER at_encl_unit;

   PARAMS[1].at_param_no  := PARAM.at_param_no + PARAMS[2].at_param_no;

   PARAMS[2].at_env_in   := PARAM.at_env_out;

   PARAMS[1].at_env_out  := PARAMS[2].at_env_out;

   PARAM.at_env_in        := PARAMS[1].at_env_in;

END;
%- - - - - - - - - - - - - - - - - - - - - - - - - - - - - - - - - - - -
RULE   r_184 :
PARAM_S                 ::= param_s PARAMS
STATIC

   TRANSFER;

END;
%- - - - - - - - - - - - - - - - - - - - - - - - - - - - - - - - - - - -
RULE   r_185:
PARAM_ASSOCS            ::=
STATIC

   PARAM_ASSOCS.at_assocs := tp_assoc_list ();

END;
%- - - - - - - - - - - - - - - - - - - - - - - - - - - - - - - - - - - -
RULE   r_186 :
PARAM_ASSOCS            ::= PARAM_ASSOC PARAM_ASSOCS
STATIC

   TRANSFER at_env_in;
```

```
   PARAM_ASSOCS[1].at_assocs := tp_assoc_list (PARAM_ASSOC.at_assoc) +
                                    PARAM_ASSOCS[2].at_assocs;

END;
%- - - - - - - - - - - - - - - - - - - - - - - - - - - - - - - - - - -
RULE   r_187 :
PARAM_ASSOC_S            ::= param_assoc_s PARAM_ASSOCS
STATIC

   TRANSFER;

END;
%- - - - - - - - - - - - - - - - - - - - - - - - - - - - - - - - - - -
RULE   r_188 :
PARAM_ASSOC              ::= ASSOC
STATIC

   TRANSFER at_env_in;

   ASSOC.at_expected_in := c_empty_descrs;

   ASSOC.at_others_allowed := FALSE;

   PARAM_ASSOC.at_assoc := ASSOC.at_valid;

   ASSOC.at_valid := ASSOC.at_allowed2;

END;
%- - - - - - - - - - - - - - - - - - - - - - - - - - - - - - - - - - -
RULE   r_189 :
PARAM_ASSOC              ::= EXP
STATIC

   TRANSFER at_env_in;

   EXP.at_context := sc_id_not_visible;

   EXP.at_others_allowed := FALSE;

   EXP.at_expected := c_no_expected;

   EXP.at_with_use := f_use_required (EXP.at_allowed1);

   EXP.at_valid := c_error_descr_set;          %SUPPRESS ERROR MESSAGES

   PARAM_ASSOC.at_assoc := tp_comp_assoc
                              (tp_choice_list (),
                               EXP.at_allowed2);

END;
%- - - - - - - - - - - - - - - - - - - - - - - - - - - - - - - - - - -
RULE   r_190 :
SUBPROG_DECL             ::= subprog_decl DESIGNATOR HEADER SUBPROG_DEF
   %
   %  SUBPROG_DEF ::= FORMAL_SUBPROG_DEF <=>
   %  SUBPROG_DECL is GENERIC_PARAM
   %
STATIC

   HEADER.at_is_operator := DESIGNATOR IS r_169; % string
```

```
%C 4.5/1=6.7/1, 6.7/2, 6.7/5
CONDITION
DESIGNATOR IS r_168   % ID
OR (ch_operator_string (DESIGNATOR.at_designator QUA SYMB)
AND ch_param_number (DESIGNATOR.at_designator QUA SYMB,
                     HEADER.at_param_no))
   MESSAGE "Illegal operator definition.";

SUBPROG_DECL.at_keys    := f_gen_keys;

SUBPROG_DECL.at_env :=
   f_add_descr
      (DESIGNATOR.at_designator,
       HEAD (SUBPROG_DECL.at_keys),
       sc_id_established,
       sc_void_nature,
       sc_void,
       SUBPROG_DECL.at_env_in);

HEADER.at_env_in := f_empty_local_encl_state
                       (HEAD (SUBPROG_DECL.at_keys),
                        sc_in_formal_part,
                        SUBPROG_DECL.at_env);

SUBPROG_DECL.at_header := HEADER.at_header;

SUBPROG_DEF.at_env_in := f_update_descrs_by_keys
                            (SUBPROG_DECL.at_keys,
                             c_start_repr,
                             sc_id_established,
                             IF HEADER.at_header IS tp_procedure THEN
                                sc_procedure
                             ELSE sc_function
                             FI,
                             tp_subpr
                                (HEADER.at_header,
                                 sc_void,
                                 sc_no_predef_op),
                             SUBPROG_DECL.at_env);

SUBPROG_DEF.at_keys   := SUBPROG_DECL.at_keys;

SUBPROG_DECL.at_env_out :=
   f_add_n_equal_descr
      (DESIGNATOR.at_designator,
       f_gen_key,
       tp_subpr (HEADER.at_header,
                 HEAD (SUBPROG_DECL.at_keys),
                 sc_no_predef_op),
       TRUE,

       f_make_derivable
          (HEAD (SUBPROG_DECL.at_keys),
           CASE c_def : SUBPROG_DEF.at_def OF
           IS tp_instantiation :
              f_expand_instantiation
                 (c_def.s_name,
                  c_def.s_assocs,
                  IF HEADER.at_header IS tp_function THEN
                     sc_function
                  ELSE sc_procedure
```

```
                FI,
                HEAD (SUBPROG_DECL.at_keys),
                SUBPROG_DECL.at_env)
        OUT f_update_descrs_by_keys
                (SUBPROG_DECL.at_keys,

                 sc_same,

                 IF SUBPROG_DEF.at_def IS tp_void THEN
                    IF HEADER.at_header IS tp_entry OR
                       (HEADER.at_header IS tp_entry_family) THEN
                       sc_complete
                    ELSE sc_spec_complete
                    FI
                 ELSE sc_complete
                 FI,

                 CASE HEADER.at_header OF
                 IS tp_procedure    : sc_procedure;
                 IS tp_function     : sc_function;
                 IS tp_entry        : sc_entry;
                 IS tp_entry_family : sc_entry_family
                 ESAC,

                 CASE c_header : HEADER.at_header OF
                 IS tp_entry : tp_den (c_header);
                 IS tp_entry_family : tp_den (c_header);
                 IS tp_procedure : IS tp_function :
                    tp_subpr
                      (HEADER.at_header,
                       SUBPROG_DEF.at_def,
                       sc_no_predef_op)
                 ESAC,

                 SUBPROG_DECL.at_env)
        ESAC));

%C 6.7/3, C 6.7/4
CONDITION
   ch_operator_overloading (DESIGNATOR.at_designator,
                            HEADER.at_header,
                            SUBPROG_DECL.at_env_out)
   MESSAGE
   "illegal operator overloading";


%C 6.6/1 checked by f_update current;

%
% Diana Generation:
%
%  1)If the subprogram renames an entry then transform
%    DESIGNATOR to an entry_id using SUBPROG_DEF.at_keys.
%
%  2)Initialize SM_BODY of DESIGNATOR with void.
%    Initialize SM_LOCATION (SM_ADDRESS if it is an entry)
%    of DESIGNATOR to void.
%    Set SM_SPEC of DESIGNATOR to HEADER.
%
%    If SUBPROG_DEF is an instantiation, then at_def.s_name
```

```
%    of SUBPROG_DEF denotes the generic subprogram.
%    Create declarations for the generic parameters and
%    set SM_ACTUAL_DECL_S of SUBPROG_DEF using SUBPROG_DEF.at_def.
%    Then perform instantiation of the specification using
%    SUBPROG_DEF.at_def and set SM_SPEC of DESIGNATOR
%    to this new specification.
%
%
END;
%- - - - - - - - - - - - - - - - - - - - - - - - - - - - - - - - - - -
RULE  r_191 :
SUBPROG_DEF            ::= RENAME
STATIC

   SUBPROG_DEF.at_def := RENAME.at_rename;

   TRANSFER  at_env_in, at_keys;

END;
%- - - - - - - - - - - - - - - - - - - - - - - - - - - - - - - - - - -
RULE   r_192 :
SUBPROG_DEF            ::= void
STATIC

   SUBPROG_DEF.at_def := sc_void;

END;
%- - - - - - - - - - - - - - - - - - - - - - - - - - - - - - - - - - -
RULE   r_193 :
SUBPROG_DEF            ::= INSTANTIATION
STATIC

   TRANSFER at_env_in;

   SUBPROG_DEF.at_def := INSTANTIATION.at_instantiation;

END;
%- - - - - - - - - - - - - - - - - - - - - - - - - - - - - - - - - - -
RULE   r_194 :
SUBPROG_DEF            ::= FORMAL_SUBPROG_DEF
STATIC

   TRANSFER at_def, at_env_in;

END;
%- - - - - - - - - - - - - - - - - - - - - - - - - - - - - - - - - - -
RULE   r_195 :
SUBPROG_BODY           ::= subprog_body DESIGNATOR HEADER BLOCK_STUB
STATIC

   TRANSFER at_block_no;

   BLOCK_STUB.at_encl_unit :=
      tp_encl_unit (HEADER.at_encl_unit.s_nature,
                    sc_in_body);

   HEADER.at_is_operator := DESIGNATOR IS r_169;      % string

   %C 4.5/1=6.7/1, 6.7/2, 6.7/5
   CONDITION
```

```
(DESIGNATOR IS r_168)    % ID
OR (ch_operator_string (DESIGNATOR.at_designator QUA SYMB)
AND ch_param_number (DESIGNATOR.at_designator QUA SYMB,
                     HEADER.at_param_no))
   MESSAGE
   "Illegal operator definition.";

SUBPROG_BODY.at_keys1 := f_prev_def_generic
                            (DESIGNATOR.at_designator,
                             IF HEADER IS r_171 THEN
                                sc_generic_procedure
                             ELSE sc_generic_function
                             FI,
                             SUBPROG_BODY.at_env_in);

SUBPROG_BODY.at_env :=
   IF f_new_key (HEAD (SUBPROG_BODY.at_keys1),
                 SUBPROG_BODY.at_env_in) THEN
      f_add_descr
         (DESIGNATOR.at_designator,
          HEAD (SUBPROG_BODY.at_keys1),
          sc_id_established,
          IF HEADER IS r_171 THEN
             sc_procedure
          ELSE sc_function
          FI,
          sc_void,
          SUBPROG_BODY.at_env_in)
   ELSE SUBPROG_BODY.at_env_in
   FI;

HEADER.at_env_in :=
   f_new_local
     (f_make_local1
        (HEAD (SUBPROG_BODY.at_keys1),
         SUBPROG_BODY.at_env),
      HEAD (SUBPROG_BODY.at_keys1),
      SUBPROG_BODY.at_env);

%C
CONDITION
   IF f_new_key (HEAD (SUBPROG_BODY.at_keys1),
                 SUBPROG_BODY.at_env_in) THEN
      TRUE
   ELSE
      f_same_subpr_spec
         (HEADER.at_header,
          f_spec (f_select_by_key (HEAD (SUBPROG_BODY.at_keys1),
                                   SUBPROG_BODY.at_env)))
   FI
   MESSAGE
   "subprog body does not match generic declaration";

SUBPROG_BODY.at_keys2 :=
   IF f_new_key (HEAD (SUBPROG_BODY.at_keys1),
                 SUBPROG_BODY.at_env_in) THEN
      f_prev_def_subpr
         (DESIGNATOR.at_designator,
          SUBPROG_BODY.at_keys1,
          HEADER.at_header,
```

```
         f_local (SUBPROG_BODY.at_env_in))
   ELSE SUBPROG_BODY.at_keys1
   FI;

BLOCK_STUB.at_env_in :=
   IF f_new_key (HEAD (SUBPROG_BODY.at_keys2),
                 SUBPROG_BODY.at_env_in) THEN
      f_add_local_descrs
         (tp_descr_list
            (f_descr
               (DESIGNATOR.at_designator,
                HEAD (SUBPROG_BODY.at_keys2),
                c_start_repr,
                sc_in_body,

                IF HEADER.at_header IS tp_procedure THEN
                   sc_procedure
                ELSE sc_function
                FI,

                tp_subpr
                   (HEADER.at_header,
                    sc_void,
                    sc_no_predef_op),

                f_enclosing (SUBPROG_BODY.at_env_in))),

         f_add_n_equal_descr
            (DESIGNATOR.at_designator,
             f_gen_key,
             tp_subpr (HEADER.at_header,
                       HEAD (SUBPROG_BODY.at_keys2),
                       sc_no_predef_op),
             FALSE,
             SUBPROG_BODY.at_env_in))
   ELSE f_update_descrs_by_keys
           (SUBPROG_BODY.at_keys2,
            sc_same,
            sc_in_body,
            sc_same,
            sc_same,
            SUBPROG_BODY.at_env_in)
   FI;

BLOCK_STUB.at_keys := SUBPROG_BODY.at_keys2;

SUBPROG_BODY.at_env_out :=
   f_update_descrs_by_keys
      (SUBPROG_BODY.at_keys2,
       sc_same,
       sc_complete,
       sc_same,
       sc_same,
       BLOCK_STUB.at_env_in);

%C 6.7/3, C 6.7/4
CONDITION
   IF f_new_key (HEAD (SUBPROG_BODY.at_keys2),
                 SUBPROG_BODY.at_env_in) THEN
      ch_operator_overloading (DESIGNATOR.at_designator,
```

```
                                   HEADER.at_header,
                                   SUBPROG_BODY.at_env_out)
     ELSE TRUE %checked in subpr. specification
     FI
     MESSAGE
     "illegal operator overloading";

   %C 6.6/1 checked by f_update_descr_by_keys/f_update_descrs_by_keys;

   %
   % Diana Generation:
   %
   %  1)If it is a generic subprogram, transform DESIGNATOR
   %    to a generic_id/generic_op and set SM_GENERIC_PARAM_S
   %    using SUBPROG_BODY.at_keys.
   %
   %  2)Adjust SM_BODY of AS_DESIGNATOR(SUBPROG_DECL) using
   %    SUBPROG_BODY.at_keys2 to BLOCK_STUB.
   %    Set SM_BODY of DESIGNATOR to BLOCK_STUB.
   %    Set SM_SPEC of DESIGNATOR using SUBPROG_BODY.at_keys2.
   %    If it is not a generic subprogram copy value of SM_ADDRESS from
   %    AS_DESIGNATOR (SUBPROG_DECL) using SUBPROG_BODY.at_keys2.
   %
END;
```

```
%-----------------------------------------------------------------------
%
% 5.8. Visibility Rules
%
%-----------------------------------------------------------------------

%- - - - - - - - - - - - - - - - - - - - - - - - - - - - - - - - - - - -
RULE   r_196 :
RENAME                 ::= rename NAME
STATIC

   TRANSFER at_env_in;

   NAME.at_expected := c_no_expected;

   NAME.at_context := sc_string_is_name;

   NAME.at_with_use := f_use_required (NAME.at_allowed1);

   NAME.at_valid := cf_unique_descr
                     (f_valid_renamed
                         (NAME.at_allowed2,
                          f_select_by_key
                             (HEAD (RENAME.at_keys),
                              RENAME.at_env_in),
                          RENAME.at_env_in),
                      FALSE,
                      RENAME.at_env_in);
   %C 8.5/1
   CONDITION
      ch_existence_depends_not_for_obj (NAME.at_valid,
                                        NAME.at_env_in);

   RENAME.at_rename := tp_rename
                        (HEAD (NAME.at_valid.s_descrs));

END;
%- - - - - - - - - - - - - - - - - - - - - - - - - - - - - - - - - - - -
RULE   r_197 :
USE                    ::= use NAMES '%'
STATIC

   TRANSFER at_env_in;

   USE.at_env_out := f_add_imported_descrs
                      (cf_packages (NAMES.at_names),
                       USE.at_env_in)

END;
```

```
%-----------------------------------------------------------------------
%                                                                      -
% 5.9. Tasks                                                           -
%                                                                      -
%-----------------------------------------------------------------------


%- - - - - - - - - - - - - - - - - - - - - - - - - - - - - - - - - - -
RULE   r_198 :
SELECT_CLAUSE            ::= select_clause EXP_VOID STM_S '%'
STATIC

   STM_S.at_return_required := SELECT_CLAUSE.at_return_required ;

   STM_S.at_encl_unit := SELECT_CLAUSE.at_encl_unit;

   SELECT_CLAUSE.at_labels := STM_S.at_labels;

   SELECT_CLAUSE.at_loops_blocks := STM_S.at_loops_blocks;

   SELECT_CLAUSE.at_first_select := STM_S.at_first_select;

   EXP_VOID.at_expected := c_bool;

   EXP_VOID.at_others_allowed := FALSE;

   EXP_VOID.at_discrim_allowed := FALSE;

   EXP_VOID.at_env_in := SELECT_CLAUSE.at_env_in;

   STM_S.at_env_in :=
      f_make_usable (STM_S.at_usable,
                     SELECT_CLAUSE.at_env_in);

   %C 3.5.3/1, C 5.3/1  checked through EXP_VOID.at_expected :=
   %                                  and cf_unique_descr;

END;
%- - - - - - - - - - - - - - - - - - - - - - - - - - - - - - - - - - -
RULE   r_199 :
SELECT_CLAUSES           ::= SELECT_CLAUSE SELECT_CLAUSES
STATIC

   TRANSFER at_return_required, at_encl_unit, at_env_in;

   SELECT_CLAUSES[1].at_labels := SELECT_CLAUSE.at_labels
                                  + SELECT_CLAUSES[2].at_labels;

   SELECT_CLAUSES[1].at_loops_blocks :=
      SELECT_CLAUSE.at_loops_blocks
      + SELECT_CLAUSES[2].at_loops_blocks;

   SELECT_CLAUSES[2].at_select_state :=
      CASE SELECT_CLAUSE.at_first_select OF
      sc_accept :
         tp_select_state( TRUE,
                          SELECT_CLAUSES[1].at_select_state.s_delay,
                          SELECT_CLAUSES[1].at_select_state.s_terminate,
                          SELECT_CLAUSES[1].at_select_state.s_else);
```

```
     sc_delay :
       (tp_select_state (SELECT_CLAUSES[1].at_select_state.s_accept,
                         TRUE,
                         SELECT_CLAUSES[1].at_select_state.s_terminate
                         SELECT_CLAUSES[1].at_select_state.s_else)

        %C 9.7.1/2
        CONDITION
        NOT SELECT_CLAUSES[1].at_select_state.s_terminate
           MESSAGE
           "Selective wait may not contain terminate and delay.")

     OUT    % stm_terminate :
      ((tp_select_state( SELECT_CLAUSES[1].at_select_state.s_accept,
                         SELECT_CLAUSES[1].at_select_state.s_delay,
                         TRUE,
                         SELECT_CLAUSES[1].at_select_state.s_else)

        %C 9.7.1/2
        CONDITION
        NOT SELECT_CLAUSES[1].at_select_state.s_delay
           MESSAGE
           "Selective wait may not contain terminate and delay.")

        %C 9.7.1/1
        CONDITION
        NOT SELECT_CLAUSES[1].at_select_state.s_terminate
           MESSAGE
           "At most one terminate per selective wait allowed.")
     ESAC;

END;
%- - - - - - - - - - - - - - - - - - - - - - - - - - - - - - - - - - -
RULE   r_200 :
SELECT_CLAUSE_S       ::= select_clause_s SELECT_CLAUSES
STATIC

   TRANSFER

END;
%- - - - - - - - - - - - - - - - - - - - - - - - - - - - - - - - - - -
RULE   r_201 :
SELECT_CLAUSES        ::=
STATIC

   SELECT_CLAUSES.at_labels := c_no_bl_lab_loops;

   SELECT_CLAUSES.at_loops_blocks := c_no_bl_lab_loops;

   %C 9.7.1/3
   CONDITION
   NOT ((SELECT_CLAUSES.at_select_state.s_delay
       OR SELECT_CLAUSES.at_select_state.s_terminate)
      AND SELECT_CLAUSES.at_select_state.s_else)
     MESSAGE
     "Else part prohibited with delay or terminate ";

   %C 9.7.1/4
   CONDITION
   SELECT_CLAUSES.at_select_state.s_accept
```

```
    MESSAGE
    "At least one accept alternative required in selective wait.";
END;
%- - - - - - - - - - - - - - - - - - - - - - - - - - - - - - - - - -
RULE r_202 :
DECL                  ::= task_decl ID TASK_DEF
STATIC

   DECL.at_keys := f_gen_keys;

   TASK_DEF.at_env_in :=
      f_add_descr
         (ID.at_designator,
          HEAD (DECL.at_keys),
          sc_id_established,
          sc_task,
          sc_void,
          DECL.at_env_in);

   TASK_DEF.at_keys := IF TASK_DEF IS r_211 THEN
                          f_gen_keys
                       ELSE DECL.at_keys
                       FI;

   DECL.at_env_out :=
      f_add_local_descrs
         (TASK_DEF.at_impl_descrs,
          f_update_descrs_by_keys
             (DECL.at_keys,
              sc_same,
              sc_complete,
              sc_task,
              CASE c_def : TASK_DEF.at_def OF
              IS tp_rename :  c_def.s_descr.s_den;
              IS tp_constrained: tp_object
                                   (c_def,
                                    c_init)
              ESAC,
              TASK_DEF.at_env_in));

   %
   % Diana Generation:
   %
   %    Set SM_OBJ_TYPE of ID to TASK_DEF. If TASK_DEF is
   %    a rename node set SM_OBJ_TYPE using TASK_DEF.at_def.
   %    Set SM_OBJ_DEF of ID to void
   %
END;
%- - - - - - - - - - - - - - - - - - - - - - - - - - - - - - - - - -
RULE   r_203 :
STM                   ::= abort NAME_S '%'
STATIC

   TRANSFER at_env_in;

   STM.at_usable := c_no_bl_lab_loops;

   STM.at_labels := c_no_bl_lab_loops;
```

```
   STM.at_loops_blocks := c_no_bl_lab_loops;

   %C KA/1
   CONDITION
   NOT STM.at_return_required
      MESSAGE
      "Warning : Return should appear after this statement.";

   %C 9.10/1
   CONDITION
   ch_is_tasks (NAME_S.at_names, NAME_S.at_env_in)
      MESSAGE
      "task names expected here";

END;
%- - - - - - - - - - - - - - - - - - - - - - - - - - - - - - - - -
RULE   r_204 :
STM                    ::= accept NAME PARAM_S '%' STM_S '%'
STATIC

   PARAM_S.at_encl_unit := tp_encl_unit (sc_entry,
                                 STM.at_encl_unit.s_state);
   STM_S.at_encl_unit := PARAM_S.at_encl_unit;

   STM_S.at_return_required := FALSE;

   STM.at_usable := c_no_bl_lab_loops;

   STM.at_labels := STM_S.at_labels;

   STM.at_loops_blocks := STM_S.at_loops_blocks;

   %C KA/1
   CONDITION
   NOT STM.at_return_required
      MESSAGE
      "Warning : Return should appear after this statement.";

   NAME.at_expected := c_no_expected;

   NAME.at_context := sc_no_special;

   NAME.at_env_in := STM.at_env_in;

   NAME.at_with_use := f_use_required (NAME.at_allowed1);

   PARAM_S.at_env_in :=  f_empty_local_add_global
                           (f_gen_key,
                            sc_in_formal_part,
                            sc_entry,
                            STM.at_env_in);

   NAME.at_valid :=
      cf_unique_descr
         (f_prev_def_entry
            (NAME.at_allowed2,
             f_local (PARAM_S.at_env_out),
             STM.at_env_in),
          FALSE,
          NAME.at_env_in);
```

```
   %C 9.5/1
   CONDITION
      IF f_head_descr (NAME.at_valid).s_nature = sc_entry THEN
        (TRUE
            %C 9.5/2, C 9.5/3
            CONDITION
               ch_entry_of_current_task (NAME.at_valid,
                                         STM.at_env_in)
               MESSAGE
               "only entries of the enclosing task allowed")
      ELSE f_head_descr (NAME.at_valid).s_nature = sc_error_nature
      FI
      MESSAGE
      "an entry name expected here";

   STM_S.at_env_in :=
      f_make_usable
         (STM_S.at_usable,
          f_update_encl_state
             (sc_in_body,
              PARAM_S.at_env_out));

END;
%- - - - - - - - - - - - - - - - - - - - - - - - - - - - - - - - -
RULE   r_205 :
STM                  ::= cond_entry STM_S '%' STM_S '%'
STATIC

   TRANSFER at_return_required, at_encl_unit;

   STM.at_usable := c_no_bl_lab_loops;

   STM.at_labels := STM_S[1].at_labels + STM_S[2].at_labels;

   STM.at_loops_blocks := STM_S[1].at_loops_blocks +
                                          STM_S[2].at_loops_blocks;

   STM_S[1].at_env_in := f_make_usable (STM_S[1].at_usable,
                                        STM.at_env_in);

   STM_S[2].at_env_in := f_make_usable (STM_S[2].at_usable,
                                        STM.at_env_in);

   %C 9.7.2/1
   CONDITION
      STM_S[1].at_first_stm = sc_entry_call
      MESSAGE
      "first stm after select in cond_entry_call must be entry_call";

END;
%- - - - - - - - - - - - - - - - - - - - - - - - - - - - - - - - -
RULE   r_206 :
STM                  ::= terminate
STATIC

   STM.at_usable := c_no_bl_lab_loops;

   STM.at_labels := c_no_bl_lab_loops;
```

```
   STM.at_loops_blocks  := c_no_bl_lab_loops;

   %C KA/1
   CONDITION
   NOT STM.at_return_required
      MESSAGE
      "Warning : Return should appear after this statement.";

END;
%- - - - - - - - - - - - - - - - - - - - - - - - - - - - - - - - - - - - - - - -
RULE   r_207 :
STM                      ::= delay EXP
STATIC

   STM.at_usable := c_no_bl_lab_loops;

   STM.at_labels := c_no_bl_lab_loops;

   STM.at_loops_blocks  := c_no_bl_lab_loops;

   %C KA/1
   CONDITION
   NOT STM.at_return_required
      MESSAGE
      "Warning : Return should appear after this statement.";

   EXP.at_expected := c_duration;

   EXP.at_context := sc_no_special;

   EXP.at_env_in := STM.at_env_in;

   EXP.at_with_use := f_use_required (EXP.at_allowed1);

   EXP.at_valid := cf_unique_descr (EXP.at_allowed2,
                                    FALSE,
                                    EXP.at_env_in);

   %C 9.6/1  checked by f_allowed_expected

   EXP.at_others_allowed := FALSE;

END;
%- - - - - - - - - - - - - - - - - - - - - - - - - - - - - - - - - - - - - - - -
RULE   r_208 :
STM                      ::= select SELECT_CLAUSE_S '%' STM_S '%'
STATIC

   TRANSFER at_return_required, at_encl_unit;

   STM.at_usable := c_no_bl_lab_loops;

   STM.at_labels := SELECT_CLAUSE_S.at_labels + STM_S.at_labels;

   STM.at_loops_blocks := SELECT_CLAUSE_S.at_loops_blocks +
                                             STM_S.at_loops_blocks;

   SELECT_CLAUSE_S.at_select_state :=
      tp_select_state
```

```
        (FALSE, FALSE, FALSE, STM_S.at_first_select =/ sc_empty);

    SELECT_CLAUSE_S.at_env_in := STM.at_env_in;

    STM_S.at_env_in := f_make_usable (STM_S.at_usable, STM.at_env_in);

END;
%- - - - - - - - - - - - - - - - - - - - - - - - - - - - - - - - - -
RULE   r_209 :
STM                    ::= timed_entry STM_S '%' STM_S '%'
STATIC

    TRANSFER at_return_required, at_encl_unit;

    STM.at_usable := c_no_bl_lab_loops;

    STM.at_labels := STM_S[1].at_labels + STM_S[2].at_labels;

    STM.at_loops_blocks := STM_S[1].at_loops_blocks +
                                      STM_S[2].at_loops_blocks;

    STM_S[1].at_env_in := f_make_usable (STM_S[1].at_usable,
                                      STM.at_env_in);

    STM_S[2].at_env_in := f_make_usable (STM_S[2].at_usable,
                                      STM.at_env_in);
    %C 9.7.3/1
    CONDITION
    STM_S[1].at_first_stm = sc_entry_call
       MESSAGE
       "first stm after select in timed_entry_call must be entry_call";

END;
%- - - - - - - - - - - - - - - - - - - - - - - - - - - - - - - - - -
RULE r_210 :
TASK_DEF               ::= RENAME
STATIC

    TRANSFER at_env_in, at_keys;

    TASK_DEF.at_impl_descrs := c_empty_descrs;

    TASK_DEF.at_def := RENAME.at_rename;

END;
%- - - - - - - - - - - - - - - - - - - - - - - - - - - - - - - - - -
RULE r_211 :
TASK_DEF               ::= TASK_SPEC
STATIC

    TRANSFER at_keys;

    TASK_SPEC.at_env_in := f_add_descr
                             (sc_anonymous,
                              HEAD (TASK_DEF.at_keys),
                              sc_in_visible,
                              sc_type,
                              sc_void,
                              TASK_DEF.at_env_in);
```

```
   TASK_DEF.at_impl_descrs :=
      tp_descr_list
         (f_descr (sc_anonymous,
                   HEAD (TASK_DEF.at_keys),
                   c_start_repr,
                   sc_spec_complete,
                   sc_type,
                   tp_type_den
                      (TASK_SPEC.at_spec,
                       c_empty_keys),
                   f_enclosing (TASK_SPEC.at_env_in)));

   TASK_DEF.at_def := tp_constrained
                         (HEAD (TASK_SPEC.at_keys),
                          sc_void);

END;
%- - - - - - - - - - - - - - - - - - - - - - - - - - - - - - - - - - -
RULE   r_212 :
TASK_BODY               ::= task_body ID BLOCK_STUB
STATIC

   TRANSFER at_block_no;

   BLOCK_STUB.at_encl_unit := tp_encl_unit (sc_task, sc_in_body);

   TASK_BODY.at_keys := f_prev_def_task
                           (ID.at_designator,
                            TASK_BODY.at_env_in);


   %C GAP
   CONDITION
   NOT f_new_key (HEAD (TASK_BODY.at_keys),
                  TASK_BODY.at_env_in)
      MESSAGE
      "missing task specification for this task body";

   BLOCK_STUB.at_env_in :=
      f_update_add_descrs
         (TASK_BODY.at_keys,
          tp_designator_list (ID.at_designator),
          sc_in_body,
          sc_type,
          sc_same,
          TASK_BODY.at_env_in);

   BLOCK_STUB.at_keys := TASK_BODY.at_keys;

   TASK_BODY.at_env_out :=
      f_update_descrs_by_keys
         (TASK_BODY.at_keys,
          sc_same,
          sc_complete,
          sc_same,
          sc_same,
          BLOCK_STUB.at_env_in);
```

```
%
% Diana Generation:
%
%     Set SM_BODY of ID to BLOCK_STUB.
%     Set SM_TYPE_SPEC of ID using TASK_BODY.at_keys.
%     Adjust SM_BODY of TASK_SPEC in task declaration
%     to BLOCK_STUB using TASK_BODY.at_keys.
%
END;
```

```
%----------------------------------------------------------------------------
%
% 5.10. Program Structure
%
%----------------------------------------------------------------------------

%- - - - - - - - - - - - - - - - - - - - - - - - - - - - - - - - - - - - - -
RULE   r_213 :
COMP_UNIT               ::= comp_unit PRAGMA_S '%' CONTEXT '%' UNIT_BODY
STATIC

   COMP_UNIT.at_env := c_start_env;

   PRAGMA_S.at_env_in := COMP_UNIT.at_env;

   CONTEXT.at_env_in := PRAGMA_S.at_env_out;

   UNIT_BODY.at_env_in := CONTEXT.at_env_out;

END;
%- - - - - - - - - - - - - - - - - - - - - - - - - - - - - - - - - - - - - -
RULE   r_214 :
CONTEXT                 ::= context CONTEXT_ELEMS
STATIC

   TRANSFER;

END;
%- - - - - - - - - - - - - - - - - - - - - - - - - - - - - - - - - - - - - -
RULE   r_215:
CONTEXT_ELEMS           ::=
STATIC

   CONTEXT_ELEMS.at_env_out := CONTEXT_ELEMS.at_env_in;

END;
%- - - - - - - - - - - - - - - - - - - - - - - - - - - - - - - - - - - - - -
RULE   r_216 :
CONTEXT_ELEMS           ::= CONTEXT_ELEM CONTEXT_ELEMS
STATIC

   TRANSFER at_env_in;

   CONTEXT_ELEMS[1].at_env_out := CONTEXT_ELEMS[2].at_env_out
      %handling of separate compilation not described within the AG

END;
%- - - - - - - - - - - - - - - - - - - - - - - - - - - - - - - - - - - - - -
RULE   r_217 :
CONTEXT_ELEM            ::= with NAMES  '%'
STATIC

   TRANSFER at_env_in;

END;
%- - - - - - - - - - - - - - - - - - - - - - - - - - - - - - - - - - - - - -
RULE   r_218 :
CONTEXT_ELEM            ::= USE
STATIC
```

```
   TRANSFER at_env_in;

END;
%- - - - - - - - - - - - - - - - - - - - - - - - - - - - - - - - - - - -
RULE   r_219 :
PRAGMA                    ::= pragma ID PARAM_ASSOC_S '%'
STATIC

   TRANSFER at_env_in;

   PRAGMA.at_env_out :=
      IF ID.at_designator QUA SYMB = 'interface' THEN
         IF LENGTH (PARAM_ASSOC_S.at_assocs) < 2 THEN
            PRAGMA.at_env_in              %ERROR, cf. ch_params
         ELSE f_complete_subpr_spec
               (f_head_descr (HEAD (TAIL (PARAM_ASSOC_S.at_assocs))
                  QUA tp_comp_assoc.s_actual),
                PRAGMA.at_env_in)
         FI
      ELSE PRAGMA.at_env_in
      FI;

   CONDITION
   ch_pragma (ID.at_designator,
              PARAM_ASSOC_S.at_assocs,
              PRAGMA.at_env_in)   AND

   CASE ID.at_designator QUA SYMB OF
   'controlled' : 'inline' : 'interface' :
   'pack' : 'priority' :
      ((PRAGMA IS r_019)   %DECL ::= PRAGMA
       CONDITION IT
          MESSAGE
          "pragma must appear within a declarative part");
   'suppress' : 'optimize' :
      (IF PRAGMA IS r_019 THEN          %DECL ::= PRAGMA
          INCLUDING (DECL.at_is_item)
       ELSE FALSE
       FI
       CONDITION IT
       MESSAGE
       "pragma must appear within the decl-part of a block or body")
   OUT TRUE
   ESAC;

   %
   % Diana Generation:
   %
   %    Adjust SM_CONTROLLED, SM_PACKING, SM_LOCATION, SM_BODY
   %    respectively (depending on ID) of the corresponding type
   %    specifications or names using PARAM_ASSOC_S.at_def.
   %
END;
%- - - - - - - - - - - - - - - - - - - - - - - - - - - - - - - - - - - -
RULE   r_220:
PRAGMAS                   ::=
STATIC

   PRAGMAS.at_env_out := PRAGMAS.at_env_in;
```

```
END;
%- - - - - - - - - - - - - - - - - - - - - - - - - - - - - - - - - - - - -
RULE   r_221 :
PRAGMAS                  ::= PRAGMA PRAGMAS
STATIC

   PRAGMA.at_env_in := PRAGMAS[1].at_env_in;

   PRAGMAS[2].at_env_in := PRAGMA.at_env_out;

   PRAGMAS[1].at_env_out := PRAGMAS[2].at_env_out;

END;
%- - - - - - - - - - - - - - - - - - - - - - - - - - - - - - - - - - - - -

RULE   r_222 :
PRAGMA_S                 ::= pragma_s PRAGMAS
STATIC

   TRANSFER;

END;
%- - - - - - - - - - - - - - - - - - - - - - - - - - - - - - - - - - - - -
RULE r_223 :
SUBUNIT_BODY             ::= SUBPROG_BODY
STATIC

   TRANSFER at_env_in;

   SUBPROG_BODY.at_block_no := 0;

   SUBUNIT_BODY.at_keys := SUBPROG_BODY.at_keys2;

END;
%- - - - - - - - - - - - - - - - - - - - - - - - - - - - - - - - - - - - -
RULE r_224 :
SUBUNIT_BODY             ::= PACKAGE_BODY
STATIC

   TRANSFER at_env_in, at_keys;

   PACKAGE_BODY.at_block_no := 0;

END;
%- - - - - - - - - - - - - - - - - - - - - - - - - - - - - - - - - - - - -
RULE r_225:
UNIT_BODY                ::= GENERIC
STATIC

   TRANSFER

END;
%- - - - - - - - - - - - - - - - - - - - - - - - - - - - - - - - - - - - -
RULE r_226 :
SUBUNIT_BODY             ::= TASK_BODY
STATIC

   TRANSFER at_env_in, at_keys;
```

```
   TASK_BODY.at_block_no := 0;

END;
%- - - - - - - - - - - - - - - - - - - - - - - - - - - - - - - - - - - -
RULE   r_227 :
UNIT_BODY                ::= PACKAGE_BODY
STATIC

   TRANSFER;

   PACKAGE_BODY.at_block_no := 0;

END;
%- - - - - - - - - - - - - - - - - - - - - - - - - - - - - - - - - - - -
RULE   r_228 :
UNIT_BODY                ::= PACKAGE_DECL
STATIC

   TRANSFER;

END;
%- - - - - - - - - - - - - - - - - - - - - - - - - - - - - - - - - - - -
RULE   r_229 :
UNIT_BODY                ::= SUBPROG_BODY
STATIC

   TRANSFER at_env_in;

   SUBPROG_BODY.at_block_no := 0;

   UNIT_BODY.at_keys := SUBPROG_BODY.at_keys2;

END;
%- - - - - - - - - - - - - - - - - - - - - - - - - - - - - - - - - - - -
RULE   r_230 :
UNIT_BODY                ::= SUBPROG_DECL
STATIC

   TRANSFER;

END;
%- - - - - - - - - - - - - - - - - - - - - - - - - - - - - - - - - - - -
RULE   r_231 :
UNIT_BODY                ::= TASK_BODY
STATIC

   TRANSFER;

   TASK_BODY.at_block_no := 0;

END;
%- - - - - - - - - - - - - - - - - - - - - - - - - - - - - - - - - - - -
RULE   r_232 :
UNIT_BODY                ::= subunit NAME SUBUNIT_BODY
STATIC

   TRANSFER;

   NAME.at_expected := c_no_expected;
```

```
   NAME.at_context := sc_no_special;

   NAME.at_with_use := f_use_required (NAME.at_allowed1);

   NAME.at_valid := cf_unique_descr (NAME.at_allowed2,
                                     FALSE,
                                     UNIT_BODY.at_env_in);

END;
```

```
%----------------------------------------------------------------------
%                                                                     -
% 5.11. Exceptions                                                    -
%                                                                     -
%----------------------------------------------------------------------


%- - - - - - - - - - - - - - - - - - - - - - - - - - - - - - - - - - -
RULE   r_233 :
DECL                  ::= exception ID_S '%' EXCEPTION_DEF
STATIC

   DECL.at_keys := f_gen_keylist (ID_S.at_designators);

   EXCEPTION_DEF.at_env_in :=
      f_add_descrs (ID_S.at_designators,
                    DECL.at_keys,
                    sc_id_established,
                    sc_exception,
                    sc_void,
                    DECL.at_env_in);

   EXCEPTION_DEF.at_keys :=tp_key_list (HEAD (DECL.at_keys));

   DECL.at_env_out := f_update_descrs_by_keys
                        (DECL.at_keys,
                         sc_same,
                         sc_complete,
                         sc_same,
                         sc_same,
                         EXCEPTION_DEF.at_env_in);

   %C 8.3/1:     checked through f_update_current;

   %
   % Diana Generation:
   %
   %   Set SM_EXCEPTION_DEF of all ID_S to EXCEPTION_DEF
   %
END;
%- - - - - - - - - - - - - - - - - - - - - - - - - - - - - - - - - - -
RULE   r_234 :
EXCEPTION_DEF          ::= RENAME
STATIC

   TRANSFER  at_env_in, at_keys;

   %C 8.5 checked in f_valid_renamed;

END;
%- - - - - - - - - - - - - - - - - - - - - - - - - - - - - - - - - - -
RULE   r_235 :
EXCEPTION_DEF          ::= void
END;
%- - - - - - - - - - - - - - - - - - - - - - - - - - - - - - - - - - -
RULE   r_236 :
STM                    ::= raise NAME_VOID
STATIC

   STM.at_usable := c_no_bl_lab_loops;
```

```
   STM.at_labels := c_no_bl_lab_loops;

   STM.at_loops_blocks := c_no_bl_lab_loops;

   %C 11.3/2
   CONDITION
   IF NAME_VOID IS r_130 THEN              % void
      STM.at_encl_unit.s_state = sc_in_handler
   ELSE
      TRUE
   FI
      MESSAGE
      "Raise without name only in handlers.";

   NAME_VOID.at_context := sc_no_special;

   NAME_VOID.at_expected := c_no_expected;

   NAME_VOID.at_env_in := STM.at_env_in;

   %C 11.3/1
   CONDITION
   IF NAME_VOID IS r_129 THEN
      HEAD (NAME_VOID.at_valid QUA tp_descr_set .s_descrs)
          .s_nature = sc_exception
   ELSE TRUE
   FI
      MESSAGE
      "an exception name expected";

END;
```

```
%-------------------------------------------------------------------
%                                                                  -
% 5.12. Generics                                                   -
%                                                                  -
%-------------------------------------------------------------------

%- - - - - - - - - - - - - - - - - - - - - - - - - - - - - - - - - -
RULE r_237 :
DECL                   ::= GENERIC
STATIC

   TRANSFER

END;
%- - - - - - - - - - - - - - - - - - - - - - - - - - - - - - - - - -
RULE   r_238 :
FORMAL_SUBPROG_DEF     ::= box
STATIC

   FORMAL_SUBPROG_DEF.at_def := sc_box;

END;
%- - - - - - - - - - - - - - - - - - - - - - - - - - - - - - - - - -
RULE   r_239 :
FORMAL_SUBPROG_DEF     ::= NAME
STATIC

   NAME.at_expected := c_no_expected;

   NAME.at_context := sc_string_is_name;

   NAME.at_env_in := FORMAL_SUBPROG_DEF.at_env_in;

   NAME.at_with_use := f_use_required (NAME.at_allowed1);

   NAME.at_valid := cf_unique_descr
                       (f_matching_subpr
                           (INCLUDING SUBPROG_DECL.at_header,
                            NAME.at_allowed2),
                        FALSE,
                        FORMAL_SUBPROG_DEF.at_env_in);

   FORMAL_SUBPROG_DEF.at_def :=
      f_head_descr (NAME.at_valid).s_key;

END ;
%- - - - - - - - - - - - - - - - - - - - - - - - - - - - - - - - - -
RULE   r_240 :
FORMAL_SUBPROG_DEF     ::= no_default
STATIC

   FORMAL_SUBPROG_DEF.at_def := sc_no_default;

END;
%- - - - - - - - - - - - - - - - - - - - - - - - - - - - - - - - - -
RULE   r_241 :
FORMAL_TYPE_SPEC       ::= formal_discrt
STATIC
```

```
   FORMAL_TYPE_SPEC.at_type := sc_formal_discrt;

END;
%- - - - - - - - - - - - - - - - - - - - - - - - - - - - - - - - - - - - - - - -
RULE   r_242 :
FORMAL_TYPE_SPEC       ::= formal_fixed
STATIC

   FORMAL_TYPE_SPEC.at_type := sc_formal_fixed;

END;
%- - - - - - - - - - - - - - - - - - - - - - - - - - - - - - - - - - - - - - - -
RULE   r_243 :
FORMAL_TYPE_SPEC       ::= formal_float
STATIC

   FORMAL_TYPE_SPEC.at_type := sc_formal_float;

END;
%- - - - - - - - - - - - - - - - - - - - - - - - - - - - - - - - - - - - - - - -
RULE   r_244 :
FORMAL_TYPE_SPEC       ::= formal_integer
STATIC

   FORMAL_TYPE_SPEC.at_type := sc_formal_integer;

END;
%- - - - - - - - - - - - - - - - - - - - - - - - - - - - - - - - - - - - - - - -
RULE r_245 :
GENERIC      ::= generic DESIGNATOR GENERIC_PARAM_S '%' GENERIC_HEADER
STATIC

   GENERIC_HEADER.at_is_operator := DESIGNATOR IS r_169;  % string

   GENERIC.at_keys := f_gen_keys;

   GENERIC.at_env  :=
      f_add_descr
         (DESIGNATOR.at_designator,
          HEAD (GENERIC.at_keys),
          sc_id_established,
          sc_void_nature,
          sc_void,
          GENERIC.at_env_in);

   GENERIC_PARAM_S.at_env_in := f_empty_local_encl_state
                                   (HEAD (GENERIC.at_keys),
                                    sc_in_generic_part,
                                    GENERIC.at_env);

   GENERIC_HEADER.at_env_in :=
      f_update_generic_params (GENERIC_PARAM_S.at_env_out);

   GENERIC.at_env_out :=
      f_update_descrs_by_keys
         (GENERIC.at_keys,
          sc_same,
          CASE c_header : GENERIC_HEADER.at_header OF
          IS tp_package :
             IF NOT f_body_required (c_header) THEN
```

```
            sc_complete
         ELSE sc_spec_complete
         FI
      OUT sc_spec_complete
      ESAC,

      CASE c_header:GENERIC_HEADER.at_header OF
      IS tp_header :
         IF c_header IS tp_procedure THEN
            sc_generic_procedure
         ELSE sc_generic_function
         FI;
      IS tp_package : sc_package
      ESAC,

      tp_generic
         (f_local (GENERIC_PARAM_S.at_env_out),
          CASE c_header:GENERIC_HEADER.at_header OF
          IS tp_package : c_header;
          IS tp_header  : tp_subpr (c_header, sc_void,
                                     sc_no_predef_op)
          ESAC),
      GENERIC.at_env);

   %
   % Diana Generation:
   %
   %    Set SM_GENERIC_PARAM_S of DESIGNATOR to GENERIC_PARAM_S
   %    Set SM_SPEC of DESIGNATOR to GENERIC_HEADER
   %    Initialize SM_BODY of DESIGNATOR with void.
   %
END;
%- - - - - - - - - - - - - - - - - - - - - - - - - - - - - - - - - -
RULE   r_246 :
GENERIC_HEADER          ::= PACKAGE_SPEC
STATIC

   PACKAGE_SPEC.at_env_in :=
      f_update_encl
         (sc_same,
          sc_package,
          sc_same,
          GENERIC_HEADER.at_env_in);

   GENERIC_HEADER.at_header := PACKAGE_SPEC.at_spec;

END;
%- - - - - - - - - - - - - - - - - - - - - - - - - - - - - - - - - -
RULE   r_247 :
GENERIC_HEADER          ::= HEADER
STATIC

   TRANSFER at_env_in, at_is_operator;

   GENERIC_HEADER.at_header := HEADER.at_header;

END;
%- - - - - - - - - - - - - - - - - - - - - - - - - - - - - - - - - -
RULE   r_248 :
GENERIC_PARAM           ::= PARAM
```

```
STATIC

   TRANSFER at_encl_unit;

   %C 12.1/1
   CONDITION
   NOT (PARAM IS r_181)
      MESSAGE
      "no generic out parameters allowed";

   PARAM.at_env_in            := GENERIC_PARAM.at_env_in;

   GENERIC_PARAM.at_env_out := PARAM.at_env_out;

END;
%- - - - - - - - - - - - - - - - - - - - - - - - - - - - - - - - - - - - - - - - -
RULE   r_249 :
GENERIC_PARAM          ::= SUBPROG_DECL
STATIC

   TRANSFER

END;
%- - - - - - - - - - - - - - - - - - - - - - - - - - - - - - - - - - - - - - - - -
RULE   r_250 :
GENERIC_PARAM          ::= TYPE_DECL
STATIC

   TRANSFER

END;
%- - - - - - - - - - - - - - - - - - - - - - - - - - - - - - - - - - - - - - - - -
RULE   r_251:
GENERIC_PARAMS         ::=
STATIC

   GENERIC_PARAMS.at_env_out := GENERIC_PARAMS.at_env_in;

END;
%- - - - - - - - - - - - - - - - - - - - - - - - - - - - - - - - - - - - - - - - -
RULE   r_252 :
GENERIC_PARAMS         ::= GENERIC_PARAM GENERIC_PARAMS
STATIC

   TRANSFER at_encl_unit;

   GENERIC_PARAMS[2].at_env_in := GENERIC_PARAM.at_env_out;
   GENERIC_PARAMS[1].at_env_out := GENERIC_PARAMS[2].at_env_out;
   GENERIC_PARAM.at_env_in      := GENERIC_PARAMS[1].at_env_in;

END;
%- - - - - - - - - - - - - - - - - - - - - - - - - - - - - - - - - - - - - - - - -
RULE   r_253 :
GENERIC_PARAM_S        ::= generic_param_s GENERIC_PARAMS
STATIC

   TRANSFER;

   GENERIC_PARAMS.at_encl_unit :=
      tp_encl_unit (sc_void_nature, sc_in_generic_part);
```

```
END;
%- - - - - - - - - - - - - - - - - - - - - - - - - - - - - - - - - - - - -
RULE   r_254 :
GENERIC_ASSOC           ::= ACTUAL
STATIC

   TRANSFER at_env_in;

   ACTUAL.at_discrim_allowed := FALSE;

   ACTUAL.at_expected :=
      f_first_not_impl_type (GENERIC_ASSOC.at_expected_in);

   ACTUAL.at_context :=
     IF ACTUAL.at_expected =/ sc_void THEN

        CASE c_descr : f_select_by_key1
                          (ACTUAL.at_expected QUA tp_key,
                           GENERIC_ASSOC.at_expected_in) OF
        IS tp_void : sc_no_special;
        IS tp_descr :
           CASE c_descr.s_nature OF
           sc_type:
           sc_subtype : sc_subtype_ind;
           sc_predefined_op : sc_common_op : sc_universal_op :
           sc_procedure : sc_function : sc_string_is_name
           OUT          sc_no_special
           ESAC
        ESAC
     ELSE sc_no_special
     FI;

   ACTUAL.at_with_use := f_use_required1 (ACTUAL.at_allowed1);

   GENERIC_ASSOC.at_valid :=
      f_generic_allowed_expected
        (tp_comp_assoc
           (tp_choice_list (),
            ACTUAL.at_allowed2 QUA tp_descr_set),
         GENERIC_ASSOC.at_expected_in,
         GENERIC_ASSOC.at_env_in);

   %C 12.1.1/2
   CONDITION
      ch_variable_for_out_in_out
         (GENERIC_ASSOC.at_valid,
          GENERIC_ASSOC.at_env_in)
     MESSAGE
      "actual parameter should be a variable";

   ACTUAL.at_valid := GENERIC_ASSOC.at_valid.s_actual;

   ACTUAL.at_others_allowed := FALSE;

END;
%- - - - - - - - - - - - - - - - - - - - - - - - - - - - - - - - - - - - -
RULE   r_255 :
GENERIC_ASSOC           ::= ASSOC
STATIC
```

```
   TRANSFER at_env_in, at_expected_in;

   GENERIC_ASSOC.at_valid :=
      f_generic_allowed_expected
         (ASSOC.at_allowed2,
          GENERIC_ASSOC.at_expected_in,
          GENERIC_ASSOC.at_env_in);

   %C 12.1.1/2
   CONDITION
      ch_variable_for_out_in_out
         (GENERIC_ASSOC.at_valid,
          GENERIC_ASSOC.at_env_in)
     MESSAGE
     "actual parameter should be a variable";


   ASSOC.at_valid := GENERIC_ASSOC.at_valid;

   ASSOC.at_others_allowed := FALSE;

END;
%- - - - - - - - - - - - - - - - - - - - - - - - - - - - - - - - - - - - - - -
RULE   r_256:
GENERIC_ASSOCS          ::=
STATIC

   GENERIC_ASSOCS.at_valid := tp_assoc_list ();

   GENERIC_ASSOCS.at_expected_out := GENERIC_ASSOCS.at_expected_in;

END;
%- - - - - - - - - - - - - - - - - - - - - - - - - - - - - - - - - - - - - - -
RULE   r_257 :
GENERIC_ASSOCS          ::= GENERIC_ASSOC GENERIC_ASSOCS
STATIC

   TRANSFER at_env_in;

   GENERIC_ASSOCS[2].at_positional_allowed :=
      GENERIC_ASSOCS[1].at_positional_allowed AND
      NOT (GENERIC_ASSOC IS r_255);                          % assoc

   %C 12.3/3
   CONDITION
   GENERIC_ASSOCS[1].at_positional_allowed
   OR (GENERIC_ASSOC IS r_255)
     MESSAGE
     "Positional parameters must occur first.";

   GENERIC_ASSOC.at_expected_in :=
      IF EMPTY (GENERIC_ASSOCS[1].at_expected_in) THEN
         (c_error_descr_list
         %C 12.3/2
         CONDITION FALSE
            MESSAGE
            "too many actual generic parameters")
      ELSE GENERIC_ASSOCS[1].at_expected_in
      FI;
```

```
   GENERIC_ASSOCS[2].at_expected_in :=
      f_adjust_generics
         (f_choices_out (GENERIC_ASSOC.at_valid.s_choices,
                         GENERIC_ASSOC.at_expected_in),
          GENERIC_ASSOC.at_valid,
          GENERIC_ASSOCS[1].at_env_in);

   GENERIC_ASSOCS[1].at_valid :=
      tp_assoc_list (GENERIC_ASSOC.at_valid) +
      GENERIC_ASSOCS[2].at_valid;

   GENERIC_ASSOCS[1].at_expected_out :=
      GENERIC_ASSOCS[2].at_expected_out;

END;
%- - - - - - - - - - - - - - - - - - - - - - - - - - - - - - - - - - -
RULE   r_258 :
GENERIC_ASSOC_S         ::= generic_assoc_s GENERIC_ASSOCS
STATIC

   TRANSFER;

   GENERIC_ASSOCS.at_positional_allowed := TRUE;

END;
%- - - - - - - - - - - - - - - - - - - - - - - - - - - - - - - - - - -
RULE   r_259 :
INSTANTIATION           ::= instantiation NAME GENERIC_ASSOC_S '%'
STATIC

   TRANSFER at_env_in;
   NAME.at_expected := c_no_expected;

   NAME.at_context := sc_no_special;

   NAME.at_with_use := f_use_required (NAME.at_allowed1);

   NAME.at_valid := cf_unique_descr (NAME.at_allowed2,
                                     FALSE,
                                     NAME.at_env_in);

   GENERIC_ASSOC_S.at_expected_in :=
      f_generic_params (NAME.at_valid);

   %C 12.3/2
   CONDITION
   ch_have_default (GENERIC_ASSOC_S.at_expected_out)
      MESSAGE
      "actual parameters missing";

   %C 12.1.1/3
   CONDITION
   ch_existence_depends_not (GENERIC_ASSOC_S.at_valid,
                             INSTANTIATION.at_env_in);

   INSTANTIATION.at_instantiation :=
      tp_instantiation
         (f_head_descr (NAME.at_valid),
          GENERIC_ASSOC_S.at_valid);

END;
```

```
%-------------------------------------------------------------------------
%
% 5.13. Representation Specifications
%
%-------------------------------------------------------------------------

%- - - - - - - - - - - - - - - - - - - - - - - - - - - - - - - - - - - - -
RULE   r_260 :
COMP_REP                    ::= comp_rep NAME EXP RANGE
STATIC

   TRANSFER at_env_in;

   NAME.at_expected := c_no_expected;

   NAME.at_context := sc_id_not_visible;
   NAME.at_with_use := f_use_required (NAME.at_allowed1);

   NAME.at_valid :=
      f_descr_set3
         (f_select_by_designator00
            (f_head_descr (NAME.at_allowed2).s_designator,
             COMP_REP.at_expected_in,
             NAME.at_env_in));

   %C 13.4/5
   CONDITION
      ch_has_static_constraint2 (NAME.at_valid, COMP_REP.at_env_in)
      MESSAGE
     "locations may only be specified for comp with static constraints"

   %C 13.4/6
   CONDITION
      NOT (f_is_error_or_empty (NAME.at_valid))
      MESSAGE
      "THIS is not a rec-comp or has been already specified";

   EXP.at_expected := c_no_expected;

   EXP.at_context := sc_no_special;

   EXP.at_with_use := f_use_required (EXP.at_allowed1);

   EXP.at_valid := cf_unique_descr (EXP.at_allowed2,
                                    TRUE,
                                    EXP.at_env_in);

   %C 13/4.1
   CONDITION
      ch_static_int (EXP.at_valid, COMP_REP.at_env_in)
      MESSAGE
      "a static integer expression required";

   EXP.at_others_allowed := FALSE;

   RANGE.at_expected := c_no_expected;

   RANGE.at_with_use := f_use_required (RANGE.at_allowed1);
```

```
   RANGE.at_valid :=  f_valid_range_constr (RANGE.at_allowed2,
                                            COMP_REP.at_env_in);

   %C 13.4/2
   CONDITION
      ch_static_int_range (RANGE.at_valid, COMP_REP.at_env_in)
      MESSAGE
      "an integer static range required";

   RANGE.at_discrim_allowed := FALSE;

   COMP_REP.at_rep :=
      tp_comp_rep
         (f_head_descr (NAME.at_valid).s_key,
          EXP.at_valid,
          tp_range_constr
             (RANGE.at_valid QUA tp_range_constr .s_lower_bound,
              RANGE.at_valid QUA tp_range_constr .s_upper_bound));

END;
%- - - - - - - - - - - - - - - - - - - - - - - - - - - - - - - - - - - -
RULE   r_261:
COMP_REPS               ::=
STATIC

   COMP_REPS.at_reps := tp_comp_rep_list ();

END;
%- - - - - - - - - - - - - - - - - - - - - - - - - - - - - - - - - - - -
RULE   r_262 :
COMP_REPS               ::= COMP_REP COMP_REPS
STATIC

   TRANSFER at_env_in;

   COMP_REP.at_expected_in := COMP_REPS[1].at_expected_in;

   COMP_REPS[2].at_expected_in :=
      f_comp_rep_out (COMP_REP.at_rep,
                      COMP_REPS[1].at_expected_in);

   COMP_REPS[1].at_reps :=
      tp_comp_rep_list (COMP_REP.at_rep) +
      COMP_REPS[2].at_reps;

END;
%- - - - - - - - - - - - - - - - - - - - - - - - - - - - - - - - - - - -
RULE   r_263 :
COMP_REP_S              ::= comp_rep_s COMP_REPS
STATIC

   TRANSFER;

END;
%- - - - - - - - - - - - - - - - - - - - - - - - - - - - - - - - - - - -
RULE   r_264 :
REP                     ::= address NAME EXP
STATIC
```

```
   TRANSFER at_env_in;

   REP.at_user_rep := c_empty_user_reps;

   NAME.at_expected := c_no_expected;

   NAME.at_context := sc_no_special;

   NAME.at_with_use := f_use_required (NAME.at_allowed1);

   NAME.at_valid := cf_unique_descr (NAME.at_allowed2,
                                     FALSE,
                                     NAME.at_env_in);

   %C 13.5/2
   CONDITION
      ch_static_int (EXP.at_valid, REP.at_env_in)
      MESSAGE
      "an integer static expression required";

   EXP.at_expected := c_no_expected;

   EXP.at_context := sc_no_special;

   EXP.at_with_use := f_use_required (EXP.at_allowed1);

   EXP.at_valid := cf_unique_descr (EXP.at_allowed2,
                                    FALSE,
                                    EXP.at_env_in);

   %C 13.5/4
   CONDITION
      ch_is_obj_subp_pack_task_entr (NAME.at_valid,
                                     REP.at_env_in)
      MESSAGE
      "address specification not allowed for this entity";

   EXP.at_others_allowed := FALSE;

   REP.at_keys := c_empty_keys;

   REP.at_env_out :=
      f_enter_rep (f_head_descr (NAME.at_valid).s_key,
                   tp_address_spec (EXP.at_valid),
                   REP.at_env_in);

   %C 13.1/1, 13.1/2 and 13.1/3 checked through f_update_rep
   %                                and  through f_add_reps;

   %
   % Diana Generation:
   %
   %    Adjust SM_ADDRESS, SM_LOCATION respectively of the
   %    name described by NAME.at_valid to EXP
   %
END;
%- - - - - - - - - - - - - - - - - - - - - - - - - - - - - - -
RULE   r_265 :
REP                    ::= simple_rep NAME EXP
STATIC
```

```
REP.at_user_rep := NAME.at_user_rep;

NAME.at_expected := c_no_expected;

NAME.at_context := IF NAME IS r_122 THEN  % attribute : length_spec
                      sc_attr_name
                   ELSE sc_no_special
                   FI;

NAME.at_env_in := REP.at_env_in;

NAME.at_with_use := f_use_required (NAME.at_allowed1);

NAME.at_valid :=
   IF NAME IS r_122 THEN              %attribute : length_spec
      cf_unique_descr (NAME.at_allowed2,
                       FALSE,
                       NAME.at_env_in)
   ELSE cf_unique_type_descr (NAME.at_allowed2)
   FI;

%C 13.1/4, %C 13.1/5
CONDITION
   ch_repr_spec_deriv (NAME.at_valid,
                       LAST (NAME CONSTITUENTS ID.at_designator),
                       REP.at_env_in);

REP.at_keys := IF NAME IS r_122 THEN
                  c_empty_keys
               ELSE f_gen_keys
               FI;

EXP.at_expected :=
   IF NAME IS r_122 THEN        %attribute : length_spec
      c_no_expected             %any integer type
   ELSE HEAD (REP.at_keys)      %implicitly declared array type
   FI;

EXP.at_context := sc_no_special;

EXP.at_env_in :=
   IF NAME IS r_122 THEN  %attribute : length_spec
      REP.at_env_in
   ELSE f_add_descr
           (sc_anonymous,
            HEAD (REP.at_keys),
            sc_complete,
            sc_type,
            tp_type_den
               (tp_array
                  (tp_dscrt_range_list
                     (tp_index
                        (tp_constrained
                           (f_base_type
                              (f_head_descr (NAME.at_valid)),
                           sc_void))),
                   c_univ_int_constr),
                c_empty_keys),
           REP.at_env_in)
```

```
   FI;

EXP.at_with_use :=
   IF NAME IS r_122 THEN          %attribute : length_spec
      NOT f_is_int_type2
            (f_object_type
               (f_head_descr (EXP.at_allowed1)),
             REP.at_env_in)
   ELSE f_use_required (EXP.at_allowed1)
   FI;

EXP.at_valid :=
   cf_unique_descr (EXP.at_allowed2,
                    FALSE,
                    EXP.at_env_in);

EXP.at_others_allowed := FALSE;

REP.at_env_out :=
   IF EXP.at_valid /= c_error_descr_set THEN
      f_calculate_repr
         (f_head_descr (NAME.at_valid).s_key,
          TRUE,
          f_update_repr
            (f_head_descr (NAME.at_valid).s_key,
             REP.at_user_reps,
             f_enter_rep
               (f_head_descr (NAME.at_valid).s_key,
                IF NAME IS r_122 THEN      %attribute : length_spec
                   f_length_spec
                      (LAST (NAME CONSTITUENTS ID.at_designator),
                       NAME.at_valid,
                       EXP.at_valid,
                       REP.at_env_in)
                ELSE
                   f_enum_rep
                      (HEAD
                           (EXP CONSTITUENTS COMP_ASSOCS.at_valid),
                       NAME.at_valid,
                       REP.at_env_in)
                FI,
                REP.at_env_in)))
   ELSE REP.at_env_in
   FI;

%C 13.1/1, 13.1/2 and 13.1/3 checked through f_enter_rep
%                              and  through f_add_reps;

%C 13.1/3
CONDITION
   f_rep_state (f_head_descr (NAME.at_valid).s_key,
                REP.at_env_out) = sc_user_rep OR
   (f_new_repr_state
       (f_head_descr (NAME.at_valid).s_key,
        REP.at_env_out) =/ sc_user_rep)
   MESSAGE
   "illegal rep-spec because of later rep-spec";

%C 13.3/1, C 13.3/1, C 13.3/4, C 13.3/5  in f_enum_rep;
```

```
  %C 13.2/1, C 13.2/2, C 13.2/3, C 13.2/4, C 13.2/5, C 13.2/6
  %C 13.2/7, C 13.2/8, C 13.2/9  in f_length_spec;
  %
  % Diana Generation:
  %
  %    If it is a length specification (NAME is an attribute)
  %    then adjust SM_SIZE, SM_STORAGE_SIZE or SM_ACTUAL_DELTA
  %    respectively (depending on the attribute's name AS_ID (NAME))
  %    of the type specification described by NAME.at_valid to EXP.
  %
  %    If it is a enumeration type specification then
  %    adjust SM_REP of the single enumeration literals
  %    using NAME.at_valid to the values provided by the
  %    aggregate (EXP).
  %
END;
%- - - - - - - - - - - - - - - - - - - - - - - - - - - - - - - - - -
RULE   r_266 :
REP                    ::= record_rep NAME EXP_VOID COMP_REP_S '%'
STATIC

  TRANSFER at_env_in, at_user_rep;

  NAME.at_expected := c_no_expected;

  NAME.at_context := sc_no_special;

  NAME.at_with_use := f_use_required (NAME.at_allowed1);

  NAME.at_valid := cf_unique_descr (NAME.at_allowed2,
                                    FALSE,
                                    NAME.at_env_in);

  EXP_VOID.at_expected := c_no_expected;

  EXP_VOID.at_others_allowed := FALSE;

  EXP_VOID.at_discrim_allowed := FALSE;

  %C 13.4/1
  CONDITION
     CASE c_exp : EXP_VOID.at_valid OF
     IS tp_void : TRUE;
     IS tp_descr_set : ch_static_int (c_exp, REP.at_env_in)
     ESAC
     MESSAGE
     "a static integer expression required for alignement";

  COMP_REP_S.at_expected_in := f_comps_of_record (NAME.at_valid,
                                                  NAME.at_env_in);

  REP.at_keys := c_empty_keys;

  REP.at_env_out :=
     f_calculate_repr
        (f_head_descr (NAME.at_valid).s_key,
         TRUE,
         f_update_repr
            (f_head_descr (NAME.at_valid).s_key,
```

```
            REP.at_user_reps,
            f_enter_rep
               (f_head_descr (NAME.at_valid).s_key,
                tp_record_rep
                   (CASE c_exp : EXP_VOID.at_valid OF
                    IS tp_descr_set   :
                       c_exp
                    OUT f_descr_set2 (c_1_int_descr)
                    ESAC,
                    COMP_REP_S.at_reps),
                REP.at_env_in)));

  %C 13.1/3
  CONDITION
     f_rep_state (f_head_descr (NAME.at_valid).s_key,
                  REP.at_env_out) = sc_user_rep OR
     (f_new_repr_state (f_head_descr (NAME.at_valid).s_key,
                        REP.at_env_out) =/ sc_user_rep)
     MESSAGE
     "illegal rep-spec because of later rep-spec";

  %C13.4/2   checked through f_comps_of_record;

END;
%- - - - - - - - - - - - - - - - - - - - - - - - - - - - - - - - - -
RULE r_267 :
STM                    ::= code NAME EXP
STATIC

   TRANSFER at_env_in;

   STM.at_usable := c_no_bl_lab_loops;

   STM.at_labels := c_no_bl_lab_loops;

   STM.at_loops_blocks := c_no_bl_lab_loops;

   NAME.at_expected := c_no_expected;

   NAME.at_context := sc_no_special;

   NAME.at_with_use := f_use_required (NAME.at_allowed1);

   NAME.at_valid := cf_unique_descr (NAME.at_allowed2,
                                     FALSE,
                                     STM.at_env_in);

   EXP.at_expected := c_no_expected;

   EXP.at_context := sc_no_special;

   EXP.at_with_use := f_use_required (EXP.at_allowed1);

   EXP.at_valid := cf_unique_descr (EXP.at_allowed2,
                                    FALSE,
                                    STM.at_env_in);

   EXP.at_others_allowed := FALSE;

END;
```

```
%%%%%%%%%%%%%%%%%%%%%%%%%%%%%%%%%%%%%%%%%%%%%%%%%%%%%%%%%%%%%%%%%%%%%%%%%%
%                                                                        %
% AG6. Semantic    Functions                                             %
%                                                                        %
%%%%%%%%%%%%%%%%%%%%%%%%%%%%%%%%%%%%%%%%%%%%%%%%%%%%%%%%%%%%%%%%%%%%%%%%%%
%                                                                        %
% The functions of the Attribute Grammar are grouped into three          %
% classes :                                                              %
%                                                                        %
% - functions, used to perform checks          (ch_)                     %
% - functions, used to calculate a result      (f_)                      %
% - functions, used for both purposes          (cf_)                     %
%                                                                        %
%%%%%%%%%%%%%%%%%%%%%%%%%%%%%%%%%%%%%%%%%%%%%%%%%%%%%%%%%%%%%%%%%%%%%%%%%%


%%%%%%%%%%%%%%%%%%%%%%%%%%%%%%%%%%%%%%%%%%%%%%%%%%%%%%%%%%%%%%%%%%%%%%%%%%
%
%       cf_        F U N C T I O N S
%
%%%%%%%%%%%%%%%%%%%%%%%%%%%%%%%%%%%%%%%%%%%%%%%%%%%%%%%%%%%%%%%%%%%%%%%%%%

FUNCTION cf_existent_entity (p_value : tp_descr_set,
                             p_env   : tp_env) tp_descr_set :

     % Called from evaluation of static attributes (pred, succ, val),
     % to check whether the result is within the type range.
     % Necessary for e.g.  integer'first'pred + 10

   IF ch_value_in_constraint (p_value, p_env) THEN
     p_value
   ELSE f_descr_set_val
          (f_obj_constrained1 (f_head_descr (p_value)),
           tp_init (sc_constraint_error,
                    sc_no_exp))
   FI;

FUNCTION cf_not_empty (p_descr_set : tp_descr_set) tp_descr_set :

     % called for evaluating NAME/EXP.at_allowed2

   IF EMPTY (p_descr_set.s_descrs) THEN
     (c_error_descr_set
     CONDITION FALSE
       MESSAGE
       "name/exp incompatible with expected type or meaningless")
   ELSE p_descr_set
   FI;

FUNCTION cf_packages (p_names : tp_descr_list)
                     tp_descr_list :

     % check names in use clauses
```

```
   IF EMPTY (p_names) THEN
      p_names
   ELSE IF HEAD (p_names).s_den IS tp_package THEN
           tp_descr_list (HEAD (p_names)) +
             cf_packages (TAIL (p_names))
        ELSE (cf_packages (TAIL (p_names))
               CONDITION HEAD (p_names) = c_error_descr
                  MESSAGE "(non-generic) package name expected")
        FI
   FI;

 FUNCTION cf_type_task (p_descr      : tp_descr,
                        p_env        : tp_env) tp_type :

      % Check condition from 13.2: name must be a type or a task.

   CASE c_den : p_descr.s_den OF
   IS tp_object :
     (f_type (c_den.s_type.s_base_type, p_env)
      %C 13.2/5
      CONDITION
      p_descr.s_nature = sc_task
        MESSAGE
         "a task or a type name expected");
   IS tp_type_den : f_parent_base_type1 (c_den.s_type, p_env);
   IS tp_constrained :
        (f_type (c_den.s_base_type, p_env)
         CONDITION
         f_select_by_key (c_den.s_base_type, p_env).s_designator
         = sc_anonymous     %implicitly declared derived type
           MESSAGE
            "a task or a type name expected")
   OUT c_error_type
   ESAC;

      %*************************************************************%
      %                                                             %
      %        cf_unique_...                                        %
      %                                                             %
      %        Used to calculate at_valid;                          %
      %        check that the set of allowed meanings consists      %
      %        of exactly one element.                              %
      %                                                             %
      %*************************************************************%

 FUNCTION cf_unique_choice (p_choice : tp_choice,
                            p_env    : tp_env) tp_choice:

   CASE c_choice : p_choice OF
   IS tp_descr :
   IS tp_others : c_choice;
   IS tp_descr_set : tp_choice
                      (cf_unique_descr (c_choice,
                                        TRUE,
                                        p_env));
   IS tp_dscrt_range :
        CASE c_range : c_choice OF
        IS tp_constrained : c_choice;
        IS tp_range : CASE c_range : c_range OF
```

```
                    IS tp_void : (c_error_dscrt_range
                                 CONDITION FALSE
                                 MESSAGE "compiler error");
                    IS tp_range_constr :
                       tp_choice (tp_dscrt_range
                          (tp_range_constr
                             (cf_unique_descr
                                (c_range.s_lower_bound,
                                 TRUE,
                                 p_env),
                              cf_unique_descr
                                (c_range.s_upper_bound,
                                 TRUE,
                                 p_env))))
                   ESAC;
      IS tp_index : (c_error_dscrt_range CONDITION FALSE MESSAGE
                                        "compiler error")
      ESAC
   ESAC;

FUNCTION cf_unique_choices (p_choices : tp_choice_list,
                            p_env     : tp_env)
                           tp_choice_list :

   IF EMPTY (p_choices) THEN
      p_choices
   ELSE tp_choice_list (cf_unique_choice (HEAD (p_choices), p_env)) +
          cf_unique_choices (TAIL (p_choices), p_env)
   FI;

FUNCTION cf_unique_descr1 (p_descr_set : tp_descr_set)
                          tp_descr_set :

     % check addidionally whether entity is already usable

   IF EMPTY (p_descr_set.s_descrs) THEN
      (c_error_descr_set
      CONDITION
         FALSE
         MESSAGE
         "Expression incompatible with expected type")
   ELSE IF EMPTY (TAIL (p_descr_set.s_descrs)) THEN
      IF f_head_descr (p_descr_set).s_state = sc_id_established THEN
         (c_error_descr_set
         CONDITION
            FALSE
            MESSAGE
            "name is not yet usable")
      ELSE p_descr_set
      FI
   ELSE (f_descr_set2 (f_head_descr (p_descr_set))
         CONDITION
            FALSE
            MESSAGE
            "ambiguous name or exp")
   FI FI;

FUNCTION cf_unique_descr (p_descr_set      : tp_descr_set,
                          p_discr_allowed  : BOOL,
                          p_env            : tp_env)
```

```
                          tp_descr_set :

   IF f_is_error_descr_set (p_descr_set) THEN
      c_error_descr_set
   ELSE (cf_unique_descr1 (p_descr_set)
        CONDITION %C 6.1/2, C 3.7.1/2, C 3.7.1/3, C 3.7.1/6, C 12.1/1
           ch_dependencies (f_head_descr (p_descr_set),
                            p_discr_allowed,
                            p_env)
           MESSAGE
           "this name must not be mentioned here")
   FI;

FUNCTION cf_unique_type_descr (p_type : tp_descr_set)
                               tp_descr_set :

   IF IF f_is_error_or_empty (p_type) THEN
         FALSE
      ELSE
         (CASE c_den : f_head_descr (p_type).s_den OF
          IS tp_type_den : IS tp_constrained : TRUE
          OUT (FALSE
              CONDITION FALSE
                 MESSAGE "type-name expected")
          ESAC
         CONDITION
            EMPTY (TAIL (p_type.s_descrs))
            MESSAGE
            "ambiguous name for type")   AND
         ch_usable (f_head_descr (p_type))
      FI THEN
      tp_descr_set (tp_descr_list
                       (HEAD (p_type.s_descrs)),
                    sc_no_add)
   ELSE c_error_type_descr_set
   FI;


%%%%%%%%%%%%%%%%%%%%%%%%%%%%%%%%%%%%%%%%%%%%%%%%%%%%%%%%%%%%%%%%%%%%
%
%      ch_      F U N C T I O N S
%
%%%%%%%%%%%%%%%%%%%%%%%%%%%%%%%%%%%%%%%%%%%%%%%%%%%%%%%%%%%%%%%%%%%%


FUNCTION ch_aggreg (p_assocs : tp_assoc_list,
                    p_exp    : tp_descr_set,
                    p_env    : tp_env) BOOL :

      % check array aggreagate :
      % - positional associations must not be mixed with
      %       named associations (except OTHERS)
      % - all choices must be static (except only one single choice
      %      is given)
      % - for named array aggregates, all choices must
      %      form a compact interval
      % - a choice value must not occur more than once
      % exhaustive choices must be checked dynamically
```

```
  %C 4.3.2/3
  IF f_object_parent_base_type (p_exp, p_env) IS tp_array OR
     (f_head_descr (p_exp).s_den IS tp_dummy_aggr) THEN
     (IF f_has_pos_comp (p_assocs) THEN
         ch_no_named_ex_others (p_assocs)
      ELSE TRUE
      FI
     CONDITION IT
        MESSAGE
         "no named (except others) allowed, using positional assocs")
     AND
     %C 4.3/1
     (IF f_has_pos_comp (p_assocs) THEN   % only positionals
         TRUE
      ELSE IF (LENGTH (p_assocs) = 1 AND
              (LENGTH (HEAD (p_assocs) QUA tp_comp_assoc
                   .s_choices) = 1)) THEN
         TRUE
      ELSE %above CONDITION is checked in ch_multiple_choices
         ch_multiple_choices
           (f_order_choices (f_assoc_choices (p_assocs),
                             tp_range_val_list ())) AND
         IF f_has_others_comp (p_assocs) THEN
            TRUE
         ELSE
            ch_compact_choices
              (f_order_choices (f_assoc_choices (p_assocs),
                                tp_range_val_list ()))
         FI
      FI FI
     CONDITION IT
        MESSAGE "C 4.3/1 invalid choices")
  ELSE TRUE
  FI;

FUNCTION ch_all_bodies_appeared (p_descrs : tp_descr_list) BOOL:

    % called at the end of a declarative part (in the sense of
    % visibility rules) and checks that for every unit specification
    % a body is provided

   IF EMPTY (p_descrs) THEN
      TRUE
   ELSE (NOT (HEAD (p_descrs).s_state = sc_spec_complete)
        CONDITION
          IT
          MESSAGE
          "this pack/subr/task has no body") AND
        ch_all_bodies_appeared (TAIL (p_descrs))
   FI;

FUNCTION ch_all_private_completed (p_descrs : tp_descr_list) BOOL:

    % called at the end of a private part and checks that
    % all (limited) private types and all deferred constants have
    % a corresponding complete declaration

   IF EMPTY (p_descrs) THEN
      TRUE
   ELSE (HEAD (p_descrs).s_state =/ sc_deferred     AND
```

```
        (HEAD (p_descrs).s_state =/ sc_incompl_private)
       CONDITION
          IT
          MESSAGE
          "this const/priv type has no full decl") AND
       ch_all_private_completed (TAIL (p_descrs))
   FI;

FUNCTION ch_all_types_completed (p_local : tp_descr_list) BOOL:

    % called at the end of a (syntactic) declarative
    % part, resp. at the end of a list of declarative items
    % and checks that all incomplete types have
    % a corresponding complete type declaration.

   IF EMPTY (p_local) THEN
      TRUE
   ELSE (HEAD (p_local).s_state /= sc_incomplete
       CONDITION IT
          MESSAGE
          "missing full decl of THIS incomplete type") AND
       ch_all_types_completed (TAIL (p_local))
   FI;

FUNCTION ch_alternatives (p_choices : tp_choice_list) BOOL :

    % check that no exception appears more than once

   IF EMPTY (p_choices) THEN
      TRUE
   ELSE CASE c_choice : HEAD (p_choices) OF
        IS tp_descr_set :
           IF f_head_descr (c_choice).s_nature = sc_exception THEN
              ch_alternatives1
                 (f_head_descr (c_choice).s_key,
                  TAIL (p_choices))
           ELSE TRUE
           FI
        OUT TRUE
        ESAC      AND
        ch_alternatives (TAIL (p_choices))
   FI;

FUNCTION ch_alternatives1 (p_exception : tp_key,
                           p_choices   : tp_choice_list) BOOL :

   IF EMPTY (p_choices) THEN
      TRUE
   ELSE CASE c_choice : HEAD (p_choices) OF
        IS tp_descr_set :
           IF f_head_descr (c_choice).s_key = p_exception THEN
              (FALSE CONDITION FALSE
                     MESSAGE "Exception appears more than once")
           ELSE TRUE
           FI
        OUT TRUE
        ESAC      AND
        ch_alternatives1 (p_exception, TAIL (p_choices))
   FI;
```

```
FUNCTION ch_compact_choices (p_l : tp_range_val_list) BOOL :

     % Input is a list of ordered choices (cf. f_order_choices).
     % Check that all choices within the minimum and the maximum
     % of this list are present.

   IF EMPTY (p_l)    THEN TRUE
   ELSE ch_compact_choices1 (p_l, HEAD (p_l).s_min-1, LAST (p_l).s_max)
   FI;


FUNCTION ch_compact_choices1 (p_l : tp_range_val_list,
                              p_min, p_max : INT)          BOOL :

   IF EMPTY (p_l)   THEN
      (p_min >= p_max CONDITION IT MESSAGE "choices missing") %p_min+1..
   ELSE IF p_min = (HEAD (p_l).s_min - 1)   THEN
      ch_compact_choices1 (TAIL (p_l), HEAD (p_l).s_max, p_max)
   ELSE IF p_min < HEAD (p_l).s_min     THEN
      (ch_compact_choices1 (TAIL (p_l), HEAD (p_l).s_max,p_max)AND FALSE
       CONDITION   %C 4.3/1
          FALSE
          MESSAGE  "choices missing") % p_min .. HEAD (p_l).s_min-1
   ELSE
      ch_compact_choices1 (TAIL (p_l),
                           IF p_min > HEAD (p_l).s_max    THEN p_min
                           ELSE HEAD (p_l).s_max
                           FI, p_max)
   FI FI FI;


FUNCTION ch_compatibl_ranges (p_new_range,
                              p_old_range : tp_range) BOOL:

     % Check that p_new_range is within p_old_range.

  CASE c_old : p_old_range OF
  IS tp_range_constr :
       CASE c_new : p_new_range OF
       IS tp_range_constr :
          f_eval_less_equal (c_old.s_lower_bound,
                             c_new.s_lower_bound) AND
          f_eval_less_equal (c_new.s_upper_bound,
                             c_old.s_upper_bound)
       OUT TRUE
       ESAC
    OUT TRUE
    ESAC;


FUNCTION ch_constraint (p_type    : tp_descr_set,
                        p_constr  : tp_constraint,
                        p_env     : tp_env) BOOL :

     % Check properties of constraint, which are not relevant
     % for overloading recolution, e.g. that no array constraint
     % is imposed on an already constrained array type.

  ch_constraint1 (f_head_descr (p_type),
                  p_constr,
```

```
             p_env);

FUNCTION ch_constraint1 (p_type   : tp_descr,
                         p_constr : tp_constraint,
                         p_env    : tp_env) BOOL :

   CASE c_type : f_parent_base_type2
                   (p_type.s_key,
                    p_env) OF
   IS tp_array : CASE c_constr : p_constr OF
                 IS tp_assoc_list :
                     ch_index_constr (c_type.s_indices,
                                      c_constr) AND
                    %C 3.3/1, C 3.6.1/1
                    ((f_constraint (p_type, p_env) IS tp_void)
                    CONDITION IT
                      MESSAGE
                      "constr illegal for alrd. constrd array type")
                 OUT (FALSE CONDITION FALSE MESSAGE "compiler error")
                 ESAC;
   IS tp_record : IS tp_private : IS tp_l_private : IS tp_incompl_type
                  CASE c_assocs : p_constr OF
                  IS tp_assoc_list :
                    ch_discr_constraint
                       (f_discriminants (tp_type (c_type)),
                        c_assocs,
                        p_env)              AND

                    %C 3.3/1, C 3.7.2/3
                    (f_constraint (p_type, p_env) IS tp_void
                     CONDITION IT
                       MESSAGE
                       "illegal constr for alr. constrd record type"
                  OUT (FALSE CONDITION FALSE MESSAGE "compiler error")
                  ESAC;
   IS tp_access :
      ((ch_constraint1
          (f_select_by_key (c_type.s_accessed.s_base_type,
                            p_env),
           p_constr,
           p_env)
        %C 3.3/1, C 3.6.1/1, C 3.7.2/3
        CONDITION (c_type.s_accessed.s_constraint IS tp_void)
            AND (f_constraint (p_type, p_env) IS tp_void)
          MESSAGE
          "constraint illegal on already constr type")
            AND
            CASE f_parent_base_type2 (c_type.s_accessed.s_base_type,
                                      p_env) OF
            IS tp_array : IS tp_record : IS tp_private :
            IS tp_l_private : IS tp_incompl_type : FALSE
            OUT TRUE
            ESAC
            CONDITION IT
              MESSAGE
              "only discrim/index constr. allowed on access type")
   OUT CASE c_constr : p_constr OF
       IS tp_range_constr :
          (ch_compatibl_ranges
             (c_constr,
```

```
            f_range_constr (p_type, p_env))
        CONDITION IT
           MESSAGE
           "new range incompatible with old")    AND
        %C 3.5.7/3
        (f_is_scalar_type (p_type, p_env)
        CONDITION IT
           MESSAGE
           "range constr only for scalar types");
    IS tp_fixed : ch_fixed_constr
                    (p_type,
                     c_constr,
                     p_env)    AND
                 (f_is_fixed_type (p_type,p_env)
                 CONDITION IT
                    MESSAGE
                    "fixed point constr only for fixed types");
    IS tp_float :  ch_float_constr
                       (p_type,
                        c_constr,
                        p_env)    AND
                  (f_is_float_type (p_type, p_env)
                  CONDITION IT
                     MESSAGE
                     "float type constr only for float types")
    OUT (FALSE
         CONDITION FALSE
            MESSAGE
            "index/discrim constraint illegal for this type")
    ESAC
  ESAC;

FUNCTION ch_control (p_name : tp_descr,
                     p_encl : tp_descr,
                     p_env  : tp_env) BOOL:

    % Check whether control is transfered out of a body or
    % an accept statement.
    % p_name denotes the enclosing entity, to which control is
    % transfered.

  IF p_encl.s_key = p_name.s_key THEN
     TRUE
  ELSE IF p_encl.s_nature = sc_loop OR
         (p_encl.s_nature = sc_block) THEN
     ch_control (p_name,
                 f_encl_descr1 (p_encl,p_env),
                 p_env)
  ELSE FALSE
  FI FI;

FUNCTION ch_deferred_constants (p_keys : tp_key_list,
                                p_type : tp_constrained,
                                p_is_init : BOOL,
                                p_env : tp_env) BOOL :

    % Incomplete and complete declarations of deferred constants
    % must have the same type.
    % The complete declaration must include an initialization.
```

```
   IF EMPTY (p_keys) THEN
      TRUE
   ELSE ch_deferred_constant (HEAD (p_keys),
                              p_type,
                              p_is_init,
                              p_env)           AND
        ch_deferred_constants (TAIL (p_keys),
                               p_type,
                               p_is_init,
                               p_env)
   FI;

FUNCTION ch_deferred_constant (p_key     : tp_key,
                               p_type    : tp_constrained,
                               p_is_init : BOOL,
                               p_env     : tp_env) BOOL:

   IF f_new_key (p_key, p_env) THEN
      TRUE
   ELSE (f_same_constrained
            (f_obj_constrained (p_key, p_env),
             p_type)
          CONDITION
             IT
          MESSAGE
             "THIS const. must have the same type as deferred const")
        AND
        (p_is_init CONDITION IT
          MESSAGE "Declaration of ^ hides previous declaration ...")
   FI;

FUNCTION ch_dependencies (p_descr          : tp_descr,
                          p_discr_allowed  : BOOL,
                          p_env            : tp_env) BOOL :

    % Check for unallowed use of
    %   - (generic) parameters in own formal part
    %   - record components in own record declaration.
    % However, - use in the own initialization part is allowed.
    %          - discriminants may be used in certain contexts.

   ch_usable (p_descr) AND
   IF (p_descr.s_enclosing = c_unaccessible) OR
      (p_descr.s_enclosing = c_standard)     OR
      (p_descr.s_enclosing = c_enclosing)    OR
      (p_descr.s_state = sc_in_init) THEN
      TRUE
   ELSE  CASE  f_select_by_key (p_descr.s_enclosing,
                                p_env).s_state OF
        sc_in_formal_part :
           (p_descr.s_state = sc_complete_generic
            %C 6.1/2
            CONDITION IT
               MESSAGE
               "don't mention params in their own formal part");
        sc_in_record : sc_in_discr_part :
           (IF p_discr_allowed THEN
               p_descr.s_nature = sc_discriminant
            ELSE FALSE
            FI
```

```
            %C 3.7.1/2,3,6
            CONDITION IT
               MESSAGE
               "don't mention record components in same record");
         sc_in_generic_part :
            (p_descr.s_den IS tp_type_den
            %C 12.1/1
            CONDITION IT
               MESSAGE
               "only gen-type-par may be mentioned by gen-par")
         OUT TRUE
         ESAC
   FI;

FUNCTION ch_discr_constraint (p_discrs : tp_descr_list,
                              p_assocs : tp_assoc_list,
                              p_env    : tp_env) BOOL:

      % Check properties of discriminant constraint, which are
      % not relevant for overloading resolution.

   IF EMPTY (p_assocs) THEN
      (EMPTY (p_discrs)
       %C 3.6.1/2
       CONDITION IT MESSAGE
          "missing constraint for discriminants")
   ELSE CASE c_assoc : HEAD (p_assocs) OF
         IS tp_comp_assoc :
            CASE c_choices : f_valid_record_choices
                                (c_assoc.s_choices,
                                 p_discrs,
                                 p_env) OF
            IS tp_void :
               (FALSE CONDITION FALSE MESSAGE
                        "this discrim does not belong to rec_type") AND
                ch_discr_constraint
                                  (p_discrs,
                                   TAIL (p_assocs),
                                   p_env);
            IS tp_choice_list :
               ch_discr_constraint
                  (f_choices_out (c_choices,
                                  p_discrs),
                   TAIL (p_assocs),
                   p_env)
            ESAC
         OUT (FALSE CONDITION FALSE MESSAGE
                      "illegal syntax for discrimiant constraint")
         ESAC
   FI;


FUNCTION ch_entry_of_current_task (p_entry : tp_descr_set,
                                   p_env   : tp_env) BOOL:

      % Check that an entry, (corresponding to an accept statement)
      % is declared within the current task and that the accept
      % statement does not occur within an exception handler.

   ch_entry_of_current_task1 (p_entry,
```

```
                              f_encl_descr (p_env),
                              p_env);

FUNCTION ch_entry_of_current_task1 (p_entry : tp_descr_set,
                                    p_encl  : tp_descr,
                                    p_env   : tp_env) BOOL:

   IF p_encl = c_standard_descr THEN
      (FALSE
       CONDITION FALSE
          MESSAGE
          "Accept stm does not correspond to any entry of this task")
   ELSE IF f_is_task (f_descr_set2 (p_encl), p_env) THEN
         ELEM_IN_LIST (f_head_descr (p_entry).s_key,
                   f_keys (f_task_entries (p_encl, p_env)))
         AND
         (p_encl.s_state /= sc_in_handler
          %C 9.5/2
          CONDITION IT MESSAGE
               "Accept stm must not appear within an exception handler"
   ELSE
      CASE p_encl.s_nature OF
      sc_generic_function : sc_generic_procedure :
      sc_package : sc_function : sc_procedure : sc_task :
      sc_type :   %task_type
        (FALSE
         %C 9.5.2/2
         CONDITION FALSE
            MESSAGE
            "Accept stm does not correspond to any entry of this task"
      OUT ch_entry_of_current_task1 (p_entry,
                                     f_encl_descr1 (p_encl,
                                                    p_env),
                                     p_env)
      ESAC
   FI FI;

FUNCTION ch_exhaustive_choices (p_type    : tp_type,
                                p_choices : tp_choice_list,
                                p_env     : tp_env) BOOL:

      % Called for choices in case statements and variant parts.
      % P_type describes the range for which each value must be
      % given (exactly once) : Either the type has a static constraint
      % or the range of the original type must be taken into account.

   CASE c_type : p_type OF
   IS tp_constrained :
      CASE c_constr : c_type.s_constraint OF
      IS tp_range_constr :
         IF f_is_static
               (f_object_value_kind (c_constr.s_lower_bound)) AND
            f_is_static
               (f_object_value_kind (c_constr.s_upper_bound)) THEN
            ch_exhaustive_choices1
               (f_object_value (c_constr.s_lower_bound) QUA INT,
                f_object_value (c_constr.s_upper_bound) QUA INT,
               p_choices)
         ELSE ch_exhaustive_choices
               (f_parent_base_type1 (c_type, p_env),
```

```
                p_choices,
                p_env)
        FI
     OUT TRUE  %no dscrt type
     ESAC;
   IS tp_integer :
     ch_exhaustive_choices1
        (f_object_value (c_type.s_range
           QUA tp_range_constr.s_lower_bound) QUA INT,
         f_object_value (c_type.s_range
           QUA tp_range_constr.s_upper_bound) QUA INT,
         p_choices);
   IS tp_enum_type : ch_exhaustive_choices1
                       (f_select_by_key
                          (HEAD (c_type.s_literals),
                           p_env).s_den QUA tp_enum_literal
                                  .s_pos,
                        f_select_by_key
                          (LAST (c_type.s_literals),
                           p_env).s_den QUA tp_enum_literal
                                  .s_pos,
                        p_choices)
   OUT TRUE  %no dscrt type
   ESAC;

FUNCTION ch_exhaustive_choices1 (p_min,
                                 p_max     : INT,
                                 p_choices : tp_choice_list) BOOL:

   ch_multiple_choices1
      (f_order_choices (p_choices,
                        tp_range_val_list ()),
       p_min,
       p_max)    AND
   IF IF EMPTY (p_choices) THEN
        FALSE
      ELSE LAST (p_choices) IS tp_others
      FI THEN
      TRUE
   ELSE ch_compact_choices1
          (f_order_choices (p_choices,
                            tp_range_val_list ()),
           p_min,
           p_max)
   FI;

FUNCTION ch_existence_depends_not (p_assocs : tp_assoc_list,
                                   p_env    : tp_env) BOOL:

     % for object renaming and actual in out parameters in generic
     % instantiations, the existence of an object must not depend
     % on discriminant-values (8.5 / 12.1.1).

   IF EMPTY (p_assocs) THEN
      TRUE
   ELSE IF HEAD (HEAD (p_assocs) QUA tp_comp_assoc.s_choices)
             QUA tp_descr.s_nature /= sc_in_out THEN
          TRUE
        ELSE ch_existence_depends_not_for_obj
               (HEAD (p_assocs) QUA tp_comp_assoc .s_actual,
```

```
                 p_env)
        FI AND
        ch_existence_depends_not
           (TAIL (p_assocs),
            p_env)
   FI;

FUNCTION ch_existence_depends_not_for_obj (p_obj : tp_descr_set,
                                           p_env : tp_env) BOOL :

  (CASE c_origin : f_head_descr (p_obj) s_origin OF
   IS tp_type_orig :
   IS tp_no_orig : TRUE;
   IS tp_entity_orig :
      CASE c_den : c_origin.s_descr.s_den OF
      IS tp_object :
         IF c_den.s_type.s_constraint /= sc_void THEN
            TRUE
         ELSE CASE c_type : f_object_parent_base_type1
                              (c_origin.s_descr,
                               p_env) OF
              IS tp_record :
                 IF EMPTY (f_discriminants (c_type)) THEN
                    TRUE
                 ELSE NOT f_variant_comp
                            (f_head_descr (p_obj).s_key,
                             c_type.s_comps)
                 FI
              OUT TRUE
              ESAC
         FI
      OUT TRUE
      ESAC
   ESAC
   CONDITION IT
      MESSAGE "Existence of object must not depend on discriminant");

FUNCTION ch_fixed_constr (p_type  : tp_descr,
                          p_fixed : tp_fixed,
                          p_env   : tp_env) BOOL :

      % Check properties of accuracy constraint for fixed type, which
      % are not relevant for overloading resolution

    %C 3.5.9/4
    (f_eval_less_equal
       (f_digits_delta (p_type,p_env),
        p_fixed.s_delta)
    CONDITION IT  MESSAGE
       "new delta smaller than old")      AND
    CASE c_range : p_fixed.s_range OF
    IS tp_void : TRUE;
    IS tp_range_constr :
       CASE c_new_range: f_make_range_void
                           (f_base_type (p_type),
                            c_range,
                            p_env) OF
       IS tp_void : TRUE;
       IS tp_range_constr :
            %C 3.5.9/4
```

```
          (ch_compatibl_ranges
              (c_new_range,
               f_range_constr (p_type, p_env))
           CONDITION IT  MESSAGE
              "new range incompatible with old")
      ESAC
   ESAC;

FUNCTION ch_float_constr (p_type  : tp_descr,
                          p_float : tp_float,
                          p_env   : tp_env) BOOL :

      % Check properties of accuracy constraint for float type, which
      % are not relevant for overloading resolution

   %C 3.5.7/4
   (f_eval_less_equal
      (p_float.s_digits,
       f_digits_delta (p_type, p_env))
   CONDITION IT MESSAGE
      "new digits bigger than old")  AND
   CASE c_range : p_float.s_range OF
   IS tp_void : TRUE;
   IS tp_range_constr :
      CASE c_new_range: f_make_range_void
                          (f_base_type (p_type),
                           c_range,
                           p_env)  OF
      IS tp_void  : TRUE;
      IS tp_range_constr :
         %C 3.5.7/4
         (ch_compatibl_ranges
            (c_new_range,
             f_range_constr (p_type, p_env))
         CONDITION IT MESSAGE
            "new range incompatible with old")
      ESAC
   ESAC;


FUNCTION ch_growing_values (p_ints : tp_enum_rep) BOOL :

      % For enumeration type representations check, that the integer
      % codes satisfy the ordering relation.

   IF EMPTY (p_ints) THEN
      TRUE
   ELSE IF EMPTY (TAIL (p_ints)) THEN
      TRUE
   ELSE ch_growing_values (TAIL (p_ints)) AND
      (%C 13.4/5
      NOT  f_eval_less_equal1 (HEAD (p_ints),
                               HEAD (TAIL (p_ints)))
      CONDITION IT
         MESSAGE
         "this enum rep value too big")
   FI FI;

FUNCTION ch_has_static_constraint1 (p_type  : tp_descr,
                                    p_env   : tp_env) BOOL:
```

```
      % Check whether p_type has a static constraint

   CASE c_den : p_type.s_den OF
   IS tp_constrained :
        IF c_den.s_constraint = sc_void
           THEN ch_has_static_constraint1
                (f_select_by_key (c_den.s_base_type, p_env),
                 p_env)
        ELSE ch_static_constraint (c_den.s_constraint)
        FI;
   IS tp_type_den :
      CASE c_type : c_den.s_type OF
      IS tp_array : IS tp_incompl_type : IS tp_private :
      IS tp_l_private : IS tp_task_spec : IS tp_error_type :
      IS tp_void : IS tp_formal_type : FALSE;
      IS tp_record : EMPTY (f_discriminants (c_type))
      OUT TRUE
      ESAC
   OUT TRUE
   ESAC;

FUNCTION ch_has_static_constraint2 (p_object : tp_descr_set,
                                    p_env    : tp_env) BOOL:

      % Check whether a record component has a static constraint

   CASE c_den : f_head_descr (p_object).s_den OF
   IS tp_object :
      ch_has_static_constraint1
         (f_select_by_key (c_den.s_type.s_base_type, p_env),
          p_env) OR
      IF c_den.s_type.s_constraint /= sc_void THEN
         ch_static_constraint
            (c_den.s_type.s_constraint)
      ELSE FALSE
      FI
   OUT TRUE
   ESAC;

FUNCTION ch_have_default (p_descrs : tp_descr_list) BOOL :

      % Check that for a generic instantiation all not specified
      % parameters have default values.

   IF EMPTY (p_descrs) THEN
      TRUE
   ELSE ch_have_default (TAIL (p_descrs))   AND
       (CASE c_den : HEAD (p_descrs).s_den OF
        IS tp_object : c_den.s_init =/ c_no_init;
        IS tp_subpr :  (c_den.s_def IS tp_key)
        OUT TRUE
        ESAC
        CONDITION IT MESSAGE
           "THIS parameter has no default value")
   FI;

FUNCTION ch_in_range (p_value : tp_value,
                      p_range : tp_range) BOOL:
```

```
    % Check whether p_value is within p_range

   CASE c_range : p_range OF
   IS tp_void : FALSE;
   IS tp_range_constr :
      (f_eval_less_equal1 (p_value,
                           f_object_value (c_range.s_upper_bound))
        CONDITION IT MESSAGE "W: value too big") AND
      (f_eval_less_equal1 (f_object_value (c_range.s_lower_bound),
                           p_value)
        CONDITION IT MESSAGE "W: value too small")
   ESAC;

FUNCTION ch_index_constr (p_indices : tp_dscrt_range_list,
                          p_assocs  : tp_assoc_list) BOOL :

    % Check properties of an index constraint, which are not
    % relevant for overloading resolution.

   IF EMPTY (p_indices) AND EMPTY (p_assocs) THEN
      TRUE
   ELSE IF EMPTY (p_indices) THEN
      (ch_index_constr (p_indices, TAIL (p_assocs))
      %C 3.6.1/2
      CONDITION FALSE MESSAGE
         "superfluous index constraint")
   ELSE IF EMPTY (p_assocs) THEN
      (ch_index_constr (TAIL (p_indices), p_assocs)
      %C 3.6/1
      CONDITION FALSE MESSAGE
         "missing index constraint")
   ELSE ch_index_constr (TAIL (p_indices), TAIL (p_assocs))
   FI FI FI;

FUNCTION ch_is_assign_allowed (p_name : tp_descr_set,
                               p_env  : tp_env) BOOL :

    % Assignment is allowed only for (converted) variables of a type
    % that allowes for assignment.

   CASE c_den : f_head_descr (p_name).s_den OF
   IS tp_object :
      CASE f_head_descr (p_name).s_nature OF
      sc_constant : sc_in : sc_number : sc_value :
      sc_discriminant : FALSE
      OUT TRUE
      ESAC                                          AND
      ch_is_assign_allowed_for_type
         (f_type
             (f_object_type1 (c_den),
              p_env),
          p_env)
   OUT (TRUE CONDITION FALSE MESSAGE
              "the name of an object expected here")
   ESAC;

FUNCTION ch_is_assign_allowed_for_type (p_type : tp_type,
                                        p_env  : tp_env) BOOL:

   CASE c_type : f_parent_base_type1 (p_type, p_env) OF
```

```
   IS tp_l_private : (FALSE CONDITION FALSE MESSAGE
      "assign/comp prohibited for limited private types");
   IS tp_task_spec : (FALSE CONDITION FALSE MESSAGE
      "assign/comp prohibited for task types");
   IS tp_incompl_type : (FALSE CONDITION FALSE MESSAGE
      "assign/comp prohibited for incomplete types")
   OUT (f_is_assign_allowed_for_type (p_type, p_env)
        CONDITION IT MESSAGE "Type does not allow for assignment")
   ESAC;

FUNCTION ch_is_obj_subp_pack_task_entr (p_entity : tp_descr_set,
                                        p_env    : tp_env) BOOL :

      % Check valid name in address representation specification

   CASE c_den : f_head_descr (p_entity).s_den OF
   IS tp_object : IS tp_subpr : IS tp_package : TRUE;
   IS tp_entry_family : (FALSE
                        %C 13.5/3
                        CONDITION FALSE MESSAGE
                           "no entry families allowed in addr spec");
   IS tp_entry : (NOT (f_select_by_key
                        (f_head_descr (p_entity).s_key,
                         p_env).s_den IS tp_entry_family)
                  %C 13.5/3
                  CONDITION IT MESSAGE
                     "no entry of a family allowed in addr spec")
   OUT FALSE
   ESAC;

FUNCTION ch_is_positive (p_exp : tp_descr_set) BOOL :

   NOT f_eval_less_equal1 (f_object_value (p_exp), 0);

FUNCTION ch_is_tasks (p_names : tp_descr_list,
                      p_env   : tp_env) BOOL :

      % Check that all names appearing in an abort statement are tasks

   IF EMPTY (p_names) THEN
      TRUE
   ELSE ch_is_tasks (TAIL (p_names), p_env)       AND
        (HEAD (p_names).s_nature = sc_task        OR
         CASE c_den : HEAD (p_names).s_den OF
         IS tp_object :
            f_type (c_den.s_type.s_base_type,
                    p_env)
         IS tp_task_spec
         OUT FALSE
         ESAC)
   FI;

FUNCTION ch_literal_exp (p_exp : tp_descr_set) BOOL:

   f_object_init (p_exp).s_exp_kind = sc_literal;

FUNCTION ch_local_hiding (p_designator : tp_designator,
                          p_den        : tp_den,
                          p_key        : tp_key,
                          p_local      : tp_descr_list,
```

```
                          p_env          : tp_env) BOOL:

     % Check whether the entity with p_designator, p_key and p_den
     % hides any other entity in p_local.

IF p_designator IS tp_anonymous
   THEN TRUE
ELSE
   CASE c_den : p_den OF
   IS tp_enum_literal :
        ch_local_overl1
           (f_select_by_designator2
               (p_designator,
                p_local));
   IS tp_entry : IS tp_subpr :
        ch_local_overl
          (f_spec1 (c_den),
           p_key,
           f_select_by_designator2
              (p_designator,
               p_local),
           p_env)
   OUT  LENGTH (f_select_by_designator2
                  (p_designator,
                   p_local))< 2
   ESAC
FI;

FUNCTION ch_local_overl (p_spec      : tp_header,
                          p_key       : tp_key,
                          p_descrs    : tp_descr_list,
                          p_env       : tp_env) BOOL:

     % Check whether a subprogram or an entry (with p_key and p_spec)
     % overloads al other entities in p_descrs.

   IF EMPTY (p_descrs) THEN
      TRUE
   ELSE ((HEAD (p_descrs).s_key = p_key)
         OR
         %A 3.4/1
         (HEAD (p_descrs).s_state = sc_implicitly_declared)
         OR
         CASE c_den : HEAD (p_descrs).s_den OF
         IS tp_entry : IS tp_subpr :
             NOT f_hiding_specs
                  (p_spec,
                   f_spec1 (c_den),
                   TRUE,
                   p_env);
         IS tp_enum_literal : TRUE
         OUT FALSE
         ESAC)
                                                         AND
        ch_local_overl (p_spec,
                        p_key,
                        TAIL (p_descrs),
                        p_env)
  FI;
```

```
FUNCTION ch_local_overl1 (p_descrs : tp_descr_list)
                          BOOL :

    % Check whether all entities in p_descrs are overloadable,
    % i.e. enumeration literals, subprograms or entries.

   IF EMPTY (p_descrs) THEN
      TRUE
   ELSE f_is_overloadable (HEAD (p_descrs)) AND
        ch_local_overl1 (TAIL (p_descrs))
   FI;

FUNCTION ch_matching_discr_parts (p_type1,
                                  p_type2 : tp_type) BOOL :

    % Check equality of discriminant parts for
    % - incomplete / (limited) private type and complete type
    %   declaration
    % - formal and actual generic parameter
    % according to 7.4.1

   ch_matching_discr_parts1 (f_discriminants (p_type1),
                             f_discriminants (p_type2));

FUNCTION ch_matching_discr_parts1 (p_discrs1,
                                   p_discrs2 : tp_descr_list)
                                               BOOL :

   IF EMPTY (p_discrs1) AND EMPTY (p_discrs2) THEN
      TRUE
   ELSE IF EMPTY (p_discrs1) OR EMPTY (p_discrs2) THEN
      (FALSE CONDITION FALSE MESSAGE
               "Discriminant part too short or too long")
   ELSE (HEAD (p_discrs1).s_designator =
         HEAD (p_discrs2).s_designator
         CONDITION IT MESSAGE %C 7.4/1
            "THIS discrim has wrong name")          AND
        (f_object_type (HEAD (p_discrs1)) =
         f_object_type (HEAD (p_discrs2))
         CONDITION IT MESSAGE %C 7.4/1
            "THIS discrim has wrong type")          AND
        (f_object_init1 (HEAD (p_discrs1)) /= c_no_init AND
        (f_object_init1 (HEAD (p_discrs2)) /= c_no_init) OR
        (f_object_init1 (HEAD (p_discrs1)) =
         f_object_init1 (HEAD (p_discrs2)))
         CONDITION IT MESSAGE  %C 7.4/1
            "Missing or superfluous discriminant initialization") AND
        (f_tree_same_value
            (f_object_init1 (HEAD (p_discrs1)).s_value,
             f_object_init1 (HEAD (p_discrs2)).s_value)
         CONDITION IT MESSAGE %C 7.4/1
            "THIS discriminant has wrong initial value")  AND
         ch_matching_discr_parts1
            (TAIL (p_discrs1),
             TAIL (p_discrs2))
   FI FI;

FUNCTION ch_matching_indices (p_formals,
                              p_actuals : tp_dscrt_range_list,
                              p_env     : tp_env) BOOL :
```

```
    % Check that indices of actual and formal generic array
    % types match.

  IF EMPTY (p_formals) AND EMPTY (p_actuals) THEN
     TRUE
  ELSE IF EMPTY (p_formals) OR EMPTY (p_actuals) THEN
     (FALSE
      %C 12.3.4./1
      CONDITION FALSE
         MESSAGE
         "same number of indices required")
  ELSE ch_matching_indices
         (TAIL (p_formals),
          TAIL (p_actuals),
          p_env)                           AND
       CASE c_formal : HEAD (p_formals) OF
       IS tp_index :
          CASE c_actual : HEAD (p_actuals) OF
          IS tp_index :
             (c_formal.s_type.s_base_type =
              c_actual.s_type.s_base_type
              %C 12.3.4/3
              CONDITION IT
                 MESSAGE
                 "Same index types required")
          OUT (TRUE CONDITION FALSE MESSAGE "compiler error")
          ESAC
       OUT (TRUE CONDITION FALSE MESSAGE "compiler error")
       ESAC
  FI FI;

FUNCTION ch_matching_types0 (p_formal   : tp_den,
                             p_actual   : tp_descr,
                             p_expected : tp_descr_list,
                             p_env      : tp_env) BOOL:

    % Check matching formal and actual generic types.

  CASE c_formal : p_formal OF
  IS tp_type_den :
     ch_matching_types (c_formal.s_type,
                        p_formal,
                        p_actual,
                        p_env);
  IS tp_constrained :  % a constrained array type
     ch_matching_types (f_type1
                         (f_select_by_key11
                            (c_formal.s_base_type,
                             p_expected)),
                        p_formal,
                        p_actual,
                        p_env)
  OUT FALSE
  ESAC;

FUNCTION ch_matching_types (p_f_type : tp_type,
                            p_formal : tp_den,
                            p_actual : tp_descr,
                            p_env    : tp_env) BOOL:
```

```
CASE c_den : p_actual.s_den OF
IS tp_type_den : IS tp_constrained :
   CASE c_act_type : f_parent_base_type2
                        (p_actual.s_key,
                         p_env) OF
   IS tp_error_type :  TRUE
   OUT CASE c_form_type : p_f_type OF
        IS tp_private : IS tp_l_private :
           (%C 12.3.2/1
            IF c_form_type IS tp_private THEN
               (ch_is_assign_allowed_for_type
                  (c_act_type,
                   p_env)
                CONDITION IT
                   MESSAGE
                   "Actual type should allow assignment/comparison")
            ELSE TRUE
            FI) AND
           (%C 12.3.2/3
            (NOT (c_act_type IS tp_array))  OR
            (NOT (f_constraint (p_actual, p_env) IS tp_void))
            CONDITION IT MESSAGE
               "unconstr. array types prohibited here");
        IS tp_formal_type :
           CASE c_form_type : c_form_type OF
           sc_formal_discrt :
              (%C 12.3.3/1
               f_is_discrete_type (p_actual, p_env)
               CONDITION IT MESSAGE
                  "actual type should be a discrete type ");
           sc_formal_fixed :
              (%C 12.3.3/1
               f_is_fixed_type (p_actual, p_env)
               CONDITION IT MESSAGE
                  "actual type should be a fixed type");
           sc_formal_float :
              (%C 12.3.3/1
               f_is_float_type (p_actual, p_env)
               CONDITION IT MESSAGE
                  "actual type should be float type");
           sc_formal_integer :
              (%C 12.3.3/1
               f_is_int_type (p_actual,p_env)
               CONDITION IT MESSAGE
                  "actual type should be an integer type")
           ESAC;
        IS tp_array:
           CASE c_act_type : c_act_type OF
           IS tp_array :
              (IF p_formal IS tp_constrained THEN
                  (c_den IS tp_constrained
                   CONDITION IT
                      MESSAGE "Constrained array type expected")
               ELSE (NOT (c_den IS tp_constrained)
                     CONDITION IT
                        MESSAGE "Unconstrained array type expected")
               FI)    AND
              (%C 12.3.4/2
               c_act_type.s_comp_type.s_base_type =
```

```
               c_form_type.s_comp_type.s_base_type
               CONDITION IT MESSAGE
                  "wrong matching of form/act comp type")
              AND
              %C 12.3.4/3
               ch_matching_indices
                  (c_form_type.s_indices,
                   c_act_type.s_indices,
                   p_env)
           OUT (FALSE
               CONDITION FALSE MESSAGE
                  "actual type should be an array type")
           ESAC;
         IS tp_access :
           CASE c_act_type : c_act_type OF
           IS tp_access :
           (%C 12.3.5/1
               c_act_type.s_accessed.s_base_type =
               c_form_type.s_accessed.s_base_type
               CONDITION IT MESSAGE
                  "form/act access type should access same type")
           OUT (FALSE CONDITION FALSE MESSAGE
                      "actual type should be an access type")
           ESAC
        OUT (TRUE CONDITION FALSE MESSAGE
                  "compiler error")
        ESAC          AND
        (ch_matching_discr_parts
           (c_act_type,
            p_f_type)
          %C 12.3.5/2
          CONDITION IT
             MESSAGE
             "act_type must have same discriminants with form_type")
     ESAC
   OUT (FALSE
       CONDITION FALSE
          MESSAGE
          "actual parameter should be a type")
   ESAC;

FUNCTION ch_multiple_choices (p_l : tp_range_val_list) BOOL :

      % Check that no choice contained in p_l occurs more than once.

   IF EMPTY (p_l)    THEN TRUE
   ELSE ch_multiple_choices1 (p_l, HEAD (p_l).s_min-1, LAST (p_l).s_max)
   FI;

FUNCTION ch_multiple_choices1 (p_l : tp_range_val_list,
                               p_min, p_max : INT)        BOOL :
   IF EMPTY (p_l) THEN
     (p_min <= p_max CONDITION IT MESSAGE "choices out of range")
                                                 % p_max+1 .. p_min
   ELSE IF p_min < HEAD (p_l).s_min    THEN
      ch_multiple_choices1 (TAIL (p_l), HEAD (p_l).s_max, p_max)
   ELSE
     (ch_multiple_choices1 (TAIL (p_l),
                            IF p_min > HEAD (p_l).s_max    THEN p_min
                            ELSE HEAD (p_l).s_max
```

```
                       FI, p_max) AND FALSE
      CONDITION    %C 4.3/1
          FALSE
          MESSAGE
          "multiple choices") % p_min..MIN (p_min,HEAD (p_l).s_min)
   FI FI;

FUNCTION ch_no_named_ex_others (p_assocs : tp_assoc_list) BOOL :

       % Check that in an array aggregate with positional associations
       % no named association must occur except with the choice OTHERS

    IF EMPTY (p_assocs) THEN
       TRUE
    ELSE IF EMPTY (HEAD (p_assocs) QUA tp_comp_assoc .s_choices) THEN
           TRUE   %positional assoc
        ELSE HEAD (HEAD (p_assocs) QUA tp_comp_assoc .s_choices)
              IS tp_others
        FI    AND
        ch_no_named_ex_others (TAIL (p_assocs))
    FI;

FUNCTION ch_no_recursion (p_type_key  : tp_key,
                          p_type      : tp_type,
                          p_env       : tp_env) BOOL :

       % Check that p_type_key is not the key of a type on which p_type
       % depends. Otherwise p_type is defined recursively.

   ch_no_recursion1 (p_type_key,
                     f_used_types (p_type, p_env),
                     p_env);

FUNCTION ch_no_recursion1 (p_type   : tp_key,
                           p_types  : tp_key_list,
                           p_env    : tp_env) BOOL :

     IF EMPTY (p_types) THEN
        TRUE
     ELSE IF ELEM_IN_LIST (p_type, p_types) THEN
            FALSE
          ELSE ch_no_recursion1 (p_type,
                                 TAIL (p_types),
                                 p_env)                     AND

               ch_no_recursion1 (p_type,
                                 f_used_types (f_type (HEAD (p_types),
                                                        p_env),
                                               p_env),
                                 p_env)
          FI
     FI;

FUNCTION ch_non_null_range (p_range : tp_range) BOOL :

       % Check that for integer type definitions no null range is used.

    CASE c_range : p_range OF
    IS tp_void : TRUE;
```

```
  IS tp_range_constr :
     f_eval_less_equal (c_range.s_lower_bound,
                  c_range.s_upper_bound)
  ESAC;

FUNCTION ch_operator_overloading (p_designator : tp_designator,
                                  p_header     : tp_header,
                                  p_env        : tp_env) BOOL :

     % Check that equality is explicitly defined only for limited
     % private types, that the result is of type boolean and
     % that the operator definition contains exactly two parameters.

  IF f_is_operator (p_designator) THEN
       CASE p_designator QUA SYMB OF
         c_equal_desi :
               (f_l_private1 (f_parameters1 (p_header),
                              p_env)
                CONDITION IT MESSAGE
                  "the parameters must be /composite/limited private")
                                                      AND
               (f_result1 (p_header).s_base_type = c_bool
                CONDITION IT MESSAGE
                   "the result must be boolean")
                                                      AND
               IF LENGTH (f_parameters1 (p_header)) = 2 THEN
                  (HEAD (f_parameters1 (p_header)).s_den
                           QUA tp_object .s_type.s_base_type =
                      HEAD (TAIL (f_parameters1 (p_header))).s_den
                           QUA tp_object .s_type.s_base_type
                      CONDITION IT MESSAGE
                     "the two parameters must be of the same type")
                ELSE TRUE
                FI
         OUT TRUE
         ESAC
  ELSE TRUE
  FI;

FUNCTION ch_operator_string (op : SYMB) BOOL :

     % Checks that S is overloadable operator string ('/=' is not!).
     % String is assumed to consist only of upper case letters.

     (op = 'AND') OR (op = 'OR') OR (op ='XOR') OR (op = '=')
  OR (op = '<')   OR (op = '<=') OR (op = '>')   OR (op = '>=')
  OR (op = '+')   OR (op = '-')  OR (op = '&')   OR (op = 'NOT')
  OR (op = '*')   OR (op = '/')  OR (op = 'REM') OR (op = 'MOD')
  OR (op = '**');

FUNCTION ch_param_number (op : SYMB, n : INT) BOOL :

     % Checks that OP is defined with correct parameter number

  IF        op ='NOT'                    THEN n=1
  ELSE IF (op = '+') OR (op = '-') THEN (n=1) OR (n=2)
  ELSE                                        n=2
  FI FI;
```

```
FUNCTION ch_pragma (p_designator : tp_designator,
                    p_assocs     : tp_assoc_list,
                    p_env        : tp_env) BOOL :

    % Check - length of parameter list
    %       - (forbidden) choices
    %       - occurence in the appropriate declarative part
    %       - valid parameters

  %CHECK LENGTH OF PARAMETER LIST

  IF CASE p_designator QUA SYMB OF
     'controlled' : 'include' : 'list' :
     'memory_size' : 'optimize' : 'pack' : 'priority' :
     'storage_unit' : 'system' :
     (LENGTH (p_assocs) = 1
      CONDITION IT
      MESSAGE "exactly one parameter required");
     'interface' : (LENGTH (p_assocs) = 2
                    CONDITION IT
                    MESSAGE "exactly two parameters required");
     'suppress' : ((LENGTH (p_assocs) = 1)  OR (LENGTH (p_assocs) = 2
                    CONDITION IT
                    MESSAGE "one or two parameters reqired");
     'inline' : 'project' : TRUE
    OUT (FALSE CONDITION FALSE MESSAGE "pragma not handled")
    ESAC THEN

  %CHECK CHOICES
  CASE p_designator QUA SYMB OF
     'controlled' : 'include': 'list' :
     'memory_size' : 'optimize' : 'pack' : 'priority' :
     'storage_unit' : 'system' : 'suppress' :
     (EMPTY (HEAD (p_assocs) QUA tp_comp_assoc .s_choices)
      CONDITION IT
      MESSAGE "no named parameter associations allowed");
     'interface' :
        ((EMPTY (HEAD (p_assocs) QUA tp_comp_assoc.s_choices)
              AND
           EMPTY (LAST (p_assocs) QUA tp_comp_assoc.s_choices))
           CONDITION IT
           MESSAGE "no named parameter associations allowed")
    OUT TRUE
    ESAC
                         AND
  %CHECK LEGAL ENCLOSING
  CASE p_designator QUA SYMB OF
  'memory_size' : 'storage_unit' : 'suppress' :
     ((f_enclosing (p_env) = c_standard)
      CONDITION IT
      MESSAGE "pragma must appear in the outermost declarative part")
  'controlled' : 'interface' : 'pack' :
     (f_head_descr
        (LAST (p_assocs) QUA tp_comp_assoc .s_actual).s_enclosing
      = f_enclosing (p_env) AND
      (f_enclosing (p_env) /= c_standard)
      CONDITION IT
      MESSAGE
```

```
   "pragma does not appear in the appropriate declarative part");
'priority' : ((f_encl_descr (p_env).s_state = sc_in_visible) AND
              ((f_encl_descr (p_env).s_nature = sc_variable) OR
                (f_encl_descr (p_env).s_nature = sc_type)) OR
                (f_encl_descr (p_env).s_enclosing = c_standard)
              CONDITION IT
              MESSAGE "pragma not allowed in this context")
OUT TRUE
ESAC

                 AND

%CHECK PARAMETERS
CASE p_designator QUA SYMB OF
'controlled' :
   (CASE c_den : f_head_descr
            (HEAD (p_assocs) QUA tp_comp_assoc .s_actual)
            .s_den OF
    IS tp_type_den : c_den.s_type IS tp_access
    OUT FALSE
    ESAC
    CONDITION IT
    MESSAGE "access type name expected");
'inline' : ch_subpr_den (p_assocs, p_env);
'list' :
   CASE f_head_descr (HEAD (p_assocs) QUA tp_comp_assoc .s_actual)
        .s_designator QUA SYMB OF
   'on' : 'off' : TRUE
   OUT (FALSE CONDITION FALSE
              MESSAGE "parameter must be 'ON' or 'OFF'")
   ESAC;
'memory_size' : 'storage_unit' :
   (CASE c_den : f_head_descr (HEAD (p_assocs) QUA tp_comp_assoc
                                 .s_actual) .s_den OF
    IS tp_object : c_den.s_type.s_base_type = c_univ_int
    OUT FALSE
    ESAC
    CONDITION IT
    MESSAGE "integer number required");
'optimize' :
   CASE f_head_descr (HEAD (p_assocs) QUA tp_comp_assoc .s_actual)
        .s_designator QUA SYMB OF
   'time' : 'space' : TRUE
   OUT (FALSE CONDITION FALSE
             MESSAGE "parameter must be 'SPACE' or 'TIME'")
   ESAC;
'pack' :
   (CASE c_den : f_head_descr (HEAD (p_assocs) QUA tp_comp_assoc
                                 .s_actual) .s_den OF
    IS tp_type_den : c_den.s_type IS tp_record OR
                   (c_den.s_type IS tp_array);
    IS tp_constrained : f_type (c_den.s_base_type, p_env)
                          IS tp_record OR
                     (f_type (c_den.s_base_type, p_env)
                          IS tp_array)
    OUT FALSE
    ESAC
    CONDITION IT
    MESSAGE "record or array type name expected");
'priority' :
```

```
    (CASE c_den : f_head_descr (HEAD (p_assocs) QUA tp_comp_assoc
                  .s_actual) .s_den OF
     IS tp_object : c_den.s_type.s_base_type = c_int AND
                  (c_den.s_init.s_exp_kind = sc_static OR
                  (c_den.s_init.s_exp_kind = sc_literal))
     OUT FALSE
     ESAC
     CONDITION IT
     MESSAGE "static integer expression expected");
  'suppress' :
    CASE f_head_descr (HEAD (p_assocs) QUA tp_comp_assoc .s_actual)
         .s_designator QUA SYMB OF
    'access_check' : 'index_check' : 'length_check' : 'range_check'
    'discriminant_check' : 'division_check' : 'overflow_check' :
    'storage_check' : TRUE
    OUT (FALSE CONDITION FALSE MESSAGE "illegal check name")
    ESAC AND
    IF LENGTH (p_assocs) = 2 THEN
       IF EMPTY (LAST (p_assocs) QUA tp_comp_assoc.s_choices) THEN
           TRUE
         ELSE (f_head_descr (HEAD (LAST (p_assocs) QUA tp_comp_assoc
              .s_choices) QUA tp_descr_set).s_designator = 'on'
              CONDITION IT
              MESSAGE "second parameter must be '[ON =>] <name>'")
         FI  AND
         CASE f_head_descr (LAST (p_assocs) QUA tp_comp_assoc
              .s_actual) .s_nature OF
         sc_variable : sc_constant : sc_type : sc_subtype : TRUE
         OUT (FALSE CONDITION FALSE
              MESSAGE "object or type name expected")
         ESAC
     ELSE TRUE
     FI
  OUT TRUE
  ESAC

  ELSE FALSE
  FI;

FUNCTION ch_repr_spec_deriv (p_name : tp_descr_set,
                             p_attr : tp_designator,
                             p_env  : tp_env) BOOL :

     % Check that
     %       - no representation specification may be given for a typ
     %         derived from an access type
     %       - only length specifications are allowed for a type
     %         that has derived user defined subprograms

   ch_repr_spec_deriv1 (CASE c_den : f_head_descr (p_name).s_den OF
                        IS tp_type_den : c_den;
                        IS tp_constrained : f_type_den
                                            (c_den.s_base_type,
                                             p_env)
                       OUT c_error_type_den
                       ESAC,
                       f_is_length_attribute (p_attr),
                       p_env);
```

```
FUNCTION ch_repr_spec_deriv1 (p_type          : tp_type_den,
                              p_is_length_spec : BOOL,
                              p_env           : tp_env) BOOL:

  CASE c_type : p_type.s_type OF
  IS tp_derived :
     %C 13.1/4
     (NOT (f_type (c_type.s_parent_type, p_env) IS tp_access)
      CONDITION IT
        MESSAGE
        "repr spec false for derived from access")  AND
     %C 13.1/5
     (f_has_no_user_subprs (p_type.s_derivable_subprogs, p_env) OR
      p_is_length_spec
      CONDITION IT
        MESSAGE
        "repr spec false for derived with user subprogs")
  OUT TRUE
  ESAC;

FUNCTION ch_repr_spec_length (p_attr     : tp_designator,
                              p_type     : tp_descr,
                              p_exp      : tp_descr_set,
                              p_env      : tp_env) BOOL:

     % Check conditions for length specifications

  CASE c_attr : p_attr QUA SYMB OF
  c_size_desi :
     (%C 13.2/2
     NOT (cf_type_task (p_type,
                       p_env) IS tp_task_spec)
     CONDITION IT
        MESSAGE "size spec false for task types")             AND
     (%C 13.2/3
     ch_static_int (p_exp, p_env)
     CONDITION IT
        MESSAGE "static integer expression required")         AND
     (%C 13.2/4
     ch_has_static_constraint1 (p_type, p_env)
     CONDITION IT
        MESSAGE "type should have static constraint");
  c_stor_size_desi :
     (%C 13.2/5
     CASE c_type : cf_type_task (p_type,
                                 p_env) OF
     IS tp_access : IS tp_task_spec : TRUE
     OUT FALSE
     ESAC
     CONDITION IT
        MESSAGE "access or task type expected") AND
     (%C 13.2/6
     f_is_int_type2 (f_object_type (f_head_descr (p_exp)),
                     p_env)
     CONDITION IT
        MESSAGE "an integer type expected");
  c_act_delta_desi :
     %C 13.2/7
     CASE c_type : cf_type_task (p_type,
                                 p_env) OF
```

```
      IS tp_fixed : %C 13.2/8
                     (ch_literal_exp (p_exp)
                      CONDITION IT MESSAGE
                          "a literal expression required") AND
                      %C 13.2/8
                      (ch_static_real (p_exp)
                       CONDITION IT MESSAGE
                           "a real expression required") AND
                      %C 13.2/9
                       (f_eval_less_equal
                            (p_exp,
                             c_type.s_delta)
                         CONDITION IT MESSAGE
                             "actual_delta too big")
      %C 13.2/7
      OUT (FALSE CONDITION FALSE MESSAGE
                     "a fixed type required")
      ESAC
   OUT TRUE
   ESAC;

FUNCTION ch_static_assocs (p_assocs : tp_assoc_list) BOOL:

   IF EMPTY (p_assocs) THEN
      FALSE
   ELSE ch_static_assocs1 (p_assocs)
   FI;

FUNCTION ch_static_assocs1 (p_assocs : tp_assoc_list) BOOL:

   IF EMPTY (p_assocs) THEN
      TRUE
   ELSE CASE c_assoc : HEAD (p_assocs) OF
        IS tp_comp_assoc : ch_static_choices (c_assoc.s_choices) AND
                           ch_static_descr_set (c_assoc.s_actual);
        IS tp_dscrt_range : ch_static_dscrt_range (c_assoc)
        ESAC                                                    AND
        ch_static_assocs1 (TAIL (p_assocs))
   FI;

FUNCTION ch_static_choice (p_choice : tp_choice) BOOL:

   CASE c_choice : p_choice OF
   IS tp_descr :
   IS tp_others : TRUE;
   IS tp_descr_set : ch_static_descr_set (c_choice);
   IS tp_dscrt_range : ch_static_dscrt_range (c_choice)
   ESAC;

FUNCTION ch_static_choices (p_choices : tp_choice_list) BOOL:

   IF EMPTY (p_choices) THEN
      TRUE
   ELSE ch_static_choice (HEAD (p_choices)) AND
        ch_static_choices (TAIL (p_choices))
   FI;


FUNCTION ch_static_constraint (p_constr : tp_constraint) BOOL:
```

```
   CASE c_constr : p_constr OF
   IS tp_void : TRUE;
   IS tp_range_constr : ch_static_range (c_constr);
   IS tp_fixed : ch_static_descr_set (c_constr.s_delta) AND
                 ch_static_range (c_constr.s_range);
   IS tp_float : ch_static_descr_set (c_constr.s_digits) AND
                 ch_static_range (c_constr.s_range);
   IS tp_dscrt_range_list :
                 ch_static_dscrt_ranges (c_constr);
   IS tp_assoc_list :
                 ch_static_assocs (c_constr)
   ESAC;

FUNCTION ch_static_descr_set (p_descr_set : tp_descr_set) BOOL:

   IF f_is_object (p_descr_set) THEN
     f_object_value_kind (p_descr_set) = sc_static  OR
    (f_object_value_kind (p_descr_set) = sc_literal)
   ELSE TRUE
   FI;

FUNCTION ch_static_discrim_array (p_name : tp_descr_set,
                                  p_env  : tp_env) BOOL :

     % Check that in records dynamic arrays may only appear
     % if the dynamic bounds are discriminants of the record.

   CASE c_type : f_parent_base_type2
                  (f_head_descr (p_name).s_key,
                   p_env) OF
   IS tp_array :
          CASE c_constr : f_constraint (f_head_descr (p_name),
                                        p_env) OF
          IS tp_dscrt_range_list:
               ch_static_discrim_ranges (c_constr,
                                         p_env)
          OUT FALSE
          ESAC
   OUT TRUE
   ESAC;

FUNCTION ch_static_discrim_ranges (p_ranges : tp_dscrt_range_list,
                                   p_env    : tp_env) BOOL :

   IF EMPTY (p_ranges)
     THEN TRUE
   ELSE ch_static_discrim_ranges (TAIL (p_ranges), p_env) AND
        ch_static_discrim_range (HEAD (p_ranges), p_env)
   FI;

FUNCTION ch_static_discrim_range (p_range : tp_dscrt_range,
                                  p_env   : tp_env) BOOL:

   CASE c_range : p_range OF
   IS tp_index : FALSE;
   IS tp_constrained :
        CASE c_range1 : c_range.s_constraint OF
        IS tp_range_constr :  ch_static_discrim_range1 (c_range1,
                                                        p_env)
        OUT ch_has_static_constraint1
```

```
                (f_select_by_key (c_range.s_base_type, p_env),
                 p_env)
        ESAC;
    IS tp_range :
        ch_static_discrim_range1 (c_range,
                                   p_env)
    ESAC;

FUNCTION ch_static_discrim_range1 (p_range : tp_range,
                                    p_env   : tp_env) BOOL:

    CASE c_range : p_range OF
    IS tp_void : FALSE;
    IS tp_range_constr :
         ch_static_discrim_exp (c_range.s_lower_bound,
                                 p_env) AND
         ch_static_discrim_exp (c_range.s_upper_bound,
                                 p_env)
    ESAC;

FUNCTION ch_static_discrim_exp (p_exp  : tp_descr_set,
                                 p_env  : tp_env) BOOL:

    ch_static_descr_set (p_exp) OR
  ((f_head_descr (p_exp).s_nature = sc_discriminant)    AND
     (f_head_descr (p_exp).s_enclosing = f_enclosing (p_env)));

FUNCTION ch_static_dscrt_ranges (p_ranges : tp_dscrt_range_list) BOOL:

    IF EMPTY (p_ranges)
       THEN TRUE
    ELSE ch_static_dscrt_range (HEAD (p_ranges)) AND
        ch_static_dscrt_ranges (TAIL (p_ranges))
    FI;

FUNCTION ch_static_dscrt_range (p_range   : tp_dscrt_range) BOOL:

    CASE c_range : p_range OF
    IS tp_constrained : ch_static_constraint (c_range.s_constraint);
    IS tp_index : TRUE; %never
    IS tp_range : ch_static_range (c_range)
    ESAC;

FUNCTION ch_static_int (p_exp : tp_descr_set, p_env : tp_env) BOOL:

    f_object_value (p_exp) IS INT
    OR f_is_int_type2 (f_object_type (f_head_descr (p_exp)),
                       p_env);

FUNCTION ch_static_int_range (p_range : tp_range, p_env : tp_env) BOOL

    CASE c_range : p_range OF
    IS tp_range_constr : ch_static_int (c_range.s_upper_bound, p_env) AN
                         ch_static_int (c_range.s_lower_bound, p_env);
    IS tp_void : TRUE
    ESAC;

FUNCTION ch_static_range (p_range : tp_range) BOOL:

    CASE c_range : p_range OF
```

```
   IS tp_void : FALSE;
   IS tp_range_constr : ch_static_descr_set (c_range.s_upper_bound) AND
                        ch_static_descr_set (c_range.s_lower_bound)
   ESAC;

FUNCTION ch_static_real (p_exp : tp_descr_set) BOOL:

   f_object_init (p_exp).s_value IS tp_real_val;

FUNCTION ch_static_real_range (p_range : tp_range) BOOL:

   CASE c_range : p_range OF
   IS tp_range_constr : ch_static_real (c_range.s_upper_bound) AND
                        ch_static_real (c_range.s_lower_bound);
   IS tp_void : TRUE
   ESAC;

FUNCTION ch_subpr_den (p_assocs : tp_assoc_list,
                       p_env    : tp_env) BOOL :

      % Check the parameters of pragma inline.

   IF EMPTY (p_assocs) THEN
      TRUE
   ELSE (EMPTY (HEAD (p_assocs) QUA tp_comp_assoc .s_choices)
        CONDITION IT MESSAGE "No named parameter association allowed")
        AND
       (NOT EMPTY (f_subprs_in_decl_part
                   (HEAD (p_assocs)
                         QUA tp_comp_assoc .s_actual.s_descrs,
                    f_enclosing (p_env)))
        CONDITION IT
        MESSAGE "name of subprog declared in this decl-part expected")
        AND ch_subpr_den (TAIL (p_assocs), p_env)
   FI;

      %*********************************************************%
      %                                                         %
      %     ch_syntax_...                                       %
      %                                                         %
      %     Used to check the syntax of constructions which are %
      %     described by APPLY ::= NAME GENERAL_ASSOCS          %
      %     after resolution of the syntactic ambiguity.        %
      %                                                         %
      %*********************************************************%

FUNCTION ch_syntax_converted (p_assocs : tp_assoc_list) BOOL :

  IF LENGTH (p_assocs) = 1 THEN
     CASE c_assoc : HEAD (p_assocs) OF
       IS tp_comp_assoc : (EMPTY (c_assoc.s_choices)
                           CONDITION IT
                           MESSAGE "no choices allowed in conversion")
       OUT (FALSE CONDITION FALSE MESSAGE
                 "no ranges allowed in type conversions")
       ESAC
  ELSE (FALSE CONDITION FALSE MESSAGE
                "exactly one expression required in type conversions")
  FI;
```

```
FUNCTION ch_syntax_indexed (p_assocs : tp_assoc_list) BOOL :
   IF EMPTY (p_assocs) THEN
      TRUE
   ELSE (CASE c_assoc : HEAD (p_assocs) OF
         IS tp_comp_assoc : (EMPTY (c_assoc.s_choices)
                             CONDITION IT %C 4.1.1/4
                             MESSAGE "no choices allowed in indexed")
         OUT (FALSE CONDITION FALSE %C 4.1.1/4
              MESSAGE "no ranges allowed in indexed components")
         ESAC)                           AND
         ch_syntax_indexed (TAIL (p_assocs))
   FI;

FUNCTION ch_syntax_params (p_assocs : tp_assoc_list) BOOL :

   IF EMPTY (p_assocs) THEN
      TRUE
   ELSE CASE c_assoc : HEAD (p_assocs) OF
        IS tp_comp_assoc :((LENGTH (c_assoc.s_choices) <= 1)
                           CONDITION IT %C 6.4/1
                           MESSAGE "at most one choice per act_param")
        IS tp_dscrt_range :(FALSE
                            CONDITION FALSE %C 6.4/1
                            MESSAGE "actual params must not be ranges"
        ESAC
   FI;

FUNCTION ch_syntax_slice (p_assocs : tp_assoc_list) BOOL:

   CASE c_assoc : HEAD (p_assocs) OF
   IS tp_comp_assoc : (EMPTY (c_assoc.s_choices)
                      CONDITION IT %C 4.1.2/4
                         MESSAGE "no choices allowed in slices");
   IS tp_dscrt_range :
      (NOT (c_assoc IS tp_index)
       CONDITION IT %C 4.1.2/4
          MESSAGE "compiler error")
   ESAC                                            AND
   (EMPTY (TAIL (p_assocs))
    CONDITION IT %C 4.1.2/4
      MESSAGE "only one dscrt_range allowed in slices");

FUNCTION ch_usable (p_descr : tp_descr) BOOL :

     % Check whether an identifier is already usable as the name an
     % entity, according to the rules of declaration elaboration.

   (CASE  p_descr.s_state OF
    sc_id_established : sc_in_record : sc_in_discr_part : FALSE
    OUT TRUE
    ESAC
    CONDITION IT
       MESSAGE
       "Name is not yet usable");

FUNCTION ch_value_in_constraint (p_obj : tp_descr_set,
                                 p_env : tp_env) BOOL:

     % Check whether for an object of a scalar type, its value is
```

```
     % within the object's range constraint.

   ch_value_in_constraint1 (f_head_descr (p_obj),
                            p_env);

FUNCTION ch_value_in_constraint1 (p_obj          : tp_descr,
                                  p_env          : tp_env) BOOL:

  (CASE c_value : f_object_init1 (p_obj).s_value OF
   IS tp_exception : IS tp_no_val : IS tp_assoc_list : TRUE;
   IS INT : CASE c_constr : f_obj_constraint1 (p_obj) OF
          IS tp_range_constr :
              ch_in_range (c_value,
                           c_constr);
          IS tp_void :
              ch_in_range
                 (c_value,
                  tp_range_constr
                     (f_attr_first
                        (f_obj_constrained1 (p_obj),
                         p_env),
                      f_attr_last
                        (f_obj_constrained1 (p_obj),
                         p_env)))
          OUT TRUE
          ESAC;
  IS tp_real_val: CASE c_constr : f_obj_constraint1 (p_obj) OF
                  IS tp_range_constr:
                     ch_in_range (c_value,
                                  c_constr);
                  IS tp_fixed: ch_in_range (c_value, c_constr.s_range);
                  IS tp_float: ch_in_range (c_value, c_constr.s_range)
                  OUT TRUE
                  ESAC;
  IS tp_string_val : TRUE
  ESAC
  CONDITION
  IT
     MESSAGE
     "W : Constraint error");


FUNCTION ch_variable_for_out_in_out (p_assoc : tp_assoc,
                                     p_env   : tp_env) BOOL:

     % Check whether (converted) variables are supplied for all
     % actual (in-) out parameters.

  CASE c_assoc : p_assoc OF
  IS tp_dscrt_range : TRUE;
  IS tp_comp_assoc :
       IF f_variable_choices (c_assoc.s_choices,
                              p_env) THEN
          CASE c_den : f_head_descr (c_assoc.s_actual).s_den OF
            IS tp_object :
                 CASE f_head_descr (c_assoc.s_actual).s_nature OF
                  sc_constant : sc_in : sc_number : sc_value :
                  sc_discriminant : FALSE
                  OUT TRUE
                  ESAC
```

```
        OUT (TRUE CONDITION FALSE MESSAGE
             "the name of an object expected here")
        ESAC
    ELSE TRUE
    FI
ESAC;

%%%%%%%%%%%%%%%%%%%%%%%%%%%%%%%%%%%%%%%%%%%%%%%%%%%%%%%%%%%%%%%%%%%%%%%%%%%%%%%%%%%%
%
%               f_          F U N C T I O N S
%
%%%%%%%%%%%%%%%%%%%%%%%%%%%%%%%%%%%%%%%%%%%%%%%%%%%%%%%%%%%%%%%%%%%%%%%%%%%%%%%%%%%%

FUNCTION f_acc_constr_is_constraint (p_assocs : tp_assoc_list,
                                     p_type   : tp_descr_set,
                                     p_env    : tp_env) BOOL:

    % ACCESS_CONSTRAINT can be a parenthesized expression,
    % an aggregate or an index-/discriminant constraint.
    % (Note that one-component-aggreagates must be named.)
    %
    % The result is true if the first component is a discrete range
    % (index constraint) or if p_type is an unconstrained type
    % with discriminants, p_assocs do not contain the
    % OTHERS and the number and the number of associations
    % equal to the number of discriminants (discriminant
    % constraint).
    % Note that in the second case a discriminant constraint
    % cannot be distinguished from a record aggregate, if no
    % components exist but discriminants.

  IF EMPTY (p_assocs) THEN
    FALSE
  ELSE f_is_index_constraint (p_assocs) OR
      (NOT (f_is_constrained (f_head_descr (p_type).s_den))
       AND f_is_discr_constr (p_type,
                              p_assocs,
                              p_env))
  FI;

FUNCTION f_acc_constr_is_exp (p_assocs : tp_assoc_list,
                              p_type   : tp_descr_set,
                              p_env    : tp_env) BOOL:

   IF f_acc_constr_is_constraint (p_assocs, p_type, p_env) THEN
     FALSE
   ELSE IF LENGTH (p_assocs)=1 THEN
          EMPTY (HEAD (p_assocs)QUA tp_comp_assoc.s_choices)
   ELSE FALSE
   FI  FI;

FUNCTION f_acc_constr_is_aggreg (p_assocs : tp_assoc_list,
                                 p_type   : tp_descr_set,
                                 p_env    : tp_env) BOOL:

   IF EMPTY (p_assocs) THEN
     FALSE
   ELSE NOT (f_acc_constr_is_constraint (p_assocs, p_type, p_env) OR
             f_acc_constr_is_exp (p_assocs, p_type, p_env))
   FI;
```

```
FUNCTION f_add_defaults (p_allowed    : tp_assoc_list,
                         p_expected   : tp_descr_list,
                         p_env        : tp_env)
                        tp_assoc_list :

     % identify subprograms for generic formal "<>"-subprograms in the
     % environment at the point of the instantiation.

   IF EMPTY (p_expected) THEN
      p_allowed
   ELSE
     CASE c_den : HEAD (p_expected).s_den OF
     IS tp_subpr   : CASE c_def : c_den.s_def OF
                     IS tp_box :
                        tp_assoc_list
                           (tp_comp_assoc
                               (tp_choice_list
                                   (HEAD (p_expected)),
                                f_matching_subpr
                                   (c_den.s_spec,
                                    f_identify
                                       (HEAD (p_expected).s_designator,
                                        p_env))))
                     OUT tp_assoc_list ()
                     ESAC
     OUT tp_assoc_list()
     ESAC +
     f_add_defaults (p_allowed, TAIL (p_expected), p_env)
   FI;

FUNCTION f_add_descr (p_designator  : tp_designator,
                      p_key         : tp_key,
                      p_state       : tp_state,
                      p_nature      : tp_nature,
                      p_den         : tp_den,
                      p_env         : tp_env) tp_env :

     % Add a description with p_designator, ..., p_den to the local
     % environment.

   f_add_local_descrs
      (tp_descr_list
          (f_descr (p_designator,
                    p_key,
                    c_start_repr,
                    p_state,
                    p_nature,
                    p_den,
                    f_enclosing (p_env))),
       p_env);

FUNCTION f_add_descrs (p_designators : tp_designator_list,
                       p_keys        : tp_key_list,
                       p_state       : tp_state,
                       p_nature      : tp_nature,
                       p_den         : tp_den,
                       p_env         : tp_env) tp_env :

     % For all designators/keys add one description to the
```

```
    % local environment.

  IF EMPTY (p_keys) THEN
    p_env
  ELSE f_add_descrs (TAIL (p_designators),
                     TAIL (p_keys),
                     p_state,
                     p_nature,
                     p_den,
                     f_add_descr
                        (HEAD (p_designators),
                         HEAD (p_keys),
                         p_state,
                         p_nature,
                         p_den,
                         p_env))
  FI;

FUNCTION f_add_dummy_aggr (p_really : BOOL,
                           p_assocs : tp_assoc_list,
                           p_descrs : tp_descr_set)
                          tp_descr_set :

    % Add an anonymous dummy-value-description to the description
    % list of p_descrs. This new description contains the
    % structure of p_assocs. It is used for the analysis
    % of multidimensional array aggregates.

  IF NOT p_really THEN
    p_descrs
  ELSE tp_descr_set
        (p_descrs.s_descrs +
         tp_descr_list
            (f_temp_descr (sc_anonymous,
                           c_key,
                           c_start_repr,
                           sc_void_state,
                           sc_void_nature,
                           tp_dummy_aggr (p_assocs),
                           c_enclosing)),
        p_descrs.s_add)
  FI;

FUNCTION f_add_imported_descrs (p_names : tp_descr_list,
                                p_env   : tp_env)   tp_env :

  f_env (f_imported (p_env) + f_keys (p_names),
         f_global (p_env),
         f_local (p_env),
         f_enclosing (p_env));

FUNCTION f_add_local_descrs (p_descrs : tp_descr_list,
                             p_env    : tp_env) tp_env:

  f_update_local (p_env, f_local (p_env) + p_descrs);

FUNCTION f_add_n_equal_descr (p_desi    : tp_designator,
                              p_key     : tp_key,
                              p_den     : tp_subpr,
                              p_is_spec : BOOL,
```

```
                              p_env          : tp_env) tp_env :

    % For a user defined "=" operator add the corresponding
    % "/=" operator to the local environment.

  IF p_desi /= c_equal_desi THEN
     p_env
  ELSE IF p_is_spec THEN
       f_make_derivable
           (p_key,
            f_add_descr (c_n_equal_desi,
                         p_key,
                         sc_implicitly_declared,
                         sc_function,
                         p_den,
                         p_env))
     ELSE f_add_descr (c_n_equal_desi,
                       p_key,
                       sc_implicitly_declared,
                       sc_function,
                       p_den,
                       p_env)
     FI
  FI;

FUNCTION f_add_reps (p_reps        : tp_rep_list,
                     p_rep         : tp_rep) tp_rep_list :

    % Add rep to reps and check for multiple specification of the
    % same representation aspect.

  IF EMPTY (p_reps) THEN
     tp_rep_list (p_rep)
  ELSE
     CASE c_rep : HEAD (p_reps) OF
     IS tp_length_spec :
        IF p_rep IS tp_length_spec THEN
           (p_reps
            %C 13.1/2
            CONDITION FALSE
               MESSAGE
                 "this representation aspect has already been specified")
         ELSE  tp_rep_list (c_rep) + f_add_reps (TAIL (p_reps), p_rep)
         FI;
     IS tp_enum_rep :
        IF p_rep IS tp_enum_rep THEN
           (p_reps
            %C 13.1/2
            CONDITION FALSE
               MESSAGE
                 "this representation aspect has already been specified")
         ELSE tp_rep_list (c_rep) + f_add_reps (TAIL (p_reps), p_rep)
         FI;
     IS tp_record_rep :
        IF p_rep IS tp_record_rep THEN
           (p_reps
            %C 13.1/2
            CONDITION FALSE
               MESSAGE
                 "this representation aspect has already been specified")
```

```
        ELSE tp_rep_list (c_rep) + f_add_reps (TAIL (p_reps), p_rep)
        FI;
     IS tp_address_spec :
        IF p_rep IS tp_address_spec THEN
           (p_reps
           %C 13.1/2
           CONDITION FALSE
              MESSAGE
              "this representation aspect has already been specified")
        ELSE tp_rep_list (c_rep)+ f_add_reps (TAIL (p_reps), p_rep)
        FI
     OUT p_reps
     ESAC
  FI;

FUNCTION f_adjust_comp_list (p_comps : tp_comp_list,
                             p_encl  : tp_key,
                             p_maps  : tp_map_list,
                             p_env   : tp_env) tp_comp_list :

     % Construct a list of record component descriptions
     % similar to p_comps but using the descriptions
     % from p_maps.

  IF EMPTY (p_comps) THEN
     p_comps
  ELSE
     tp_comp_list
       (CASE c_comp : HEAD (p_comps) OF
        IS tp_variant_part :
           tp_variant_part
              (f_map (c_comp.s_discr,
                      p_maps) QUA tp_descr.s_key,
               f_adjust_variant_list
                  (c_comp.s_variants,
                   p_encl,
                   p_maps,
                   p_env));
        IS tp_descr_list : (c_error_descr
                            CONDITION FALSE
                               MESSAGE "compiler error");
        IS tp_void : sc_void;
        IS tp_descr :
           CASE c_map : f_map (c_comp.s_key,
                               p_maps) OF
           IS tp_void : (c_error_descr
                         CONDITION FALSE
                            MESSAGE "compiler error");
           IS tp_descr :
              f_descr
                 (c_map.s_designator,
                  c_map.s_key,
                  c_map.s_repr,
                  c_map.s_state,
                  c_map.s_nature,
                  f_adjust_den (c_map.s_den,
                                p_encl,
                                p_maps,
                                p_env),
                  p_encl)
```

```
            ESAC
         ESAC) +
      f_adjust_comp_list
         (TAIL (p_comps),
         p_encl,
         p_maps,
         p_env)
   FI;

FUNCTION f_adjust_constr (p_constr : tp_constrained,
                          p_maps   : tp_map_list,
                          p_env    : tp_env) tp_constrained :

      % If the base type of p_constr is associated to a new key
      % by p_maps, create a new constrained,where the base type
      % is replaced by the associated type.
      % If the parent base type of p_constr is associated to a
      % subtype by p_maps and if p_constr does not contain a constraint
      % set the constraint of the result to the constraint of the
      % associated subtype.

   CASE c_map : f_map (p_constr.s_base_type,
                       p_maps) OF
   IS tp_void : p_constr;
   IS tp_descr :
      tp_constrained
         (CASE c_den : c_map.s_den OF
          IS tp_constrained : c_den.s_base_type
          OUT c_map.s_key
          ESAC,
          IF p_constr.s_constraint =/ sc_void THEN
             p_constr.s_constraint
          ELSE
             CASE c_parent_map :
                     f_map
                        (f_parent_base_type
                           (p_constr.s_base_type,
                            p_env),
                         p_maps) OF
             IS tp_void : sc_void;
             IS tp_descr :
                CASE c_den : c_parent_map.s_den OF
                IS tp_constrained : c_den.s_constraint
                OUT sc_void
                ESAC
             ESAC
          FI)
   ESAC;

FUNCTION f_adjust_den (p_den  : tp_den,
                       p_encl : tp_key,
                       p_maps : tp_map_list,
                       p_env  : tp_env) tp_den :

      % Create a new denotation for p_den is it refers to copied
      % descriptions in p_maps.

   CASE c_den : p_den OF
   IS tp_package :
      tp_package
```

```
      (f_adjust_descr_list
          (c_den.s_visible,
           p_encl,
           p_maps,
           p_env),
       c_empty_descrs,
       c_empty_keys,
       TRUE);
 IS tp_subpr :
    tp_subpr
      (CASE c_spec : c_den.s_spec OF
        IS tp_function :
           tp_function
              (f_adjust_descr_list
                  (c_spec.s_params,
                   p_encl,
                   p_maps,
                   p_env),
               f_adjust_constr
                  (c_spec.s_result,
                   p_maps,
                   p_env));
        IS tp_procedure :
           tp_procedure
              (f_adjust_descr_list
                  (c_spec.s_params,
                   p_encl,
                   p_maps,
                   p_env))
        OUT (tp_procedure (c_empty_descrs)
             CONDITION FALSE
                 MESSAGE "compiler error")
        ESAC,
        sc_void,
        c_den.s_op);
 IS tp_entry :
    tp_entry
      (f_adjust_descr_list
          (c_den.s_params,
           p_encl,
           p_maps,
           p_env));
 IS tp_entry_family :
    tp_entry_family
      (f_adjust_constr
          (c_den.s_dscrt_range QUA tp_constrained,
           p_maps,
           p_env),
       tp_entry
          (f_adjust_descr_list
              (c_den.s_entry.s_params,
               p_encl,
               p_maps,
               p_env)));
 IS tp_type_den :
    tp_type_den
      (CASE c_type : c_den.s_type OF
        IS tp_record :
           tp_record
              (f_adjust_descr_list
```

```
        (c_type.s_descrs,
         p_encl,
         p_maps,
         p_env),
      f_adjust_comp_list
        (c_type.s_comps,
         p_encl,
         p_maps,
         p_env));
IS tp_private :
   tp_private
     (f_adjust_descr_list
        (c_type.s_discriminants,
         p_encl,
         p_maps,
         p_env));
IS tp_l_private :
   tp_l_private
     (f_adjust_descr_list
        (c_type.s_discriminants,
         p_encl,
         p_maps,
         p_env));
IS tp_incompl_type :
   tp_incompl_type
     (f_adjust_descr_list
        (c_type.s_discriminants,
         p_encl,
         p_maps,
         p_env));
IS tp_task_spec :
   tp_task_spec
     (f_adjust_descr_list
        (c_type.s_visible,
         p_encl,
         p_maps,
         p_env));
IS tp_derived :
   tp_derived
     (f_map_type
        (c_type.s_parent_type,
         p_maps));
IS tp_array :
   tp_array
     (f_adjust_dscrt_ranges
        (c_type.s_indices,
         p_maps,
         p_env),
      f_adjust_constr
        (c_type.s_comp_type,
         p_maps,
         p_env));
IS tp_access :
   tp_access
     (f_adjust_constr
        (c_type.s_accessed,
         p_maps,
         p_env));
IS tp_enum_type :
   tp_enum_type
```

```
                (f_map_impls
                    (c_type.s_literals,
                     p_maps),
                 c_type.s_char)
           OUT c_type
           ESAC,
           f_map_impls
              (c_den.s_derivable_subprogs,
               p_maps));
   IS tp_enum_literal :
      tp_enum_literal
         (f_map (c_den.s_type,
                 p_maps) QUA tp_descr.s_key,
          c_den.s_pos,
          c_den.s_char);
   IS tp_generic :
      tp_generic
         (f_adjust_descr_list
             (c_den.s_generic_params,
              p_encl,
              p_maps,
              p_env),
          f_adjust_den
             (c_den.s_den,
              p_encl,
              p_maps,
              p_env));
   IS tp_object :
      tp_object
         (f_adjust_constr
             (c_den.s_type,
              p_maps,
              p_env),
          c_den.s_init);
   IS tp_constrained :
      f_adjust_constr
         (c_den,
          p_maps,
          p_env)
   OUT p_den
   ESAC;

FUNCTION f_adjust_descr_list (p_descrs : tp_descr_list,
                              p_encl   : tp_key,
                              p_maps   : tp_map_list,
                              p_env    : tp_env) tp_descr_list :

    % Build a description list similar to p_descrs but with the
    % descriptions associated to p_descrs by p_maps.
    % For descriptions of composite entities (package, records, ...)
    % adjust the constituents.

   IF EMPTY (p_descrs) THEN
      c_empty_descrs
   ELSE
      tp_descr_list
        (CASE c_descr : f_map (HEAD (p_descrs).s_key,
                               p_maps) OF
           IS tp_void : (c_error_descr CONDITION FALSE MESSAGE
                                      "compiler error");
```

```
        IS tp_descr :
           f_descr
              (IF f_map_derived (HEAD (p_descrs),
                                 p_maps,
                                 p_env) IS tp_void THEN
                 c_descr.s_designator
               ELSE sc_anonymous
               FI,
               c_descr.s_key,
               c_descr.s_repr,
               c_descr.s_state,
               c_descr.s_nature,
               f_adjust_den
                  (c_descr.s_den,
                   c_descr.s_key,
                   p_maps,
                   p_env),
               p_encl)
        ESAC)    +
     f_adjust_descr_list
        (TAIL (p_descrs),
         p_encl,
         p_maps,
         p_env)   +
     CASE c_constr : f_map_derived (HEAD (p_descrs),
                                    p_maps,
                                    p_env) OF
     IS tp_void : c_empty_descrs
     OUT tp_descr_list
           (f_descr
               (HEAD (p_descrs).s_designator,
                f_gen_key,
                c_start_repr,
                sc_complete,
                sc_subtype,
                tp_constrained
                  (f_map (HEAD (p_descrs).s_key,
                          p_maps) QUA tp_descr.s_key,
                   c_constr),
                p_encl))
     ESAC
   FI;

FUNCTION f_adjust_dscrt_ranges (p_ranges : tp_dscrt_range_list,
                                p_maps   : tp_map_list,
                                p_env    : tp_env)
                               tp_dscrt_range_list :

     % Adjust the discrete ranges in p_ranges according to
     % p_maps.

   IF EMPTY (p_ranges) THEN
     p_ranges
   ELSE
     tp_dscrt_range_list
       (CASE c_range : HEAD (p_ranges) OF
        IS tp_index :
           tp_index
              (f_adjust_constr
                 (c_range.s_type,
```

```
                    p_maps,
                    p_env))
          OUT (tp_index (c_error_type) CONDITION FALSE MESSAGE
                                        "compiler error")
          ESAC) +
       f_adjust_dscrt_ranges (TAIL (p_ranges),
                              p_maps,
                              p_env)
    FI;

FUNCTION f_adjust_generics (p_descrs    : tp_descr_list,
                            p_assoc     : tp_comp_assoc,
                            p_env       : tp_env) tp_descr_list :

      % Adjust the descriptions in p_descrs according to
      % p_assoc if this is a type association, i.e. replace
      % all key references to the formal type by the actual one.

    IF EMPTY (p_descrs) THEN
      p_descrs
    ELSE CASE HEAD (p_assoc.s_choices) QUA tp_descr.s_nature OF
         sc_type : sc_subtype :
            f_adjust_descr_list
               (p_descrs,
                HEAD (p_descrs).s_enclosing,
                f_map_ident (p_descrs) +
                f_init_type_map
                   (tp_assoc_list (p_assoc),
                    p_env),
                p_env)
         OUT p_descrs
         ESAC
    FI;

FUNCTION f_adjust_local_env (p_old   : tp_key,
                             p_new   : tp_descr,
                             p_env   : tp_env) tp_env :
      % Creates a new local environment where all key - refererences
      % to descriptions are adjusted according to p_maps
      % (cf. f_adjust_descr_list)
    f_update_local
      (p_env,
       f_adjust_descr_list
          (p_env.s_local,
           f_enclosing (p_env),
           tp_map_list
              (tp_map
                  (f_select_by_key (p_old, p_env),
                   p_new)) +
           f_map_ident (f_local (p_env)),
           p_env));

FUNCTION f_adjust_variant_list (p_variants  : tp_variant_list,
                                p_encl      : tp_key,
                                p_maps      : tp_map_list,
                                p_env       : tp_env) tp_variant_list :
      % Create a new list of variants similar to p_variants but
      % using the descriptions from p_maps.

    IF EMPTY (p_variants) THEN
```

```
    p_variants
  ELSE tp_variant_list
        (tp_variant
           (HEAD (p_variants).s_choices,
            f_adjust_comp_list
               (HEAD (p_variants).s_comps,
                p_encl,
                p_maps,
                p_env))) +
       f_adjust_variant_list
          (TAIL (p_variants),
           p_encl,
           p_maps,
           p_env)
  FI;

     %***********************************************************%
     %                                                           %
     %        f_all_..._types                                    %
     %                                                           %
     %        Search all ... types in the environment, i.e. all  %
     %         ... types which are currently usable (not necessary %
     %        visible).                                          %
     %                                                           %
     %***********************************************************%
FUNCTION f_all_acc_types (p_accessed : tp_key,
                          p_env      : tp_env)tp_key_list:

    f_all_acc_types1 (p_accessed,
                      f_all_types (p_env),
                      p_env);

FUNCTION f_all_acc_types1 (p_accessed : tp_key,
                           p_descrs   : tp_descr_list,
                           p_env      : tp_env)tp_key_list:

  IF EMPTY (p_descrs) THEN
     c_empty_keys
  ELSE CASE c_type : f_parent_base_type2 (HEAD (p_descrs).s_key,
                                          p_env) OF
       IS tp_access : IF f_parent_base_type
                           (c_type.s_accessed.s_base_type, p_env) =
                        p_accessed THEN
                        tp_key_list
                           (HEAD (p_descrs).s_key)
                      ELSE c_empty_keys
                      FI
       OUT c_empty_keys
       ESAC                                                   +
       f_all_acc_types1 (p_accessed, TAIL (p_descrs), p_env)
  FI;

FUNCTION f_all_aggregate_types (p_env : tp_env) tp_key_list:

  f_all_aggregate_types1 (f_all_types (p_env));

FUNCTION f_all_aggregate_types1 (p_descrs : tp_descr_list)
                                 tp_key_list :
```

```
   IF EMPTY (p_descrs) THEN
      c_empty_keys
   ELSE CASE f_type1 (HEAD (p_descrs)) OF
          IS tp_record : tp_array :
               tp_key_list (HEAD (p_descrs).s_key)
          OUT c_empty_keys
        ESAC                                  +
        f_all_aggregate_types1 (TAIL (p_descrs))
   FI;

FUNCTION f_all_deriv_types (p_father : tp_key,
                            p_env    : tp_env)tp_key_list:

    tp_key_list (p_father)       +
    f_all_deriv_types1 (p_father,
                        f_all_types (p_env),
                        p_env);

FUNCTION f_all_deriv_types1 (p_father : tp_key,
                             p_descrs : tp_descr_list,
                             p_env    : tp_env) tp_key_list:
   IF EMPTY (p_descrs) THEN
      c_empty_keys
   ELSE CASE c_type : f_type1 (HEAD (p_descrs)) OF
        IS tp_derived : IF f_parent_base_type (c_type.s_parent_type,
                                               p_env) = p_father
                        THEN tp_key_list
                               (HEAD (p_descrs).s_key) +
                             f_all_deriv_types1
                               (HEAD (p_descrs).s_key,
                                f_all_types (p_env),
                                p_env)
                        ELSE c_empty_keys
                        FI
        OUT c_empty_keys
        ESAC                                            +
        f_all_deriv_types1 (p_father, TAIL (p_descrs), p_env)
   FI;

FUNCTION f_all_string_types (p_env : tp_env) tp_descr_list:

   f_all_string_types1 (f_all_types (p_env), p_env);

FUNCTION f_all_string_types1 (p_types : tp_descr_list,
                              p_env   : tp_env) tp_descr_list:

   IF EMPTY (p_types) THEN
      c_empty_descrs
   ELSE IF  CASE c_array : f_type1 (HEAD (p_types)) OF
            IS tp_array : (LENGTH (c_array.s_indices) = 1) AND
               CASE c_enum : f_type (c_array.s_comp_type.s_base_type,
                                     p_env) OF
               IS tp_enum_type : c_enum.s_char
               OUT FALSE
               ESAC
            OUT FALSE
            ESAC THEN
           tp_descr_list (HEAD (p_types))
        ELSE c_empty_descrs
```

```
        FI                                              +
        f_all_string_types1 (TAIL (p_types), p_env)
   FI;

FUNCTION f_all_types (p_env : tp_env) tp_descr_list :

   f_all_types1 (f_local (p_env) + f_global (p_env));

FUNCTION f_all_types1 (p_descrs : tp_descr_list) tp_descr_list :

   IF EMPTY (p_descrs) THEN
      c_empty_descrs
   ELSE CASE c_den : HEAD (p_descrs).s_den OF
        IS tp_type_den : tp_descr_list (HEAD (p_descrs)) +
                         CASE c_type : c_den.s_type OF
                         IS tp_record : f_all_types1 (c_type.s_descrs)
                         OUT c_empty_descrs
                         ESAC;
        IS tp_package : CASE HEAD (p_descrs).s_state OF
                        sc_in_visible : sc_in_private :
                        sc_in_body : sc_in_handler :
                        c_empty_descrs
                        OUT f_all_types1 (c_den.s_visible)
                        ESAC
        OUT c_empty_descrs
        ESAC                                                  +
        f_all_types1 (TAIL (p_descrs))
   FI;

      %**********************************************************%
      %                                                          %
      %        f_allowed_...                                     %
      %                                                          %
      %        Used to evaluate at_allowed1 / 2.                 %
      %                                                          %
      %        Often uses f_valid_...1, which yields sc_void     %
      %        in case of invalid constructions.                 %
      %                                                          %
      %        If one of the constituents of a composite         %
      %        construction denotes or contains an error value,  %
      %        the result is an error value, which satisfies the %
      %        requirements imposed by the context.              %
      %                                                          %
      %        f_allowed_...1 generally is used for iteration    %
      %        over the list of allowed meanings of a constituent%
      %        construction.                                     %
      %                                                          %
      %**********************************************************%

FUNCTION f_allowed_aggregates (p_expected : tp_key_void,
                               p_assocs   : tp_assoc_list,
                               p_env      : tp_env)
                              tp_descr_set   :

   IF f_error_aggregate (p_assocs) THEN
      c_error_descr_set
   ELSE
      tp_descr_set
        (f_allowed_aggregates1
```

```
        (CASE c_expected : p_expected OF
          IS tp_void : f_all_aggregate_types (p_env);
          IS tp_key  : tp_key_list (f_parent_base_type
                                     (c_expected,
                                      p_env))
          ESAC,
          p_assocs,
          p_env),
      IF p_expected IS tp_void THEN
         sc_add_deriv
      ELSE sc_no_add
      FI)
  FI;

FUNCTION f_allowed_aggregates1 (p_expected : tp_key_list,
                                p_assocs   : tp_assoc_list,
                                p_env      : tp_env)
                               tp_descr_list :

  IF EMPTY (p_expected) THEN
     c_empty_descrs
  ELSE CASE c_assocs : f_valid_aggregate1
                         (HEAD (p_expected),
                          p_assocs,
                          p_env) OF
       IS tp_void : c_empty_descrs;
       IS tp_assoc_list :
          tp_descr_list
             (f_temp_descr
                 (c_designator,
                  c_key,
                  c_start_repr,
                  sc_void_state,
                  sc_value,
                  tp_object
                     (tp_constrained
                        (HEAD (p_expected),
                         sc_void),
                      tp_init
                        (c_assocs,
                         f_exp_kind_assocs (c_assocs))),
                  c_enclosing))
       ESAC +
       f_allowed_aggregates1 (TAIL (p_expected), p_assocs, p_env)
  FI;

FUNCTION f_allowed_all (p_name : tp_descr_set,
                        p_env  : tp_env)
                       tp_descr_set    :

  IF f_is_error_or_empty (p_name) THEN
     c_error_descr_set
  ELSE CASE c_additional : p_name.s_add OF
          sc_add_access :
             tp_descr_set (f_update_nature_descrs
                              (p_name.s_descrs,
                               sc_variable),
                           sc_no_add)
       OUT  tp_descr_set (f_allowed_all1 (p_name.s_descrs,
                                          p_env),
```

```
                                        sc_no_add)
       ESAC
   FI;

FUNCTION f_allowed_all1 (p_descrs : tp_descr_list,
                         p_env    : tp_env)
                        tp_descr_list :

   IF EMPTY (p_descrs) THEN
      c_empty_descrs
   ELSE CASE c_type : f_object_parent_base_type1
                        (HEAD (p_descrs),
                         p_env) OF
       IS tp_access :  tp_descr_list
         (f_temp_descr
             (HEAD (p_descrs).s_designator,
              HEAD (p_descrs).s_key,
              HEAD (p_descrs).s_repr,
              HEAD (p_descrs).s_state,
              sc_variable,
              tp_object
                 (IF f_obj_constraint1 (HEAD (p_descrs)) /= sc_void
                  THEN
                  tp_constrained
                     (c_type.s_accessed.s_base_type,
                      f_obj_constraint1 (HEAD (p_descrs)))
                ELSE
                  c_type.s_accessed
                FI,
              c_init),
             HEAD (p_descrs).s_enclosing))
       OUT  tp_descr_list ()
       ESAC +
       f_allowed_all1 (TAIL (p_descrs), p_env)
   FI;

FUNCTION f_allowed_allocator (p_expected : tp_key_void,
                              p_type     : tp_descr_set,
                              p_assocs   : tp_assoc_list,
                              p_env      : tp_env) tp_descr_set :

   IF f_is_error_or_empty (p_type) OR f_is_error_empty_assocs (p_assocs)
      THEN c_error_descr_set
   ELSE IF
      f_head_descr (p_type).s_nature /= sc_type AND
     (f_head_descr (p_type).s_nature /= sc_subtype) THEN
      c_empty_descr_set
   ELSE IF
     CASE c_expected : p_expected OF
      IS tp_void : TRUE;
      IS tp_key :
        CASE c_type : f_parent_base_type2
                         (c_expected, p_env) OF
        IS tp_access :
           f_implicitly_convertable1
              (c_type.s_accessed.s_base_type,
               f_base_type
                  (f_head_descr (p_type)),
                   p_env)
        OUT FALSE
```

```
      ESAC
   ESAC                                       AND
   IF EMPTY (p_assocs) THEN
      TRUE
   ELSE IF f_acc_constr_is_constraint (p_assocs, p_type, p_env)
      THEN NOT (f_valid_constraint
                   (p_type,
                    p_assocs,
                    p_env)  IS tp_void)
   ELSE IF f_acc_constr_is_exp (p_assocs,
                                p_type,
                                p_env) THEN
      f_make_void_descrs
        (f_valid_descr_set
            (HEAD (p_assocs) QUA tp_comp_assoc.s_actual,
             f_base_type (f_head_descr (p_type)),
             p_env)) IS tp_descr_set
   ELSE f_valid_aggregate1  % it is an aggregate
          (f_base_type (f_head_descr (p_type)),
           p_assocs,
           p_env) IS tp_assoc_list
   FI FI FI THEN
      f_descr_set (c_key,
                   sc_value,
                   tp_object
                     (tp_constrained
                         (CASE c_expected : p_expected OF
                          IS tp_key : c_expected;
                          IS tp_void :  f_base_type
                                          (f_head_descr (p_type))
                          ESAC,
                          sc_void),
                      c_init),
                   CASE c_exp : p_expected OF
                   IS tp_key :  sc_no_add;
                   IS tp_void : sc_add_access
                   ESAC)
  ELSE c_empty_descr_set
  FI FI FI;

FUNCTION f_allowed_apply (p_name      : tp_descr_set,
                          p_assocs    : tp_assoc_list,
                          p_context   : tp_context,
                          p_env       : tp_env) tp_descr_set:

     % Select between
     %      - procedure / entry call        context = sc_call
     %      - subtype_indication            name is type and
     %                                      context = sc_subtype_ind
     %      - converted                     name is type and
     %                                      context /= sc_subtype_in
     %      - indexed                       name is object and assoc
     %                                      are expressions or name
     %                                      is entry family
     %      - slice                         name is object and assoc
     %                                      are discrete ranges
     %      - function call                 name is overloadable and
     %                                      context /= sc_call .
     %
```

```
IF f_is_error_or_empty (p_name) OR f_is_error_empty_assocs (p_assocs)
   THEN c_error_descr_set
ELSE IF
   p_context = sc_call THEN
   IF (ch_syntax_params (p_assocs)
       CONDITION IT
          MESSAGE
            "wrong syntax for proc/entry calls") THEN
      f_allowed_proc_entry (p_name,
                            p_assocs,
                            p_env)
   ELSE c_empty_descr_set
   FI
ELSE CASE f_head_descr (p_name).s_nature OF
     sc_type : sc_subtype :
        CASE p_context OF
        sc_subtype_ind : sc_access :
           IF (EMPTY (p_assocs)
               CONDITION NOT IT
                  MESSAGE
                  "Defective construction of subtype indication")
              THEN c_empty_descr_set
           ELSE
              CASE c_constr : f_valid_constraint (p_name,
                                                  p_assocs,
                                                  p_env) OF
              IS tp_void : c_empty_descr_set
              OUT f_descr_set2
                    (f_mark_origin2
                       (f_temp_descr
                          (f_head_descr (p_name).s_designator,
                           c_key,
                           c_start_repr,
                           sc_void_state,
                           sc_subtype,
                           tp_constrained
                              (f_base_type
                                    (f_head_descr (p_name)),
                               c_constr),
                           c_enclosing),
                        f_origin (f_head_descr (p_name))))
              ESAC
           FI
        OUT IF (ch_syntax_converted (p_assocs)
                CONDITION IT
                   MESSAGE
                   "wrong syntax for type conversion") THEN
               f_allowed_converted (p_name,
                                    p_assocs,
                                    p_env)
            ELSE c_empty_descr_set
            FI
        ESAC;
    sc_constant : sc_variable : sc_in : sc_in_out : sc_out :
    sc_value :
       IF EMPTY (p_assocs) THEN
          c_empty_descr_set
       ELSE IF CASE c_assoc : HEAD (p_assocs) OF
               IS tp_comp_assoc :
                  CASE f_head_descr (c_assoc.s_actual).s_nature OF
```

```
                  sc_type : sc_subtype : FALSE
                  OUT TRUE
                  ESAC;
                IS tp_dscrt_range : FALSE
                ESAC THEN
            IF (ch_syntax_indexed (p_assocs)
                 CONDITION IT
                   MESSAGE
                     "wrong syntax of indexed expression") THEN
               f_allowed_indexed (p_name,
                                  p_assocs,
                                  p_env)
            ELSE c_empty_descr_set
            FI
          ELSE IF (ch_syntax_slice (p_assocs)
                  CONDITION IT
                     MESSAGE
                     "wrong syntax of slice expression") THEN
                f_allowed_slice (p_name,
                                 p_assocs,
                                 p_env)
          ELSE c_empty_descr_set
          FI FI FI;
        sc_predefined_op : sc_common_op : sc_universal_op :
        sc_procedure : sc_entry : sc_enum_literal : sc_entry_family :
        sc_function:   %context =/ sc_call : only functions and
                       %entry families allowed
          IF f_head_descr (p_name).s_nature = sc_entry_family THEN
            IF (ch_syntax_indexed (p_assocs)
                 CONDITION IT
                    MESSAGE
                     "wrong syntax of indexed expression") THEN
                f_allowed_funct_entry (p_name,
                                       p_assocs,
                                       p_env)
            ELSE c_empty_descr_set
            FI
          ELSE IF (ch_syntax_params (p_assocs)
                  CONDITION IT
                     MESSAGE
                     "wrong syntax for subprogram call") THEN
                f_allowed_funct_entry (p_name,
                                       p_assocs,
                                       p_env)
          ELSE c_empty_descr_set
          FI FI
        OUT (c_empty_descr_set CONDITION FALSE MESSAGE
                        "Name ^ not allowed in this context")
        ESAC
   FI FI;

FUNCTION f_allowed_attr_apply (p_attr    : tp_descr_set,
                               p_design  : SYMB,
                               p_assocs  : tp_assoc_list,
                               p_env     : tp_env)
                             tp_descr_set :

   IF f_is_error_or_empty (p_attr) OR f_is_error_empty_assocs (p_assoc
      THEN c_error_descr_set
   ELSE
```

```
CASE p_design OF
'image' : 'value' :
   IF f_is_scalar_type (f_head_descr (p_attr), p_env) THEN
      IF p_design = 'image' THEN
         f_descr_set_val (c_string_constr, c_init)
      ELSE
         CASE f_head_descr (p_attr).s_nature OF
         sc_type : sc_subtype :
            f_descr_set_val
               (f_constrained
                   (f_head_descr (p_attr).s_key,
                    p_env),
                c_init)
         OUT  c_error_descr_set
         ESAC
      FI
   ELSE (c_empty_descr_set
         CONDITION FALSE
            MESSAGE
            "a scalar type expected for IMAGE, VALUE attributes")
   FI;

'first' : 'last' : 'range' : 'length':
   IF f_is_error_or_empty
         (f_first_comp_assoc_actual
             (p_assocs,
              c_int,
              p_env)) THEN
      c_empty_descr_set
   ELSE
      f_allowed_attr_apply1
         (p_attr,

          CASE c_den:f_head_descr (p_attr).s_den OF
          IS tp_object :
             CASE c_type : f_object_parent_base_type1
                              (f_head_descr (p_attr),
                               p_env) OF
             IS tp_array :
                CASE c_indices : f_obj_constraint (p_attr) OF
                IS tp_dscrt_range_list : c_indices
                OUT (tp_dscrt_range_list ()
                     %C A
                     CONDITION FALSE MESSAGE
                        "a constrained array object required")
                ESAC
             OUT (tp_dscrt_range_list ()
                  %C A
                  CONDITION FALSE
                     MESSAGE "array object expected")
             ESAC;
          IS tp_type_den : IS tp_constrained :
             CASE c_type : f_parent_base_type1
                              (CASE c_den : c_den OF
                               IS tp_type_den : c_den.s_type
                               OUT c_den QUA tp_constrained
                               ESAC,
                                p_env) OF
             IS tp_array :
                CASE c_indices : f_constraint
```

```
                              (f_head_descr (p_attr),
                               p_env) OF
            IS tp_dscrt_range_list : c_indices
            OUT (tp_dscrt_range_list ()
                 %C A
                 CONDITION FALSE MESSAGE
                   "constrained array type required")
            ESAC
          OUT (tp_dscrt_range_list ()
               CONDITION FALSE
                 MESSAGE "array type expected")
          ESAC
        OUT (tp_dscrt_range_list ()
             CONDITION FALSE
               MESSAGE "type or object name expected")
        ESAC,

        p_design,

        CASE c_int : f_object_value
                      (f_first_comp_assoc_actual
                         (p_assocs,
                          c_int,
                          p_env)) OF
        IS INT : c_int
        OUT 0
        ESAC,

        p_env)
   FI;

'pos' : 'val' : 'pred' : 'succ' :
   IF f_is_discrete_type (f_head_descr (p_attr),
                          p_env) THEN
     CASE p_design OF
     'val' : IF f_is_error_or_empty
                  (f_first_comp_assoc_actual
                     (p_assocs,
                      c_int,
                      p_env)) THEN
                c_error_descr_set
             ELSE
                f_attr_val
                  (f_head_descr (p_attr).s_key,
                   f_object_init
                     (f_first_comp_assoc_actual
                        (p_assocs,
                         c_int,
                         p_env)),
                   p_env)
             FI
     OUT f_allowed_attr_apply2
           (f_first_comp_assoc_actual
              (p_assocs,
               f_base_type
                 (f_head_descr (p_attr)),
                  p_env),
               p_design,
               p_env)
     ESAC
```

```
      ELSE (c_error_descr_set
            CONDITION FALSE MESSAGE
               "a discrete type expected")
      FI
    OUT (c_error_descr_set
         %C
         CONDITION FALSE MESSAGE
            "this attribute does not take any parameters")
    ESAC
  FI;

FUNCTION f_allowed_attr_apply1 (p_attr    : tp_descr_set,
                                p_indices : tp_dscrt_range_list,
                                p_design  : SYMB,
                                p_n       : INT,
                                p_env     : tp_env)
                               tp_descr_set :

  IF EMPTY (p_indices) OR (p_n = 0) THEN
     c_empty_descr_set
  ELSE IF HEAD (p_indices) IS tp_index THEN
    (c_error_descr_set
     CONDITION FALSE
        MESSAGE "no unconstrained array (type) allowed")
  ELSE
     f_allowed_attribute1
       (p_design,
        f_n_th_index (p_indices, p_n),
        p_env)
  FI FI;

FUNCTION f_allowed_attr_apply2 (p_value  : tp_descr_set,
                                p_design : SYMB,
                                p_env    : tp_env) tp_descr_set :

  IF f_is_error_or_empty (p_value) THEN
     c_empty_descr_set
  ELSE
     CASE p_design OF
     'pos'  : f_attr_pos (p_value, p_env);
     'pred' : f_attr_pred (p_value, p_env);
     'succ' : f_attr_succ (p_value, p_env)
     OUT (c_error_descr_set CONDITION FALSE MESSAGE "compiler error")
     ESAC
  FI;

FUNCTION f_allowed_attribute1 (p_design      : SYMB,
                               p_constrained : tp_constrained,
                               p_env         : tp_env)
                              tp_descr_set :

  CASE p_design  OF
  'first'  :     f_attr_first
                   (p_constrained,
                    p_env);
  'last'   :     f_attr_last
                   (p_constrained,
                    p_env);
  'length' :     f_attr_length
                   (p_constrained,
```

```
                    p_env);
  'range' : f_descr_set4
                        (sc_subtype,
                         p_constrained)
   OUT (c_error_descr_set CONDITION FALSE MESSAGE "compiler error")
   ESAC;


FUNCTION f_allowed_attribute (p_designator : SYMB,
                              p_allowed    : tp_descr_set,
                              p_env        : tp_env)
                             tp_descr_set :

   IF f_is_error_or_empty (p_allowed) THEN
      c_error_descr_set
   ELSE
     (CASE p_designator OF

       'address' : 'storage_size' :
           f_descr_set_val
              (c_univ_int_constr,
               f_repr_spec_init (p_allowed, p_designator, p_env));
       'last_bit' : 'first_bit' : 'position' :
       'size'
          f_descr_set_val
             (c_int_constr,
              f_repr_spec_init (p_allowed, p_designator, p_env));
       'base' :
          CASE f_head_descr (p_allowed).s_nature OF
          sc_type : sc_subtype :
             f_descr_set2
                (f_select_by_key
                    (f_base_type (f_head_descr (p_allowed)),
                     p_env))
          OUT (c_error_descr_set
               CONDITION FALSE
                  MESSAGE "type name expected")
          ESAC;

       'count' :  f_descr_set_val (c_int_constr, c_init);

       'digits' : 'delta' :
          f_descr_set_val
             (c_univ_real_constr,
              f_object_init
                 (f_digits_delta (f_head_descr (p_allowed),
                                  p_env)));
       'actual_delta' :
          f_descr_set_val
             (c_univ_real_constr,
              f_repr_spec_init (p_allowed, p_designator, p_env));
       'large' : 'small' : 'epsilon' :
          f_descr_set_val (c_univ_real_constr, c_init);

       'bits' :
       'mantissa' : 'emax' : 'machine_radix' : 'machine_mantissa' :
       'machine_emax' : 'machine_emin' :
       'priority' :
          f_descr_set_val (c_univ_int_constr, c_init);
```

```
'machine_rounds' : 'machine_overflows' :
'terminated' :
   f_descr_set_val (c_bool_constr, c_init);

'constrained' :
   f_attr_constrained (p_allowed, p_env);

'failure' : c_exception_descr_set;

'first' : 'last' : 'length' : 'range' :
   IF CASE f_head_descr (p_allowed).s_den OF
      IS tp_type_den : IS tp_constrained :
         f_is_discrete_type (f_head_descr (p_allowed), p_env)
         AND ((p_designator = 'first') OR
              (p_designator = 'last'))
      OUT FALSE
      ESAC
   THEN f_allowed_attribute1
           (p_designator,
            f_constrained
               (f_head_descr (p_allowed).s_key,
                p_env),
            p_env)
   ELSE
      f_allowed_attr_apply
         (p_allowed,
          p_designator,
          tp_assoc_list
             (tp_comp_assoc
               (tp_choice_list (),
                f_descr_set2 (c_1_int_descr))),
        p_env)
   FI;
'image' : 'value' : 'pos' : 'val' : 'succ' : 'pred' :
   IF NOT (f_head_descr (p_allowed).s_den IS tp_type_den) AND
     (NOT (f_head_descr (p_allowed).s_den IS tp_constrained)) THEN
     (c_empty_descr_set
      CONDITION FALSE
         MESSAGE "Type name expected")
   ELSE
      f_attribute_function
         (f_gen_key,
          IF p_designator /= c_value_desi AND
             (p_designator /= c_val_desi) THEN
              f_gen_constrained
                 (f_head_descr (p_allowed),
                  sc_void)
          ELSE IF p_designator = c_value_desi THEN
              f_gen_constrained
               (c_string_descr,
                sc_void)
          ELSE f_gen_constrained
                  (c_int_descr,
                   sc_void)
          FI FI,
          IF p_designator /= c_image_desi AND
             (p_designator /= c_pos_desi) THEN
             f_gen_constrained
                (f_head_descr (p_allowed),
                 sc_void)
```

```
          ELSE IF p_designator = c_image_desi THEN
             f_gen_constrained
                (c_string_descr,
                 sc_void)
          ELSE f_gen_constrained
                 (c_int_descr,
                  sc_void)
          FI FI)
   FI
OUT (c_empty_descr_set
     CONDITION FALSE
        MESSAGE "Attribute not known")
ESAC

CONDITION

CASE p_designator OF

'address' : f_head_descr (p_allowed).s_den IS tp_object OR
           (f_head_descr (p_allowed).s_den IS tp_subpr);

'base' : (NOT f_is_task (p_allowed,
                         p_env)
          CONDITION IT
             MESSAGE "no tasks for BASE attribute");

'size' :((f_head_descr (p_allowed).s_den IS tp_object)      OR
         (f_head_descr (p_allowed).s_den IS tp_constrained) OR
         (f_head_descr (p_allowed).s_den IS tp_type_den)) AND
        (NOT (f_is_task (p_allowed,
                         p_env))
        CONDITION IT
           MESSAGE "no tasks for SIZE attribute");

'pos' : 'val' : 'pred' : 'succ' : 'image' : 'value' :
   (TRUE
    CONDITION FALSE
       MESSAGE
       "an indexed required for those attributes");
'delta' :
'actual_delta' :
'bits' :
   f_is_fixed_type (f_head_descr (p_allowed),
                    p_env);

'large' :
'machine_rounds' :
   f_is_fixed_type (f_head_descr (p_allowed),
                                  p_env)  OR
   f_is_float_type (f_head_descr (p_allowed),
                                  p_env);
'digits' :
'mantissa' :
'emax' :
'small' :
'epsilon' :
'machine_radix' :
'machine_mantissa' :
```

```
'machine_emax' :
'machine_emin' :
'machine_overflows' :
   f_is_float_type (f_head_descr (p_allowed),
                                 p_env);
'length' :
   CASE c_den : f_head_descr (p_allowed).s_den OF
   IS tp_type_den : f_is_array_type1 (c_den.s_type, p_env);
   IS tp_constrained : f_is_array_type1 (c_den, p_env);
   IS tp_object :
      f_is_array (f_head_descr (p_allowed), p_env)
   OUT FALSE
   ESAC;
'constrained' :
   CASE c_type : f_object_parent_base_type (p_allowed,
                                            p_env) OF
   IS tp_record : (TRUE CONDITION
                        NOT EMPTY (f_discriminants (c_type))
                           MESSAGE
                           "record type must have discriminants")
   OUT (FALSE CONDITION FALSE MESSAGE "record object required")
   ESAC;

'position' :
'first_bit' :
'last_bit' :
   f_head_descr (p_allowed).s_nature = sc_discriminant OR
  (f_head_descr (p_allowed).s_nature = sc_rec_comp);

'storage_size' :
   f_is_task (p_allowed, p_env)        OR
   f_is_access_type (f_head_descr (p_allowed).s_key,
                     p_env);
'terminated' :
'priority' :
'failure' : IF f_head_descr (p_allowed).s_den IS tp_object THEN
               f_is_task (p_allowed, p_env)
            ELSE FALSE
            FI;
'count' : f_head_descr (p_allowed).s_den IS tp_entry
OUT TRUE
ESAC

   MESSAGE "attribute not allowed for that name")
FI;

   %*********************************************************%
   %                                                         %
   %     f_allowed_common_...                                %
   %                                                         %
   %     Used for operator identification.                   %
   %     Operators which are user defined or which are       %
   %     declared by the mechanism of derived subprograms    %
   %     are already contained in p_found.                   %
   %                                                         %
   %     Operators which are additionally described in       %
   %     chapter 4.4 of [Ada80], not contained               %
   %     in p_found and not hidden by an operator in         %
   %     p_found are added to p_found.                       %
   %                                                         %
   %*********************************************************%
```

```
FUNCTION f_allowed_common_op (p_desi   : tp_designator,
                              p_assocs : tp_assoc_list,
                              p_env    : tp_env,
                              p_found  : tp_descr_list)
                             tp_descr_list :

    IF f_is_universal (p_found) THEN
       c_empty_descrs
    ELSE IF NOT EMPTY (f_assoc_choices (p_assocs)) THEN
       c_empty_descrs
    ELSE CASE p_desi QUA SYMB OF
         'abs' :
            IF LENGTH (p_assocs) = 1 THEN
               f_allowed_common_abs
                 (p_desi,
                  HEAD (p_assocs)  QUA tp_comp_assoc
                       .s_actual.s_descrs,
                  p_env,
                  p_found)
            ELSE c_empty_descrs
            FI;
         '+' : '-' :
            IF LENGTH (p_assocs) = 2 THEN
               f_allowed_common_add
                 (p_desi,
                  HEAD (p_assocs)  QUA tp_comp_assoc
                       .s_actual.s_descrs,
                  LAST (p_assocs)  QUA tp_comp_assoc
                       .s_actual.s_descrs,
                  p_env,
                  p_found)
            ELSE IF LENGTH (p_assocs) = 1 THEN
               f_allowed_common_sign
                 (p_desi,
                  HEAD (p_assocs)  QUA tp_comp_assoc
                       .s_actual.s_descrs,
                  p_env,
                  p_found)
            ELSE c_empty_descrs
            FI FI;
         '*' : IF LENGTH (p_assocs) = 2 THEN
                  f_allowed_common_mult
                    (p_desi,
                     HEAD (p_assocs)  QUA tp_comp_assoc
                          .s_actual.s_descrs,
                     LAST (p_assocs)  QUA tp_comp_assoc
                          .s_actual.s_descrs,
                     p_env,
                     p_found)
               ELSE c_empty_descrs
               FI;
          '/' : IF LENGTH (p_assocs) = 2 THEN
                  f_allowed_common_div
                    (p_desi,
                     HEAD (p_assocs)  QUA tp_comp_assoc
                          .s_actual.s_descrs,
                     LAST (p_assocs)  QUA tp_comp_assoc
```

```
                    .s_actual.s_descrs,
                p_env,
                p_found)
         ELSE c_empty_descrs
         FI;
   '**' : IF LENGTH (p_assocs) = 2 THEN
           f_allowed_common_exp
             (p_desi,
                HEAD (p_assocs) QUA tp_comp_assoc
                    .s_actual.s_descrs,
                LAST (p_assocs) QUA tp_comp_assoc
                    .s_actual.s_descrs,
                p_env,
                     p_found)
         ELSE c_empty_descrs
         FI;
   '&' : IF LENGTH (p_assocs) = 2 THEN
          f_allowed_common_concat
            (p_desi,
             HEAD (p_assocs)  QUA tp_comp_assoc
                .s_actual.s_descrs,
             LAST (p_assocs)  QUA tp_comp_assoc
                .s_actual.s_descrs,
             p_env,
             p_found)
        ELSE c_empty_descrs
        FI;
   'and' : 'or' : 'xor' :
      IF LENGTH (p_assocs) = 2 THEN
        f_allowed_common_logical
          (p_desi,
           HEAD (p_assocs) QUA tp_comp_assoc
              .s_actual.s_descrs,
           LAST (p_assocs)  QUA tp_comp_assoc
              .s_actual.s_descrs,
           p_env,
           p_found)
      ELSE c_empty_descrs
      FI;
   'not' :
      IF LENGTH (p_assocs) = 1 THEN
        f_allowed_common_not
          (p_desi,
                   HEAD (p_assocs)  QUA tp_comp_assoc
                     .s_actual.s_descrs,
                   p_env,
                   p_found)
      ELSE c_empty_descrs
      FI;
   '>=' : '>' : '<=' : '<' :
      IF LENGTH (p_assocs) = 2 THEN
        f_allowed_common_compare
          (p_desi,
           HEAD (p_assocs) QUA tp_comp_assoc
              .s_actual.s_descrs,
           LAST (p_assocs) QUA tp_comp_assoc
              .s_actual.s_descrs,
           p_env,
           p_found)
      ELSE c_empty_descrs
```

```
        FI;
      '=' : '/=' :
        IF LENGTH (p_assocs) = 2 THEN
           f_allowed_common_equal
              (p_desi,
               HEAD (p_assocs)  QUA tp_comp_assoc
                  .s_actual.s_descrs,
               HEAD (p_assocs)  QUA tp_comp_assoc
                  .s_actual.s_add,
               LAST (p_assocs)  QUA tp_comp_assoc
                  .s_actual.s_descrs,
               LAST (p_assocs)  QUA tp_comp_assoc
                  .s_actual.s_add,
               p_env,
               p_found)
        ELSE c_empty_descrs
        FI
      OUT (c_empty_descrs CONDITION FALSE MESSAGE "compiler error"
      ESAC
  FI FI;

FUNCTION f_allowed_common_abs (p_desi   : tp_designator,
                               p_left   : tp_descr_list,
                               p_env    : tp_env,
                               p_found  : tp_descr_list)
                              tp_descr_list :

  IF EMPTY (p_left) THEN
     c_empty_descrs
  ELSE IF f_is_fixed_type
            (f_select_by_key
               (f_object_type (HEAD (p_left)),
                p_env),
             p_env) THEN
          f_hide_by_user_def1
             (p_desi,
              sc_co_abs_op,
              c_common_abs,
              f_object_type (HEAD (p_left)),
              f_object_init1 (HEAD (p_left)),
              p_env,
              p_found)
       ELSE c_empty_descrs
       FI +
       f_allowed_common_abs
             (p_desi,
              TAIL (p_left),
              p_env,
              p_found)
  FI;

FUNCTION f_allowed_common_add (p_desi    : tp_designator,
                               p_left,
                               p_right   : tp_descr_list,
                               p_env     : tp_env,
                               p_found   : tp_descr_list)
                              tp_descr_list :

  IF EMPTY (p_left) THEN
     c_empty_descrs
```

```
   ELSE IF f_is_fixed_type
           (f_select_by_key
               (f_object_type (HEAD (p_left)),
                p_env),
            p_env) THEN
           f_allowed_common_add1
              (p_desi,
               f_object_type (HEAD (p_left)),
               f_object_init1 (HEAD (p_left)),
               p_right,
               p_env,
               p_found)
        ELSE c_empty_descrs
        FI +
        f_allowed_common_add
            (p_desi,
             TAIL (p_left),
             p_right,
             p_env,
             p_found)
   FI;

FUNCTION f_allowed_common_add1 (p_desi       : tp_designator,
                                p_left_type  : tp_key,
                                p_left_init  : tp_init,
                                p_right      : tp_descr_list,
                                p_env        : tp_env,
                                p_found      : tp_descr_list)
                               tp_descr_list :

   IF EMPTY (p_right) THEN
      c_empty_descrs
   ELSE IF f_object_type (HEAD (p_right)) = p_left_type OR
           (p_left_type = c_univ_real) OR
           (f_object_type (HEAD (p_right)) = c_univ_real) THEN
           f_hide_by_user_def2
              (p_desi,
               IF p_desi = '+' THEN sc_co_plus_op
                               ELSE sc_co_minus_op FI,
               IF p_desi = '+' THEN c_common_plus
                               ELSE c_common_minus FI,
               IF p_left_type = c_univ_real THEN
                  f_object_type (HEAD (p_right))
               ELSE p_left_type
               FI,
               IF p_left_type = c_univ_real THEN
                  f_object_type (HEAD (p_right))
               ELSE p_left_type
               FI,
               IF p_left_type = c_univ_real THEN
                  f_object_type (HEAD (p_right))
               ELSE p_left_type
               FI,
               p_left_init,
               f_object_init1 (HEAD (p_right)),
               p_env,
               p_found)
        ELSE c_empty_descrs
        FI +
        f_allowed_common_add1
```

```
          (p_desi,
           p_left_type,
           p_left_init,
           TAIL (p_right),
           p_env,
           p_found)
   FI;

FUNCTION f_allowed_common_sign (p_desi   : tp_designator,
                                p_left   : tp_descr_list,
                                p_env    : tp_env,
                                p_found  : tp_descr_list)
                               tp_descr_list :

   IF EMPTY (p_left) THEN
      c_empty_descrs
   ELSE IF f_is_fixed_type
            (f_select_by_key
                (f_object_type (HEAD (p_left)),
                 p_env),
             p_env) THEN
           f_hide_by_user_def1
              (p_desi,
               IF p_desi = '+' THEN sc_co_plus_op
                               ELSE sc_co_minus_op FI,
               IF p_desi = '+' THEN c_common_plus
                               ELSE c_common_minus FI,
               f_object_type (HEAD (p_left)),
               f_object_init1 (HEAD (p_left)),
               p_env,
               p_found)
        ELSE c_empty_descrs
        FI +
        f_allowed_common_sign
              (p_desi,
               TAIL (p_left),
               p_env,
               p_found)
   FI;

FUNCTION f_allowed_common_mult (p_desi    : tp_designator,
                                p_left,
                                p_right   : tp_descr_list,
                                p_env     : tp_env,
                                p_found   : tp_descr_list)
                               tp_descr_list :

   IF EMPTY (p_left) THEN
      c_empty_descrs
   ELSE IF f_is_fixed_type
            (f_select_by_key
                (f_object_type (HEAD (p_left)),
                 p_env),
             p_env)
        OR f_is_int_type
            (f_select_by_key
               (f_object_type (HEAD (p_left)),
                p_env),
             p_env) THEN
          f_allowed_common_mult1
```

```
              (f_is_fixed_type
                 (f_select_by_key
                    (f_object_type (HEAD (p_left)),
                     p_env),
                  p_env),
               p_desi,
               f_object_type (HEAD (p_left)),
               f_object_init1 (HEAD (p_left)),
               p_right,
               p_env,
               p_found)
      ELSE c_empty_descrs
      FI +
      f_allowed_common_mult
           (p_desi,
            TAIL (p_left),
            p_right,
            p_env,
            p_found)
   FI;

FUNCTION f_allowed_common_mult1 (p_is_fixed  : BOOL,
                                  p_desi      : tp_designator,
                                  p_left_type : tp_key,
                                  p_left_init : tp_init,
                                  p_right     : tp_descr_list,
                                  p_env       : tp_env,
                                  p_found     : tp_descr_list)
                                 tp_descr_list :

   IF EMPTY (p_right) THEN
      c_empty_descrs
   ELSE IF f_is_fixed_type
            (f_select_by_key
               (f_object_type (HEAD (p_right)),
                p_env),
             p_env) OR
          (f_is_int_type
            (f_select_by_key
               (f_object_type (HEAD (p_right)),
                p_env),
             p_env) AND p_is_fixed) THEN
        f_hide_by_user_def2
            (p_desi,
             sc_co_mult_op,
             c_common_mult,
             p_left_type,
             f_object_type (HEAD (p_right)),
             IF p_is_fixed THEN
                IF f_is_int_type
                      (f_select_by_key
                         (f_object_type (HEAD (p_right)),
                          p_env),
                       p_env) THEN
                   p_left_type
                ELSE c_univ_fixed
                FI
             ELSE f_object_type (HEAD (p_right))
             FI,
             p_left_init,
```

```
                f_object_init1 (HEAD (p_right)),
                p_env,
                p_found)
        ELSE c_empty_descrs
        FI +
        f_allowed_common_mult1
            (p_is_fixed,
             p_desi,
             p_left_type,
             p_left_init,
             TAIL (p_right),
             p_env,
             p_found)
   FI;

FUNCTION f_allowed_common_div (p_desi    : tp_designator,
                               p_left,
                               p_right   : tp_descr_list,
                               p_env     : tp_env,
                               p`found   : tp_descr_list)
                              tp_descr_list :

   IF EMPTY (p_left) THEN
      c_empty_descrs
   ELSE IF f_is_fixed_type
            (f_select_by_key
                (f_object_type (HEAD (p_left)),
                 p_env),
             p_env) THEN
           f_allowed_common_div1
               (p_desi,
                f_object_type (HEAD (p_left)),
                f_object_init1 (HEAD (p_left)),
                p_right,
                p_env,
                p_found)
        ELSE c_empty_descrs
        FI +
        f_allowed_common_div
            (p_desi,
             TAIL (p_left),
             p_right,
             p_env,
             p_found)
   FI;

FUNCTION f_allowed_common_div1 (p_desi      : tp_designator,
                                p_left_type : tp_key,
                                p_left_init : tp_init,
                                p_right     : tp_descr_list,
                                p_env       : tp_env,
                                p_found     : tp_descr_list)
                               tp_descr_list :

   IF EMPTY (p_right) THEN
      c_empty_descrs
   ELSE IF f_is_fixed_type
            (f_select_by_key
                (f_object_type (HEAD (p_right)),
                 p_env),
```

```
            p_env) OR
         f_is_int_type
           (f_select_by_key
              (f_object_type (HEAD (p_right)),
               p_env),
            p_env) THEN
         f_hide_by_user_def2
             (p_desi,
              sc_co_div_op,
              c_common_div,
              p_left_type,
              f_object_type (HEAD (p_right)),
              IF f_is_int_type
                   (f_select_by_key
                      (f_object_type (HEAD (p_right)),
                       p_env),
                    p_env) THEN
                 p_left_type
              ELSE c_univ_fixed
              FI,
              p_left_init,
              f_object_init1 (HEAD (p_right)),
              p_env,
              p_found)
      ELSE c_empty_descrs
      FI +
      f_allowed_common_div1
          (p_desi,
           p_left_type,
           p_left_init,
           TAIL (p_right),
           p_env,
           p_found)
   FI;

FUNCTION f_allowed_common_exp (p_desi    : tp_designator,
                               p_left,
                               p_right   : tp_descr_list,
                               p_env     : tp_env,
                               p_found   : tp_descr_list)
                              tp_descr_list :

   IF EMPTY (p_left) THEN
      c_empty_descrs
   ELSE IF f_is_float_type
           (f_select_by_key
              (f_object_type (HEAD (p_left)),
               p_env),
            p_env)
      OR f_is_int_type
           (f_select_by_key
              (f_object_type (HEAD (p_left)),
               p_env),
            p_env) THEN
         f_allowed_common_exp1
             (p_desi,
              f_object_type (HEAD (p_left)),
              f_object_init1 (HEAD (p_left)),
              p_right,
              p_env,
```

```
               p_found)
         ELSE c_empty_descrs
         FI +
         f_allowed_common_exp
              (p_desi,
               TAIL (p_left),
               p_right,
               p_env,
               p_found)
   FI;

FUNCTION f_allowed_common_exp1 (p_desi       : tp_designator,
                                 p_left_type  : tp_key,
                                 p_left_init  : tp_init,
                                 p_right      : tp_descr_list,
                                 p_env        : tp_env,
                                 p_found      : tp_descr_list)
                                tp_descr_list :

   IF EMPTY (p_right) THEN
      c_empty_descrs
   ELSE IF f_is_int_type
             (f_select_by_key
                 (f_object_type (HEAD (p_right)),
                  p_env),
              p_env) THEN
           f_hide_by_user_def2
              (p_desi,
               sc_co_exp_op,
               c_common_exp,
               p_left_type,
               f_object_type (HEAD (p_right)),
               p_left_type,
               p_left_init,
               f_object_init1 (HEAD (p_right)),
               p_env,
               p_found)
        ELSE c_empty_descrs
        FI +
        f_allowed_common_exp1
             (p_desi,
              p_left_type,
              p_left_init,
              TAIL (p_right),
              p_env,
              p_found)
   FI;

FUNCTION f_allowed_common_concat (p_desi      : tp_designator,
                                   p_left,
                                   p_right     : tp_descr_list,
                                   p_env       : tp_env,
                                   p_found     : tp_descr_list)
                                  tp_descr_list :

   IF EMPTY (p_left) THEN
      c_empty_descrs
   ELSE f_allowed_common_concat1
          (f_is_array_type1
              (f_obj_constrained1 (HEAD (p_left)),
```

```
          p_env),
        p_desi,
        HEAD (p_left),
        f_object_init1 (HEAD (p_left)),
        p_right,
        p_env,
        p_found) +
      f_allowed_common_concat
        (p_desi,
          TAIL (p_left),
          p_right,
          p_env,
          p_found)
  FI;

FUNCTION f_allowed_common_concat1 (p_is_array  : BOOL,
                                   p_desi      : tp_designator,
                                   p_left      : tp_descr,
                                   p_left_init : tp_init,
                                   p_right     : tp_descr_list,
                                   p_env       : tp_env,
                                   p_found     : tp_descr_list)
                                  tp_descr_list :

  IF EMPTY (p_right) THEN
     c_empty_descrs
  ELSE IF IF f_is_array_type1
            (f_obj_constrained1 (HEAD (p_right)),
             p_env) THEN

          f_implicitly_convertable1
            (f_object_type (p_left),
             f_parent_base_type1 (f_obj_constrained1
                                    (HEAD (p_right)),
                                  p_env)
              QUA tp_array .s_comp_type.s_base_type,
             p_env)
        ELSE FALSE
        FI              OR
        IF p_is_array THEN

          f_implicitly_convertable1
             (f_object_type (HEAD (p_right)),
              f_parent_base_type1
                 (f_obj_constrained1 (p_left), p_env)
               QUA tp_array .s_comp_type.s_base_type,
              p_env)
        ELSE FALSE
        FI              OR
        (f_object_type (p_left) = f_object_type (HEAD (p_right)) AND
         p_is_array) THEN
        f_hide_by_user_def2
           (p_desi,
            sc_co_concat_op,
            c_common_concat,
            IF p_is_array THEN
               f_object_type (p_left)
            ELSE f_parent_base_type1 (f_obj_constrained1
                                        (HEAD (p_right)),
                                      p_env)
```

```
                  QUA tp_array .s_comp_type.s_base_type
               FI,
               IF f_is_array_type1
                  (f_obj_constrained1 (HEAD (p_right)),
                  p_env) THEN
                  f_object_type (HEAD (p_right))
               ELSE f_parent_base_type1
                     (f_obj_constrained1 (p_left), p_env)
                  QUA tp_array .s_comp_type.s_base_type
               FI,
               IF p_is_array THEN
                  f_object_type (p_left)
               ELSE f_object_type (HEAD (p_right))
               FI,
               p_left_init,
               f_object_init1 (HEAD (p_right)),
               p_env,
               p_found)
         ELSE c_empty_descrs
         FI +
         f_allowed_common_concat1
            (p_is_array,
             p_desi,
             p_left,
             p_left_init,
             TAIL (p_right),
             p_env,
             p_found)
   FI;

FUNCTION f_allowed_common_logical (p_desi    : tp_designator,
                                   p_left,
                                   p_right   : tp_descr_list,
                                   p_env     : tp_env,
                                   p_found   : tp_descr_list)
                                  tp_descr_list :

   IF EMPTY (p_left) THEN
      c_empty_descrs
   ELSE IF f_is_boolean_array_type
             (f_object_type (HEAD (p_left)),
              p_env) THEN
           f_allowed_common_logical1
              (p_desi,
               f_object_type (HEAD (p_left)),
               f_object_init1 (HEAD (p_left)),
               p_right,
               p_env,
               p_found)
        ELSE c_empty_descrs
        FI +
        f_allowed_common_logical
            (p_desi,
             TAIL (p_left),
             p_right,
             p_env,
             p_found)
   FI;
```

```
FUNCTION f_allowed_common_logical1 (p_desi       : tp_designator,
                                    p_left_type  : tp_key,
                                    p_left_init  : tp_init,
                                    p_right      : tp_descr_list,
                                    p_env        : tp_env,
                                    p_found      : tp_descr_list)
                                   tp_descr_list :

   IF EMPTY (p_right) THEN
      c_empty_descrs
   ELSE IF f_object_type (HEAD (p_right)) = p_left_type THEN
         f_hide_by_user_def2
            (p_desi,
             CASE p_desi QUA SYMB OF
             'and' : sc_co_and_op;
             'or'  : sc_co_or_op
             OUT     sc_co_xor_op
             ESAC,
             CASE p_desi QUA SYMB OF
             'and' : c_common_and;
             'or'  : c_common_or
             OUT     c_common_xor
             ESAC,
             p_left_type,
             f_object_type (HEAD (p_right)),
             p_left_type,
             p_left_init,
             f_object_init1 (HEAD (p_right)),
             p_env,
             p_found)
        ELSE c_empty_descrs
        FI +
        f_allowed_common_logical1
             (p_desi,
              p_left_type,
              p_left_init,
              TAIL (p_right),
              p_env,
              p_found)
   FI;

FUNCTION f_allowed_common_not (p_desi    : tp_designator,
                               p_left    : tp_descr_list,
                               p_env     : tp_env,
                               p_found   : tp_descr_list)
                              tp_descr_list :

   IF EMPTY (p_left) THEN
      c_empty_descrs
   ELSE IF f_is_boolean_array_type
            (f_object_type (HEAD (p_left)),
             p_env) THEN
         f_hide_by_user_def1
            (p_desi,
             sc_co_not_op,
             c_common_not,
             f_object_type (HEAD (p_left)),
             f_object_init1 (HEAD (p_left)),
             p_env,
             p_found)
```

```
          ELSE c_empty_descrs
          FI +
          f_allowed_common_not
               (p_desi,
                TAIL (p_left),
                p_env,
                p_found)
     FI;

FUNCTION f_allowed_common_compare (p_desi    : tp_designator,
                                   p_left,
                                   p_right   : tp_descr_list,
                                   p_env     : tp_env,
                                   p_found   : tp_descr_list)
                                  tp_descr_list :

     IF EMPTY (p_left) THEN
        c_empty_descrs
     ELSE IF f_is_discrete_array_type
               (f_object_type (HEAD (p_left)),
                p_env) OR
             f_is_scalar_type
               (f_select_by_key
                  (f_object_type (HEAD (p_left)),
                   p_env),
                p_env) THEN
             f_allowed_common_compare1
                (f_is_discrete_array_type
                    (f_object_type (HEAD (p_left)),
                     p_env),
                 p_desi,
                 f_object_type (HEAD (p_left)),
                 f_object_init1 (HEAD (p_left)),
                 p_right,
                 p_env,
                 p_found)
          ELSE c_empty_descrs
          FI +
          f_allowed_common_compare
               (p_desi,
                TAIL (p_left),
                p_right,
                p_env,
                p_found)
     FI;

FUNCTION f_allowed_common_compare1 (p_is_array  : BOOL,
                                    p_desi      : tp_designator,
                                    p_left_type : tp_key,
                                    p_left_init : tp_init,
                                    p_right     : tp_descr_list,
                                    p_env       : tp_env,
                                    p_found     : tp_descr_list)
                                   tp_descr_list :

     IF EMPTY (p_right) THEN
        c_empty_descrs
     ELSE IF (f_object_type (HEAD (p_right)) = p_left_type
              AND p_is_array) OR
             f_implicitly_convertable
```

```
            (f_object_type (HEAD (p_right)),
             p_left_type,
             p_env) THEN
         f_hide_by_user_def2
             (p_desi,
              CASE p_desi QUA SYMB OF
               '<'  : sc_co_less_op;
               '<=' : sc_co_le_equal_op;
               '>'  : sc_co_greater_op
              OUT    sc_co_gr_equal_op
              ESAC,
              CASE p_desi QUA SYMB OF
               '<'  : c_common_less;
               '<=' : c_common_le_equal;
               '>'  : c_common_greater
              OUT    c_common_gr_equal
              ESAC,
              IF p_is_array THEN
                 p_left_type
              ELSE IF f_implicitly_convertable1
                         (f_object_type (HEAD (p_right)),
                          p_left_type,
                          p_env) THEN
                      p_left_type
                   ELSE f_object_type (HEAD (p_right))
                   FI
              FI,
              IF p_is_array THEN
                 p_left_type
              ELSE IF f_implicitly_convertable1
                         (f_object_type (HEAD (p_right)),
                          p_left_type,
                          p_env) THEN
                      p_left_type
                   ELSE f_object_type (HEAD (p_right))
                   FI
              FI,
              c_bool,
              p_left_init,
              f_object_init1 (HEAD (p_right)),
              p_env,
              p_found)
      ELSE c_empty_descrs
      FI +
      f_allowed_common_compare1
           (p_is_array,
            p_desi,
            p_left_type,
            p_left_init,
            TAIL (p_right),
            p_env,
          - p_found)
  FI;

FUNCTION f_allowed_common_equal (p_desi      : tp_designator,
                                 p_left      : tp_descr_list,
                                 p_left_add  : tp_additional,
                                 p_right     : tp_descr_list,
                                 p_right_add : tp_additional,
                                 p_env       : tp_env,
```

```
                                        p_found     : tp_descr_list)
                                       tp_descr_list :

   IF EMPTY (p_left) THEN
      c_empty_descrs
   ELSE IF f_is_assign_allowed_for_type
            (f_type
               (f_object_type (HEAD (p_left)),
                p_env),
             p_env) THEN
          f_allowed_common_equal1
              (p_desi,
               f_object_type (HEAD (p_left)),
               f_object_init1 (HEAD (p_left)),
               p_left_add,
               p_right_add,
               p_right,
               p_env,
               p_found)
        ELSE c_empty_descrs
        FI +
        f_allowed_common_equal
             (p_desi,
              TAIL (p_left),
              p_left_add,
              p_right,
              p_right_add,
              p_env,
              p_found)
   FI;

FUNCTION f_allowed_common_equal1 (p_desi        : tp_designator,
                                  p_left_type  : tp_key,
                                  p_left_init  : tp_init,
                                  p_left_add,
                                  p_right_add  : tp_additional,
                                  p_right      : tp_descr_list,
                                  p_env        : tp_env,
                                  p_found      : tp_descr_list)
                                 tp_descr_list :

   IF EMPTY (p_right) THEN
      c_empty_descrs
   ELSE IF f_implicitly_convertable
            (IF p_right_add = sc_add_deriv THEN
                f_parent_base_type
                   (p_left_type,
                    p_env)
             ELSE IF p_right_add = sc_add_access THEN
                     f_deref_type
                        (p_left_type,
                         p_env)
                  ELSE p_left_type
                  FI
             FI,
             IF p_left_add = sc_add_deriv THEN
                f_parent_base_type
                   (f_object_type (HEAD (p_right)),
                    p_env)
             ELSE IF p_left_add = sc_add_access THEN
```

```
                    f_deref_type
                         (f_object_type (HEAD (p_right)),
                          p_env)
                  ELSE f_object_type (HEAD (p_right))
                  FI
              FI,
              p_env) THEN
          f_hide_by_user_def2
            (p_desi,
             CASE p_desi QUA SYMB OF
             '='  : sc_co_equal_op
             OUT    sc_co_n_equal_op
             ESAC,
             CASE p_desi QUA SYMB OF
             '='  : c_common_equal
             OUT    c_common_n_equal
             ESAC,
             IF p_left_add = sc_add_deriv THEN
                f_object_type (HEAD (p_right))
             ELSE IF p_right_add = sc_add_deriv THEN
                p_left_type
             ELSE IF f_implicitly_convertable1
                        (f_object_type (HEAD (p_right)),
                         p_left_type,
                         p_env) THEN
                p_left_type
             ELSE f_object_type (HEAD (p_right))
             FI FI FI,
             IF p_left_add = sc_add_deriv THEN
                f_object_type (HEAD (p_right))
             ELSE IF p_right_add = sc_add_deriv THEN
                p_left_type
             ELSE IF f_implicitly_convertable1
                        (f_object_type (HEAD (p_right)),
                         p_left_type,
                         p_env) THEN
                p_left_type
             ELSE f_object_type (HEAD (p_right))
             FI FI FI,
             c_bool,
             p_left_init,
             f_object_init1 (HEAD (p_right)),
             p_env,
             p_found)
       ELSE c_empty_descrs
       FI +
       f_allowed_common_equal1
            (p_desi,
             p_left_type,
             p_left_init,
             p_left_add,
             p_right_add,
             TAIL (p_right),
             p_env,
             p_found)
   FI;

FUNCTION f_allowed_converted (p_name   : tp_descr_set,
                              p_assocs : tp_assoc_list,
                              p_env    : tp_env) tp_descr_set :
```

```
   IF f_is_error_or_empty (p_name) OR EMPTY (p_assocs)
          OR f_is_error_empty_assocs (p_assocs) THEN
      c_error_descr_set
   ELSE CASE c_assoc : HEAD (p_assocs) OF
        IS tp_comp_assoc :
             tp_descr_set
               (f_allowed_converted1
                  (f_head_descr (p_name),
                   c_assoc.s_actual.s_descrs,
                   c_assoc.s_actual.s_add,
                   p_env),
                sc_no_add);
        IS tp_dscrt_range : c_error_descr_set
        ESAC
   FI;

FUNCTION f_allowed_converted1 (p_type : tp_descr,
                               p_exps : tp_descr_list,
                               p_add  : tp_additional,
                               p_env  : tp_env)
                              tp_descr_list :

   IF EMPTY (p_exps) THEN
      c_empty_descrs
   ELSE IF (f_valid_converted1
              (p_type.s_key,
               f_expand_additional (tp_descr_list (HEAD (p_exps)),
                                    p_add,
                                    p_env),
            p_env) =/ c_empty_descrs) THEN
           tp_descr_list
             (f_mark_origin2
                (f_temp_descr
                   (c_designator,
                    c_key,
                    c_start_repr,
                    sc_void_state,
                    IF HEAD (p_exps).s_nature = sc_variable THEN
                       sc_converted_var
                    ELSE sc_value
                    FI,
                    tp_object (f_constrained (p_type.s_key, p_env),
                               f_eval_converted
                                  (p_type.s_key,
                                   HEAD (p_exps),
                                   p_env)),
                    c_enclosing),
                 f_origin (p_type)))
        ELSE c_empty_descrs
        FI                                                +
        f_allowed_converted1 (p_type,
                              TAIL (p_exps),
                              p_add,
                              p_env)
    FI;

 FUNCTION f_allowed_expected (p_allowed  : tp_descr_set,
                              p_expected : tp_key_void,
```

```
                                p_env        : tp_env) tp_descr_set :

     % Called after evaluation of at_allowed_...1 / 2 to
     % check whether the allowed meanings conflict with an expected
     % type (if any).

           CASE c_expected : p_expected OF
           IS tp_void :
               IF EMPTY (p_allowed.s_descrs) THEN
                  c_empty_descr_set
               ELSE p_allowed
               FI;
           IS tp_key :
               f_valid_descr_set (p_allowed,
                                  c_expected,
                                  p_env)
           ESAC;

FUNCTION f_allowed_exp_in_range (p_exp   : tp_descr_set,
                                 p_type  : tp_type_range,
                                 p_env   : tp_env)
                                tp_descr_set :

     % Build intersection of the types of p_exp and p_type (possibly
     % lower and upper bound) and yield such meanings in exp
     % compatible with one of these types.

   CASE c_type : p_type OF
   IS tp_constrained  : f_allowed_expected
                          (p_exp,
                           c_type.s_base_type,
                           p_env);
   IS tp_range_constr : f_allowed_expected
                          (p_exp,
                           f_same_type
                             (tp_descrs_list
                                (p_exp,
                                 c_type.s_lower_bound,
                                 c_type.s_upper_bound),
                              p_env),
                           p_env)
   ESAC;

FUNCTION f_allowed_funct_entry (p_name   : tp_descr_set,
                                p_assocs : tp_assoc_list,
                                p_env    : tp_env) tp_descr_set :

     % Function call or indexed entry family

   tp_descr_set
      (f_universal
         (f_allowed_funct_entry1
            (p_name.s_descrs,
             p_assocs,
             p_env)) +
       IF f_is_common_op (p_name.s_descrs) THEN
          f_allowed_common_op
            (f_head_descr (p_name) .s_designator,
             p_assocs,
```

```
          p_env,
            f_universal
               (f_allowed_funct_entry1
                  (p_name.s_descrs,
                   p_assocs,
                   p_env)))
      ELSE c_empty_descrs
      FI,
      sc_no_add);

FUNCTION f_allowed_funct_entry1 (p_names   : tp_descr_list,
                                 p_assocs  : tp_assoc_list,
                                 p_env     : tp_env) tp_descr_list:

   IF EMPTY (p_names) THEN
      c_empty_descrs
   ELSE  CASE c_params :
              IF CASE c_den : HEAD (p_names).s_den OF
                 IS tp_subpr  : c_den.s_spec IS tp_function
                 OUT FALSE
                 ESAC THEN
                 IF HEAD (p_names).s_state = sc_in_formal_part OR
                    (HEAD (p_names).s_state = sc_in_generic_part)
                   THEN sc_void
                 ELSE f_valid_params1
                         (f_parameters (HEAD (p_names)),
                          p_assocs,
                          p_env)
                 FI
              ELSE sc_void
              FI                    OF
        IS tp_assoc_list :
           tp_descr_list (f_mark_origin2
                     (f_temp_descr (c_designator,
                           c_key,
                           c_start_repr,
                           sc_void_state,
                           sc_value,
                           tp_object
                             (f_result (HEAD (p_names)),
                              f_eval_function
                                 (HEAD (p_names),
                                  c_params,
                                  p_env)),
                           c_enclosing),
                      f_origin (HEAD (p_names))));
        IS tp_void :IF HEAD (p_names).s_den IS tp_entry_family THEN
                       IF f_valid_indices1
                             (tp_dscrt_range_list
                                (HEAD (p_names).s_den QUA
                                   tp_entry_family .s_dscrt_range),
                              p_assocs,
                              p_env) IS tp_assoc_list THEN
                          tp_descr_list
                            (f_mark_origin2
                               (f_temp_descr
                                  (HEAD (p_names).s_designator,
                                   HEAD (p_names).s_key,
                                   HEAD (p_names).s_repr,
                                   HEAD (p_names).s_state,
```

```
                                        HEAD (p_names).s_nature,
                                        HEAD (p_names).s_den
                                         QUA tp_entry_family .s_entry,
                                        HEAD (p_names).s_enclosing),
                                     f_origin (HEAD (p_names))))
                           ELSE c_empty_descrs
                           FI
                      ELSE c_empty_descrs
                      FI
         ESAC +
         f_allowed_funct_entry1 (TAIL (p_names), p_assocs, p_env)
   FI;

FUNCTION f_allowed_indexed (p_name    : tp_descr_set,
                            p_assocs  : tp_assoc_list,
                            p_env     : tp_env)tp_descr_set:

        tp_descr_set (f_allowed_indexed1 (p_name.s_descrs,
                                          p_assocs,
                                          p_env),
                      sc_no_add);

FUNCTION f_allowed_indexed1 (p_names  : tp_descr_list,
                             p_assocs : tp_assoc_list,
                             p_env    : tp_env) tp_descr_list:

   IF EMPTY (p_names) THEN
      c_empty_descrs
   ELSE CASE c_type : f_object_parent_deref_type
                           (HEAD (p_names),
                            p_env) OF
        IS tp_array :
           CASE c_indices : f_valid_indices1 (c_type.s_indices,
                                              p_assocs,
                                              p_env)OF
           IS tp_void : c_empty_descrs;
           IS tp_assoc_list :
              tp_descr_list (f_mark_origin2
                     (f_temp_descr (c_designator,
                                    c_key,
                                    c_start_repr,
                                    sc_void_state,
                                    IF f_object_parent_base_type1
                                          (HEAD (p_names),
                                           p_env)
                                                 IS tp_access THEN
                                       sc_variable
                                    ELSE HEAD (p_names).s_nature
                                    FI,
                                    tp_object
                                       (c_type.s_comp_type,
                                        f_eval_indexed
                                           (HEAD (p_names),
                                            c_indices,
                                            p_env)),
                                    c_enclosing),
                                 f_origin (HEAD (p_names))))
           ESAC
        OUT c_empty_descrs
        ESAC                                      +
```

```
        f_allowed_indexed1 (TAIL (p_names), p_assocs, p_env)
   FI;
FUNCTION f_allowed_membership (p_exp          : tp_descr_set,
                              p_type_range : tp_type_range,
                              p_op         : tp_op,
                              p_env        : tp_env)
                             tp_descr_set :

   IF f_is_error_or_empty (p_exp) OR
     CASE c_range : p_type_range OF
     IS tp_range_constr : f_is_error_empty_range (tp_range (c_range))
     OUT FALSE
     ESAC THEN
     c_error_descr_set
   ELSE f_descr_set_val
           (c_bool_constr,
            f_eval_membership
                 (f_head_descr (p_exp),
                  p_type_range,
                  p_op,
                  p_env))
   FI;
FUNCTION f_allowed_parenthesized (p_exp : tp_descr_set,
                                  p_env : tp_env)
                                 tp_descr_set :

   tp_descr_set (f_allowed_parenthesized1 (p_exp.s_descrs,
                                           p_env),
                 sc_no_add);

FUNCTION f_allowed_parenthesized1 (p_descrs : tp_descr_list,
                                   p_env    : tp_env)
                                  tp_descr_list :

   IF EMPTY (p_descrs) THEN
      p_descrs
   ELSE tp_descr_list
          (f_mark_origin2
             (f_temp_descr
                (sc_anonymous,
                 c_key,
                 HEAD (p_descrs).s_repr,
                 HEAD (p_descrs).s_state,
                 sc_value,
                 HEAD (p_descrs).s_den,
                 HEAD (p_descrs).s_enclosing),
           f_origin (HEAD (p_descrs))))
        + f_allowed_parenthesized1 (TAIL (p_descrs), p_env)
   FI;

FUNCTION f_allowed_proc_entry (p_name   : tp_descr_set,
                               p_assocs : tp_assoc_list,
                               p_env    : tp_env) tp_descr_set :

   tp_descr_set (f_allowed_proc_entry1 (p_name.s_descrs,
                                        p_assocs,
                                        p_env),
                 sc_no_add);
```

```
FUNCTION f_allowed_proc_entry1 (p_descrs : tp_descr_list,
                                p_assocs : tp_assoc_list,
                                p_env    : tp_env) tp_descr_list :

   IF EMPTY (p_descrs) THEN
      c_empty_descrs
   ELSE CASE c_params :
                 IF CASE c_den : HEAD (p_descrs).s_den OF
                    IS tp_subpr : CASE c_den.s_spec OF
                                  IS tp_procedure : TRUE
                                  OUT FALSE
                                  ESAC;
                    IS tp_entry : TRUE
                    OUT FALSE
                    ESAC THEN
                    f_valid_params1
                          (f_parameters (HEAD (p_descrs)),
                           p_assocs,
                           p_env)
                 ELSE IF HEAD (p_descrs).s_den IS tp_entry_family THEN
                         IF f_valid_indices1
                               (tp_dscrt_range_list
                                  (HEAD (p_descrs).s_den QUA
                                     tp_entry_family .s_dscrt_range),
                                p_assocs,
                                p_env) IS tp_assoc_list THEN
                            f_valid_params1
                                  (HEAD (p_descrs).s_den
                                     QUA tp_entry_family .s_entry
                                     .s_params,
                                   tp_assoc_list (),
                                   p_env)
                         ELSE sc_void
                         FI
                      ELSE sc_void
                      FI
                 FI               OF
      IS tp_assoc_list :
            tp_descr_list
              (f_mark_origin2
                 (f_temp_descr (c_designator,
                                c_key,
                                c_start_repr,
                                sc_void_state,
                                IF (HEAD (p_descrs).s_nature =
                                       sc_entry) THEN
                                       sc_entry
                                ELSE sc_void_nature
                                FI,
                                sc_void,
                                HEAD (p_descrs).s_enclosing),
                  f_origin (HEAD (p_descrs))))
      OUT c_empty_descrs
      ESAC           +
      f_allowed_proc_entry1 (TAIL (p_descrs), p_assocs, p_env)
  FI;

FUNCTION f_allowed_qualified (p_allowed  : tp_descr_set,
                              p_expected : tp_descr,
```

```
                                   p_env        : tp_env)
                                  tp_descr_set :

   tp_descr_set
     (f_allowed_qualified1
          (f_is_fixed_type (p_expected, p_env),
           p_allowed.s_descrs,
           f_base_type (p_expected),
           f_constrained (p_expected.s_key,
                          p_env),
           p_env),
       sc_no_add);

FUNCTION f_allowed_qualified1 (p_is_fixed      : BOOL,
                               p_descrs        : tp_descr_list,
                               p_expected      : tp_key,
                               p_constrained   : tp_constrained,
                               p_env           : tp_env)
                              tp_descr_list :

   IF EMPTY (p_descrs) THEN
      p_descrs
   ELSE CASE c_den : HEAD (p_descrs).s_den OF
        IS tp_object :
             IF NOT p_is_fixed OR
                (c_den.s_type.s_base_type = c_univ_fixed) OR
                (c_den.s_type.s_base_type = c_univ_real) OR
                (c_den.s_type.s_base_type = p_expected) THEN
               tp_descr_list
                  (f_mark_origin2
                     (f_temp_descr
                        (sc_anonymous,
                         c_key,
                         HEAD (p_descrs).s_repr,
                         HEAD (p_descrs).s_state,
                         HEAD (p_descrs).s_nature,
                          tp_object
                            (p_constrained,
                             c_den.s_init),
                         HEAD (p_descrs).s_enclosing),
                  f_origin (HEAD (p_descrs))))
             ELSE c_empty_descrs
             FI
        OUT c_empty_descrs
        ESAC +
        f_allowed_qualified1 (p_is_fixed,
                              TAIL (p_descrs),
                              p_expected,
                              p_constrained,
                              p_env)
   FI;

FUNCTION f_allowed_selected (p_name      : tp_descr_set,
                             p_designator : tp_designator,
                             p_env : tp_env) tp_descr_set :

   IF f_is_error_or_empty (p_name) THEN
      c_error_descr_set
   ELSE IF CASE f_head_descr (p_name).s_state OF
           sc_spec_complete : sc_void_state : sc_deferred : TRUE;
```

```
        sc_complete : sc_complete_generic : sc_in_init :
            IF f_head_descr (p_name).s_nature = sc_task THEN
               CASE f_select_by_key
                       (f_object_type
                           (f_head_descr (p_name)),
                        p_env).s_state OF
                  sc_in_body : sc_in_handler : FALSE
                  OUT TRUE
                  ESAC
            ELSE TRUE
            FI
        OUT FALSE
        ESAC THEN
         tp_descr_set
            (f_allowed_selected1 (p_name.s_descrs,
                                  p_designator,
                                  p_env),
            sc_no_add)
      ELSE IF EMPTY (p_name.s_descrs) THEN

           tp_descr_set
            (f_mark_origin1
               (f_select_by_designator0
                  (p_designator,
                   f_enclosed_descrs
                      (IF f_head_descr (p_name).s_nature = sc_task
                          THEN f_object_type
                                 (f_head_descr (p_name))
                       ELSE f_head_descr (p_name).s_key
                       FI,
                       p_env),
                   p_env),
                f_origin (HEAD (p_name.s_descrs))),
             sc_no_add)
         ELSE (c_empty_descr_set CONDITION FALSE MESSAGE
               "ambiguous selected component")
         FI
      FI
   FI;

FUNCTION f_allowed_selected1 (p_names      : tp_descr_list,
                              p_designator : tp_designator,
                              p_env        : tp_env)
                             tp_descr_list  :

   IF EMPTY (p_names) THEN
      c_empty_descrs
   ELSE f_update_nature_descrs
          (f_update_init
             (f_mark_origin1
                (f_select_by_designator0
                    (p_designator,
                     CASE c_den : HEAD (p_names).s_den OF
                     IS tp_object :
                        CASE c_type : f_object_parent_deref_type
                                         (HEAD (p_names),
                                          p_env) OF
                        IS tp_record : c_type.s_descrs;
                        IS tp_task_spec : c_type.s_visible
                        OUT c_empty_descrs
```

```
                    ESAC;
                  IS tp_package: c_den.s_visible
                  OUT c_empty_descrs
                  ESAC,
                  p_env),
               f_origin (HEAD (p_names))),
            f_eval_selected
               (HEAD (p_names),
                p_designator,
                p_env)),
         CASE c_type : f_object_parent_deref_type
                          (HEAD (p_names),
                           p_env) OF
         IS tp_record : IF f_object_parent_base_type1
                             (HEAD (p_names),
                              p_env) IS tp_access
                        THEN sc_variable
                        ELSE HEAD (p_names).s_nature
                        FI
         OUT sc_same
         ESAC)                                          +
      f_allowed_selected1 (TAIL (p_names),
                           p_designator,
                           p_env)
   FI;

FUNCTION f_allowed_short_circuit (p_exp_1,
                                  p_exp_2 : tp_descr_set,
                                  p_op    : tp_op,
                                  p_env   : tp_env)
                                 tp_descr_set :

   IF f_is_error_or_empty (p_exp_1) OR f_is_error_or_empty (p_exp_2)
     THEN c_error_descr_set
   ELSE f_descr_set_val
          (c_bool_constr,
           f_eval_short_circuit
                 (f_head_descr (p_exp_1),
                  f_head_descr (p_exp_2),
                  p_op,
                  p_env))
   FI;


FUNCTION f_allowed_slice (p_name   : tp_descr_set,
                          p_assocs : tp_assoc_list,
                          p_env    : tp_env) tp_descr_set:

   IF f_is_error_or_empty (p_name) OR EMPTY (p_assocs)
      OR f_is_error_empty_assocs (p_assocs) THEN
     c_error_descr_set
   ELSE tp_descr_set
        (f_allowed_slice1 (p_name.s_descrs,
                           p_assocs,
                           p_env),
         sc_no_add)
   FI;

FUNCTION f_allowed_slice1 (p_names  : tp_descr_list,
                           p_assocs : tp_assoc_list,
```

```
                    p_env : tp_env) tp_descr_list :

  IF EMPTY (p_names) THEN
     c_empty_descrs
  ELSE CASE c_type : f_object_parent_deref_type
                          (HEAD (p_names),
                           p_env) OF
       IS tp_array :
          IF LENGTH (c_type.s_indices) = 1 THEN
             CASE c_slice : f_valid_slice1 (HEAD (c_type.s_indices),
                                            p_assocs,
                                            p_env)OF
                 IS tp_assoc_list :
                    tp_descr_list
                     (f_mark_origin2
                       (f_temp_descr (c_designator,
                                      c_key,
                                      f_repr (f_deref_type
                                               (f_object_type
                                                 (HEAD (p_names)),
                                              p_env),
                                            p_env),
                                      sc_complete,
                                      IF f_object_parent_base_type1
                                          (HEAD (p_names),
                                           p_env)
                                                 IS tp_access
                                         THEN sc_variable
                                      ELSE HEAD (p_names).s_nature
                                      FI,
                                      tp_object
                                         (tp_constrained
                                            (f_deref_type
                                              (f_object_type
                                                 (HEAD (p_names)),
                                             p_env),
                                             tp_dscrt_range_list
                                               (HEAD (c_slice)
                                                 QUA tp_dscrt_range)),
                                          c_init),
                                      c_enclosing),
                        f_origin (HEAD (p_names))))
                OUT c_empty_descrs
                ESAC
           ELSE c_empty_descrs
           FI
      OUT c_empty_descrs
      ESAC +
      f_allowed_slice1 (TAIL (p_names),
                        p_assocs,
                        p_env)
  FI;

FUNCTION f_assoc_choices (p_assocs : tp_assoc_list) tp_choice_list :

     % The list of all choices in p_assocs.

  IF EMPTY (p_assocs) THEN
     tp_choice_list ()
```

```
   ELSE CASE c_assoc : HEAD (p_assocs) OF
        IS tp_comp_assoc : c_assoc.s_choices
        OUT tp_choice_list ()
        ESAC +
        f_assoc_choices (TAIL (p_assocs))
   FI;

     %*************************************************************%
     %                                                             %
     %       f_attr_...                                            %
     %                                                             %
     %       Evaluate the attribute ...                            %
     %                                                             %
     %*************************************************************%

FUNCTION f_attr_constrained (p_obj : tp_descr_set,
                             p_env : tp_env) tp_descr_set :

   f_descr_set_val
     (c_bool_constr,
      IF (f_obj_constraint (p_obj) /= sc_void)
         OR (f_head_descr (p_obj).s_nature = sc_in)
         THEN IF (f_head_descr (p_obj).s_nature = sc_out) OR
                 (f_head_descr (p_obj).s_nature = sc_in_out)
              THEN c_init
              ELSE tp_init (0, sc_static)
              FI
      ELSE c_int_1_init
      FI);

FUNCTION f_attr_first (p_type : tp_constrained,
                       p_env  : tp_env) tp_descr_set :

   f_descr_set_val
     (p_type,
      CASE c_constr : p_type.s_constraint OF
      IS tp_range_constr :
         f_literal_to_static
           (f_object_init
              (c_constr.s_lower_bound));
      IS tp_fixed :
         CASE c_range : c_constr.s_range OF
         IS tp_range_constr :
            f_literal_to_static
              (f_object_init
                 (c_range.s_lower_bound));
         IS tp_void : f_attr_first1
                        (f_parent_base_type2
                           (p_type.s_base_type,
                            p_env))
         ESAC;
      IS tp_float :
         CASE c_range : c_constr.s_range OF
         IS tp_range_constr :
            f_literal_to_static
              (f_object_init
                 (c_range.s_lower_bound));
         IS tp_void : f_attr_first1
                        (f_parent_base_type2
```

```
                                (p_type.s_base_type,
                                 p_env))
        ESAC;
     IS tp_void : f_attr_first1
                    (f_parent_base_type2
                        (p_type.s_base_type,
                         p_env))
     OUT c_init
     ESAC);

FUNCTION f_attr_first1 (p_type : tp_type) tp_init :

   CASE c_type : p_type OF
   IS tp_integer : f_literal_to_static
                    (f_object_init
                       (c_type.s_range QUA tp_range_constr
                         .s_lower_bound));
   IS tp_enum_type : tp_init (0, sc_static)
   OUT c_init
   ESAC;

FUNCTION f_attr_last (p_type : tp_constrained,
                      p_env  : tp_env) tp_descr_set :

   f_descr_set_val
     (p_type,
      CASE c_constr : p_type.s_constraint OF
      IS tp_range_constr :
         f_literal_to_static
            (f_object_init
               (c_constr.s_upper_bound));
      IS tp_fixed :
         CASE c_range : c_constr.s_range OF
         IS tp_range_constr :
            f_literal_to_static
               (f_object_init
                  (c_range.s_upper_bound));
         IS tp_void : f_attr_last1
                        (f_parent_base_type2
                            (p_type.s_base_type,
                             p_env))
         ESAC;
      IS tp_float :
         CASE c_range : c_constr.s_range OF
         IS tp_range_constr :
            f_literal_to_static
               (f_object_init
                  (c_range.s_upper_bound));
         IS tp_void : f_attr_last1
                        (f_parent_base_type2
                            (p_type.s_base_type,
                             p_env))
         ESAC;
      IS tp_void : f_attr_last1
                     (f_parent_base_type2
                         (p_type.s_base_type,
                          p_env))
      OUT c_init
      ESAC);
```

```
FUNCTION f_attr_last1 (p_type : tp_type) tp_init :

   CASE c_type : p_type OF
   IS tp_integer : f_literal_to_static
                        (f_object_init
                            (c_type.s_range QUA tp_range_constr
                                .s_upper_bound));
   IS tp_enum_type : tp_init
                        (LENGTH (c_type.s_literals),
                         sc_static)
   OUT c_init
   ESAC;

FUNCTION f_attr_length (p_type : tp_constrained,
                        p_env  : tp_env) tp_descr_set:

    f_descr_set_val
       (c_int_constr,
        f_int_plus_init
           (tp_init (1, sc_literal),
            f_int_minus_init
               (f_object_init
                   (f_attr_last (p_type, p_env)),
                f_object_init
                   (f_attr_first (p_type, p_env)))));

FUNCTION f_attr_pos (p_value : tp_descr_set,
                     p_env   : tp_env) tp_descr_set :

    f_descr_set_val
       (tp_constrained
          (c_univ_int,
           sc_void),
        f_object_init (p_value));

FUNCTION f_attr_pred (p_entity : tp_descr_set,
                      p_env    : tp_env) tp_descr_set :

    cf_existent_entity
       (f_descr_set_val
           (f_obj_constrained1
               (f_head_descr (p_entity)),
            f_int_minus_init
               (f_object_init (p_entity),
                c_int_1_init)),
        p_env);

FUNCTION f_attr_succ (p_entity : tp_descr_set,
                      p_env    : tp_env) tp_descr_set :

    cf_existent_entity
       (f_descr_set_val
           (f_obj_constrained1
               (f_head_descr (p_entity)),
            f_int_plus_init
               (f_object_init (p_entity),
                c_int_1_init)),
        p_env);
```

```
FUNCTION f_attr_val (p_type   : tp_key,
                     p_pos    : tp_init,
                     p_env    : tp_env) tp_descr_set :

   cf_existent_entity
     (f_descr_set_val
        (tp_constrained
           (p_type,
            sc_void),
         p_pos),
      p_env);

FUNCTION f_attribute_function (p_key    : tp_key,
                               p_param  : tp_constrained,
                               p_result : tp_constrained)
                             tp_descr_set :

     % Return the description of a function described by
     % an attribute (e.g. 'POS).

   f_descr_set2
     (f_descr
        (sc_anonymous,
         p_key,
         c_start_repr,
         sc_complete,
         sc_function,
         f_standard_function1
           (p_key,
            p_param,
            p_result,
            sc_no_predef_op),
         c_unaccessible));

FUNCTION f_base_type (p_descr  : tp_descr) tp_key :

     % Only applicable to descriptions of types or subtypes.

   CASE c_den : p_descr.s_den OF
   IS tp_constrained : c_den.s_base_type;
   IS tp_type_den : p_descr.s_key
   OUT (c_error_type_key CONDITION FALSE MESSAGE "compiler error")
   ESAC;

FUNCTION f_base_type1 (p_type  : tp_key,
                       p_env   : tp_env) tp_key :

   f_base_type (f_select_by_key (p_type, p_env));

FUNCTION f_body_required (p_pack : tp_package_def) BOOL :

   CASE c_pack : p_pack OF
   IS tp_instantiation : IS tp_rename : FALSE;
   IS tp_package :
         f_body_required1 (c_pack.s_visible)
   ESAC;

FUNCTION f_body_required1 (p_descrs : tp_descr_list) BOOL:
```

```
    % The result is true if the declarations of a package
    % specification (p_descrs) contain a specification, which
    % requires a body (i.e. task(-type), subprogram, or
    % package which requires a body).

  IF EMPTY (p_descrs) THEN
     FALSE
  ELSE (HEAD (p_descrs).s_state = sc_spec_complete)    OR
       f_body_required1 (TAIL (p_descrs))
  FI;

FUNCTION f_calculate_repr (p_entity   : tp_key,
                           p_user_rep : BOOL,
                           p_env      : tp_env) tp_env :

    % Calculate the representation attributes for the given entity
    % and for all entities, this entity depends on, e.g.
    % parent types.
    %
    % The calculation is done by calling functions
    % of the type mapping interface.
    %
    % The results are entered into the entity's descriptions
    % contained in p_env.

  IF (f_rep_state (p_entity, p_env) = sc_start_rep) THEN
     f_calculate_repr1 (p_entity,
                        p_user_rep,
                        f_calculate_reprs
                           (f_used_types3 (p_entity,
                                           p_env),
                            p_env))
  ELSE p_env
  FI;

FUNCTION f_calculate_repr1 (p_entity   : tp_key,
                            p_user_rep : BOOL,
                            p_env      : tp_env) tp_env :

  CASE c_rep_state : f_new_repr_state (p_entity, p_env) OF
  sc_static_rep : sc_dynamic_rep :
     f_update_repr1 (p_entity,
                     IF c_rep_state = sc_static_rep
                        THEN tp_repr (sc_static_rep,
                                      f_type_map
                                         (p_entity,
                                          p_user_rep,
                                          p_env))
                     ELSE tp_repr (sc_dynamic_rep,
                                   f_reps (p_entity, p_env))
                     FI,
                     p_env)
  OUT p_env
  ESAC;

FUNCTION f_calculate_reprs (p_entities : tp_key_list,
                            p_env      : tp_env) tp_env :

  IF EMPTY (p_entities) THEN
     p_env
```

```
   ELSE f_calculate_reprs (TAIL (p_entities),
                           f_calculate_repr (HEAD (p_entities),
                                             FALSE,
                                             p_env))
   FI;

FUNCTION f_choice_out (p_choice : tp_choice,
                       p_descrs : tp_descr_list)
                      tp_descr_list :

     % Delete p_choice from p_descrs.

   IF EMPTY (p_descrs) THEN
      p_descrs
   ELSE CASE c_choice : p_choice OF
        IS tp_others : c_empty_descrs;
        IS tp_descr  : IF HEAD (p_descrs).s_key = c_choice.s_key THEN
                         TAIL (p_descrs)
                       ELSE tp_descr_list (HEAD (p_descrs)) +
                         f_choice_out (p_choice,
                                       TAIL (p_descrs))
                       FI;
        IS tp_descr_set : IF HEAD (c_choice.s_descrs).s_designator  =
                             HEAD (p_descrs).s_designator THEN
                             TAIL (p_descrs)
                          ELSE tp_descr_list (HEAD (p_descrs)) +
                              f_choice_out (p_choice,
                                            TAIL (p_descrs))
                          FI
        OUT p_descrs
        ESAC
   FI;

FUNCTION f_choices_out (p_choices : tp_choice_list,
                        p_descrs  : tp_descr_list)
                       tp_descr_list:

     % Delete choices from p_descrs.

   IF EMPTY (p_choices) THEN
      TAIL (p_descrs)
   ELSE f_choices_out1 (p_choices, p_descrs)
   FI;

FUNCTION f_choices_out1 (p_choices : tp_choice_list,
                         p_descrs  : tp_descr_list)
                        tp_descr_list :

   IF EMPTY (p_choices) THEN
      p_descrs
   ELSE f_choices_out1 (TAIL (p_choices),
                        f_choice_out (HEAD (p_choices), p_descrs))
   FI;

FUNCTION f_common_descrs (p_designators : tp_designator_list,
                          p_keys        : tp_key_list,
                          p_ops         : tp_op_list)
                         tp_descr_list :

     % Used for building  the start environment.
```

```
   IF EMPTY (p_designators) THEN
      c_empty_descrs
   ELSE tp_descr_list
          (tp_descr (HEAD (p_designators),
                     HEAD (p_keys),
                     c_start_repr,
                     sc_complete,
                     sc_common_op,
                     tp_operation (HEAD (p_ops)),
                     sc_no_orig,
                     c_unaccessible))
        + f_common_descrs (TAIL (p_designators),
                           TAIL (p_keys),
                           TAIL (p_ops))
   FI;

FUNCTION f_comp_rep_out (p_rep    : tp_comp_rep,
                         p_descrs : tp_descr_list) tp_descr_list:

    % Deletes the component for which a component representation
    % is given (within a record specification) from p_descrs.

   IF EMPTY (p_descrs) THEN
      c_empty_descrs
   ELSE IF HEAD (p_descrs).s_key = p_rep.s_comp THEN
      TAIL (p_descrs)
   ELSE tp_descr_list (HEAD (p_descrs)) +
      f_comp_rep_out (p_rep,
                      TAIL (p_descrs))
   FI FI;

FUNCTION f_compatible_range_lists (p_list1,
                                   p_list2 : tp_dscrt_range_list,
                                   p_env   : tp_env) BOOL :

    % Check whether the array type with indices p_list1 is
    % convertable into the array type with indices p_list2
    % by a type conversion (4.6 (b) [Ada80]).

   IF EMPTY (p_list1) AND EMPTY (p_list2) THEN
      TRUE
   ELSE IF EMPTY (p_list1) OR EMPTY (p_list2) THEN
      FALSE
   ELSE IF f_is_directly_derived
            (f_range_type (HEAD (p_list1), p_env),
             f_range_type (HEAD (p_list2), p_env),
             p_env)                  OR
         (f_range_type (HEAD (p_list1), p_env) =
          f_range_type (HEAD (p_list2), p_env)) THEN
      f_compatible_range_lists (TAIL (p_list1),
                                TAIL (p_list2),
                                p_env)
   ELSE FALSE
   FI FI FI;

FUNCTION f_complete_subpr_spec (p_subpr : tp_descr,
                                p_env   : tp_env) tp_env :

    % Called for pragma interface
```

```
    %       - to indicate in the environment, that a no further
    %         body must be provided for the subprogram
    %       - to check that p_subpr is a legal subprogram name.

  IF NOT (p_subpr.s_den IS tp_subpr) THEN
     (p_env
        CONDITION FALSE
        MESSAGE "subprogram name expected")
  ELSE IF p_subpr.s_enclosing /= f_enclosing (p_env) THEN
          (p_env
           CONDITION FALSE
              MESSAGE
     "subprogram specification must appear in this declarative part")
  ELSE IF p_subpr.s_state /= sc_spec_complete THEN
          (p_env
           CONDITION FALSE
              MESSAGE "body is already provided")
  ELSE f_update_descr_by_key
          (p_subpr.s_key,
           sc_same,
           sc_complete,
           sc_same,
           sc_same,
           p_env)
  FI FI FI;

FUNCTION f_comps_of_record (p_record : tp_descr_set,
                            p_env    : tp_env) tp_descr_list :

    % Check that p_record denotes a record base type and yield
    % the components, including discriminants and anonymous
    % type definitions.

  CASE c_den : f_head_descr (p_record).s_den OF
  IS tp_type_den :
     CASE c_type : c_den.s_type OF
     IS tp_record : c_type.s_descrs;
     IS tp_constrained : (c_empty_descrs CONDITION FALSE MESSAGE
        "The name of a type not a subtype expected");
     IS tp_derived :
           f_comps_of_record
              (f_descr_set2
                  (f_select_by_key
                     (f_parent_base_type
                         (c_type.s_parent_type, p_env),
                      p_env)),
              p_env)
     OUT (c_empty_descrs
          CONDITION FALSE MESSAGE
             "A record type expected")
     ESAC
  OUT (c_empty_descrs
       CONDITION FALSE MESSAGE
          "Name of a type expected")
  ESAC;

FUNCTION f_constrained (p_type : tp_key,
                        p_env  : tp_env) tp_constrained :

    % P_type must denote a type. In the case of a base type
```

```
    % it is expanded to a subtype of its own.

   CASE c_den : f_select_by_key (p_type, p_env).s_den OF
   IS tp_type_den : tp_constrained (p_type, sc_void);
   IS tp_constrained : c_den
   OUT (c_constrained CONDITION FALSE MESSAGE "compiler error")
   ESAC;

FUNCTION f_constraint (p_type : tp_descr,
                      p_env  : tp_env) tp_constraint :

    % The constraint of p_type. For access types the constraint
    % refers to the accessed type.

   CASE c_den : p_type.s_den OF
   IS tp_constrained :
      c_den.s_constraint
   OUT sc_void
   ESAC;

FUNCTION f_copy_descr_list (p_descrs     : tp_descr_list,
                            p_encl       : tp_key,
                            p_type_map   : tp_map_list,
                            p_env        : tp_env)
                           tp_descr_list :

    % Build a mapping list from keys of descriptions directly and
    % indirectly contained in p_descrs to new descriptions.
    % Subsequently copy p_descrs and adjust the references to
    % copied descriptions according to the previously built
    % mapping list.

   f_adjust_descr_list
     (p_descrs,
      p_encl,
      p_type_map +
         f_map_descr_list (p_descrs),
      p_env);

FUNCTION f_declare_implicit (p_implicit : tp_descr_list,
                            p_env      : tp_env) tp_env :

    % Used for declaring labels, loop- and block names and
    % check forbidden hiding of entities from the same
    % declarative part.

   IF EMPTY (p_implicit) THEN
      p_env
   ELSE f_declare_implicit
          (TAIL (p_implicit),
          (f_add_local_descrs (tp_descr_list (HEAD (p_implicit)),
                               p_env)
          %C 8.3/1
          CONDITION
          ch_local_hiding (HEAD (p_implicit).s_designator,
                           HEAD (p_implicit).s_den,
                           HEAD (p_implicit).s_key,
                           f_local (p_env),
                           p_env)
             MESSAGE
```

```
             "THIS implicit decl hides previous one  "))
   FI;

FUNCTION f_deref_type (p_type : tp_key,
                       p_env  : tp_env) tp_key :

      % For access types the result is the accessed type else
      % the identity.

   CASE c_type : f_parent_base_type2 (p_type, p_env) OF
   IS tp_access : c_type.s_accessed.s_base_type
   OUT p_type
   ESAC;

      %*************************************************************%
      %                                                             %
      %       f_derive_...                                          %
      %                                                             %
      %       Used to construct the list of derived subprograms     %
      %       for the son type by replacing the parent type by      %
      %       the son type in parameter and result description.     %
      %                                                             %
      %*************************************************************%

FUNCTION f_derive_params (p_params      : tp_descr_list,
                          p_parent_type,
                          p_son_type    : tp_key)
                         tp_descr_list :

   IF EMPTY (p_params) THEN
      c_empty_descrs
   ELSE tp_descr_list
         (CASE c_den : HEAD (p_params).s_den OF
          IS tp_object : IF c_den.s_type
                              .s_base_type = p_parent_type THEN
                           f_descr
                              (HEAD (p_params).s_designator,
                               f_gen_key,
                               HEAD (p_params).s_repr,
                               HEAD (p_params).s_state,
                               HEAD (p_params).s_nature,
                               tp_object
                                  (tp_constrained
                                      (p_son_type,
                                       c_den.s_type
                                           .s_constraint),
                                   c_den.s_init),
                               HEAD (p_params).s_enclosing)
                         ELSE HEAD (p_params)
                         FI
          OUT HEAD (p_params)
          ESAC) +
          f_derive_params (TAIL (p_params),
                           p_parent_type, p_son_type)
   FI;

FUNCTION f_derive_subprs (p_parent_type,
                          p_son_type    : tp_key,
                          p_env         : tp_env)
```

```
                tp_descr_list :

   f_derive_subprs1 (p_parent_type,
                     p_son_type,
                     f_subpr_list
                       (f_select_by_key
                          (p_parent_type,
                           p_env).s_den QUA tp_type_den
                         .s_derivable_subprogs,
                        p_env),
                     p_env);

FUNCTION f_derive_subprs1 (p_parent_type,
                           p_son_type    : tp_key,
                           p_subprs      : tp_descr_list,
                           p_env         : tp_env) tp_descr_list :

   IF EMPTY (p_subprs) THEN
      c_empty_descrs
   ELSE tp_descr_list
         (f_derive_subpr (p_parent_type,
                          p_son_type,
                          HEAD (p_subprs),
                          p_env))+
        f_derive_subprs1 (p_parent_type,
                          p_son_type,
                          TAIL (p_subprs),
                          p_env)
   FI;

FUNCTION f_derive_subpr (p_parent_type,
                         p_son_type   : tp_key,
                         p_subpr      : tp_descr,
                         p_env        : tp_env) tp_descr :

   f_descr
      (p_subpr.s_designator,
       f_gen_key,
       c_start_repr,
       sc_implicitly_declared,
       p_subpr.s_nature,
       tp_subpr
          (CASE c_spec : p_subpr.s_den QUA tp_subpr .s_spec OF
           IS tp_procedure :
              tp_procedure
                 (f_derive_params (c_spec.s_params,
                                   p_parent_type,
                                   p_son_type));
          IS tp_function :
              tp_function
                (f_derive_params (c_spec.s_params,
                                  p_parent_type,
                                  p_son_type),
                 IF c_spec.s_result.s_base_type = p_parent_type THEN
                    tp_constrained
                       (p_son_type,
                        c_spec.s_result.s_constraint)
                 ELSE c_spec.s_result
                 FI)
          OUT tp_procedure (c_empty_descrs)
```

```
        ESAC,
        p_subpr.s_key,
        p_subpr.s_den QUA tp_subpr.s_op),
     f_enclosing (p_env));

FUNCTION f_descr (p_designator  : tp_designator,
                  p_key         : tp_key,
                  p_repr        : tp_repr,
                  p_state       : tp_state,
                  p_nature      : tp_nature,
                  p_den         : tp_den,
                  p_enclosing   : tp_key)
                 tp_descr :

     % Used to create a description which is entered into the
     % environment (entity description) and which may be referred to
     % by p_key.
     %
     % f_descr is textually equivalent to f_temp_descr, however
     % f_temp_descr creates a description which is used for
     % describing the meaning of a name/expression (tp_descr_set)
     % and which cannot be referred to by p_key.
     %
     % For a pointer implementation of tp_key, f_descr creates the
     % description which is referred to by p_key, while a description
     % created by f_temp_descr is not referrable by the pointer p_key.

  tp_descr (p_designator,
            p_key,
            p_repr,
            p_state,
            p_nature,
            p_den,
            c_no_origin,
            p_enclosing);

     %*************************************************************%
     %                                                             %
     %        f_descr_set...                                       %
     %                                                             %
     %        Used to construct values of type tp_descr_set.       %
     %                                                             %
     %*************************************************************%

FUNCTION f_descr_set (p_key       : tp_key,
                      p_nature    : tp_nature,
                      p_den       : tp_den,
                      p_add       : tp_additional)tp_descr_set   :

tp_descr_set
  (tp_descr_list
     (f_temp_descr (c_designator,
                    p_key,
                    c_start_repr,
                    sc_void_state,
                    p_nature,
                    p_den,
                    c_enclosing)),
   p_add);
```

```
FUNCTION f_descr_set_val (p_type : tp_constrained,
                          p_init : tp_init) tp_descr_set :

   f_descr_set4
      (sc_value,
       tp_object (p_type, p_init));

FUNCTION f_descr_set2 (p_descr : tp_descr) tp_descr_set :

   tp_descr_set
      (tp_descr_list (p_descr),
       sc_no_add);

FUNCTION f_descr_set3 (p_descrs : tp_descr_list) tp_descr_set :

   tp_descr_set
       (p_descrs,
        sc_no_add);

FUNCTION f_descr_set4 (p_nature : tp_nature,
                       p_den    : tp_den) tp_descr_set :

   f_descr_set2
     (IF p_den IS tp_object THEN
         f_temp_descr (sc_anonymous,
                       c_key,
                       c_start_repr,
                       sc_complete,
                       p_nature,
                       p_den,
                       c_error_key)
      ELSE
         f_descr (sc_anonymous,
                  f_gen_key,
                  c_start_repr,
                  sc_complete,
                  p_nature,
                  p_den,
                  c_error_key)
      FI);

FUNCTION f_desig_key_in_choices (p_designator : tp_designator,
                                 p_key        : tp_key,
                                 p_choices    : tp_choice_list)
                                BOOL :

     % Check whether a choice with either p_designator or p_key
     % occurs in p_choices.

    IF EMPTY (p_choices) THEN
       FALSE
    ELSE CASE c_choice : HEAD (p_choices) OF
         IS tp_others : TRUE;
         IS tp_descr_set    : HEAD (c_choice.s_descrs).s_designator =
                              p_designator;
         IS tp_descr : p_key = c_choice.s_key
         OUT FALSE
         ESAC  OR
         f_desig_key_in_choices
           (p_designator,
```

```
            p_key,
            TAIL (p_choices))
   FI;

FUNCTION f_digits_delta (p_type : tp_descr,
                         p_env  : tp_env) tp_descr_set:

   CASE c_den : p_type.s_den OF
   IS tp_constrained :
      CASE c_constr : c_den.s_constraint OF
      IS tp_fixed : c_constr.s_delta;
      IS tp_float : c_constr.s_digits
      OUT f_digits_delta
            (f_select_by_key (c_den.s_base_type, p_env),
             p_env)
      ESAC;
   IS tp_type_den :
      CASE c_type : c_den.s_type OF
      IS tp_fixed : c_type.s_delta;
      IS tp_float : c_type.s_digits
      OUT c_error_descr_set
      ESAC
   OUT (c_error_descr_set
        CONDITION FALSE
           MESSAGE "compiler error")
   ESAC;

FUNCTION f_discriminants (p_type : tp_type) tp_descr_list :

   CASE c_type : p_type OF
   IS tp_record : f_discrs(c_type.s_descrs);
   IS tp_private : c_type.s_discriminants;
   IS tp_l_private : c_type.s_discriminants;
   IS tp_incompl_type : c_type.s_discriminants
   OUT c_empty_descrs
   ESAC;

FUNCTION f_discrs (p_descrs : tp_descr_list)
                   tp_descr_list :

      % Select the discriminants from the components of a record type.
      % Note that discriminant description occur first and without
      % intermediate implicit array type descriptions.

   IF EMPTY (p_descrs) THEN
      c_empty_descrs
   ELSE IF HEAD (p_descrs).s_nature = sc_discriminant THEN
           tp_descr_list (HEAD (p_descrs))
           + f_discrs (TAIL (p_descrs))
        ELSE c_empty_descrs
        FI
   FI;

FUNCTION f_empty_local_add_global (p_key    : tp_key,
                                   p_state  : tp_state,
                                   p_nature : tp_nature,
                                   p_env    : tp_env) tp_env :

      % Build a new environment :
      %     - enter an anonymous description with p_key, p_state and
```

```
    %       p_nature to the current local environment
    %     - open a new scope with this description as enclosing

  f_empty_local_encl_state
     (p_key,
      p_state,
      f_add_descr
         (sc_anonymous,
          p_key,
          p_state,
          p_nature,
          sc_void,
          p_env));

FUNCTION f_empty_local_encl_state (p_new_encl : tp_key,
                                   p_state    : tp_state,
                                   p_env      : tp_env) tp_env:

    % Open a new scope with p_new_encl as enclosing.

  f_new_local (c_empty_descrs,
               p_new_encl,
               f_update_descr_by_key
                  (p_new_encl,
                   sc_same,
                   p_state,
                   sc_same,
                   sc_same,
                   p_env));

FUNCTION f_encl_descr (p_env : tp_env) tp_descr :

    % The description of the current enclosing unit, block or loop.

  f_select_by_key (f_enclosing (p_env), p_env);

FUNCTION f_encl_descr1 (p_descr : tp_descr,
                        p_env   : tp_env) tp_descr :

    % Description of the unit, block or loop enclosing the declarati
    % of p_descr.

  IF (p_descr.s_enclosing = c_key)   OR
     (p_descr.s_enclosing = c_error_key) THEN
     c_error_descr
  ELSE f_select_by_key (p_descr.s_enclosing, p_env)
  FI;

FUNCTION f_encl_except_bl_loop (p_env : tp_env) tp_den :

    % Denotation of the innermost enclosing unit (except blocks and
    % loops).

  CASE c_den : f_encl_except_bl_loop1
                  (f_encl_descr (p_env),
                   p_env).s_den  OF
    IS tp_entry :
    IS tp_subpr : c_den;
    IS tp_generic : c_den.s_den;
    IS tp_object : IS tp_package : IS tp_type_den : c_den
```

```
    OUT (c_den
         CONDITION
         FALSE
            MESSAGE
            "compiler error")
  ESAC;

FUNCTION f_encl_except_bl_loop1 (p_descr : tp_descr,
                                 p_env   : tp_env) tp_descr:

   CASE c_den : p_descr.s_den OF
      IS tp_void : f_encl_except_bl_loop1
                     (f_encl_descr1 (p_descr,p_env),
                      p_env)
      OUT p_descr
   ESAC;

FUNCTION f_encl_state (p_env : tp_env) tp_state :

   f_encl_descr (p_env).s_state;

FUNCTION f_enclosed_descrs (p_key    : tp_key,
                            p_env    : tp_env) tp_descr_list :

      % The list of descriptions which are enclosed by the entity
      % denoted by p_key.

   f_enclosed_descrs1 (p_key,
                       f_global (p_env)+f_local (p_env));


FUNCTION f_enclosed_descrs1 (p_key   : tp_key,
                             p_list  : tp_descr_list) tp_descr_list :

   IF EMPTY (p_list) THEN
      c_empty_descrs
   ELSE IF HEAD (p_list).s_enclosing = p_key THEN
           tp_descr_list (HEAD (p_list)) +
              f_enclosed_descrs1 (p_key, TAIL (p_list))
        ELSE f_enclosed_descrs1 (p_key, TAIL (p_list))
        FI
   FI;

FUNCTION f_enclosing (p_env : tp_env) tp_key:

   p_env.s_enclosing;

FUNCTION f_enter_rep (p_key      : tp_key,
                      p_rep      : tp_rep,
                      p_env      : tp_env) tp_env :

      % Add p_rep to the representation component of the description
      % denoted by p_key. Check that the declaration of the
      % corresponding entity occurs in the current declarative part
      % and that the representation aspect specified by p_rep
      % has not already been specified for this entity (f_add_reps).

   IF p_key = c_error_key OR
     (p_key = c_error_type_key) THEN
      p_env
```

```
   ELSE
      (f_update_descr_by_key
          (p_key,
           tp_repr (sc_start_rep,
                    f_add_reps (f_reps (p_key, p_env),
                                p_rep)),
           sc_same,
           sc_same,
           sc_same,
           p_env)
      %C 13.1/1
      CONDITION
      f_enclosing (p_env) =
      f_select_by_key (p_key, p_env).s_enclosing
         MESSAGE
         "repr_spec may only be given for items from same decl part")
   FI;

FUNCTION f_enter_subprs (p_subprs : tp_key_list,
                         p_type   : tp_key,
                         p_env    : tp_env) tp_env :

      % Add p_subprs as derivable subprograms to p_type.
      % (cf. f_update_descr!)

   f_update_descr_by_key
      (p_type,
       sc_same,
       sc_same,
       sc_same,
       tp_type_den
          (f_select_by_key (p_type, p_env).s_den QUA tp_type_den
                .s_type,
           p_subprs),
       p_env);

FUNCTION f_enum_rep (p_assocs : tp_assoc_list,
                     p_type   : tp_descr_set,
                     p_env    : tp_env) tp_enum_rep :

      % Contruct an enumeration representation from p_assocs for
      % the enumeration type p_type.
      % Check all conditions of chapter 13.3 [Ada80]

   (f_enum_rep1 (p_assocs, f_literals (p_type, p_env), p_env)
    %C 13.3/5
    CONDITION
    ch_growing_values (IT)
       MESSAGE
       "int values must satisfy ordering of enum literals");

FUNCTION f_enum_rep1 (p_assocs   : tp_assoc_list,
                      p_literals : tp_key_list,
                      p_env      : tp_env) tp_enum_rep :

   IF EMPTY (p_literals) THEN
      c_empty_enum_rep
   ELSE CASE c_assoc : f_enum_rep_assoc (p_assocs,
                                         HEAD (p_literals),
                                         p_env) OF
```

```
        IS tp_void : (c_empty_enum_rep
                      %C 13.3/2
                      CONDITION FALSE MESSAGE
                        "missing integer code for this literal");
        IS tp_assoc_list :
           IF ch_static_int (HEAD (c_assoc) QUA tp_comp_assoc.s_actual,
                             p_env) THEN
              tp_enum_rep
                (f_object_init (HEAD (c_assoc) QUA tp_comp_assoc
                               .s_actual).s_value QUA INT)
           ELSE (c_empty_enum_rep
                 %C 13.4/3
                 CONDITION FALSE MESSAGE
                   "a static int expression required")
                 FI
        ESAC  +
        f_enum_rep1 (p_assocs, TAIL (p_literals), p_env)
   FI;

FUNCTION f_enum_rep_assoc (p_assocs  : tp_assoc_list,
                           p_literal : tp_key,
                           p_env     : tp_env) tp_assoc_list_void :

   IF EMPTY (p_assocs) THEN
      sc_void
   ELSE IF f_enum_rep_assoc1 (HEAD (p_assocs) QUA tp_comp_assoc.
                                         s_choices,
                              p_literal,
                              p_env) THEN
      tp_assoc_list (HEAD (p_assocs))
   ELSE f_enum_rep_assoc (TAIL (p_assocs), p_literal, p_env)
   FI FI;

FUNCTION f_enum_rep_assoc1 (p_choices : tp_choice_list,
                            p_literal : tp_key,
                            p_env     : tp_env) BOOL :

   IF EMPTY (p_choices) THEN
      TRUE
   ELSE (CASE c_choice : HEAD (p_choices) OF
        IS tp_descr : c_choice.s_key = p_literal;
        IS tp_dscrt_range : IS tp_others :
           (FALSE
            %C 13.3/4
            CONDITION FALSE MESSAGE
              "enum literals must have distinct codes");
        IS tp_descr_set : f_object_init (c_choice) =
                          f_object_init1 (f_select_by_key
                                               (p_literal,
                                                p_env))
        ESAC
        %C 13.3/2
        CONDITION
        EMPTY (TAIL (p_choices))
           MESSAGE
        "enum literals must have distinct codes")
   FI;

FUNCTION f_env (p_imported  : tp_key_list,
                p_global,
```

```
              p_local      : tp_descr_list,
              p_enclosing  : tp_key) tp_env :

   tp_env (p_imported, p_global, p_local, p_enclosing);

FUNCTION  f_error_aggregate (p_assocs : tp_assoc_list) BOOL :

      % Decide whether p_assocs denote an error value in the
      % context of an aggregate component.
      % In contrast to f_is_error_empty_assocs, dummy aggregate
      % descriptions are considered to have a valid meaning.

   IF EMPTY (p_assocs) THEN
      FALSE
   ELSE
      CASE c_assoc : HEAD (p_assocs) OF
      IS tp_comp_assoc : f_error_aggr1 (c_assoc.s_choices) OR
                         f_error_aggr2 (c_assoc.s_actual);
      IS tp_dscrt_range : f_error_aggr3 (c_assoc)
      ESAC   OR
      f_error_aggregate (TAIL (p_assocs))
   FI;

FUNCTION f_error_aggr1 (p_choices : tp_choice_list) BOOL :

   IF EMPTY (p_choices) THEN
      FALSE
   ELSE CASE c_choice : HEAD (p_choices) OF
        IS tp_descr_set : f_error_aggr2 (c_choice);
        IS tp_dscrt_range : f_error_aggr3 (c_choice);
        IS tp_others : IS tp_descr : FALSE
        ESAC        OR
        f_error_aggr1 (TAIL (p_choices))
   FI;

FUNCTION f_error_aggr2 (p_descrs : tp_descr_set) BOOL :

   LENGTH (p_descrs.s_descrs) = 1 AND
   (f_head_descr (p_descrs) = c_error_descr);

FUNCTION f_error_aggr3 (p_dscrt_range : tp_dscrt_range) BOOL :

   CASE c_range : p_dscrt_range OF
   IS tp_range :
      CASE c_range : c_range OF
      IS tp_range_constr : f_error_aggr2 (c_range.s_lower_bound) OR
                           f_error_aggr2 (c_range.s_upper_bound);
      IS tp_void : FALSE
      ESAC;
   IS tp_constrained : c_range.s_base_type = c_error_type_key;
   IS tp_index : FALSE
   ESAC;

FUNCTION f_error_assocs (p_assocs : tp_assoc_list) tp_assoc_list :

      % Used for error recovery. Result is an assoc list consisting
      % of error descriptions only. The structure of the created
      % assoc list ,i.e kind and number of choices and associations
      % is equal to p_assocs.
```

```
  IF EMPTY (p_assocs) THEN
    p_assocs
  ELSE CASE c_assoc : HEAD (p_assocs) OF
       IS tp_dscrt_range : tp_assoc_list (c_error_dscrt_range);
       IS tp_comp_assoc :
              tp_assoc_list
                (tp_comp_assoc
                   (f_error_choices (c_assoc.s_choices),
                    c_error_descr_set))
       ESAC  +
       f_error_assocs (TAIL (p_assocs))
  FI;

FUNCTION f_error_choices (p_choices : tp_choice_list) tp_choice_list :

  IF EMPTY (p_choices) THEN
    p_choices
  ELSE tp_choice_list
        (CASE HEAD (p_choices) OF
         IS tp_dscrt_range : tp_choice (c_error_dscrt_range);
         IS tp_descr_set : tp_choice (c_error_descr_set);
         IS tp_descr : tp_choice (c_error_descr);
         IS tp_others : HEAD (p_choices)
         ESAC) +
      f_error_choices (TAIL (p_choices))
  FI;

FUNCTION f_error_constraint (p_constr : tp_constraint) tp_constraint :

     % Error value for a constraint which is compatible with
     % all types.

  CASE c_constr : p_constr OF
  IS tp_range_constr : IS tp_void : c_error_range;
  IS tp_fixed : tp_constraint
                  (tp_fixed
                     (c_error_descr_set,
                      c_error_range));
  IS tp_float : tp_float
                 (c_error_descr_set,
                  c_error_range)
  OUT (c_constr CONDITION FALSE MESSAGE "compiler error")
  ESAC;

FUNCTION f_error_dscrt_ranges (p_assocs : tp_assoc_list)
                               tp_dscrt_range_list :

     % Error value for a discrete range which is compatible with
     % all types.

  IF EMPTY (p_assocs) THEN
     tp_dscrt_range_list ()
  ELSE tp_dscrt_range_list (c_error_dscrt_range) +
       f_error_dscrt_ranges (TAIL (p_assocs))
  FI;

     %**********************************************************%
     %                                                          %
     %       f_eval_...                                         %
     %                                                          %
```

```
%        Interface to evaluation of static expressions.      %
%        In cases which allow to decide whether an expression%
%        is static or not independent from the constituent   %
%        expressions, this information is contained in       %
%        the result.                                         %
%                                                            %
%************************************************************%

FUNCTION f_eval (p_op : tp_op,
                 p_left, p_right : tp_init) tp_init :

   c_init; %>MACHINE<

FUNCTION f_eval_converted (p_type  : tp_key,
                           p_descr : tp_descr,
                           p_env   : tp_env) tp_init :

  tp_init (sc_no_val,  %>MACHINE<
          f_object_value_kind1 (p_descr));

FUNCTION f_eval_function (p_function : tp_descr,
                          p_assocs   : tp_assoc_list,
                          p_env      : tp_env) tp_init :
  tp_init (sc_no_val,                %>MACHINE<
          IF f_is_user_defined_funct (p_function, p_env) THEN
             sc_not_static
          ELSE f_exp_kind_assocs (p_assocs)
          FI);

FUNCTION f_eval_indexed (p_name   : tp_descr,
                         p_assocs : tp_assoc_list,
                         p_env    : tp_env) tp_init :

   tp_init (sc_no_val,                   %>MACHINE<
           f_exp_kind_new
              (f_object_value_kind1 (p_name),
               f_exp_kind_assocs (p_assocs)));

FUNCTION f_eval_less_equal (p_obj1,
                            p_obj2 : tp_descr_set) BOOL:

   f_eval_less_equal1
      (f_object_value (p_obj1),
       f_object_value (p_obj2));

FUNCTION f_eval_less_equal1 (p_value1,      %>MACHINE<
                             p_value2 : tp_value) BOOL:

   CASE c_val1 : p_value1 OF
   IS INT : CASE c_val2 : p_value2 OF
            IS INT : c_val1 <= c_val2
            OUT TRUE
            ESAC
   OUT TRUE
   ESAC;

FUNCTION f_eval_membership (p_name       : tp_descr,
                            p_type_range : tp_type_range,
                            p_op         : tp_op,
                            p_env        : tp_env) tp_init :
```

```
  c_init; %>MACHINE<

FUNCTION f_eval_selected (p_name : tp_descr,
                          p_desi : tp_designator,
                          p_env  : tp_env) tp_init :

   tp_init (sc_no_val,   %>MACHINE<
            f_object_value_kind1 (p_name));

FUNCTION f_eval_short_circuit (p_exp1,
                               p_exp2 : tp_descr,
                               p_op   : tp_op,
                               p_env  : tp_env) tp_init :

  c_init; %>MACHINE<

     %**************************************************************%
     %                                                              %
     %        f_exp_kind_...                                        %
     %                                                              %
     %        Get the "weakest" kind of a composit construction,    %
     %        where the order is 'literal', 'static', 'not static'%
     %        and 'no exp'.                                         %
     %                                                              %
     %**************************************************************%

FUNCTION f_exp_kind_assocs (p_assocs : tp_assoc_list) tp_exp_kind:

   IF EMPTY (p_assocs) THEN
      sc_static
   ELSE IF EMPTY (TAIL (p_assocs)) THEN
           f_exp_kind_assoc (HEAD (p_assocs))
        ELSE f_exp_kind_new
                (f_exp_kind_assoc (HEAD (p_assocs)),
                 f_exp_kind_assocs (TAIL (p_assocs)))
        FI
   FI;

FUNCTION f_exp_kind_assoc (p_assoc : tp_assoc) tp_exp_kind :

   CASE c_assoc : p_assoc OF
   IS tp_comp_assoc :
         f_exp_kind_new
             (f_exp_kind_choices (c_assoc.s_choices),
              f_object_value_kind (c_assoc.s_actual));
   IS tp_dscrt_range : sc_not_static
   ESAC;

FUNCTION f_exp_kind_choices (p_choices : tp_choice_list)
                             tp_exp_kind :

  IF EMPTY (p_choices)
     THEN sc_static
  ELSE f_exp_kind_new
          (f_exp_kind_choice (HEAD (p_choices)),
           f_exp_kind_choices (TAIL (p_choices)))
  FI;
```

```
FUNCTION f_exp_kind_choice (p_choice : tp_choice) tp_exp_kind :

   CASE c_choice : p_choice OF
   IS tp_descr : sc_static;
   IS tp_dscrt_range : f_exp_kind_range (c_choice);
   IS tp_descr_set : f_object_value_kind (c_choice);
   IS tp_others : sc_static
   ESAC;

FUNCTION f_exp_kind_new (p_kind1,
                         p_kind2 : tp_exp_kind) tp_exp_kind :

   CASE p_kind1 OF
   sc_literal : p_kind2;
   sc_static : IF p_kind2 = sc_literal
                  THEN sc_static
               ELSE p_kind2
               FI;
   sc_not_static : IF p_kind2 = sc_no_exp
                      THEN sc_no_exp
                   ELSE sc_not_static
                   FI;
   sc_no_exp : sc_no_exp
   ESAC;

FUNCTION f_exp_kind_range (p_range : tp_dscrt_range) tp_exp_kind :

   CASE c_range : p_range OF
   IS tp_range_constr :
        f_exp_kind_new
            (f_object_value_kind (c_range.s_lower_bound),
             f_object_value_kind (c_range.s_upper_bound))
   OUT sc_literal
   ESAC;

      %*********************************************************%
      %                                                         %
      %        f_expand_additional...                           %
      %                                                         %
      %        Transform the representation of description      %
      %        within tp_descr_set. Additional descriptions     %
      %        denoted by s_add are explicitly included in      %
      %        s_descrs.                                        %
      %                                                         %
      %*********************************************************%

FUNCTION f_expand_additional (p_descrs : tp_descr_list,
                              p_add    : tp_additional,
                              p_env    : tp_env) tp_descr_list:

   CASE c_add : p_add OF
   sc_no_add : p_descrs
   OUT f_expand_additional1
             (p_descrs,
              p_add,
              p_env)
   ESAC;

FUNCTION f_expand_additional1 (p_descrs : tp_descr_list,
                               p_add    : tp_additional,
```

```
                                  p_env     : tp_env) tp_descr_list :

  IF EMPTY (p_descrs)
     THEN p_descrs
  ELSE f_expand_additional1 (TAIL (p_descrs),
                             p_add,
                             p_env) +
       f_expand_additional2 (HEAD (p_descrs),
                             f_expand_additional_to_keys1
                                   (f_object_type (HEAD (p_descrs)),
                                    p_add,
                                    p_env),
                             p_env)
  FI;

FUNCTION f_expand_additional2 (p_descr  : tp_descr,
                               p_types  : tp_key_list,
                               p_env    : tp_env) tp_descr_list :

  IF EMPTY (p_types) THEN
     c_empty_descrs
  ELSE tp_descr_list
            (f_temp_descr (p_descr.s_designator,
                           c_key,
                           f_repr (HEAD (p_types), p_env),
                           p_descr.s_state,
                           p_descr.s_nature,
                           tp_object
                              (f_constrained (HEAD (p_types),
                                              p_env),
                               f_object_init1 (p_descr)),
                           p_descr.s_enclosing))
                     +
       f_expand_additional2 (p_descr, TAIL (p_types), p_env)
  FI;

FUNCTION f_expand_additional_to_keys (p_descrs : tp_descr_list,
                                      p_add    : tp_additional,
                                      p_env    : tp_env)
                                     tp_key_list :

  IF EMPTY (p_descrs) THEN
     c_empty_keys
  ELSE f_expand_additional_to_keys1
           (f_object_type (HEAD (p_descrs)),
            p_add,
            p_env)       +
       f_expand_additional_to_keys
           (TAIL (p_descrs),
            p_add,
            p_env)
  FI;

FUNCTION f_expand_additional_to_keys1 (p_type : tp_key,
                                       p_add  : tp_additional,
                                       p_env  : tp_env) tp_key_list:

  tp_key_list (p_type) +
  CASE p_add OF
      sc_no_add      : c_empty_keys;
      sc_add_deriv   : f_all_deriv_types
```

```
                        (p_type,
                         p_env);
     sc_add_access : f_all_acc_types
                        (p_type,
                         p_env)
   ESAC;

FUNCTION f_expand_instantiation (p_name    : tp_descr,
                                 p_assocs  : tp_assoc_list,
                                 p_nature  : tp_nature,
                                 p_new     : tp_key,
                                 p_env     : tp_env) tp_env :

     % Generate the description of the instantiated entity
     % and enter it into the environment.
     % Check that p_name denotes an appropriate generic unit.
     % p_name is the description of the generic unit, p_assocs
     % the generic associations in the instantiation, p_nature
     % the required nature (sc_package, sc_function, sc_procedure)
     % p_new the key of the instantiated entity.

  (f_expand_instantiation1 (p_name,
                            p_assocs,
                            p_nature,
                            p_new,
                            f_init_type_map (p_assocs, p_env),
                            p_env)
   CONDITION p_name.s_state = sc_complete
      MESSAGE "Body of generic unit must occur before instantiation");

FUNCTION f_expand_instantiation1 (p_name          : tp_descr,
                                  p_assocs        : tp_assoc_list,
                                  p_nature        : tp_nature,
                                  p_new           : tp_key,
                                  p_init_type_map : tp_map_list,
                                  p_env           : tp_env) tp_env :

   f_update_descr_by_key
      (p_new,
       sc_same,
       sc_complete,
       p_nature,

       IF IF NOT (p_name.s_den IS tp_generic) THEN
             (FALSE
              %12.3/1
              CONDITION FALSE
                 MESSAGE "Generic unit expected")
          ELSE IF p_nature = sc_function THEN
             (p_name.s_nature = sc_generic_function
              CONDITION IT
                 MESSAGE "Generic function expected")
          ELSE IF p_nature = sc_procedure THEN
             (p_name.s_nature = sc_generic_procedure
              CONDITION IT
                 MESSAGE "Generic procedure expected")
          ELSE
             (p_name.s_nature = sc_package
              CONDITION IT
                 MESSAGE "Generic package expected")
```

```
            FI FI FI  THEN
            IF p_nature = sc_function THEN
               tp_subpr
                  (tp_function
                      (f_copy_descr_list
                          (p_name.s_den QUA tp_generic
                              .s_den QUA tp_subpr.s_spec
                             QUA tp_function.s_params,
                           p_new,
                           p_init_type_map,
                           p_env),
                       f_adjust_constr
                          (p_name.s_den QUA tp_generic
                              .s_den QUA tp_subpr.s_spec
                             QUA tp_function.s_result,
                           p_init_type_map,
                           p_env)),
                   sc_void,
                   p_name.s_den QUA tp_generic
                      .s_den QUA tp_subpr.s_op)
            ELSE IF p_nature = sc_procedure THEN
               tp_subpr
                  (tp_procedure
                      (f_copy_descr_list
                          (p_name.s_den QUA tp_generic
                              .s_den QUA tp_subpr.s_spec
                             QUA tp_procedure.s_params,
                           p_new,
                           p_init_type_map,
                           p_env)),
                   sc_void,
                   p_name.s_den QUA tp_generic
                      .s_den QUA tp_subpr.s_op)
            ELSE
               tp_package
                  (f_copy_descr_list
                      (p_name.s_den QUA tp_generic
                          .s_den QUA tp_package.s_visible,
                       p_new,
                       p_init_type_map,
                       p_env),
                   c_empty_descrs,
                   c_empty_keys,
                   TRUE)
            FI FI
         ELSE IF p_nature = sc_function THEN
            c_function_den
         ELSE IF p_nature = sc_procedure THEN
            c_proc_den
         ELSE c_package_den
         FI FI FI,
         p_env);

FUNCTION f_expand_others (p_descrs : tp_descr_list)
                         tp_choice_list :

      % Expand the choice OTHERS in a record aggregate to all
      % remaning choices (might be no choices).
```

```
   IF EMPTY (p_descrs) THEN
      tp_choice_list ()
   ELSE tp_choice_list
          (tp_choice
             (HEAD (p_descrs)))
        + f_expand_others (TAIL (p_descrs))
   FI;

FUNCTION f_first_comp_assoc_actual (p_assocs : tp_assoc_list,
                                     p_type   : tp_key,
                                     p_env    : tp_env) tp_descr_set:

      % Yields the parameter of an attribute call. The valid syntax
      % of attribute call parameters is checked by f_valid_attr_param.

   IF LENGTH (p_assocs) < 1 THEN
      c_error_descr_set
   ELSE CASE c_assoc : HEAD (p_assocs) OF
        IS tp_dscrt_range : c_error_descr_set;
        IS tp_comp_assoc :
             f_valid_descr_set
                        (c_assoc.s_actual,
                         p_type,
                         p_env)
        ESAC
   FI;

FUNCTION f_first_not_impl (p_expected : tp_descr_list)
                            tp_choice_list :

      % The next description from p_expected that is no implicitly
      % declared type. p_expected is the list of formal generic
      % parameters including implicitly declared array types.

   IF EMPTY (p_expected) THEN
      tp_choice_list (c_error_descr)
   ELSE IF HEAD (p_expected).s_designator /= sc_anonymous AND
          (HEAD (p_expected).s_state /= sc_implicitly_declared) THEN
      tp_choice_list (HEAD (p_expected))
   ELSE f_first_not_impl (TAIL (p_expected))
   FI FI;

FUNCTION f_first_not_impl_type (p_expected : tp_descr_list)
                                 tp_key_void :

      % If the next not implicitly declared description in p_expected
      % denotes an object, the result is the object's type.

   IF EMPTY (p_expected) THEN
      c_no_expected
   ELSE IF HEAD (p_expected).s_designator /= sc_anonymous AND
          (HEAD (p_expected).s_state /= sc_implicitly_declared) THEN
      IF HEAD (p_expected).s_den IS tp_object THEN
         f_object_type1
            (HEAD (p_expected).s_den)
      ELSE c_no_expected
      FI
   ELSE f_first_not_impl_type (TAIL (p_expected))
   FI FI;
```

```
FUNCTION f_further_derivable (p_impl_subprs : tp_descr_list)
                              tp_key_list :

      % Further derivable are subprograms that are implicitly
      % declared for a derived type without the predefined operators.
      % Such operators are considered separately.
      % (cf. f_impl_subprs)

   IF EMPTY (p_impl_subprs) THEN
      c_empty_keys
   ELSE IF HEAD (p_impl_subprs).s_nature = sc_predefined_op THEN
           c_empty_keys
        ELSE tp_key_list (HEAD (p_impl_subprs).s_key)
        FI +
        f_further_derivable (TAIL (p_impl_subprs))
   FI;

FUNCTION f_gen_constrained (p_type        : tp_descr,
                            p_constraint  : tp_constraint)
                            tp_constrained :

      % p_type is restricted by p_constraint (if this is not void)
      % and possibly expanded to a subtype of its own.

   CASE c_type : p_type.s_den OF
   IS tp_constrained : IF p_constraint = sc_void THEN
                          c_type
                       ELSE tp_constrained
                              (c_type.s_base_type,
                               p_constraint)
                       FI
   OUT tp_constrained
         (p_type.s_key,
          p_constraint)
   ESAC;

FUNCTION f_gen_key   tp_key :

      % For each call a new key is generated.
      %
      % For an implementation this function must be expanded.
      % ALADIN does not allow the generation of distinct
      % keys within functions.

c_key;

FUNCTION f_gen_keylist (p_designators : tp_designator_list)
                        tp_key_list :

      % Generate a list of new keys, one for each designator.

   IF   EMPTY (p_designators) THEN
      c_empty_keys
   ELSE tp_key_list (f_gen_key) +
        f_gen_keylist (TAIL (p_designators))
   FI;

FUNCTION f_gen_keys  tp_key_list :

   tp_key_list (f_gen_key);
```

```
FUNCTION f_generate_imported (p_designator : tp_designator,
                              p_names      : tp_key_list,
                              p_found      : tp_descr_list,
                              p_env        : tp_env)
                              tp_descr_list :

    % Generate the list of descriptions which are made directly
    % visible by use clauses (=imported entities), not regarding
    % otherwise visible entities (cf f_identify_with_use,
    % f_select_with_use).
    % p_names are the names of packages introduces in use clauses.
    % p_found are the already imported entities, starting with an
    % empty list.

  IF EMPTY (p_names) THEN
    f_generate_imported1 (p_found,
                          p_found,
                          p_env)
  ELSE f_generate_imported
         (p_designator,
          TAIL (p_names),
          p_found+
          CASE c_den : f_select_by_key
                         (HEAD (p_names),
                          p_env).s_den OF
          IS tp_package : f_select_by_designator0
                            (p_designator,
                             c_den.s_visible,
                             p_env)
          OUT c_empty_descrs
          ESAC,
          p_env)
  FI;

FUNCTION f_generate_imported1 (p_found,
                               p_rest   : tp_descr_list,
                               p_env    : tp_env)
                               tp_descr_list :

    % Delete those descriptions from p_rest, which are not compatibl
    % with those in p_found according to chapter 8.4 of [Ada80].
    % Entities which are 'otherwise visible'
    % are considered in f_select_with_use.

  IF EMPTY (p_rest) THEN
    p_rest
  ELSE f_out_hidden
         (HEAD (p_rest),
          p_found,
          p_env) +
       f_generate_imported1
         (p_found,
          TAIL (p_rest),
          p_env)
  FI;

FUNCTION f_generic_allowed_expected (p_allowed  : tp_comp_assoc,
                                     p_expected : tp_descr_list,
                                     p_env      : tp_env)
```

```
                          tp_comp_assoc :

    % For subprogram associations select a subprogram from p_allowed
    % which matches the formal subprogram.
    % Check that the actual parameter (p_allowed) matches the formal
    % one (first of p_expected).

  f_generic_allowed_expected1
    (p_allowed,
     p_expected,
     IF EMPTY (p_allowed.s_choices) THEN
        tp_choice_list (f_first_not_impl (p_expected))
     ELSE p_allowed.s_choices
     FI,
     p_env);

FUNCTION f_generic_allowed_expected1 (p_allowed  : tp_comp_assoc,
                                      p_expected : tp_descr_list,
                                      p_choices  : tp_choice_list,
                                      p_env      : tp_env)
                                     tp_comp_assoc :

  tp_comp_assoc
    (p_choices,
     CASE c_den : f_select_by_key11
                     (HEAD (p_choices) QUA tp_descr.s_key,
                      p_expected).s_den OF
     IS tp_object :
        p_allowed.s_actual;
     IS tp_type_den : IS tp_constrained :
        (cf_unique_type_descr (p_allowed.s_actual)
         CONDITION
         ch_matching_types0
            (c_den,
             f_head_descr (IT),
             p_expected,
             p_env)
             MESSAGE
             "illegal matching of actual and formal types");
     IS tp_subpr :
        cf_unique_descr1
           (f_matching_subpr
              (c_den.s_spec,
               p_allowed.s_actual))
     OUT (c_descr_set CONDITION FALSE
             MESSAGE "compiler error")
     ESAC);

FUNCTION f_generic_params (p_generic : tp_descr_set)
                          tp_descr_list :

    % The generic parameters from p_generic without implicitly
    % declared types.

  CASE c_den : f_head_descr (p_generic).s_den OF
  IS tp_generic : f_generic_params1 (c_den.s_generic_params)
  OUT c_empty_descrs
  ESAC;

FUNCTION f_generic_params1 (p_generics : tp_descr_list)
```

```
                        tp_descr_list :

   IF EMPTY (p_generics)
      THEN p_generics
   ELSE CASE c_den : HEAD (p_generics).s_state OF
        sc_implicitly_declared : c_empty_descrs
        OUT tp_descr_list (HEAD (p_generics))
        ESAC +
        f_generic_params1 (TAIL (p_generics))
   FI;

FUNCTION f_global (p_env : tp_env)
                   tp_descr_list :

   p_env.s_global;

FUNCTION f_has_default (p_descr : tp_descr) BOOL:

     % Subprogram parameter is initialized.

   p_descr.s_den QUA tp_object.s_init =/ c_no_init;

FUNCTION f_has_no_user_subprs (p_keys : tp_key_list,
                               p_env  : tp_env) BOOL :

     % p_keys are the implicitly derivable subprograms of a type.
     % Check whether they contain user defined subprograms.
     % Note that predefined subprograms are not entered into the
     % list of derivable subprograms.

   EMPTY (p_keys);

FUNCTION f_has_others_comp (p_assocs : tp_assoc_list) BOOL :

     % p_assocs must not be empty. Check whether p_assocs
     % contain the choice OTHERS. For valid associations
     % it can only be the last choice of the last association.

   IF EMPTY (LAST (p_assocs) QUA tp_comp_assoc.s_choices) THEN
      FALSE
   ELSE HEAD (LAST (p_assocs)
             QUA tp_comp_assoc .s_choices) IS tp_others
   FI;

FUNCTION f_has_pos_comp (p_assocs : tp_assoc_list) BOOL :

     % Check whether an aggregate has positional components.
     % p_assocs must only consist of component_associations.

   IF EMPTY (p_assocs) THEN
      FALSE
   ELSE EMPTY (HEAD (p_assocs) QUA tp_comp_assoc .s_choices) OR
        f_has_pos_comp (TAIL (p_assocs))
   FI;

FUNCTION f_have_default (p_descrs : tp_descr_list) BOOL :

     % Check whether all p_descrs are initialized.

   IF EMPTY (p_descrs) THEN
```

```
   TRUE
  ELSE f_have_default (TAIL (p_descrs))    AND
       (f_object_init1 (HEAD (p_descrs)) =/ c_no_init)
  FI;

FUNCTION f_head_descr (p_descr_set : tp_descr_set) tp_descr :

     % Applied to at_valid, the result is description of the
     % denoted entity.

  IF EMPTY (p_descr_set.s_descrs) THEN
     (c_error_descr CONDITION FALSE MESSAGE "compiler error")
  ELSE HEAD (p_descr_set.s_descrs)
  FI;

FUNCTION f_hide_by_user_def1 (p_desi       : tp_designator,
                              p_operation  : tp_op,
                              p_op_key     : tp_key,
                              p_type       : tp_key,
                              p_init       : tp_init,
                              p_env        : tp_env,
                              p_found      : tp_descr_list)
                             tp_descr_list :

     % Used for operator identification: If the operator with one
     % parameter and result both of p_type is not hidden by one of the
     % user defined operator contained in the origins of p_found
     % (cf. f_origins), then the result is the description of this
     % operator. Else an empty list is returned.

  IF f_overloadable
       (tp_function
          (tp_descr_list
             (f_make_value_descr (c_no_init, p_type)),
           tp_constrained (p_type, sc_void)),
        f_origins (p_found),
        TRUE,
        p_env) THEN
     tp_descr_list
        (f_mark_origin2
           (f_make_value_descr
              (f_eval (p_operation,
                       p_init, c_no_init),
               p_type),
            tp_entity_orig
              (f_temp_descr
                 (p_desi,
                  p_op_key,
                  c_start_repr,
                  sc_complete,
                  sc_common_op,
                  tp_subpr
                    (tp_function
                       (tp_descr_list
                          (f_make_value_descr (c_no_init, p_type)),
                        tp_constrained (p_type, sc_void)),
                     sc_void,
                     p_operation),
                  c_unaccessible)))
  ELSE c_empty_descrs
```

```
FI;

FUNCTION f_hide_by_user_def2 (p_desi       : tp_designator,
                              p_operation  : tp_op,
                              p_op_key     : tp_key,
                              p_type1,
                              p_type2,
                              p_result     : tp_key,
                              p_init1,
                              p_init2      : tp_init,
                              p_env        : tp_env,
                              p_found      : tp_descr_list)
                             tp_descr_list :

    % Similar to f_hide_by_user_def1.

  IF f_overloadable
      (tp_function
         (tp_descr_list
            (f_make_value_descr (c_no_init, p_type1),
             f_make_value_descr (c_no_init, p_type2)),
          tp_constrained (p_result, sc_void)),
       f_origins (p_found),
       TRUE,
       p_env) THEN
    tp_descr_list
      (f_mark_origin2
         (f_make_value_descr
            (f_eval (p_operation,
                     p_init1, p_init2),
             p_result),
          tp_entity_orig
            (f_temp_descr
               (p_desi,
                p_op_key,
                c_start_repr,
                sc_complete,
                sc_common_op,
                tp_subpr
                  (tp_function
                     (tp_descr_list
                        (f_make_value_descr (c_no_init, p_type1),
                         f_make_value_descr (c_no_init, p_type2)),
                      tp_constrained (p_result, sc_void)),
                   sc_void,
                   p_operation),
                c_unaccessible))))
  ELSE c_empty_descrs
  FI;

      %*****************************************************%
      %                                                     %
      %       f_hiding_...                                  %
      %                                                     %
      %       checks whether two subprograms hide each other %
      %       (f_hiding_specs). For hiding, the parameter lists %
      %       must 'hide' each other (f_hiding_params) and the %
      %       result types must be the same                 %
      %       (f_hiding_constrained).                       %
      %                                                     %
      %*****************************************************%
```

```
FUNCTION f_hiding_constrained (p_constr1,
                               p_constr2 : tp_constrained,
                               p_env     : tp_env) BOOL :

    f_base_type1 (p_constr1.s_base_type, p_env) =
    f_base_type1 (p_constr2.s_base_type, p_env);

FUNCTION f_hiding_param (p_param1,
                         p_param2 : tp_descr,
                         p_not_names: BOOL,
                         p_env     : tp_env) BOOL :

    IF p_not_names THEN
       TRUE
    ELSE p_param1.s_designator = p_param2.s_designator
    FI
                                              AND
    f_hiding_constrained (p_param1.s_den QUA tp_object.s_type,
                          p_param2.s_den QUA tp_object.s_type,
                          p_env)
                                              AND
   (f_has_default (p_param1) = f_has_default (p_param2));

FUNCTION f_hiding_params (p_params1,
                          p_params2  : tp_descr_list,
                          p_not_names: BOOL,
                          p_env      : tp_env) BOOL :

   IF EMPTY (p_params1) AND EMPTY (p_params2) THEN
      TRUE
   ELSE IF EMPTY (p_params1) OR EMPTY (p_params2) THEN
        FALSE
      ELSE f_hiding_params (TAIL (p_params1),
                            TAIL (p_params2),
                            p_not_names,
                            p_env)
           AND
           f_hiding_param (HEAD (p_params1),
                           HEAD (p_params2),
                           p_not_names,
                           p_env)

      FI
   FI;

FUNCTION f_hiding_specs (p_spec1,
                         p_spec2 : tp_header,
                         p_not_names: BOOL,
                         p_env   : tp_env) BOOL :

   CASE c_spec1 : p_spec1 OF
   IS tp_function :
        CASE c_spec2 : p_spec2 OF
        IS tp_function :
             f_hiding_params (c_spec1.s_params,
                              c_spec2.s_params,
                              p_not_names,
```

```
                                p_env) AND
           f_hiding_constrained (c_spec1.s_result,
                                 c_spec2.s_result,
                                 p_env);
        IS tp_procedure : FALSE;
        IS tp_entry_family : TRUE;
        IS tp_entry : (TRUE CONDITION FALSE MESSAGE "compiler error")
        ESAC;
   IS tp_procedure :
        CASE c_spec2 : p_spec2 OF
        IS tp_entry_family : TRUE;
        IS tp_entry : (TRUE CONDITION FALSE MESSAGE "compiler error")
        IS tp_function : FALSE;
        IS tp_procedure :
             f_hiding_params (c_spec1.s_params,
                              c_spec2.s_params,
                              FALSE,
                              p_env)
        ESAC;
   IS tp_entry_family : TRUE;
   IS tp_entry : (TRUE CONDITION FALSE MESSAGE "compiler error")
   ESAC;

FUNCTION f_identify (p_designator : tp_designator,
                     p_env        : tp_env) tp_descr_set:

     % Select all directly visible entities in p_env,
     % not considering use clauses (cf f_select_by_designator).
     % Enumeration literals are transformed
     % to static values of the enumeration type they belong to.
     % For overloadable entities (i.e. especially for enumeration
     % literals - subprograms do not matter) literals of derived
     % types are not identified - they are not included in the
     % environment. sc_add_deriv indicates, that they must
     % be considered additionally.

  tp_descr_set
   (f_make_value
      (f_select_by_designator
         (p_designator,
          p_env)),
     IF EMPTY (f_select_by_designator
                (p_designator,
                 p_env))
        THEN sc_no_add
     ELSE
        IF f_is_overloadable (HEAD (f_select_by_designator
                                     (p_designator,
                                      p_env)))
                             THEN
           sc_add_deriv
        ELSE sc_no_add
        FI
     FI);

FUNCTION f_identify_with_use (p_designator : tp_designator,
                              p_env        : tp_env)
                             tp_descr_set :

     % Similar to f_identify, but with consideration of use clauses.
```

```
    % (Cf. f_generate_imported, f_select_with_use).

 tp_descr_set
    (f_make_value
       (f_select_by_designator
          (p_designator,
           p_env)+
        f_select_with_use
          (p_designator,
           f_select_by_designator
              (p_designator,
               p_env),
           f_generate_imported
              (p_designator,
               f_make_set (c_empty_keys,
                           f_imported (p_env)),
           c_empty_descrs,
           p_env),
        p_env)),
     IF EMPTY (f_select_by_designator
                  (p_designator,
                   p_env)) THEN
        sc_no_add
     ELSE IF
        f_is_overloadable (HEAD (f_select_by_designator
                                    (p_designator,
                                     p_env))) THEN
        sc_add_deriv
     ELSE sc_no_add
     FI FI);

FUNCTION f_impl_subprs (p_type,
                        p_parent_type : tp_key,
                        p_env   : tp_env) tp_descr_list:

    % Calcualate all subprograms, which are derived from p_parent
    % type for p_type.
    % Predefined operators are considered separately.

  IF f_select_by_key
       (f_parent_base_type (p_parent_type,
                            p_env),
        p_env) .s_enclosing =
     c_standard
     THEN  f_derive_subprs
       (f_parent_base_type (p_parent_type,
                            p_env),
        p_type,
        p_env)
  ELSE c_empty_descrs
  FI +
  IF f_is_compl_package
       (f_encl_descr1
          (f_select_by_key (p_parent_type, p_env),
           p_env))    AND NOT
    (f_select_by_key (p_parent_type, p_env).s_enclosing = c_standard)
     THEN f_derive_subprs
       (p_parent_type,
        p_type,
```

```
            p_env)
    ELSE c_empty_descrs
    FI;

FUNCTION f_implicitly_convertable (p_type1,
                                   p_type2  : tp_key,
                                   p_env    : tp_env) BOOL :

        % Central check for type equality.

    f_implicitly_convertable1 (p_type1, p_type2, p_env) OR
    f_implicitly_convertable1 (p_type2, p_type1, p_env);

FUNCTION f_implicitly_convertable1 (p_type1,
                                    p_type2  : tp_key,
                                    p_env    : tp_env)BOOL:

    p_type1 = p_type2 OR
    (p_type1 = c_error_type_key) OR
    (p_type2 = c_error_type_key) OR
    (p_type1 = c_univ_int AND f_is_int_type2 (p_type2, p_env)) OR
    (p_type1 = c_univ_real AND f_is_real_type2 (p_type2, p_env) OR
    (p_type1 = c_any_access AND f_is_access_type (p_type2, p_env)));

FUNCTION f_imported (p_env : tp_env) tp_key_list:
    p_env.s_imported;

FUNCTION f_init_type_map (p_assocs : tp_assoc_list,
                          p_env    : tp_env) tp_map_list :

        % Construct a mapping list for formal and actual type
        % parameters.

    IF EMPTY (p_assocs) THEN
        tp_map_list ()
    ELSE
        CASE c_formal : HEAD (HEAD (p_assocs) QUA tp_comp_assoc
                                 .s_choices) QUA tp_descr.s_den OF
        IS tp_type_den :
            CASE c_actual : f_head_descr (HEAD (p_assocs)
                                         QUA tp_comp_assoc.s_actual)
                              .s_den OF
            IS tp_constrained :
                IF c_actual.s_constraint /= sc_void THEN
                    tp_map_list
                      (tp_map
                          (HEAD (HEAD (p_assocs) QUA tp_comp_assoc
                                  .s_choices) QUA tp_descr,
                           f_descr
                              (sc_anonymous,
                               f_gen_key,
                               c_start_repr,
                               sc_complete,
                               sc_subtype,
                               c_actual,
                               f_enclosing (p_env))))
                ELSE tp_map_list
                      (tp_map
                          (HEAD (HEAD (p_assocs) QUA tp_comp_assoc
                                  .s_choices) QUA tp_descr,
```

```
                    f_select_by_key
                       (c_actual.s_base_type,
                        p_env)))
          FI
       OUT tp_map_list
             (tp_map
                 (HEAD (HEAD (p_assocs) QUA tp_comp_assoc
                              .s_choices) QUA tp_descr,
                  f_head_descr (HEAD (p_assocs) QUA tp_comp_assoc
                                      .s_actual)))
       ESAC;
    IS tp_constrained :
       tp_map_list
         (tp_map
             (f_select_by_key
                 (c_formal.s_base_type,
                  p_env),
              f_select_by_key
                 (f_base_type
                     (f_head_descr (HEAD (p_assocs) QUA tp_comp_assoc
                                            .s_actual)),
                  p_env)))
    OUT tp_map_list()
    ESAC +
    f_init_type_map (TAIL (p_assocs), p_env)
  FI;

FUNCTION f_insert_choice (p_r : tp_range_val,
                          p_l : tp_range_val_list) tp_range_val_list :

    % Insert p_r into p_l according to the order of the lower
    % bound of a range_val.

    IF EMPTY (p_l)    THEN
       tp_range_val_list (p_r)
    ELSE IF p_r.s_min <= HEAD (p_l).s_min THEN
       tp_range_val_list (p_r) + p_l
    ELSE
       tp_range_val_list (HEAD (p_l))+
       f_insert_choice (p_r, TAIL (p_l))
    FI FI;

FUNCTION f_int_minus_init (p_init1,
                           p_init2 : tp_init) tp_init :

    % Integer minus operator for tp_init.

  CASE c_exp_kind : f_exp_kind_new
                       (p_init1.s_exp_kind,
                        p_init2.s_exp_kind) OF
  sc_literal : sc_static :
     CASE c_value1 : p_init1.s_value OF
     IS INT :
        CASE c_value2 : p_init2.s_value OF
        IS INT :  tp_init
                    (c_value1 - c_value2,
                     c_exp_kind)
        OUT c_init
        ESAC
     OUT c_init
```

```
      ESAC
    OUT c_init
    ESAC;

FUNCTION f_int_plus_init (p_init1,
                          p_init2 : tp_init) tp_init :

    % Integer plus operator for tp_init.

    CASE c_exp_kind :
      f_exp_kind_new (p_init1.s_exp_kind,
                      p_init2.s_exp_kind) OF
    sc_literal : sc_static :
      IF (p_init1.s_value IS INT)        AND
         (p_init2.s_value IS INT) THEN
         tp_init
           (p_init1.s_value QUA INT + p_init2.s_value QUA INT,
            c_exp_kind)
      ELSE c_init
      FI
    OUT c_init
    ESAC;

FUNCTION f_intersect_types (p_list1,
                            p_list2 : tp_key_list,
                            p_env   : tp_env)
                           tp_key_list :

    % The intersection of p_list1 and p_list2.

    IF EMPTY (p_list1) THEN
      c_empty_keys
    ELSE f_intersect_types1 (HEAD (p_list1), p_list2, p_env) +
         f_intersect_types (TAIL (p_list1), p_list2, p_env)
    FI;

FUNCTION f_intersect_types1 (p_type : tp_key,
                             p_list : tp_key_list,
                             p_env  : tp_env)
                            tp_key_list :

    IF EMPTY (p_list) THEN
      c_empty_keys
    ELSE f_same_type2 (p_type, HEAD (p_list), p_env)
         + f_intersect_types1 (p_type, TAIL (p_list), p_env)
    FI;

FUNCTION f_in_loop (p_encl : tp_descr,
                    p_env  : tp_env) BOOL :

      % Check whether an exit without name transfers control
      % out of a loop and does not transfer control out of a body
      % or accept statement.

    IF p_encl.s_key = c_standard THEN
       FALSE
    ELSE IF p_encl.s_nature = sc_error_nature OR
          (p_encl.s_nature = sc_loop) THEN
       TRUE
    ELSE IF p_encl.s_nature = sc_block THEN
```

```
    f_in_loop (f_encl_descr1 (p_encl, p_env),
               p_env)
 ELSE (TRUE
       CONDITION FALSE
          MESSAGE
          "Exit must not transfer control out of body or accept stm")
 FI FI FI;

    %***********************************************************%
    %                                                           %
    %        f_is_. . .                                         %
    %                                                           %
    %        checks certain properties of a description.        %
    %                                                           %
    %***********************************************************%

FUNCTION f_is_access_type (p_key : tp_key,
                           p_env : tp_env) BOOL :

   f_parent_base_type2 (p_key, p_env) IS tp_access;

FUNCTION f_is_array (p_descr : tp_descr,
                     p_env   : tp_env) BOOL :

   f_object_parent_base_type1 (p_descr,
                               p_env) IS tp_array;

FUNCTION f_is_array_type1 (p_type : tp_type,
                           p_env  : tp_env) BOOL:

   f_parent_base_type1 (p_type, p_env) IS tp_array;

FUNCTION f_is_assign_allowed_for_type (p_type : tp_type,
                                       p_env  : tp_env) BOOL:

     % Check whether a type is limited private or a task type
     % or incomplete containts components of such a type.

   CASE c_type : f_parent_base_type1 (p_type, p_env) OF
   IS tp_l_private :
   IS tp_task_spec :
   IS tp_incompl_type : FALSE;
   IS tp_record : f_is_assign_allowed_for_record
                  (c_type.s_descrs, p_env);
   IS tp_array : f_is_assign_allowed_for_type
                 (f_parent_base_type1
                    (c_type.s_comp_type, p_env), p_env)
   OUT TRUE
   ESAC;

FUNCTION f_is_assign_allowed_for_record (p_descrs : tp_descr_list,
                                         p_env    : tp_env)
                                        BOOL :

   IF EMPTY (p_descrs) THEN
      TRUE
   ELSE CASE c_den : HEAD (p_descrs).s_den OF
        IS tp_object : f_is_assign_allowed_for_type
                       (f_parent_base_type1
                          (c_den.s_type, p_env), p_env)
```

```
        OUT TRUE
        ESAC AND
        f_is_assign_allowed_for_record (TAIL (p_descrs),p_env)
   FI;

FUNCTION f_is_boolean_array_type (p_type : tp_key,
                                  p_env  : tp_env)
                                 BOOL :

   CASE c_type : f_parent_base_type2 (p_type, p_env) OF
   IS tp_array : c_type.s_comp_type.s_base_type = c_bool
   OUT FALSE
   ESAC;

FUNCTION f_is_common_op (p_descrs : tp_descr_list)
                        BOOL :

   IF EMPTY (p_descrs) THEN
      FALSE
   ELSE IF HEAD (p_descrs) .s_nature = sc_common_op THEN
      TRUE
   ELSE f_is_common_op (TAIL (p_descrs))
   FI FI;

FUNCTION f_is_compl_package (p_descr : tp_descr) BOOL:

      % Decide whether subprograms are further derived from a type
      % declared within p_descr.

      p_descr.s_nature =/ sc_package OR
      (p_descr.s_state = sc_complete) OR
      (p_descr.s_state = sc_complete_generic) OR
      (p_descr.s_state = sc_spec_complete) OR
      (p_descr.s_state = sc_in_body);


FUNCTION f_is_constr_arr (p_type : tp_descr,
                          p_env  : tp_env) BOOL :

   IF f_parent_base_type2 (p_type.s_key, p_env) IS tp_array
      THEN f_is_constrained (p_type.s_den)
   ELSE FALSE
   FI;


FUNCTION f_is_constr_arr1 (p_object : tp_descr,
                           p_env    : tp_env) BOOL :

   CASE c_den : p_object.s_den OF
   IS tp_object : IF f_is_array (p_object, p_env) THEN
                     c_den.s_type.s_constraint =/ sc_void
                  ELSE FALSE
                  FI
   OUT FALSE
   ESAC;

FUNCTION f_is_constrained (p_den : tp_den)
                          BOOL :

   IF p_den IS tp_constrained THEN
```

```
    p_den QUA tp_constrained.s_constraint =/ sc_void
  ELSE FALSE
  FI;

FUNCTION f_is_derived_from (p_type1, p_type2 : tp_key,
                            p_env            : tp_env)
                            BOOL:

  CASE c_type : f_type (p_type2, p_env) OF
  IS tp_derived : p_type1 = c_type.s_parent_type OR
                  f_is_derived_from (p_type1, c_type.s_parent_type,
                                     p_env)
  OUT FALSE
  ESAC;

FUNCTION f_is_directly_derived1 (p_type1,
                                 p_type2 : tp_key,
                                 p_env   : tp_env) BOOL :

  CASE c_type : f_type (f_base_type1 (p_type2, p_env), p_env) OF
  IS tp_derived : c_type.s_parent_type = f_base_type1 (p_type1, p_env)
  OUT FALSE
  ESAC;

FUNCTION f_is_directly_derived (p_type1,
                                p_type2 : tp_key,
                                p_env   : tp_env) BOOL :

  f_is_directly_derived1 (p_type1, p_type2, p_env) OR
  f_is_directly_derived1 (p_type2, p_type1, p_env);

FUNCTION f_is_discr_constr (p_type   : tp_descr_set,
                            p_assocs : tp_assoc_list,
                            p_env    : tp_env)
                           BOOL :
  CASE c_type : f_type
                 (f_base_type (HEAD (p_type.s_descrs)),
                  p_env) OF
  IS tp_private : IS tp_l_private :
  IS tp_record : LENGTH (f_discriminants (c_type)) =
                 f_number_of_assocs (p_assocs) AND NOT
                 f_has_others_comp (p_assocs)
  OUT FALSE
  ESAC;

FUNCTION f_is_discrete_array_type (p_type : tp_key,
                                   p_env  : tp_env)
                                  BOOL :

  CASE c_type : f_parent_base_type2 (p_type, p_env) OF
  IS tp_array : f_is_discrete_type
                  (f_select_by_key
                     (c_type.s_comp_type.s_base_type,
                      p_env),
                   p_env) AND
                (LENGTH (c_type.s_indices) = 1)
  OUT FALSE
  ESAC;
```

```
FUNCTION f_is_discrete_type (p_type : tp_descr,
                             p_env  : tp_env) BOOL:

   p_type.s_key = c_univ_int OR (p_type.s_key = c_error_type_key) OR
   f_is_discrete_type1 (f_type (p_type.s_key, p_env),
                        p_env);

FUNCTION f_is_discrete_type1 (p_type : tp_type,
                              p_env  : tp_env) BOOL:

   f_is_int_type1 (p_type,p_env) OR
   CASE c_type : f_parent_base_type1 (p_type, p_env) OF
   IS tp_enum_type :
   IS tp_error_type : TRUE;
   IS tp_formal_type : c_type = sc_formal_discrt
   OUT FALSE
   ESAC;

FUNCTION f_is_error_descr_set (p_descr_set : tp_descr_set)
                               BOOL :
   p_descr_set = c_error_descr_set     OR
  (p_descr_set = c_error_type_descr_set);

FUNCTION f_is_error_empty_range (p_range : tp_dscrt_range) BOOL :

   CASE c_range : p_range OF
   IS tp_constrained : c_range.s_base_type = c_error_key;
   IS tp_range :
      CASE c_range : c_range OF
      IS tp_range_constr:
         f_is_error_or_empty (c_range.s_lower_bound) OR
         f_is_error_or_empty (c_range.s_upper_bound);
      IS tp_void : FALSE
      ESAC;
   IS tp_index : (FALSE CONDITION FALSE MESSAGE "compiler error")
   ESAC;

FUNCTION f_is_error_empty_assocs (p_assocs : tp_assoc_list) BOOL:

   IF EMPTY (p_assocs)
    THEN FALSE
   ELSE f_is_error_empty_assocs (TAIL (p_assocs)) OR
        CASE c_assoc : HEAD (p_assocs) OF
        IS tp_comp_assoc   : f_is_error_empty2 (c_assoc.s_choices) OR
                             f_is_error_or_empty (c_assoc.s_actual);
        IS tp_dscrt_range : f_is_error_empty_range (c_assoc)
        ESAC
   FI;

FUNCTION f_is_error_empty1 (p_choice : tp_choice) BOOL :

   CASE c_choice : p_choice OF
   IS tp_others : IS tp_descr : FALSE;
   IS tp_descr_set : f_is_error_or_empty (c_choice);
   IS tp_dscrt_range : f_is_error_empty_range (c_choice)
   ESAC;

FUNCTION f_is_error_empty2 (p_choices : tp_choice_list) BOOL:
```

```
   IF EMPTY (p_choices)
      THEN FALSE
   ELSE f_is_error_empty1 (HEAD (p_choices)) OR
        f_is_error_empty2 (TAIL (p_choices))
   FI;

FUNCTION f_is_error_or_empty (p_descr_set : tp_descr_set)
                             BOOL :

   f_is_error_descr_set (p_descr_set) OR
   EMPTY (p_descr_set.s_descrs);

FUNCTION f_is_fixed_type (p_type : tp_descr,
                          p_env  : tp_env) BOOL:

   CASE c_type : f_parent_base_type2 (p_type.s_key, p_env) OF
   IS tp_fixed : TRUE;
   IS tp_formal_type : c_type = sc_formal_fixed
   OUT FALSE
   ESAC                              OR
   (p_type.s_key = c_univ_real);

FUNCTION f_is_float_type (p_type : tp_descr,
                          p_env  : tp_env) BOOL:

   CASE c_type : f_parent_base_type2 (p_type.s_key, p_env) OF
   IS tp_float : TRUE;
   IS tp_formal_type : c_type = sc_formal_float
   OUT FALSE
   ESAC                              OR
   (p_type.s_key = c_univ_real);

FUNCTION f_is_index_constraint (p_assocs : tp_assoc_list)
                               BOOL :

   CASE c_assoc : HEAD (p_assocs) OF
   IS tp_dscrt_range : TRUE;
   IS tp_comp_assoc :
      HEAD (c_assoc.s_actual.s_descrs).s_nature = sc_type
      OR (HEAD (c_assoc.s_actual.s_descrs).s_nature= sc_subtype)
   ESAC;

FUNCTION f_is_int_type (p_type : tp_descr,
                        p_env  : tp_env) BOOL:

   f_is_int_type1 (f_type (p_type.s_key, p_env),
                  p_env) OR
  (p_type.s_key = c_univ_int);

FUNCTION f_is_int_type1 (p_type : tp_type,
                         p_env  : tp_env) BOOL:

   CASE c_type : f_parent_base_type1 (p_type, p_env) OF
   IS tp_integer : TRUE;
   IS tp_formal_type : c_type = sc_formal_integer
   OUT FALSE
   ESAC                                   OR
   IF p_type IS tp_constrained THEN
      p_type QUA tp_constrained .s_base_type = c_univ_int
   ELSE FALSE
```

```
   FI;

FUNCTION f_is_int_type2 (p_type : tp_key,
                          p_env  : tp_env) BOOL:

   f_is_int_type1 (f_type (p_type, p_env),
                   p_env) OR (p_type = c_univ_int);

FUNCTION f_is_l_private_type1 (p_type : tp_type,
                                p_env  : tp_env) BOOL:

   CASE c_type: f_parent_base_type1 (p_type,p_env) OF
   IS tp_l_private : TRUE;
   IS tp_array : f_is_l_private_type1
                    (f_type (c_type.s_comp_type.s_base_type,
                                                      p_env),
                     p_env);
   IS tp_record :  f_l_private3 (c_type.s_descrs, p_env)
   OUT FALSE
   ESAC;

FUNCTION f_is_length_attribute (p_attr : tp_designator) BOOL:

   CASE c_attr : p_attr QUA SYMB OF
   c_stor_size_desi : c_size_desi : c_act_delta_desi : TRUE
   OUT FALSE
   ESAC;

FUNCTION f_is_numeric_type (p_type : tp_key,
                            p_env  : tp_env) BOOL :

   f_is_int_type2 (p_type, p_env)                             OR
   f_is_fixed_type (f_select_by_key (p_type, p_env), p_env)   OR
   f_is_float_type (f_select_by_key (p_type, p_env), p_env);

FUNCTION f_is_object (p_descr_set : tp_descr_set) BOOL :

   HEAD (p_descr_set.s_descrs).s_den IS tp_object;

FUNCTION f_is_of_char_type (p_enums     : tp_descr_list,
                            p_char_type : tp_key) BOOL :

     % Check whether p_enums contain a description of an enumeration
     % literal of p_char_type.

   IF    EMPTY (p_enums) THEN
      FALSE
   ELSE  CASE c_enum : HEAD (p_enums).s_den OF
         IS tp_enum_literal :   c_enum.s_char     AND
                               (c_enum.s_type = p_char_type)
         OUT FALSE
         ESAC                                                OR
         f_is_of_char_type (TAIL (p_enums), p_char_type)
   FI;

FUNCTION f_is_of_string_type (p_string      : tp_string_val,
                              p_string_type : tp_descr,
                              p_env         : tp_env) BOOL :

     % Check whether p_string has only characters contained
```

```
    % in the component type of p_string type.

   IF EMPTY (p_string) THEN
      TRUE
   ELSE IF NOT (f_parent_base_type2 (p_string_type.s_key, p_env)
            IS tp_array) THEN
      FALSE
   ELSE f_is_of_char_type
         (f_select_by_designator
            (tp_designator (HEAD (p_string)),
             p_env),
          f_parent_base_type
             (f_type1 (p_string_type) QUA tp_array
                  .s_comp_type.s_base_type,
             p_env)) AND
        f_is_of_string_type (TAIL (p_string), p_string_type, p_env)
   FI FI;

FUNCTION f_is_operator (p_designator : tp_designator) BOOL :

   CASE c_desi : p_designator OF
   IS SYMB : CASE c_desi OF
             c_not_desi   : c_and_desi   : c_or_desi   : c_xor_desi :
             c_plus_desi  : c_minus_desi : c_abs_desi  : c_mult_desi:
             c_div_desi   : c_rem_desi   : c_mod_desi  : c_exp_desi :
             c_equal_desi:c_n_equal_desi:c_greater_desi:c_gr_equal_desi:
             c_less_desi:c_le_equal_desi:c_concat_desi:
                                  TRUE
             OUT FALSE
             ESAC
   OUT FALSE
   ESAC;

FUNCTION f_is_overloadable (p_descr : tp_descr) BOOL:

   CASE p_descr.s_nature OF
   sc_predefined_op : sc_common_op : sc_universal_op :
   sc_procedure : sc_function :
   sc_enum_literal :
   sc_entry : TRUE
   OUT FALSE
   ESAC;

FUNCTION f_is_real_type (p_type : tp_descr,
                         p_env  : tp_env) BOOL:

  f_is_fixed_type (p_type,p_env) OR f_is_float_type (p_type,p_env);

FUNCTION f_is_real_type2 (p_type   : tp_key,
                          p_env    : tp_env) BOOL:

   f_is_real_type (f_select_by_key (p_type,p_env),
                   p_env);

FUNCTION f_is_repr_attribute (p_attr : tp_designator) BOOL :

   CASE c_attr : p_attr QUA SYMB OF
   c_size_desi : c_position_desi : c_stor_size_desi :
   c_act_delta_desi : c_first_bit_desi : c_last_bit_desi : TRUE
   OUT FALSE
```

```
   ESAC;

FUNCTION f_is_scalar_type (p_type : tp_descr,
                           p_env  : tp_env) BOOL:

  f_is_discrete_type (p_type,p_env)  OR  f_is_real_type (p_type,p_env).

FUNCTION f_is_static (p_kind : tp_exp_kind) BOOL:

   p_kind = sc_static OR (p_kind = sc_literal);

FUNCTION f_is_static_descr (p_descr : tp_descr) BOOL :

   CASE c_den : p_descr.s_den OF
   IS tp_object : f_is_static (c_den.s_init.s_exp_kind)
   OUT FALSE
   ESAC;

FUNCTION f_is_task (p_task : tp_descr_set,
                    p_env  : tp_env) BOOL :

      % Check whether p_task is a task or a task type.

   (f_object_parent_base_type
      (p_task,
       p_env)  IS tp_task_spec)      OR
   (f_parent_base_type2 (f_head_descr (p_task).s_key,
                         p_env) IS tp_task_spec);

FUNCTION f_is_task_type (p_type : tp_type,
                         p_env  : tp_env)
                       BOOL :

   f_parent_base_type1 (p_type, p_env) IS tp_task_spec;

FUNCTION f_is_unconstr_arr (p_type : tp_descr,
                            p_env  : tp_env) BOOL :

   IF f_parent_base_type2 (p_type.s_key, p_env) IS tp_array
      THEN NOT f_is_constrained (p_type.s_den)
   ELSE FALSE
   FI;

FUNCTION f_is_universal (p_descrs : tp_descr_list)
                        BOOL :

      % Check whether p_descrs contain a description for a value
      % of a universal (integer/real) type.

   IF EMPTY (p_descrs) THEN
      FALSE
   ELSE IF HEAD (p_descrs).s_origin QUA tp_entity_orig .s_descr
           .s_nature = sc_universal_op THEN
      TRUE
   ELSE f_is_universal (TAIL (p_descrs))
   FI FI;

FUNCTION f_is_user_defined_funct (p_name : tp_descr,
                                  p_env  : tp_env) BOOL :
```

```
   p_name.s_nature = sc_function;

FUNCTION f_is_user_repr (p_key        : tp_key,
                         p_user_reps  : tp_user_reps,
                         p_env        : tp_env) BOOL:

     % Check whether a representation specification is provided
     % for p_key.

   ELEM_IN_LIST (f_select_by_key (p_key, p_env).s_designator,
                 p_user_reps);

FUNCTION f_keys (p_descrs : tp_descr_list) tp_key_list:

     % The list of keys of p_descrs.

   IF EMPTY (p_descrs) THEN
      c_empty_keys
   ELSE tp_key_list (HEAD (p_descrs).s_key) +
        f_keys (TAIL (p_descrs))
   FI;

FUNCTION f_l_private1 (p_params : tp_descr_list,
                       p_env    : tp_env) BOOL:

     % Check whether p_params only contains descriptions of parameters
     % of a limited private type or of a type which has components
     % of such a type.

   IF EMPTY (p_params) THEN
      TRUE
   ELSE f_l_private2 (HEAD (p_params).s_den QUA tp_object.s_type,
                      p_env) AND
        f_l_private1 (TAIL (p_params), p_env)
   FI;

FUNCTION f_l_private2 (p_constr : tp_constrained,
                       p_env    : tp_env) BOOL:

   CASE c_type : f_parent_base_type2
                 (p_constr.s_base_type,
                  p_env) OF
   IS tp_l_private : TRUE;
   IS tp_array     : f_l_private2 (c_type.s_comp_type, p_env);
   IS tp_record    : f_l_private3 (c_type.s_descrs, p_env)
   OUT FALSE
   ESAC;

FUNCTION f_l_private3 (p_comps : tp_descr_list,
                       p_env   : tp_env) BOOL:

   IF EMPTY (p_comps) THEN
      FALSE
   ELSE CASE c_den : HEAD (p_comps).s_den OF
        IS tp_object : f_l_private2 (c_den.s_type, p_env)
        OUT FALSE
        ESAC                                        OR
        f_l_private3 (TAIL (p_comps), p_env)
   FI;
```

```
FUNCTION f_legal_type_conversion (p_type1,
                                  p_type2 : tp_key,
                                  p_env   : tp_env)BOOL:

     % Check whether p_type1 may be converted to p_type2 using a
     % type conversion (cf. 4.4 of [Ada80]).

   IF f_is_directly_derived (p_type1, p_type2, p_env) OR
      (f_is_numeric_type (p_type1, p_env) AND
       f_is_numeric_type (p_type2, p_env)) THEN
      TRUE
   ELSE CASE c_type1: f_type (p_type1,p_env) OF
        IS tp_array :
           CASE c_type2: f_type (p_type2,p_env) OF
           IS tp_array :
              f_compatible_range_lists (c_type1.s_indices,
                                        c_type2.s_indices,
                                        p_env)
                     AND
             (f_is_directly_derived
                (c_type1.s_comp_type.s_base_type,
                 c_type2.s_comp_type.s_base_type,
                 p_env)
                     OR
             (c_type1.s_comp_type.s_base_type =
              c_type2.s_comp_type.s_base_type))
           OUT FALSE
           ESAC
        OUT FALSE
        ESAC
   FI;
FUNCTION f_length_spec (p_attr : tp_designator,
                        p_type : tp_descr_set,
                        p_exp  : tp_descr_set,
                        p_env  : tp_env) tp_length_spec :

     % Construct a length representation specification from :
     % FOR p_type'p_attr USE p_exp
     % Check all conditions of chapter 13.2 [Ada80]

   (tp_length_spec
       (CASE p_attr QUA SYMB OF
        c_size_desi : sc_obj_size;
        c_stor_size_desi : CASE f_head_descr (p_type).s_nature OF
                              sc_type : sc_subtype : sc_collection_size
                           OUT sc_task_size
                           ESAC;
        c_act_delta_desi : sc_actual_delta
        OUT (sc_obj_size CONDITION FALSE MESSAGE
                           "wrong attribute in length spec")
        ESAC,
        p_exp)
    CONDITION
    ch_repr_spec_length (p_attr,
                         f_head_descr (p_type),
                         p_exp,
                         p_env));
```

```
FUNCTION f_literal_to_static (p_init : tp_init) tp_init :

     % A literal expression is changed to be only static.

   IF p_init.s_exp_kind = sc_literal THEN
      tp_init (p_init.s_value, sc_static)
   ELSE p_init
   FI;

FUNCTION f_literals (p_type : tp_descr_set,
                     p_env  : tp_env) tp_key_list :

     % Check that p_type is an enumeration type.
     % Yield the literals of p_type.

   CASE c_type : cf_type_task (f_head_descr (p_type), p_env) OF
   IS tp_enum_type : c_type.s_literals
   OUT (c_empty_keys
        %C 13.3/1
        CONDITION FALSE MESSAGE
        "an enumeration type required")
   ESAC;

FUNCTION f_local (p_env : tp_env) tp_descr_list :

   p_env.s_local;

FUNCTION f_make_assocs (p_constraint : tp_constraint)
                       tp_assoc_list :

     % p_constraint denotes an index- or discriminant constraint.
     % In the case of an index constraint transform the discrete
     % range list to a list of associations, which are discrete
     % ranges.

   IF p_constraint IS tp_assoc_list THEN
      p_constraint QUA tp_assoc_list
   ELSE IF EMPTY (p_constraint QUA tp_dscrt_range_list) THEN
         tp_assoc_list ()
   ELSE tp_assoc_list (HEAD (p_constraint QUA tp_dscrt_range_list))
      + f_make_assocs (TAIL (p_constraint QUA tp_dscrt_range_list))
   FI FI;

FUNCTION f_make_comps (p_comp : tp_comp)
                      tp_comp_list :

     % Transform a component denoting a list of entities
     % (tp_descr_list) into a list of components, each denoting
     % one entity.

   CASE c_comp : p_comp OF
   IS tp_descr_list : IF EMPTY (c_comp) THEN
                         tp_comp_list ()
                      ELSE tp_comp_list
                           (tp_comp (HEAD (c_comp)))
                                     +
                         f_make_comps (tp_comp (TAIL (c_comp)))
                      FI
   OUT tp_comp_list (p_comp)
   ESAC;
```

```
FUNCTION f_make_constrained (p_descr_set : tp_descr_set)
                            tp_choice :

    % The representation of a type name in the context CHOICE
    % is transformed from tp_descr_set to tp_dscrt_range

  IF f_is_error_or_empty (p_descr_set) THEN
    tp_choice (p_descr_set)
  ELSE
    CASE f_head_descr (p_descr_set).s_nature OF
    sc_type : tp_dscrt_range
              (tp_constrained
                 (f_head_descr (p_descr_set).s_key,
                  sc_void));
    sc_subtype : f_head_descr (p_descr_set).s_den QUA tp_constrained
    OUT tp_choice (p_descr_set)
    ESAC
  FI;

FUNCTION f_make_constraineds (p_choices : tp_choice_list)
                              tp_choice_list :

  IF EMPTY (p_choices) THEN
    p_choices
  ELSE CASE c_choice : HEAD (p_choices) OF
       IS tp_descr_set : tp_choice_list
                         (f_make_constrained (c_choice))
       OUT tp_choice_list (c_choice)
       ESAC  +
       f_make_constraineds (TAIL (p_choices))
  FI;

FUNCTION f_make_derivable (p_subpr_key : tp_key,
                           p_env       : tp_env) tp_env:

    % Add p_subpr_key to the derivable subprograms of those types,
    % which
    %     - are parameter or result type of this subprogram
    %     - are declared in the same package specification as this
    %       subprogram

  IF (f_encl_state (p_env) = sc_in_visible) OR
     (f_encl_state (p_env) = sc_in_private) THEN
     CASE c_den : f_select_by_key (p_subpr_key, p_env).s_den OF
     IS tp_subpr :
        CASE  c_spec : c_den.s_spec OF
        IS tp_procedure : f_make_derivable1 (c_spec.s_params,
                                             p_subpr_key,
                                             p_env);
        IS tp_function  : f_make_derivable2
                            (c_spec.s_result,
                             p_subpr_key,
                             f_make_derivable1 (c_spec.s_params,
                                                p_subpr_key,
                                                p_env))
        OUT p_env
        ESAC
     OUT p_env
     ESAC
```

```
  ELSE p_env
  FI;

FUNCTION f_make_derivable1 (p_params     : tp_descr_list,
                            p_subpr_key  : tp_key,
                            p_env        : tp_env) tp_env :

  IF EMPTY (p_params) THEN
     p_env
  ELSE f_make_derivable1
        (TAIL (p_params),
         p_subpr_key,
         CASE c_den : HEAD (p_params).s_den OF
         IS tp_object :
            IF f_select_by_key
                 (c_den.s_type.s_base_type,
                  p_env).s_enclosing =
               f_enclosing (p_env) THEN
               f_update_local
                 (p_env,
                  f_update_derivable
                   (c_den.s_type.s_base_type,
                    p_subpr_key,
                    f_local (p_env)))
            ELSE p_env
            FI
         OUT p_env
         ESAC)
  FI;

FUNCTION f_make_derivable2 (p_result     : tp_constrained,
                            p_subpr_key  : tp_key,
                            p_env        : tp_env) tp_env :

  IF f_select_by_key
       (p_result.s_base_type,
        p_env).s_enclosing = f_enclosing (p_env) THEN
     f_update_local
        (p_env,
         f_update_derivable
           (p_result.s_base_type,
            p_subpr_key,
            f_local (p_env)))
  ELSE p_env
  FI;

FUNCTION f_make_descrs (p_bl_lab_loops : tp_bl_lab_loops,
                        p_enclosing    : tp_key) tp_descr_list:

     % Construct a description for a label, block or loop
     % from s_designator, s_key and s_nature of each
     % element in p_bl_lab_loops.

  IF EMPTY (p_bl_lab_loops) THEN
     c_empty_descrs
  ELSE tp_descr_list
        (f_descr (HEAD (p_bl_lab_loops).s_designator,
                  HEAD (p_bl_lab_loops).s_key,
                  c_start_repr,
                  sc_spec_complete,
```

```
                   HEAD (p_bl_lab_loops).s_nature,
                   sc_void,
                   p_enclosing))
                     +
      f_make_descrs (TAIL (p_bl_lab_loops), p_enclosing)
    FI;

FUNCTION f_make_dummy (p_designator : tp_designator,
                       p_descrs     : tp_descr_set,
                       p_context    : tp_context) tp_descr_set:

      % Dummy descriptions are used for record aggregate choices
      % and formal parameters in procedure calls.
      % These contexts are described by p_context = sc_id_not_visible.
      % The designator of this description is used to analyze      .
      % the complete aggreagate.

    IF (p_context = sc_id_not_visible)  AND
       f_is_error_or_empty (p_descrs)
      THEN tp_descr_set (%inline
           tp_descr_list
             (f_temp_descr
               (p_designator,
                c_key,
                c_start_repr,
                sc_void_state,
                sc_void_nature,
                sc_dummy,
                c_enclosing)),
           sc_no_add)
    ELSE p_descrs
    FI;

 FUNCTION f_make_index_constr (p_indices : tp_dscrt_range_list,
                               p_init    : tp_init,
                               p_env     : tp_env)
                              tp_dscrt_range_list :

      % Construct an index constraint from the initial value of an
      % constant of an unconstrained array type.

    IF EMPTY (p_indices)
      THEN p_indices
    ELSE IF EMPTY (HEAD (p_init.s_value QUA tp_assoc_list)
                   QUA tp_comp_assoc .s_choices) THEN
      f_make_index_constr2 (p_indices, p_init, p_env)
    ELSE f_make_index_constr1 (p_indices, p_init, p_env)
    FI FI;

 FUNCTION f_make_index_constr1 (p_indices : tp_dscrt_range_list,
                                p_init    : tp_init,
                                p_env     : tp_env)
                               tp_dscrt_range_list :

    IF EMPTY (p_indices) THEN
       tp_dscrt_range_list ()
    ELSE CASE c_init : p_init.s_value OF
         IS tp_assoc_list :
              tp_dscrt_range_list
                (tp_dscrt_range
```

```
            (tp_constrained
               (HEAD (p_indices) QUA tp_index.s_type.s_base_type,
                tp_range_constr
                 (f_min_choice
                   (c_init,
                    c_descr_set,
                    p_env),
                  f_max_choice
                   (c_init,
                    c_descr_set,
                    p_env)))))
                       +
         f_make_index_constr
           (TAIL (p_indices),
            HEAD (HEAD (c_init)
                 QUA tp_comp_assoc .s_actual.s_descrs)
             .s_den QUA tp_object .s_init,
            p_env)
     OUT (tp_dscrt_range_list ()
           CONDITION FALSE MESSAGE "compiler error")
     ESAC
  FI;

FUNCTION f_make_index_constr2 (p_indices : tp_dscrt_range_list,
                               p_init    : tp_init,
                               p_env     : tp_env)
                              tp_dscrt_range_list :

  IF EMPTY (p_indices) THEN
     tp_dscrt_range_list ()
  ELSE tp_dscrt_range_list
       (tp_dscrt_range
         (tp_constrained
           (HEAD (p_indices) QUA tp_index.s_type.s_base_type,
            tp_range_constr
             (f_attr_first (HEAD (p_indices) QUA tp_index.s_type,
                           p_env),
              f_attr_val
               (HEAD (p_indices) QUA tp_index.s_type.s_base_type,
                CASE c_pos : f_object_init
                              (f_attr_pos
                                (f_attr_first
                                  (HEAD (p_indices)
                                     QUA tp_index.s_type,
                                   p_env),
                                 p_env)).s_value OF
                IS INT : tp_init
                          (c_pos + LENGTH
                                (p_init.s_value
                                   QUA tp_assoc_list) + 1,
                           sc_literal)
                OUT c_init
                ESAC,
                p_env)))))
                    +
      f_make_index_constr (TAIL (p_indices),
                           f_object_init
                            (HEAD (p_init.s_value
                                    QUA tp_assoc_list)
                                QUA tp_comp_assoc
```

```
                                        .s_actual),
                                    p_env)
   FI;

 FUNCTION f_make_index_list (p_ranges : tp_dscrt_range_list)
                             tp_dscrt_range_list :

      % Extract the base types from p_ranges and build the
      % indices of an unconstrained array type, which is the
      % implicitly declared base type of the array type
      % declared with p_ranges as constraint.

   IF EMPTY (p_ranges) THEN
      p_ranges
   ELSE tp_dscrt_range_list
        (tp_index
            (tp_constrained
                (HEAD (p_ranges) QUA tp_constrained.s_base_type,
                 sc_void)))
                      +
        f_make_index_list (TAIL (p_ranges))
   FI;

 FUNCTION f_make_local1 (p_key : tp_key,
                         p_env  : tp_env) tp_descr_list:

      % Create the local environment for the formal part of a
      % subprogram, making directly visible the generic parameters
      % of the subprogram.

   CASE c_den : f_select_by_key (p_key, p_env).s_den OF
   IS tp_generic : c_den.s_generic_params
   OUT c_empty_descrs
   ESAC;

 FUNCTION f_make_local (p_den : tp_den)
                        tp_descr_list :

      % Create the local environment for a unit body, making directly
      % visible the entities, declared within the unit's specification

   CASE c_den : p_den OF
   IS tp_generic : f_make_local (c_den.s_den) +
                   c_den.s_generic_params;
   IS tp_package   : c_den.s_pack_spec;
   IS tp_type_den: CASE c_type : c_den.s_type OF
                   IS tp_task_spec : c_type.s_visible
                   OUT c_empty_descrs
                   ESAC;
   IS tp_subpr   : CASE c_header : c_den.s_spec  OF
                   IS tp_function : c_header.s_params;
                   IS tp_procedure : c_header.s_params
                   OUT c_empty_descrs
                   ESAC
   OUT c_empty_descrs
   ESAC;

 FUNCTION f_make_range (p_range   : tp_range_constr,
                        p_type    : tp_key,
                        p_env     : tp_env)tp_range_constr:
```

```
    % Adjust the bounds of p_range to p_type.

  tp_range_constr (f_valid_descr_set (p_range.s_lower_bound,
                                      p_type,
                                      p_env),
                   f_valid_descr_set (p_range.s_upper_bound,
                                      p_type,
                                      p_env));

FUNCTION f_make_range_void (p_type   : tp_key,
                            p_constr : tp_range_constr,
                            p_env    : tp_env) tp_range :

    % If the types of the bounds of p_range are compatible with
    % p_type, adjust the types of the bounds of p_range to p_type.

  IF f_is_error_or_empty
        (f_make_range (p_constr, p_type, p_env).s_lower_bound)
    OR
    f_is_error_or_empty
        (f_make_range (p_constr, p_type, p_env).s_upper_bound) THEN
    tp_range (sc_void)
  ELSE f_make_range (p_constr, p_type, p_env)
  FI;

FUNCTION f_make_set (p_set, p_list : tp_key_list) tp_key_list :

    % Delete multiple occurences from p_list.

  IF EMPTY (p_list) THEN
    p_set
  ELSE f_make_set
       (p_set +
        IF ELEM_IN_LIST (HEAD (p_list), p_set) THEN
          c_empty_keys
        ELSE tp_key_list (HEAD (p_list))
        FI,
        TAIL (p_list))
  FI;

FUNCTION f_make_string_aggregate (p_designator : SYMB,
                                  p_expected   : tp_key_void,
                                  p_env        : tp_env)
                                  tp_descr_set:

    % Analyze the string denoted by p_designator as an aggregate.

  tp_descr_set
     (f_make_string_aggregate1
        (p_designator,
         f_symb_string (p_designator),
         CASE c_expected : p_expected OF
         IS tp_void : f_all_string_types (p_env);
         IS tp_key : tp_descr_list
                       (f_select_by_key
                          (c_expected,
                           p_env))
         ESAC,
         p_env),
```

```
      sc_add_deriv);

FUNCTION f_make_string_aggregate1 (p_designator   : SYMB,
                                   p_string       : tp_string_val,
                                   p_string_types : tp_descr_list,
                                   p_env          : tp_env)
                                  tp_descr_list :

   IF EMPTY (p_string_types) THEN
      c_empty_descrs
   ELSE f_make_string_aggregate1 (p_designator,
                                  p_string,
                                  TAIL (p_string_types),
                                  p_env) +
        IF f_is_of_string_type
              (p_string,
               HEAD (p_string_types),
               p_env) THEN
           tp_descr_list
              (f_temp_descr (p_designator,
                             c_key,
                             c_start_repr,
                             sc_complete,
                             sc_value,
                             tp_object
                                (tp_constrained
                                    (HEAD (p_string_types).s_key,
                                     sc_void),
                                 tp_init (p_string, sc_static)),
                             f_enclosing (p_env)))
        ELSE c_empty_descrs
        FI
   FI;

FUNCTION f_make_usable (p_usable : tp_bl_lab_loops,
                        p_env    : tp_env) tp_env :

      % The label names denoted by p_usable are marked as usable.
      % Using s_state of the label's description, the condition
      % that a goto must not transfer control into a sequence of
      % statements.

   IF EMPTY (p_usable) THEN
      p_env
   ELSE
      f_make_usable
         (TAIL (p_usable),
          f_update_descr_by_key (HEAD (p_usable).s_key,
                                 sc_same,
                                 sc_complete,
                                 sc_same,
                                 sc_same,
                                 p_env))
   FI;

FUNCTION f_make_value (p_descrs : tp_descr_list)
                      tp_descr_list :

      % Transform the entity description of an enumeration literal
      % into a value description , i.e a value of the enumeration
```

```
      % type denoting this literal.

   IF EMPTY (p_descrs) THEN
      p_descrs
   ELSE f_make_value1 (HEAD (p_descrs)) +
         f_make_value (TAIL (p_descrs))
   FI;

FUNCTION f_make_value1 (p_descr : tp_descr) tp_descr_list:

   tp_descr_list
      (IF p_descr.s_den IS tp_enum_literal THEN
          f_temp_descr
             (p_descr.s_designator,
              c_key,
              p_descr.s_repr,
              p_descr.s_state,
              sc_value,
              tp_object
                 (tp_constrained
                     (p_descr.s_den QUA tp_enum_literal .s_type,
                      sc_void),
                  f_object_init1 (p_descr)),
              p_descr.s_enclosing)
       ELSE p_descr
       FI);

FUNCTION f_make_value_descr (p_init : tp_init,
                             p_type : tp_key)
                            tp_descr :

   f_temp_descr
      (c_designator,
       f_gen_key,
       c_start_repr,
       sc_void_state,
       sc_value,
       tp_object
          (tp_constrained (p_type, sc_void),
           p_init),
       c_enclosing);

FUNCTION f_make_void_descrs (p_descrs : tp_descr_set) tp_descr_set_void:

   IF EMPTY (p_descrs.s_descrs) THEN
      tp_descr_set_void (sc_void)
   ELSE p_descrs
   FI;

FUNCTION f_map (p_key  : tp_key,
                p_maps : tp_map_list) tp_descr_void :

      % Yields the description which is mapped to p_key by p_maps,
      % if such a description exists else sc_void.

   IF EMPTY (p_maps) THEN
      sc_void
   ELSE IF HEAD (p_maps).s_old.s_key = p_key THEN
      HEAD (p_maps).s_new
   ELSE f_map (p_key, TAIL (p_maps))
```

```
FI FI;

FUNCTION f_map_den (p_den   : tp_den) tp_map_list :

    % Generate new keys for descriptions contained in p_den.

  CASE c_den : p_den OF
  IS tp_package :
     f_map_descr_list (c_den.s_visible);
  IS tp_subpr :
     CASE c_spec : c_den.s_spec OF
     IS tp_function :
        f_map_descr_list (c_spec.s_params);
     IS tp_procedure :
        f_map_descr_list (c_spec.s_params)
     OUT (tp_map_list () CONDITION FALSE MESSAGE "compiler error")
     ESAC;
  IS tp_entry :
     f_map_descr_list (c_den.s_params);
  IS tp_entry_family :
     f_map_descr_list (c_den.s_entry.s_params);
  IS tp_type_den :
     CASE c_type : c_den.s_type OF
     IS tp_record :
        f_map_descr_list (c_type.s_descrs);
     IS tp_private :
        f_map_descr_list (c_type.s_discriminants);
     IS tp_l_private :
        f_map_descr_list (c_type.s_discriminants);
     IS tp_incompl_type :
        f_map_descr_list (c_type.s_discriminants);
     IS tp_task_spec :
        f_map_descr_list (c_type.s_visible)
     OUT tp_map_list ()
     ESAC;
  IS tp_generic :
     f_map_descr_list (c_den.s_generic_params) +
     f_map_den (c_den.s_den)
  OUT tp_map_list ()
  ESAC;

FUNCTION f_map_derived (p_descr : tp_descr,
                        p_maps  : tp_map_list,
                        p_env   : tp_env) tp_constraint :

    % If p_descr denotes a type, whose parent base type
    % is mapped to a subtype, the result is the constraint
    % of this subtype, else void.

  CASE c_den : p_descr.s_den OF
  IS tp_type_den :
     CASE c_type : c_den.s_type OF
     IS tp_derived :
        CASE c_map : f_map (f_parent_base_type
                              (c_type.s_parent_type,
                               p_env),
                            p_maps) OF
        IS tp_void : sc_void;
        IS tp_descr :
           CASE c_constr : c_map.s_den OF
```

```
          IS tp_constrained : c_constr.s_constraint
          OUT sc_void
          ESAC
       ESAC
    OUT sc_void
    ESAC
  OUT sc_void
  ESAC;

FUNCTION f_map_descr_list (p_descrs : tp_descr_list) tp_map_list :

    % Generate for each description directly or indirectly
    % contained in p_descrs a new description and enter it
    % into p_maps.

  IF EMPTY (p_descrs) THEN
     tp_map_list ()
  ELSE tp_map_list
          (tp_map
             (HEAD (p_descrs),
              f_descr
                 (HEAD (p_descrs).s_designator,
                  f_gen_key,
                  HEAD (p_descrs).s_repr,
                  HEAD (p_descrs).s_state,
                  HEAD (p_descrs).s_nature,
                  HEAD (p_descrs).s_den,
                  HEAD (p_descrs).s_enclosing))) +
       f_map_den (HEAD (p_descrs).s_den)      +
       f_map_descr_list (TAIL (p_descrs))
  FI;

FUNCTION f_map_ident (p_descrs : tp_descr_list) tp_map_list :

    % Creates a mapping list which contains only identities,
    % i.e new = old.

  IF EMPTY (p_descrs) THEN
     tp_map_list ()
  ELSE tp_map_list
          (tp_map
             (HEAD (p_descrs),
              HEAD (p_descrs))) +
       f_map_ident_den (HEAD (p_descrs).s_den) +
       f_map_ident (TAIL (p_descrs))
  FI;

FUNCTION f_map_ident_den (p_den  : tp_den) tp_map_list :

    % Create a mapping list for descriptions contained in p_den,
    % where s_old = s_new

  CASE c_den : p_den OF
  IS tp_package :
     f_map_ident (c_den.s_visible);
  IS tp_subpr :
     CASE c_spec : c_den.s_spec OF
     IS tp_function :
        f_map_ident (c_spec.s_params);
     IS tp_procedure :
```

```
            f_map_ident (c_spec.s_params)
         OUT (tp_map_list () CONDITION FALSE MESSAGE "compiler error")
         ESAC;
      IS tp_entry :
         f_map_ident (c_den.s_params);
      IS tp_entry_family :
         f_map_ident (c_den.s_entry.s_params);
      IS tp_type_den :
         CASE c_type : c_den.s_type OF
         IS tp_record :
            f_map_ident (c_type.s_descrs);
         IS tp_private :
            f_map_ident (c_type.s_discriminants);
         IS tp_l_private :
            f_map_ident (c_type.s_discriminants);
         IS tp_incompl_type :
            f_map_ident (c_type.s_discriminants);
         IS tp_task_spec :
            f_map_ident (c_type.s_visible)
         OUT tp_map_list ()
         ESAC;
      IS tp_generic :
         f_map_ident (c_den.s_generic_params) +
         f_map_den (c_den.s_den)
      OUT tp_map_list ()
      ESAC;

FUNCTION f_map_impls (p_impls : tp_key_list,
                      p_maps  : tp_map_list) tp_key_list :

      % Returns the list of keys which is associated to p_impls
      % according to p_maps.

      IF EMPTY (p_impls) THEN
         p_impls
      ELSE
         tp_key_list
            (f_map (HEAD (p_impls),
                    p_maps) QUA tp_descr.s_key) +
         f_map_impls (TAIL (p_impls), p_maps)
      FI;

FUNCTION f_map_type (p_type : tp_key,
                     p_maps : tp_map_list) tp_key :

      % If p_type is mapped to a subtype yield the base type
      % else the associated type itself.

      CASE c_map : f_map (p_type, p_maps) OF
      IS tp_void : p_type;
      IS tp_descr : CASE c_den : c_map.s_den OF
                    IS tp_constrained : c_den.s_base_type
                    OUT c_map.s_key
                    ESAC
      ESAC;

FUNCTION f_mark_body_prov (p_package : tp_key_list,
                           p_env     : tp_env)
                           tp_env :
```

```
    % The information that a body is provided for a package is entered
    % into the description of the package.

  f_update_local (p_env,
                  f_mark_body_prov1 (HEAD (p_package),
                                     f_local (p_env)));

FUNCTION f_mark_body_prov1 (p_package : tp_key,
                            p_local   : tp_descr_list)
                            tp_descr_list :

  IF HEAD (p_local).s_key = p_package THEN
     tp_descr_list
        (f_update_descr
           (HEAD (p_local),
            sc_same,
            sc_complete,
            sc_same,
            CASE c_den  : HEAD (p_local).s_den OF
            IS tp_package :
               tp_package (c_den.s_visible,
                           c_den.s_pack_spec,
                           c_den.s_imported,
                           TRUE);
            IS tp_generic :
               tp_generic
                  (c_den.s_generic_params,
                   tp_package (c_den.s_den QUA tp_package.s_visible,
                               c_den.s_den QUA tp_package.s_pack_spec,
                               c_den.s_den QUA tp_package.s_imported,
                               TRUE))
            OUT (c_error_pack_den CONDITION FALSE MESSAGE
                                  "compiler error")
            ESAC))
            + TAIL (p_local)
  ELSE tp_descr_list (HEAD (p_local)) +
       f_mark_body_prov1 (p_package, TAIL (p_local))
  FI;

FUNCTION f_mark_origin1 (p_descrs  : tp_descr_list,
                         p_origin  : tp_origin) tp_descr_list:

    % Set the component s_origin of all descirptions in p_descrs
    % to p_origin.

  IF EMPTY (p_descrs) THEN
     p_descrs
  ELSE tp_descr_list (f_mark_origin2 (HEAD (p_descrs),
                                      p_origin))
       + f_mark_origin1 (TAIL (p_descrs), p_origin)
  FI;

FUNCTION f_mark_origin2 (p_descr    : tp_descr,
                         p_origin   : tp_origin) tp_descr :

  tp_descr (p_descr.s_designator,
            p_descr.s_key,
            p_descr.s_repr,
            p_descr.s_state,
            p_descr.s_nature,
```

```
            p_descr.s_den,
            p_origin,
            p_descr.s_enclosing);


FUNCTION f_matching_param (p_param1,
                           p_param2 : tp_descr) BOOL :

   p_param1.s_nature  = p_param2.s_nature                    AND
   f_same_constrained (p_param1.s_den QUA tp_object.s_type,
                       p_param2.s_den QUA tp_object.s_type);

FUNCTION f_matching_params (p_params1,
                            p_params2 : tp_descr_list) BOOL :

   IF EMPTY (p_params1) AND EMPTY (p_params2) THEN
      TRUE
   ELSE IF EMPTY (p_params1) OR EMPTY (p_params2) THEN
      FALSE
   ELSE f_matching_param (HEAD (p_params1), HEAD (p_params2)) AND
        f_matching_params (TAIL (p_params1), TAIL (p_params2))
   FI FI;

FUNCTION f_matching_subpr (p_header : tp_header,
                           p_actual : tp_descr_set) tp_descr_set :

     % Select from p_actual the descriptions that match p_header
     % according to the rules of renaming respectively
     % generic parameter associations.

   f_descr_set3
      (f_matching_subpr1
         (p_header,
          p_actual.s_descrs));

FUNCTION f_matching_subpr1 (p_header : tp_header,
                            p_descrs : tp_descr_list) tp_descr_list :

   IF EMPTY (p_descrs) THEN
      p_descrs
   ELSE f_matching_subpr1 (p_header, TAIL (p_descrs)) +
        CASE c_den : HEAD (p_descrs).s_den OF
        IS tp_subpr :
           IF f_matching_subpr_spec (p_header, f_spec1 (c_den)) THEN
              tp_descr_list (HEAD (p_descrs))
           ELSE c_empty_descrs
           FI
        OUT c_empty_descrs
        ESAC
   FI;

FUNCTION f_matching_subpr_spec (p_spec1,
                                p_spec2 : tp_header) BOOL :

   CASE c_spec1 : p_spec1 OF
   IS tp_function :
      CASE c_spec2 : p_spec2 OF
      IS tp_function :
         f_matching_params (c_spec1.s_params,
                            c_spec2.s_params) AND
```

```
          f_same_constrained (c_spec1.s_result,
                              c_spec2.s_result);
        IS tp_procedure : IS tp_entry_family : FALSE;
        IS tp_entry : (TRUE CONDITION FALSE MESSAGE
                        "compiler error") %cf. spec1
        ESAC;
     IS tp_procedure :
          CASE c_spec2 : p_spec2 OF
          IS tp_function : IS tp_entry_family : FALSE;
          IS tp_entry : (TRUE CONDITION FALSE MESSAGE
                          "compiler error"); %cf. spec1
          IS tp_procedure : f_matching_params (c_spec1.s_params,
                                               c_spec2.s_params)
          ESAC;
     IS tp_entry : tp_entry_family : (TRUE CONDITION FALSE
                                       MESSAGE "compiler error")
     ESAC;

FUNCTION f_max_choice (p_aggregate : tp_assoc_list,
                       p_max       : tp_descr_set,
                       p_env       : tp_env)
                      tp_descr_set   :

     IF EMPTY (p_aggregate) THEN
        p_max
     ELSE f_max_choice
           (TAIL (p_aggregate),
            f_maximum
             (p_max,
              CASE c_choice : HEAD (HEAD (p_aggregate) QUA tp_comp_assoc
                                     .s_choices) OF
              IS tp_descr_set : c_choice;
              IS tp_dscrt_range : c_choice QUA tp_constrained
                                   .s_constraint
                                  QUA tp_range_constr .s_upper_bound
              OUT c_error_descr_set
              ESAC,
              p_env),
            p_env)
     FI;

FUNCTION f_max_choice_val (p_choice : tp_choice) INT :

    CASE c_choice : p_choice OF
    IS tp_dscrt_range :
         CASE c_upper : HEAD (c_choice QUA tp_constrained
                               .s_constraint QUA tp_range_constr
                               .s_upper_bound.s_descrs).s_den
                         QUA tp_object .s_init.s_value OF
         IS INT : c_upper
         OUT (0 CONDITION FALSE
              MESSAGE "static expression expected")
         ESAC;
    IS tp_descr_set :
         CASE c_value : HEAD (c_choice.s_descrs).s_den QUA tp_object
                         .s_init.s_value OF
         IS INT : c_value
         OUT (0 CONDITION FALSE
              MESSAGE "static expression expected")
         ESAC
```

```
   OUT (0 CONDITION FALSE MESSAGE "compiler error")
   ESAC;

FUNCTION f_maximum (p_descrs_1,
                    p_descrs_2  : tp_descr_set,
                    p_env       : tp_env) tp_descr_set :

   IF p_descrs_1 = c_descr_set THEN
      p_descrs_2
   ELSE IF f_eval_less_equal (p_descrs_1, p_descrs_2)
           THEN p_descrs_2
        ELSE p_descrs_1
        FI
   FI;

FUNCTION f_min_choice (p_aggregate : tp_assoc_list,
                       p_min       : tp_descr_set,
                       p_env       : tp_env)tp_descr_set:

   IF EMPTY (p_aggregate) THEN
      p_min
   ELSE f_min_choice
          (TAIL (p_aggregate),
           f_minimum
            (p_min,
             CASE c_choice : HEAD (HEAD (p_aggregate) QUA tp_comp_ass
                                   .s_choices) OF
             IS tp_descr_set : c_choice;
             IS tp_dscrt_range : c_choice QUA tp_constrained
                                   .s_constraint
                                 QUA tp_range_constr .s_lower_bound
             OUT c_error_descr_set
             ESAC,
             p_env),
          p_env)
   FI;

FUNCTION f_min_choice_val (p_choice : tp_choice) INT :

   CASE c_choice : p_choice OF
   IS tp_dscrt_range :
        CASE c_lower : HEAD (c_choice QUA tp_constrained
                             .s_constraint QUA tp_range_constr
                             .s_lower_bound.s_descrs).s_den
                       QUA tp_object .s_init.s_value OF
        IS INT : c_lower
        OUT (0 CONDITION FALSE
              MESSAGE "static expression expected")
        ESAC;
   IS tp_descr_set :
        CASE c_value : HEAD (c_choice.s_descrs).s_den QUA tp_object
                       .s_init.s_value OF
        IS INT : c_value
        OUT (0 CONDITION FALSE
              MESSAGE "static expression expected")
        ESAC
   OUT (0 CONDITION FALSE MESSAGE "compiler error")
   ESAC;

FUNCTION f_minimum (p_descrs_1,
```

```
                     p_descrs_2   : tp_descr_set,
                     p_env        : tp_env)tp_descr_set:

   IF p_descrs_1 = c_descr_set THEN
     p_descrs_2
   ELSE IF f_eval_less_equal (p_descrs_1, p_descrs_2)
          THEN p_descrs_1
        ELSE p_descrs_2
        FI
   FI;

FUNCTION f_n_th_index (p_indices  : tp_dscrt_range_list,
                        n          : INT)
                       tp_constrained :

   IF n < 1 OR EMPTY (p_indices) THEN
     (c_error_type
      CONDITION FALSE
         MESSAGE "index does not exist")
   ELSE IF n = 1 THEN
      CASE c_index : HEAD (p_indices) OF
      IS tp_constrained : c_index
      OUT (c_error_type CONDITION FALSE
                      MESSAGE "compiler error")
      ESAC
   ELSE f_n_th_index (TAIL (p_indices), n-1)
   FI FI;

FUNCTION f_new_imported (p_descr  : tp_descr,
                         p_env    : tp_env) tp_env :

      % If p_descr is a package desription then add the names appearing
      % in use clauses within the specification of that package
      % to the list of current use clauses (env.s_imported) of the
      % environment of the corresponding package body.

   f_env
      (CASE c_den : p_descr.s_den OF
       IS tp_package : c_den.s_imported + f_imported (p_env)
       OUT f_imported (p_env)
       ESAC,
       f_global (p_env),
       f_local (p_env),
       f_enclosing (p_env));

FUNCTION f_new_key (p_key      : tp_key,
                    p_env      : tp_env) BOOL:

      % Decide whether p_key is the key of a description in the local
      % environment. (Otherwise p_key is a key of a description
      % which will be entered into the local environment.)

   f_new_key1 (p_key, f_local (p_env));

FUNCTION f_new_key1 (p_key     : tp_key,
                     p_local   : tp_descr_list) BOOL:

   IF EMPTY (p_local) THEN
      TRUE
   ELSE IF HEAD (p_local).s_key = p_key THEN
```

```
      FALSE
    ELSE f_new_key1 (p_key, TAIL (p_local))
    FI FI;

 FUNCTION f_new_local (p_new_local : tp_descr_list,
                       p_new_encl  : tp_key,
                       p_env       : tp_env) tp_env :

      % Central function for opening a new environment scope.

    f_env (f_imported (p_env),
           f_local (p_env) + f_global (p_env),
           p_new_local,
           p_new_encl);

 FUNCTION f_new_repr_state (p_key : tp_key,
                            p_env : tp_env) tp_rep_state :

      % Evaluate the new representation state for p_key, if
      % a representation is not already determined and
      % if no representation specifications follow for
      % the entity denoted by p_key.
      % This state is determined by the state of entities on which
      % the given entity depends and by the definitions
      % of those entities (e.g. on whether their constraints
      % are static).

    CASE c_rep_state : f_rep_state (p_key, p_env) OF
    sc_user_rep : sc_dynamic_rep : sc_static_rep : c_rep_state
    OUT CASE c_den : f_select_by_key (p_key, p_env).s_den OF
        IS tp_type_den :
           CASE c_type : c_den.s_type OF
           IS tp_private : tp_l_private : IS tp_incompl_type :
              sc_incompl_rep;
           IS tp_void : IS tp_error_type : sc_user_rep
           OUT f_new_repr_state2
                (sc_static_rep,
                 f_used_types (c_type, p_env),
                 p_env)
           ESAC;
        IS tp_constrained : f_repr_state_constr (c_den, p_env);
        IS tp_object : f_repr_state_constr (c_den.s_type, p_env);
        IS tp_subpr  : CASE c_spec : c_den.s_spec OF
                       IS tp_function : f_repr_state_constr
                                        (c_spec.s_result, p_env)
                       OUT sc_start_rep
                       ESAC
        OUT sc_start_rep
        ESAC
    ESAC;

 FUNCTION f_new_repr_state1 (p_state1,
                             p_state2 : tp_rep_state) tp_rep_state :

      % Select the 'weakest' state of p_state1 and p_state2 with
      % the order sc_static_rep, sc_dynamic_rep, sc_incomplete_rep,
      % sc_user_rep.

    CASE p_state1 OF
    sc_static_rep  : p_state2;
```

```
  sc_dynamic_rep : IF p_state2 = sc_static_rep THEN
                        sc_dynamic_rep
                   ELSE p_state2
                   FI;
  sc_incompl_rep : IF p_state2 = sc_user_rep THEN
                        sc_user_rep
                   ELSE sc_incompl_rep
                   FI;
  sc_user_rep    : sc_user_rep;
  sc_start_rep   : sc_start_rep
  ESAC;

FUNCTION f_new_repr_state2 (p_state : tp_rep_state,
                            p_types : tp_key_list,
                            p_env   : tp_env) tp_rep_state:

    % The 'weakest' state of p_state and the representation states
    % of all p_types.

  IF EMPTY (p_types) THEN
    p_state
  ELSE f_new_repr_state2
         (f_new_repr_state1
             (p_state,
              f_new_repr_state (HEAD (p_types), p_env)),
          TAIL (p_types),
          p_env)
  FI;

FUNCTION f_no_unconstr_arr_rec (p_type : tp_type,
                                p_env  : tp_env)
                               BOOL :

    % Check whether p_type denotes an unconstrained array type
    % or an unconstrained type which has discriminants without
    % default values.

  CASE c_type   : f_parent_base_type1 (p_type, p_env) OF
  IS tp_array   : CASE c_type : p_type OF
                  IS tp_constrained : c_type.s_constraint =/ sc_void
                  OUT FALSE
                  ESAC;
  IS tp_private : IS tp_l_private :
  IS tp_record  : CASE c_type : p_type OF
                  IS tp_constrained : c_type.s_constraint =/ sc_void
                  OUT FALSE
                  ESAC    OR
                  f_have_default (f_discriminants (c_type))
  OUT TRUE
  ESAC;

FUNCTION f_number_of_assocs (p_assocs : tp_assoc_list) INT :

    % Number of choices appearing within the accociation list.
    % OTHERS is counted as one choice. Positional associtiations
    % are considered to have a single choice.

  IF EMPTY (p_assocs) THEN
    0
  ELSE CASE c_length : LENGTH (HEAD (p_assocs) QUA tp_comp_assoc
```

```
                        .s_choices) OF
      0 : 1
      OUT c_length
      ESAC +
      f_number_of_assocs (TAIL (p_assocs))
   FI;

    %**************************************************************%
    %                                                              %
    %       f_obj...                                               %
    %                                                              %
    %       Select properties of object descriptions.              %
    %                                                              %
    %**************************************************************%

FUNCTION f_obj_constrained (p_obj : tp_key,
                            p_env : tp_env) tp_constrained :

   f_obj_constrained1 (f_select_by_key (p_obj, p_env));

FUNCTION f_obj_constrained1 (p_obj : tp_descr) tp_constrained :

   CASE c_den : p_obj.s_den OF
   IS tp_object : c_den.s_type;
   IS tp_enum_literal : tp_constrained (c_den.s_type, sc_void)
   OUT c_error_type
   ESAC;

FUNCTION f_obj_constraint (p_obj : tp_descr_set) tp_constraint :

   f_obj_constraint1 (f_head_descr (p_obj));

FUNCTION f_obj_constraint1 (p_obj : tp_descr) tp_constraint :

   CASE c_obj : p_obj.s_den OF
   IS tp_object : c_obj.s_type.s_constraint
   OUT sc_void
   ESAC;

FUNCTION f_object_init (p_descrs : tp_descr_set) tp_init :

   f_object_init1 (HEAD (p_descrs.s_descrs));

FUNCTION f_object_init1 (p_descr : tp_descr) tp_init :
   CASE c_den : p_descr.s_den OF
   IS tp_dummy : IS tp_dummy_aggr : c_no_init;
   IS tp_object : c_den.s_init;
   IS tp_enum_literal : tp_init (c_den.s_pos,
                                 sc_static)
   OUT c_init
   ESAC;

FUNCTION f_object_parent_base_type (p_descr_set : tp_descr_set,
                                    p_env       : tp_env)tp_type:

   f_object_parent_base_type1 (f_head_descr (p_descr_set),
                               p_env);

FUNCTION f_object_parent_base_type1 (p_descr : tp_descr,
```

```
                                                p_env   : tp_env) tp_type :
   f_parent_base_type2
         (f_object_type (p_descr),
          p_env);

FUNCTION f_object_parent_deref_type (p_descr : tp_descr,
                                                p_env   : tp_env) tp_type :

   f_parent_base_type2
      (f_deref_type
         (f_object_type
               (p_descr),
          p_env),
       p_env);

FUNCTION f_object_type (p_descr : tp_descr) tp_key :

   f_object_type1 (p_descr.s_den);

FUNCTION f_object_type1 (p_den : tp_den) tp_key :

   CASE c_den : p_den OF
   IS tp_object : c_den.s_type.s_base_type;
   IS tp_enum_literal : c_den.s_type
   OUT c_no_type_key
   ESAC;

FUNCTION f_object_value (p_object : tp_descr_set) tp_value :

   f_object_init (p_object).s_value;

FUNCTION f_object_value_kind (p_obj : tp_descr_set) tp_exp_kind :

   f_object_init (p_obj).s_exp_kind;

FUNCTION f_object_value_kind1 (p_obj : tp_descr) tp_exp_kind :

   f_object_init1 (p_obj).s_exp_kind;

FUNCTION f_only_enums_or_subprs (p_descrs : tp_descr_list) BOOL :

      % Check whether p_descrs only contain enumeration literal -
      % or subprogram - descriptions.

   IF EMPTY (p_descrs) THEN
      TRUE
   ELSE CASE HEAD (p_descrs).s_den OF
        IS tp_enum_literal : IS tp_subpr : IS tp_operation :
           f_only_enums_or_subprs (TAIL (p_descrs))
        OUT FALSE
        ESAC
   FI;

FUNCTION f_order_choices (p_choices : tp_choice_list,
                          p_choice_ranges : tp_range_val_list)
                          tp_range_val_list :

     % Order the choices in p_choices (and change their representation)
```

```
   IF EMPTY (p_choices) THEN
      p_choice_ranges
   ELSE IF HEAD (p_choices) IS tp_others THEN   % must be last choice
      p_choice_ranges
   ELSE
      f_order_choices (TAIL (p_choices),
         f_insert_choice (tp_range_val
                             (f_min_choice_val (HEAD (p_choices)),
                              f_max_choice_val (HEAD (p_choices))),
                         p_choice_ranges))
   FI FI;

FUNCTION f_origin (p_descr : tp_descr) tp_origin :

    % Decide whether p_descr is a description denoting an entity
    % described in the environment or a description denoting
    % a value. Accordingly this description (as one of the
    % description in a descr_set) is referenced by an entity -
    % respectively a type origin.

   IF p_descr.s_key = c_key THEN
      tp_type_orig (f_object_type (p_descr))
   ELSE  tp_entity_orig (p_descr)
   FI;

FUNCTION f_origins (p_descrs : tp_descr_list)
                    tp_descr_list :

    % Applied to to the decriptions of the results of a function cal
    % the result are the descriptions of the corresponding functions

   IF EMPTY (p_descrs) THEN
      c_empty_descrs
   ELSE tp_descr_list
         (HEAD (p_descrs).s_origin QUA tp_entity_orig .s_descr) +
      f_origins (TAIL (p_descrs))
   FI;

FUNCTION f_out_hidden (p_descr  : tp_descr,
                       p_found  : tp_descr_list,
                       p_env    : tp_env)
                      tp_descr_list :

    % Return p_descr if it is compatible with all entities in p_foun
    % according to the rules of use clauses in 8.4, [Ada80].

   IF EMPTY (p_found) THEN
      tp_descr_list (p_descr)
   ELSE IF p_descr = HEAD (p_found) THEN
      f_out_hidden (p_descr, TAIL (p_found), p_env)
   ELSE IF NOT f_is_overloadable (p_descr) THEN
      c_empty_descrs
   ELSE IF p_descr.s_den IS tp_enum_literal THEN
      tp_descr_list (p_descr)
   ELSE CASE c_den1 : p_descr.s_den OF
         IS tp_subpr :
            CASE c_den2 : HEAD (p_found).s_den OF
            IS tp_subpr :
               IF NOT f_hiding_specs
```

```
                      (c_den1.s_spec,
                       c_den2.s_spec,
                       TRUE,
                       p_env)
                THEN f_out_hidden
                       (p_descr,
                        TAIL (p_found),
                        p_env)
             ELSE IF HEAD (p_found).s_state = sc_implicitly_declared
                    AND (p_descr.s_enclosing =
                         HEAD (p_found).s_enclosing) THEN
                f_out_hidden
                   (p_descr,
                    TAIL (p_found),
                    p_env)
             ELSE  c_empty_descrs
             FI FI;
          IS tp_enum_literal :
             f_out_hidden
               (p_descr,
                TAIL (p_found),
                p_env)
          OUT c_empty_descrs
          ESAC
       OUT (c_empty_descrs CONDITION FALSE MESSAGE "compiler error")
       ESAC
  FI FI FI FI;

FUNCTION f_overloadable (p_spec        : tp_header,
                         p_descrs      : tp_descr_list,
                         p_not_names   : BOOL,
                         p_env         : tp_env)
                        BOOL :

    % Check whether the subprogram described by p_spec is overloadable
    % with all entities described by p_descrs. p_not_names indicates,
    % whether parameter names are considered for overloading.

  IF EMPTY (p_descrs) THEN
     TRUE
  ELSE IF HEAD (p_descrs).s_den IS tp_enum_literal
          OR (HEAD (p_descrs).s_enclosing = c_unaccessible) THEN
     f_overloadable (p_spec,
                     TAIL (p_descrs),
                     p_not_names,
                     p_env)
  ELSE IF f_hiding_specs
            (p_spec,
             f_spec (HEAD (p_descrs)),
             p_not_names,
             p_env) THEN
     FALSE
  ELSE f_overloadable (p_spec,
                       TAIL (p_descrs),
                       p_not_names,
                       p_env)
  FI FI FI;

FUNCTION f_own_entry (p_name : tp_descr_set,
```

```
                         p_env   : tp_env) BOOL:

      % Check whether p_name (name of an entry) is declared within
      % an enclosing unit. (This can only be a task)

   IF f_head_descr (p_name).s_nature = sc_entry THEN
      f_own_entry1
         (f_head_descr (p_name).s_enclosing,
          f_encl_descr (p_env),
          p_env)
   ELSE FALSE
   FI;

FUNCTION f_own_entry1 (p_task : tp_key,
                       p_encl : tp_descr,
                       p_env  : tp_env) BOOL :

   IF p_encl = c_unaccessible_descr THEN
      FALSE
   ELSE IF p_encl.s_key = p_task THEN
      TRUE
   ELSE f_own_entry1 (p_task,
                      f_encl_descr1 (p_encl,
                                     p_env),
                      p_env)
   FI FI;

FUNCTION f_parameters (p_descr : tp_descr) tp_descr_list:

      % The list of parameters of an entry (family) - or subprogram.

   CASE c_den : p_descr.s_den OF
   IS tp_subpr : f_parameters1 (c_den.s_spec);
   IS tp_entry : c_den.s_params;
   IS tp_entry_family : c_empty_descrs
   OUT (c_empty_descrs CONDITION FALSE MESSAGE "compiler error")
   ESAC;

FUNCTION f_parameters1 (p_header : tp_header) tp_descr_list:

   CASE c_header : p_header OF
   IS tp_function : c_header.s_params;
   IS tp_procedure : c_header.s_params;
   IS tp_entry_family : (c_header.s_entry.s_params
                         CONDITION FALSE MESSAGE "compiler error");
   IS tp_entry : (c_header.s_params CONDITION FALSE
                                     MESSAGE "compiler error")
   ESAC;

FUNCTION f_parent_base_type (p_type : tp_key,
                             p_env  : tp_env) tp_key:

      % The origin type of p_type, i.e. not a subtype and not a
      % derived type.

   CASE c_den : f_select_by_key (p_type, p_env).s_den OF
   IS tp_type_den : CASE c_type : c_den.s_type OF
                    IS tp_derived : f_parent_base_type
                                       (c_type.s_parent_type,
                                        p_env);
```

```
                IS tp_constrained: f_parent_base_type
                                      (c_type.s_base_type,
                                       p_env)
                OUT p_type
                ESAC;
   IS tp_constrained : f_parent_base_type
                        (c_den.s_base_type,
                         p_env)
   OUT c_error_type_key
   ESAC;

FUNCTION f_parent_base_type1 (p_type : tp_type,
                              p_env  : tp_env) tp_type :

   CASE c_type : p_type OF
   IS tp_derived       :
      f_parent_base_type2 (c_type.s_parent_type, p_env);
   IS tp_constrained :
      f_parent_base_type2 (c_type.s_base_type, p_env)
   OUT c_type
   ESAC;


FUNCTION f_parent_base_type2 (p_type : tp_key,
                              p_env  : tp_env) tp_type :

   f_type (f_parent_base_type (p_type, p_env),
          p_env);

      %*************************************************************%
      %                                                             %
      %       f_prev_def...                                         %
      %                                                             %
      %       Yield the key corresponding to a description          %
      %       of a previous declaration for p_designator, if        %
      %       such a declaration exists, otherwise generate         %
      %       a new key.                                            %
      %                                                             %
      %*************************************************************%

FUNCTION f_prev_def (p_designator : tp_designator,
                     p_nature     : tp_nature,
                     p_local      : tp_descr_list) tp_key:

   IF EMPTY (p_local) THEN
      f_gen_key
   ELSE IF HEAD (p_local).s_designator = p_designator AND
          CASE p_nature OF
          sc_type : sc_subtype :
             HEAD (p_local).s_state = sc_incomplete OR
            (HEAD (p_local).s_state = sc_incompl_private);
          sc_constant : HEAD (p_local).s_state = sc_deferred;
          sc_package : HEAD (p_local).s_nature = sc_package AND
                      (HEAD (p_local).s_state = sc_spec_complete)
                  AND (HEAD (p_local).s_nature = sc_package)
                   OR IF HEAD (p_local).s_den IS tp_package THEN
                         NOT HEAD (p_local).s_den QUA tp_package
                                          .s_body_prov
                      ELSE FALSE
                      FI
```

```
        OUT FALSE
        ESAC THEN
    HEAD (p_local).s_key
  ELSE f_prev_def (p_designator,
                   p_nature,
                   TAIL (p_local))
  FI FI;

FUNCTION f_prev_defs (p_designators : tp_designator_list,
                      p_nature      : tp_nature,
                      p_env         : tp_env)
                     tp_key_list:

  IF EMPTY (p_designators) THEN
     c_empty_keys
  ELSE tp_key_list
          (f_prev_def
              (HEAD (p_designators),
               p_nature,
               f_local (p_env)))
                       +
       f_prev_defs (TAIL (p_designators),
                    p_nature,
                    p_env)
  FI;

FUNCTION f_prev_def_entry (p_allowed : tp_descr_set,
                           p_params  : tp_descr_list,
                           p_env     : tp_env) tp_descr_set :

  IF f_is_error_or_empty (p_allowed) THEN
     c_error_descr_set
  ELSE f_descr_set3
        (f_prev_def_entry1 (p_allowed.s_descrs,
                            p_params,
                            p_env))
  FI;

FUNCTION f_prev_def_entry1 (p_allowed : tp_descr_list,
                            p_params  : tp_descr_list,
                            p_env     : tp_env) tp_descr_list :

  IF EMPTY (p_allowed) THEN
     c_empty_descrs
  ELSE CASE c_den : HEAD (p_allowed).s_den OF
       IS tp_entry : IF f_same_params
                          (p_params,
                           f_parameters (HEAD (p_allowed))) THEN
                        tp_descr_list (HEAD (p_allowed))
                     ELSE c_empty_descrs
                     FI
       OUT c_empty_descrs
       ESAC +
       f_prev_def_entry1 (TAIL (p_allowed), p_params, p_env)
  FI;

FUNCTION f_prev_def_generic (p_designator : tp_designator,
                             p_nature     : tp_nature,
                             p_env        : tp_env)
                            tp_key_list:
```

```
   f_prev_def_generic1 (p_designator,p_nature,f_local (p_env));

FUNCTION f_prev_def_generic1 (p_designator : tp_designator,
                              p_nature     : tp_nature,
                              p_local      : tp_descr_list)
                             tp_key_list:

   IF EMPTY (p_local) THEN
      f_gen_keys
   ELSE IF p_designator =/ HEAD (p_local).s_designator THEN
        f_prev_def_generic1 (p_designator,
                             p_nature,
                             TAIL (p_local))
   ELSE IF (HEAD (p_local).s_den IS tp_generic) AND
           (HEAD (p_local).s_nature = p_nature) THEN
      tp_key_list (HEAD (p_local).s_key)
   ELSE f_gen_keys
   FI FI FI;

FUNCTION f_prev_def_subpr (p_designator : tp_designator,
                           p_old_key    : tp_key_list,
                           p_spec       : tp_header,
                           p_local      : tp_descr_list)
                          tp_key_list :

   IF EMPTY (p_local) THEN
      p_old_key
   ELSE IF HEAD (p_local).s_designator =/ p_designator THEN
      f_prev_def_subpr
         (p_designator,
          p_old_key,
          p_spec,
          TAIL (p_local))
   ELSE CASE c_den: HEAD (p_local).s_den OF
      IS tp_subpr : IF f_same_subpr_spec
                          (c_den.s_spec,
                           p_spec) AND
                       (HEAD (p_local).s_state = sc_spec_complete)
                    THEN tp_key_list
                             (HEAD (p_local).s_key)
                 ELSE f_prev_def_subpr
                          (p_designator,
                           p_old_key,
                           p_spec,
                           TAIL (p_local))
                 FI;
      IS tp_generic : (p_old_key
                       %C 6.3/2
                       CONDITION FALSE  MESSAGE
                          "generic body doesn't match gen decl");
      IS tp_entry_family : p_old_key;
      IS tp_entry : f_prev_def_subpr
                       (p_designator,
                        p_old_key,
                        p_spec,
                        TAIL (p_local))
      OUT p_old_key
      ESAC
  FI FI;
```

```
FUNCTION f_prev_def_task (p_designator : tp_designator,
                          p_env        : tp_env)
                         tp_key_list :

   f_prev_def_task1 (p_designator,
                     f_local (p_env),
                     p_env);

FUNCTION f_prev_def_task1 (p_designator : tp_designator,
                           p_local      : tp_descr_list,
                           p_env        : tp_env)
                          tp_key_list:

   IF EMPTY (p_local) THEN
      f_gen_keys
   ELSE IF HEAD (p_local).s_designator =/ p_designator THEN
      f_prev_def_task1 (p_designator,
                        TAIL (p_local),
                        p_env)
   ELSE IF (HEAD (p_local).s_state = sc_spec_complete) AND
           (HEAD (p_local).s_nature = sc_type) THEN
      tp_key_list (HEAD (p_local).s_key)
   ELSE IF HEAD (p_local).s_nature = sc_task AND
          (f_select_by_key
              (f_object_type1 (HEAD (p_local).s_den),
               p_env).s_state = sc_spec_complete) THEN
      tp_key_list (f_object_type1 (HEAD (p_local).s_den))
   ELSE f_prev_def_task1 (p_designator,
                          TAIL (p_local),
                          p_env)
   FI FI FI FI;

FUNCTION f_private_from_same_decl_part (p_type : tp_type,
                                        p_env  : tp_env) BOOL :

      % Check, whether p_type is a (limited) private type declared
      % in the current declarative part and the actual declarative
      % part is the visible part of a package (not e.g. a generic
      % parameter list)

   CASE c_type : p_type OF
   IS tp_constrained :
      CASE c_type1 : f_type (c_type.s_base_type, p_env) OF
      IS tp_private : IS tp_l_private :
         f_select_by_key (c_type.s_base_type, p_env).s_enclosing
         = f_enclosing (p_env)
         AND (f_encl_state (p_env) = sc_in_visible)
      OUT FALSE
      ESAC
   OUT FALSE
   ESAC;

FUNCTION f_range_constr (p_type : tp_descr,
                         p_env  : tp_env) tp_range :

      % The range of p_type, if p_type has a range or accuracy
      % constraint or is a numeric type.

   CASE c_den : p_type.s_den OF
```

```
  IS tp_constrained :
     CASE c_constr  : c_den.s_constraint OF
     IS tp_fixed    : c_constr.s_range;
     IS tp_float    : c_constr.s_range;
     IS tp_range_constr :  c_constr
     OUT f_range_constr
           (f_select_by_key (c_den.s_base_type,
                                   p_env),
            p_env)
     ESAC;
  IS tp_type_den :
     CASE c_type    : c_den.s_type OF
     IS tp_fixed    : c_type.s_range;
     IS tp_float    : c_type.s_range;
     IS tp_integer  : c_type.s_range
     OUT tp_range (sc_void)
     ESAC
  OUT tp_range (sc_void)
  ESAC;

FUNCTION f_range_type (p_range : tp_dscrt_range,
                       p_env   : tp_env) tp_key:

     % The base type of p_range.

  CASE c_range : p_range OF
  IS tp_constrained : c_range.s_base_type;
  IS tp_range : f_base_type1
                  (f_object_type
                     (f_head_descr
                        (c_range
                           QUA tp_range_constr.s_upper_bound)),
                      p_env);
  IS tp_index : c_range.s_type.s_base_type
  ESAC;

FUNCTION f_recent_local (p_old_env,
                         p_new_env : tp_env) tp_descr_list:

     % local (new_env) - local (old_env)
     % E.g. used to gain the list of non-generic parameters
     % in a generic subprogram declaration (all parameters
     % - generic parameters) or the list of declarations in
     % the private part of a package (all declarations - visible part)

  f_recent_local1 (f_local (p_old_env),
                   f_local (p_new_env));

FUNCTION f_recent_local1 (p_old_local  : tp_descr_list,
                          p_new_local  : tp_descr_list) tp_descr_list:
  IF EMPTY (p_old_local)
     THEN p_new_local
  ELSE f_recent_local1 (TAIL (p_old_local), TAIL (p_new_local))
  FI;

FUNCTION f_rep_state (p_key : tp_key,
                      p_env : tp_env) tp_rep_state :

  f_repr (p_key, p_env).s_rep_state;
```

```
FUNCTION f_repr (p_key : tp_key,
                 p_env : tp_env) tp_repr :

   f_select_by_key (p_key, p_env).s_repr;

FUNCTION f_repr_spec_init (p_entity : tp_descr_set,
                           p_attr   : SYMB,
                           p_env    : tp_env) tp_init :

      % Evaluate the representations attribute p_attr of p_entity.

   f_repr_spec_init1
      (p_entity,
       f_reps
         (CASE p_attr OF
          'position' : 'first_bit' : 'last_bit' :
             f_head_descr (p_entity).s_enclosing
          OUT f_head_descr (p_entity).s_key
          ESAC,
          p_env),
      p_attr);

FUNCTION f_repr_spec_init1 (p_record_comp : tp_descr_set,
                            p_reps        : tp_rep_list,
                            p_attr        : SYMB) tp_init :

   IF EMPTY (p_reps)
      THEN c_init
   ELSE CASE c_rep : HEAD (p_reps) OF
        IS tp_length_spec :
           IF  CASE c_rep.s_kind OF
               sc_obj_size : (p_attr = 'size');
               sc_collection_size : sc_task_size :
                  (p_attr = 'storage_size');
               sc_actual_delta :(p_attr = 'actual_delta')
               ESAC THEN
               f_object_init (c_rep.s_val)
           ELSE f_repr_spec_init1 (p_record_comp,
                                   TAIL (p_reps),
                                   p_attr)
           FI;
        IS tp_enum_rep :
           f_repr_spec_init1 (p_record_comp,
                              TAIL (p_reps),
                              p_attr);
        IS tp_record_rep :
           CASE p_attr OF
           'position' : 'first_bit' : 'last_bit' :
              f_repr_spec_init2
                (f_head_descr (p_record_comp).s_key,
                 c_rep.s_comp_reps,
                 p_attr)
           OUT f_repr_spec_init1 (p_record_comp,
                                  TAIL (p_reps),
                                  p_attr)
           ESAC;
        IS tp_address_spec :
           IF p_attr = 'address' THEN
              f_object_init (c_rep.s_address)
           ELSE f_repr_spec_init1
```

```
                (p_record_comp,
                 TAIL (p_reps),
                 p_attr)
          FI
        OUT c_init
        ESAC
   FI;

FUNCTION f_repr_spec_init2 (p_record_comp : tp_key,
                           p_comp_reps  : tp_comp_rep_list,
                           p_attr : SYMB) tp_init :

   IF EMPTY (p_comp_reps) THEN
      c_init
   ELSE IF HEAD (p_comp_reps).s_comp = p_record_comp THEN
      CASE p_attr OF
      'position'  : f_object_init
                    (HEAD (p_comp_reps).s_relative);
      'first_bit' : f_object_init
                    (HEAD (p_comp_reps).s_range_constr
                 .s_lower_bound);
      'last_bit'  : f_object_init
                    (HEAD (p_comp_reps).s_range_constr
                 .s_upper_bound)
      OUT (c_init CONDITION FALSE MESSAGE "compiler error")
      ESAC
   ELSE f_repr_spec_init2 (p_record_comp,
                           TAIL (p_comp_reps),
                           p_attr)
   FI FI;

FUNCTION f_repr_state_constr (p_constrained : tp_constrained,
                              p_env         : tp_env) tp_rep_state :

     % The representation state of the base type of p_constrained,
     % but not static_rep, if the constraint of p_constraint
     % is not static.

   f_new_repr_state1
      (IF ch_static_constraint (p_constrained.s_constraint) THEN
         sc_static_rep
       ELSE sc_dynamic_rep
       FI,
       f_rep_state (p_constrained.s_base_type, p_env));

FUNCTION f_reps (p_key : tp_key,
                 p_env : tp_env) tp_rep_list :

   f_repr (p_key, p_env).s_reps;


FUNCTION f_result (p_descr : tp_descr) tp_constrained :

   CASE c_den : p_descr.s_den OF
   IS tp_subpr  : f_result1 (c_den.s_spec);
   IS tp_entry  : c_no_type
   OUT c_no_type
   ESAC;

FUNCTION f_result1 (p_header : tp_header) tp_constrained :
```

```
   CASE c_header : p_header OF
   IS tp_function : c_header.s_result
   OUT c_no_type
   ESAC;

FUNCTION f_same_choice_types (p_type     : tp_key,
                              p_choices  : tp_choice_list,
                              p_env      : tp_env) BOOL:

     % Check, whether all p_choices are of the type p_type.
     % The choice OTHERS does not appear in p_choices;
     % it is previously expanded.

   IF EMPTY (p_choices) THEN
      TRUE
   ELSE f_same_choice_types (p_type,
                             TAIL (p_choices),
                             p_env) AND
        f_implicitly_convertable1
            (f_object_type1
                (HEAD (p_choices) QUA tp_descr.s_den),
             p_type,
             p_env)
   FI;

FUNCTION f_same_constrained (p_constrained1,
                             p_constrained2 : tp_constrained) BOOL:

   (p_constrained1.s_base_type  =  p_constrained2.s_base_type) AND
   f_tree_same_constraint (p_constrained1.s_constraint,
                           p_constrained2.s_constraint);

FUNCTION f_same_default (p_init1,
                         p_init2 : tp_init) BOOL :

   IF p_init1 = c_no_init OR (p_init2= c_no_init) THEN
      p_init1 = p_init2
   ELSE f_tree_same_value (p_init1.s_value,
                           p_init2.s_value)
   FI;

FUNCTION f_same_param (p_param1,
                       p_param2 : tp_descr) BOOL :

  ((p_param1.s_designator = p_param2.s_designator AND
   (p_param1.s_nature     = p_param2.s_nature))   AND
   f_same_constrained (p_param1.s_den QUA tp_object.s_type,
                       p_param2.s_den QUA tp_object.s_type)) AND
   f_same_default (p_param1.s_den QUA tp_object.s_init,
                   p_param2.s_den QUA tp_object.s_init);

FUNCTION f_same_params (p_params1,
                        p_params2 : tp_descr_list) BOOL :

   IF EMPTY (p_params1) AND EMPTY (p_params2) THEN
      TRUE
   ELSE IF EMPTY (p_params1) OR EMPTY (p_params2) THEN
      FALSE
   ELSE f_same_param (HEAD (p_params1), HEAD (p_params2)) AND
```

```
      f_same_params (TAIL (p_params1), TAIL (p_params2))
  FI FI;

FUNCTION f_same_subpr_spec (p_spec1,
                            p_spec2 : tp_header) BOOL:

    % Check that the specification of a body is equivalent to a
    % previously given specification.

  CASE c_spec1 : p_spec1 OF
  IS tp_function :
     CASE c_spec2 : p_spec2 OF
     IS tp_function :
        f_same_params (c_spec1.s_params,
                       c_spec2.s_params) AND
        f_same_constrained (c_spec1.s_result,
                            c_spec2.s_result);
     IS tp_procedure : IS tp_entry : IS tp_entry_family : FALSE
     ESAC;
  IS tp_procedure :
     CASE c_spec2 : p_spec2 OF
     IS tp_function : IS tp_entry_family : IS tp_entry : FALSE;
     IS tp_procedure : f_same_params (c_spec1.s_params,
                                      c_spec2.s_params)
     ESAC;
  IS tp_entry :
  IS tp_entry_family : FALSE
  ESAC;

FUNCTION f_same_type (p_descrs : tp_descrs_list,
                      p_env   : tp_env) tp_key:

    % The intersection of the sets of types of objects denoted
    % by the descr_sets of p_descrs.

  IF EMPTY (f_same_type1 (p_descrs, p_env)) THEN
     c_error_type_key
  ELSE (HEAD (f_same_type1 (p_descrs, p_env))
       CONDITION EMPTY (TAIL (f_same_type1 (p_descrs, p_env)))
          MESSAGE "ambiguous range")
  FI;

FUNCTION f_same_type1 (p_descrs : tp_descrs_list,
                       p_env   : tp_env) tp_key_list:
  IF EMPTY (TAIL (p_descrs))
     THEN f_expand_additional_to_keys
            (HEAD (p_descrs).s_descrs,
             HEAD (p_descrs).s_add,
             p_env)
  ELSE f_intersect_types
          (f_expand_additional_to_keys
              (HEAD (p_descrs).s_descrs,
               HEAD (p_descrs).s_add,
               p_env),
           f_same_type1
              (TAIL (p_descrs),
               p_env),
           p_env)
  FI;
```

```
FUNCTION f_same_type2 (p_type1, p_type2   : tp_key,
                       p_env              : tp_env)
                      tp_key_list :

   IF f_implicitly_convertable1 (p_type1, p_type2, p_env) THEN
      tp_key_list (p_type2)
   ELSE IF f_implicitly_convertable1 (p_type2, p_type1, p_env) THEN
      tp_key_list (p_type1)
   ELSE c_empty_keys
   FI FI;

FUNCTION f_same_type3 (p_descrs : tp_descrs_list,
                       p_env    : tp_env) tp_key:

    % Check that the intersection of types of values denoted by
    % the descr_sets of p_descrs consists of exactly one element.

   IF EMPTY (f_same_type1 (p_descrs,p_env)) THEN
      (c_error_type_key CONDITION FALSE MESSAGE "no common type")
   ELSE (HEAD (f_same_type1 (p_descrs,p_env))
        CONDITION EMPTY (TAIL (f_same_type1 (p_descrs,p_env)))
        MESSAGE "ambiguous type")
   FI;

FUNCTION f_select_assoc (p_designator : tp_designator,
                         p_key        : tp_key,
                         p_assocs     : tp_assoc_list)
                        tp_comp_assoc_void :

    % Select an association from p_assocs whitc has a choice denotin
    % an entity with p_designator or p_key. If no such association
    % exists in p_assocs return sc_void.

   IF EMPTY (p_assocs) THEN
      sc_void
   ELSE IF f_desig_key_in_choices (p_designator,
                                   p_key,
                                   HEAD (p_assocs) QUA tp_comp_assoc
                                          s_choices) THEN
      HEAD (p_assocs) QUA tp_comp_assoc
   ELSE f_select_assoc (p_designator, p_key, TAIL (p_assocs))
   FI FI;

FUNCTION f_select_by_type (p_type   : tp_key,
                           p_descrs : tp_descr_list) tp_descr_list:

    % Select all descriprions from p_descrs which denote an object
    % of p_type.

   IF EMPTY (p_descrs) THEN
      c_empty_descrs
   ELSE IF f_object_type (HEAD (p_descrs)) = p_type THEN
              tp_descr_list (HEAD (p_descrs))
        ELSE c_empty_descrs
        FI +
        f_select_by_type (p_type, TAIL (p_descrs))
   FI;

FUNCTION f_select_by_designator (p_designator : tp_designator,
```

```
                                          p_env        : tp_env)
                                          tp_descr_list :

     % Yield descriptions of all entities with p_designator,
     % which are directly visible (not_hidden) in p_env.

   f_select_by_designator1 (p_designator,
                            f_global (p_env) + f_local (p_env),
                            c_empty_descrs,
                            p_env);

FUNCTION f_select_by_designator0 (p_designator : tp_designator,
                                  p_descrs     : tp_descr_list,
                                  p_env        : tp_env)
                                  tp_descr_list :

   f_select_by_designator1 (p_designator,
                            p_descrs,
                            c_empty_descrs,
                            p_env);

FUNCTION f_select_by_designator00 (p_designator : tp_designator,
                                   p_descrs     : tp_descr_list,
                                   p_env        : tp_env)
                                   tp_descr_list :

   IF EMPTY (f_select_by_designator0 (p_designator,p_descrs,p_env))
      THEN c_error_descr_list
   ELSE f_select_by_designator0 (p_designator, p_descrs,p_env)
   FI;

FUNCTION f_select_by_designator1 (p_designator : tp_designator,
                                  p_descrs,
                                  p_found      : tp_descr_list,
                                  p_env        : tp_env)
                                  tp_descr_list :

  IF EMPTY (p_descrs) THEN
     p_found
  ELSE IF p_designator =/ LAST (p_descrs).s_designator THEN
     f_select_by_designator1
        (p_designator,
         FRONT (p_descrs),
         p_found,
         p_env)
  ELSE IF f_is_overloadable (LAST (p_descrs)) THEN
     IF IF (LAST (p_descrs).s_den IS tp_enum_literal) OR
           (LAST (p_descrs).s_den IS tp_operation) THEN
           TRUE
        ELSE f_overloadable
               (f_spec (LAST (p_descrs)),
                p_found,
                f_is_operator
                   (LAST (p_descrs).s_designator),
                p_env)
        FI THEN
        f_select_by_designator1
           (p_designator,
            FRONT (p_descrs),
```

```
            tp_descr_list (LAST (p_descrs)) + p_found,
            p_env)
       ELSE f_select_by_designator1
              (p_designator,
               FRONT (p_descrs),
               p_found,
               p_env)
       FI
    ELSE IF EMPTY (p_found) THEN
           tp_descr_list (LAST (p_descrs))
    ELSE p_found
    FI FI FI FI;

FUNCTION f_select_by_designator2 (p_designator   : tp_designator,
                                  p_descrs       : tp_descr_list)
                                 tp_descr_list:

    IF EMPTY (p_descrs) THEN
       c_empty_descrs
    ELSE IF HEAD (p_descrs).s_designator = p_designator THEN
           tp_descr_list (HEAD (p_descrs))
         ELSE c_empty_descrs
         FI +
         f_select_by_designator2 (p_designator,
                                  TAIL (p_descrs))
    FI;

FUNCTION f_select_by_key (p_key : tp_key,
                          p_env : tp_env) tp_descr :

       % Yield the unique description in p_env with p_key.
       % For a pointer implementation of tp_key, this function
       % implements dereferencing.

    CASE c_descr : f_select_by_key1 (p_key, f_local (p_env) +
                                     f_global (p_env)) OF
    IS tp_descr : c_descr;
    IS tp_void  : (c_error_type_descr CONDITION FALSE
                                      MESSAGE "compiler error")
    ESAC;

FUNCTION f_select_by_keys (p_keys : tp_key_list,
                           p_env  : tp_env) tp_descr_list :

    IF EMPTY (p_keys) THEN
       c_empty_descrs
    ELSE tp_descr_list (f_select_by_key (HEAD (p_keys), p_env)) +
       f_select_by_keys (TAIL (p_keys), p_env)
    FI;

FUNCTION f_select_by_key1 (p_key    : tp_key,
                           p_descrs : tp_descr_list) tp_descr_void:

    IF EMPTY (p_descrs) THEN
       sc_void
    ELSE IF HEAD (p_descrs).s_key = p_key THEN
       HEAD (p_descrs)
    ELSE f_select_by_key1
           (p_key,
            CASE c_den : HEAD (p_descrs).s_den OF
```

```
           IS tp_generic :
              c_den.s_generic_params +
              CASE c_generic : c_den.s_den OF
              IS tp_subpr : f_make_local (c_generic);
              IS tp_package : c_generic.s_visible
              OUT c_empty_descrs
              ESAC;
           IS tp_subpr    : f_make_local (c_den);
           IS tp_package  : c_den.s_visible;
           IS tp_type_den : CASE c_type : c_den.s_type OF
                            IS tp_task_spec : c_type.s_visible;
                            IS tp_record : c_type.s_descrs;
                            IS tp_incompl_type :
                               c_type.s_discriminants;
                            IS tp_private : c_type.s_discriminants;
                            IS tp_l_private :
                               c_type.s_discriminants
                            OUT c_empty_descrs
                            ESAC;
           IS tp_entry : c_den.s_params;
           IS tp_entry_family : c_den.s_entry.s_params
           OUT c_empty_descrs
           ESAC +
           TAIL (p_descrs))
   FI FI;

FUNCTION f_select_by_key11 (p_key    : tp_key,
                            p_descrs : tp_descr_list) tp_descr :

   IF EMPTY (p_descrs) THEN
      c_error_descr
   ELSE IF HEAD (p_descrs).s_key = p_key THEN
      HEAD (p_descrs)
   ELSE f_select_by_key11 (p_key, TAIL (p_descrs))
   FI FI;

FUNCTION f_select_descr (p_key    : tp_key,
                         p_descrs : tp_descr_list)
                         tp_descr :

   IF HEAD (p_descrs).s_key = p_key THEN
      HEAD (p_descrs)
   ELSE f_select_descr (p_key, TAIL (p_descrs))
   FI;

FUNCTION f_select_discrs (p_discrs : tp_descr_list,
                          p_assocs : tp_assoc_list,
                          p_env    : tp_env)
                          tp_descr_list_void :

     % Returns the list of discriminants (p_discrs), where the
     % initial values are adjusted to the associated values
     % in p_assocs, provided that p_assocs contains associations
     % for all of p_discrs. Else the result is sc_void.

   IF EMPTY (p_discrs) THEN
      p_discrs
   ELSE IF EMPTY (p_assocs) THEN
      sc_void
   ELSE CASE c_actual :
```

```
          CASE c_assoc :
                 IF EMPTY (HEAD (p_assocs)
                             QUA tp_comp_assoc .s_choices) THEN
                   HEAD (p_assocs) QUA tp_comp_assoc
                 ELSE f_select_assoc
                        (HEAD (p_discrs).s_designator,
                         HEAD (p_discrs).s_key,
                         p_assocs)
                 FI OF
          IS tp_void : sc_void;
          IS tp_comp_assoc :
             f_make_void_descrs
               (f_valid_descr_set
                  (c_assoc.s_actual,
                   f_object_type (HEAD (p_discrs)),
                   p_env))
          ESAC OF
     IS tp_void : sc_void;
     IS tp_descr_set :
        CASE c_assocs :
             f_select_discrs
               (TAIL (p_discrs),
                IF EMPTY (HEAD (p_assocs)
                            QUA tp_comp_assoc.s_choices) THEN
                  TAIL (p_assocs)
                ELSE p_assocs
                FI,
                p_env) OF
        IS tp_void : tp_descr_list_void (sc_void);
        IS tp_descr_list :
           tp_descr_list
             (f_temp_descr
                (HEAD (p_discrs).s_designator,
                 HEAD (p_discrs).s_key,
                 HEAD (p_discrs).s_repr,
                 HEAD (p_discrs).s_state,
                 HEAD (p_discrs).s_nature,
                 f_head_descr (c_actual).s_den,
                 HEAD (p_discrs).s_enclosing))   +
           c_assocs
        ESAC
     ESAC
  FI FI;

FUNCTION f_select_dummy_aggr (p_descrs : tp_descr_list)
                              tp_den :

  IF EMPTY (p_descrs) THEN
     sc_void
  ELSE CASE c_den : HEAD (p_descrs).s_den OF
     IS tp_dummy_aggr : c_den
     OUT f_select_dummy_aggr (TAIL (p_descrs))
     ESAC
  FI;

FUNCTION f_select_generic_assoc (p_key    : tp_key,
                                 p_assocs : tp_assoc_list) tp_descr:

  IF EMPTY (p_assocs) THEN
     c_error_descr
```

```
ELSE IF p_key =
        HEAD (HEAD (p_assocs) QUA tp_comp_assoc.s_choices)
            QUA tp_descr.s_key THEN
    f_head_descr (HEAD (p_assocs) QUA tp_comp_assoc .s_actual)
ELSE f_select_generic_assoc (p_key,
                             TAIL (p_assocs))
FI FI;

    %******************************************************************%
    %                                                                  %
    %        f_seclect_record...                                       %
    %                                                                  %
    %        Build a record description without variant parts          %
    %        using the values of discriminants to select the           %
    %        appropriate variants.                                     %
    %                                                                  %
    %******************************************************************%

FUNCTION f_select_record_comps (p_discrs : tp_descr_list,
                                p_comps  : tp_comp_list,
                                p_env    : tp_env)
                               tp_descr_list_void :

  IF EMPTY (p_comps) THEN
    c_empty_descrs
  ELSE CASE c_comp : f_select_record_comp
                      (p_discrs,
                       HEAD (p_comps),
                       p_env) OF
      IS tp_void : sc_void
      OUT CASE c_variants : f_select_record_comps
                             (p_discrs,
                              TAIL (p_comps),
                              p_env) OF
          IS tp_void : tp_descr_list_void (sc_void);
          IS tp_descr_list : c_comp QUA tp_descr_list + c_variants
          ESAC
      ESAC
  FI;

FUNCTION f_select_record_comp (p_discrs : tp_descr_list,
                               p_comp   : tp_comp,
                               p_env    : tp_env)
                              tp_descr_list_void :

  CASE c_comp : p_comp OF
  IS tp_void : c_empty_descrs;
  IS tp_descr_list : (c_empty_descrs CONDITION FALSE
                                      MESSAGE "compiler error");
  IS tp_descr : IF c_comp.s_nature = sc_type OR
                   (c_comp.s_nature = sc_subtype) THEN
                  c_empty_descrs
                ELSE tp_descr_list (c_comp)
                FI;
  IS tp_variant_part : CASE c_comps : f_select_record_variant
                                        (c_comp,
                                         p_discrs,
                                         p_env) OF
                         IS tp_void : sc_void;
                         IS tp_comp_list : f_select_record_comps
```

```
                                                  (p_discrs,
                                                   c_comps,
                                                   p_env)
                              ESAC
   ESAC;

FUNCTION f_select_record_variant (p_variant_part : tp_variant_part,
                                  p_discrs       : tp_descr_list,
                                  p_env          : tp_env)
                                 tp_comp_list_void :

   f_select_record_variant1
      (f_select_by_key1
         (p_variant_part.s_discr,
          p_discrs) QUA tp_descr,
       p_variant_part.s_variants,
       p_env);

FUNCTION f_select_record_variant1 (p_value    : tp_descr,
                                   p_variants : tp_variant_list,
                                   p_env      : tp_env)
                                  tp_comp_list_void :

   IF EMPTY (p_variants) THEN
      (sc_void CONDITION FALSE MESSAGE "invalid discriminant value")
   ELSE IF NOT f_is_static_descr (p_value) THEN
      (sc_void CONDITION FALSE
               MESSAGE "static expression required")
   ELSE IF f_value_in_choices (p_value,
                               HEAD (p_variants).s_choices,
                               p_env) THEN
      HEAD (p_variants).s_comps
   ELSE f_select_record_variant1 (p_value,
                                  TAIL (p_variants),
                                  p_env)
   FI FI FI;

FUNCTION f_select_with_use (p_designator        : tp_designator,
                            p_otherwise_visible : tp_descr_list,
                            p_imported          : tp_descr_list,
                            p_env               : tp_env)
                           tp_descr_list :

      % Identification under cosideration of use clauses :
      % Add to p_otherwise_visible those entities of p_imported,
      % which do not conflict with an entity contained in
      % p_otherwise visible (according to the rules of use clauses,
      % chapter 8.4 [Ada80]).

   IF IF EMPTY (p_otherwise_visible) THEN
         FALSE
      ELSE NOT f_only_enums_or_subprs (p_otherwise_visible)
      FI THEN
      c_empty_descrs
   ELSE IF EMPTY (p_imported) THEN
         p_imported
   ELSE IF p_designator = HEAD (p_imported).s_designator THEN
         IF NOT f_is_overloadable (HEAD (p_imported)) THEN
            IF EMPTY (p_otherwise_visible) THEN
               tp_descr_list (HEAD (p_imported))
```

```
            ELSE c_empty_descrs
            FI
         ELSE CASE c_den : HEAD (p_imported).s_den OF
              IS tp_enum_literal :
                 IF EMPTY (p_otherwise_visible) OR
                    c_den.s_char THEN
                    tp_descr_list (HEAD (p_imported))
                 ELSE c_empty_descrs
                 FI;
              IS tp_subpr :
                 IF f_overloadable
                       (c_den.s_spec,
                        p_otherwise_visible,
                        TRUE,
                        p_env) THEN
                    tp_descr_list (HEAD (p_imported))
                 ELSE c_empty_descrs
                 FI
              OUT (c_empty_descrs CONDITION FALSE
                                  MESSAGE "compiler error")
              ESAC
         FI
      ELSE c_empty_descrs
      FI +
      f_select_with_use
         (p_designator,
          p_otherwise_visible,
          TAIL (p_imported),
          p_env)
   FI FI;

FUNCTION f_spec (p_descr : tp_descr) tp_header:

     % The specification of a subprogram or an entry.
     % Entry specifications are transformed to procedure
     % specifications (to be compatible with procedures e.g. in the
     % case of renaming).

   f_spec1 (p_descr.s_den);

FUNCTION f_spec1 (p_den : tp_den)
              tp_header :

   CASE c_den : p_den OF
   IS tp_subpr           : c_den.s_spec;
   IS tp_entry_family    : c_den;
   IS tp_entry           : tp_procedure (c_den.s_params);
   IS tp_generic         : f_spec1 (c_den.s_den);
   IS tp_void            : (c_error_header CONDITION FALSE
                              MESSAGE "name is not yet usable")
   OUT (c_error_header CONDITION FALSE MESSAGE "compiler error")
   ESAC;

FUNCTION f_standard_descr (p_designator : tp_designator,
                           p_key        : tp_key,
                           p_nature     : tp_nature,
                           p_den        : tp_den) tp_descr :

    % Build a description for the standard environment.
```

```
   f_descr (p_designator,
            p_key,
            c_start_repr,
            sc_complete,
            p_nature,
            p_den,
            c_standard);

FUNCTION f_standard_function1 (p_function     : tp_key,
                               p_param_type,
                               p_result_type  : tp_constrained,
                               p_op           : tp_op) tp_subpr:

   tp_subpr
     (tp_function
         (tp_descr_list
            (f_descr (c_x_desi,
                      f_gen_key,
                      c_start_repr,
                      sc_complete,
                      sc_in,
                      tp_object (p_param_type,
                                 c_no_init),
                      p_function)),
          p_result_type),
      sc_void,
      p_op);

FUNCTION f_standard_function2 (p_function     : tp_key,
                               p_param_type1,
                               p_param_type2,
                               p_result_type  : tp_constrained,
                               p_op           : tp_op) tp_subpr:
   tp_subpr
     (tp_function
        (tp_descr_list
          (f_descr (c_x_desi,
                    f_gen_key,
                    c_start_repr,
                    sc_complete,
                    sc_in,
                    tp_object (p_param_type1, c_no_init),
                    p_function),
           f_descr (c_y_desi,
                    f_gen_key,
                    c_start_repr,
                    sc_complete,
                    sc_in,
                    tp_object (p_param_type2, c_no_init),
                    p_function)),
      p_result_type),
     sc_void,
     p_op);

FUNCTION f_subpr_list (p_keys  : tp_key_list,
                       p_env   : tp_env) tp_descr_list:

     % tp_key_list -> tp_descr_list

   IF EMPTY (p_keys) THEN
```

```
    c_empty_descrs
  ELSE tp_descr_list (f_select_by_key (HEAD (p_keys), p_env)) +
       f_subpr_list (TAIL (p_keys), p_env)
  FI;

FUNCTION f_subprs_in_decl_part (p_descrs : tp_descr_list,
                                p_encl   : tp_key)
                               tp_descr_list :

    % All descriptions of subprograms in p_descr, which are declared
    % in the declarative part of p_encl.

  IF EMPTY (p_descrs) THEN
    p_descrs
  ELSE IF HEAD (p_descrs).s_den IS tp_subpr AND
         (HEAD (p_descrs).s_enclosing = p_encl) THEN
          tp_descr_list (HEAD (p_descrs))
       ELSE tp_descr_list ()
       FI  +
       f_subprs_in_decl_part (TAIL (p_descrs), p_encl)
  FI;

FUNCTION f_subtr_n (p_list : tp_key_list,
                    p_n    : INT) tp_key_list :

    % Delete the first p_n elements from p_list.

  IF p_n = 0 THEN
    p_list
  ELSE f_subtr_n (TAIL (p_list), p_n - 1)
  FI;

FUNCTION f_symb_string (p_string : SYMB) tp_string_val :

  tp_string_val ();                         %% EXTERNAL

FUNCTION f_task_entries (p_task : tp_descr,
                         p_env  : tp_env) tp_descr_list:

    % Entries of p_task.

  CASE c_den : p_task.s_den OF
  IS tp_object : f_task_entries
                   (f_select_by_key (c_den.s_type.s_base_type,
                                     p_env),
                 p_env);
  IS tp_type_den : c_den.s_type QUA tp_task_spec.s_visible
  OUT (c_empty_descrs CONDITION FALSE MESSAGE "compiler error")
  ESAC;

FUNCTION f_temp_descr (p_designator  : tp_designator,
                       p_key         : tp_key,
                       p_repr        : tp_repr,
                       p_state       : tp_state,
                       p_nature      : tp_nature,
                       p_den         : tp_den,
                       p_enclosing   : tp_key)
                      tp_descr :

    % cf. FUNCTION f_descr.
```

```
   tp_descr (p_designator,
             p_key,
             p_repr,
             p_state,
             p_nature,
             p_den,
             c_no_origin,
             p_enclosing);

     %************************************************************%
     %                                                            %
     %       f_tm_...                                             %
     %                                                            %
     %       Functions for type mapping, which must be            %
     %       implemented by calls target machine dependent        %
     %       modules.                                             %
     %                                                            %
     %************************************************************%

FUNCTION f_tm_map_derived (p_key      : tp_key,
                           p_user_rep : BOOL,
                           p_env      : tp_env) tp_rep_list :

   c_empty_reps;  %>MACHINE<

FUNCTION f_tm_map_subtype (p_key : tp_key,
                           p_env : tp_env) tp_rep_list:

   c_empty_reps;  %>MACHINE<

FUNCTION f_tm_map_type (p_key : tp_key,
                        p_user_rep : BOOL,
                        p_env      : tp_env) tp_rep_list :

   c_empty_reps;  %>MACHINE<

FUNCTION f_tree_same_constraint (p_constraint1,
                                 p_constraint2 : tp_constraint) BOOL

   %>INCOMPLETE<
   p_constraint1 = p_constraint2;

FUNCTION f_tree_same_value (p_value1,
                            p_value2 : tp_value) BOOL :

   %>INCOMPLTE<
   TRUE;

FUNCTION f_type (p_type : tp_key,
                 p_env  : tp_env) tp_type :

   f_type1 (f_select_by_key (p_type, p_env));

FUNCTION f_type1 (p_type : tp_descr) tp_type :

   CASE c_den : p_type.s_den OF
   IS tp_type_den : c_den.s_type;
   IS tp_constrained : tp_type (c_den)
   OUT tp_type (c_error_type)
 %
 %. . . . . . . . . . . . . . . . . . . . . . . . . . . . . . . . . . .
```

```
  ESAC;

FUNCTION f_type_den (p_type : tp_key,
                     p_env  : tp_env) tp_type_den :

  CASE c_den : f_select_by_key (p_type, p_env).s_den OF
  IS tp_type_den : c_den
  OUT c_error_type_den
  ESAC;

FUNCTION f_type_map (p_key      : tp_key,
                     p_user_rep : BOOL,
                     p_env      : tp_env) tp_rep_list:

    CASE c_den : f_select_by_key (p_key, p_env).s_den OF
    IS tp_type_den :
       CASE c_type : c_den.s_type OF
       IS tp_access : IS tp_array : IS tp_enum_type : IS tp_record :
       IS tp_fixed : IS tp_float : IS tp_integer :
          f_tm_map_type (p_key, p_user_rep, p_env);
       IS tp_constrained : f_tm_map_subtype (p_key, p_env);
       IS tp_derived : f_tm_map_derived (p_key, p_user_rep, p_env)
       OUT c_empty_reps
       ESAC;
    IS tp_subpr: CASE c_spec : c_den.s_spec OF
                 IS tp_function : f_tm_map_subtype (p_key, p_env)
                 OUT c_empty_reps
                 ESAC;
    IS tp_object : f_tm_map_subtype (p_key, p_env)
    OUT f_reps (p_key, p_env)
    ESAC;

FUNCTION f_unaccessible_descr (p_designator : tp_designator,
                               p_key        : tp_key,
                               p_nature     : tp_nature,
                               p_den        : tp_den) tp_descr :

    % Build a description for the 'unaccessible' environment.

  f_descr (p_designator,
           p_key,
           tp_repr (sc_static_rep, tp_rep_list ()),
           sc_complete,
           p_nature,
           p_den,
           c_unaccessible);

FUNCTION f_univ_to_int (p_constr : tp_constrained,
                        p_env    : tp_env)
                       tp_constrained :

    % If p_constr is universal integer, convert it to integer.

  IF p_constr.s_base_type = c_univ_int THEN
     tp_constrained
        (c_int,
         tp_range_constr
            (f_valid_descr_set
                (p_constr.s_constraint QUA tp_range_constr
                    .s_lower_bound,
```

```
                c_int,
                p_env),
            f_valid_descr_set
               (p_constr.s_constraint QUA tp_range_constr
                   .s_upper_bound,
                c_int,
                p_env)))
   ELSE p_constr
   FI;

FUNCTION f_universal (p_descrs : tp_descr_list)
                      tp_descr_list :

     % If p_descrs contain the description of a value of a universal
     % (integer/real) type, then select all universal values from
     % p_descrs, else return all p_descrs.

   IF NOT f_is_universal (p_descrs) THEN
      p_descrs
   ELSE f_universal1 (p_descrs)
   FI;

FUNCTION f_universal1 (p_descrs : tp_descr_list)
                      tp_descr_list :

   IF HEAD (p_descrs).s_origin QUA tp_entity_orig.s_descr
         .s_nature = sc_universal_op THEN
      tp_descr_list (HEAD (p_descrs))
   ELSE f_universal1 (TAIL (p_descrs))
   FI;

     %*****************************************************************%
     %                                                                 %
     %          f_update_...                                           %
     %                                                                 %
     %          Construct a new environment in which one or            %
     %          more descriptions (denoted by keys) have the given     %
     %          components. Description(s) with the given keys         %
     %          are already contained in p_env. The new environment    %
     %          is equal to p_env, except that these descriptions      %
     %          are 'updated'.                                         %
     %                                                                 %
     %          f_update_add_...                                       %
     %                                                                 %
     %          Similar to f_update_... but descriptions with the      %
     %          given key(s) are not necessarily contained in p_env    %
     %          and are added to p_env in that case.                   %
     %                                                                 %
     %*****************************************************************%

FUNCTION f_update_add_descr (p_key          : tp_key,
                             p_designator   : tp_designator,
                             p_state        : tp_state,
                             p_nature       : tp_nature,
                             p_den          : tp_den_same,
                             p_env          : tp_env) tp_env :

   IF f_new_key (p_key, p_env) THEN
      f_add_local_descrs
```

```
        (tp_descr_list
           (f_descr (p_designator,
                     p_key,
                     c_start_repr,
                     p_state,
                     p_nature,
                     CASE c_den : p_den OF
                     IS tp_same :
               %error handling for task/package bodies
               %without specification
                        IF p_state = sc_in_body THEN
                           IF p_nature = sc_task THEN
                              c_error_task_den
                           ELSE IF p_nature = sc_package THEN
                              c_error_pack_den
                           ELSE sc_void
                           FI FI
                        ELSE sc_void
                        FI;
                     IS tp_den : c_den
                     ESAC,
                     f_enclosing (p_env))),
         p_env)
  ELSE f_update_descr_by_key (p_key,
                              f_repr (p_key, p_env),
                              IF p_state = sc_id_established THEN
                                 sc_same
                              ELSE p_state
                              FI,
                              p_nature,
                              IF p_den = sc_void THEN
                                 sc_same
                              ELSE p_den
                              FI,
                              p_env)
  FI;

FUNCTION f_update_add_descrs (p_keys        : tp_key_list,
                              p_designators : tp_designator_list,
                              p_state       : tp_state,
                              p_nature      : tp_nature,
                              p_den         : tp_den_same,
                              p_env         : tp_env)
                             tp_env :

  IF EMPTY (p_keys) THEN
     p_env
  ELSE f_update_add_descrs (TAIL (p_keys),
                            TAIL (p_designators),
                            p_state,
                            p_nature,
                            p_den,
                            f_update_add_descr (HEAD (p_keys),
                                                HEAD (p_designators),
                                                p_state,
                                                p_nature,
                                                p_den,
                                                p_env))
  FI;
```

```
FUNCTION f_update_derivable (p_type,
                             p_subpr : tp_key,
                             p_local : tp_descr_list)
                            tp_descr_list :

    % Add p_subprs to the list of derivable subprograms of p_type,
    % if it is not yet contained in this list.

   IF HEAD (p_local).s_key = p_type THEN
      tp_descr_list
         (f_update_descr
            (HEAD (p_local),
             sc_same,
             sc_same,
             sc_same,
             tp_type_den
                (f_type1 (HEAD (p_local)),
                 IF ELEM_IN_LIST
                       (p_subpr,
                        HEAD (p_local).s_den QUA tp_type_den
                            .s_derivable_subprogs) THEN
                     c_empty_keys
                 ELSE tp_key_list (p_subpr)
                 FI)))
                   +
      TAIL (p_local)
   ELSE tp_descr_list (HEAD (p_local)) +
        f_update_derivable (p_type, p_subpr, TAIL (p_local))
   FI;

FUNCTION f_update_descr (p_descr          : tp_descr,
                         p_repr           : tp_repr_same,
                         p_state          : tp_state_same,
                         p_nature         : tp_nature_same,
                         p_den            : tp_den_same)
                        tp_descr :

    % Specialities : If the updated description denotes a type,
    % the derivable subprograms of this type are added to the
    % derivable subprograms of the new denotation.

   tp_descr
     (p_descr.s_designator,
      p_descr.s_key,
      CASE p_repr OF
      IS tp_same : p_descr.s_repr;
      IS tp_repr : THIS
      ESAC,
      CASE p_state OF
      IS tp_same : p_descr.s_state;
      IS tp_state : THIS
      ESAC,
      CASE p_nature OF
      IS tp_same : p_descr.s_nature;
      IS tp_nature : THIS
      ESAC,
      CASE c_den : p_den OF
      IS tp_same : p_descr.s_den;
      IS tp_den :
         CASE c_old : p_descr.s_den OF
```

```
        IS tp_type_den :
            CASE c_new : c_den OF
            IS tp_type_den :
                tp_type_den
                    (c_new.s_type,
                     c_old.s_derivable_subprogs +
                        c_new.s_derivable_subprogs)
            OUT c_den
            ESAC
        OUT c_den
        ESAC
    ESAC,
    p_descr.s_origin,
    p_descr.s_enclosing);

FUNCTION f_update_descr_by_key (p_key         : tp_key,
                                p_repr        : tp_repr_same,
                                p_state       : tp_state_same,
                                p_nature      : tp_nature_same,
                                p_den         : tp_den_same,
                                p_env         : tp_env) tp_env:

  (f_update_local
     (p_env,
      f_update_descr_by_key1 (p_key,
                              p_repr,
                              p_state,
                              p_nature,
                              p_den,
                              f_local (p_env)))
   %C 8.3/1
   CONDITION
      CASE c_state : p_state OF
      IS tp_same : TRUE;
      IS tp_state :
         CASE c_state OF
         sc_complete : sc_incomplete : sc_spec_complete :
         sc_deferred : sc_incompl_private :
               ch_local_hiding (f_select_by_key (p_key, p_env)
                                              .s_designator,
                                CASE c_den : p_den OF
                                IS tp_same :
                                    f_select_by_key (p_key, p_env).s_den;
                                IS tp_den : c_den
                                ESAC,
                                p_key,
                                f_local (p_env),
                                p_env)
         OUT TRUE
         ESAC
      ESAC
   MESSAGE
      "THIS new decl hides decl from same decl-part");

FUNCTION f_update_descr_by_key1
                         (p_key          : tp_key,
                          p_repr         : tp_repr_same,
                          p_state        : tp_state_same,
                          p_nature       : tp_nature_same,
                          p_den          : tp_den_same,
```

```
                         p_descrs      : tp_descr_list) tp_descr_list:

   IF EMPTY (p_descrs) THEN
      c_empty_descrs
   ELSE IF p_key = HEAD (p_descrs).s_key THEN
      tp_descr_list
         (f_update_descr
             (HEAD (p_descrs),
              p_repr,
              p_state,
              p_nature,
              p_den)) +
      TAIL (p_descrs)
   ELSE tp_descr_list (HEAD (p_descrs)) +
        f_update_descr_by_key1 (p_key,
                                p_repr,
                                p_state,
                                p_nature,
                                p_den,
                                TAIL (p_descrs))
   FI FI;

FUNCTION f_update_descrs_by_keys
                         (p_keys       : tp_key_list,
                          p_repr       : tp_repr_same,
                          p_state      : tp_state_same,
                          p_nature     : tp_nature_same,
                          p_den        : tp_den_same,
                          p_env        : tp_env)tp_env :

IF    EMPTY (p_keys) THEN
   p_env
ELSE  f_update_descrs_by_keys
              (TAIL (p_keys),
               p_repr,
               p_state,
               p_nature,
               p_den,
               f_update_descr_by_key (HEAD (p_keys),
                                      p_repr,
                                      p_state,
                                      p_nature,
                                      p_den,
                                      p_env))
   FI;

FUNCTION f_update_encl (p_state  : tp_state_same,
                        p_nature : tp_nature_same,
                        p_den    : tp_den_same,
                        p_env    : tp_env) tp_env :

 f_update_global
       (f_update_descr_by_key1
                (f_enclosing (p_env),
                 sc_same,
                 p_state,
                 p_nature,
                 p_den,
                 f_global (p_env)),
        p_env);
```

```
FUNCTION f_update_encl_state (p_state : tp_state,
                              p_env   : tp_env) tp_env :

   f_update_encl (p_state, sc_same, sc_same, p_env);

FUNCTION f_update_generic_params (p_env : tp_env) tp_env :

   tp_env (p_env.s_imported,
           p_env.s_global,
           f_update_generic_params1 (p_env.s_local),
           p_env.s_enclosing);

FUNCTION f_update_generic_params1 (p_descrs : tp_descr_list)
                                   tp_descr_list :

   IF EMPTY (p_descrs) THEN
      p_descrs
   ELSE tp_descr_list
     (IF HEAD (p_descrs).s_state /= sc_implicitly_declared THEN
         f_update_descr
           (HEAD (p_descrs),
            sc_same,
            sc_complete_generic,
            sc_same,
            sc_same)
      ELSE HEAD (p_descrs)
      FI) +
      f_update_generic_params1 (TAIL (p_descrs))
   FI;

FUNCTION f_update_global (p_global : tp_descr_list,
                          p_env    : tp_env) tp_env :

   f_env (f_imported (p_env),
          p_global,
          f_local (p_env),
          f_enclosing (p_env));

FUNCTION f_update_init (p_descrs : tp_descr_list,
                        p_init   : tp_init) tp_descr_list :

   IF EMPTY (p_descrs) THEN
      p_descrs
   ELSE CASE c_den : HEAD (p_descrs).s_den OF
        IS tp_object :
           tp_descr_list
              (f_update_descr
                  (HEAD (p_descrs),
                   sc_same,
                   sc_same,
                   sc_same,
                   tp_object
                      (c_den.s_type,
                       p_init)))
        OUT tp_descr_list (HEAD (p_descrs))
        ESAC +
        f_update_init (TAIL (p_descrs), p_init)
   FI;
```

```
FUNCTION f_update_local (p_env   : tp_env,
                         p_local : tp_descr_list) tp_env :

   f_env (f_imported (p_env),
          f_global (p_env),
          p_local,
          f_enclosing (p_env));

FUNCTION f_update_nature_descrs (p_descrs : tp_descr_list,
                                 p_nature : tp_nature_same)
                                 tp_descr_list :

     % 'Update' the nature of p_descrs, except for descriptions
     % which denote discriminants.

   CASE c_nature : p_nature OF
   IS tp_same : p_descrs;
   IS tp_nature :
     IF EMPTY (p_descrs) THEN
        c_empty_descrs
     ELSE IF HEAD (p_descrs).s_nature = sc_discriminant THEN
             tp_descr_list (HEAD (p_descrs))
          ELSE tp_descr_list
                  (f_update_descr (HEAD (p_descrs),
                                   sc_same,
                                   sc_same,
                                   c_nature,
                                   sc_same))
          FI  +
          f_update_nature_descrs (TAIL (p_descrs), p_nature)
     FI
   ESAC;

FUNCTION f_update_repr (p_key       : tp_key,
                        p_user_reps : tp_user_reps,
                        p_env       : tp_env) tp_env :

   f_update_repr1
        (p_key,
         IF  f_is_user_repr (p_key, p_user_reps, p_env) THEN
            tp_repr (sc_user_rep, f_reps (p_key, p_env))
         ELSE tp_repr (sc_start_rep, f_reps (p_key, p_env))
         FI,
         p_env);

FUNCTION f_update_repr1 (p_entity : tp_key,
                         p_repr   : tp_repr,
                         p_env    : tp_env) tp_env :

   f_update_descr_by_key
        (p_entity,
         p_repr,
         sc_same,
         sc_same,
         sc_same,
         p_env);

FUNCTION f_use_required (p_allowed : tp_use_decide) BOOL :

      % Decide whether p_allowed denotes an error value or has
```

```
      % no valid meaning, so that use clauses must be considered
      % for the analysis of the name/expression.

   CASE c_decide : p_allowed OF
   IS tp_choice :
         f_is_error_empty1 (c_decide);
   IS tp_fixed :
         f_is_error_or_empty (c_decide.s_delta) OR
         f_is_error_empty_range (c_decide.s_range);
   IS tp_float :
         f_is_error_or_empty (c_decide.s_digits) OR
         f_is_error_empty_range (c_decide.s_range)
   ESAC;

FUNCTION f_use_required1 (p_allowed : tp_actual) BOOL:

   CASE c_actual : p_allowed OF
   IS tp_descr_set : f_is_error_or_empty (c_actual);
   IS tp_dscrt_range : f_is_error_empty_range (c_actual)
   ESAC;

FUNCTION f_used_types (p_type : tp_type,
                       p_env  : tp_env) tp_key_list :

      % The list of all types on which p_type depends (transitive
      % closure).

   CASE c_type : p_type OF
   IS tp_record : f_used_types1 (c_type.s_descrs);
   IS tp_array  : tp_key_list (c_type.s_comp_type.s_base_type) +
                  f_used_types2 (c_type.s_indices, p_env);
   IS tp_derived: tp_key_list (c_type.s_parent_type)
   OUT c_empty_keys
   ESAC;

FUNCTION f_used_types1 (p_descrs : tp_descr_list) tp_key_list :

   IF EMPTY (p_descrs) THEN
      c_empty_keys
   ELSE CASE c_den : HEAD (p_descrs).s_den OF
        IS tp_object : tp_key_list (c_den.s_type.s_base_type)
        OUT            tp_key_list ()
        ESAC +
        f_used_types1 (TAIL (p_descrs))
   FI;

FUNCTION f_used_types2 (p_ranges : tp_dscrt_range_list,
                        p_env    : tp_env)
                       tp_key_list:

   IF EMPTY (p_ranges) THEN
      c_empty_keys
   ELSE CASE c_range : HEAD (p_ranges) OF
        IS tp_constrained : tp_key_list (c_range.s_base_type);
        IS tp_range       : (c_empty_keys CONDITION FALSE
                              MESSAGE "compiler error");
        IS tp_index       : tp_key_list (c_range.s_type.s_base_type)
        ESAC                             +
        f_used_types2 (TAIL (p_ranges), p_env)
   FI;
```

```
FUNCTION f_used_types3 (p_entity : tp_key,
                        p_env    : tp_env) tp_key_list:

  CASE c_den : f_select_by_key (p_entity, p_env).s_den OF
  IS tp_type_den : f_used_types (c_den.s_type, p_env);
  IS tp_constrained : f_used_types (f_type (c_den.s_base_type,p_env),
                                    p_env);
  IS tp_object : f_used_types
             (f_type (c_den.s_type.s_base_type, p_env), p_env)
  OUT c_empty_keys
  ESAC;

FUNCTION f_valid (p_valid  : tp_descr_set,
                  p_descrs : tp_descr_list) tp_descr_set :

    % Select from p_descrs the description denoted by the
    % origin of the description contained in p_valid.

   IF f_is_error_descr_set (p_valid) THEN
      c_error_descr_set
   ELSE tp_descr_set
        (CASE c_origin : f_head_descr (p_valid).s_origin OF
         IS tp_entity_orig:
            tp_descr_list (c_origin.s_descr);
         IS tp_type_orig :
            f_select_by_type (c_origin.s_key,
                              p_descrs);
         IS tp_no_orig : (c_error_descr_list  CONDITION FALSE
            MESSAGE "compiler error")
         ESAC,
         sc_no_add)
   FI;

     %*************************************************************%
     %                                                             %
     %         f_valid_...                                         %
     %                                                             %
     %         Used to calulate at_valid.                          %
     %                                                             %
     %         f_valid_...1 is called from f_valid_... as well     %
     %         as from f_allowed_... . In the case of a call       %
     %         from f_valid it is assured that the result of       %
     %         f_valid_...1 is not sc_void, for in the case        %
     %         of an error, f_valid_...1 is not called, but an     %
     %         error_value is returned.                            %
     %                                                             %
     %*************************************************************%

 FUNCTION f_valid_aggregate1 (p_type   : tp_key,
                              p_assocs : tp_assoc_list,
                              p_env    : tp_env)
                             tp_assoc_list_void :

   CASE c_type : f_type (p_type, p_env) OF
   IS tp_array : f_valid_array_aggr (c_type, p_assocs, p_env);
   IS tp_record : f_valid_record_aggr (c_type, p_assocs, p_env)
   OUT tp_assoc_list_void (sc_void)
   ESAC;
```

```
FUNCTION f_valid_aggregate (p_exp     : tp_descr_set,
                            p_assocs  : tp_assoc_list,
                            p_env     : tp_env) tp_assoc_list :

   IF f_is_error_descr_set (p_exp) THEN
      f_error_assocs (p_assocs)
   ELSE CASE c_den : f_head_descr (p_exp).s_den OF
        IS tp_dummy_aggr : c_den.s_assocs
        OUT  f_valid_aggregate1
                 (f_object_type (f_head_descr (p_exp)),
                  p_assocs,
                  p_env) QUA tp_assoc_list
        ESAC
   FI;

FUNCTION f_valid_all (p_valid,
                      p_allowed : tp_descr_set) tp_descr_set :

   IF f_is_error_descr_set (p_valid) THEN
      c_error_descr_set
   ELSE tp_descr_set
          (tp_descr_list
             (f_select_descr (HEAD (p_valid.s_descrs).s_key,
                              p_allowed.s_descrs)),
           sc_no_add)
   FI;

FUNCTION f_valid_array_aggr (p_type    : tp_array,
                             p_assocs  : tp_assoc_list,
                             p_env     : tp_env)
                            tp_assoc_list_void :

   IF EMPTY (p_assocs) THEN
      p_assocs
   ELSE CASE c_assoc : f_valid_array_assoc
                         (HEAD (p_type.s_indices),
                          IF EMPTY (TAIL (p_type.s_indices)) THEN
                             p_type.s_comp_type
                          ELSE tp_array
                                 (TAIL (p_type.s_indices),
                                  p_type.s_comp_type)
                          FI,
                          HEAD (p_assocs) QUA tp_comp_assoc,
                          p_env) OF
        IS tp_void : sc_void
        OUT CASE c_assocs : f_valid_array_aggr
                              (p_type,
                               TAIL (p_assocs),
                               p_env) OF
            IS tp_void : tp_assoc_list_void (sc_void);
            IS tp_assoc_list : c_assoc QUA tp_assoc_list + c_assocs
            ESAC
        ESAC
   FI;

FUNCTION f_valid_array_assoc (p_index      : tp_dscrt_range,
                              p_comp_type  : tp_type,
                              p_assoc      : tp_assoc,
```

```
                              p_env          : tp_env)
                              tp_assoc_list_void :

   CASE c_choices : f_valid_array_choices
                      (p_index QUA tp_index.s_type.s_base_type,
                       f_make_constraineds
                         (p_assoc QUA tp_comp_assoc .s_choices),
                       p_env) OF
   IS tp_void : sc_void
   OUT CASE c_value : f_valid_array_comp
                       (p_comp_type,
                        p_assoc QUA tp_comp_assoc .s_actual,
                        p_env) OF
       IS tp_void : tp_assoc_list_void (sc_void);
       IS tp_descr_set    : tp_assoc_list
                             (tp_assoc
                               (tp_comp_assoc
                                 (c_choices QUA tp_choice_list,
                                  c_value)))
       ESAC
   ESAC;

FUNCTION f_valid_array_choices (p_type      : tp_key,
                                p_choices   : tp_choice_list,
                                p_env       : tp_env)
                               tp_choice_list_void :

   IF EMPTY (p_choices) THEN
      tp_choice_list ()
   ELSE CASE c_choices : f_valid_array_choices
                           (p_type,
                            TAIL (p_choices),
                            p_env) OF
        IS tp_void : tp_choice_list_void (sc_void);
        IS tp_choice_list :
           CASE c_choice : HEAD (p_choices) OF
           IS tp_others : tp_choice_list (c_choice) +
                          c_choices;
           IS tp_dscrt_range :
                IF c_choice IS tp_constrained THEN
                   IF p_type = c_choice QUA tp_constrained
                                            .s_base_type THEN
                      tp_choice_list (c_choice) +
                        c_choices
                   ELSE sc_void
                   FI
                ELSE CASE c_range : f_make_range_void
                                      (p_type,
                                       c_choice QUA tp_range
                                                QUA tp_range_constr,
                                       p_env) OF
                   IS tp_void : sc_void;
                   IS tp_range_constr :
                      tp_choice_list (tp_choice
                        (tp_constrained (p_type, c_range)))
                      + c_choices
                   ESAC
                FI;
          IS tp_descr_set    :
                CASE c_descrs : f_make_void_descrs
```

```
                                   (f_valid_descr_set
                                      (c_choice,
                                       p_type,
                                       p_env)) OF
                   IS tp_void : sc_void;
                   IS tp_descr_set :
                       tp_choice_list (tp_choice (c_descrs)) +
                       c_choices
                   ESAC
             OUT sc_void
             ESAC
         ESAC
    FI;

 FUNCTION f_valid_array_comp (p_type    : tp_type,
                              p_comp    : tp_descr_set,
                              p_env     : tp_env)
                             tp_descr_set_void :

    CASE c_type : p_type OF
    IS tp_constrained : f_make_void_descrs
                         (f_valid_descr_set
                           (p_comp,
                            c_type.s_base_type,
                            p_env));
    IS tp_array : IF EMPTY (p_comp.s_descrs) THEN
                     sc_void
                  ELSE CASE c_den : f_select_dummy_aggr (p_comp.s_descrs)
                      OF
                      IS tp_dummy_aggr :
                          CASE c_aggr : f_valid_array_aggr
                                         (c_type,
                                          c_den.s_assocs,
                                          p_env) OF
                          IS tp_void : tp_descr_set_void (sc_void);
                          IS tp_assoc_list :
                                f_descr_set
                                  (c_key,
                                   sc_value,
                                   tp_dummy_aggr
                                     (c_aggr),
                                   sc_no_add)
                          ESAC
                      OUT sc_void
                      ESAC
                  FI
    OUT sc_void
    ESAC;


FUNCTION f_valid_assocs (p_apply   : tp_descr_set,
                         p_name    : tp_descr_set,
                         p_assocs  : tp_assoc_list,
                         p_context : tp_context,
                         p_env     : tp_env) tp_assoc_list:

IF f_is_error_descr_set (p_apply) OR
   f_is_error_empty_assocs (p_assocs) THEN
   p_assocs
ELSE
```

```
   CASE f_head_descr (p_name).s_nature OF
   sc_type :
   sc_subtype : CASE p_context OF
                 sc_subtype_ind : sc_access :
                     (f_make_assocs (f_valid_constraint
                                          (p_name,
                                           p_assocs,
                                           p_env))
                                     CONDITION
                                     ch_constraint (p_name,
                                                    IT,
                                                    p_env)
                                        MESSAGE
                                        "illegal constraint")
                 OUT f_valid_converted (p_name,
                                        p_assocs,
                                        p_env)
                 ESAC;
   sc_constant : sc_variable :
   sc_in : sc_in_out : sc_out : sc_value :
      IF    CASE c_assoc : HEAD (p_assocs) OF
            IS tp_comp_assoc :
                 CASE f_head_descr (c_assoc.s_actual).s_nature OF
                 sc_type : sc_subtype : FALSE
                 OUT TRUE
                 ESAC;
            IS tp_dscrt_range : FALSE
            ESAC THEN
          f_valid_indices (p_name, p_assocs, p_env) QUA tp_assoc_list
      ELSE  f_valid_slice (p_name, p_assocs, p_env)
      FI;
   sc_predefined_op : sc_common_op : sc_universal_op :
   sc_function : sc_procedure : f_valid_params (p_apply,
                                                p_name,
                                                p_assocs,
                                                p_env);
   sc_entry      :       f_valid_params (p_apply,
                                         p_name,
                                         p_assocs,
                                         p_env);
   sc_entry_family :    f_valid_indices (p_name,
                                         p_assocs,
                                         p_env)QUA tp_assoc_list

   OUT p_assocs
   ESAC
FI;

FUNCTION f_valid_attr_param (p_assocs : tp_assoc_list,
                             p_name   : tp_descr_set,
                             p_design : tp_designator,
                             p_env    : tp_env)
                            tp_assoc_list :

CASE c_assoc : HEAD (p_assocs) OF
IS tp_dscrt_range : (p_assocs CONDITION FALSE
                              MESSAGE "no dscrt range allowed");
IS tp_comp_assoc:
     tp_assoc_list
       (tp_comp_assoc
          ((f_error_choices (c_assoc.s_choices)
```

```
          CONDITION EMPTY (IT)
          MESSAGE "no choice (s) allowed"),
         CASE p_design QUA SYMB OF
         'image' :
         'pos' :
         'pred' :
         'succ' : f_valid_descr_set
                    (c_assoc.s_actual,
                     CASE c_den : f_head_descr (p_name).s_den OF
                     IS tp_type_den : IS tp_constrained :
                        f_base_type (f_head_descr (p_name))
                     OUT c_error_type_key
                     ESAC,
                     p_env);
         'val' :
         'first' :
         'last' :
         'range' :
         'length' : (c_assoc.s_actual
                     CONDITION
                        CASE c_den : f_head_descr (c_assoc.s_actual)
                                                         .s_den OF
                        IS tp_object : f_is_int_type2
                                        (f_object_type1 (c_den),
                                         p_env)
                        OUT FALSE
                        ESAC
                     MESSAGE
                      "integer expression expected");
         'value'   : f_valid_descr_set
                      (c_assoc.s_actual,
                       c_string,
                       p_env)
         OUT (c_error_descr_set CONDITION FALSE MESSAGE
                                  "compiler error")
         ESAC)) +
     (f_error_assocs (TAIL (p_assocs))
      CONDITION EMPTY (IT)
      MESSAGE "exactly one parameter required")
ESAC;


FUNCTION f_valid_constraint (p_type   : tp_descr_set,
                             p_constr : tp_constraint,
                             p_env    : tp_env) tp_constraint :

  f_valid_constraint1 (f_head_descr (p_type),
                       p_constr,
                       p_env);

FUNCTION f_valid_constraint1 (p_type   : tp_descr,
                              p_constr : tp_constraint,
                              p_env    : tp_env) tp_constraint :

   CASE c_type : f_parent_base_type2
                    (p_type.s_key,
                     p_env) OF
   IS tp_array : CASE c_constr : p_constr OF
                 IS tp_assoc_list :
```

```
                f_valid_index_constr (c_type.s_indices,
                                      c_constr,
                                      p_env)
            OUT p_constr
            ESAC;
    IS tp_record : IS tp_private : IS tp_l_private : IS tp_incompl_type
            CASE c_assocs : p_constr OF
            IS tp_assoc_list :
                f_valid_discr_constraint
                  (f_discriminants (tp_type (c_type)),
                   c_assocs,
                   p_env)
            OUT p_constr
            ESAC;
    IS tp_access :
            f_valid_constraint1
                (f_select_by_key (c_type.s_accessed.s_base_type,
                                  p_env),
                 p_constr,
                 p_env)
    OUT CASE c_constr : p_constr OF
        IS tp_range_constr :
            CASE c_range : f_make_range_void (f_base_type (p_type),
                                              c_constr,
                                              p_env) OF
            IS tp_void : tp_constraint (sc_void);
            IS tp_range_constr :
                         tp_constraint (c_range)
            ESAC;
        IS tp_fixed :    f_valid_fixed_constr
                          (p_type,
                           c_constr,
                           p_env);
        IS tp_float : f_valid_float_constr
                          (p_type,
                           c_constr,
                           p_env)
        OUT p_constr
        ESAC
    ESAC;

FUNCTION f_valid_converted (p_name    : tp_descr_set,
                            p_assocs  : tp_assoc_list,
                            p_env     : tp_env)tp_assoc_list :

    IF f_is_error_descr_set (p_name) OR
       EMPTY (p_assocs) THEN
       p_assocs
    ELSE CASE c_assoc : HEAD (p_assocs) OF
        IS tp_comp_assoc :
            tp_assoc_list (tp_assoc (tp_comp_assoc
                (tp_choice_list (),
                 tp_descr_set
                   (f_valid_converted1
                       (f_head_descr (p_name).s_key,
                        f_expand_additional
                            (c_assoc.s_actual.s_descrs,
                             c_assoc.s_actual.s_add,
                             p_env),
                        p_env),
```

```
               sc_no_add))));
        IS tp_dscrt_range : c_error_assocs
        ESAC
  FI;

FUNCTION f_valid_converted1 (p_type   : tp_key,
                             p_descrs: tp_descr_list,
                             p_env    : tp_env)tp_descr_list:

   IF EMPTY (p_descrs) THEN
      c_empty_descrs
   ELSE IF f_legal_type_conversion
              (f_base_type1 (p_type,p_env),
               f_object_type (HEAD (p_descrs)),
               p_env) THEN
          tp_descr_list (HEAD (p_descrs))
        ELSE c_empty_descrs
        FI                                          +
        f_valid_converted1 (p_type,
                            TAIL (p_descrs),
                            p_env)
   FI;

FUNCTION f_valid_descr_set (p_descrs : tp_descr_set,
                            p_type   : tp_key,
                            p_env    : tp_env) tp_descr_set:

      % Yield a descr_set which contains only descriptions
      % for values of p_type. s_add of the result is sc_no_add, i.e.
      % s_descrs contains exaclty the descriptions which are
      % represented by the descr_set.
      % Note that s_descrs of s_descrs need not be completely expanded
      % even if s_add /= sc_no_add.

   IF f_is_error_descr_set (p_descrs) THEN
      p_descrs
   ELSE
      tp_descr_set
        (CASE c_add : p_descrs.s_add OF
         sc_no_add  : f_valid_descr_set1 (p_descrs.s_descrs,
                                          p_type,
                                          p_env);

         sc_add_deriv :
            f_valid_descr_set2 (p_descrs.s_descrs,
                                p_type,
                                p_env);
         sc_add_access : f_valid_descr_set3 (p_descrs.s_descrs,
                                             p_type,
                                             p_env)

         ESAC,
      sc_no_add)
   FI;

FUNCTION f_valid_descr_set1 (p_descrs : tp_descr_list,
                             p_type   : tp_key,
                             p_env    : tp_env)
                           tp_descr_list:

   IF EMPTY (p_descrs) THEN
      p_descrs
```

```
ELSE CASE c_den : HEAD (p_descrs).s_den OF
      IS tp_object :
         IF f_implicitly_convertable1
              (f_object_type1 (c_den),
               p_type,
               p_env) THEN
            tp_descr_list
              (IF HEAD (p_descrs) = c_error_descr THEN
                  HEAD (p_descrs)
               ELSE
                  f_mark_origin2
                     (f_temp_descr
                        (HEAD (p_descrs).s_designator,
                         HEAD (p_descrs).s_key,
                         HEAD (p_descrs).s_repr,
                         HEAD (p_descrs).s_state,
                         HEAD (p_descrs).s_nature,
                         tp_object (tp_constrained
                                      (p_type,
                                       c_den.s_type.s_constraint)
                                    c_den.s_init),
                         HEAD (p_descrs).s_enclosing),
                      HEAD (p_descrs).s_origin)
               FI)
         ELSE c_empty_descrs
         FI
      OUT c_empty_descrs
      ESAC +
      f_valid_descr_set1 (TAIL (p_descrs), p_type, p_env)
  FI;

FUNCTION f_valid_descr_set2 (p_descrs   : tp_descr_list,
                             p_type     : tp_key,
                             p_env      : tp_env)
                            tp_descr_list :

   IF EMPTY (p_descrs) THEN
      p_descrs
   ELSE CASE c_den : HEAD (p_descrs).s_den OF
      IS tp_object:
         IF f_implicitly_convertable1
              (f_object_type1 (c_den),
               p_type,
               p_env) THEN
            tp_descr_list (HEAD (p_descrs))
         ELSE IF f_is_derived_from
                   (f_object_type1 (c_den),
                    p_type,
                    p_env) THEN
            tp_descr_list
              (f_temp_descr
                  (HEAD (p_descrs).s_designator,
                   c_key,
                   HEAD (p_descrs).s_repr,
                   HEAD (p_descrs).s_state,
                   HEAD (p_descrs).s_nature,
                   tp_object
                      (tp_constrained
                          (p_type,
                           c_den.s_type.s_constraint),
```

```
                c_den.s_init),
             c_enclosing))
      ELSE f_valid_descr_set2
           (TAIL (p_descrs),
            p_type,
            p_env)
      FI FI
    OUT f_valid_descr_set2
         (TAIL (p_descrs),
          p_type,
          p_env)
    ESAC
  FI;

FUNCTION f_valid_descr_set3 (p_descrs : tp_descr_list,
                             p_type   : tp_key,
                             p_env    : tp_env) tp_descr_list :

  IF EMPTY (p_descrs) THEN
     p_descrs
  ELSE f_valid_descr_set31 (HEAD (p_descrs), p_type, p_env) +
       f_valid_descr_set3 (TAIL (p_descrs), p_type, p_env)
  FI;

FUNCTION f_valid_descr_set31 (p_descr   : tp_descr,
                              p_type    : tp_key,
                              p_env     : tp_env)tp_descr_list:

  CASE c_type : f_parent_base_type2 (p_type, p_env) OF
  IS tp_access : IF p_descr.s_den IS tp_object THEN
                   IF f_object_type1 (p_descr.s_den)
                      = c_type.s_accessed.s_base_type THEN
                     tp_descr_list
                       (f_temp_descr
                          (p_descr.s_designator,
                           c_key,
                           p_descr.s_repr,
                           p_descr.s_state,
                           p_descr.s_nature,
                           tp_object
                              (tp_constrained
                                  (p_type,
                                   sc_void),
                               c_init),
                           c_enclosing))
                   ELSE c_empty_descrs
                   FI
                 ELSE c_empty_descrs
                 FI
  OUT c_empty_descrs
  ESAC;

FUNCTION f_valid_discr_constraint (p_discrs  : tp_descr_list,
                                   p_assocs  : tp_assoc_list,
                                   p_env     : tp_env)
                                 tp_constraint :

  IF EMPTY (p_assocs) THEN
     tp_assoc_list ()
  ELSE
```

```
  IF HEAD (p_assocs) IS tp_dscrt_range THEN
     sc_void
  ELSE
     CASE c_assoc : f_valid_discr_assoc
                       (p_discrs,
                        HEAD (p_assocs),
                        p_env) OF
      IS tp_assoc_list :
           CASE c_assocs : f_valid_discr_constraint
                             (f_choices_out
                                (HEAD (c_assoc)
                                  QUA tp_comp_assoc .s_choices,
                                 p_discrs),
                              TAIL (p_assocs),
                              p_env) OF
           IS tp_assoc_list : c_assoc + c_assocs
           OUT tp_constraint (sc_void)
           ESAC
      OUT tp_constraint (sc_void)
      ESAC
    FI
 FI;

FUNCTION f_valid_discr_assoc (p_discrs : tp_descr_list,
                              p_assoc  : tp_assoc,
                              p_env    : tp_env) tp_constraint:

  (CASE c_choices : f_valid_record_choices
                      (p_assoc QUA tp_comp_assoc .s_choices,
                       p_discrs,
                       p_env) OF
   IS tp_void : tp_constraint (tp_assoc_list (p_assoc));
   IS tp_choice_list :
       CASE c_value : f_make_void_descrs
                        (f_valid_descr_set
                           (p_assoc QUA tp_comp_assoc .s_actual,
                            f_object_type1
                               (f_select_by_key1
                                  (HEAD (c_choices) QUA tp_descr
                                        .s_key,
                                   p_discrs)
                                QUA tp_descr.s_den),
                            p_env)) OF
        IS tp_void : tp_constraint (sc_void);
        IS tp_descr_set :
               tp_constraint
                    (tp_assoc_list
                        (tp_comp_assoc
                           (c_choices,
                            c_value)))
        ESAC
   ESAC
   CONDITION
      IF EMPTY (p_assoc QUA tp_comp_assoc.s_choices) THEN
        TRUE
      ELSE NOT (HEAD (p_assoc QUA tp_comp_assoc.s_choices) IS tp_other
      FI
      MESSAGE
      "OTHERS not allowed in discriminant constraints");
```

```
FUNCTION f_valid_dscrt_range (p_range : tp_dscrt_range,
                              p_env   : tp_env) tp_dscrt_range:
   CASE c_range : p_range OF
   IS tp_range :
      CASE c_range : c_range OF
      IS tp_void : tp_dscrt_range (tp_range (sc_void));
      IS tp_range_constr :
          f_univ_to_int
           (tp_constrained
              (f_object_type1
                 (f_head_descr
                    (f_valid_range_constr
                       (c_range,
                        p_env)QUA tp_range_constr .s_lower_bound)
                            .s_den),
               f_valid_range_constr (c_range,
                                     p_env) QUA tp_range_constr),
             p_env)
      ESAC;
   IS tp_index : c_range;
   IS tp_constrained :
         tp_constrained
            (c_range.s_base_type,
             CASE c_constraint : c_range.s_constraint OF
             IS tp_range_constr:
                tp_constraint
                     (f_valid_range_constr (c_constraint,
                                            p_env) QUA tp_range_constr)
             OUT (tp_constraint (sc_void)
                   CONDITION FALSE
                   MESSAGE "compiler error")
             ESAC)
   ESAC;
FUNCTION f_valid_fixed_constr (p_type  : tp_descr,
                               p_fixed : tp_fixed,
                               p_env   : tp_env) tp_constraint :

   CASE c_range : p_fixed.s_range OF
   IS tp_void :
            tp_fixed
                (p_fixed.s_delta,
                 f_range_constr (p_type, p_env));
   IS tp_range_constr :
            CASE c_new_range: f_make_range_void
                                  (f_base_type (p_type),
                                   c_range,
                                   p_env) OF
            IS tp_void : tp_constraint (sc_void);
            IS tp_range_constr :
                     tp_fixed
                         (p_fixed.s_delta,
                          tp_range (c_new_range))
            ESAC
   ESAC;

FUNCTION f_valid_float_constr (p_type  : tp_descr,
                              p_float : tp_float,
                              p_env   : tp_env) tp_constraint:
```

```
   CASE c_range : p_float.s_range OF
   IS tp_void :
        tp_float
             (p_float.s_digits,
              f_range_constr (p_type, p_env));
   IS tp_range_constr :
             CASE c_new_range: f_make_range_void
                                    (f_base_type (p_type),
                                     c_range,
                                     p_env) OF
             IS tp_void :
                tp_constraint (sc_void);
             IS tp_range_constr :
                tp_float
                   (p_float.s_digits,
                    tp_range (c_new_range))
                ESAC
   ESAC;

FUNCTION f_valid_index_assoc (p_index   : tp_dscrt_range,
                              p_assoc   : tp_assoc,
                              p_env     : tp_env) tp_constraint :

   CASE c_index : p_index OF
   IS tp_index :
      CASE c_assoc : p_assoc OF
      IS tp_dscrt_range :
            CASE c_assoc : c_assoc OF
            IS tp_constrained :
                IF  f_implicitly_convertable1
                      (c_assoc.s_base_type,
                       c_index.s_type.s_base_type,
                       p_env) THEN
                   tp_constraint (tp_dscrt_range_list (c_assoc))
                ELSE tp_constraint (sc_void)
                FI;
            IS tp_range :
                CASE c_range : f_make_range_void
                                  (c_index.s_type.s_base_type,
                                   c_assoc QUA tp_range_constr,
                                   p_env) OF
                IS tp_range_constr : tp_dscrt_range_list
                  (tp_dscrt_range
                     (tp_constrained
                        (c_index.s_type.s_base_type,
                         c_range)))
                OUT tp_constraint (sc_void)
                ESAC;
            IS tp_index : tp_constraint (sc_void)
            ESAC;
      IS tp_comp_assoc : tp_dscrt_range_list (tp_dscrt_range
                          (f_gen_constrained
                             (f_head_descr (c_assoc.s_actual),
                              sc_void)))
      ESAC
   OUT tp_constraint (sc_void)
   ESAC;
 FUNCTION f_valid_index_constr (p_indices   : tp_dscrt_range_list,
                                p_assocs    : tp_assoc_list,
                                p_env       : tp_env)
```

```
                         tp_constraint :
   IF EMPTY (p_indices) OR EMPTY (p_assocs)
      THEN f_error_dscrt_ranges (p_assocs)
   ELSE CASE c_index : f_valid_index_assoc (HEAD (p_indices),
                                            HEAD (p_assocs),
                                            p_env) OF
        IS tp_dscrt_range_list :
                CASE c_indices : f_valid_index_constr
                                      (TAIL (p_indices),
                                       TAIL (p_assocs),
                                       p_env)OF
                IS tp_dscrt_range_list :
                                c_index + c_indices
                OUT tp_constraint (sc_void)
                ESAC
        OUT tp_constraint (sc_void)
        ESAC
   FI;

FUNCTION f_valid_index (p_index : tp_dscrt_range,
                        p_assoc : tp_assoc,
                        p_env   : tp_env) tp_assoc_list_void:

   CASE c_assoc : p_assoc OF
   IS tp_comp_assoc :
      CASE c_actual :
            f_make_void_descrs
              (f_valid_descr_set (c_assoc.s_actual,
                                  f_range_type (p_index, p_env),
                                  p_env)) OF
      IS tp_descr_set :
         tp_assoc_list_void (tp_assoc_list (tp_assoc
            (tp_comp_assoc (c_assoc.s_choices, c_actual))));
      IS tp_void : tp_assoc_list_void (sc_void)
      ESAC;
   IS tp_dscrt_range : tp_assoc_list_void (sc_void)
   ESAC;

FUNCTION f_valid_indices (p_name   : tp_descr_set,
                          p_assocs : tp_assoc_list,
                          p_env    : tp_env) tp_assoc_list_void:

   IF  f_is_error_descr_set (p_name) THEN
       f_error_assocs (p_assocs)
   ELSE f_valid_indices1
     (CASE c_den : f_head_descr (p_name).s_den OF
      IS tp_entry_family : tp_dscrt_range_list (c_den.s_dscrt_range);
      IS tp_object :
           CASE c_type : f_object_parent_deref_type
                           (f_head_descr (p_name),
                            p_env) OF
           IS tp_array : c_type.s_indices
           OUT (tp_dscrt_range_list () CONDITION FALSE MESSAGE
                                           "compiler error")
           ESAC
      OUT (tp_dscrt_range_list () CONDITION FALSE MESSAGE
                                     "compiler error")
      ESAC,
      p_assocs,
      p_env)
```

```
FI;

FUNCTION f_valid_indices1 (p_indices: tp_dscrt_range_list,
                           p_assocs : tp_assoc_list,
                           p_env    : tp_env)tp_assoc_list_void:

   IF EMPTY (p_indices) AND EMPTY (p_assocs) THEN
      tp_assoc_list ()
   ELSE IF EMPTY (p_indices) OR EMPTY (p_assocs) THEN
         tp_assoc_list_void (sc_void)
        ELSE CASE c_index : f_valid_index (HEAD (p_indices),
                                           HEAD (p_assocs),
                                           p_env) OF
             IS tp_assoc_list :
                CASE c_indices : f_valid_indices1 (TAIL (p_indices),
                                                   TAIL (p_assocs),
                                                   p_env)OF

                IS tp_assoc_list : c_index + c_indices
                OUT tp_assoc_list_void (sc_void)
                ESAC
           OUT tp_assoc_list_void (sc_void)
           ESAC
        FI
   FI;

FUNCTION f_valid_params (p_apply,
                         p_name   : tp_descr_set,
                         p_assocs : tp_assoc_list,
                         p_env    : tp_env) tp_assoc_list:

   IF f_is_error_descr_set (p_name) THEN
      p_assocs
   ELSE CASE c_params : f_valid_params1
            (f_parameters (f_head_descr (p_name)),
             p_assocs,
             p_env) OF
        IS tp_void : (c_error_assocs CONDITION FALSE MESSAGE
                                     "compiler error");

        IS tp_assoc_list : c_params
        ESAC
   FI;

FUNCTION f_valid_params1 (p_params : tp_descr_list,
                          p_assocs : tp_assoc_list,
                          p_env    : tp_env) tp_assoc_list_void :

   IF EMPTY (p_assocs) AND f_have_default (p_params) THEN
      tp_assoc_list ()
   ELSE IF EMPTY (p_params) OR EMPTY (p_assocs) THEN
         sc_void
        ELSE CASE c_param : f_valid_param
                            (p_params,
                             HEAD (p_assocs),
                             p_env) OF
             IS tp_assoc_list :
                CASE c_params : f_valid_params1
                                (f_choices_out
                                   (HEAD (c_param)QUA tp_comp_assoc.
                                           s_choices,
                                    p_params),
```

```
                                TAIL (p_assocs),
                                p_env) OF
              IS tp_assoc_list : c_param + c_params;
              IS tp_void       : tp_assoc_list_void (sc_void)
              ESAC;
           IS tp_void : tp_assoc_list_void (sc_void)
           ESAC
       FI
   FI;
 FUNCTION f_valid_param (p_params : tp_descr_list,
                         p_assoc  : tp_assoc,
                         p_env    : tp_env) tp_assoc_list_void:

   CASE c_assoc : p_assoc OF
   IS tp_comp_assoc :
   (CASE c_param : f_valid_record_choices (c_assoc.s_choices,
                                           p_params,
                                           p_env) OF
    IS tp_void : tp_assoc_list_void (sc_void);
    IS tp_choice_list :
           CASE c_value : f_make_void_descrs
                          (f_valid_descr_set
                              (c_assoc.s_actual,
                               f_object_type
                                  (HEAD (c_param) QUA tp_descr),
                               p_env))
                                             OF
           IS tp_void : tp_assoc_list_void (sc_void);
           IS tp_descr_set : tp_assoc_list_void (tp_assoc_list
                             (tp_assoc (tp_comp_assoc
                                          (c_param,
                                           c_value))))
           ESAC
   ESAC
   CONDITION
      IF EMPTY (c_assoc.s_choices) THEN
         TRUE
      ELSE NOT (HEAD (c_assoc.s_choices) IS tp_others)
      FI
      MESSAGE
      "OTHERS not allowed in parameter associations")
  OUT tp_assoc_list_void (sc_void)
  ESAC;


FUNCTION f_valid_predef_float (p_constr : tp_float,
                               p_env    : tp_env) tp_key :

      % Select the predefined floating point type which includes
      % p_constr according to chapter 3.5.7 [Ada80]

   c_float;

FUNCTION f_valid_predef_int (p_constr : tp_range_constr,
                             p_env    : tp_env) tp_key :

      % Select the predefined integer type which includes
      % p_constr according to chapter 3.5.4 [Ada80]
```

```
  c_int;

FUNCTION f_valid_range_constr (p_range : tp_range,
                               p_env   : tp_env) tp_range :

    % Construct a range from p_range for which no type is
    % given by the context (Numeric type definition,
    % discrete range, record type representation).
    % Check that the type uf the constructed range is
    % completely determined by the two bounds.

  CASE c_range : p_range OF
  IS tp_range_constr :
    tp_range_constr
      (f_valid_descr_set
         (c_range.s_lower_bound,
          f_same_type3
            (tp_descrs_list (c_range.s_lower_bound,
                             c_range.s_upper_bound),
             p_env),
          p_env),
       f_valid_descr_set
         (c_range.s_upper_bound,
          f_same_type3
            (tp_descrs_list (c_range.s_lower_bound,
                             c_range.s_upper_bound),
             p_env),
          p_env))
  OUT p_range
  ESAC;

FUNCTION f_valid_record_aggr (p_type   : tp_record,
                              p_assocs : tp_assoc_list,
                              p_env    : tp_env)
                             tp_assoc_list_void :

  CASE c_discrs : f_select_discrs
                    (f_discrs (p_type.s_descrs),
                     p_assocs,
                     p_env) OF
  IS tp_void : sc_void;
  IS tp_descr_list : CASE c_comps : f_select_record_comps
                                      (c_discrs,
                                       p_type.s_comps,
                                       p_env)  OF

                     IS tp_void : sc_void;
                     IS tp_descr_list : f_valid_record_aggr1
                                          (f_discrs (p_type.s_descrs),
                                           c_comps,
                                           p_type,
                                           p_assocs,
                                           p_env)

                     ESAC
  ESAC;

FUNCTION f_valid_record_aggr1 (p_descrs : tp_descr_list,
                               p_type   : tp_record,
                               p_assocs : tp_assoc_list,
                               p_env    : tp_env)
                              tp_assoc_list_void :
```

```
IF EMPTY (p_assocs) THEN
   IF EMPTY (p_descrs)
        THEN tp_assoc_list ()
      ELSE tp_assoc_list_void (sc_void)
      FI
ELSE CASE c_assoc : f_valid_record_assoc
                    (p_descrs,
                     HEAD (p_assocs),
                     p_env) OF
      IS tp_void : sc_void;
      IS tp_assoc_list :
           CASE c_assocs : f_valid_record_aggr1
                           (IF EMPTY (HEAD (c_assoc) QUA
                                   tp_comp_assoc.s_choices)
                               THEN p_descrs
                            ELSE
                              f_choices_out
                                (HEAD (c_assoc)
                                   QUA tp_comp_assoc .s_choices,
                                 p_descrs)
                            FI,
                            p_type,
                            TAIL (p_assocs),
                            p_env) OF
           IS tp_void : tp_assoc_list_void (sc_void);
           IS tp_assoc_list : tp_assoc_list (c_assoc) + c_assocs
           ESAC
     ESAC
  FI;

FUNCTION f_valid_record_assoc (p_descrs : tp_descr_list,
                               p_assoc  : tp_assoc,
                               p_env    : tp_env)
                              tp_assoc_list_void:

  CASE c_choices : f_valid_record_choices
                   (p_assoc QUA tp_comp_assoc .s_choices,
                    p_descrs,
                    p_env) OF
  IS tp_void : sc_void;
  IS tp_choice_list :
       CASE c_value : f_make_void_descrs
                      (IF EMPTY (c_choices)
                          THEN p_assoc QUA tp_comp_assoc .s_actual
                       ELSE
                         f_valid_descr_set
                           (p_assoc QUA tp_comp_assoc .s_actual,
                            f_object_type1
                              (f_select_by_key1
                                 (HEAD (c_choices) QUA tp_descr
                                     .s_key,
                                  p_descrs) QUA tp_descr
                                    .s_den),
                            p_env)
                       FI) OF
       IS tp_void : tp_assoc_list_void (sc_void);
       IS tp_descr_set : tp_assoc_list
                         (tp_comp_assoc
                            (IF EMPTY (c_choices) THEN  % OTHERS
```

```
                                   p_assoc QUA tp_comp_assoc
                                     .s_choices
                                ELSE c_choices
                                FI,
                                c_value))
        ESAC
    ESAC;

FUNCTION f_valid_record_choice (p_choice  : tp_choice,
                                p_descrs  : tp_descr_list,
                                p_env     : tp_env)
                               tp_choice_list_void :

    CASE c_choice : p_choice OF
    IS tp_dscrt_range  : sc_void;
    IS tp_descr_set    :
        CASE c_descrs : f_make_void_descrs
                          (tp_descr_set
                            (f_select_by_designator0
                               (f_head_descr (c_choice).s_designator
                                p_descrs,
                                p_env),
                             sc_no_add)) OF
         IS tp_void : sc_void;
         IS tp_descr_set  : tp_choice_list
                              (HEAD (c_descrs.s_descrs))
         ESAC;
    IS tp_others  : f_expand_others (p_descrs);
    IS tp_descr    : CASE f_select_by_key1
                          (c_choice.s_key,
                           p_descrs) OF
                     IS tp_void : (sc_void CONDITION FALSE
                                          MESSAGE "compiler error")
                     OUT tp_choice_list (c_choice)
                     ESAC
    ESAC;

FUNCTION f_valid_record_choices (p_choices : tp_choice_list,
                                 p_descrs  : tp_descr_list,
                                 p_env     : tp_env)
                                tp_choice_list_void :

    IF EMPTY (p_choices) THEN
       IF EMPTY (p_descrs) THEN
           sc_void
       ELSE tp_choice_list (HEAD (p_descrs))
       FI
    ELSE CASE c_choices : f_valid_record_choices1
                            (p_choices, p_descrs, p_env)
                                                   OF
         IS tp_void : sc_void;
         IS tp_choice_list : IF EMPTY (c_choices) %OTHERS
                                THEN c_choices
                             ELSE
                                IF f_same_choice_types
                                     (f_object_type1
                                        (f_select_by_key1
                                         (HEAD (c_choices) QUA tp_desc
                                              .s_key,
                                          p_descrs) QUA tp_descr.
                                              s_den),
```

```
                                   TAIL (c_choices),
                                   p_env) THEN
                                  c_choices
                             ELSE sc_void
                             FI
                        FI
        ESAC
   FI;

FUNCTION f_valid_record_choices1 (p_choices : tp_choice_list,
                                  p_descrs  : tp_descr_list,
                                  p_env     : tp_env)
                                 tp_choice_list_void :

   IF EMPTY (p_choices) THEN
      tp_choice_list ()
   ELSE CASE c_choice : f_valid_record_choice
                         (HEAD (p_choices),
                          p_descrs,
                          p_env) OF
        IS tp_void : sc_void;
        IS tp_choice_list :
             CASE c_choices : f_valid_record_choices1
                              (TAIL (p_choices),
                               IF EMPTY (c_choice)  % EMPTY OTHERS
                                  THEN p_descrs
                               ELSE
                                  f_choices_out
                                   (c_choice,
                                    p_descrs)
                               FI,
                               p_env) OF
             IS tp_void : sc_void;
             IS tp_choice_list : c_choice + c_choices
             ESAC
        ESAC
   FI;

FUNCTION f_valid_renamed (p_name  : tp_descr_set,
                          p_descr : tp_descr,
                          p_env   : tp_env) tp_descr_set :

      % Select a description from p_name which matches p_descr.
      % Check matching rules.

   CASE c_den : p_descr.s_den OF
   IS tp_object :
      CASE   c_obj : f_head_descr (p_name).s_den OF
      IS tp_object :
         (p_name
          CONDITION %C 8.5
          f_object_type1 (c_den) =
          f_object_type1 (c_obj)
             MESSAGE
             "renamed obj. must be of the indicated type")
      OUT (c_error_descr_set
           CONDITION FALSE MESSAGE
              "an object required")
      ESAC;
   IS tp_void :
```

```
     CASE c_nature : p_descr.s_nature OF
     sc_exception :
        IF f_head_descr (p_name).s_nature = sc_exception THEN
           p_name
        ELSE (c_exception_descr_set
              CONDITION FALSE MESSAGE %C 8.5
                 "an exception name  expected here")
        FI;
     sc_task :
        IF f_is_task (p_name, p_env)
           THEN p_name
        ELSE (c_task_descr_set
              CONDITION FALSE MESSAGE %C 8.5
                 "name of a task expected here")
        FI
     OUT (c_error_descr_set CONDITION FALSE MESSAGE "compiler error")
     ESAC;
   IS tp_package :
     IF f_head_descr (p_name).s_nature = sc_package THEN
        p_name
     ELSE (c_error_descr_set
           CONDITION FALSE MESSAGE  %C 8.5
              "the name of a package expected")
     FI;
   IS tp_subpr :
     IF EMPTY (f_matching_subpr (f_spec1 (c_den), p_name).s_descrs)
        THEN (CASE c_den.s_spec OF
              IS tp_function  : c_error_descr_set;
              IS tp_procedure : c_error_descr_set;
              IS tp_entry : IS tp_entry_family : (c_proc_descr_set
                            CONDITION FALSE MESSAGE "compiler error")
              ESAC
              CONDITION FALSE MESSAGE
                 "no matching subprograms")
     ELSE
        f_matching_subpr (c_den.s_spec, p_name)
     FI
   OUT (c_error_descr_set CONDITION FALSE
                          MESSAGE "compiler error")
  ESAC;

FUNCTION f_valid_slice (p_name     : tp_descr_set,
                        p_assocs   : tp_assoc_list,
                        p_env      : tp_env) tp_assoc_list :

   IF f_is_error_descr_set (p_name) OR EMPTY (p_assocs) THEN
      p_assocs
   ELSE CASE c_type : f_object_parent_deref_type
                       (f_head_descr (p_name),
                        p_env) OF
        IS tp_array :
           f_valid_slice1 (HEAD (c_type.s_indices),
                           p_assocs,
                           p_env) QUA tp_assoc_list
        OUT (p_assocs CONDITION FALSE MESSAGE "compiler error")
        ESAC
   FI;

FUNCTION f_valid_slice1 (p_index   : tp_dscrt_range,
                         p_assocs  : tp_assoc_list,
```

```
                                    p_env : tp_env) tp_assoc_list_void:

    CASE c_assoc : HEAD (p_assocs) OF
    IS tp_comp_assoc :
        IF f_implicitly_convertable1
              (f_range_type (p_index, p_env),
               CASE c_den : f_head_descr (c_assoc.s_actual).s_den OF
               IS tp_constrained : c_den.s_base_type;
               IS tp_type_den : f_head_descr (c_assoc.s_actual).s_key
               OUT (c_error_type_key
                    CONDITION FALSE
                    MESSAGE "dscrt range required")
               ESAC,
               p_env) THEN
           tp_assoc_list
              (CASE c_den : f_head_descr (c_assoc.s_actual).s_den OF
               IS tp_constrained : c_den;
               IS tp_type_den : tp_constrained
                                    (f_head_descr (c_assoc.s_actual).s_key,
                                     sc_void)
               OUT tp_constrained (c_error_type_key, sc_void)
               ESAC)
        ELSE tp_assoc_list (sc_void)
        FI;
    IS tp_dscrt_range :
        CASE c_assoc : c_assoc OF
        IS tp_constrained :
           IF f_implicitly_convertable1 (c_assoc.s_base_type,
                                          f_range_type (p_index, p_env),
                                          p_env)
             THEN tp_assoc_list_void (p_assocs)
           ELSE tp_assoc_list_void (sc_void)
           FI;
        IS tp_range :
           CASE c_assoc : c_assoc OF
           IS tp_range_constr :
              CASE c_range : f_make_range_void
                                 (f_range_type (p_index,p_env),
                                  c_assoc,
                                  p_env)  OF

              IS tp_range_constr :
                        tp_assoc_list_void (tp_assoc_list
                           (tp_constrained
                              (f_range_type (p_index, p_env),
                               c_range)));
              IS tp_void : tp_assoc_list_void (sc_void)
              ESAC;
           IS tp_void : tp_assoc_list_void (sc_void)
           ESAC;
        IS tp_index : tp_assoc_list_void (sc_void)
        ESAC
   ESAC;

FUNCTION f_valid_type_range (p_exp   : tp_descr_set,
                             p_type  : tp_type_range,
                             p_env   : tp_env)tp_type_range:
  CASE c_type : p_type OF
  IS   tp_constrained  : IF f_implicitly_convertable1
                                (c_type.s_base_type,
```

```
                                f_object_type (f_head_descr (p_exp)),
                                p_env) THEN
                            p_type
                        ELSE (c_error_type_range
                             CONDITION FALSE
                             MESSAGE "type and exp incompatible")
                        FI;
   IS   tp_range_constr :
        CASE c_range : f_make_range_void
                          (f_same_type3
                             (tp_descrs_list
                                (p_exp,
                                 c_type.s_lower_bound,
                                 c_type.s_upper_bound),
                              p_env),
                           c_type,
                           p_env) OF
          IS tp_void : (c_error_type_range
                        CONDITION FALSE
                        MESSAGE " type and exp incompatible");
          IS tp_range_constr : tp_type_range (c_range)
          ESAC
   ESAC;


FUNCTION f_value_in_choices (p_value   : tp_descr,
                             p_choices : tp_choice_list,
                             p_env     : tp_env)
                            BOOL :

     % Check whether p_value occurs within p_choices.

   IF EMPTY (p_choices) THEN
      FALSE
   ELSE CASE c_choice : HEAD (p_choices) OF
        IS tp_others : TRUE;
        IS tp_descr : f_value_in_choices
                        (p_value,
                         TAIL (p_choices),
                         p_env);
        IS tp_descr_set   : f_object_init1 (p_value) =
                            f_object_init (c_choice) OR
                            f_value_in_choices
                               (p_value,
                                TAIL (p_choices),
                                p_env);
        IS tp_dscrt_range :
           f_eval_less_equal
              (f_attr_pos
                  (c_choice QUA tp_constrained .s_constraint
                     QUA tp_range_constr .s_lower_bound,
                   p_env),
               f_attr_pos
                  (f_descr_set2 (p_value),
                   p_env))
           AND
           f_eval_less_equal
              (f_attr_pos
                  (f_descr_set2 (p_value),
                   p_env),
```

```
            f_attr_pos
               (c_choice QUA tp_constrained .s_constraint
                  QUA tp_range_constr .s_upper_bound,
               p_env))
        OR  f_value_in_choices (p_value,
                                TAIL (p_choices),
                                p_env)
     ESAC
  FI;

FUNCTION f_variable_choices (p_choices : tp_choice_list,
                             p_env     : tp_env)BOOL :

     % Check whether p_choices contain a formal [in-] out parameter.

  IF EMPTY (p_choices) THEN
     FALSE
  ELSE CASE c_choice : HEAD (p_choices) OF
       IS tp_others : tp_dscrt_range : FALSE;
       IS tp_descr_set :
          CASE c_nature : f_head_descr (c_choice).s_nature OF
          sc_out : sc_in_out : TRUE
          OUT FALSE
          ESAC;
       IS tp_descr :
          CASE c_nature : c_choice.s_nature OF
          sc_out : sc_in_out : TRUE
          OUT FALSE
          ESAC
       ESAC                                    OR
       f_variable_choices (TAIL (p_choices),
                           p_env)
  FI;

FUNCTION f_variant_choices (p_variants : tp_variant_list)
                           tp_choice_list :

     % All choices in a variant part.

  IF EMPTY (p_variants) THEN
     tp_choice_list ()
  ELSE HEAD (p_variants).s_choices +
       f_variant_choices (TAIL (p_variants))
  FI;

FUNCTION f_variant_comp (p_key   : tp_key,
                         p_comps : tp_comp_list)
                        BOOL :

     % p_key is the key of a record component. The result is true
     % if this component occurs in a variant part of the record.

  CASE c_comp : HEAD (p_comps) OF
  IS tp_descr : IF c_comp.s_key = p_key THEN
                   FALSE
                ELSE f_variant_comp (p_key, TAIL (p_comps))
                FI
  OUT (TRUE CONDITION c_comp IS tp_variant_part MESSAGE
           "compiler error")
  ESAC;
```

AG7. Syntax Cross Reference

abort	:	r_203
accept	:	r_204
access	:	r_059
address	:	r_264
aggregate	:	r_099
allocator	:	r_100
all	:	r_121
alternative_s	:	r_139
alternative	:	r_136
and_then	:	r_132
apply	:	r_084
array	:	r_061
assign	:	r_150
assoc	:	r_085
attribute	:	r_122
binary	:	r_101
block	:	r_140
box	:	r_238
case	:	r_153
char	:	r_037 r_102
choice_s	:	r_093
code	:	r_267
comp_rep_s	:	r_263
comp_rep	:	r_260
comp_unit	:	r_213
cond_clause	:	r_143
cond_entry	:	r_205
constant	:	r_013
constrained	:	r_005
context	:	r_214
decl_rep_s	:	r_027
decl_s	:	r_022
delay	:	r_207
derived	:	r_062
dscrt_range_s	:	r_033
entry	:	r_172
enum_literal_s	:	r_063
exception	:	r_233
exit	:	r_155
fixed	:	r_040
float	:	r_041
formal_discrt	:	r_241
formal_fixed	:	r_242
formal_float	:	r_243
formal_integer	:	r_244
for	:	r_146
function	:	r_170
general_assoc_s	:	r_115
generic_assoc_s	:	r_258
generic_param_s	:	r_253
generic	:	r_245
goto	:	r_156
id_s	:	r_118
id	:	r_001 r_036
if	:	r_154

in_op	:	r_119
in_out	:	r_180
index	:	r_030
inner_record	:	r_077
instantiation	:	r_259
integer	:	r_066
in	:	r_179
item_s	:	r_049
l_private	:	r_072
labeled	:	r_157
loop	:	r_158
membership	:	r_104
name_s	:	r_128
named_stm	:	r_159
named	:	r_131
no_default	:	r_240
not_in	:	r_120
null_access	:	r_105
null_comp	:	r_002
null_stm	:	r_160
number_decl	:	r_015
numeric_literal	:	r_103
or_else	:	r_133
others	:	r_090
out	:	r_181
package_body	:	r_178
package_decl	:	r_173
package_spec	:	r_177
param_assoc_s	:	r_187
param_s	:	r_184
parenthesized	:	r_106
pragma_s	:	r_222
pragma	:	r_219
private	:	r_071
procedure	:	r_171
qualified	:	r_107
raise	:	r_236
range	:	r_052
record_rep	:	r_266
record	:	r_067
rename	:	r_196
return	:	r_161
reverse	:	r_147
select_clause	:	r_198
select_clause_s	:	r_200
selected	:	r_125
select	:	r_208
simple_rep	:	r_265
stm_s	:	r_165
string	:	r_169
stub	:	r_142
subprog_body	:	r_195
subprog_decl	:	r_190
subtype	:	r_016
subunit	:	r_232
task_body	:	r_212
task_decl	:	r_202
task_spec	:	r_069
terminate	:	r_206
timed_entry	:	r_209

type	: r_057
use	: r_197
var_decl_s	: r_076
var_decl	: r_073
variant_part	: r_003
variant_s	: r_080
variant	: r_077
void	: r_008 r_035 r_054 r_070 r_109 r_130 r_148 r_192 r_235
while	: r_149
with	: r_217
ACCESS_CONSTRAINT	: r_081 r_100
ACTUAL	: r_082 r_083 r_085 r_110 r_254
ALTERNATIVE_S	: r_139 r_140 r_153
ALTERNATIVES	: r_137 r_138 r_139
ALTERNATIVE	: r_136 r_138
APPLY	: r_084 r_124
ASSOC	: r_085 r_188 r_255
BINARY_OP	: r_086 r_101
BLOCK_STUB	: r_141 r_142 r_178 r_195 r_212
BLOCK	: r_140 r_141 r_151
CHOICE_S	: r_077 r_093 r_131 r_136
CHOICES	: r_091 r_092 r_092 r_093
CHOICE	: r_087 r_088 r_089 r_090 r_092
COMP_ASSOCS	: r_096 r_097 r_099
COMP_ASSOC	: r_094 r_095 r_097
COMP_REP_S	: r_263 r_266
COMP_REPS	: r_261 r_262 r_262 r_263
COMP_REP	: r_260 r_262
COMP_UNIT	: r_213
COMP	: r_002 r_003 r_004 r_055
COND_CLAUSES	: r_144 r_145 r_154
COND_CLAUSE	: r_143 r_144
CONSTRAINED_1	: r_005 r_006 r_083 r_088
CONSTRAINED_VOID	: r_008 r_009 r_170
CONSTRAINED	: r_006 r_007 r_009 r_016 r_028 r_058 r_059 r_061 r_062 r_135 r_179 r_180 r_181
CONSTRAINT	: r_005 r_010 r_011 r_012
CONTEXT_ELEMS	: r_214 r_215 r_216
CONTEXT_ELEM	: r_216 r_217 r_218
CONTEXT	: r_213 r_214
DECL_REP_S	: r_027 r_069 r_177
DECL_REPS	: r_025 r_026 r_027
DECL_REP	: r_023 r_024 r_026
DECL_S	: r_022 r_177
DECLS	: r_020 r_021 r_022
DECL	: r_013 r_014 r_015 r_016 r_017 r_018 r_019 r_021 r_023 r_042 r_166 r_167 r_202 r_233 r_237
DESIGNATOR	: r_123 r_125 r_168 r_169 r_190 r_195 r_245
DSCRT_RANGE_S	: r_033 r_061
DSCRT_RANGE_VOID	: r_034 r_035 r_172
DSCRT_RANGES	: r_031 r_032 r_033
DSCRT_RANGE	: r_028 r_029 r_030 r_032 r_034 r_146 r_147
ENUM_LITERAL	: r_036 r_037 r_038
ENUM_LITERALS	: r_038 r_039 r_063
EXCEPTION_DEF	: r_233 r_234 r_235
EXP_VOID	: r_050 r_108 r_109 r_143 r_155 r_161 r_179 r_180 r_181 r_198 r_266

EXP	:	r_015 r_040 r_041 r_052 r_082 r_089 r_095 r_098 r_099 r_100 r_101 r_102 r_103 r_104 r_105 r_106 r_107 r_108 r_131 r_149 r_150 r_153 r_189 r_207 r_260 r_264 r_265 r_267
FIXED	:	r_010 r_040 r_064
FLOAT	:	r_011 r_041 r_065
FORMAL_SUBPROG_DEF	:	r_194 r_238 r_239 r_240
FORMAL_TYPE_SPEC	:	r_060 r_241 r_242 r_243 r_244
GENERAL_ASSOC_S	:	r_081 r_084 r_115
GENERAL_ASSOC	:	r_110 r_111 r_112 r_114
GENERAL_ASSOCS	:	r_113 r_114 r_115
GENERIC_ASSOC	:	r_254 r_255 r_257
GENERIC_ASSOCS	:	r_256 r_257 r_258
GENERIC_ASSOC_S	:	r_258 r_259
GENERIC_HEADER	:	r_245 r_246 r_247
GENERIC_PARAM_S	:	r_245
GENERIC_PARAM	:	r_248 r_249 r_250 r_252
GENERIC_PARAMS	:	r_251 r_252 r_253
GENERIC_PARAM_S	:	r_253
GENERIC	:	r_225 r_237 r_245
HEADER	:	r_170 r_171 r_172 r_190 r_195 r_247
ID_S	:	r_013 r_015 r_073 r_118 r_179 r_180 r_181 r_233
IDS	:	r_116 r_117 r_118
ID	:	r_001 r_016 r_057 r_085 r_117 r_122 r_146 r_147 r_157 r_159 r_168 r_173 r_178 r_202 r_212 r_219
INSTANTIATION	:	r_175 r_193 r_259
ITEM_S	:	r_049 r_140
ITEMS	:	r_047 r_048 r_049
ITEM	:	r_042 r_043 r_044 r_045 r_046 r_048
ITERATION	:	r_146 r_147 r_148 r_149 r_158
MEMBERSHIP_OP	:	r_104 r_119 r_120
NAME_S	:	r_128 r_203
NAME_VOID	:	r_129 r_130 r_155 r_236
NAMED	:	r_094 r_112 r_131
NAMES	:	r_126 r_127 r_128 r_197 r_217
NAME	:	r_003 r_005 r_007 r_030 r_084 r_098 r_100 r_107 r_121 r_122 r_123 r_124 r_125 r_126 r_129 r_150 r_152 r_156 r_196 r_204 r_232 r_239 r_259 r_260 r_264 r_265 r_266 r_267
OBJECT_DEF	:	r_013 r_050 r_051 r_073
PACKAGE_BODY	:	r_044 r_178 r_224 r_227
PACKAGE_DECL	:	r_166 r_173 r_228
PACKAGE_DEF	:	r_173 r_174 r_175 r_176
PACKAGE_SPEC	:	r_176 r_177 r_246
PARAM_ASSOC_S	:	r_187 r_219
PARAM_ASSOCS	:	r_185 r_186 r_187
PARAM_ASSOC	:	r_186 r_188 r_189
PARAM_S	:	r_170 r_171 r_172 r_184 r_204
PARAMS	:	r_182 r_183 r_184
PARAM	:	r_179 r_180 r_181 r_183 r_248
PRAGMA_S	:	r_213 r_222
PRAGMAS	:	r_220 r_221 r_222
PRAGMA	:	r_019 r_162 r_219 r_221
RANGE_VOID	:	r_040 r_041 r_053 r_054
RANGE	:	r_012 r_029 r_052 r_053 r_066 r_087 r_111 r_134 r_260
RECORD	:	r_055 r_056 r_067 r_077
RENAME	:	r_051 r_174 r_191 r_196 r_210 r_234

```
REP                   :   r_024 r_043 r_264 r_265 r_266
SELECT_CLAUSE         :   r_198 r_199
SELECT_CLAUSES        :   r_199 r_200 r_201
SELECT_CLAUSE_S       :   r_200 r_208
SHORT_CIRCUIT_OP      :   r_086 r_132 r_133
STM_S                 :   r_136 r_140 r_143 r_158 r_165 r_198 r_204
                          r_205 r_208 r_209
STMS                  :   r_163 r_164 r_164 r_165
STM                   :   r_150 r_151 r_152 r_153 r_154 r_155 r_156
                          r_157 r_157 r_158 r_159 r_160 r_161 r_162
                          r_164 r_203 r_204 r_205 r_206 r_207 r_208
                          r_209 r_236 r_267
SUBPROG_BODY          :   r_045 r_195 r_223 r_229
SUBPROG_DECL          :   r_167 r_190 r_230 r_249
SUBPROG_DEF           :   r_190 r_191 r_192 r_193 r_194
SUBUNIT_BODY          :   r_223 r_224 r_226 r_232
TASK_BODY             :   r_046 r_212 r_226 r_231
TASK_DEF              :   r_202 r_210 r_211
TASK_SPEC             :   r_068 r_069 r_211
TYPE_DECL             :   r_017 r_057 r_250
TYPE_RANGE            :   r_104 r_134 r_135
TYPE_SPEC             :   r_013 r_057 r_058 r_059 r_060 r_061 r_062
                          r_063 r_064 r_065 r_066 r_067 r_068 r_070
                          r_071 r_072 r_073
UNIT_BODY             :   r_213 r_225 r_227 r_228 r_229 r_230 r_231
                          r_232
USE                   :   r_018 r_197 r_218
VAR_DECL_S            :   r_057 r_076
VAR_DECLS             :   r_074 r_075 r_076
VAR_DECL              :   r_004 r_014 r_073 r_075
VARIANT_S             :   r_003 r_080
VARIANTS              :   r_078 r_079 r_080
VARIANT               :   r_077 r_079
```

References

[Ada79] J.D. Ichbiah et al.
Preliminary Ada Reference Manual
ACM Sigplan Notices, vol. 14, no. 6, Part A, June 79

[Ada80] US Department of Defense
Ada Reference Manual
Proposed Standard Document
available as LNCS, Vol 106, Springer Verlag

[BjOe80] D. Bjoerner, O. N. Oest (ed.)
Towards a Formal Definition of Ada
LNCS, vol. 98, Springer 1980

[Dau79] M. Dausmann, G. Persch, G. Winterstein
Ada-O Reference Manual
Universität Karlsruhe, Inst. f. Informatik II
Bericht Nr. 20/79, 1979

[Dau80] M. Dausmann, S. Drossopoulou,
G. Persch, G. Winterstein
Preliminary AIDA Reference Manual
Universität Karlsruhe, Inst. f. Informatik II
Bericht Nr. 2/80, February 1980

[Dau81] M. Dausmann, S. Drossopoulou
G. Persch, G. Winterstein
A Separate Compilation System for Ada
Proc. GI Tagung: Werkzeuge der Programmiertechnik, Karlsruhe, March 1981

[Denc77] P. Dencker
PGS: ein neues LALR(1) - System
Universität Karlsruhe,
Inst für Informatik II,
Diplomarbeit, September 1977

[Denc80] P. Dencker
Benutzerbeschreibung des PGS
Universität Karlsruhe,
Institut für Informatik II,
Bericht Nr. 8/80, March 1980

[Diana81] G. Goos, W. Wulf ed.
Diana Reference Manual
Universität Karlsruhe, Inst. f. Informatik II
Bericht Nr. 1/8.1, March 1981

[Dro82] S. Drossopoulou, J. Uhl, G. Persch,
G. Goos, M. Dausmann, G. Winterstein
An Attribute Grammar for Ada
ACM Symposium on Compiler Construction, Boston June 1982

[FD80] Formal Definition for the Programming Language Ada, Preliminary Version for Public Review, Nov 80
Honeywell Inc, Minneapolis
Cii Honeywell Bull, 78430 Louveciennes, France,
INRIA, 78150 Lechesnay, France

[GoWa82] G. Goos, W. Waite
Translator Engineering
Springer Verlag, New York
- to appear -

[GoWi80] G. Goos, G. Winterstein
Towards a Compiler Front-End for Ada
Proc. Ada Symposium, Boston 1980
ACM SIGPLAN Notices 15 (Nov. 1980), pp. 36 - 46

[GoWi81] G. Goos, G. Winterstein
Problems in Compiling Ada
ECI - Conference, October 1981,
LNCS, vol. 123, Springer 1980

[IG80] J. Goodenough
Ada Compiler Validation - Implementor's Guide,
Version October 1980
SOFTECH Inc. Waltham Ma 02154

[Kast76] U. Kastens
Ein Übersetzer-erzeugendes System auf der Basis attributierter Grammatiken
Dissertation
Universität Karlsruhe, Inst. f. Informatik II
Bericht Nr. 10/76, 1976

[Kast79] U. Kastens
ALADIN - Eine Definitionssprache für attributierte Grammatiken
Universität Karlsruhe, Inst. f. Informatik II
Bericht Nr. 7/79, 1979

[Kast80] U. Kastens
Ordered Attributed Grammars
Acta Informatica 13 (1980), pp 229-256

[KaZi80] U. Kastens, E. Zimmermann
GAG - A Generator based on Attributed Grammars
Universität Karlsruhe, Inst. f. Informatik II
Bericht Nr. 14/80, 1980

[KAZ81] U. Kastens, B. Asbrock, E. Zimmermann
Generating a Pascal Analyzer from an Attributed Grammar
Universität Karlsruhe,
Institut f. Informatik II
Bericht Nr. 16/81, 1981

[Knuth68] D.E. Knuth
Semantics of context-free languages
Math. Syst. Theory 2, 2, 127-145, 1968

[Knuth71] D.E. Knuth
Semantics of context-free languages:correction
Math. Syst. Theory 5, 1, 95-96, 1971

[LIS78] J. D. Ichbiah et al.
LIS Reference Manual
SIEMENS A.G. UB D Dv WS SP31
Munich

[Pearl80] DIN 66251 Teil 2:
Programmiersprache Pearl,
Normentwurf
November 1980

[Per79] G. Persch, G. Winterstein
M. Dausmann, S. Drossopoulou
Overloading in Ada
Proc. Ada Symposium, Boston 1980
ACM SIGPLAN Notices 15-11-80, pp. 47 - 56

[Per81a] G. Persch, G. Winterstein
M. Dausmann, S. Drossopoulou
(Revised) Ada-O Reference Manual
Universität Karlsruhe, Inst. f. Informatik II
Bericht Nr. 9/81

[Per81b] G. Persch, G. Winterstein
M. Dausmann, S. Drossopoulou
An LALR(1) Grammar for (Revised) Ada
ACM Sigplan Notices, 16-3-81, 85-94

[Roe78] J. Roehrich
Methods for the Automatic Construction of
Error Correcting Parsers
Acta Informatica 13, 115-139 (1980)

[Uhl81] J. Uhl
An Attributed Grammar for Ada
Diplomarbeit
Universität Karlsruhe, Inst. f. Informatik II
Bericht Nr. 25/1981, März 1981